Socialism Goes Global

Socialism Goes Global

The Soviet Union and Eastern Europe in the Age of Decolonization

A collectively researched and written monograph,
co-ordinated by

JAMES MARK
PAUL BETTS

OXFORD
UNIVERSITY PRESS

OXFORD

UNIVERSITY PRESS

Great Clarendon Street, Oxford, OX2 6DP,
United Kingdom

Oxford University Press is a department of the University of Oxford.
It furthers the University's objective of excellence in research, scholarship,
and education by publishing worldwide. Oxford is a registered trade mark of
Oxford University Press in the UK and in certain other countries

© Oxford University Press 2022

The moral rights of the authors have been asserted

First Edition published in 2022

Impression: 1

Published in the United States of America by Oxford University Press
198 Madison Avenue, New York, NY 10016, United States of America

British Library Cataloguing in Publication Data

Data available

Library of Congress Control Number: 2021951437

ISBN 978-0-19-284885-7

DOI: 10.1093/oso/9780192848857.001.0001

Printed and bound by
CPI Group (UK) Ltd, Croydon, CR0 4YY

Acknowledgements

First of all, we would like to thank the Arts and Humanities Research Council (UK) for their funding of the 'Socialism Goes Global: Cold War Connections Between the 'Second' and 'Third Worlds'' project (AH/M001830/10), which enabled most of the research and writing time necessary to complete this book. The project was based at the University of Exeter and directed by James Mark. The team would like to express its deep gratitude to James for overseeing the project so ably and energetically from start to finish. James also acknowledges the support of a Netherlands Institute for Advanced Study (NIAS) fellowship, which provided time to complete the analysis and writing. We would also like to note the generous support of the Hungarian National Research, Development and Innovation Office (Grant no. NN 115711, 2015–2018), which kindly covered Bogdan C. Iacob's expenses, along with additional research costs in Romania and Hungary. A grant from the DFG (German Research Council) in the framework of SFB 1199 helped subsidise further research in Germany.

We would like to recall the conversations at meetings we held between 2014 and 2018, the richness of which still continue to inspire and inform our writing. Special thanks go to Kristin Roth-Ey, Małgorzata Mazurek, Natasha Telepneva, Nemanja Radonjić and Zoltán Ginelli for their support, intellectual engagement and, in some cases, the research material that they shared. Individual research contributions are noted at the start of each chapter. Their authored contributions are represented in our companion volume, edited by Kristin Roth-Ey: *Second-Third World Spaces in the Cold War: Global Socialism and the Gritty Politics of the Particular* (London: Bloomsbury, 2022). Sections of the Culture chapter were first published in Paul Betts, Ruin and Renewal: Civilising Europe after the Second World War (London: Profile Books, 2020) and thanks to Profile for providing permission to reproduce them. We would like to thank the Museum of Yugoslavia's director, Neda Kneževic, and her staff, for their great assistance in helping to organise and host a spin-off project of the research—the *Tito in Africa: Picturing Solidarity* photography show—and for producing the accompanying bilingual English and Serbian exhibition catalogues. Thanks too should be expressed to Philip Grover at the Pitt Rivers Museum in Oxford and Justin Jampol and Joes Segal at the Wende Museum in Los Angeles for their cooperation with the travelling exhibition. The proceeds from the sales of the exhibition catalogue were donated to the London-based charity the Swawou School Foundation, which builds girls' schools in Sierra Leone. Many thanks to its director Callum Campbell for making this possible.

Further thanks to Cathryn Steele at Oxford University Press for shepherding the project so expertly. We are greatly indebted to Martin Thom, whose detailed and imaginative copy-editing and proofreading helped raise the level of the writing in many places. We were very privileged to have Arnia van Vuuren as our indexer; despite her illness, she remained committed to the book and produced an index of great quality based on an insightful grasp of its arguments. It is a great loss to the profession that that there will not be indexes after this one, and we are terribly sad that she was not able to see the final result published.

Contents

Introduction

James Mark and Paul Betts

When Socialism Went Global

In the summer of 1961, Marshal Josip Broz Tito of Yugoslavia embarked on a grand six-week tour of newly independent African nations, arriving in style by state yacht and airplane at various national capitals. The purpose of the tour was to drum up support among fledgling decolonized states for the first Non-Aligned Conference, to be held that autumn in Belgrade. Tito and his wife Jovanka, in the guise of the First Couple of the Non-Aligned World, visited over a dozen countries, and were sumptuously feted everywhere they went. His trip to Egypt and India in 1954–55 was the first by a non-Asian head of state to these new independent countries; the 1961 journey was the first visit by a Communist head of state to sub-Saharan Africa. In the African press coverage of the Yugoslav leader's state visits around the continent, Tito was often described as the one white European that Africans could trust. He was the first state leader from the Communist world to tour Latin America, with stopovers in Brazil, Bolivia, Chile and Mexico in 1963. These tours were an integral part of this dramatic global encounter between the Soviet Union, Eastern Europe and a now rapidly decolonizing world; European Communists looked to develop new relationships in the spheres of trade, development, public health, warfare, culture and education.

In the wake of the collapse of Communism (1989–91), such episodes came to be considered, at best, historical curiosities, or, at worst, evidence of nefarious dictatorships which had torn Eastern European populations from their true home in European civilization. As a post-Cold War western orientation was consolidated, the idea that Eastern Europe's history was not just a story of nations' struggle for independence from the region's German, Habsburg, Ottoman and Russian Empires, but might be connected to a global story of colonialism and anti-colonialism, had little appeal. Yet the idea that the region was defined through its position between the colonial West and anti-colonial peripheries had a long history. In the late nineteenth century, burdened with debt to German banks, and with extensive, underdeveloped agricultural hinterlands, Balkan countries had feared *becoming* Africa in a world dominated by western empires. To their north,

James Mark and Paul Betts, *Introduction* In *Socialism Goes Global: The Soviet Union and Eastern Europe in the Age of Decolonization*. Edited by James Mark and Paul Betts, Oxford University Press. © Oxford University Press 2022.
DOI: 10.1093/oso/9780192848857.003.0001

Polish, Czech and Hungarian nationalist movements drew inspiration from African anti-imperial revolts or Native American resistance for their own independence struggles, whilst simultaneously dreaming about obtaining their own colonies to preserve nations that had no political home in Europe. After the First World War, as the Russian, Hohenzollern, Hapsburg and Ottoman Empires were swept away, Eastern Europe became the site of the first major decolonization of the twentieth century.[1] Whilst some new national elites fantasized about becoming part of an white imperial Europe, both the Soviet Union—proclaimed as the world's first anti-imperialist state—and the region's smaller nation states marked out a path for independence movements forming across the Afro-Asian world. With the rising threat of German and Italian imperialism in the 1930s, ever more political and cultural groups began to see the region as part of a wider anti-colonial world.

The experience of Nazi occupation during the Second World War, the Communist takeovers in its wake, and the acceleration of decolonization in Africa and Asia further deepened these relationships. Eastern Europe was a region of nations that had twice liberated themselves from empires. Tito himself traded on his past as an anti-fascist partisan who had stood up to the Wehrmacht as he crafted a message of common anti-imperialist solidarity and socialist development. Moreover, as a leader of a Communist non-aligned state that had broken free of Moscow's influence, he also became a fierce champion of small states who stood up to hegemons of every stripe. Bonded in a common anti-imperialism and desire to escape their own economic and cultural marginalization, the states of Eastern Europe and what later became known as the 'global South' found common cause in the struggle to forge a new world as western European Empires collapsed. Tito's 'safari diplomacy' may have been unusually energetic and elaborate, but similar links and initiatives multiplied. High-profile state visits proliferated, as Khrushchev, Brezhnev, Ceaușescu, Pieck, Honecker and other Eastern Bloc figures made high-profile trips to Africa, Asia, the Middle East and Latin America and hosted leaders from the developing world in their national capitals: Nyerere, Nkrumah, Ben Bella, Selassie and later Mandela were much feted visitors to Moscow and around the Eastern Bloc. Trade and arms deals were negotiated, development projects in technology, health, housing and military training were initiated, literary festivals and art shows were co-sponsored, and student exchanges and then labour mobility were institutionalized.

Yet there were always ambiguities and tensions at the heart of these new relationships. During what Tanzanian President Julius Nyerere once sardonically

---

[1] James Mark and Quinn Slobodian, 'Eastern Europe in the Global History of Decolonization', in Martin Thomas and Andrew S. Thompson (eds.), *The Oxford Handbook of the Ends of Empire* (Oxford: OUP, 2018), 352–3.

called a 'Second Scramble for Africa', were Soviets and Eastern Europeans really different from other white Europeans? To what extent was their commitment to an anti-colonial world also driven by the desire to obtain the privileges that other whites had long been afforded, or, at the very least, as a claim to equality as Europeans, and to overcome their peripheralization on their own continent? Tito adopted of the garb of nineteenth-century European hunter, dressed in a white explorer's suit, posing with the big game he had shot.[2] This emphasis on whiteness could demonstrate that the Non-Aligned Movement, which he led alongside Nehru and Nasser, embodied the idea of a newly equitable racial order. Yet he was also one of many Eastern European Communists pictured aping the styles of aristocratic European hunters: images which were seldom publicized for fear of political embarrassment back home. This colonial mimicry that fascinated some European Communists suggested that their anti-colonialism was also a diplomatic route to gain global status, an aspiration long frustrated by the dominance of Western European empires.

Questions over the nature of Eastern Europeans' ideological commitment only grew in the last decades of the Cold War. In 1980, on the occasion of Tito's funeral—attended by a galaxy of world leaders from Margaret Thatcher to Robert Mugabe to Indira Gandhi—the reach of the socialist world was unprecedented in its extent. It encompassed roughly one third of the global population and western politicians still took its challenge very seriously indeed.[3] Yet the world that Tito had helped to forge was also in crisis. Although economic relations were still growing—Yugoslav enterprises were amongst the biggest in Europe and were still expanding off the back of non-alignment across Africa, the Middle East and the Soviet Union—the values that underpinned them were rapidly shifting. The search for hard currency often replaced relationships formerly based on political solidarity. With the exception of Romania, whose President Nicolae Ceaușescu sought to prove his independence from Moscow by cultivating relationships with African states from the 1970s, socialist states became more reluctant to publicize imagery of their leaders connected to the global South. The experiences and expertise accumulated through an anti-colonial global project in some cases prepared the groundwork for a growing accommodation with a new world order based on financialized capitalist globalization.

---

[2] Radina Vučetić, 'Tito's Africa: Representation of Power during Tito's African Journeys', in Radina Vučetić and Paul Betts (eds.), *Tito in Africa. Picturing Solidarity* (Belgrade: Museum of Yugoslavia: 2017), 42.

[3] For contemporaries' concerns, see, e.g., Ramond L. Garthoff, *Détente and Confrontation: American-Soviet Relations from Nixon to Reagan* (Washington: Brookings Institution, 1985).

Departure Points

This is a collaboratively written book based on a four-year ten-person research project. Although there have been specific country studies and edited collections on this topic in the last few years, this monograph is among the first books to provide a broad history of the relationship between Eastern Europe and the extra-European world in the age of decolonization. It begins in the late nineteenth century, arguing that Communists' engagement with a world escaping empire was part of a longer-term history of the region's positioning between the colonial and anti-colonial worlds. At its core, however, is the encounter of the post-1945 period, when socialism's importance as a globalizing force accelerated and drew together what contemporaries called the 'Second' and 'Third Worlds'.

Many histories of contemporary globalization start in the early 1970s with the rise of a western-led deterritorialized finance capitalism: this western-centric history ignores the dramatic expansion of the socialist world following the end of European colonial empires. This work, by contrast, identifies new internationalizing impulses that emerged as the collapse of European empires accelerated in the postwar period, and the opportunities this offered non-western peripheries to remake the world. The socialist world was not simply a victim of these processes. Eastern European socialist states, undergoing their own form of decolonization with the end of Stalinism, drove new forms of economic, political and cultural interconnectedness that linked the region to the world's peripheries as much as it did to the West—in arenas ranging from economics to culture to public health. Whilst a belief in the power of modernization was common to both sides in the Cold War, the socialist idea and practice of development was fuelled by a vision of modernity distinct from that of its liberal rival, which socialist experts condemned as destructive, socially iniquitous and insensitive to local needs and traditions. This anti-imperialist globalization—in contrast to a western-centred capitalist form—was taken very seriously across the world as a viable model of internationalism until very late in the Cold War.

There have been numerous attempts in recent years to shift the focus of Cold War history away from superpower conflict, taking it beyond a bipolar account that relegates the rest of the world to the status of 'proxies' or 'peripheries'.[4] This brought Moscow and its historical relationship with the 'Third World' back into focus.[5] Some went further, arguing that too much emphasis was being placed on East–West conflict, and that the principal cleavage in the world of the second half

---

[4] For the best known text: Odd Arne Westad, *The Global Cold War: Third World Intervention and the Making of Our Time* (Cambridge: CUP, 2007).

[5] For an overview, see David Engerman, 'The Second World's Third World', *Kritika* 12/1 (2011), 183–211; Oscar Sanchez-Sibony, *Red Globalization: The Political Economy of the Soviet Cold War from Stalin to Khrushchev* (Cambridge: CUP, 2014).

of the twentieth century was between the colonial and anti-colonial worlds.[6] Yet these works mainly focused on the Soviet–Third World story, and until very recently, neglected the smaller Eastern European nations' global engagements.[7] After all, the socialist world was both expanding and fracturing at the same time. Given the Yugoslav–Soviet split, the Maoist Revolution and then the Sino–Soviet split, overly crude notions of an intractable two-camp model of world affairs are not very helpful. Even within the Eastern Bloc, countries competed for the hearts and minds of newly decolonized Africans and Asians, and this book seeks to describe the often surprising effects of this sense of competition in the realms of politics, economics, health, education and culture. Underneath claims to 'international solidarity' that bound often disparate worlds lay complex processes of cultural engagement. Actors on various sides rethought questions of race, tradition, development, national culture and civilization as they sought to make sense of their new roles. Yet even as anti-colonialism and socialism opened up the possibility of building a new world after empire, the question remained of whether Eastern Europeans were capable of overcoming traditions of European colonialism in their politics and culture, transcending the political meanings of their white skin, or weaning themselves away from the West.

A Forgotten History

The question as to whether the development of Eastern Europe should be understood as part of a history of global empires and their disintegration has been long debated. With the rise of fascism in the 1930s, many anti-colonial leaders and intellectuals—from Nehru to W.E.B. Du Bois to Aimé Césaire—encouraged the Soviets and Eastern Europeans to view their experiences of both liberation from and violence at the hands of empires as part of a shared historical experience that connected the 'other Europe' to non-European worlds. Likewise, Communist popular histories written for Eastern European publics from the 1950s urged citizens to recognize connections between the postwar struggle in Africa and Asia against collapsing Western European empires, and their own earlier liberation

---

[6] Matthew Connelly, 'Rethinking the Cold War and Decolonization: The Grand Strategy of the Algerian War for Independence', *International Journal of Middle East Studies*, 33/2 (2001), 221–45.

[7] For this shift, see e.g. Philip E. Muehlenbeck, *Czechoslovakia in Africa, 1945–1968* (Basingstoke, New York: Palgrave MacMillan, 2015); Philip E. Muehlenbeck and Natalia Telepneva (eds.), *Warsaw Pact Intervention in the Third World: Aid and Influence in the Cold War* (London: I.B. Tauris, 2019); James Mark, Artemy M. Kalinovsky and Steffi Marung (eds.), *Alternative Globalizations. Eastern Europe and the Postcolonial World* (Bloomington, IN: Indiana University Press, 2020); Łukasz Stanek, *Architecture in Global Socialism: Eastern Europe, West Africa, and the Middle East in the Cold War* (Princeton, NJ: Princeton University Press, 2020); Theodora Dragostinova, *The Cold War from the Margins. A Small Socialist State on the Global Cultural Scene* (Ithaca: Cornell University Press, 2021); Anna Calori et al. (eds.), *Between East and South: Spaces of Interaction in the Globalizing Economy of the Cold War* (Berlin: De Gruyter Oldenbourg, 2019).

from the Habsburg, German, Ottoman or Russian Empires.[8] And from the 1970s, 'world systems theory' situated Eastern Europe as a so-called semi-periphery in the global system, its history defined by waves of advancing towards, and distancing itself from, a western imperial core.[9]

The detachment of Eastern Europe from the global has a long history too: from the early Cold War, Western liberals and conservatives argued that the region had been captured by 'Oriental Bolshevism' and needed to be reclaimed for European civilization. With the lessening appeal of the anti-colonial project, and with the advent of European détente from the early 1960s, calls for the bloc countries to return to their 'European home' became ever more pronounced. And as the collapse of socialism in both Europe and Africa marked the end of the Cold War, the Iron Curtain moved, as UN Secretary General Boutros-Boutros Ghali observed, to the middle of the Mediterranean, dividing Europe from Africa.[10] In this new world, the very notion that Eastern European history could be understood through in-betweenness—caught between European colonialism and the appeal of anti-colonialism—lost all purchase. Ousted as the region had purportedly been from its real political home in democratic Europe and its economic base in Euro-Atlantic capitalism, the collapse of Communism became, in this account, the moment of real liberation from an oriental trap and despotic Soviet-imposed ideology. Historians of Eastern Europe have followed suit by presenting these nations' stories as a series of liberation struggles *from* regional empires or federations[11], or have fashioned its twentieth-century history as a warning about the evils of totalitarianism and genocide 'between empires' that only a turn to the liberal West had finally overcome.[12]

This is not to say that the idea of Eastern Europe as a colonized region disappeared altogether. A new right-wing provincial 'post-colonialism' manifested itself particularly powerfully in Poland and the Baltic states in the 1990s. Its intellectuals condemned the pre-1989 period as one of criminal Soviet occupation, and connected their experiences to longer-term histories of their nations' suppression

---

[8] James Mark and Péter Apor, 'Socialism Goes Global: Decolonization and the Making of a New Culture of Internationalism in Socialist Hungary 1956–1989', *Journal of Modern History*, 87 (2015), 866–7.

[9] World-systems theorists have been particularly interested in the 'catching up' role played by socialist states within the broader global economy: not only Immanuel Wallerstein, *The Capitalist World-Economy* (Cambridge: CUP, 1979), 284, but also the Eastern European thinkers who inspired him, e.g. Marian Małowist: an influence addressed in Adam F. Kola, 'A Prehistory of Postcolonialism in Socialist Poland' in Mark et al. (eds.), *Alternative Globalizations*, 278–9; Manuela Boatcă, 'Semiperipheries in the World-System. Reflecting Eastern European and Latin American Experiences', *Journal of World-Systems Research*, 2 (2006), 322; József Böröcz, 'Dual Dependency and Property Vacuum: Social Change on the State Socialist Semiperiphery', *Theory and Society*, 1 (1992), 77–104.

[10] Boutros Boutros-Ghali, 'The Marginalisation of Africa', in Nikolaos A. Stavrou (ed.), *Mediterranean Security at the Crossroads: A Reader* (Durham, NC: Duke University Press, 1999), 24–5.

[11] E.g. John Connelly, *From Peoples into Nations: A History of Eastern Europe* (Princeton: Princeton University Press, 2020).

[12] E.g. Timothy Snyder, *Bloodlands: Europe between Hitler and Stalin* (London: Vintage, 2015).

by European empires.[13] Communists were classified as collaborators or traitors, and their extra-European internationalism recast as a criminal activity. In post-Communist Bulgaria, for instance, former General Secretary Zhivkov, former Prime Minister Lukanov along with twenty Communist Party officials were accused in 1992 of economic sabotage, on the grounds that between 1986 and 1989 they had approved financial aid and loans to the Cuban, Nicaraguan and Laotian Communist parties. Unlike most post-colonial theorizing, this right-wing version of it showed no interest in thinking *across* anti-colonial experiences: thus it did not, for example, draw comparisons between the struggle of decolonizing Africa and their own against Soviet socialism, as a previous generation of both left and rightist oppositionists had done. Rather, it appropriated post-colonial language to assert victimhood as white European nations captured by an 'Oriental' dictatorship. Such Eurocentric ways of remembering were reinforced in the institutions that post-Communist elites sought to join. The European Union, which turned to history and memory to cement its legitimacy after the Cold War, incorporated Eastern European experiences into a tale of European integration produced through a continental struggle against the horrors of fascism and Communism. Such accounts commonly sidelined any discussion of Europe's colonial past, and invoked Eastern Europe's absence of colonial experience overseas to justify this exclusion.[14] In doing so, they erased not only the East's rich history of international engagement, but also the ways in which a broader European imperialism shaped Eastern Europe's own development.

Eastern Europe has also been absent from histories of twentieth-century globalization. The term itself came to prominence in the early 1990s at a moment of post-Cold War capitalist triumphalism. Emerging intellectual disciplines were shaped by their birth at this conjuncture: the newly influential discipline of 'transitology' for instance assessed the success of states in Latin America, southern and eastern Europe and then Africa in entrenching the political structures and legal frameworks necessary to engineer 'transitions' and thus converge towards western democratic liberalism.[15] Such approaches erased the opposition between

---

[13] Violeta Kelertas (ed.), *Baltic Postcolonialism* (Amsterdam: Rodopi, 2006); Steven Tötösy De Zepetnek, 'Configurations of Postcoloniality and National Identity: Inbetween Peripherality and Narratives of Change', *The Comparatist*, 23 (May 1999), 89. Clare Cavanagh, 'Postcolonial Poland', *Common Knowledge*, 10/2 (Winter 2004), 84–92; David Chioni Moore, 'Is the Post- in Postcolonial the Post- in Post-Soviet? Toward a Global Postcolonial Critique', *PMLA*, 116/1 (2001), 118–24. Diana T. Kudaibergenova, 'The Use and Abuse of Postcolonial Discourses in Post-independent Kazakhstan', *Europe-Asia Studies*, 68/5 (2016), 917–35.

[14] On these exclusions, see Aline Sierp, 'EU Memory Politics and Europe's Forgotten Colonial Past', *Interventions*, 22/6 (2020), 686–702; Fatima El-Tayeb, *European Others: Queering Ethnicity in Postnational Europe* (Minneapolis: University of Minnesota Press, 2011); Peo Hansen, 'European Integration, European Identity and the Colonial Connection', *European Journal of Social Theory*, 5/4 (2002) 483–98.

[15] See, e.g., Guillermo O'Donnell and Philippe Schmitter (eds.), *Transitions from Authoritarianism: Comparative Perspectives* (Baltimore: The Johns Hopkins University Press, 1986); Juan Linz and Alfred Stepan, *Democratic Transitions and Consolidation: Eastern Europe, Southern Europe and Latin America*

colonialism and anti-colonialism that had defined a history of non-western global interconnections, and instead placed dictatorship, planning and illiberalism on one side, and western liberal multi-party democracy, markets and civil society on the other, in order to assess the success of countries emerging from authoritarian rule.

This historical revision had profound effects. An interest in connections between Eastern European, Latin American and African countries which had often turned to socialist or non-capitalist modernization during postwar decolonization was now replaced by a flattened, unidirectional 'from the west to the rest' model. This served to suppress the complex, contested nature and multiple forms of *mondialization*—a term first coined to describe the multifarious forms of world-making, of which globalization was only one.[16] When forms of socialist global integration were recognized, these were seen as blind alleys, oddities outstripped by history, or connections which had no legacies or relevance to the present. More commonly, the Communist world was pictured as bordered by walls and barbed wire—barriers that had only fallen away with the collapse of Communist regimes and the spread of liberal capitalism.

A revival of the idea that Eastern Europe was a space 'in-between' re-emerged as the inevitability of the westernization of the region was increasingly placed in doubt. This turn was first discernible from the early 2000s under the first presidency of Vladimir Putin. His government rejected Gorbachev's idea of Russia as an ordinary nation state in a 'common European home' in favour of reclaiming a great power status, pursuing a foreign policy in explicitly anti-western alliances and becoming a global player once again in Asia and Africa. It was only from the late 2000s that the criticism of the region's convergence with a western liberalism, which had hitherto been only a minority intellectual pursuit, went mainstream in those Eastern European states that had joined the European Union (or were still hoping to do so). The financial crisis of 2008 put western developmental models into question, and the achievement of long sought after EU membership enabled regional elites to develop new political languages and to seek new relationships beyond Europe, free from the pressures to conform to the accession process. The Right's provincial post-colonialism soon became part of everyday political rhetoric: after 1989, they claimed, their cosmopolitan 'comprador' elites had engaged

(Baltimore: Johns Hopkins University Press, 1996); Kathryn Stoner and Michael McFaul (eds.), *Transitions to Democracy: A Comparative Perspective* (Baltimore: Johns Hopkins University Press, 2013).

[16] For a discussion, see Stuart Elden, 'Mondialisation before Globalization. Lefebvre and Axelos', in Kanishka Goonewardena, Stefan Kipfer, Richard Milgrom and Christian Schmid (eds.), *Space, Difference, Everyday Life: Reading Henri Lefebvre* (Abingdon: Routledge, 2008), 80–93; Łukasz Stanek, 'Socialist Worldmaking: Architecture and Global Urbanization in the Cold War', in Mark et al. (eds.), *Alternative Globalizations*, 166–86. For 'globalization' as a form of western imperialism: Andreas Eckert and Shalini Randeira, *Vom Imperialismus zum Empire. Nicht-westliche Perspektiven auf Globalisierung* (Frankfurt: Suhrkamp, 2009).

in a deferential mimicry of western liberalism. Much like Eastern Europe's Communist elites' subservience to Moscow before them, they had effectively enabled a new political and cultural colonization of a region, which now needed to be defended from the grip of the West.[17] In so doing, they echoed Communists' earlier claim that the East represented the 'better Europe', free from guilt for the sins of the continent's colonialism. Yet such arguments were no longer deployed in the name of a more equitable and less racist world order, but rather were directed against Western Europe's liberalism, unbridled individualism, multiculturalism and 'gender ideology'—in the name of preserving the imperilled cultural nation, a generous welfare state and white Christian civilization. This position gained significant traction during the migration of people from the Middle East and Africa to Europe in 2015, when nativist leaders claimed that the region had no responsibility to take in desperate refugees: they maintained that their Eastern European countries had never had empires and hence, unlike the west of the continent, had no bad conscience to assuage by the performance of humanitarian gestures.

It also led elites across the region to return to the embrace of older partners—from China to Africa—to offset their economic and cultural dependency on the West. In 2010, the populist right-wing FIDESZ government in Hungary announced a 'keleti nyitás', or 'opening to the East': the authoritarian capitalist models of Singapore, China and Central Asia replaced a supposedly sclerotic European Union as political and economic models. Whilst invoking the defence of a white Christian Europe, Hungarian Prime Minister Viktor Orbán also sought to discover the country's Turkic roots, and argued that power needed to be centralized in Hungary—a natural state of affairs, he contended, for a 'half-Asian nation'.[18] An impetus to recover older relationships came from East Asia too. Under President Xi Jinping, the Chinese government divided the continent into so-called 'Europe 1', generally consisting of the more economically developed western parts of the European Union, and 'Europe 2'—the target of Beijing's '16+1 initiative' which sought to deepen investment, trade, cultural and educational links with more historically and culturally familiar former Communist European countries.[19]

[17] Ivan Krastev and Stephen Holmes, *The Light that Failed: A Reckoning* (UK: Allen Lane, 2019); James Mark, Bogdan C. Iacob, Tobias Rupprecht and Ljubica Spaskovska, *1989: A Global History of Eastern Europe* (Cambridge: CUP, 2019), chapter 6.

[18] Chris Moreh, 'The Asianization of National Fantasies in Hungary: A Critical Analysis of Political Discourse', *International Journal of Cultural Studies*, 19/3 (2016), 346–8.

[19] Susan Bayly coined the term 'socialist ecumene' to describe the endurance of socialist-era values in forms of trade and assistance between parts of the world in a similar peripheral position in the neoliberal world order. Susan Bayly, 'Vietnamese Narratives of Tradition, Exchange and Friendship in the Worlds of the Global Socialist Ecumene', in Harry West and Parvathi Raman (eds.), *Enduring Socialism. Explorations of Revolution and Transformation, Restoration and Continuation* (Oxford: Berghahn, 2008), 125–47.

On the political Left, the question of whether westernization would really address questions of the region's economic peripherality returned: would EU and NATO membership turn Eastern European countries into 'insignificant colonies on the periphery of the Euro-Atlantic Empire'?[20] The answer was ambiguous inbetweenness; as Piro Rexhepi put it: 'the (post)socialist world cannot resolve its (geo)political position: [whether to remain] in a pact with, and in the proximity of, Euro-American coloniality, or be its defying periphery.'[21] This growing ambivalence towards the West was reflected in public opinion too. In a survey conducted in 2019, people in the Czech Republic, Poland, Slovakia and Hungary were asked the question 'would you like your country to be a part of the West, a part of the East, or somewhere in-between?' In each case, around a half of respondents declared 'somewhere in-between'. Those saying that their homeland should be 'part of the West' ranged from a high of 45% in Hungary to a low of 23% in Slovakia.[22]

Escaping Peripherality: Eastern Europe as a Region between the Colonial and the Anti-colonial

Thus the story we tell here of Communist internationalism no longer appears as an excavation of a lost world or as an 'oriental aberration', but rather one episode in a longer-term history of a region marked by the question, posed since the early nineteenth century, of how to escape political, cultural and economic marginalization in a western-dominated world system.[23] In other words, it was defined by

---

[20] On the region as 'doubly postcolonial'—the object of both Soviet imperialism and Western 'peripheralizing capitalism'—see Dorota Kołodziejczyk and Cristina Șandru, 'Introduction: On Colonialism, Communism and East-central Europe—Some Reflections', *Journal of Postcolonial Writing*, 48/2 (2012), 115. On peripheralization, see also Dušan I. Bjelić (ed.), *Balkan Transnationalism at the Time of Neoliberal Catastrophe* (Routledge, 2019); Dorothee Bohle, *Europas neue Peripherie. Polens Transformation und transnationale Integration* (Münster: Westfälisches Dampfboot, 2002); Vera Šćepanović and Dorothee Bohle, 'The Institutional Embeddedness of Transnational Corporations: Dependent Capitalism in Central and Eastern Europe', in Andreas Nölke and Christian May (eds.), *Handbook of the International Political Economy of the Corporation* (Northampton, MA: Edward Elgar Pub., 2018), 152–66.

[21] Marina Gržinić, Tjaša Kancler and Piro Rexhepi, 'Decolonial Encounters and the Geopolitics of Racial Capitalism', *Eastern European Journal of Feminist and Queer Studies* (2020) https://feminist.krytyka.com/en/articles/decolonial-encounters-and-geopolitics-racial-capitalism (last accessed 1 September 2021).

[22] Timothy Garton Ash, 'Thirty Years On: Time for a New Liberation?', in his *The Magic Lantern: The Revolution of '89 Witnessed in Warsaw, Budapest, Berlin and Prague* (London: Atlantic, 2019), 184.

[23] On Eastern Europe as semi-periphery, Manuela Boatcă, 'Semi-peripheries in the World-System: Reflecting Eastern European and Latin American Experiences', *Journal of World-Systems Research*, 12/2 (2006), 321–46; Marta Grzechnik, 'The Missing Second World: On Poland And Postcolonial Studies', *Interventions. International Journal of Postcolonial Studies*, 21/7 (2019), 1002–3; Balázs Trencsényi et al., 'Introduction', in idem. (eds.), *A History of Modern Political Thought in East Central Europe. Volume I Negotiating Modernity in the 'Long Nineteenth Century'* (Oxford: OUP, 2018), especially 3–5; Katherine Lebow, Małgorzata Mazurek and Joanna Wawrzyniak, 'Making Modern Social

its status inbetween the colonial and anti-colonial worlds: associating with the core and often seeking to ape its values and achievements, whilst also fearing colonization and identifying with others who resisted it and seeking to provide its own more vital alternative.[24] In the late nineteenth century, both Russian and Habsburg elites aped the practices of western imperialism in their contiguous empires whilst claiming to be above it: Moscow professed the spiritual superiority of its civilization, whilst Vienna declared that its forms of governing, harmonious, and lacking the rapacity and violence of a now degraded western European imperial project, explained their lack of extra-European territories.[25] By the early twentieth century, some emerging Eastern European nationalisms fantasized about colonies, whilst simultaneously identifying with anti-colonial resistance of the Americas and Africa, as they sought to throw off their own imperial subjugation and to prove their worth as Europeans and fitness as nation states.[26] The desire for leadership of a global anti-colonial project which spread from Moscow to the smaller countries of Eastern Europe after the Second World War only underlined the validity of such questions. Was internationalist solidarity in an age of global imperial disintegration also a chance to gain a status previously denied as Europeans: to catch up, whilst also redeeming the continent's fallen imperial project? The history we tell here charts this complex navigation, exploring how a range of actors from within and without—from Eastern European nationalists to Cominternians, anti-colonial activists, Nazi occupiers, United Nations' developmentalists, African and Asian students, and labour migrants—made sense of a region caught between the colonial and anti-colonial worlds.

Our story begins with imperial disintegration in Eastern Europe itself. In the chapter *Origins*, we consider how the countries that were established from the wreckage of the German, Habsburg, Ottoman and Russian Empires attempted to navigate a world dominated by powerful yet weakening Western European empires. The liberation of nations from empire appeared to mark a pathway

---

Science: The Global Imagination in East Central and Southeastern Europe after Versailles', *Contemporary European History* (2019), 3–4.

[24] On the relationship of the region to European colonialism, see e.g. Madina Tlostanova, 'Postsocialist ≠ Postcolonial? On post-Soviet Imaginary and Global Coloniality', *Journal of Postcolonial Writing*, 48/2 (2012), 130–42; she puts it thus: 'The subaltern empire, even when claiming a global spiritual and transcendental superiority, has always been looking for approval/envy and love/hatred from the west, never questioning the main frame of western modernity, only changing the superfluous details' (136–7); also her 'The South of the Poor North: Caucasus Subjectivity and the Complex of Secondary "Australism"', *The Global South*, 5/1 (2011), 71; Sharad Chari and Katherine Verdery, 'Thinking between the Posts: Postcolonialism, Postsocialism, and Ethnography after the Cold War', *Comparative Studies in Society and History*, 51/1 (2009), 6–34; Filip Herza, 'Colonial Exceptionalism: Post-colonial Scholarship and Race in Czech and Slovak Historiography', *Slovenský národopis*, 68/2 (2020), 175–87.

[25] E.g. Ulrich E. Bach, *Tropics of Vienna: Austrian Colonial Utopias, 1870–1900* (New York: Berghahn, 2016), 2.

[26] E.g. Lenny A. Ureña Valerio, *Colonial Fantasies, Imperial Realities: Race Science and the Making of Polishness on the Fringes of the German Empire, 1840–1920* (Athens: Ohio University Press, 2019); Grzechnik, 'Missing Second World', 1009.

for many future movements: the term *counter-colonization*, the antecedent of *decolonization*, was coined in the early 1930s to connect what had happened in Eastern Europe with that which seemed likely to transpire in Africa and Asia. The Soviet Union, with the founding of the Comintern, became the first world power to provide international support for anti-colonial struggles; by the 1930s, however, it had retreated, and in the wake of the Second World War returned to great power imperialism. The smaller Eastern European states had to survive in an international environment in which their own sovereignty was still vulnerable. Some elites sought to work through a broader white imperial world to fortify their fragile new polities and, in a few cases such as Czechoslovakia and Poland, fantasized about gaining overseas possessions themselves and becoming 'superior colonizers', enlightened by their own experience of suppression under imperial rule in Europe. For others, long before the Communist takeovers, the region's marginality would only be overcome by developing non-western or anti-imperial relationships through a vast array of expanding internationalisms. With the collapse of the liberal international order in the mid-1930s, the question of how to address the threat of recolonization became central in the region; some, especially on the left, sought out a global solidarity; others spied an opportunity to realize their national projects under the protection of Nazi Germany and Mussolini's Italy.

It was only after the Second World War that we can really talk of a much more extensive and cohesive *Eastern European* engagement with a wider world fighting against empires. The Nazi recolonization of large parts of the region during the Second World War had demonstrated that sovereignty for countries east of the Elbe was fragile and reversible. With the support of Moscow in many—but not all—countries, the reach of Communism now spread from Siberia to Berlin. Rejecting the idea that the presence of Red Army troops was evidence of a new colonization, the elites in newly Communist countries rather presented themselves as part of a global progressive anti-colonial space, characterized, in different iterations, as the 'socialist camp', or 'non-aligned world'.[27] Securing this world against western imperialism was central: *Rights* and *Culture* explore how Eastern Europeans hoped that their assistance to fragile decolonized nations in Africa and Asia would be reciprocated in support for the defence of their own sovereignty—Poland's western borders, for instance, were not recognized by many western states until 1970. Such links would be important in challenging the exclusion of these nations from the international system too: both the GDR, which was not recognized by the UN until 1973, and Hungary, which was excluded from the

---

[27] Socialist revolutions often occurred in what world-system theorists called 'semi-peripheral' or 'peripheral' locations as they offered strong state-led developmental pathways that promised catch-up with, or even challenge to, the dominant capitalist core. Manfred Kossok, 'Das 20. Jahrhundert—eine Epoche der peripheren Revolution?', in Katharina Middell and Matthias Middell (eds.), *Manfred Kossok, Ausgewählte Schriften, Bd. 3: Zwischen Reform und Revolution. Übergänge von der Universal- zur Globalgeschichte* (Leipzig: Leipziger Universitätsverlag, 2000), 289–96.

international community following the suppression of the 1956 revolt, fostered such overseas links with a view to obtaining international recognition.[28] *War and Peace* addresses how the memory of struggle of the Soviet Red Army, the Yugoslav partisans or even the nationalist Polish Home Army during the Second World War was integrated into a professed commitment to defend a hard-won anti-fascist and anti-imperialist world. In awe of the Soviet contribution to the allied victory, officers from armed liberation movements across Africa went to the Soviet Union and Czechoslovakia to train under those 'heroes' who had defeated fascism. Humanitarian missions featured too. Yugoslavia sent psychiatrists who specialized in war trauma to Algeria to help in the rebuilding of society after the 'liberation war'. Socialist states' militaries took part in peace missions following the conflict in Vietnam, and Eastern Europe gave refuge to displaced North Korean children during the Korean War.[29]

A rapidly changing world opened out possibilities for the region to advance hitherto frustrated attempts to develop global economic and cultural links. As *Development* argues, this episode was part of a longer-term history of endeavours to escape the status of continental hinterland: at moments of severe economic crisis the continent's East had its very Europeanness questioned, imagined as part of an agricultural world that extended into Asia or Africa. Much of the region had been excluded from extra-European opportunities for trade, settlement and extraction that had long been available to the imperial Western European powers: in the interwar period, new Polish, Czechoslovak and Hungarian states had either sought colonies or to work through western imperial systems—but with limited success. The Soviets feared isolation from the global economy, but then purposefully de-internationalized, to build at home in response to the rise of fascism in the 1930s. After the Second World War, however, with their rise to superpower status, they sought to export centralized planning, industrialization and agrarian expertise globally—first to China after 1949, then to South Asia and Africa. For many smaller Eastern European Communist states, lacking as they did the Soviet Union's vast resources, it was also a way to escape an economic dependence on Moscow, and isolation rendered still more deleterious by their exclusion from the nascent European Community.

In this sense, a collapsing western-dominated imperial system provided the smaller Eastern European Communist states with fresh opportunities to internationalize in ways that had not been available to a previous generation of

---

[28] On escaping isolation, see Paul Betts, James Mark, Kim Christiaens and Idesbald Goddeeris, 'Race, Socialism and Solidarity: Anti-Apartheid in Eastern Europe', in Robert Skinner and Anna Konieczna (eds.), *A Global History of Anti-apartheid: 'Forward to Freedom' in South Africa* (Basingstoke: Palgrave, 2019), 155–62.

[29] Péter Apor, 'The School. Schools as Liminal Spaces: Integrating North Korean Children Within Socialist Eastern Europe, 1951-1959', in Kristin Roth-Ey (ed.), *Second-Third World Spaces in the Cold War: Global Socialism and the Gritty Politics of the Particular* (London: Bloomsbury, 2022).

regional elites—and which did not require the support or approval of Western Europeans. The world seemed to be 'going their way'.[30] The 1949 Chinese Revolution and the 1959 Cuban Revolution were hailed as dramatic indications that the dynamics of history were on the side of Communism—or at least non-capitalist development. By 1960 'world communism' could count on 830 million additional members since the war, including around 260 million citizens from the Soviet Union and Eastern Europe.[31] Decolonization in the late 1950s and 1960s in Africa and Asia promised a red 'wind of change', and the Communist world shifted its attention southwards to take advantage of a more ideologically sympathetic world. Eastern European states could begin to imagine a new global geography—of a common 'anti-colonial world' or 'socialist camp', connected by a Marxist conception of time, expansion and development. As the celebrations of the fiftieth anniversary of the Russian Revolution neared, commemorations across the bloc recounted a story that connected the establishment of Communism in Europe to the achievements of decolonized states across the world: what had been won in the former Russian Empire after the First World War, and in Eastern Europe after the Second, was now finding new homes across the globe, imparting life to a process that had now led to the end of empires and to independent states across Asia and Africa.[32] In this sense, both decolonization and the expansion of the Communist world in the 1950s were important launching pads for the region's globalization.[33]

Soviet and Eastern European planning became for a few decades one of the main globalizing forces, proving attractive to decolonizing states in the global South looking to build their own economic sovereignty.[34] After all, one third of all projects in China's first five-year-plan were financed and implemented by bloc states. Tens of thousands of advisors and technicians from the socialist world flocked to all parts of the country.[35] Large parts of the region were still heavily

---

[30] Christopher M. Andrew, *The World Was Going Our Way: The KGB and the Battle for the Third World* (New York: Basic Books, 2005).

[31] Zbigniew Brzezinski, 'Introduction', in idem (ed.), *Africa and the Communist World* (London: OUP, 1964), 5.

[32] The October Revolution figured prominently as a watershed in the organization of global history accounts by both Soviet and African writers. J.B. Marks, 'October, Africa and National Liberation', *African Communist*, 31 (1967), 15–37; and later, A. A Gromyko and N. D. Kosukhin, *The October Revolution and Africa* (Moscow: Progress Publishers, 1983).

[33] See also Johanna Bockman, 'Socialist Globalization against Capitalist Neocolonialism: The Economic Ideas behind the New International Economic Order', *Humanity*, 6/1 (2015), 109–28; James Mark and Tobias Rupprecht, 'The Socialist World in Global History: From Absentee to Victim to Co-Producer', in Matthias Middell (ed.), *The Practice of Global History: European Perspectives* (London; New York, NY: Bloomsbury Academic, 2019), 81–114.

[34] Sanchez-Sibony, *Red Globalization*, chapter 5; Massimiliano Trentin, 'Modernization as State Building: The Two Germanies in Syria, 1963–1972', *Diplomatic History*, 33/3 (2009), 487–505. Alessandro Iandolo, 'The Rise and Fall of the "Soviet Model of Development" in West Africa, 1957–6', *Cold War History*, 12/4 (2012), 683–704.

[35] Austin Jersild, *The Sino-Soviet Alliance. An International History* (Chapel Hill: University of North Carolina Press, 2014), especially Introduction and chapter 2; Thomas Bernstein and Hua-Yu Li

agrarian, and agricultural development, rural health and village and folk culture made for meaningful connections and exchange across these worlds. From 1964, medical education in Cuba was based on a Czechoslovak model. Market socialism developed in Hungary, Poland and Yugoslavia sparked new interest in East Asia and Africa in the 1970s. This expertise extended to building the authoritarian surveillance states serving to enable such rapid transformations: China in the 1950s was influenced by Soviet models ranging from the army to the party, and from cultural institutions to labour camps. The KGB and Stasi in particular helped develop secret police forces and surveillance for states across Africa and the Middle East.[36]

As *Health* and *Development* explore, this response was possible in part because the region had faced questions of state-building and development after the First World War that prefigured many of the challenges faced by new states in the African and Asian world after 1945.[37] Smaller Eastern European states had been laboratories for improvement and intervention by western powers: an experience of compromised sovereignty which had nevertheless also helped to further enhance already substantial local traditions of developmental expertise. A range of experts in Eastern Europe—from economists to social scientists to epidemiologists to archaeologists—who had served national projects in the interwar, later turned their attention to the extra-European world.[38] Such specialists promoted their knowledge as grounded in a deep experience of the challenges of nation-building under conditions of external surveillance and invasion, and in some cases played leading roles within those international organizations whose influence massively expanded with the arrival of large numbers of newly decolonized nation states from the late 1950s. *Health* explores how expertise in disease eradication and basic health services that had been developed in interwar Eastern Europe—often with the assistance of the League of Nations—became part of the basis for new socialist health interventions globally at the World Health Organization (WHO). *Development* relates how economists who had been involved in combating rural poverty in Eastern Europe in the interwar period played important roles—alongside Latin American dependency theorists—in UN economic development programmes.

(eds.), *China Learns From the Soviet Union, 1949–Present* (Cambridge, MA: Harvard UP, 2011); Lorenz Lüthi, *The Sino-Soviet Split. Cold War in the Communist World* (Princeton: Princeton UP, 2008), 19–87; Odd Arne Westad (ed.), *Brothers in Arms. The Rise and Fall of the Sino-Soviet Alliance* (Stanford: Stanford UP, 1998).

[36] See for example, Joseph Sassoon, 'The East German Ministry for State Security and Iraq, 1968–1989', *Journal of Cold War Studies*, 16/1 (2014), 4–23.

[37] Moritz Bonn, 'The Age of Counter-Colonisation', *International Affairs*, 13/6 (1934), 846. See also Joseph Love, *Crafting the Third World: Theorizing Underdevelopment in Romania and Brazil* (Stanford, CA: Stanford University Press, 1996), especially Introduction.

[38] Małgorzata Mazurek, 'Polish Economists in Nehru's India: Making Science for the Third World in an Era of De-Stalinization and Decolonization', *Slavic Review*, 77/3 (2018), 588–610.

Socialism seemed for a time to offer a different pathway to modernization.[39] The bloc understood itself as the better Europe which had never held colonies, and was now the champion of a more humane socialist modernity, which was thus capable of an authentic solidarity.[40] As *Culture* explores, the appeal of their modernization paradigms lay in their combination of economic betterment with a respect for the recovery of national traditions and histories—as well as the claim to be able to integrate minority cultures and religious plurality, drawing on a tradition going back to Lenin's support for indigenization within the Soviet Union in the 1920s. For the Soviets, the economic and cultural advancement of their own internal 'Third World'—namely Central Asia and the Caucasus—was used to sell their project as an equitable union of nations rather than as the reproduction of Russian imperial rule at the periphery.[41] Even the ancient past became a vibrant site of identity-formation in the wake of decolonization.[42] In sub-Saharan Africa, for instance, Eastern European archaeologists, anthropologists and art historians promoted a new socialist humanity rooted in linking ancient African traditions with a non-capitalist post-colonial African present. Ideas of 'socialist antiquity' often clashed with both UNESCO-style ideals of universal civilization as well as ongoing African conceptions of distinctly new national heritages. As *Rights* discusses, the representatives of decolonized states formed new coalitions that often included smaller Eastern European countries, fighting for the right to self-determination and against racial and religious discrimination in the 1960s, and then for women's rights in the 1970s.

Whilst Eastern Europeans were asserting their anti-colonial identity on the international stage, the question of whether the bloc was itself a colonial formation of only nominally independent nations under the thumb of Moscow was frequently employed to undermine Communist claims to represent a truly anti-imperialist world order. Yet how far did the power of Moscow shape this history of encounter? The postwar formation of a Communist political and economic bloc in the region ensured a certain commonality of response. Although so-called 'satellite states' were often coordinated within Comecon and the Warsaw Pact, this should not be overstated.[43] The smaller states of Eastern Europe were in fact

---

[39] For historical analyses of the differing offers of modernization, see e.g. Hubertus Büschel, *Hilfe zur Selbsthilfe. Deutsche Entwicklungsarbeit in Afrika 1960–1975* (Frankfurt: Campus, 2014); Antonio Giustozzi and Artemy M. Kalinovsky, *Missionaries of Modernity: Advisory Missions and the Struggle for Hegemony in Afghanistan and Beyond* (London: Hurst, 2016).

[40] Tlostanova, 'Postsocialist ≠ Postcolonial?', 130–42.

[41] Artemy M. Kalinovsky, 'Writing the Soviet South into the History of the Cold War and Decolonization', in Mark et al. (eds.), *Alternative Globalizations*, 189–208.

[42] Paul Betts, 'The Warden of World Heritage: UNESCO and the Rescue of the Nubian Monuments', *Past and Present*, 226 (2015), 100–25; Dragostinova, *The Cold War from the Margins*, chapter 5.

[43] On the value of exploring difference, see Theodora Dragostinova and Malgorzata Fidelis, 'Introduction', *Slavic Review*, 77/3 (2018), 577–87.

often at the vanguard of engagement, having had much more globalized interwar cultures of expertise, more developed overseas markets and more internationalized business elites to support them, and a longer-term experience of engagement with international organizations. Moreover, many had a subsisting urban cultural cosmopolitanism which was either absent or weakly developed in the Soviet Union, which in the postwar still bore the legacies of Stalin's socialism-in-one-country policies of the 1930s.[44] Soviet experts regarding the non-European world had been widely purged in the late 1930s, and their traditions of expertise took longer to recover.[45] Certainly, Khrushchev's rejection of an earlier Stalinist-era Eurocentrism and his 'turn to the South' in the mid-1950s enhanced the bloc's realignment with the decolonizing world—but this was a moment of significant consolidation rather than a point of departure. In this sense, similarities in out-reach were rooted as much in the broader regional experience of marginalization, isolation and anti-colonialism, now channeled in various different ways through national Communist parties, as in the dominance of Moscow. Moreover, varieties of engagement also reflected longer-term differences in relationships with European colonialism that divided the region internally. In south-eastern Europe, for instance, where there had been no movements for colonial expansionism, and wider anti-colonial solidarities prior to the Communist period, there was often a quicker recognition of a common anti-colonialism, a swifter rejection of Moscow's 'imperialism' and a longer-term commitment to the global South.[46] Yugoslavia—following the Tito–Stalin split in 1948—used its position in the Non-Aligned Movement to build up its own prestige as an independently minded socialist state. Tito engaged at Bandung, and the Soviets followed. From the 1970s, Ceaușescu's Romania would also use African connections to assert greater independence within the bloc, and its commitments continued through the 1980s as those of the other states waned.

The region's globalization was not one familiar to western eyes; mobility was limited, multilateral cooperation often eschewed, and links between national revolutionary projects were the key drivers. Thus this story is primarily a history of nation states that resisted regionalism in their attempts to cope with the pres-sures of a globally integrating world in an era of imperial disintegration. Even at the international level—to the frustration of many anti-colonial figures—Eastern European states often refused to act together, even where it might have provided greater ideological clout. Raúl Prebisch, the first head of UNCTAD at the United

---

[44] On Soviets learning from central Europeans, see e.g. Jersild, *Sino-Soviet Alliance*, chapter 2.

[45] Steffi Marung, 'The Provocation of Empirical Evidence: Soviet African Studies Between Enthusiasm and Discomfort', *African Identities*, 16/2 (2018), 176–90.

[46] On south-eastern Europe as a liminal Europe where anti-colonialism thus had a special appeal, see Bogdan C. Iacob, 'Southeast by Global South: The Balkans, UNESCO, and the Cold War', in Mark et al. (eds.), *Alternative Globalizations*, 251–70.

Nations, often complained about 'eastern European bilateralism' as he tried to organize peripheral areas regionally to take on the might of a western-dominated world economy.[47] Whilst there were some examples of trans-Eastern European cooperation in the South—especially after the expansion of Comecon in the 1970s—this encounter was for the most part a series of bilateral national exchanges. Yet this failure to coordinate in many cases drove the intensity of exchange, fuelled by competition between Eastern European states for influence and prestige on one side, and the appeal of nationalizing autarkic projects as models for post-colonial development to the sensibilities of the first post-independence leaderships in Africa on the other. Moreover, by the 1970s, the Soviets no longer wished to take the lead: seeking to extract themselves from the role of supplier of raw materials and energy, which continued to develop the peripheries of the bloc to the detriment of the centre, they encouraged Eastern European states to develop freer relationships with the South in order to reduce this dependency.[48]

Histories of this encounter are often written as an export story: this is due not only to the richness of Eastern European archives, but also to the divisions between area studies scholarship, the national and regional framing of histories of socialism, and the persisting Eurocentrism of much of the region's history. Whilst centred in the Eastern European archive, this work also draws in voices from the South through the writings of its leaders and intellectuals, archival work on specific encounters, notably in South Africa and Ghana, and the archives of international organizations (League of Nations, United Nations, UNCTAD, UNESCO and so on). We explore how some Eastern European countries' attempts to fashion themselves as 'more developed developing countries' were received in the South, and how they had to battle with other socialist and anti-colonial visions for the world after empire. *Health* addresses how the bloc competed with seemingly more committed forms of Chinese and Cuban rural medicine. *Race* addresses the challenge of racial politics to the agendas of the Eastern Bloc. Despite the abandonment of Stalinist-era conceptions that had linked race to backwardness, Eastern European countries were initially reluctant to confront the issue. They often did so only through pressure from the outside, most notably after Bandung when it became increasingly clear that, in order to be an important player in the global South, a commitment to a global racial equality was a prerequisite. Nevertheless, the philosophy of *négritude* remained a perennial challenge for European Communists eager to emphasize class over race.

---

[47] Raúl Prebisch, 'Statement at Informal Meeting of the Second Committee' (1963) Report. Myrdal Papers—General Files—UNCTAD 1963–4, GF 93 95 (UN archive, Geneva).
[48] James Mark and Iakov Feygin, 'The Soviet Union, Eastern Europe, and Alternative Visions of a Global Economy 1950s–1980s', in Mark et al. (eds.), *Alternative Globalizations*, 44.

Other chapters address how the region's engagement was part of complex circulations across a socialist world. *Mobility* for example explores how Eastern Europe functioned as part of a system of labour exchange that linked the Far East and Africa. It is also important to stress that Eastern Europeans were transformed by the experience too. Histories of socialism remained very regionally or nationally bound immediately after the Cold War; thus the declining faith in European socialism of the late twentieth century has usually been written as a very Eurocentric history, stressing moments of crisis, such as Hungary in 1956, Prague in 1968 or Poland in the early 1980s. Here we seek to globalize this story, showing how transformations in beliefs about socialism were part of global flows that stretched between Africa, the Far and Middle Easts, Latin America and Eastern Europe. The internationalization that accompanied decolonization provided the region's elites with the links and intellectual tools through which they could make sense of the limitations of their own development in a global context. The failures of their own extra-European projects, and the growing knowledge of other more successful attempts at economic catch-up on the (semi-) periphery, meant that the extra-European world played an important role in shaping the transformation that grew out of the crisis of European state socialism in the late Cold War.

Challenges: Were Eastern Europeans Really Anti-colonial?

Across the Cold War, many from the global South questioned whether Eastern European socialists were genuinely committed to a new post-imperial world order. The region seemed to many still marked by an ambiguous in-betweenness: had Soviet elites really thrown off the imperial impulses from their Tsarist forebears? Was anti-colonialism still underpinned by fantasies of imperial power under the guise of anti-colonialism? *Race* explores how even without overseas empires, the region shared in many aspects of wider European colonial culture— evident in native shows of the late nineteenth century; or the fascination with taming the US frontier, or imperial adventure literature, which continued into the socialist period.[49] Eastern European skin colour would be a key point of contention: could these new relationships signal the beginnings of a new post-racial world order based on a common socialism, or were the racial hierarchies, and the privilege derived from a whiteness which took its power from a broader European

---

[49] On earlier colonial cultures, Irina Novikova, 'Imagining Africa and Blackness in the Russian Empire: From Extra-Textual Arapka and Distant Cannibals to Dahomey Amazon Shows—Live in Moscow and Riga', *Social Identities*, 19/5 (2013), 571–91. On their revival, see Eric Burton, Zoltán Ginelli, James Mark and Nemanja Radonjic, 'The Colonial in the Anti-Colonial: Travel Writing and the Global Imagination in Socialist Eastern Europe', in Kristin Roth-Ey (ed.), *Second-Third World Spaces in the Cold War: Global Socialism and the Gritty Politics of the Particular* (London: Bloomsbury, 2022).

colonialism, too entrenched to be meaningfully overcome?[50] *Development* and *Culture* explore whether, for example, economists, geographers, archaeologists could throw off the colonial roots of their disciplines, or whether museums distinguish themselves as sites of international solidarity with progressive and humanist displays that rejected European civilizational superiority. And was in fact their commitment to anti-colonialism equally driven by a desire for status, reach and mobility? Might therefore anti-coloniality equally be a route to becoming recognized as full Europeans, to escape a second-class status vis-à-vis the West, and to overcome its status as continental hinterland? And for all those who advocated solidarity, there were often those from within—from trade ministries to arms manufacturers—who criticized anti-colonialism as economically irrational and a threat to sovereignty.[51]

Outside Europe, the region's allies and opponents fought over the position of Eastern Europe in the world: was it an essentially anti-colonial region or a part of a wider white global North? Whilst centred in the eastern European archive, this volume also integrates the voices of the decolonizing world, and close attention is paid to the ambivalences inherent in the negotiation of these new relationships. Some feared the remnants of imperial behaviours: after the Red Army invasion and suppression of the Hungarian Uprising in 1956, Nehru commented that the actions of the Soviets in Budapest and the British and French at Suez shared a melancholy symmetry, revivals of 'old colonial methods, which we had thought, in our ignorance, belonged to a more unenlightened age'.[52] *Race* and *Rights* explore whether the Soviets and Eastern Europeans, even under Communism, had ever really freed themselves from the habits of western imperialism, or were capable, as Europeans, from expressing real solidarity in an economically and racially divided world. After the Sino–Soviet split in the late 1950s, Beijing's racialized propaganda claimed that the bloc was part of a broader white world that had no right to lead. Whilst Communists claimed themselves to be the 'white negroes' of Europe, African students in Eastern Europe challenged their hosts' reluctance to recognize the remnants of racism within their own societies.

---

[50] On this question, see e.g. Jelena Subotic and Srdjan Vucetic, 'Performing Solidarity: Whiteness and Status-Seeking In the Non-Aligned World', *Journal of International Relations and Development*, 22 (2019), 722–43; on non-colonial whiteness, see, Anikó Imre, 'Whiteness in Post-Socialist Eastern Europe: The Time of the Gypsies, the End of Race', in Alfred J. López (ed.), *Postcolonial Whiteness: A Critical Reader on Race and Empire* (Albany: SUNY Press, 2005), 79–102; on marginal Eastern European whiteness as contested or conditional, Dušan I. Bjelić, 'Introduction', in idem. (ed.), *Balkan Transnationalism at the Time of Neoliberal Catastrophe* (Abingdon: Routledge, 2018), 17; Catherine Baker, 'Postcoloniality Without Race? Racial Exceptionalism and Southeast European Cultural Studies', *Interventions*, 20/6 (2018), 772.

[51] Daniela Richterova, Mikuláš Pešta and Natalia Telepneva, 'Banking on Military Assistance: Czechoslovakia's Struggle for Influence and Profit in the Third World 1955–1968', *The International History Review*, 43/1 (2020), 90–108.

[52] Quoted in Nataša Mišković, 'Between Idealism and Pragmatism: Tito, Nehru and the Hungarian Crisis, 1956', in Nataša Mišković, Harald Fischer-Tiné and Nada Boškovska (eds.), *The Non-Aligned Movement and the Cold War: Delhi, Bandung, Belgrade* (Abingdon and New York: Routledge, 2014), 125.

Mobility addresses these challenges from within. While in non-state-socialist contexts, migrants are frequently considered in terms of individualism and self-realization, the socialist states privileged collective forms of mobility that were brokered by institutions and organizations. For states in the global South, these mobilities, born out of solidarity, enabled them to export unemployment, and gain skills to build capacity for their own revolutionary projects. Arrivals who experienced Eastern European socialism first-hand were well aware of the tensions between the promises and realities of the internationalist project. Students from the global South were long considered a threat too—variously for their heterodox political opinions, their preparedness to critique socialism, or as embodiments of an international mobility that could invoke disquiet amongst populations less free to travel. By the 1980s, the effects of solidarity were distanced from Eastern European societies: Cuban and Vietnamese labour migrants' presence was kept quiet at industrial locations distant from population centres; Mozambiquan children in the GDR were educated in separate segregated institutions.

Home Front addresses the unsettling effects of this internationalism. After 1989, as 'Third Worldism' rapidly withered, anti-colonial solidarity became characterized as cynical propaganda or a set of practices imposed from above that had elicited only grudging, ritualized responses from unimpressed populations.[53] Here we argue against this restrictive history. Most did not experience an anti-colonial world through physical encounter. Rather, it was mediated through many forms of socialist-era culture, ranging from travel writing to film to museum exhibits to folk and pop culture fascination with Third World revolutionary heroes. Such culture was certainly exploited to legitimize socialist regimes—particularly important in the wake of the disillusionment with Stalinism. However, its appeal went well beyond the machinations of the state, precisely because it drew on longer-term traditions of anti-colonial feeling that had extended far beyond any Communist movement. It was precisely for this reason that it could be politically disruptive: it provided exemplars and languages of critique that could be turned against domestic authoritarianism, the seeming abandonment of revolution by consumerist Eastern European regimes, or indeed against the 'imperialism' of the Soviet Union itself.[54]

Reperipheralization and the End of Anti-colonialism?

Over the course of the 1970s and 1980s, at varying speeds in different countries, socialist internationalism and a 'strategic in-betweenness' no longer seemed to

---

[53] For this argument, see Toni Weis, 'The Politics Machine: On the Concept of 'Solidarity' in East German Support for SWAPO', *Journal of Southern African Studies*, 37/2 (2011), 351–67.

[54] For subversive readings, see e.g. James Mark, Péter Apor, Radina Vučetić, and Piotr Osęka, '"We Are with You, Vietnam": Transnational Solidarities in Socialist Hungary, Poland and Yugoslavia', *Journal of Contemporary History*, 50/3 (2015), 439–64.

answer the problem of Eastern Europe's peripheralization—on the contrary, solidarity with this alternative anti-colonial global project appeared only to entrench it. The commitment to build a different world that had fascinated postwar elites was gradually replaced by an East–West reorientation, a slow cultural realignment towards a 'common European home' and white western civilization. From this perspective, the last decades of the Cold War in fact saw the de-globalization of the region and a retreat from the claims to leadership on the global stage.

The *Race, Rights, Culture* and *Development* chapters all chart the nature of this reorientation and retreat that occurred long before the collapse of European Communist states in 1989–91. *Development* explores the turn away from the economics of North–South trade and developmental solidarity by the mid-1970s; only Romania and Yugoslavia supported the claims for global economic justice put forward in the New International Economic Order (NIEO). Its proponents began referring to Eastern Europe as part of the 'global North', criticizing the seeming preference for western integration over anti-colonial solidarity, and pointing out the unsettling similarities in exploitative programmes of resource extraction that now came from both their capitalist *and* their Communist partners in Europe. Eastern European technocrats, in parallel, started more commonly to refer to their relationship with the 'Third World'—a term always used with scare quotes whose invocation nevertheless denoted the distance they were increasingly placing between themselves and the radical economic claims of the South. Anti-colonial partners, especially in Africa, cautioned Eastern Europeans that this abandonment would be likely to lead to the reperipheralization of the region as a low-wage hinterland to the West.

The internationalization of the bloc's expertise and mission through decolonization eventually provided tools through which the Communist system was critiqued, transformed and eventually fell. As we chart in *Development* and *Health*, bloc experts saw the limitations of their economic and political projects in the South: the failure of central planning, agricultural collectivization and regional cooperation in their outreach gave ammunition to reformist critics at home. Western and Eastern European firms from the early 1970s worked together in Africa: from this perspective, European cooperation was partly discovered in the 'Third World'. And the direction of the flow of expertise in fact reversed: already internationalized and cosmopolitan Eastern European experts, especially on the western fringes of the European socialist world, increasingly looked to other (semi-) peripheries, notably Latin America and East Asia, for models of how to overcome their enduring peripheralization.[55] The East Asian Tigers' and Chile under Pinochet's successful integration into the world economy in the late Cold War appeared to demonstrate that 'semi-peripheries' akin to Eastern Europe

---

[55] Ibid., 48, 51; Odd Arne Westad, 'Conclusion' in George Lawson et al. (eds.), *The Global 1989. Continuity and Change in World Politics* (Cambridge: CUP, 2010), 273.

could globalize without remarginalizing themselves—while still retaining authoritarian leadership of single parties.[56]

Cultures of solidarity were hollowed out in many countries too—despite the growth in exchange in the 1970s and 1980s. *Mobility* demonstrates that there were still rising numbers of labour migrants and students coming from the South; they were, however, less the objects of solidarity and more a source of hard currency, to be earned through migrants' work in export industries, or through student fees. *Development, War and Peace* and *Health* variously explore the expansion of socialist multilateral collaboration, national arms industries and world-leading medical enterprises in Africa and the Middle East.[57] Yet a new generation of technocratic experts who had not experienced the struggles against fascism and of the Second World War assessed the value of these relationships in terms of technocratic and economistic evaluations of mutual benefit and profitability. Poorer African socialist states were less and less viewed as the object of Eastern European states' solidarity-based developmental largesse.[58] Weapons initially supplied as expressions of solidarity were now business opportunities; large sums were earned from arms exports from the Eastern Bloc to Africa in the 1980s, which were, in part, used to pay off their debts to the West. Nor—with the exception of Yugoslavia and Romania—did Eastern European states call for solidarity with African and Latin American states suffering from the IMF-led demands for structural adjustment and repayment in the 1980s. Debt forgiveness, many feared, would contribute further to the economic crisis in Eastern Europe.

The region's elites increasingly retreated into the European sphere. *Rights* explores how the universalized notion of human rights fractured in the 1970s, in part due to the declining international appeal of common social and economic rights. Just as some outside Europe turned to the idea of e.g. African or Islamic rights, so European socialists' rights work was increasingly focused on collective security in the European sphere, and their commitment to collective justice and anti-racist work at international institutions sharply declined. *Culture* explores how regions which had once been connected through a common anti-colonial

---

[56] James Mark and Tobias Rupprecht, 'Europe's 1989 in Global Context', in Silvio Pons, Juliane Fürst and Mark Selden (eds.), *The Cambridge History of Communism. Volume 3, Endgames? Late Communism in Global Perspective, 1968 to the Present* (Cambridge: CUP, 2017), 226–7. Tobias Rupprecht, 'Formula Pinochet. Chilean Lessons for Russian Liberal Reformers during the Soviet Collapse, 1970–2000', *Journal of Contemporary History*, 51/1 (2016), 165–86; Chris Miller, *The Struggle to Save the Soviet Economy* (Chapel Hill: University of North Carolina Press, 2017), 2.

[57] Mark Kramer, 'The Decline in Soviet Arms Transfers to the Third World, 1986–1991', in Artemy M. Kalinovsky and Sergey Radchenko (eds.), *The End of the Cold War and The Third World: New Perspectives on Regional Conflict* (Abingdon: Routledge, 2011), 56–7. On East Germany, see Klaus Storkmann, *Geheime Solidarität: Militärbeziehungen und Militärhilfen der DDR in die 'Dritte Welt'* (Berlin: Christoph Links, 2012).

[58] For an early account of this shift, see László Csaba, *Eastern Europe in the World Economy* (Cambridge: CUP, 1990), 127–9. Pál Germuska, 'Failed Eastern Integration and a Partly Successful Opening Up to the West: The Economic Re-Orientation of Hungary During the 1970s', *European Review of History*, 21/2 (2014), 278.

socialist imaginary now emphasized civilizational difference based on irreconcilable histories and culture. *War and Peace* explores how a violence which had once been accepted as legitimate by a generation that had lived through the Second World War was more and more associated with the supposedly excessive demands of liberation movements, or with Islamic terrorism. By the last decades of the Cold War, Eastern Bloc states were increasingly divided on these questions— whilst the Soviets and the GDR still saw revolutionary violence as acceptable in some circumstances, other elites preferred to propagate peace, solutions based in international law, and trade.

Both reform Communists and dissidents increasingly positioned their countries as part of a peaceful, tempered European civilization. As *Race* demonstrates, such actors negatively associated an irrational socialist internationalism with blackness.[59] New forms of boundary-making were equally a part of the end of Communism, as alternative anti-Eurocentric, less bordered visions of Europe in the East collapsed.[60] Former African leftist allies saw in this moment the affirmation of an essentially white continent allied to the neoliberal Washington Consensus built around a revived sense of hard civilizational and racialized boundaries.

Nevertheless, the processes set in train by the 1989 revolutions were widely heralded as breaking down borders and enabling the globalization of Eastern Europe. From the perspective of this encounter, the fall of state socialism in 1989–91 was rather a moment that crystallized the choice over how to globalize. The big offer of integration that western political and economic institutions made to the East around 1989 brought an end to many internationalist paradigms and linkages. Eastern European states lost the Third World as a place for their investment and supply of raw materials. In this sense, this loss not only represented the confirmation of Eastern Europe's journey towards a western-led globalization and European politics, but also as a process of de-internationalization from a world which had opened up through the decolonization of Western European empires. Its elites no longer asserted the importance of their region as a leading representative of an alternative modernity, but rather accepted a new status as integrating adjunct on the periphery of a Euro-Atlantic world.

---

[59] Ian Law and Nikolaj Zakharov, 'Race and Racism in Eastern Europe: Becoming White, Becoming Western', in Philomena Essed, Karen Farquharson, Kathryn Pillay and Elisa Joy White (eds.), *Relating Worlds of Racism. Dehumanisation, Belonging, and the Normativity of European Whiteness* (Cham: Palgrave Macmillan, 2019), 114.

[60] Daniela Vicherat Mattar, 'Did Walls Really Come Down? Contemporary B/ordering Walls in Europe', in Marc Silberman, Karen E. Till and Janet Ward (eds.), *Walls, Borders, Boundaries: Spatial and Cultural Practices in Europe* (New York: Berghahn, 2012), 77–94.

1

Origins

James Mark and Steffi Marung

The political settlements that followed the First World War marked the beginning of a century of disintegrating empires. In 1919, Eastern Europe became the site of the century's first collapse:[1] Latvia, Lithuania, Estonia, Hungary, Czechoslovakia and Poland emerged immediately from the dismembered Central European and Russian Empires. Here they joined the older nation states of Romania and Bulgaria, increasingly autonomous since 1878. The newly established Kingdom of Serbs, Croats and Slovenes (later Yugoslavia) welded Serbia to areas liberated from the Austro-Hungarian Empire. The Soviet Union was built from the ruins of the Russian Empire: despite casting itself as the world's first anti-imperialist state, Ukrainian, Armenian and Azerbaijani nationalists would soon petition the League of Nations to recognize their subjection to it, although their claims to statehood would have to wait seven long decades.[2] Yet the postwar settlement that had shattered the German, Russian, Habsburg and Ottoman Empires deferred independence for the Asian and African colonies of the Western European powers. US President Woodrow Wilson's 'Fourteen Points' speech delivered on 8 January 1918 became a symbol for the start of a process to establish the self-determining nation state as the dominant political form worldwide, but at this moment the right to such states would only be granted to 'civilized' European nations deemed ready for self-government. This Wilson applied enthusiastically to the lands of the former Austria-Hungary, although halting at the Bosphorus, where, he unsuccessfully argued, an American authority should be established.[3] The United States did not challenge the legitimacy of Western European colonial

The authors wish to thank Bogdan C. Iacob, Nemanja Radonjić, Maria Dembek, Zoltán Ginelli and Alena Alamgir for providing research assistance for this chapter; and to Paul Hanebrink and Manuela Boatcă for their insightful comments and suggestions.

[1] Natasha Wheatley, 'Central Europe as Ground Zero of the New International Order', *Slavic Review*, 78/4 (2019), 901.

[2] Alexander Shulgin, 'Ukraine and Its Political Aspirations', *The Slavonic and East European Review*, 13/38 (1935), 350–62; Lilian M. Friedlander, 'The Admission of States to the League of Nations', *British Yearbook of International Law*, 9 (1928), 84–100.

[3] Larry Wolff, *Woodrow Wilson and the Reimagining of Eastern Europe* (Stanford: Stanford University Press, 2020), 17. The US Senate rejected this proposal, as they did much of this Wilsonian vision.

James Mark and Steffi Marung, *Origins* In *Socialism Goes Global: The Soviet Union and Eastern Europe in the Age of Decolonization*. Edited by James Mark and Paul Betts, Oxford University Press. © Oxford University Press 2022. DOI: 10.1093/oso/9780192848857.003.0002

rule in the aftermath of the First World War:[4] the so-called Mandates system, established in 1920, meant the long-term oversight of international bodies and imperial powers over a number of colonies, through which, it was argued, they might eventually develop the economic and political capacities to stand alone.[5]

Yet the fragile postwar circumstance of Eastern Europe could be taken as proof that it had been a grave error to enable imperial dissolution. Not only had it led to the establishment of the world's first Communist state, which posed a threat to Europe and its colonies, but it had also created a swathe of small and brittle states beset by territorial disputes and conflicts regarding the rights of minorities. South African statesman Jan Smuts deemed the region to consist of 'embryo states and derelict territories' with leaders who were 'untrained...deficient in power'.[6] When doubt was cast on their capacities for self-government, Eastern Europeans were no longer fully white Europeans: for Smuts they were 'kaffir', while Lord Robert Cecil referred to the Poles as 'orientalized Irish'. As far as they were concerned, Mandates should have been established in Eastern Europe too.[7] In its full-blooded form this option was rejected, and some prominent German intellectuals, the liberal imperialist Friedrich Naumann amongst them, argued that Poland should not be a site for western colonization, and was capable of becoming a proper European nation that might eventually compete with Germany for influence in the Baltic region.[8] However, the idea of there being a close equivalence between a brittle post-colonial Eastern Europe and a colonial world needing to be shepherded towards self-sufficiency persisted in the everyday assumptions of international politics in the interwar period. Even without the full supervision of the Mandates system, the League of Nations had been granted the right to interfere in the minority policies of these smaller states.[9] The League's financial experts were vested with the authority to intervene in the region's reconstruction and financial stabilization.[10] For its economists, both the Soviet Union and many of the smaller Eastern states stood outside the developed 'real Europe'; much of the region was

[4] Uriel Abulof, 'We the Peoples? The Strange Demise of Self-Determination', *European Journal of International Relations*, 22/3 (2015), 536–65; Erez Manela, *The Wilsonian Moment: Self-Determination and the Origins of Anticolonial Nationalism* (Oxford: OUP, 2007).

[5] Mandates were divided into three categories according to their long-term prospects for independence.

[6] Adam Tooze, *The Deluge: The Great War, America and the Remaking of the Global Order, 1916-1931* (New York: Allen Lane, 2015), 555. For a more sympathetic account of Smuts' role in reconstruction in Eastern Europe and the Middle East after the First and Second World Wars, see Saul Dubow, 'Smuts, the United Nations and the Rhetoric of Race and Rights', *Journal of Contemporary History*, 43/1 (2008), 52–3.

[7] Jan Christiaan Smuts, *The League of Nations: A Practical Suggestion* (London: Hodder and Stoughton, 1918), especially 10–13.

[8] Mark T. Kettler, 'Designing Empire for the Civilized East: Colonialism, Polish Nationhood, and German War Aims in the First World War', *Nationalities Papers*, 47/6 (2019), 949–50.

[9] Tooze, *The Deluge*, 555–6.

[10] Jamie Martin, 'The Colonial Origins of the Greek Bailout', *Exeter Imperial and Global History Blog*, July 2015 http://imperialglobalexeter.com/2015/07/27/the-colonial-origins-of-the-greek-bailout/ (last accessed March 2020).

considered rather to be a marginal agricultural hinterland that had more in common with Asia or Africa than the Atlantic world.[11]

Contemporaries wondered whether this moment signalled a new global future in which all European empires would fall. In 1920, Harry H. Johnston, prolific British explorer and writer, saw in the liberation of the eastern European nations—which he designated as '97% or 98%' civilized[12]—a future for Africa. 'If we are to say, what we do sentimentally, but rightly, about restoring Polish nationality, about giving reparation to Ireland's separatist aspirations, about what should be done for the oppressed peoples of Europe, we cannot possibly exclude the African countries from that consideration', he wrote.[13] The antecedent of the term 'decolonization'—*Gegenkolonisation* (countercolonization)—was first popularized in 1934 by the German Moritz Bonn to describe exactly this connection. What had been granted to Eastern Europe had now set the world on a path that would lead to the end of empire globally.[14] The Soviet Union for its part, declaring itself the world's first truly anti-imperialist state, challenged Wilsonian complacency: the more radical Leninist concept of self-determination offered an alternative that provided both beacon and refuge for those battling imperialism across the world. The smaller states of interwar Eastern Europe led the way too, as the Romanian leftist newspaper *Facla* announced in 1925: 'The time of Empire has passed. We believe that the generations of tomorrow will no longer have to learn in school the complicated list of colonies and dominions.'[15] Leaders of anti-colonial movements from Korea through India to West Africa soon recognized that the future of their own projects was connected to the survival of independent Eastern European states.[16]

Yet what role would Eastern Europeans in fragile new polities, vulnerable to the European imperialists on their doorstep who still viewed their sovereignty as negotiable, play in this wider world of weakening world empires? Was their survival best achieved by accepting the dynamics of a still powerful imperial system and by trying, as fellow Europeans, to work within the framework of the continent's remaining empires? Or could the region's marginality only be overcome by developing new non-western or anti-imperial relationships through the vast array of burgeoning interwar internationalisms and their organizations—from the

---

[11] See the extensive discussion in the chapter *Development*. Also: Patricia Clavin, *Securing the World Economy: The Reinvention of the League of Nations, 1920–1946* (Oxford: OUP, 2013), 169, 181–2.

[12] Sir Harry Johnston, *The Backward Peoples and our Relations with Them* (Oxford: OUP, 1920), 8.

[13] Quoted in W.E.B. Du Bois, *Darkwater: Voices from within the Veil* (New York: Harcourt Brace, 1921), 26.

[14] Moritz Bonn, 'The Age of Counter-Colonisation', *International Affairs*, 13/6 (1934), 846.

[15] Constantin Botoran and Gheorghe Unc, *Tradiții de solidaritate ale mișcării muncitorești și democratice din România cu lupta de emancipare națională și socială a popoarelor din Asia, Africa și America Latină* (București: Editura Politica, 1977), 42.

[16] On Korea, Manela, *Wilsonian Moment*, 133; for India, Benoy Kumar Sarkar, *The Social Philosophy of Masaryk* (Calcutta: Oriental Book Agency, 1937); Manu Goswami, 'Imaginary Futures and Colonial Internationalisms', *American Historical Review*, 117/5 (2012), 1469–70.

League of Nations to the Comintern?[17] As non-European anti-colonial actors began to integrate themselves into such international bodies, they made it diffi-cult for Europeans of all political persuasions to keep questions concerning the fate of the continent as the exclusive preserve of Europeans. Afro-Asian and Afro-American leaders encouraged Eastern Europeans to see themselves as part of a 'quasi-colonized' region over which the great powers fought, and to be conscious of their connections to a wider colonized world in ways that could transcend divisions defined by ideas of race or civilization. From this perspec-tive, the later alliances of the Cold War—as most of Eastern Europe became Communist, and decolonization in Africa and Asia accelerated—were neither entirely novel nor altogether a break with the region's often supposed Eurocentrism and parochialism. Rather, they were a continuation of struggles over Eastern Europe's place in a world of declining European empires that had begun decades earlier.

Eastern Europe: An Anti-colonial Colonialism?

In early 1919, the Czech Dr. V. Forster argued that the new Eastern European states—namely Poland, partitioned between the German, Russian and Habsburg Empires since the late eighteenth century, and Czechoslovakia, formerly part of Austria-Hungary—should be given new overseas territory. 'By having colonies', he argued, 'we would become part of the centre of the world, whereas now we find ourselves on the margins.'[18] Lobbies from Czechoslovakia and Poland sought territory from the now collapsed German Empire in Africa: Polish colonial advocates argued for this right as one of the successor states to the German Empire, or as compensation for the 'Reich's destruction and looting on Polish soil'.[19] Some Czechs argued for a 'miniature United States' in Africa, and colonies in Kamchatka and New Guinea too: this was fair reward for the oppression they had suffered at the hands of Germans and Austrians, and for the wartime service provided by the Czechoslovak Legion in Siberia.[20] Economic extraction from such territory would help build the economic base of fragile new states, and con-tribute to Europe's overall stability by bolstering a region that could act as an effective counterweight to Germany.[21] Forster nevertheless distanced himself

---

[17] Glenda Sluga and Patricia Clavin (eds.), *Internationalisms. A Twentieth-Century History* (Cambridge: CUP, 2016).

[18] Dr. V. Forster, 'Je nám třeba koloniálního území?', *Národní listy*, 29 January and 5 February 1919.

[19] K. Warchałowski, 'Przyczynek do historii polskiej akcji kolonialnej', *Morze*, 9 (1932), 24–5; Marta Grzechnik, 'Ad Maiorem Poloniae Gloriam!' Polish Inter-colonial Encounters in Africa in the Interwar Period', *The Journal of Imperial and Commonwealth History*, 48/5 (2020), 827.

[20] Forster, 'Je nám třeba koloniálního území?'

[21] Marek Arpad Kowalski, *Dyskurs Kolonialny w Drugiej Rzeczypospolitej* (Warszawa: DiG, 2009), 39; Sarah Lemmen, 'The 'Return to Europe': Intellectual Debates on the Global Place of Czechoslovakia in the Interwar Period', *European Review of History*, 23/4 (2016), 613–14.

from what he considered the violent and inherently oppressive western variant of colonialism: the concern to obtain Czechoslovak colonies did not reflect 'a desire for power, nor imperialism, nor a hunger for profit that is forcing us to demand overseas settlements, but rather a prudent concern about the future of the nation'. Their own experience of imperial subjugation, he argued, had given their new elites a sensitivity towards subaltern civilizations: hence 'their colonialism' would be less rapacious, and more humane than the degraded form imposed by Western Europeans.[22]

In arguing thus, Forster provided one of many different answers to a urgent question facing Eastern European nationalists after the First World War: how to construct a viable nation state that not only could no longer easily be rendered a European periphery vulnerable to colonization, but might also become a 'centre of the world'. Three decades later, with the region under Communist rule, these histories would be used to bolster the idea that Eastern Europe was a naturally anti-colonial space whose earlier struggles for sovereignty had anticipated those of Asia and Africa. And there was raw material to construct such arguments: from the mid-nineteenth century, Hungarians resisting Habsburg control looked to the Latin American struggles for independence; Polish nationalists seeking liberation from three empires raised money for emancipation causes in the US, and would later celebrate the revolts of the San Bushmen, the Zulu and then the Boers against the British.[23] By the early twentieth century, a rising left would call on Eastern Europeans to view themselves as part of a common global anti-imperial struggle. At the Seventh Congress of the Second International, in August 1907, Christian Rakovsky, the head of the Romanian socialist delegation and future Soviet ambassador to London and Paris, noted 'the simple motive that our country, which does not have colonies, is herself taken to be a colony, as are all Balkan countries, by the great powers. That is why I voted against the principle of colonial policy.'[24]

Yet this was not the only story: even where their polities did not possess overseas empires, some Eastern Europeans came to participate in, and identify with, the continent's expansionist colonialism of the nineteenth century—albeit at the margins, and with only partial access granted on other Europeans' terms. Their emigrants had benefited from passage to the US: three and a half million left from Austria-Hungary alone between 1876 and 1910, and sent significant remittances back home.[25] Nevertheless, they would on their arrival be denigrated, like the Irish, as lesser

---

[22] Michael Dean, 'Czech Togo? Czech New Guinea? The Campaign for Czechoslovak Colonial Mandates on the Eve of the Paris Peace Conference' (manuscript kindly shared with authors).

[23] P. Zajas, 'Polacy jako Burowie', in J. Axer and T. Bujnicki (eds.), Wokół 'W pustyni i w puszczy'. W stulecie pierwodruku powieści (Kraków Universitas, 2012), 33. Memories of sympathy for the Boer cause were repressed under Communism, but revived after 1989.

[24] Botoran and Unc, Tradiţii, 27.

[25] Ulf Brunnbauer, Globalizing Southeastern Europe: Emigrants, America, and the State since the Late Nineteenth Century (Lanham: Lexington Books, 2016), 28, 45.

whites. Such notions of racialized hierarchy came back with the many who returned.[26] And the imperial display used to make sense of, and validate, that rapid expansion for colonizing Europeans also came to those 'colonized' in the German, Austro-Hungarian and western part of the Russian Empires too. From the 1880s, travelling human zoos of Nubians, Samoyeds, Sinhalese, Bella-Coola Indians, Sioux and Lapps arrived in Budapest; the 'African village' at the capital's zoological gardens was founded in 1896.[27] The reactions of the more educated urban audiences to touring 'Buffalo Bill' shows in partitioned Poland hint at the complexities of the region's relationship to this expanding European world. These performances could be seen as, variously, a lament for a heroic (but dying) native American civilization, rightly tamed by a colonial-settler European civilization to which audiences felt that they belonged, or as an inspiration for Poles resisting the particularly harsh assimilation policies under Prussian rule. Conversely, they might be condemned as expensive spectacles from a colonial West that was now economically profiting from its own violence, the shows' unaffordable prices being emblematic of the wider extraction of wealth from a poorer Eastern European hinterland.[28]

The anti-colonialism of Eastern European national movements cannot be separated from a broader identification, no matter how ambivalent, with overseas empire. The very preservation of their subjugated nations was envisaged as part of a world of European supremacy and expansion. Following the failed revolts against Austrian rule in 1848–49, Hungarian nationalists sought to create a 'free national colony' similar to the US-founded Liberia—a diasporic time capsule, to preserve the emigré nation until the moment came to return and claim independence. Following the 1867 power sharing Compromise, Budapest elites in the new Kingdom of Hungary sought to break their own economic dependency on Vienna. The Scramble for Africa inspired dreams of new borderland expansions from Eastern Europe too: following Austria-Hungary's award of Bosnia in 1878, Budapest sought to build on the Balkan colony in order to reach the Adriatic, from where they might develop a trade-based maritime colonialism—the

---

[26] James R. Barrett and David Roediger, 'Inbetween Peoples: Race, Nationality and the "New Immigrant" Working Class', *Journal of American Ethnic History*, 16/3 (1997), 3–44; Robert M. Zecker, *Race and America's Immigrant Press: How the Slovaks Were Taught to Think Like White People* (London: Bloomsbury Academic, 2013).

[27] László Kontler, 'Relocating the "Human Zoo": Exotic Displays, Metropolitan Identity, and Ethnographic Knowledge in Late Nineteenth-Century Budapest', *East Central Europe*, 47 (2020), 187, 190–2; Irina Novikova, 'Imagining Africa and Blackness in the Russian Empire: From Extra-Textual Arapka and Distant Cannibals to Dahomey Amazon Shows—Live in Moscow and Riga', *Social Identities*, 19/5 (2013), 571–91.

[28] Kamila Baraniecka-Olszewska, 'Buffalo Bill and Patriotism: Criticism of the Wild West Show in the Polish-Language Press in Austrian Galicia in 1906', *East Central Europe*, 47 (2020), 313–33; Dagnosław Demski, 'Spaces of Modernity: Ethnic Shows in Poznań, 1879–1914', *East Central Europe*, 47 (2020), 215.

'Hungarian Sea'.[29] Such projects generally failed. Yet even when they partially succeeded, they could only do so on other states' terms. Between the 1880s and 1918, in a fit of what contemporaries called 'Brazilian fever', 120,000 Poles settled in the south of that country, many in 'New Poland'; such emigration created a space where Polish culture and language could develop free from pressures to assimilate.[30] Without territory in the Americas, however, their position was always insecure. Considered a potential reserve of national strength, such communities would in fact soon assimilate into German settlements, and the wider American or Brazilian 'melting pots'.[31]

By the turn of the twentieth century, nationalist movements had come to see the intensification of western territorial expansion beyond Europe as a threat to their own eventual independence. They increasingly associated a full claim to European nationhood with the capacity to undertake imperialism overseas—a project in which their region had failed. Moreover, the civilizational hierarchies that overseas expansion had further reinforced threatened to exacerbate the peripheralization of colonized peoples in Europe's East. Imagery from a global colonial palate was used to make sense of backwardness: German imperialists came to equate 'darker skinned' Poles in their 'wild East' with both Native Americans and Africans.[32] Without colonies, they could be consigned to a space beyond European civilization.

At the turn of the twentieth century, Eastern European nationalists also began to question Western Europeans' right to claim a superior Europeanness, given the moral degradation of their own imperialist projects. The massacres of the Herero (1904–8) in German South-West Africa or the violent treatment of the Boers by the British in South Africa was marshalled as evidence of the barbarization of Western Europe.[33] Such arguments were employed by Habsburg elites to legitimate their own imperial rule, and explain away their failure to seize colonies, unlike their fellow imperial latecomer and neighbour, the German Empire.[34] The colonization of Bosnia-Herzegovina from 1878 was in particular presented by

[29] Zoltán Ginelli, 'Global Colonialism and Hungarian Semiperipheral Imperialism in the Balkans', in Manuela Boatca (ed.), *De-Linking: Critical Thought and Radical Politics. Political Economy of the World-System Annuals* (London: Routledge, forthcoming).

[30] Lenny A. Ureña Valerio, *Colonial Fantasies, Imperial Realities: Race Science and the Making of Polishness on the Fringes of the German Empire, 1840–1920* (Athens: Ohio University Press, 2019), 152.

[31] Ibid., 160. For these reasons, Roman Dmowski and the National Democracy Party would later advocate against Polish migration.

[32] Patrick Bernhard, 'Hitler's Africa in the East: Italian Colonialism as a Model for German Planning in Eastern Europe', *Journal of Contemporary History*, 51/1 (2016), 61–90.

[33] Zajas, 'Polacy', 33.

[34] The failure to seize earmarked northern African territories undermined their sense of being part of a collective European expansionism in which their civilization was as exportable as that of other Europeans; Alison Frank, 'The Children of the Desert and the Laws of the Sea: Austria, Great Britain, the Ottoman Empire, and the Mediterranean Slave Trade in the Nineteenth Century', *The American Historical Review*, 117/2 (2012), 410–444; Walter Sauer, 'Habsburg Colonial: Austria-Hungary's Role in European Overseas Expansion Reconsidered', *Austrian Studies*, 20 (2012), 5–23.

Vienna as evidence of its supposedly more enlightened form of imperial rule, too harmonious and peaceful and lacking the brutality required to obtain colonies overseas.[35] This was a model, they claimed, that other more 'successful' European imperialists in Africa and Asia would do well to imitate.[36] Yet this invocation of others' barbarism could also be turned to the anti-imperial cause: Polish nationalists celebrated Boer resistance, and highlighted how German colonial massacres were simply unthinkable in Europe, concluding that the ever-greater resort to violence in Africa signalled imperial exhaustion and hence increased the likelihood of their own independence.[37] Moreover, their subaltern status within Europe, which rendered them subject to the scorn of Westerners, was in fact becoming an advantage on the global scale: similarly colonized, but also heirs to the European Enlightenment, they could become, given the chance, the superior colonizers, more acutely attuned to the needs of populations they might rule. Accounts of the Polish explorer of Cameroon Stefan Szolc-Rogoziński, or the Henryk Sienkiewicz novel *In Desert and Wilderness* (1910) were hugely popular amongst Polish readers precisely because they encapsulated this fantasy.[38] The granting of colonies to new Eastern European nation states, whose experts were already circulating in western Europeans' colonies, thus had the potential to reclaim and renew a corrupted European imperial project.

These were not realistic claims on territory: in March 1919, when the Polish 'mandate policy' was formulated by Prince Janusz Radziwiłł, Chairman of the Foreign Commission of the *Sejm*, it was rejected by the new Polish government as impractical. Indeed, Poland's de facto leader Marshal Piłsudski dismissed, for much of the 1920s, such fantastical expansionism as a distraction from the urgent task of securing the fragile new state within Europe. It was initially a fantasy of immense political utility, however: a prism through which Polish and Czechoslovak lobbies at the Peace conferences could present themselves as full members of the European club-to-be, and hence as viable nation states, whose European territory was no longer colonizable. It sharply distinguished their claims from those of African or Asian nationalists: key at a time when Western Europeans would not contemplate the dissolution of imperial holdings outside Europe, and when a regional left was connecting Eastern European liberation struggles to those of a wider world in ways that threatened to soften this distinction. Austro-Hungarian

---

[35] On the equating of Africa and Bosnia in this 'Ersatz-colonialization', see Clemens Ruthner, 'Bosnia- Herzegovina, 1878–1918: A Colony of a Multinational Empire', in Róisín Healy and Enrico Dal Lago (eds.), *The Shadow of Colonialism on Europe's Modern Past* (Basingstoke: Palgrave Macmillan, 2014), 160.

[36] Ulrich E. Bach, *Tropics of Vienna: Austrian Colonial Utopias, 1870–1900* (New York: Berghahn Books, 2016), 2.

[37] Polish nationalists were nevertheless concerned—as Solidarność would be almost a century later in the face of anti-apartheid's global appeal—that Boer resistance distracted the world's attention from the plight of Polish economic oppression in the Prussian partition.

[38] Valerio, *Colonial Fantasies*, chapter 4.

troops had fought alongside colonial soldiers in Foreign Legions; nationalists sought to distance themselves from the claims of North Africans and Arabs their compatriots had stood with, whereas socialists and Communists remembered these wartime solidarities when seeking to promote parallel national liberations.[39] Some emphasized their prospective polities' status as historic nations, with rights to such claims embedded within the constitutions of the imperial polities they were escaping from: their new countries had a legal-historical basis for existence which extra-European nationalisms, or indeed competitor nationalisms in Eastern Europe, did not.[40] Polish and Czechoslovak claims regarding their superior ability to govern Mandates were by the same token a demonstration that their nations could be full members of a still-colonial Europe, or a still expanding white world, and hence were worthy of being constituted as independent states.[41]

Such aspirations did not disappear with these states' foundation.[42] In Hungary, where interwar politics focused on the overturning of the huge territorial losses of the postwar settlement, an external colonialism was less urgent[43]—although Asian cultural and racial connections were promoted as an important counter to dependency on western powers that, following the Treaty of Trianon, could no longer be relied upon. Nevertheless, even here the fantasy of a superior colonialism continued in popular fiction and travel writing.[44] In Poland, it took a political form: from 1924, the Maritime and Colonial League promoted the idea of the 'Polish sea', the construction of trade routes around the modernization of backward coastal areas, that would connect Polish emigrants and settlers across the world, and set Poland on the path to 'superpower' status.[45] In the 1930s the League petitioned the League of Nations for concessions in Cameroon, Angola, Brazil and Liberia.[46] The idea of a morally superior colonialism persisted:

---

[39] Zecker, *Race*, 159–60.   [40] Wheatley, 'Central Europe', 910.

[41] Marta Grzechnik, 'The Missing Second World: On Poland and Postcolonial Studies', *Interventions* (2019), 12; Lemmen, 'The "Return to Europe"', 615.

[42] Kowalski, *Dyskurs Kolonialny*, 99.

[43] Szilvia Váradi, 'A Páneurópa-mozgalom és hatása Magyarországon', *Acta Universitatis Szegediensis*, 6/1 (2006), 196.

[44] P. Howard (Jenő Rejtő, 1905–1943), writer of the most popular novels of the interwar period, told stories of Eastern Europeans finding freedom and meaning as adventurers or legionnaires, fighting side by side with colonial troops in French colonial Africa and South East Asia. See also the popular works of Catholic missionaries Béla Bangha and Zoltán Nyisztor, which sold a vital Catholic colonialism as a force morally superior to the rapacity of its hegemonic Western European Protestant capitalist form.

[45] Kazimierz Głuchowski, 'Idźmy za morza!', *Morze*, 3 (1928), 31.

[46] On Cameroon: A. Dębczyński, 'Kolonie dźwignią rozwoju Polski, lecz nie załatwieniem sprawy emigracji', *Ilustrowany Kurier Codzienny*, 91 (1929), 1–2; Piotr Puchalski, 'The Polish Mission to Liberia, 1934–1938: Constructing Poland's Colonial Identity', *The Historical Journal*, 60/4 (2017), 1071–96; Bolaji Balogun, 'Polish Lebensraum: The Colonial Ambition to Expand on Racial Terms', *Ethnic and Racial Studies*, 41/14 (2018), 2561–79.

These [black] races, subjugated for centuries, regard a white man, that is, primarily an Englishman, a German, a Frenchman etc., as an oppressor .... An authorized representative of African races has said that because Poland itself has experienced the bitterness of slavery, she knows what a foreign yoke is. A coloured person would see a protector, a great friend in a Pole, and not a hated oppressor. Here lies, it seems, the great moral force of Poland...Poles have a high degree of aptitude for the economic management of uninhabited areas.[47]

When Poland gained a commercial (and attempted military) foothold in Liberia in the late 1930s, it rejected the idea that it aspired to a colony of direct political control, instead claiming that the Polish mission was to gain an economic foothold in order to encourage 'free maritime commerce'. Anti-colonial African activists, whose territories had not obtained their independence at the Paris peace conferences after the First World War, were shocked. Nnamdi Azikiwe, who would later become independent Nigeria's president, wrote:

And so Poland, which until 1914 was a colonial territory of three different countries and which has been allowed to exercise the Wilsonian right of self-determination, now needs colonies, and not in Europe but in Africa....The former servant of the Austrian empress Maria Theresa, the Russian empress Catherine II and the Prussian king Frederick the Great now wants to be a master in an African country.[48]

By contrast, there had been no colonial lobbies from the Balkans after the First World War. The cores of the Romanian, Bulgarian and Serbian states were already being consolidated from 1878: hence their elites had no need to fantasize over diasporic homelands. Whilst the Polish intelligentsia, even under conditions of occupation, could imagine a future Polish nation state as an imperial power, elites in south-eastern Europe saw their already established sovereignty as vulnerable and reversible. Their states had been founded in an era of high imperialism, a moment at which the very idea of the Balkans was invented as a backward, savage region, Europe's own Africa or Asia, held up as a mirror to reflect the West's superiority.[49] National movements were well aware of the parallel cultural and political processes that rendered both Africa and the Balkans colonizable; after all, the Congress of Berlin had simultaneously divided up Africa and given Vienna the right to administer a Balkan territory—namely a Habsburg Protectorate in Bosnia-Herzegovina. Its eventual military annexation in 1908 was

---

[47] Edward Ligocki, 'Czarne lądy a Polska', *Ilustrowany Kurier Codzienny*, 64 (1937), 2–3; Kowalski, *Dyskurs Kolonialny*, 258–9.

[48] 'National Mythology, Suitcase Trade, and Blank Spaces. Janek Simon in conversation with Michał Woliński', *Piktogram*, 13 (2009), 50.

[49] Maria Todorova, 'The Balkans: From Discovery to Invention', *Slavic Review*, 53/2 (1994), 479.

a warning that the Balkans were still vulnerable. Moreover, the massive loans raised to fund programmes of modernization had left the region the largest debt-ors in Europe, mainly to German and French banks. Apprehensive at the thought of being stuck as an indebted agricultural periphery, nationalist elites feared the region becoming Africa: the newspaper *Macedonia* cautioned that 'it won't be long before we find ourselves, much to our regret, empty-handed and as naked and starving on dry hills as the Africans in their deserts.'[50] Nor was there a social base for imperial visions. Some of the aristocracy, and an expanding urban bourgeoisie, in parts of historic Poland, Hungary and Bohemia, could imagine themselves as joining the ranks of European imperialists, consumed a western imperial culture, and served as experts in their empires. In the still peasant-dominated and far less industrialized and urbanized Balkans, by contrast, imperial shows did not tour, colonial genres such as travel writing did not develop until the interwar period, and the circulation of experts in Western European empires was far more limited.

Colonialism was instead enacted closer to home. Modernizing urban elites may have criticized the exploitation of their economy by westerners as akin to the latters' treatment of Indians, Africans, and Native Americans, but nevertheless had internalized the idea that the nation's 'backward' rural territories were their own terra incognita, needing to be mapped, and then tamed through national integration.[51] From 1878, inspired by French practice, the Serbian national move-ment sought to drive out Albanian Muslims—variously described as 'lazy savages' and 'European Indians'—from the country's southern provinces and replace them with Christian Serbs and Montenegrins.[52] The Kingdom of Yugoslavia had been created by the Versailles treaties; Romania had gained large swathes of territory; both were thus committed to protecting it. Their elites rather focussed on issues of internal stability and the assimilation of minorities. Romania did have an 'Office for Colonization', but this was designed to transfer citizens from over-populated regions to underpopulated ones within its own national borders. The newly established Kingdom of Yugoslavia sought to extend its civilizing mission and settler colonialism to its poorer southern hinterland, namely, Macedonia and Kosovo.[53] Local critics of European empire were aghast at how its values had been imported into the region. Serbian Social Democrat Dimitrije Tucović noted:

[50] Marie-Janine Calic, *The Great Cauldron: A History of Southeastern Europe* (Cambridge, MA: Harvard University Press, 2019), 354.

[51] Dessislava Lilova, 'The Homeland as Terra Incognita. Geography and Bulgarian National Identity, 1830s–1870s', in Timothy Snyder and Katherine Younger (eds.), *The Balkans as Europe, 1821–1914* (Rochester, NY: University of Rochester Press, 2018), 46.

[52] Djordje Stefanović, 'Seeing the Albanians through Serbian Eyes: The Inventors of the Tradition of Intolerance and Their Critics, 1804–1939', *European History Quarterly*, 35/3 (2005), 469–72; Dušan I. Bjelić, 'The Balkans: Radical Conservatism and Desire', *South Atlantic Quarterly*, 108/2 (2009), 53–72.

[53] Catherine Baker, *Race and the Yugoslav Region Postsocialist, Post-conflict, Postcolonial?* (Manchester, MUP: 2018), 62–4.

'Serbian capitalists have opened their account of colonial murders and horrors and now they can proudly join the capitalist company with the English, the Dutch, the French, the Germans, the Italians, and the Russians.'[54] In so far as interwar Romanian and Bulgarian states did imagine colonialism beyond their borders, it was contiguously: fantasies of expansion were targeted at lands lost through the postwar settlement and geographically adjacent to them—namely Transnistria, Macedonia and Thrace—rather than extra-European territories.[55]

For the new interwar states of central-eastern Europe, nation-building was no longer a struggle against empires but rather concerned, as was already the case in the Balkans, the consolidation and homogenization of territory. Here too ideas drawn from an imperialist palette beyond Europe were intertwined with nationalist fantasies about colonizing and taming their own poorer, 'unruly' and ethnically other 'Easts'.[56] Even if central-eastern European nations were to be denied colonies outside Europe, they could demonstrate their Europeanizing and civilizing prowess in their own domestic 'darkest Africas'. Anthropologists were often the conduit for the return to Europe of such ideas: as Czech elites took their mission to Slovakia and sub-Carpathian Ruthenia, Vojtěch Suk, a distinguished Czech anthropologist, who had previously conducted fieldwork in South Africa, Canada and Ukraine, racialized his mission. For him, the Czechs were the British civilizers, and Jews the rich Indians in eastern and southern Africa, who blocked 'less developed' Slavic minorities—thus equated with black Africans—from accumulation and development.[57] Such visions of the colonization of an ethnically diverse and 'backward' periphery by a dominant national group often predated independence. In the Polish case, it was the Scramble for Africa, and images of heroic Boer defence of their farmstead settlements against the British, which helped intensify the longing for the agricultural Polish East, or *Kresy*:[58] the Ukrainian-, Lithuanian- and Belorussian-speaking territories of the Polish-Lithuanian Commonwealth that Polish nationalists claimed had been 'temporarily

---

[54] Dimitrije Tucović, 'Srbija i Arbanija', quoted in Stefanović, 'Seeing the Albanians', 477.

[55] On Romania: Vladimir Solonari, *A Satellite Empire: Romanian Rule in Southwestern Ukraine, 1941-1944* (Ithaca, NY: Cornell University Press, 2019); on Macedonia: Nadège Ragaru, 'Contrasting Destinies: The Plight of Bulgarian Jews and the Jews in Bulgarian-occupied Greek and Yugoslav Territories during World War Two', *SciencesPo*, 15 March 2017 https://www.sciencespo.fr/mass-violence-war-massacre-resistance/en/document/contrasting-destinies-plight-bulgarian-jews-and-jews-bulgarian-occupied-greek-and-yugoslav- (last accessed March 2020).

[56] Milica Bakić-Hayden, 'Nesting Orientalisms: The Case of Former Yugoslavia', *Slavic Review*, 54/4 (1995), 917–31. On internal colonization in Europe, see Healy and Dal Lago, *The Shadow of Colonialism*.

[57] Victoria Shmidt, 'The Politics of Surveillance in the Interwar Czechoslovak Periphery: The Role of Campaigns Against Infectious Diseases', *Zeitschrift für Ostmitteleuropa-Forschung*, 68/1 (2019), 37; idem, 'Public Health as an Agent of Internal Colonialism in Interwar Czechoslovakia: Shaping the Discourse About the Nation's Children', *Patterns of Prejudice*, 52/4 (2018), 355–87. Suk would nevertheless go on to oppose Nazi biological conceptions of race.

[58] Paweł Zajas, 'In het land der Boeren: de receptie van de Anglo-Boerenoorlog in de Poolse jeugdliteratuur', *Tydskrif vir Letterkunde*, 47/1 (2010), 66–78. Von Barfus, *W kraju dzielnych Burów* (Warszawa, 1901).

kidnapped' by the Russian Empire and needed to be returned to Poland. Following its incorporation into the independent state in 1918, racialized ideas of inferiority and degeneracy were projected by anthropologists on to this poorer hinterland, and Warsaw proselytized its cultural civilizing mission amongst its new 'citizen-savages'.[59]

Whilst Cold War-era Communist regimes would subsequently place great emphasis on the need to restrict mobility in order to strengthen the nation, inter-war economists and demographers, faced with hunger and economic distress after the First World War, argued the opposite: living space was required for 'excess' populations. Thus targeted emigration policies were designed to clear out poor, rural, dependent and less nationalized communities, whose removal would 'improve' the health and homogeneity of the nation. The Kingdom of Yugoslavia pursued ethnically differentiated policies with a view to hastening the departure of 'anational' non-Slavic Muslims to Turkey, whilst restricting 'national' Slavic emigration to the Americas.[60]

Some intellectuals and politicians in the new states of Poland and Czechoslovakia envisaged emigration through collective European colonialism: a 'Eurafrican' project in which Eastern European nations could provide labour drawn from their 'excess' populations. In 1924, as US immigration restrictions put an end to the mass exodus across the Atlantic, the advantages of Africa were increasingly discussed. Here, poor and minority communities that had been recently incorporated into new Eastern European states could better develop an allegiance to their new nation when surrounded by a 'more alien' civilization—without the temptation to shed older identities in the American 'melting pot'.[61] Rudolf Cicvárek, Czech landowner and Orientalist, argued that in subtropical Africa 'our reserves continue to multiply in a purely national spirit, unmixed, and it would be of help to us in times of need'.[62] Western powers were undermining Europe by denying overpopulated parts of the European East the opportunity to create a 'wider base for the white race', whilst also exacerbating intra-European conflict, as overpopulation was driving desires for national expansion.[63] Roman

---

[59] For this conception, see Kathryn Ciancia, *On Civilization's Edge: A Polish Borderland in the Interwar World* (New York: OUP, 2020), Introduction; Olga Linkiewicz, 'Applied Modern Science and the Self-Politicization of Racial Anthropology in Interwar Poland', *Ab Imperio*, 2 (2016), 153–81.

[60] Ulf Brunnbauer, 'Emigration Policies and Nation-building in Interwar Yugoslavia', *European History Quarterly*, 42/4 (2012), 616–18.

[61] See debates in the Polish Sejm in 1929, which called for the government to advocate for colonies in Latin America to take Polish emigrants. The foreign ministry considered this unrealistic: 'Sprawa uzyskania kolonii dla Polski', 1929, sygn. 322/9579, 4.

[62] Rudolf Cicvárek, *Asijské problémy a naše vystěhovalectví* (Praha: Česká grafická unie, 1927), especially the chapter 'Our Migration'. Others were less sure: a journal close to the Polish National Democratic Party, *Mysl Narodowa*, frequently published articles on the dangers of potential intermixing.

[63] Jan Havlasa, *České kolonie zámořské* (Praha: Nakladatelství spisů, 1919); Tara Zahra, *The Great Departure: Mass Migration from Eastern Europe and the Making of the Free World* (New York and London: Norton, 2016), 129–30.

Dmowski, the nationalist ideologue of the *Endecja* movement in Poland was more critical. He had visited 'New Poland' in Brazil in 1899, and, having witnessed illiteracy, poverty and the failures of assimilation first-hand there, became convinced that such migration politics were nationalist day-dreaming.[64]

Nevertheless, Dmowski embraced the idea that a white colonial Christian continent now under threat both from Soviet Bolshevism and the 'yellow peril' needed to be defended: 'Europe is retreating, Asia is advancing [...] Today Europe is only talking to itself, but in a short space of time it will start to look at Asia with eyes open wide in fear.'[65] Leon Radzikowski argued in an article *Eurafrica* in the Colonial and Maritime League's journal for a renunciation of the 'colonial egoisms' of individual states, which now had to work together in Africa to ensure the survival of the continent in a soon-to-be tripartite world: 'Africa is destined to provide a beginning to the unity of Europe and... to become, after America... and Asia governed by Japan... the third self-sufficient economic unit in the world.'[66] Collective colonialism was attractive to those states that did not possess colonies: one of the founders of the European movement, Count Coudenhove-Kalergi, came from Austro-Hungarian aristocratic stock, and felt keenly the marginalization of central Europe's new, smaller nations; he argued that, as part of 'Pan-Europa', Czechoslovakia and Poland should be given a 'stake' in a European colonialism—together with Germany.[67] Africa could become an economic provider and a population outlet that would ensure the preservation and revitalization of the European continent beyond 'national selfishness'.[68] In 1929, Coudenhove-Kalergi somewhat presciently warned of a coming European civil war between its colony-possessing West, led by London, and a colony-deprived East, which would end up led by Communist Moscow. In his vision, the East would garner global sympathies due to its anti-colonialism, which could be effectively deployed to force Westerners out of Africa, after which Eastern Europeans would take their place.[69] But not all embraced this Pan-Europeanism, viewing it as an already outdated colonial mindset panicked by the racial threat represented by the awakening of the Asian peoples.[70] Hungarian

---

[64] M. Starczewski, 'Mrzonki racjonalnej kolonizacji w duchu narodowym. Roman Dmowski i polska emigracja do Brazylii', *Przegląd Humanistyczny*, 2 (2015), 63–74.

[65] Roman Dmowski, 'Azja', *Gazeta Warszawska*, 392 (1933), 3. On Dmowski's fascination with Japan: 'Ex Oriente Lux', *Przegląd Wszechpolski*, X, 1904.

[66] Leon Radzikowski, 'Eur-Afryka', *Morze*, 4 (1931), 24.

[67] On the colonial origins of European integration: Peo Hansen and Stefan Jonsson, *Eurafrica: The Untold History of European Integration and Colonialism* (London: Bloomsbury, 2014), especially chapter 2. Eastern European contributions are almost entirely missing from their account, however. See: Benjamin Thorpe, 'Eurafrica: A Pan-European Vehicle for Central European Colonialism (1923–1939)', *European Review*, 26/3 (2018), 503–13.

[68] Janusz Lewandowski, 'Afryka terenem współpracy państw europejskich', *Morze*, 10 (1936), 6–8.

[69] Benjamin J. Thorpe, *The Time and Space of Richard Coudenhove-Kalergi's Pan-Europe, 1923–1939*, PhD thesis (University of Nottingham, 2018), 247–8.

[70] Katalin Egresi, 'Területi revízió vagy egységes Európa? A magyarországi Szociáldemokrata Párt külpolitikai nézetei az 1920-as években', *Kutatási füzetek*, 12 (2005), 119, 124.

Social Democrats argued that 'pan-Europa' made little sense. The future of anti-capitalism would be determined, they reckoned, by Afro-Asian revolutions: 'Europe is nothing else but a part of the Eurasian world. A small island that will fall back in its geopolitical importance as soon as it loses its political significance.'[71]

Polish, Hungarian and Czechoslovak nationalisms were sometimes aligned with a European imperialism abroad through a fantasy of participation, necessary to fortify the nation or to defend a religious-racial vision of Europe. Although south-eastern European governments imported colonial ideas to tame their own peripheries, they evinced little interest in a collective 'Eurafrican colonialism' that might serve to place them 'at the centre' of a colonial world. This is not to suggest a natural anti-colonial affinity: governments in south-eastern Europe often supported Western European imperial wars. In these cases, however, this was tied to territorial ambitions at their own borders rather than global visions. An expanded Romania and newly founded Yugoslavia were reliant on the French, and later the Italians, to support their states' integrity within the League of Nations' international system. And in such contexts, they not only supported these states' imperialisms, but lent credence to notions of French and Latin cultural sympathies in order to align their own countries with a pro-colonial conception of Europe. Romania's liberal government thus supported French repression during the Rif War in the 1920s: its pilots were sent to Morocco to assist a fellow 'Latin civilisation'.[72] At home, the government promoted Romanians' own Dacian links to the Roman Empire as evidence that it naturally belonged in a common European imperial project in North Africa.[73]

Nevertheless, to the extent that imperialism was presumed to limit the capacity of some peoples to devise their own alternative paths to modernity, it was condemned. Here, the notion of great power 'egotism' or 'greediness'—derived from the region's own experience—was also a source of solidarity with extra-European nationalisms, particularly with those considered more 'mature nations', such as China, India, Egypt, Turkey, Latin American peoples, Ethiopia and the Boers, which were thought to share a common experience of peripheralization and exploitation by empires.[74] Intellectual circles on both left and right embraced the notion that Balkan peoples had their own paths to statehood that were less tainted by western decadence, and through them had developed greater empathy with extra-European peoples who were likewise trying to recover marginalized

[71] László Hortobágyi, 'Lehet-e Páneurópa szocialista program?', Szocializmus (July 1926), 206.

[72] Botoran and Unc, Tradiţii, 134.

[73] Stefano Santoro, 'The Latin "Frontier of Civilization": Italian Cultural Policies and Fascist Propaganda Towards Central and Eastern Europe in the Interwar Period', Annales Universitatis Apulensis. Series Historica, 19/I (2015), 168.

[74] Charles Sabatos, 'Marginal Modernists: Claude McKay, Panait Istrati, and the "Minor Mediterranean"', in Adam Goldwyn and Renée Silverman (eds.), Mediterranean Modernism. Intercultural Exchange and Aesthetic Development (New York: Palgrave Macmillan, 2016), 62.

cultures. In Yugoslavia, the Serbian avant-garde writer Ljubomir Micić called for a Balkan anti-Europe that would surpass a West whose claims to civilization had been tarnished by colonial violence. Mircea Eliade, a prominent Romanian scholar of religion and popular intellectual, criticized the violence of British imperialism and its diminution of the humanity of the 'white man'. According to Eliade, Balkan culture, by contrast, embodied a more spiritual, and more vital alternative to a Western European rationality that had led to barbaric war.[75] This insight could lead in a number of very different ideological directions. Romanian Communists and Social Democrats were particular admirers of Gandhi and supporters of Indian independence in the 1930s.[76] Ion Pas, who would become the head of the Institute for Cultural Relations Abroad under Communist rule, wrote: 'Gandhi's people are led by an idea and this gives them a strength that, like an electric current, jolts the British metropolis…Their peace is poignant, a calm mirror of a deep lake, and grandiose as an oak with its roots deeply embedded in the ground, but its crown of leaves heading towards the sun.'[77] Yet this same insight would also be embraced by pro-fascist groupings in the 1930s, when supporting the 'alternative imperialisms' of Italy and Germany which, it was claimed, had the potential to recast a world perverted by western liberal decadence—as we shall see below.

Soviet Union: An Anti-imperialist Empire?

Whereas the Ottoman, and then the Habsburg and German Empires, broke up into smaller nation states, the vast bulk of the Russian Empire was reconstituted as the Soviet Union. The question of whether this new formation was an imperialist or anti-imperialist entity, in an era of weakening and then collapsing empires, would be revisited for much of the twentieth century.[78] For many—ranging from African-American radicals to Asian anti-colonial activists—the Soviet Union initially represented a powerful model of anti-imperialist state building both at home and abroad. The Communist International (Comintern), established in 1919 in Moscow, enabled a powerful internationalism that, despite its demise, facilitated networks that survived, developed and underpinned a socialist global connectedness after the Second World War. For some anti-colonials outside

---

[75]   Calic, *Great Cauldron*, 435–6; Raul Cârstocea, 'The Unbearable Virtues of Backwardness: Mircea Eliade's Conceptualisation of Colonialism and his Attraction to Romania's Interwar Fascist Movement', in Dorota Kołodziejczyk and Siegfried Huigen (eds.), *Central Europe Between the Colonial and the Postcolonial* (Basingstoke: Palgrave Macmillan, forthcoming).

[76]   See articles in newspapers *Lupta* and *Facla* from April and March 1931. In Botoran and Unc, *Tradiţii*, 81.

[77]   See article by leftist Ion Pas, future president of the Romanian Institute for Cultural Relations Abroad (1965–1974), in *Lumea nouă*, 23 July 1939 in Ibid., 83.

[78]   Viatcheslav Morozov, 'Subaltern Empire?', *Problems of Post-Communism*, 60/6 (2013), 16–28.

Europe, the Soviet Union—and later Eastern Europe too—would become established as an imaginary for an alternative path to development.[79] The influence was not one way, however: the presence of mobile and cosmopolitan people of colour from beyond Europe helped push the Soviet elites themselves towards a less Eurocentric anti-colonial internationalism. As in smaller Eastern European states, so too was Moscow concerned about survival—in the Soviet Union's case, as a less economically developed great power within a western-dominated global imperial system. In seeking to develop a systemic alternative to the West, the Soviets sought not only to nurture whatever international conditions would serve to promote the rise of anti-imperialism and socialism, but also worked with anti- or non-Communist parties where it suited the security of the Soviet state.[80]

Creating the 'Communist Ecumene'

The Russian Revolution brought into existence a polity that proclaimed itself to be the first truly anti-imperialist state. Even as its leaders set about reconstituting much of the territory of the former Russian Empire, they nevertheless declared this formation to be a rejection of the values of European imperialism; rather, it was a liberator and would become an equitable developer of those nations within its borders. It also proclaimed itself the world's first major state dedicated to the anti-imperialist struggle worldwide—and it would soon venture upon the creation of an international infrastructure through whose veins not only could internationalist blood circulate, but which also could act as a safety net for the fragile Soviet state. The 1919 Manifesto of the Communist International (Comintern) to the Proletariat of the Entire World argued that US President Woodrow Wilson's programme for self-determination constituted only 'a change in the form of colonial enslavement'. Their document claimed, by contrast, to offer not only support for the right of self-determination of oppressed peoples, but also a new model for economic transformation, the reordering of social relations, and for the creation of multi-ethnic and multi-religious states. This was rooted in the Soviets' own understanding of political struggle derived from what Moscow saw as the 'liberation' of Central Asia, Siberia and the Caucasus.[81] This claim, forged in the early 1920s, was used well into the Cold War to assert that it was only *their* path

---

[79] Hakim Adi, *Pan-Africanism and Communism: The Communist International, Africa and the Diaspora, 1919–1939* (Trenton, NJ: Africa World Press, 2013).

[80] Jonathan Haslam, 'Comintern and Soviet Foreign Policy, 1919–1941', in Ronald Grigor Suny (ed.), *The Cambridge History of Russia*, vol. 2 (Cambridge: CUP, 2006), 636–61.

[81] Adeeb Khalid, 'Communism on the Frontier. The Sovietization of Central Asia and Mongolia', in Silvio Pons and Stephen A. Smith, (eds.), *The Cambridge History of Communism: World Revolution and Socialism in One Country 1917–1941*, vol. 1 (New York: CUP, 2017), 594–612; Niccolò Pianciola, 'Décoloniser l'Asie centrale?', *Cahiers du monde russe*, 49/1 (2008), 101–44; Moritz Florin, 'Zentralasien, die Sowjetunion und die Globalgeschichte der Dekolonisation', in Matthias Middell

that would lead former imperial peripheries into a world free from imperial exploitation.[82]

From the Soviet perspective, the survival of the revolution depended both on the success of Communism in other countries[83]—most notably in Germany—and the eventual collapse of the European Empires. However, the Soviet and Comintern's first official call for an end to global imperialism remained Eurocentric and imputed little agency to people in the Afro-Asian world. Global revolution would require workers' takeovers in the West and the expansion of 'socialist Europe' to ensure the liberation of the 'workers and peasants of Annam, Algeria, Bengal...Persia and Armenia' from Europe's 'capitalistic whirlpool'.[84] But with the defeat of revolutionary hopes for Hungary and Germany in 1919, the Soviets began to look beyond Europe.[85] The founding of Communist Parties in China (1921), South Africa (1921), as well as in Egypt, and Vietnam, all suggested the possibility of a new revolutionary geography.[86] Asian and Afro-American activists challenged this refusal to concede that non-Europeans might be the subjects of their own revolutionary fate.[87] The Indian M.N.Roy, who had cofounded the first extra-European Communist party in Mexico (1918), and then the Communist Party of India (1920), played an important role in globalizing Communist internationalism and Soviet-sponsored infrastructures, which provided a space of manoeuvre for non-Europeans.[88] Roy additionally assisted the Soviets in their categorization of colonies according to their revolutionary potential. He saw Asia as the vanguard, called for Comintern support for the Chinese revolution, championed the revolutionary potential of the peasantry, helped establish an Eastern Department for the Comintern after its Second Congress (1920), and founded a military training school in Tashkent to prepare his continent's

and Ulrich Mählert (eds.), *Kommunismus jenseits des Eurozentrismus*, Jahrbuch für historische Kommunismusforschung (Berlin: Metropol, 2019), 67–81.

[82] Artemy M. Kalinovsky, 'Not Some British Colony in Africa: The Politics of Decolonization and Modernization in Soviet Central Asia, 1955–1964', *Ab Imperio*, 2 (2013), 191–222.

[83] V.I. Lenin, 'The Socialist Revolution and the Right of Nations to Self-Determination', in ibid. (ed.), *Lenin Collected Works*, vol. 22 (Moscow: State Publishing House of Political Literature, 1916), 143–56; Ronald Grigor Suny, '"Don't Paint Nationalism Red!": National Revolution and Socialist Anti-Imperialism', in Prasenjit Duara (ed.), *Decolonization: Perspectives from Now and Then* (New York: Taylor & Francis, 2004), 176–98.

[84] 'Manifesto of the Communist International', *The Revolutionary Age. A Chronicle and Interpretation of International Events*, 1, 10 May 1919.

[85] Lars T. Lih, 'Bolshevik Roots of International Communism', in Pons and Smith (eds.), *The Cambridge History of Communism*, 121–41.

[86] David Priestland, *The Red Flag: A History of Communism* (New York: Grove/Atlantic, 2016), Chapter 6.

[87] Michele Louro, *Comrades Against Imperialism. Nehru, India, and Interwar Internationalism* (New York: CUP, 2018), 5.

[88] Kris K. Manjapra, *M. N. Roy: Marxism and Colonial Cosmopolitanism* (London: Taylor & Francis, 2016); John P. Haithcox, 'The Roy-Lenin Debate on Colonial Policy: A New Interpretation', *The Journal of Asian Studies*, 23/1 (1963), 93–101.

cadres. After the Third Congress (1921), further departments focusing on the Middle and Far East were created.[89]

Non-Europeans also challenged a Eurocentric internationalism which excluded issues of race. Just as colonial migrants in Paris pressed the French Communist party to put the colonial and racial question on their agenda,[90] so Asian Communists forced the Soviets to centre colonialism on the international agenda, and African-American and Caribbean Marxists challenged the Comintern to act on the so-called 'Negro question'. The Soviets for their part had to deal with multiple anti-colonial leaderships that frequently crossed borders and had come into contact with Communist and socialist thinking in many different contexts, most notably in Paris and London.[91] Such activists therefore resisted too easy an accommodation with the Soviet world view. African-American and Caribbean Marxists helped create a Negro Bureau in 1922 to extend Comintern discussions of world revolution so as to consider the plight of blacks under US and South African capitalism and to promote the position of black Communists within their national Communist parties.[92] During the Comintern's leftist turn (1928–34), they seized the opportunity to broaden out discussions to consider prospects for pan-African liberation.[93] The Soviet Union became in their view 'an exemplary revolutionary model'[94] for anti-colonial and anti-racial activists all over the world: the careers of black radicals and future Communists such as Hubert Harrison, Cyril Briggs, George Padmore and Otto Huiswood showed how the Comintern provided an international arena for their fight for the emancipation of blacks worldwide. However, compared to the later decades of the Cold War, Africa, still imagined as backward and politically underdeveloped, would play a marginal role in the revolutionary imagination of the Soviets themselves.

In the course of the 1920s, the Comintern would help transform anti-colonialism by forging links between Communist organizations and the Soviet Union, thereby inspiring a myriad of new organizations.[95] These were later,

[89] Sobhanlal Datta Gupta, 'Communism and the Crisis of the Colonial System', in Pons and Smith (eds.), *The Cambridge History of Communism*, 189–211.
[90] Michael Goebel, *Anti-Imperial Metropolis: Interwar Paris and the Seeds of Third World Nationalism* (Cambridge: CUP, 2016), Chapter 6.
[91] Ibid.; Hakim Adi, *West Africans in Britain, 1900–1960: Nationalism, Pan-Africanism, and Communism* (London: Lawrence & Wishart, 1998); Andreas Eckert, 'Afrikanische Intellektuelle und Aktivisten in Europa und die Dekolonisation Afrikas', *Geschichte und Gesellschaft*, 37/2 (2011), 244–74.
[92] Adi, *Pan-Africanism and Communism*; Leslie James, *George Padmore and Decolonization from Below* (New York: Springer, 2014).
[93] Holger Weiss (ed.), *International Communism and Transnational Solidarity: Radical Networks, Mass Movements and Global Politics, 1919–1939* (Leiden: Brill, 2017).
[94] Theo Williams, 'George Padmore and the Soviet Model of the British Commonwealth', *Modern Intellectual History*, 16/2 (2019), 531–59; Constantin Katsakioris, 'Der Leninismus und die nationale Frage in Afrika. Kulturtransfer in der kolonialen und postkolonialen Welt', in Middell and Mählert (eds.), *Kommunismus jenseits des Eurozentrismus*, 209–22.
[95] Kris K. Manjapra, 'Communist Internationalism and Transcolonial Recognition', in Sugata Bose and Kris Manjapra (eds.), *Cosmopolitan Thought Zones: South Asia and the Global Circulation of*

during the Cold War, often characterized as 'front organizations' or 'puppet parties', but this underestimates their highly complex geographies and politics.[96] One of the most important was the International Workers Relief (IAH), founded in 1921 in Berlin by the German Communist Willi Münzenberg, in response to the famine in the Soviet Union. Becoming part of the Comintern's network in 1922, it too helped internationalize solidarity, mobilizing workers to support their counterparts in Great Britain, Japan, Syria and China.[97] The 'colonial question' became an ever more important aspect of its activities once Münzenberg had helped to set up the League against Imperialism (LAI) in 1927.[98] Soviet elites came to rely for the functioning of the Communist ecumene on actors from the colonies, in western metropoles[99] and across diaspora networks alike, often built on earlier imperial travel infrastructures, such as the maritime networks of the British, French and American merchant navies, for the distribution of Communist publications.[100] The International of Seamen and Harbour Workers (ISH) as well as the International Trade Union Committee of Negro Workers (ITUCNW)[101] became partners—albeit often awkward ones, as their African, Caribbean and Chinese activists were frequently at odds with Moscow.[102] Although they were joined by a smaller group of mobile Soviet Communists such as Mikhail Borodin, the 'worldly wisdom' of foreign actors often enabled them to shape the Soviet-led socialist project in the colonial world, a pattern which would recur during the Cold War.[103] The

Ideas (Basingstoke: Palgrave Macmillan, 2010), 159–77; Masha Kirasirova, 'The "East" as a Category of Bolshevik Ideology and Comintern Administration. The Arab Section of the Communist University of the Toilers of the East', *Kritika*, 18/1 (2017), 7–34.

[96] Kasper Brasken, 'In Pursuit of Global International Solidarity? The Transnational Networks of the International Workers' Relief, 1921–1935', in Holger Weiss (ed.), *International Communism and Transnational Solidarity: Radical Networks, Mass Movements and Global Politics, 1919–1939* (Leiden: Brill, 2017), 130–67.

[97] Ibid.

[98] Michele Louro, Carolien Stolte, Heather Streets-Salter and Sana Tannoury-Karam (eds.), *The League Against Imperialism. Lives And Afterlives* (Chicago: University of Chicago Press, 2020).

[99] Leslie James, *George Padmore and Decolonization from Below*; Holger Weiss, 'Hamburg, 8 Rothesoodstrasse. From a Global Space to a Non-place', in Matthias Middell and Steffi Marung (eds.), *Spatial Formats under the Global Condition* (Berlin, Boston: De Gruyter, 2019), 205–27.

[100] Holger Weiss, '"Vereinigt in der internationalen Solidarität!". Der Aufruf der Internationale der Seeleute und Hafenarbeiter an die "Kolonial"- und "Neger"-Seeleute in den frühen 1930er-Jahren', in Middell and Mählert (eds.), *Kommunismus jenseits des Eurozentrismus*, 15–34; Jonathan Hyslop, 'Guns, Drugs and Revolutionary Propaganda. Indian Sailors and Smuggling in the 1920s', *South African Historical Journal*, 61/4 (2009), 838–46.

[101] Weiss, '"Vereinigt in der internationalen Solidarität!"'; Weiss, 'Hamburg, 8 Rothesoodstrasse'.

[102] Holger Weiss, *Framing a Radical African Atlantic. African American Agency, West African Intellectuals, and the International Trade Union Committee of Negro Workers.* (Leiden: Brill, 2014), 292–4.

[103] Steffi Marung 'The Provocation of Empirical Evidence: Soviet African Studies Between Enthusiasm and Discomfort', *African Identities*, 16/2 (2018), 176–90.

international Communist movement was very far from being simply a monolith run by Moscow.[104]

The Soviets also sought to control the tenor of this internationalism by developing relevant educational institutions within the Soviet Union. Universities were founded to 'Bolshevize' the network, but they soon also became attractive places for students from all parts of the world seeking higher education, access to which was blocked for many of their number in the colonial context. The International Lenin School (1926–38)[105] mainly enrolled Communist cadres from Europe and the US; the more short-lived Sun Yat-sen University of the Toilers of China (1925–30) took students sent not only by the Communist Party of China, but also by the nationalist Guomindang. The final nail in its coffin was the collapse of the Communist-Guomindang alliance. The Communist University of the Toilers of the East (KUTV) was founded in 1921 specifically for students from Asia and the Middle East. It came under Comintern jurisdiction in 1923 and expanded to include students from black Africa and Latin America.[106] This university nurtured new networks between Africa, the black Atlantic and the Soviet Union and became the most important institution for African and Asian students. Jomo Kenyatta, future president of Kenya; the Turkish poet Nazim Hikmet; the anti-colonial Gold Coast activist Bankole Awoonor-Renner; the leading Indian Communist M.N. Roy; Sen Katayama, co-founder of the Communist Party of Japan; Albert Nzula and Moses Kotane, future leaders of the Communist Party of South Africa; Ho Chi Minh, future president of Vietnam; Sultan Galiev, leading Muslim national Communist, and the prominent African American Communist Harry Haywood all attended.[107]

European Communists at the KUTV were reshaped by their time there—the presence of students and comrades from across the world globalized teachers' fields of interest and helped professionalize area studies in the Soviet Union. The pioneering Africanists who did so much to develop Eastern European-African study and relations in the 1950s—among them the Russian Ivan Potekhin and the Hungarian Endre Sík—gained their first experiences at the KUTV's Africa-oriented research department, the Association on the Study of National-Colonial

---

[104] Weiss (ed.), *International Communism and Transnational Solidarity*; Fredrik Petersson, 'Hub of the Anti-Imperialist Movement', *Interventions: International Journal of Postcolonial Studies*, 16/1 (2012), 49–71; Fredrik Petersson, 'Imperialism and the Communist International', *Journal of Labor and Society*, 20/1 (2017), 23–42.

[105] Woodford McClellan, 'Africans and Black Americans in the Comintern Schools, 1925–1934', *International Journal of African Historical Studies*, 26 (1993), 371–90.

[106] Allison Blakely, 'African Imprints on Russia. An Historical Overview', in Maxim Matusevich (ed.), *Africa in Russia, Russia in Africa: Three Centuries of Encounters* (Trenton, NJ: Africa World Press, 2007), 37–60; Kirasirova, 'The "East" as a Category', 15–19.

[107] Rossen Djagalov, *From Internationalism to Postcolonialism: Literature and Cinema Between the Second and the Third Worlds* (Montreal: McGill-Queen's University Press, 2020), 44.

Problems (NIANKP).[108] Here they took on board the challenge to Eurocentric agendas: the KUTV and the various Comintern networks provided fora where the Soviet version of anti-racism and anti-imperialism, and its under-examined coloniality, could be questioned.[109] In 1928, black students complained about the failure of the curriculum to address empire. The Comintern investigated institutional 'white chauvinism' and integrated anti-imperialism and black history into its courses. Their encounters in Moscow helped non-European activists promote the emergence if not of a Communist, at any rate a 'transcolonial ecumene'.[110]

For the Soviets, the Comintern was also seen as a necessary adjunct to a wider foreign policy needed to secure a fragile Soviet state; thus their agendas often came into conflict with those of its individual activists.[111] At the first Congress of the Peoples of the East, held in Baku in 1920—the first large arena to host a debate on the relationship between the revolution in Russia and anti-colonial activism outside of Europe—Moscow elites recognized the overlap between geopolitical and ideological concerns in Asia. The new state was threatened both by the British Empire (through India, China, Iran, and Afghanistan) and by an expansionist Japan[112]—a threat later evinced by Tokyo's invasion of Manchuria in 1931. Soviet foreign policy would use the channels of the Comintern to contain risk in ways that would exacerbate tensions within Communist networks. For instance, aid was provided to 'bourgeois China' under Sun Yat-sen, to the later frustration of Mao. The Communist Party in Japan, in its turn, was initially backed in its efforts to mobilize at home so as to disarm Japanese imperialism, but was later advised to engage in pan-Asian networks in support of Chinese, Korean and Indian revolutions.[113] Local nationalists could learn how to work effectively within these tensions: Mongolian leaders seeking an independent state argued not only for their capacity for socialist development, but also knew how to frame their region as a buffer zone against imperialist Japan, in order to boost their chances of

[108] Apollon B. Davidson, 'Afrikanistika, Afrikanisti i Afrikantsy v kominterne: statia pervaia', *Vostok*, 6 (1995), 112–34; Apollon B. Davidson (ed.), *Stanovlenie otechestvenoǐ afrikanistiki: 1920-e nachalo 1960-e g.* (Moscow: Nauka, 2003); Colin Darch and Gary Littlejohn, 'Endre Sik and the Development of African Studies in the USSR: A Study Agenda from 1929', *History in Africa*, 10 (1983), 73–108.

[109] Steffi Marung, 'The October Revolution and Soviet-African Encounters. The Challenges of Entangled Internationalisms', *Contemporanea*, 21/2 (2018), 268–77.

[110] Katerina Clark, 'The Representation of the African American as Colonial Oppressed in Texts of the Soviet Interwar Years', *The Russian Review*, 75/3 (2016), 368–85, 370.

[111] Haslam, 'Comintern and Soviet foreign policy, 1919–1941', 637, 640.

[112] Cemil Aydin, 'A Global Anti-Western Moment? The Russo-Japanese War, Decolonization, and Asian Modernity', in Sebastian Conrad and Dominic Sachsenmaier (eds.), *Competing Visions of World Order: Global Moments and Movements, 1880s–1930s* (New York: Palgrave Macmillan, 2007), 213–36.

[113] Tatiana Linkhoeva, 'New Revolutionary Agenda: The Interwar Japanese Left on the Chinese Revolution', *Cross-Currents: East Asian History and Culture Review*, 6/2 (2017), 583–607; Anna Belogurova, 'Communism in South East Asia', in Stephen Anthony Smith (ed.), *The Oxford Handbook of the History of Communism* (Oxford: OUP, 2017), 236–51.

enjoying Moscow's patronage.[114] For Soviet elites there were multiple limitations to their influence in the Far East: they often had to rely on diaspora networks of Japanese, Chinese and Indian radicals. Soviet advisors faced multiple obstacles, which were not only linguistic but also an effect of their paternalistic assumptions regarding the 'backwardness' of Asia.[115]

On their southern borders, the Soviets also sought alliances with non-Communist powers, and cultivated quasi-imperial ambitions, having there to secure a state still beset by a sense of debilitating peripherality vis-à-vis the West.[116] In particular, it worked with Turkey, another new state reconstituted from the ruins of empire that sought to secure its sovereignty on the peripheries of Europe. Despite the anti-Communism of the Turkish independence movement under Kemal Attatürk, the two countries' elites found commonalities of purpose in their anti-westernism. Indeed, it was the Soviet resistance to the West that made it attractive to Pan-Asian and Pan-Islamic movements,[117] who would not always share a Marxist orientation.[118] The Soviets combined their concerns for security and their anti-imperialism at their southern borders with Afghanistan: London had refused independence to its Afghan protectorate after the First World War, and the Soviets became the first to recognize the newly decolonized state, supported the Afghan army and provided economic links for the new state through a friendship treaty. Territorial disputes and ideological cleavages between the Bolshevik and the Pashtun government, however, would not allow for a common internationalist front.[119]

In the long run, this focus on its southern and eastern borderlands meant that the Soviet Union was far less global in outlook than other Eastern European countries. Some of the latter were already developing trade and other links to Africa, the Far East and Latin America, while the legacy of older Tsarist struggles with the British in Central Asia and the Ottoman Empire led the Soviets to focus on their Union's southern borderlands. Africa and Latin America gained importance for the Soviets only after the Second World War.[120] Ethiopia, where there had been Orthodox religious ties, was the only real exception. These differences would later explain why the outreach to a decolonizing Africa from the 1950s would be

---

[114] Ivan Sablin, 'Sibirien und die Mongolei zwischen Russischem Reich und Komintern. Regionalismus, Nationalismus und Imperialismus in den Werken von Elbek-Dorži Rinčino', in Middell and Mählert (eds.), *Kommunismus jenseits des Eurozentrismus*, 53–66.

[115] Dan N. Jacobs, 'Recent Russian Material on Soviet Advisers in China: 1923–1927', *The China Quarterly*, 41 (1970), 103–12.

[116] Austin Jersild, 'The Soviet State as Imperial Scavenger. 'Catch Up and Surpass' in the Transnational Socialist Bloc, 1950–1960', *The American Historical Review*, 116/1 (2011), 109–32.

[117] Djagalov, *From Internationalism to Postcolonialism*.

[118] Cemil Aydin, *The Politics of Anti-Westernism in Asia: Visions Of World Order in Pan-Islamic and Pan-Asian Thought* (New York: Columbia University Press, 2007).

[119] Haslam, 'Comintern and Soviet Foreign Policy', 638.

[120] Robert G. Patman, *The Soviet Union in the Horn of Africa: The Diplomacy of Intervention and Disengagement* (Cambridge: CUP, 2009).

undertaken first by some of the smaller states on the western periphery of the Eastern Bloc rather than by the Soviet Union itself, which would only become active beyond its immediate geopolitical neighbourhood after the death of Stalin.

By the mid-1930s, anti-colonial activists were losing faith in the Soviet Union's commitment to anti-imperialism, seemingly lost in the state's overriding concern with self-preservation. George Padmore, for example, left the ITUCNW in 1933 in protest at the Comintern's increasing reluctance to privilege the struggles of colonized nations.[121] Padmore judged the Soviets to be abandoning internationalism, refocusing on the European scene due to concerns over security on their western flank.[122] In 1934, many anti-colonial activists condemned the Soviets for having joined the League of Nations, in order to cement alliances with non-Communist countries and thereby build opposition to Nazi Germany. In 1935, George Padmore heavily criticized the Soviets' reluctance to support Ethiopia against Italian aggression, charging them with abandoning their commitment to anti-imperialism, preferring not to antagonise Mussolini, and forging an alliance with white Europe against black Africa.[123] The National Association for the Advancement of Colored People (NAACP) in the United States likewise noted the hypocrisy of such rhetoric, and criticized the Soviets for sacrificing an independent black African nation on the altar of European security.[124] While the Soviets presented themselves as the only European player to act as a mediator in a struggle between 'black and white', Ethiopia was the 'coin' with which they tried to purchase support against the German as well as the Japanese threat—from an awkward partner, Fascist Italy.[125] They were therefore circumspect in their criticism of the Italian invasion. The Soviet leadership encouraged the Comintern to call for mass protests on behalf of Abyssinia across the world—yet made little mention of this within the Soviet Union itself.

The Comintern's abandonment of their anti-colonial and anti-racist agenda after 1934 led to often painful ruptures—followed by the loss of experience and

---

[121] James, *George Padmore and Decolonization from Below*, 3, 28.

[122] Silvio Pons, 'The Soviet Union and the International Left', in Richard J.B. Bosworth and Joseph A. Maiolo (eds.), *Cambridge History of the Second World War*, vol. 2 (Cambridge: CUP, 2015), 68–90.

[123] George Padmore, 'Ethiopia and World Politics', *The Crisis*, May 1935, 138–9 and 156–7; George Padmore, *Africa and World Peace* (London: M. Secker and Warburg, Ltd., 1937); Tom Buchanan, '"The Dark Millions in the Colonies are Unavenged". Anti-Fascism and Anti-Imperialism in the 1930s', *Contemporary European History*, 25/4 (2016), 645–65.

[124] J. Calvitt Clarke, 'Periphery and Crossroads, Ethiopia and World Diplomacy, 1934-36', in K. E. Fukui and M. Shigeta (eds.), *Ethiopia in Broader Perspective: Papers of the XIIIth International Conference of Ethiopian Studies*, vol. 1 (Kyoto: Shokado, 1997), 699–712.

[125] J. Calvitt Clarke, *Alliance of the Colored Peoples: Ethiopia and Japan before World War II* (Woodbridge: Boydell & Brewer, 2011), Chapter 6; Lowell R. Tillett, 'The Soviet Role in League Sanctions Against Italy', *American Slavic and East European Review*, 15/1 (1956), 11–16.

knowledge about global complexities through the purges of the Great Terror.[126] Many thousands of internationalists were killed in the years 1937/38—a large part of the teaching staff of the KUTV disappeared in the course of these atrocities. Specialists on Africa, for example, were decimated or forced into internal exile to such an extent that its study almost disappeared, and would only slowly be reconstituted in the 1950s.[127] For almost two decades, the Stalinist assault on internationalism severely crippled the Soviets' capacity to understand the complexities of anti- and post-colonial globalization projects.

Nevertheless, an emerging anti-fascist front bonded anti-colonialists to the Soviet Union in new, if more ambivalent, ways.[128] Even those who, like George Padmore, had broken with the Soviets, would continue to regard theirs as the most positive model available for the resolution of racial and national questions.[129] Moreover, despite this 'anti-internationalism', Moscow's position as a utopian 'Fourth Rome' had been strengthened: with the rise of the Nazi threat, diplomatic relations with the US improved, resulting in a steady increase in visits by Afro-American radicals and artists eager to witness all the latest developments in a self-proclaimed anti-racist state.[130] The black activist and writer Langston Hughes, for example, visited in 1932, in order to participate in the film project 'Black and White', designed to expose the crimes of racism and the plight of black workers in the American South—although the project was curtailed due to the Soviet concern not to endanger their recent economic rapprochement with the US.[131] And the equally celebrated singer, actor and activist Paul Robeson—who arrived in Moscow from London, where he had become fascinated with socialism and non-racism in the Soviet Union—accepted Sergei Eisenstein's invitation to play a major role in a (never realized) film on the Haitian revolt of 1791.[132] The energy which survived the decoupling showed that a dynamics of global

---

[126] Maxim Matusevich, 'Journeys of Hope: African Diaspora and the Soviet Society', *African Diaspora: A Journal of Transnational Africa in a Global World*, 1/1–2 (2008), 53–85; Joy Gleason Carew, *Blacks, Reds, and Russians: Sojourners in Search of the Soviet Promise* (New Brunswick, N.J: Rutgers University Press, 2008), 157–83.

[127] Apollon Davidson, Irina Filatova, Valentin Gorodnov and Sheridan Johns (eds.), *South Africa and the Communist International: A Documentary History* (London: Frank Cass, 2003); Davidson, *Stanovlenie.*

[128] David Featherstone, *Solidarity: Hidden Histories and Geographies of Internationalism* (London: Zed Books, 2012), 96-7.

[129] George Padmore and Dorothy Pizer, *How Russia Transformed Her Colonial Empire. A Challenge to the Imperial Powers* (London: Dennis Dobson, 1946).

[130] Katerina Clark, *Moscow, the Fourth Rome: Stalinism, Cosmopolitanism, and the Evolution of Soviet Culture, 1931–1941* (Cambridge, MA: Harvard University Press, 2011); Kate A. Baldwin, *Beyond the Color Line and the Iron Curtain: Reading Encounters between Black and Red, 1922-1963* (Durham, N.C., London: Duke University Press, 2002), especially chapters 1 and 2.

[131] Carew, *Blacks, Reds, and Russians*, 115–39.

[132] Charles Forsdick and Christian Høgsbjerg, 'Sergei Eisenstein and the Haitian Revolution. "The Confrontation between Black and White Explodes into Red"', *History Workshop Journal*, 78/1 (2014), 157–85.

anti-imperialism—to which the Soviets had contributed—could not be so readily halted. Moreover, the withdrawal of the Comintern from internationalism helped black Marxism cultivate its anti-racist and Pan-African strands free from Moscow—the trajectories of George Padmore and C.L.R. James being the most prominent in this regard.[133] In this sense, the severe weakening of anti-imperialist commitment, confirmed by the disbandment of the Comintern in 1943, also helped accelerate the pluralization of socialisms—a dynamic that would prove difficult to manage for Moscow in the wake of decolonization two decades later.

The geographical reach of public cultures of internationalism also shrank within the Soviet Union. There had been a more globalized culture in the everyday lives of Soviet citizens in the 1920s and early 1930s.[134] Broader campaigns against racism and anti-colonialism took various forms in film, the translation of literature, the publication of children's books and more general political campaigns mobilizing workers and peasants to take a stand—from the trial of two white American workers for having insulted a fellow black worker at a factory in Stalingrad, to the mobilization of public support for the falsely accused African-American Scottsboro Boys.[135] With the rise of the Nazi threat, campaigns were reoriented to the victims of fascism in Europe, most notably in the Spanish Civil War.[136] However, these transnational imaginaries of a world revolution—which were marginalized in official Soviet foreign policy but lingered on in schools and newspapers—continued to socialize generations of Soviet citizens, who were thereby led to see themselves as part of a more global movement.[137] A broader internationalist public imagination, however, would only again come to be strengthened in the 1950s and 1960s, when the population at large were co-opted into society-wide solidarity movements for Korea, Cuba and Vietnam.

Thus, just as the October Revolution helped open up Africa, Asia and Latin America to Marxist thinking and socialist experiments, it also opened the Soviet Union—and later the Eastern Bloc—to more intense and often disquieting encounters with a world beyond Europe, which had deeply significant effects on the reformulation of socialism globally. The dynamics in the wake of the October

---

[133] Christian Høgsbjerg, 'Die Roten und die Schwarzen. C L R James und die historische Idee der Weltrevolution', in Middell and Mählert (eds.), *Kommunismus jenseits des Eurozentrismus*, 35–51; Robin D. G. Kelley, 'Introduction', in C. L. R. James, *A History of Pan-African Revolt* (Chicago: PM Press, 2012), 133.

[134] Gleb J. Albert, *Das Charisma der Weltrevolution. Revolutionarer Internationalismus in Der Fruhen Sowjetgesellschaft 1917-1927* (Köln: Böhlau, 2017), especially Introduction and chapter 5.

[135] Meredith L. Roman, *Opposing Jim Crow: African Americans and the Soviet Indictment of U.S. Racism, 1928–1937* (Lincoln: University of Nebraska Press, 2012), Chapter 3.

[136] Lisa A. Kirschenbaum, *International Communism and the Spanish Civil War: Solidarity and Suspicion* (Cambridge: CUP, 2015).

[137] Irina Volkova, 'Spanish Republicans' Struggle and Its Impact on the Soviet Wartime Generation', *Kritika*, 21/2 (2020), 327–46.

Revolution had helped turn socialism into a truly global, transnational project, pluralizing it and challenging its Eurocentric orientation.

A Post-colonial Vanguard?

Was the Soviet Union a forerunner of a post-colonial world, and a model for its development? Contemporaries from the non-European colonial world were certainly fascinated by it. The challenges it faced seemingly mirrored those that they themselves would soon have to reckon with. It too had a peripheral economic position in the world economy and a predominantly agrarian character. Both Lenin and Bukharin had explored the manner in which the Russian Revolution had deviated from Marx's prediction of revolution in advanced capitalist economies with a full-fledged proletariat. Hence they had formulated a new theory, to the effect that a fully developed capitalism would not be a precondition for the achievement of socialism. Rather, a *direct* transition from pre-capitalist to socialist economic and political forms would be possible under the leadership of the advanced proletariat—the so-called non-capitalist path to socialism. This stood in contrast to the stageist view of Marxism, which would become the dominant paradigm under Stalin and would marginalize this earlier, more flexible vision of revolutionary agency.[138] Only during the 1950s, at the prompting of area studies specialists who saw the potential for revolution in Africa and Asia, would this theory be revived—and anti-colonial elites could once again engage with the Soviet models of rapid economic development.[139]

In the interwar period, however, questions of national liberation and race, not economics, took centre stage. And to that end the leaders of anti-colonial movements focused their attention on the non-European parts of the Soviet Union. Was the treatment of the Soviet peripheries by post-revolutionary elites evidence that this Communist state was a reconstitution of the Tsarist Empire and its imperialist practices, or was it rather a new type of progressive liberator of formerly marginalized hinterlands and enabler of self-determination for minority groups?[140] Hence the scrutiny by, for example, the Gold Coast activist Bankole Awoonor-Renner[141] in his *The West African Soviet Union*,[142] of Central Asia and the Far East, where the capacity of the Soviet system to solve the national

---

[138] Marung, 'Provocation of Empirical Evidence'; Jerry F. Hough, *The Struggle for the Third World: Soviet Debates and American Options* (Washington, DC: Brookings Institution, 1986).

[139] Asian anti-colonial elites were here the first to reflect on this dimension. See David Engerman, *The Price of Aid* (Cambridge: Harvard University Press, 2019) especially Chapter 3.

[140] George Padmore, 'How Russia Transformed her Colonial Empire'.

[141] Holger Weiss, 'The Making of an African Bolshevik. Bankole Awoonor Renner in Moscow, 1925–1928', *Ghana Studies*, 9 (2006), 177–220.

[142] Bankole Awoonor-Renner, *West African Soviet Union* (London: Wans Press, 1946).

question and flatten racial hierarchies was put to the test.[143] Renner sought to find lessons in the ways in which Muslims in the Soviet South were engaging with socialism for a putative revolution amongst the large Islamic populations of French and Spanish West Africa.[144]

Moscow termed an area situated beyond European Russia as their 'East'.[145] This capacious category not only covered Central Asia, the Caucasus and Siberia—but also the Arabic world and Asia beyond its borders. The Soviets claimed that their centre-periphery relationships should be wholly differentiated from western imperialism.[146] Under the Tsarist Empire, the late nineteenth-century expansion into both Siberia—'Russia's Wild East'[147]—and Central Asia aimed not only at developing indigenous peoples on these colonial peripheries but also facilitating economic and social uplift for those Russian landless peasants who settled there after the abolition of serfdom in 1865.[148] They were relocated to the East and trained to become managers of the appropriated land.[149] Yet, simultaneously, Tsarist elites did not just perceive the peoples of the East as the backward 'other' to be civilized, but also parts of the Russian population in these regions. For them, these were sites in which to test and develop an interventionist, paternalistic state with a highly modernist programme, aspects of which left their mark on the Bolsheviks.[150]

Soviet Moscow saw itself not only as the exporter of socialist progress to less developed peripheries,[151] but also as able to integrate actors from that 'East' in order to create knowledge about the non-Russian regions of the Soviet Union and beyond.[152] Soviet specialists, such as ethnographers, who assisted this project, sought to define themselves as different from their imperial forebears. They conceived of themselves as modern experts who now viewed the post-colonial fringes of the Soviet Union not as empty or alien—but as containing peoples with the potential to become part of a new socialist community. Cultures of expertise soon

---

[143] Katsakioris, 'Der Leninismus und die nationale Frage in Afrika', 212–18.

[144] Weiss, Framing a Radical African Atlantic, 73–4.

[145] Kirasirova, 'The "East" as a Category', 7–9.

[146] Khalid, 'Communism on the Frontier', 621–25.

[147] Eva-Maria Stolberg, Sibirien: Russlands 'Wilder Osten' Mythos und soziale Realität im 19. und 20. Jahrhundert (Stuttgart: Franz Steiner Verlag, 2009).

[148] Alexander Etkind, Internal Colonization. Russia's Imperial Experience (Cambridge: Polity, 2011).

[149] Alberto Masoero, 'Territorial Colonization in Late Imperial Russia. Stages in the Development of a Concept', Kritika, 14/1 (2013), 59–91.

[150] Christian Teichmann, 'Cultivating the Periphery', Comparativ, 19/1 (2017), 34–52; Niccolò Pianciola, 'Décoloniser l'Asie Centrale?', 102–106.

[151] Botakoz Kassymbekova and Christian Teichmann, 'The Red Man's Burden. Soviet European Officials in Central Asia in the 1920s and 1930s', in Maurus Reinkowski and Gregor Thum (eds.), Helpless Imperialists: Imperial Failure, Fear and Radicalization (Göttingen: Vandenhoeck & Ruprecht, 2013), 163–88.

[152] Vera Tolz, Russia's Own Orient: The Politics of Identity and Oriental Studies in the Late Imperial and Early Soviet Periods (Oxford: OUP, 2011), Chapter 6.

developed from minority intellectuals in the Soviet 'East' too.[153] Anthropological expeditions no longer counted up the 'civilized' Christians but rather the people and animals living on collectivized farms; folklore texts were invoked not as manifestations of the backwardness of 'peoples without history' but so as to highlight their potential for historical development.[154] The tension between a hierarchical gaze across the 'periphery' and claims regarding the equality of all socialist nations nevertheless persisted. And despite Bolshevik declarations that they had erased the remnants of the imperial past, Soviet advisers who were sent to the region in the 1920s and 1930s still considered themselves to be European— and Europe was the model of modernization that informed Soviet development strategies, as against the backwardness of this 'East'.[155] Newly established administrative structures often resembled western colonial institutions, such as the Central Asian Bureau. Soviet activists from the western republics were frequently sent to the 'East' as punishment for previous failures in party work, and their labour at the periphery could serve as a path back to the metropole. Their letters home suggest that they experienced this as forced labour in a region about which they had insufficient knowledge. Yet such hierarchies never went unchallenged, and in the metropole questions were raised: the fact that settlers viewed themselves as European civilizers was seen as a problem in Moscow, where leaders feared that such attitudes would both elicit resistance in the periphery and also endanger the Soviet Union's reputation abroad as an anti-colonial state.[156] It was the development of these peripheries that became a template for the Soviet Union's later engagement with a broader world of collapsing empires after the Second World War. Russian Orientalists, who had studied this 'East', became the founding fathers of post–war Soviet area studies, training future generations of Soviet specialists on Africa, China and India to become important players in outreach to the decolonizing world.[157]

[153] Hanna Jansen, *Peoples' Internationalism, Central Asian Modernisers, Soviet Oriental Studies and Cultural Revolution in the East (1936-1977)*, PhD dissertation (University of Amsterdam, 2020), 59–65.

[154] David G. Anderson, Mikhail S. Batashev and Craig Campbell, 'The Photographs of Baluev. Capturing the "Socialist Transformation" of the Krasnoyarsk Northern Frontier, 1938–1939', in Maja Kominko (ed.), *From Dust to Digital: Ten Years of the Endangered Archives Programme* (Cambridge: Open Book Publishers, 2015), 135–78.

[155] Benjamin Loring, '"Colonizers with Party Cards". Soviet Internal Colonialism in Central Asia, 1917–39', *Kritika*, 15/1 (2014), 77–102; Stephen Kotkin, 'Modern Times. The Soviet Union and the Interwar Conjuncture', *Kritika*, 2/1 (2001), 111–64.

[156] Kassymbekova and Teichmann, 'The Red Man's Burden', 167–171.

[157] Michael Kemper and Stephan Conerman (eds.), *The Heritage of Soviet Oriental Studies* (London: Routledge, 2011); Andreas Hilger, 'Area Studies in Times of Global Cold War: Indology in the Soviet Union', in Katja Naumann, Torsten Loschke, Steffi Marung and Matthias Middell (eds.), *In Search of Other Worlds: Essays towards a Cross-Regional History of Area Studies* (Leipzig: Leipziger Universitätsverlag, 2019), 51–77; Steffi Marung, 'Peculiar Encounters with the "Black Continent": Soviet Africanists in the Global 1960s and the Expansion of the Discipline', in Matthias Middell (ed.), *Self-Reflexive Area Studies* (Leipzig: Leipziger Universitätsverlag, 2013), 103–34.

And there was resistance to Soviet claims of liberation, particularly from Muslim modernizers in the Caucasus, who feared that their nations might be economically relegated to the imperial hinterland. One notable figure who embodied the complexity of this relationship was the Azerbaijani leader Mammad Amin Rasulzadeh: he resisted—with Ottoman help—the integration of Azerbaijan into the Soviet Union. After this had failed, he worked in Moscow for the Commissariat for Nationalities, before leaving in 1922, when he became one of the loudest anti-Soviet voices, living in Turkey and Poland (where he married Marshal Piłsudski's daughter). Eventually, he ended up in Nazi Germany, where he agitated for Azerbaijani nationalism, Pan-Islamism and Pan-Turkism, an anti-Soviet shift he shared with the region's Muslim diaspora living in western metropoles.[158]

Despite these domestic contestations over the relationship of the Soviet Union to colonialism, many African-American intellectuals were persuaded by the claim that the Soviets had built an anti-imperial federation whose commitment to economic uplift on the periphery was serious. From the other side of the Atlantic, the Soviet Union was often seen as a society struggling to escape economic backwardness whilst also overcoming the legacies of colonial and racial hierarchies. The African-American agricultural engineer Oliver Golden was optimistic that the USSR could secure the advancement of the 'non-European peoples of the Soviet Union—the Uzbeks, Turkmen, Chukcha—who had been colonized and who in American terms were "coloured".[159] He recruited fellow agricultural specialists to go to the Soviet Union and assist in the modernization of the cotton regions of Central Asia. Likewise, black writer and activist Langston Hughes favourably compared the Uzbek Soviet Socialist Republic with the American South, admiring the Soviet capacity to overcome racism and seeing 'a coloured land moving into orbits hitherto reserved for whites'.[160] He emphatically called for putting 'One more "S" in the U.S.A. to make it Soviet', so that 'Black and White can all be red'.[161] These visions of a non-racist, anti-colonial Soviet development were shared by a highly diverse range of other activists, the South African writer and Communist Alex La Guma[162] and the Indian anti-colonial leader Jawaharlal

[158] Zaur Gasimov and Wiebke Bachmann, 'Transnational Life in Multicultural Space: Azerbaijani and Tatar Discourses in Interwar Europe', in Bekim Agai, Umar Ryad und Mehdi Sajid (eds.), *Muslims in Interwar Europe. A Transcultural Historical Perspective* (Leiden: Brill, 2015), 205–24.

[159] Lily Golden, *My Long Journey Home* (Chicago: Third World Press, 2002), 7; see also Carew, *Blacks, Reds, and Russians.*

[160] Langston Hughes, *I Wonder as I Wander: An Autobiography* (New York: Hill and Wang, 1993 [1940]), 116; David Chioni Moore, 'Local Color, Global "Color": Langston Hughes, the Black Atlantic, and Soviet Central Asia, 1932', *Research in African Literatures*, 27/4 (1996), 49–70.

[161] The poem 'One more "S"' was first published in 1934. Arnold Rampersad and David Roessel, *The Collected Poems of Langston Hughes* (New York: Knopf, 1994).

[162] Alex La Guma, *A Soviet Journey. A Critical Annotated Edition.* Edited by Christopher J. Lee (Lanham: Rowman and Littlefield, 2017).

Nehru among them.[163] Yet during the 1930s critical voices were raised that cotton agriculture would condemn Central Asia to the economic hinterland, creating a colonial relationship with Moscow.[164] During the Second World War, Central Asia was used by Moscow to promote the image of the Soviet Union as an anti-racist state: Muslim freedoms were showcased, as from 1941 private mosques were allowed, and some prominent Muslims gained permission to go on the hajj. This was incorporated into international anti-fascist propaganda across Asia and the Middle East in order to demonstrate the superiority of Soviet civilization.[165] From the 1950s, agricultural development in Central Asia was once again employed to illustrate what Soviet leadership could offer economically to a decolonizing world.[166]

The extent to which the Soviets had overcome racialized thinking remained a live question throughout the interwar period. The African-American intellectual W.E.B. Du Bois, after visiting the Soviet Union in 1926, argued that the Russians were 'unconscious of race'. Soviet anthropologists had tried to reconceptualize race in socialist terms,[167] but the limits to the break from an imperial racialized gaze remained in evidence. Both late Tsarist and early Bolshevik society consumed a broader western colonial culture, and the Russian avant-garde would often depict eroticized African figures to be gawped at, or infantalized ones to be improved. The early Soviet fascination with American slave stories was a case in point: supposedly embodying the Soviet commitment to a culture of racial redemption, the most popular contained heroic white figures as liberators of childlike blacks from oppression. In films that denounced western racism, white and non-white Soviet figures, embodiments of a (multi-national) Soviet Union, feature as the saviours of black characters from the evils of racism or as teachers of white chauvinists who come to reconsider their mistakes.[168] One popular comedy film 'Circus', made in 1936 by Grigorii V. Aleksandrov, presented a white American woman and her black child as victims of German Nazism and American racism—from which they would be saved by the warm embrace of

---

[163] Jawaharlal Nehru, *Soviet Russia. Some Random Sketches and Impressions* (Bombay: Chetana, 1949).

[164] Artemy M. Kalinovsky, 'Writing the Soviet South into the History of the Cold War and Decolonization', in James Mark, Artemy M. Kalinovsky and Steffi Marung (eds.), *Alternative Globalizations. Eastern Europe and the Postcolonial World* (Bloomington, IN.: Indiana University Press, 2020), 191–2; Julia Obertreis, *Imperial Desert Dreams: Cotton Growing and Irrigation in Central Asia, 1860–1991* (Göttingen: Vandenhoeck & Ruprecht, 2017).

[165] Jansen, *Peoples' Internationalism*, 51–2.

[166] Kalinovsky, 'Writing the Soviet South', 192–199.

[167] Francine Hirsch, 'Race without the Practice of Racial Politics', *Slavic Review*, 61/1 (2002), 30–43; Sergej Alymov, 'World War II and the Cold War as a Context for Discipline Formation. The Case of Soviet Ethnography, 1940s–1960s', in Naumann et al. (eds.), *In Search of Other Worlds*, 23–50; Francine Hirsch, *Empire of Nations: Ethnographic Knowledge & the Making of the Soviet Union* (Ithaca, London: Cornell University Press, 2005), 21–61.

[168] Roman, *Opposing Jim Crow*, 193–206.

Soviet internationalism. These cultural products often reinscribed racial hierarchies in the name of overcoming them.[169] Yet, in any case, the Soviet retreat from internationalism in the late 1930s put pay to cultures which aspired to foreground such anti-racist sentiments—just as a popular international anti-imperialism was beginning to develop in Eastern Europe.

From Berlin to Addis: The Rise of Fascism and Eastern European Anti-colonialism

Whereas the rise of Fascism led to the de-internationalization of the Soviet Union, for many of the smaller countries of Eastern Europe, the reverse was the case. Here anti-colonial solidarities predated their institutionalization by Communist states in the 1950s—a product of the growing recognition there of the connections between the revivals of imperial intent over both Africa and Eastern Europe. The Italian invasion of Abyssinia in 1935 was a key moment in the growth of solidarity well beyond the Communist or broader left. Earlier expressions of colonial aggression had elicited far less reaction.[170] Romanian President of the League of Nations Nicolae Titulescu, for instance, did not condemn Japan after its invasion of Manchuria in 1931. In fact, when he was asked to be part of the commission that was supposed to investigate the situation, he declined as his focus was on Romania's territorial interests in Europe.[171]

Ethiopia, by contrast, raised the spectre that imperialism outside Europe might encourage revisionism within. The Romanian delegation to the League of Nations, led by Titulescu, argued that this aggression must not be considered a local, unimportant war, but 'a conflict which could break out tomorrow in Europe [too].'[172] It feared that a war in Ethiopia meant a further step on the path to revision by the fascist powers of the European territorial status-quo established in the Balkans after the First World War. According to Lucrețiu Pătrășcanu, arguably the most important Communist intellectual of twentieth-century Romania, 'Fascist Italy signals the beginning of a new fire. Started in Africa, it can quickly spread in Europe because fascist dictatorships, overt or covert, can transform our entire continent into an immense powder keg and one spark will suffice for an explosion

---

[169] Raquel Greene, 'Constructions of Africa in Early Soviet Children's Literature', *Black Perspectives: Blog of the African American Intellectual History Association*, 31 October 2017; Irina Novikova, 'Russian Blackamoors, From Grand-Manner Portraiture to Alphabet in Pictures', in Leigh Raiford and Heike Raphael-Hernandez (eds.), *Migrating the Black Body: The African Diaspora and Visual Culture* (Seattle: University of Washington Press, 2017), 30–51.

[170] Interview with Janez Stanovnik, 7–8 January 2001, 9–10 (UN Oral History Collection).

[171] Botoran and Unc, *Tradiții*, 64–5.

[172] Statement published in *Dimineata*, 7 November 1935.

that can encompass the entire world.'[173] For these reasons, Romania, along with a group of small and middle-sized states, first and foremost the allies from the Little Entente (Yugoslavia, Czechoslovakia) and the Balkan Pact (consisting of Yugoslavia, Greece, and Turkey) took up the defence of Ethiopia's independence and integrity, pressing for the strict observance of the League of Nations' Pact. By contrast, Bulgaria and Hungary, who challenged the post-Versailles settlement, rather sought to use Mussolini's enhanced stature in European and international diplomacy to promote him as arbiter in Central and Southeast European territorial disputes.[174] Hungarian Prime Minister Gyula Gömbös' refusal to give his country's support in 1935 at the League of Nations vote to condemn Italy was rooted in his hopes for Mussolini's backing to regain the territory lost after the First World War.[175]

Afro-American radicals and anti-colonial intellectuals began to promote an internationalized vision of the links between Eastern Europe and Africa. Understanding that the fates of the 'other Europe', and the colonized world beyond Europe, were related, they questioned the western powers' commitment to Eastern European independence, and demanded that these new nations—and their sovereignty—be respected.[176] It was not only Abyssinia that was imperilled. There were signs that Eastern Europe likewise was slowly being returned to the colonizable world. When the British were selecting an envoy to Prague to address the tensions between Germany and Czechoslovakia in the late 1930s, Lord Halifax suggested sending a specialist who, 'has practical experience of administration and of minority problems, such as an ex-governor of an Indian province'.[177] The German occupation of Czechoslovakia in summer 1938 was a key moment: British officials contemplated offering Nazi elites control over territory in Central Africa in exchange for self-restraint in Eastern Europe.[178] The Trinidadian campaigner George Padmore dubbed the occupation a 'new Abyssinia'.[179] Indian leader Nehru himself had been interested in the Czechoslovak struggle for a secure state since the early 1920s, and would continue to idealize the country as

[173] Botoran and Unc, Tradiţii de solidaritate, 152.

[174] The peak of this development was after 1938 when, as Holly Case pointed out, 'Nazi Germany and Fascist Italy were playing the role of minority rights watchdog for both states, in a sense picking up where the League of Nations had left off.' (Holly Case, Between States: The Transylvanian Question and the European Idea During World War II (Stanford, CA: Stanford University Press, 2009), 152.

[175] György Réti, 'The European Consequences of the Italian Aggression against Ethiopia', Rivista di Studi Politici Internazionali, 74/3 (2007), 426–31.

[176] On African American radical Cyril Briggs, see Minkah Makalani, In the Cause of Freedom: Radical Black Internationalism from Harlem to London, 1917–1939 (Chapel Hill: University of North Carolina Press, 2011), 3.

[177] E.L. Woodward and R. Butler (eds.), Documents on British Foreign Policy 1919–1939 (London, 1949), 425.

[178] Susan Pedersen, The Guardians: The League of Nations and the Crisis of Empire (Oxford: OUP, 2015), 343–5.

[179] See George Padmore, 'Czechoslovakia: A New Abyssinia', in The People (Trinidad), 15 October 1938. Thanks to Leslie James for this reference.

the last bastion of democracy in the region.[180] On his visit to London in mid-1938 he was dismayed by the lack of resolve in the face of the threat of Nazi occupation in Eastern Europe. At the London Conference of Peace and Empire held on 15–16 July 1938, he emphasized in his presidential address the globality of Fascism and its imperial designs: 'The problem of Central Europe, Czechoslovakia, Spain, China and many other problems... ought to be taken together and considered as a whole.'[181] Nehru turned down an invitation to go to Nazi Germany and instead visited Prague to show his solidarity in early autumn 1938. He encouraged his audience to see their struggle with fascist colonialism in Europe to maintain sovereignty as fundamental to the anti-colonial fight for independence globally.[182] When Germany invaded Czechoslovakia and the League of Nations did nothing, he noted that this was of course unsurprising given the international community's earlier reluctance to stop the Italian invasion of Abyssinia. The Indian National Congress continued to protest vigorously against British indifference and German aggression.[183]

And there were signs of new forms of transregional solidarity. Domestic expressions of sympathy for Abyssinia were expressed most broadly in Yugoslavia, long threatened by Mussolini who had wished to see the state dismembered. 1950s propaganda in Communist Yugoslavia remembered the war as the point at which a broader anti-fascist front was forged between the European left and Africa. Recounting the growth in Yugoslav–Ethiopian linkages, in preparation for the first visit of the emperor to Yugoslavia, in July 1954, a declaration of the Ministry of Foreign Affairs related:

> At the time, as well as during the whole of the Ethiopian-Italian war, the Yugoslav public gave mass support to the struggle of the Ethiopian peoples against fascist aggression. Throughout the country, anti-fascist rallies, lectures and protests were held. The press, without regard to political leanings, followed the heroic struggle closely.... Some volunteered for the Ethiopian army. The alliance of the Yugoslav and Ethiopian government was already forged in the battle against fascism.[184]

---

[180] Jawaharlal Nehru, *Glimpses of World History*, 4th edn (London: Lindsay Drummond, 1949), 963–4.

[181] Jawaharlal Nehru, *The Unity of India. Collected Writings 1937–40* (New York: John Day Company, 1942), 273–4.

[182] M Krása, 'Jawaharlal Nehru and Czechoslovakia at the Time of the 1938 European Crisis', *Archív Orientální*, 34 (1966), 339.

[183] Tagore, too, who had been a regular visitor to Prague in the 1920s, condemned the aggression. Miloslav Krása, 'India and Czechoslovakia Between Two World Wars: A Study of Cultural Contacts and Exchange of Ideas', in Stanislava Vavroušková (ed.), *India and Czechoslovakia Between Two World Wars: A Study of Cultural Contacts and. Exchange of Ideas* (Prague, 2006).

[184] DASMIP, PA, 1954, f-18, Etiopija, July 1954, *O ratnim vezama*, 112 (Diplomatic Archives of the Serbian Ministry of Foreign Affairs).

Not all had in fact supported this: Milan Stojadinović, the pro-German Yugoslavia Prime Minister argued that 'it is in [Yugoslavia's] interest that Italy obtains Ethiopia, since it will not attack us...and Germany obtain the restitution of its colonies, to entangle themselves materially. It was a mistake to have robbed Germany of colonies.'[185] Nevertheless, a fear of Italian revanchism was crucial for fostering sympathy for the plight of Abyssinia across both the political left and right.[186] The newspaper *Politika* led the charge: Ethiopia was shown to be an 'ancient kingdom' engaged in a 'noble struggle'. The main leftist newspapers called for volunteers in articles such as *The Abyssinian Joan of Arc goes to the front*.[187] *Radio Beograd* broadcast the Emperor's plea to the world—'Alo, alo ovde Abyssinia!'—noting that across society it was 'well received'.[188] In Bijelo Polje, the mayor and two priests founded the society 'Friends of Ethiopia'. All over Yugoslavia, citizens collected money and sent it to the Red Cross. Haile Selassie was celebrated and school children were set assignments to draw comic strips of Abyssinians killing Italians.[189] And a wider anti-colonialism developed there well before postwar Communism. Afro-Caribbean poet and politician Aimé Césaire, and Léopold Senghor, the future president of Senegal, made their first contacts with Yugoslav Communists in Paris, and, by the 1930s, Yugoslavia became a centre for African and 'negro art'. Aimé Césaire loved travelling to Yugoslavia, and it was there that he wrote one of his most famous works on négritude, *Return to My Native Land*.

Poland likewise came to the assistance of Abyssinia. A year before the conflict erupted, the two countries had signed a 'friendship, settlement and trade' agreement—Poland saw it as compensation for the restrictive trade quotas imposed

---

[185] Milan Vanku, 'La politique du gouvernement yougoslave a l'égard de l'Anchluss et de l'accord de Munich en 1938', in Nikolaj Todorov and Christina Mikova (eds.), *Les Grandes Puissances et les Balkans a la veille et au début de la deuxième guerre mondiale 1937–1941* (Sofia: Éditions de l'Académie Bulgare des Sciences, 1973), 223.

[186] Antonina Kuzmanova, 'L'agression de l'Italie fasciste contre l'Éthiopie et les pays', *Etudes balkaniques*, 22/1 (1986), 563–4.

[187] Dušan Timotijević, 'Italijanske trupe prodrle u Abisiiniju, a avioni bombardovali Aduu i Adigrat', *Politika*, 4 October 1935; Dušan Timotijević, 'G. Baldivn apeluje na Italiju da obustavi svoju akciju', *Politika*, 6 October 1935; Dušan Timotijević, 'Po sinoćnim vestima iz Rima, Italijani su juče zauzeli Aduu', *Politika*, 7 October 1935; Dušan Timotijević, 'Egipat ne želi rat, ali ga očekuje svakog trenutka', *Politika*, 11 October 1935; Dušan Timotijević, 'Prema vestima iz Adis Abebe prošle noći su Abisinci izvršili prepad na Aduu i poubijali 2.500 Italijana', *Politika*, 12 October 1935; Dušan Timotijević, 'Abisinska Jovanka Orleanka odlazi na front sa 15.000 vojnika', *Politika*, 12 October 1935; Dušan Timotijević, 'Teške borbe u oblasti Aksuma', 13 October 1935.

[188] 'Alo! Alo!...Ovde Abisinija!', *Radio Beograd*, 8 October 1935.

[189] There are many examples of postwar Africanists whose fascination with the continent began in their opposition to the Italian invasion—and whose expertise was reactivated with the region's turn to the South in the mid-1950s. For example, the Romanian travel writer Mihai Tican-Rumano, who wrote anti-colonial adventure stories, and became an interwar popularizer of the 'heroic' Ethiopian struggle, advocated during the early 1960s for the cause of African-Romanian solidarity. Mihai Tincan-Rumano, 'Drumeţ prin Africa', *Secolul*, 20/2 (February 1962), 69–75. The left-leaning Yugoslav journalist Dušan Timotijević, continued to promote the historical memory of the parallels between the anti-fascist struggles of Ethiopia and Yugoslavia during the Communist era.

by the West whereas Abyssinia sought 'non-colonial' partners to shield it from Italian aggression.[190] The Polish government, as a member of the Council of the League of Nations, voted in favour of sanctions against Italy. It was an important moment for the Polish left too: according to Stanisław Ossowski, who later became a prominent sociologist, one had to reject the hypocrisy and falsehoods inherent in Italian calls for 'white solidarity', as they purportedly set about 'defending human rights' by ridding Abyssinia of slavery. He called upon all those who were 'repulsed by the cynical morality of capitalist imperialism' to stand with Abyssinia, a country that could play a role as a model for Africa as it leapt from 'tribal Communism' to a 'modern Communistic society' based on rational organization and technologies. For Ossowski, the independence of Abyssinia would start a process that would inevitably lead to the independence of Africa as a whole.[191] Material support for Abyssinia was strongest from Czechoslovakia: its factories supplied arms and its army provided training for their Ethiopian counterparts from the early 1930s. The government sent military advisers at the start of the conflict—although soon withdrew them after pressure from Italy.[192]

Yet many in Eastern Europe—particularly on the political right—supported the colonial ambitions of Italy in Africa. For them, the threat of a revived western colonialism was less important than the boost it might give to their own specific national projects. Abyssinia was also viewed as an economic opportunity for countries that had failed to gain their own territory. In 1937, the Bulgarian government expanded its existing commercial treaty with Italy to include trade opportunities in Rome's new colonies in Africa.[193] In Hungary, large enterprises had not developed a colonial lobby, as in Poland. Rather they often cooperated with western cartels to gain access to new markets in the South.[194] Moreover, Hungarian experts in geology, agriculture, and water systems also began to work in Africa and Asia as part of Western European colonial projects: knowledge that would be retooled in the 1950s as expertise from European socialist states assisting decolonizing states.[195] In the mid-1930s, the potential opening up of eastern

---

[190] Konrad Banaś, 'Polsko-abisyńskie stosunki handlowe w latach 1918–1939', *Przegląd Orientalistyczny*, 3–4 (2018), 265–82.

[191] Stanisław Ossowski '"Misja cywilizacyjna" białego człowieka a niepodległość Etiopii', *Wiadomości Literackie*, 38 (1935), 2. Ossowski also argued for the independence of India: 'O wolność Indii', *Wiadomości Literackie*, 13 (1934), 7. 'Przeszłość i przyszłość kast indyjskich, *Wiadomości Literackie*, 21 (1934), 2.

[192] *The 20th Century Revisited: Relations between former Czechoslovakia and Ethiopia* (Ministry of Foreign Affairs of the Czech Republic, 2015), 9–12.

[193] Lüben Berov, 'Les rapports économiques entre la Bulgarie et l'Italie à la veille de la seconde guerre mondiale', in Todorov and Mikova (eds.), *Les Grandes Puissances*, 131.

[194] Mária Hidvégi, 'A Ganz-Jendrassik dízel motorkocsik Argentínában', *Aetas*, 29/4 (2014), 45–64.

[195] In the Hungarian case, see for example geologist Horst Bandat, and water experts Gyula Jolánkai and Béla Entz. Both would work extensively in Africa from the 1960s. Indeed, the experience in water management in Hungary was of great interest in interwar British colonial administration in Elemér Sajó and Árpád Trummer (eds.) *A Magyar szikesek* (Budapest: Pátria, 1934). From

Africa by Italy caused excitement because of the prospect of new opportunities for Hungarian business.[196] Mussolini had promised those countries that supported him at the League of Nations special treatment. Hungary would be granted mining and cotton concessions as the Italian Empire expanded, and in its gratitude became one of only four countries to refuse to condemn the Italian invasion of Abyssinia.[197] The 'Società Commerciale Ungaro-Etiopica' or *Hungafric* was formed in 1936, with the aim of developing 'Hungarian industrial trade and agricultural activities in Ethiopia'. The first Italian colonial consignment of bananas arrived in Hungary from Italian Somalia in October 1937.[198] Even Hungary's Social Democrats argued that Ethiopia might be a destination for their country's 'excess working population'.[199]

In Romania, Abyssinia accelerated a turn to right-wing visions of a Europe revitalized by a project of fascist imperialism.[200] Those on the moderate right to full-blown fascists widely supported Italian Fascism as a recipe for national revitalization: in 1936, an open letter was sent to Rome signed by 109 prominent Romanians (such as Nicolae Iorga, a former Prime Minister, and the economist Mihail Manoilescu) in support of Italy's 'normal' colonial appetites, counterposed to 'English greediness'.[201] Iorga drew on the notion of a shared Latinity in his support for Mussolini, a providential leader engineering the rebirth of Ancient Rome, against whom Hitler paled.[202] He believed in Latin solidarity as a bulwark against the Soviet Union and, later, Nazism. He attacked the left's condemnation of Italy's aggression, describing Rome's offensive in the Mediterranean and Africa as a conflict between civilization and barbarism. Those who criticized Italy were betraying their countries' shared Latin heritage: he told his students at the University of Bucharest that the invasion was a 'legitimate expansion of a people that lives on the land where the Romans lived and who feels within itself some of the virtues that made the Romans powerful and glorious'.[203] It was also through the Abyssinian issue that the connections between anti-Semitism and support for European colonization became very explicit.[204] Iorga's racial denigrations of 'Black Ethiopians', in the context of his belief in the Italian civilizing mission,

Zoltán Ginelli, 'Decolonization and Semiperipheral Postcoloniality: Hungarian Experts in Nkrumah's Ghana', in Eszter Szakács (ed.), Refractions of Socialist Solidarity, *Mezosfera*, 5 (Budapest: tranzit. hu, 2018).
[196] Balázs Szélinger, *Magyarország és Etiópia. Formális és informális kapcsolatok a 19. század második felétől a II. világháborúig*, Doctoral Dissertation (Szeged, 2008).
[197] Ibid., 138.   [198] Ibid., 140–1.
[199] László Ascher, 'The Fate of Abyssinia', *Szocializmus* (1935), 417–19.
[200] For this argument, see Balázs Trencsényi, *The Politics of 'National Character'. A Study in Interwar East European Thought* (London/New York: Routledge, 2012), 184.
[201] Georgiana Țăranu, *Nicolae Iorga și Italia lui Mussolini. Studii* (Cluj Napoca: Academia Română, 2015), 91.
[202] Ibid., 53–4.   [203] Ibid., 242.
[204] Shelley Baranowski, *Nazi Empire: German Colonialism and Imperialism from Bismarck to Hitler* (Cambridge: CUP, 2010), 55.

reignited an anti-Semitism and a hysteria about 'foreign bodies' polluting Europe that had been tempered since the First World War.[205]

Italy's colonial revival significantly increased interest in such matters among elite circles in Poland: in 1937, the Ministry of Foreign Affairs asked the Jagiellonian University to establish a Department of Colonial Studies; the same year saw the founding of a Colonial Museum in Lviv, and an Institute of Maritime and Colonial Studies.[206] According to the Ministry, '[o]ver the last few years, population, migration and colonial subjects have become prime issues in Poland. Finding the most appropriate solution will largely depend on scientific investigations as well as on making them familiar to the public...'.[207] The Maritime and Colonial League mobilized against Abyssinia: its leaders, often invoking Eurafrican ideas, argued that support for Italian colonialism would eventually help the Polish colonial cause in Africa too.[208] They were critical of the Italians' violence, but used it as an argument for their own superior form of 'light touch' free trade seaborne colonialism, rather than as a reason for criticizing imperialism per se. And some charged those compatriots who supported the African side with being civilizational traitors. The Polish far rightist and Mussolini supporter Marek Romański argued that moral scruples over colonial atrocities only helped the Comintern and exacerbated the Soviet threat to Europe. The unity of a superior Christian colonial continent, to which Eastern Europeans too should pledge themselves, now had to be fought for in the face of an anti-imperialist attitude that 'unnaturally' sought to dissolve sacred civilizational borders. Fearing that Poland's own past partition rendered its citizens sympathetic to Abyssinia's plight, he argued that imperialism in Africa was fundamentally different. He tried to reinforce precisely those cultural differences that the left were attempting to dissolve: Ethiopia was still feudal, uncivilized, contained remnants of slavery and did not deserve her seat at the League of Nations.[209] Ethiopian Christianity was fundamentally different from that of European Catholicism, he argued, presenting the Coptic Church as corrupted by the influence of Judaism and paganism. And Romański further acknowledged a role for Germany in Eastern Europe: he had accepted the Anschluss with Austria, whereby Germany, he argued, had been compensated for the loss of the Polish western lands and their African colonies.

---

[205] Ţăranu, *Nicolae Iorga*, 82.

[206] Diana Błońska, 'Studium kolonialne Uniwersytetu Jagiellońskiego', *Prace Historyczne*, 134 (2007), 91–104; J. Dybiec, *Uniwersytet Jagielloński 1918–1939* (Kraków: Księgarnia Akademicka, 2000), 599–601.

[207] Błońska 'Studium kolonialne', 92. On Mussolini and colonial technology, see the journalist Roman Fajans, *Na frontach Abisynii* (Warsaw: Biblioteka Polska, 1936).

[208] Piotr Rypson, 'Polish Public Opinion on Italo-Abyssinian War (1935–1936)'. Roman Piotrowicz, in his *Zagadnienia abisyńskie a polskie tezy kolonialne* (Warsaw: Zakłady Drukarskie 'Kolumna', 1935), 70.

[209] On the important role for Italians stamping out Abyssinian slavery, see Wanda Wyhowska de Andreis, 'Włochy i Abisynia', *Wiadomości Literackie*, 41 (1935), 5; Piotrowicz, *Zagadnienia abisyńskie a polskie tezy kolonialne*.

Nevertheless, even with a dominant Germany, a patriotic Poland could still play an important role as second fiddle in the region.[210]

The reinvigoration of European overseas imperialism also revived arguments about using emigration to clear out unwanted 'unhealthy' populations of Europe, rendering the expulsion of Jews conceivable—'finding a solution that would relieve Europe of its ancient infirmities', as the Polish colonial journal *The Sea* put it in January 1939.[211] Poland had the largest, and rapidly growing, Jewish minority in the region—over three million by the late 1930s. By the middle of the decade, Polish elites were taking the idea of colonialism much more seriously, and, as the liberal international order collapsed, all Poland's major political parties came to advocate Jewish migration.[212] The otherness of Africa was projected onto local religious Jewish communities to emphasize their disturbing alterity: in a series of articles in the mid-1930s entitled 'Warsaw's Black Continent', the Polish weekly *Literary News* presented visits to traditional Polish Jewish cheder as unsettlingly similar to exploration in the African jungle. Communities with a physiology rooted outside the continent would take to agricultural labour in the tropics with much more ease than those who were 'fully European'.[213] Nevertheless, Jews were 'almost white': hence their emigration to Palestine or Australia would in the long run actually help in the defence of a white world against Arabs or the 'yellow race'.[214] A global presence for Jews with connections back to Poland might prove to have economic benefits too: in late 1938, the Prime Minister Felicjan Sławoj Składkowski proposed that the government acquire land for Jewish migration, which, he argued, would benefit Poland's maritime free trade globalism too—a clinching factor, he thought, that could garner the proposal wide social support.[215] In late 1938, when the Polish parliament debated the issue, a majority argued that forced migration was an 'honourable and noble solution'. The Polish Maritime and Colonial League organized a declaration in favour of the 'liquidation of Jewish overpopulation' in Poland,[216] and called on Jews to propose territories which were 'underpopulated' such as Rhodesia, Angola, and the Belgian Congo.[217] Following the closure of Palestine to Jewish emigration in the late 1930s, the relocation of Jews 'out of the civilized world' to Madagascar continued

---

[210] Marek Romański, *Najazd cywilizacji* (Warsaw: Dom Książki Polskiej, 1936). The League's journal praised its own role in erasing anti-colonial sympathies in Poland in favour of Italy: Czesław Zagórski, 'Pionierska Praca', *Morze*, 10 (1935), 23.

[211] No author, 'Sprawy kolonialne w Sejmie', *Morze*, 2 (20 January 1939), 8–9.

[212] Tadeusz Białas, *Liga Morska i Kolonialna 1930–1939* (Gdańsk: Wydawn. Morskie, 1983), 181–2.

[213] For this discussion, see Zahra, *The Great Departure*, 163.

[214] On the colonialism in Eastern European Zionism, see Dušan I. Bjelić, 'Bulgaria's Zionism, The Colonization of Palestine and the Question of Balkan Postcoloniality', *Interventions* 19/2 (2017), 218–37.

[215] Paweł Fiktus, 'Liga Morska I Kolonialna wobec kwestii żydowskiej w latach 1938–1939', *Imponderabilia*, 1 (2010), 62.

[216] Ibid., 58.   [217] Lemanus, 'Emigracja żydowska', *Morze*, 1 (1938), 1–5.

to be under serious consideration up until the end of 1940.[218] Such 'tropical Zionisms' failed:[219] it would take another form of genocidal colonialism, brought by Nazi imperialism, to decimate Jewish life in Eastern Europe.

The Second World War and Its Aftermath

The Second World War was crucial to the deepening identification between the region and a world that would struggle in its aftermath to escape the chains of empire. On the one hand, the central role that the Soviet Union had played in defeating Nazi Empire in Europe gave it an anti-colonial reputation that would help to hide the complexity of its relationship with imperialism in the postwar world. On the other, the smaller Eastern European power imperialisms of the interwar period would be forgotten: in the wake of Nazi occupation, new spaces and feelings of affinity between the region and others seeking to oust their own occupiers gradually emerged—and would be harnessed by the Communist parties that took power across the region in the late 1940s.

The Soviet Union

The 1939 partition of Poland that followed the Molotov-Ribbentrop Pact with Nazi Germany tarnished the reputation of the Soviet project for many anti-colonial movements.[220] Not all, however: right-wing nationalists from India to the Middle East saw a Communist-Fascist fusion as a way to overcome the liberal imperial world order led by Western Europe.[221] And even ex-Cominternians such as Padmore could still insist in 1940 that, 'The destruction of Russia would give rise to such conditions of repression everywhere that it might take decades before the working class could recover its force once more.' Padmore eloquently drew the line between Stalin's betrayals of the Communist, anti-imperialist and anti-racist struggle and the dynamics of a wider internationalist movement, which would still need the first socialist state to survive.[222] The Soviet Union continued to be at the heart of global imaginaries for an anti-imperialist future beyond the war.

---

[218] Zahra, *The Great Departure*, 144–5, 156. Arkady Fielder was an advocate of Madagascar plans: see his *Jutro na Madagaskar* (Warszawa: Towarzystwo Wydawnicze Rój, 1939). Adam Rovner, *In the Shadow of Zion: Promised Lands before Israel* (New York: New York University Press, 2014), 130.

[219] Allen Wells, *Tropical Zion: General Trujillo, FDR, and the Jews of Sosúa* (Durham: Duke University Press, 2009), 37–8.

[220] Irina Filatova, 'South Africa's Soviet Connection', *History Compass*, 6/2 (2008), 389–403.

[221] David Motadel, 'The Global Authoritarian Moment', *American Historical Review*, 124/3 (2019), 860.

[222] George Padmore, 'Hands Off the Soviet Union' https://www.marxists.org/archive/padmore/1940/hands-off-soviets.htm (last accessed March 2020); on the complex trajectory of Padmore, see Leslie James, *George Padmore and Decolonization from Below*.

When the Soviets turned against Nazi Germany in 1941, and as military victories were amassed, Soviet soil itself became the heroic epicentre of a global struggle for many across the world. In South Africa, for instance, there was a great increase in interest in Soviet affairs: 'Friends of the Soviet Union' organized exhibitions, trade fairs and collected funds for the Soviet war effort.[223] Medical aid for the Soviet Union was collected across southern Africa.[224] For a time, the Soviets gained an unprecedented level of support in allied African territories, including within progressive white cultures.[225] The immense sacrifice of the country was a stamp of moral rectitude, of commitment to the broader struggle against Fascism and imperialism, which could not easily fade. Thus at the end of the war, the Soviets were viewed as heroic liberators—a reputation which would survive amongst many black activists in the US[226] and within African liberation struggles for much of the Cold War.[227]

Yet this was also an ambivalent reputation. In the first postwar years, before the 'Bandung moment' led the Soviets to revive their earlier, more committed anti-colonialism, Moscow saw their wartime victory as a chance to join the imperial powers. The Soviets argued that, given the huge contribution the Red Army had made to the war effort, they should obtain trusteeship over the imperial possessions of the defeated Axis powers, and be granted the former Italian colonies of Libya, Somalia and Eritrea. The Italians, they argued, had failed to 'prepare colonial peoples for self-government'. Africa, as far as the Stalinist elite were concerned, was not yet sufficiently proletarianized for revolution—a view that angered the continent's Communist parties. Thus even these Italian territories were not really seen as objects for revolutionary development—their acquisition was for reasons of Soviet strategic interest.[228]

Closer to home the Soviets sought a 'sphere of influence' in Eastern Europe. Fears regarding their own vulnerability following wartime devastation led them to view the region as appropriable in a world of competing imperial interests. The tension between being at one and the same time both liberators of Europe from Fascism and colonizers of its eastern part in the name of anti-Fascism—would continue to dog the Soviet outreach to the global South throughout the Cold War. Afro-American intellectual W.E.B. Du Bois in his 1945 work *Color and Democracy* expressed the fear that the Soviets had lost their revolutionary zeal. They had been rendered parochial and nationalistic by the war and had abandoned their

---

[223] Filatova, 'South Africa's Soviet Connection', 394.

[224] Donal Lowry, 'The Impact of Anti-communism on White Rhodesian Political Culture, ca.1920s–1980', *Cold War History*, 7/2 (2007), 171.

[225] Ibid., 171–2.   [226] Baldwin, *Beyond the Color Line*.

[227] Katsakioris, 'Der Leninismus und die nationale Frage in Afrika'; Williams, 'George Padmore and the Soviet Union', 536.

[228] Sergei Mazov, 'The USSR and the Former Italian Colonies, 1945–50', *Cold War History*, 3/3 (2003), 49–78.

earlier commitment to a broader internationalism. In exchange they had gained imperial desires whose contours were less and less distinct from those of the West—as their refusal after the war to withdraw from either oil-rich Iran or what Du Bois called 'the Balkans' demonstrated.[229] Moreover, the first signs of the coming wave of decolonization in the late 1940s—which was of great interest to smaller Eastern European nations—did not register so strongly with the Soviets. Their elites paid little attention to Indian independence. It was only with the challenge provided by Bandung Conference—and with it the emergence of a strong anti-colonial movement that had the potential to displace Soviet leadership on the global stage—that a new elite in Moscow under Khrushchev engineered a return to the state's earlier internationalism.

Nazi Occupation in Eastern Europe

The Polish author Antoni Słonimski argued in his 1935 article 'Black Man and Black Shirts' that support for Mussolini's expansionist aims only helped to consolidate arguments that could be turned against the European East.[230] The uncritical acceptance of Italian claims to a superior humanistic form of colonialism in Africa, he asserted, simply lent credence to German claims to be better developers of 'their East'. Such arguments could be taken up by 'people who see Poland as a barbarian country and who suggest that only Germans "could build roads and wells and electrify cities" or establish "hospitals and sanitary institutes for native people". We are all too familiar with these arguments as they are used to describe the difference between Śląsk [modern Silesia] or Poznańskie county and Polesie [less developed Eastern Poland].'[231]

With the German occupation of Czechoslovakia from 1938, the invasion of Poland in September 1939, the extension of the Eastern front across the Baltic states and then Belarus, Ukraine and deep into Russia by 1942, ideas of racial inferiority that had equated Slavs with Africans or Native Americans, forged in the German Empire's twin experiences of African and Polish colonization prior to the First World War, returned.[232] The idea of Poles as a civilized European nation was attacked in Nazi propaganda, replaced by an image of a rabble of distinct indigenous groups—Masovians, Lubliners, and so on. No longer considered fully European, imperial practices developed elsewhere became applicable in a space

---

[229] W.E.B. Du Bois, *Color and Democracy: Colonies and Peace* (New York: Harcourt, Brace and Company, 1945), 114–15.

[230] Antoni Słonimski, 'Czarny człowiek i czarne koszule', *Wiadomości Literackie*, 46 (1935), 6.

[231] Ibid.

[232] Jürgen Zimmerer, 'Der Geburt des "Ostlandes" aus dem Geiste des Kolonialismus', *Sozial Geschichte*, 19 (2004), 13. For an excellent discussion, see Edward Ross Dickinson, 'The German Empire: An Empire?', *History Workshop Journal*, 66 (2008), 129–62.

where the rules that governed relations elsewhere in Europe could be loosened or abandoned altogether.[233] Italian East African governmental structures, and its resettlement policy developed in North Africa, provided an important inspiration for the policy to move around 16 million colonists across Eastern Europe.[234] The idea that indigenous labour could be utilized at will by the colonial state arrived too: Ukraine was variously proclaimed to be the Nazis' India, a mass of population to serve Germans 'like helots', while its rich agricultural soil rendered it the 'California of Europe'.[235] As the concept of colonizing 'empty space' travelled from its origins in the German colonialism in South West Africa, its remit expanded profoundly. Its former association with agricultural development was supplemented with a heightened racial-biological planning, in which whole areas could be emptied or resettled.[236] By 1941, the racial reconstruction of the East was no longer possible only through quarantine in ghettoes or reservations—a policy itself partly based on practices towards Native Americans. Surplus populations could be exterminated: Eastern European Jews, supposedly backward compared to their 'western capitalist' counterparts, were no longer even indigenous people whose cheap labour might serve empire; rather, they were, unlike the Eastern European Slavs, an unnecessary and economically unproductive burden. Nevertheless, their survival in Eastern Europe also constituted a 'breeding ground' for a global Jewish community that, it was feared, could economically colonize Germany. It was this combination of the Eastern Jews as unassimilable pollutant and as reserve demographic supply for a Jewish global capitalist conspiracy that made mass extermination comprehensible for Nazis.[237] Their plans for the hoped-for return of African colonies to Germany in the 1930s did not

---

[233] Mark Mazower, *Hitler's Empire: Nazi Rule in Occupied Europe* (London: Penguin, 2009); Philip Ther, 'Beyond the Nation: the Relational Basis of a Comparative History of Germany and Europe', *Central European History*, 36/1 (2003), 45–73, and his chapter 'Imperial instead of National History: Positioning Modern German History on the Map of European Empires', in Alexei Miller and Alfred J. Rieber (eds.), *Imperial Rule* (Budapest: Central European University Press, 2004); Benjamin Madley, 'From Africa to Auschwitz: How German Southwest Africa Incubated Ideas and Methods Adopted and Developed by the Nazis in Europe', *European History Quarterly*, 35/3 (2005), 429–64; Birthe Kundrus, 'Kontinuitäten, Parallelen, Rezeptionen: Überlegungen zur 'Kolonialisierung' des Nationalsozialismus', *Werkstatt Geschichte*, 43 (2006), 45–62; on continuities and legacies of colonial phantasies beyond 1919, see Sara Friedrichsmeyer, Sara Lennox and Susanne Zantop (eds.), *Imperialist Imaginations: German Colonialism and Its Legacy* (Ann Arbor: University of Michigan Press, 1998).

[234] David Furber, 'Near as Far in the Colonies: The Nazi Occupation of Poland', *International History Review*, 26/3 (2004), 551–3; Kristin Kopp, 'Constructing Racial Difference in Colonial Poland', in Eric Ames, Marcia Klotz and Lora Wildenthal (eds.), *Germany's Colonial Pasts* (Lincoln and London: University of Nebraska Press, 2005), 76–96. Patrick Bernhard, 'Hitler's Africa in the East: Italian Colonialism as a Model for German Planning in Eastern Europe', *Journal of Contemporary History*, 51/1 (2016), 61–90.

[235] David Furber and Wendy Lower, 'Colonialism and Genocide in Nazi-Occupied Poland and Ukraine', in A. Dirk Moses (ed.), *Empire, Colony, Genocide. Occupation, and Subaltern Resistance in World History* (New York: Berghahn, 2008), 381, 385.

[236] Ulrike Jureit, *Das Ordnen von Räumen: Territorium und Lebensraum im 19. und 20. Jahrhundert* (Hamburg: Hamburger Edition HIS, 2016).

[237] Furber and Lower, 'Colonialism', 383–4.

have such genocidal impulses: recovered colonies would provide raw materials, but, at a distance from Germany, their indigenous populations were no threat to the biological nation.

Anti-colonial intellectuals were quick to note the links that historians of Europe would only explore decades later: George Padmore wrote in 1941 that, 'Hitler and his Gestapo sadists are merely applying, with the usual Germanic efficiency, in Poland and other conquered countries, colonial practices borrowed lock, stock and barrel from the British in southern Africa.'[238] Yet his sympathies were tempered. Some Eastern Europeans were victims too, certainly, yet their demands for liberation were supported more widely by western allies. After all, British Prime Minister Churchill had argued in 1941 that the Atlantic Charter—an Anglo-American document that promised self-determination after the war—should be applied only to those under Nazi rule within Europe, and not to western Europe's colonies. As Padmore noted: 'Hitler's victims are white...Perhaps that accounts for the reasons why the British press denounces the Nazis—and rightly so—but remains silent (with few exceptions) about the sufferings of the blacks in southern Africa.'[239]

For some Eastern European nationalists, Nazi ambitions in the East were an opportunity: they meant the realization of self-determination under the protection of Germany. This fuelled a right-wing anti-colonialism that, despite its defeat in 1945, would continue to circulate in exile throughout the Cold War as one strand of a movement to overthrow the 'Communist colonization' of Eastern Europe. Pro-fascist groupings in the late 1930s across the region had supported the 'alternative imperialisms' of Italy and Germany as a way for those with smaller numbers to recover their own sovereignty and cleanse their culture in a world 'perverted by Western decadence'. Some of those trapped, as they saw it, within the Soviet, Yugoslav and Czechoslovak federations—namely nationalist leaders in Slovakia, Croatia, Ukraine, Central Asia, Chechnya and Azerbaijan—hoped that Berlin might advance their own national self-determination. And with Germany's failure to forge a Europe-wide axis against Bolshevism, Hitler turned for support towards the end of the war to a broader anti-colonial world. Berlin became a global centre for anti-colonial nationalists from India to the Middle East who valued strong leadership and strongly racialized nation states, and saw in Fascism the hope for an alternative anti-western and anti-socialist national renewal, and the possibility of realizing dreams of self-determination.[240] Figures such as Syrian nationalist Munir al-Rayyis or the Iraqi Yunus Bahri admired and encouraged the revolt against the Soviets, especially in the Caucasus and Central Asia.[241]

---

[238] George Padmore, 'British Imperialists Treat the Negro Masses Like Nazis Treat the Jews', *Labor Action*, 5/42 (20 October 1941), 4.
[239] Ibid.
[240] Motadel, 'The Global Authoritarian Moment', 850.
[241] Ibid., 865.

Nevertheless, many anti-Soviet nationalist groups—such as the Ukrainian Insurgent Army—had turned against the Germans by the end of the war.

Elsewhere, the experience of German occupation also served to deepen cultures of anti-imperialist internationalism that had predated the Communist version of international solidarity. In Britain and France, resistance to Nazism required the preservation of empire. Imperial resources were needed to defeat Fascism. The Trinidadian socialist C.L.R. James, amongst many others, noted that the struggle against Fascism would lead to the prioritization of European interests and would hold back the demands for anti-colonial liberation.[242] Yet in the smaller countries of Eastern Europe the idea of shared struggle against fascist imperialism was already crystallizing in a way that it had not after the First World War. When Germany declared the protectorate of Bohemia-Moravia in March 1939, Czechoslovak elites noted that the distinction between civilized and less civilized peoples that had underpinned colonial rule outside Europe had now collapsed.[243] Edvard Beneš, leader of the wartime Czechoslovak government-in-exile, was amongst the first Europeans to call for an international conference to challenge a revived racial ideology that now targeted Europeans too. In Prague, a new sympathy with Beijing emerged—as students in particular recognized the parallels between their own situation under a German Protectorate and the occupation of China by the Japanese. The popular Sinophilia evident in 1950s Communist Eastern Europe derived in part from the cultures of identification formed during the war.[244]

After Occupation

The idea that Eastern Europe could be colonized did not disappear with the defeat of Fascism and 'liberation' by the Red Army. Indeed, as African-American intellectual W.E.B Du Bois noted in 1945, the new talk of 'spheres of influence' revealed how both the Soviets and the West still believed that they had the right to 'colonize' the 'free states' of Eastern Europe:

---

[242] C.L.R. James, *World Revolution, 1917–1936. The Rise and Fall of the Communist International* (London: Secker & Warburg, 1937), 13 quoted in Tom Buchanan, 'The Dark Millions in the Colonies are Unavenged': Anti-Fascism and Anti-Imperialism in the 1930s', 25/4 (2016), 645–65.

[243] Mark Mazower, *Hitler's Empire*, 587.

[244] David Tompkins, 'The East is Red? Images of China in East Germany and Poland through the Sino-Soviet Split', *Zeitschrift für Ostmitteleuropa-Forschung*, 62/3 (2013), 393–424. One of the most popular wartime books was Jaroslaw Průšek's memoir of his time in China—*My Sister China*—in which philosophy and cultural traditions as expressions of non-violence and peaceful coexistence were interpreted as a resource for passive resistance against occupation. Olga Lomová and Anna Zádrapová, 'Beyond Academia and Politics: Understanding China and Doing Sinology in Czechoslovakia after World War II', *The China Review*, 14/2 (2014), 6.

In addition to the some seven hundred and fifty millions of disenfranchised colonial peoples there are more than a half-billion persons in nations or groups who are quasi-colonials and in no sense form free and independent states. In the Balkans there are 60,000,000 persons in the 'free states' of Hungary, Romania, Bulgaria, Yugoslavia, Albania, and Greece. They form in the mass an ignorant, poor, and sick people, over whom already Europe is planning 'spheres of influence'.[245]

For Du Bois, only an international order that guaranteed small state sovereignty would prevent a return to conflict:

the nineteenth-century dream... of a world filled with peaceful but independent nations... was proclaimed by Toussaint [L'Ouverture] and Dessalines in Haiti; it was even planned in the Balkans and Far Asia. Then gradually it was over-whelmed, and with a dying gasp in 1919 it was beaten back by mounting waves of imperialism... the small free nation began to disappear from reality. The one great ideal was empire... The one sure outcome was war. If we are now going to re-establish peace... we must re-establish the right of small nations to be free.[246]

In the aftermath of war, the question of how to safeguard the sovereignty of the region's nations was a central question. The struggle to render Eastern Europe uncolonizable was central to the progressive popular fronts that preceded Communist takeovers in the late 1940s: their anti-colonial politics was usually directed not only against Moscow's territorial ambitions, but also at the reach of western capitalism which was still widely blamed for the economic impoverish-ment of the pre-war period. The prominent populist intellectual László Németh claimed that Hungarians had become a colonized people, compared Hungary to New Guinea, and put forward proposals for an independent Third Way—for a region of socialist peasantry free from an imitative westernism, national socialism and Soviet Communism alike.[247]

As Eastern European states were taken over by Communist parties—in many cases backed by the Red Army—new claims that the Soviets were the true colon-izers of the modern world took hold. This image gained ever more credence as the other European powers lost their colonies. Anti-Communists would repeat-edly claim that the Soviet Union was heir to Russian imperial traditions, a gaoler of nations, and a 'scavenger state' that chose to expand into buffer zones beyond

---

[245] W.E.B. Du Bois, *Color and Democracy: Colonies and Peace* (New York: Harcourt, Brace and Company, 1945), 67.

[246] Ibid., 69–70.

[247] Balázs Trencsényi, *A History of Modern Political Thought in East Central Europe*, Vol. 2: *Negotiating modernity in the short twentieth century* (Oxford: OUP, 2018), 154.

its borders.[248] In late 1956, during the Suez Crisis, as the British were losing influence and the Red Army cementing their power in Budapest, British Prime Minister Anthony Eden noted that the Soviets had become the most successful colonizers of the postwar period, certainly when assessed in terms of the expansion of territorial control and the sheer number and extent of its 'subject peoples'.[249] The Soviet Empire, he argued, was an amplified version of its Tsarist forerunner: it reached more than one sixth of the world's land mass, and its imperial nature was only disguised by its territorial contiguity. Empires were usually seen as thalassocratic, distant and separated by sea from the metropole—to understand the only expanding global empire left, the British Under-Secretary of State at the Colonial Office, Sir Hilton Poynton, argued, an effective anti-Communist movement had to overcome this 'salt water fallacy' in the popular mind.[250]

Communists in Eastern Europe reversed the argument. The arrival of the Red Army, combined with local anti-fascist struggle, marked the liberation of the region from its history of colonization. Institutions that had supported the region's failed colonial projects collapsed: the Polish Maritime and Colonial League disappeared with the Nazi invasion in 1939; the Hungarian Adriatic Society was swept away in 1944.[251] Some of their supporters went into exile, although others returned recast as progressive developmentalists in the 1950s. Such claims would provide the basis for the further elaboration of the relationship with a wider world battling empire in the postwar period. First, the power of these new histories helped to erase the memory of the colonial ambitions of some eastern European states. The famous Polish journalist and travel writer Ryszard Kapuściński was typical in this regard. In *The Soccer War*, set in the years of conflict between Honduras and El Salvador, he submerged the memory of colonialism in his nation's suffering under Fascism:

My country had no colonies...and there was a time when my country was a colony. I respect what you've suffered, but, we too, have suffered horrible things: there were streetcars, restaurants, districts *nur für Deutsche*. There were camps, war, executions. That was what we called fascism. It is the worst kind of colonialism.[252]

---

[248] Jersild, 'The Soviet State as Imperial Scavenger'.

[249] Martin Thomas and Richard Toye, *Arguing about Empire: Imperial Rhetoric in France and Britain 1882–1956* (Oxford: OUP, 2017), 206.

[250] George Gretton, 'Colonial Policies of Great Britain and the USSR', *Radio Free Europe Background Information USSR/East-West*, 12 February 1962.

[251] Ginelli, 'Global Colonialism'.

[252] Ryszard Kapuściński, *The Soccer War*, trans. by William Brand (New York: Viking Press, 1990), 232.

Moreover, wartime experiences contributed to a language of shared and ongoing suffering and struggle. New solidarities emerged even before the Communist takeovers of the late 1940s. The United Nations War Crimes Commission (1943–48)—which once rivalled the Nuremberg process as a space for the prosecution of war criminals but was soon forgotten—provided a context for nonwestern actors to combine their efforts. Eastern European governments—first those in exile during the war, and then postwar popular fronts, lent their support to Ethiopia in its attempts to obtain justice for war crimes committed by Italy after the invasion in 1935—despite the main Allied powers choosing to resist the claims of an African state against Europeans.[253] Eastern European leaders hoped that their own pursuit of justice would be recognized by Africans too.[254] The Commission would collapse, however, with the withdrawal of support by the western powers in 1948—in part on account of their fears that it could become a venue to prosecute their own colonial violence. Relationships forged at the UNWCC around shared national experiences of suffering under colonial occupation would be rebuilt from the late 1950s at the United Nations as the challenge from newly decolonized states in the South intensified (see *Rights*).

Communist leaders evoked genocide, mass starvation and the economic exploitation witnessed during the Second World War to retrospectively create a connection between 'Nazi imperialism' in Eastern Europe and the consequences of the western presence in African and Asian colonies—the Soviet occupation of eastern Poland in 1939–41 was not mentioned in official propaganda. Moreover, Nazi occupation had demonstrated that the abrogation of national independence after a short period of self-determination was possible and that decolonization was reversible. Thus, in the Soviet worldview, it was only with continued collective vigilance towards the heirs to Nazi imperialism in the guise of the US and the fascist successor state of West Germany that Eastern Europe and a wider world could be free to develop.[255]

Some new Communist states encouraged histories that connected their recolonization and the violence inflicted upon them to broader western colonial violence, as they sought to attract economic and political support from newly established sovereign states in Africa and Asia. Aimé Césaire was one of the most prominent voices in articulating this connection too. In his 1950 *Discourse on Colonialism*, he wrote:

[253]   Richard Pankhurst, 'Italian Fascist War Crimes in Ethiopia: A History of Their Discussion, from the League of Nations to the United Nations (1936–1949)', *Northeast African Studies*, 6/1–2 (1999), 117.

[254]   Haile Muluken, 'The Failed Ethio-Polish Cooperation to Prosecute Italian Fascist War Crime Suspects: The UNWCC Between Abstract Justice and Political Exigency, 1943–1949', conference paper, 19th International Conference of Ethiopian Studies (Warsaw, August 2015).

[255]   See, e.g., Afro-Asian Solidarity Committee of the GDR, *The Neo-Colonialism of the West German Federal Republic* (1965).

It is not the *humiliation of man as such*, it is the crime against the white man, the humiliation of the white man, and the fact that he [Hitler] applied to Europe colonialist procedures which until then had been reserved exclusively for the Arabs of Algeria, the coolies of India, and the blacks of Africa.[256]

His work was immediately translated into Polish.[257] Progressive nations needed to support each other in order to forestall a return to the principles that had undergirded both European imperialism overseas and Nazi Empire. When India's Prime Minister Jawaharlal Nehru came to Poland in June 1955—after the Soviet Union had backed the goals of the Bandung conference—he discussed with the Polish Prime Minister, Józef Cyrankiewicz, who had spent more than two years in Auschwitz as a leader of the socialist underground, how nations endured occupation.[258] These sorts of personal bond between leaders became one of the main political tools to improve Poland's geopolitical position. Polish Communists feared revanchism—West Germany did not recognize postwar Poland's altered western borders until 1970—and formed some of their first political friendships with anti-colonial leaders from Africa and Asia for whom the fragility of claims to sovereignty was most keenly felt, and who would as a matter of course support this struggle for international recognition.

The discourses of shared suffering that underpinned these burgeoning anti-colonial relationships were based on homogeneous visions of the nation that paid little attention to the experiences of minorities. W.E.B. Du Bois had visited Poland just after the war, and in his writings on the Warsaw Ghetto[259] considered the connections between imperialism and Fascism, and explored how the suffering of Africans and African-Americans could no longer be considered without reference to the tragedy of the European Jews. Yet in Poland, as across Europe, the memory of the Holocaust was subsumed into the suffering of the nation. Organizations tasked with highlighting continuing postwar anti-Semitism were shut down, and the specificity of the Jewish experience downplayed, and given scant consideration. Visitors from a decolonizing world were perplexed to encounter a region whose elites routinely highlighted colonial violence across Asia and Africa and yet forgot the Jewish genocide at home (see *Race*). This undifferentiated nationalistic version of anti-colonialism could equally be mobilized for the project of ethnic homogenization: in Poland, the persistence of Nazi ideology globally, now manifest in American imperialism, was used also to justify the

---

[256] Aimé Césaire, *Discours sur le colonialisme* (Paris: Présence Africaine, 1955). For the discussion, see Furber, 'Near as Far', 543.

[257] Aimé Césaire, *Rozprawa z kolonializmem*, transl. and foreword by Zofia Jaremko-Żytyńska (Warszawa: Czytelnik, 1950).

[258] Archiwum Ministerstwa Spraw Zagranicznych (AMSZ), 12/8/184, Notatka Jerzego Grudzińskiego, ambasadora PRL w Delhi z wizyty premiera Indii w Polsce, [after 23] June 1955, 42.

[259] Quoted in Michael Rothberg, 'W. E. B. Du Bois in Warsaw: Holocaust Memory and the Color Line, 1949–1952', *The Yale Journal of Criticism*, 14/1 (Spring 2001), 172.

de-Germanization of the so-called 'Recovered Territories' incorporated from the German Reich. Campaigns of nationalist Communists in the early 1950s deployed accounts of the brutality of what contemporary propagandists called the 'American Auschwitz' in the Korean War to justify the cleansing of an ethnic group who, for them, represented the remnants of Nazi ideology on Polish soil.[260] For postwar East European states, these were struggles conducted in the name of nations, formerly peripheralized, colonized or otherwise subjugated, in solidarity against imperialism. The experience of Nazi occupation was used to erase—with claims that would be long contested—the region's complex historical relationship with European colonialism, and formed part of the ideological basis for a new type of socialist globalization that would flourish during the Cold War.

---

[260] Adam Kola, 'A Prehistory of Postcolonialism in Socialist Poland', in James Mark, Steffi Marung and Artemy M. Kalinovsky (eds.), *Alternative Globalizations: Eastern Europe and the Postcolonial World* (Bloomington: Indiana University Press, 2020), 275.

2

Development

Eric Burton, James Mark and Steffi Marung

Histories of development most commonly highlight the story of its origins from a western perspective.[1] Often they trace the roots of the idea in interwar programmes which sought to save weakening Western European empires through the promise of social improvement by rational expert planning. In such accounts, the idea then spreads through postwar institutions at the United Nations, and through the ideological battles of the Cold War, where American leaders, from Truman onwards, appealed to a Keynesian version of capitalist development as an answer to economic backwardness and poverty across the world.[2] These western-focused histories have been instrumentalized by supporters and opponents of development alike: so-called 'post-developmentalists' have emphasized the destructive impacts of its imperial legacies in their critiques since the 1990s.[3] Yet this is only one part of the story. Anti-colonial and non-western elites and experts in formally independent but economically marginal nations—from Latin America to East Asia—have also played major roles: not only in developing ideas of domestic planning, but, as peripheries, forging creative ways to integrate into a global economy without being confined, or returned, to the margins.[4] Centring ways to overcome peripherality in a world system still dominated by imperial

The authors wish to express their gratitude to Maria Dembek (Poland), Bogdan C. Iacob (Romania), and Zoltán Ginelli (Hungary) for their material contributions to this chapter.

[1] For a review, see Artemy M. Kalinovsky, 'Sorting Out the Recent Historiography of Development Assistance: Consolidation and New Directions in the Field', *Journal of Contemporary History* 56/1 (2021), 227–239; Frederick Cooper, 'Writing the History of Development', *Journal of Modern European History*, 8/1 (2010), 5–23.

[2] On colonial origins, see Joseph M. Hodge, 'Writing the History of Development (Part 2: Longer, Deeper, Wider)', *Humanity* 7/1 (2016), 125–74; Michael Cowen and Robert W. Shenton, *Doctrines of Development* (London: Taylor & Francis, 1996). On multiple uses, David Engerman, *Price of Aid: The Economic Cold War in India* (Cambridge, MA: Harvard University Press, 2018), 10–14.

[3] Arturo Escobar, *Encountering Development: The Making and Unmaking of the Third World* (Princeton: Princeton University Press, 1995); Gilbert Rist, *The History of Development: From Western Origins to Global Faith*, 3rd edn (New York, 2008).

[4] Sara Lorenzini, *Global Development: A Cold War History* (Princeton, NJ: Princeton University Press, 2019), 9–10. On the importance of non-western contributions, see e.g. Christy Thornton, '"Mexico Has the Theories": Latin America and the Interwar Origins of Development', in Stephen Macekura and Erez Manela (eds.), *The Development Century: A Global History* (Cambridge:

Eric Burton, James Mark and Steffi Marung, *Development* In *Socialism Goes Global: The Soviet Union and Eastern Europe in the Age of Decolonization*. Edited by James Mark and Paul Betts, Oxford University Press.
© Oxford University Press 2022. DOI: 10.1093/oso/9780192848857.003.0003

structures, their varying ideas, from Latin America's dependency and *desarrollo* models, to East Asia's 'tiger economies', echoed widely across a non-western world.[5]

It is in this context of circulations across global peripheries that we should locate the Soviet and Eastern European story.[6] Examining encounters between the region and a wider world, this chapter explores how local political and economic elites came to conceptualize Eastern Europe's position as periphery, tracing an intellectual journey that informed political transformations, taking the region from the margins to the centre of debates about overcoming dependency and alternative world-making, before returning it to a periphery of the West. The highpoint of such engagements lay in the postwar period: Communism itself began in many ways as a peripheral development project, and, with its spread to East Asia, and the onset of global decolonization, Eastern Europe's experts, funds, and ideas were brought into new encounters with agricultural and industrial projects of development across the world.[7] Yet the power of this engagement was the result of much longer attempts to deal with peripheralization within a western-dominated world economy. In the late nineteenth century, long before the arrival of Communism, Europe's East appeared stuck as a backward hinterland to Europe's northwestern developed core, just as the continent's other peripheries, notably Italy, Ireland and Scandinavia, were embarking on economic take-off.[8] In this context, the region's new nation states, emerging from the dismantled Ottoman, Russian, German and Habsburg Empires, faced many questions that would later present themselves to leaders in newly decolonized Asian and African countries. Governments of Balkan countries, the first to be independent, soon found themselves confined: indebted to the West, their economic sovereignty compromised by German and French banks, and British enterprises, elites wondered if formal political independence was turning them into 'Europe's Africa'.[9]

Even the central-eastern European states that emerged from the ruins of the Habsburg and German Empires after the First World War, which contained substantial islands of wealth, notably in Bohemia, Silesia and Galicia, soon felt

Cambridge University Press, 2018), 263–82. Christy Thornton, *Revolution in development: Mexico and the governance of the global economy* (Oakland, CA: University of California Press, 2021).

[5] Thornton, *Mexico Has*, 263. More recent works on African development have noted its hybrid origins and reference to local as well as global sources, but do not explore the global influence of African ideas. See e.g. Abou B. Bamba, *African Miracle, African Mirage. Transnational Politics and the Paradox of Modernization in Ivory Coast* (Athens, OH: Ohio University Press, 2016); Priya Lal, *African Socialism in Postcolonial Tanzania. Between the Village and the World* (Cambridge: CUP, 2015).

[6] For a recent shift that includes Eastern Europe, see Lorenzini, *Global Development*.

[7] This was noted in the early 1950s: Doreen Warriner, 'Some Controversial Issues in the History of Agrarian Europe', *Slavonic and East European Review*, 32 (1953), 168–86.

[8] Iván T. Berend and György Ránki, *The European Periphery and Industrialization 1780–1914* (Cambridge: CUP, 1982); Kevin H. O'Rourke and Jeffrey G. Williamson, 'Around the European Periphery 1870–1913: Globalization, Schooling and Growth', *European Review of Economic History*, 1/2 (1997), 153–90.

[9] Marie-Janine Calic, *The Great Cauldron: A History of Southeastern Europe* (Cambridge, MA: Harvard University Press, 2019), 354.

questions of peripherality acutely. With the crisis of economy and hunger that followed their formal independence, the whole region came to be seen by western-dominated international bodies as an under-differentiated impoverished rural periphery that had as much in common with Asia as with Western Europe. Both central-eastern and south-eastern European states became the targets for substantial experimental international developmental intervention through the League of Nations—a 'proto-Third World'.[10] The region was turned into *the* inter-war locale through which to discuss overcoming poverty and marginality: not only by western experts, but also by an emerging, well-connected cohort of economists from the region itself who would later play key roles in promoting state-led development and planning on a global scale. Although the Soviet Union resisted such interventions, and proclaimed themselves the centre of a new world revolution, its post-revolutionary elites were well aware of their state's fragility— poorer than other European peripheries, with a substantially agrarian economy, and surrounded by ideologically hostile opponents.[11]

Yet this consciousness of precarity, and the impulse to escape it even in a western-dominated global economy, in turn generated traditions of economic expertise that would later speak well beyond the region. The very idea of centre to periphery development was crafted within their new nation states: facing severe rural poverty and unemployment by the 1930s, elites sought to bring the benefits of centralized state planning to overcome what contemporaries called 'backward-ness' in their own (often ethnically diverse) peripheries. This ranged across polit-ical movements—from the right-wing Serbian nationalists who brought ethnically based resettlement to the southern peripheries of a newly formed Yugoslavia, to the Soviet Union, whose claims to anti-colonial solidarity and uplift of its Central Asian Islamic republics was beginning to garner attention from nascent anti-colonial movements. Increasingly too, elites in both the Soviet Union and Eastern Europe questioned whether excessive integration into the international capitalist system in fact held back development in the periphery. Like concepts of their Latin American counterparts, their interwar programmes already anticipated aspects of the autarchic, protectionist and import-substitution development of the post-1945 period.

The Communist states that multiplied across Eastern Europe after the Second World War were thus not the first in the region to imagine an anti-western, pro-tectionist, centrally planned version of development. Yet they set it to new uses; smaller Eastern European states, which had direct experience of western develop-mental intervention, and experts more comfortable in a globalizing world of development, were first to move, claiming a progressive solidarity between

[10] For this phrase, see Joseph Love, *Crafting the Third World: Theorizing Underdevelopment in Rumania and Brazil* (Stanford: Stanford University Press, 1996), 6.

[11] Oscar Sanchez-Sibony, 'Depression Stalinism: The Great Break Reconsidered', *Kritika*, 15/1 (2014), 27.

peripheries which had commonly been held back in an imperial world system. The Soviets, having been more isolated, and still unsure of their anti-colonial commitments, were slower to follow.

Even under Communist rule, however, these globalizing moves were often ambivalent. Experts from European state socialist countries often discovered that their region was admired not for its Communism per se as its seemingly successful struggle for economic sovereignty in the face of war and western intervention or hostility, and its expertise was valued for its capacity to fortify new post-colonial nations' economic sovereignty. Moscow in particular remained suspicious of the 'bourgeois' nationalism of post-colonial projects, and oscillated between supporting only *socialist allies* and half-heartedly embracing *anti-colonial* world-making. It preferred for instance the massive developmental support for China and North Korea in the early 1950s or the global expansion of Comecon over the radicalism of the New International Economic Order of the 1970s. Tellingly, it was countries excluded from (Yugoslavia) or peripheralized within (Romania) the Eastern Bloc that were much more receptive to alternative global economic visions.

By the late Cold War, alternative visions of solidarity-based developmentalism, or even aspirations for a separate 'socialist world system', inherited from the two-world dreams of the Third International, were already in decline. Whereas western 'globalists' were able to build an international economic system that encased and constrained the nation state,[12] the Communist project—both in Europe and beyond—never overcame the nationalizing impulses of state socialism. Eastern European visions of planned economic development that had foregone any real regional coordination—approaches that in fact initially appealed to many post-colonial states in Africa and Asia attracted to autonomy in pursuit of economic sovereignty—also reinforced cultures of national self-interest that eventually undermined attempts to forge an alternative economic and financial architecture.

From Periphery to Fragile Centre: The Soviet Union and Eastern Europe as Developmental Models

The idea of Eastern Europe as a backward periphery to be developed from without accelerated after the First World War. The collapse of Austria-Hungary had destroyed the largest integrated market in Europe. Multiple imperial disintegrations had brought at least 6,000 kilometres of new borders, and nations lost ready access to neighbouring markets. Interwar Hungarian elites complained that the former empire had retarded their industrialization; nevertheless, they had had

---

[12] Quinn Slobodian, *Globalists: The End of Empire and the Birth of Neoliberalism* (Cambridge, MA: Harvard University Press, 2018), 7–16.

huge markets for their agricultural and semi-processed goods. Eighty per cent of Polish exports had been bought by the 'partitioning powers'—the German, Russian and Austro-Hungarian Empires—and these links were sundered after 1918.[13] With the creation of the Soviet Union, Polish trade with the East was lost.[14] Wartime blockades had likewise led to intense hunger and starvation from Austria through Poland and into Russia.[15] In a parlous state, the region would come to be compared with a wider economically backward, rural and unstable world that extended into Africa and Asia.[16] Despite the attainment of political sovereignty, its new polities were regarded as fragile, held back by their overpopulation, rural undercapitalization, underproductivity and underemployment, and in need of being shepherded towards economic self-sufficiency. The newly established League of Nations oversaw processes of reconstruction and financial stabilization in Hungary and Poland in the early 1920s, and provided credit for health and food programmes to Bulgaria, in a manner that for contemporaries resembled the international administration of China or the debt-ridden Ottoman Empire.[17] Hungary, Romania, Yugoslavia and Bulgaria were dependent on western loans, which financed over half of their domestic investment.[18] Strikingly, Communist internationalism developed a similar geographical imaginary. The Workers International Relief, founded in 1921 on the initiative of German Communists responding to Lenin's call for assistance, internalized a conception of Eurasian underdevelopment targeted at the immediate alleviation of hunger, and rural and urban development, in both the Soviet Union and East Asia.[19]

Yet Eastern Europe was not only subject to external intervention; its new elites constructed their own developmental traditions rooted in securing the economic sovereignty of the post-imperial nation state. Against a background of extreme rural poverty—the League of Nations estimated that a quarter of the 60 million peasants living in Eastern Europe were malnourished by 1938[20]—the modernization of rural labour was a central political preoccupation. Nationalists, fascists,

[13] Aldcroft, *Europe's Third World*.

[14] Oscar Sanchez-Sibony, *Red Globalization: The Political Economy of the Soviet Cold War from Stalin to Khrushchev* (Cambridge: CUP, 2014), 54–5.

[15] Patricia Clavin, 'The Austrian Hunger Crisis and the Genesis of International Organization after the First World War', *International Affairs*, 90/2 (2014), 265–78.

[16] On Eastern Europe as one of the five global 'backward areas', see P. N. Rosenstein-Rodan, 'The International Development of Economically Backward Areas', *International Affairs*, 20/2 (April 1944), 159; Patricia Clavin, *Securing the World Economy: The Reinvention of the League of Nations, 1920–1946* (Oxford: OUP, 2013), 180–1.

[17] Jamie Martin, 'The Colonial Origins of the Greek Bailout', *Exeter Imperial and Global History Blog*, 27 July 2015 http://imperialglobalexeter.com/2015/07/27/the-colonial-origins-of-the-greek-bailout/ (last accessed March 2020).

[18] Derek H. Aldcroft, *Europe's Third World: The European Periphery in the Interwar Years* (Aldershot, Burlington: Ashgate, 2010), 52–3.

[19] See e.g. Heinz Sommer, *Im Zeichen der Solidarität. Bibliographie von Veröffentlichungen der Internationalen Arbeiterhilfe in Deutschland, 1921–1933* (Berlin: Institut für Marxismus-Leninismus,1986).

[20] Clavin, *Securing the World Economy*, 30–3, 169, 179.

neo-Malthusians and Marxists all fought fierce political battles around the issues of agrarian poverty, rural capitalism and land reforms. Their visions ranged from agrarian garden socialism, to the Yugoslav idea of agrarian-industrial civilization, to Soviet efforts to integrate the rural population through collectivized farms—with socially catastrophic effects.[21] Agricultural modernization was directed at poor rural minorities, often in newly incorporated marginal territories whose populations were frequently deemed insufficiently receptive to the new national idea.[22] Contemporaries noted how Warsaw's policy of forced Polonization through the modernization of its Belarussian and Ukrainian-speaking eastern rural borderlands (*Kresy*), or the Kingdom of Yugoslavia's use of Serb settlement to modernize poorer south Slav lands, such as Macedonia and Kosovo, repro-duced a wider rhetoric of European colonial conquest.[23] Such traditions of inter-war development were only selectively drawn upon after the Second World War. Yugoslav Communists vowed that the non-aligned assistance they offered in Africa would not reproduce the iniquitous and unidirectional aspects of their country's interwar development, which they linked to the most deleterious imper-ial practices found in East India, Manchuria and Alsace-Lorraine.[24]

Hiding from the world the devastation caused by its agricultural collectiviza-tion, the Soviet Union forged a globally resonant progressive interpretation of the development of its rural southern peripheries, one that might speak to anti-colonial nationalist movements. Central Asia had long served as a crucial source of cotton for Tsarist Russia; starting in the late 1920s, its economy was wholly transformed to supply the Soviet industrializing core—thereby rendering it immune to the volatility of cotton prices on the world market. Ambitious irriga-tion schemes, railways and other infrastructural projects served to boost the productivity of cotton monocultures.[25] Although this would later be taken as evi-dence of Moscow's structural peripheralization of Central Asia—after all, they set plans for local industrialization aside, and left the region dependent on exporting

---

[21] Sheila Fitzpatrick, *Stalin's Peasants: Resistance and Survival in the Russian Village after Collectivization* (New York: OUP, 1996).

[22] The question of how to deal with these peripheries were part of a global debate at that time, see Raluca Muşat, 'Making the Countryside Global: The Bucharest School of Sociology and International Networks of Knowledge', *Contemporary European History*, 28/2 (2019), 205–19.

[23] Jan Sowa, *Fantomowe ciało króla: peryferyjne zmagania z nowoczesną formą* (Kraków: Towarzystwo Autorów i Wydawców Prac Naukowych Universitas, 2011), 329–30; Patrick Zylbermann, 'Mosquitos and the Komitadjis: Malaria and Borders in Macedonia (1919–1938)', in Iris Borowy and Wolf D. Gruner (eds.), *Facing Illness in Troubled Times: Health in Europe in the Interwar Years 1918–1933* (Frankfurt am Main: Peter Lang, 2005), 305–43.

[24] Vladan Jovanović, 'Rekonkvista "Stare Srbije": O kontinuitetu teritorijalne i demografske poli-tike na Kosovu', in Aleksandar Pavlović et al. (eds.), *Figura neprijatelja. Preosmišljavanje srpsko-albanskih odnosa* (Beton: Beograd, 2015), 95–111.

[25] Patryk Michal Reid, *Managing Nature, Constructing the State: The Material Foundation of Soviet Empire in Tajikistan, 1917–1937*, Phd thesis (University of Illinois, 2016).

primary agricultural products[26]—these measures were internationally promoted as an anti-colonial programme of Communist modernization. Soviet developmentalism thus claimed to be different: it promised a relationship of solidarity in which the periphery was both the object *and* the subject of its own development. Although the benefits of such modernization were still limited in the interwar period, loyal Central Asian leaders who had avoided purges were paraded to sell the idea that their republics were no longer confined to the hinterland, and that they provided a model of development beyond capitalism for the globally marginalized. In the 1930s, leftist graduates of the Tuskegee Institute in Alabama came to share technical advice on cotton growing.[27] Indians too saw in the Soviet modernization of the peasantry inspiration for their own national project once independence had been achieved. As future Prime Minister Jawaharlal Nehru stated on his return from his Soviet visit in the late 1920s, attempting to counter the anti-Communist propaganda of the British: 'Russia thus interests us because it may help to find some solution for great problems…because conditions there have not been very dissimilar to conditions in India. Both are vast agricultural countries with only the beginnings of industrialization, and both have to face poverty and illiteracy.'[28] These ideas thrived in part because some British officials in India were fascinated too, wondering how to appropriate socialist planning for developmental projects that might sustain the Indian colonial state.[29]

The Soviet Union, which presented itself as the world's first truly anti-imperialist state, was already in a position to promote such models in the 1930s; in so doing, they hitched this peripheral development theory of diverse ideological parentage to a world Communist project. Having protected its economy from external shocks, reduced its dependence on international capital flows, and having grown rapidly even as other regions were experiencing the Great Depression, the Soviets gradually became viewed as a source of economic instruction over how to industrialize at the global margins. Yet politically alone, a multilateral coordination of this challenge was all but impossible: the Soviet alternative tended rather to spread through bilateral exchange, often to states with differing ideologies which nevertheless shared a sense of fragility. Moscow developed particularly close relations with Turkey, despite the anti-Communism of the independence movement under Kemal Attatürk. These states recognized each other as

---

[26] Benjamin Loring, '"Colonizers with Party Cards": Soviet Internal Colonialism in Central Asia, 1917–39', *Kritika*, 15/1 (2014), 77–102; Adeeb Khalid, 'Communism on the Frontier: The Sovietization of Central Asia and Mongolia', in Silvio Pons and Stephen A. Smith (eds.), *The Cambridge History of Communism. Vol. 1* (Cambridge: CUP, 2017), 629–30.

[27] Maya Peterson, 'US to USSR: American Experts, Irrigation, and Cotton in Soviet Central Asia, 1929–32', *Environmental History* 21/3 (2016), 442–66.

[28] Jawaharlal Nehru, 'The Fascination of Russia' (around 1927) in idem, *Soviet Russia* (Bombay: Chetana, 1929), 3.

[29] Benjamin Zachariah, *Developing India: An Intellectual and Social History, c. 1930–50* (New Delhi: OUP, 2005), 123.

commonly reconstituted from the ruins of empire and in need of securing their sovereignty on the peripheries of Europe.[30] The Soviets helped Turkish forces in both their struggles for independence and their subsequent state-led industrialization. These exchanges provided a testing ground for later postwar engagements with post-colonial states from the 1950s.[31]

For the smaller non-Communist states in interwar Eastern Europe, the question of whether unconstrained integration into an international capitalist system held back development became a central preoccupation. By the 1930s, economists and social researchers in the region connected the persistence of what contemporaries called 'rural backwardness' and dependent low-waged work to excessive integration into the western capitalist economy.[32] The Romanian economist Mihail Manoilescu advanced influential theories on 'unequal exchange' between agrarian and industrialized countries: raw materials producers had nothing to gain from specializing in agriculture and trading primary produce for industrial goods. He argued against the international division of labour, and for the state-led development of protected industries. As Romanian minister of industry and commerce, speaking at the League of Nations in 1930, he demanded a preferential tariff regime for Eastern Europe. Due to his involvement with Romanian fascism and admiration for the Third Reich, his direct influence in postwar Europe waned. His work had however been translated into French, Portuguese and Spanish. It helped Latin American *dependencia* theorists such as Raúl Prebisch conceptualize their vision of *desarollo* (development)[33] through state-directed high tariff-protected import-substitution industrialization, for which they became the most vocal global advocates.[34] By the late 1930s, countries in both of the world's politically decolonized, but economically dependent, regional peripheries—namely Eastern Europe and Latin America—were resorting to more extreme forms of protectionism, including the use of currency controls and tariffs to promote local industries. This was to become a popular model for state-protected import substitution development after 1945.[35]

---

[30] Samuel J. Hirst, 'Anti-Westernism on the European Periphery. The Meaning of Soviet-Turkish Convergence in the 1930s', *Slavic Review*, 72/1 (2013), 32–53.

[31] Samuel J. Hirst, 'Transnational Anti-Imperialism and the National Forces. Soviet Diplomacy and Turkey, 1920–23', *Comparative Studies of South Asia, Africa and the Middle East*, 33/2 (2013), 214–26.

[32] Raluca Mușat, 'Making the Countryside Global: The Bucharest School of Sociology and International Networks of Knowledge', *Contemporary European History*, 28/2 (2019), 218.

[33] Octavian Gh. Botez, 'European and Latin-American Appreciation', *Revista Română de Statistică* (II/2012), 361–5.

[34] On these links, see Jacob Viner, *International Trade and Economic Development* (Glencoe: Free Press, 1952), 60–4; Joseph L. Love, 'The Latin American Contribution to Center-Periphery Perspectives', in Peter Hanns Reill and Balázs A. Szelényi (eds.), *Cores, Peripheries, and Globalization* (Budapest: Central European University Press, 2011), 26–7.

[35] Ivan T. Berend, *Decades of Crisis: Central and Eastern Europe before World War II* (Berkeley: University of California Press, 1998), 271; Mária Hidvégi, 'Crises and Responses: Government Policies and the Machine-Building Cartels in Hungary, 1919–1949', *Enterprise & Society*, 20/1 (2019), 107–9.

The Romanian Communist Lucrețiu Pătrășcanu turned such arguments about interwar impoverishment into a call for revolution in the dependent European periphery. Writing at the end of the Second World War, he argued that capitalism in the Balkans had, 'woven together new and old forms of exploitation, deepened conflicts and ultimately gave them a more violent form.'[36] Economic depression and the collapse in living standards had been caused by a global system in a monopolist stage that had resulted in the more extreme exploitation of Europe's agrarian peripheries; the suppression of the population's wages and consumption abilities, he argued, had thrown intellectual elites into disarray, pushing them toward Fascism.[37] Balkan societies' deeper peripherialization within the western-dominated global economy had rendered whole nations 'proletarians': it was their 'classed location' in the international division of labour that rendered them ripe for an anti-western and anti-capitalist Communist revolution.[38] Political fantasies of protecting Eastern Europe economically from the West were powerful well before the arrival of the Red Army and Communist dominance in the region.

It was those economists who had connections with the Eastern European agrarian areas reorganized after the First World War who would later became globally influential, as the pioneers of development economics after 1945. This was partly because the region's cosmopolitan multilingual experts responsible for the League's interventions or British-led development planning in interwar Eastern Europe—such as Nicholas Kaldor, Thomas Balogh, Ragnar Nurkse, Hans W. Singer, Peter T. Bauer and Michał Kalecki—had been forced out of the region as right-wing movements consolidated their hold. Taking refuge in western universities or international organizations, they played important roles in advocating development. They extensively lobbied, alongside representatives from European colonies, for state-led development to be a key feature of the postwar global economic architecture at Bretton Woods.[39] In their arguments, interwar Eastern Europe was a key locality to discuss rural poverty, illustrative of *any* world region where peasant farming was widespread.[40] As one of the founders of developmental economics, the Jewish Pole Paul Rosenstein-Rodan, put it in 1944: the 'international development of Eastern and South-Eastern Europe...provides a

---

[36] Lucrețiu Pătrășcanu, *Un veac de frământări sociale 1821–1907* (București: Cartea Rusă, 1947), 287.

[37] Balázs Trencsényi et al., *Negotiating Modernity in the 'Short Twentieth Century' and Beyond, Part I: 1918–1968* (Oxford: OUP, 2018), 287–8; Love, *Crafting the Third World*, 55–6.

[38] Manuela Boatcă, 'Peripheral Solutions to Peripheral Development: The Case of Early 20th Century Romania', *Journal of World-Systems Research*, 11/1 (2005), 21–2; idem, *Laboratoare ale modernității. Europa de Est și America Latină în (co)relație* (Cluj: IDEA Design+Print, 2020).

[39] Eric Helleiner, *Forgotten Foundations of Bretton Woods: International Development and the Making of the Postwar Order* (Ithaca, NY: Cornell University Press, 2014), chapter 9.

[40] Michele Alacevich, 'Planning Peace: The European Roots of the Post-War Global Development Challenge', *Past & Present*, 239/1 (2018), 224; Love, *Crafting the Third World*, 6.

model presenting all the problems which are relevant to the reconstruction and development of backward areas [i.e. across the world].'[41]

Yet it was still common after the Second World War to view Eastern Europe as part of a global agricultural periphery. Kurt Mandelbaum, whose work on Eastern European development would prove influential from the 1950s in both the Economic Commission for Europe and the UN Commission for Trade and Development (UNCTAD),[42] argued in 1945 that 'there are vast and densely crowded areas, such as China, India and Eastern Europe, where almost the whole active population has remained in agriculture .... Industrial progress has bypassed these territories which between them contain over half the world's population. Large numbers...eke out a precarious existence on submarginal land.'[43] In 1945 one representative of US interests at the UN, in a memo entitled 'Standard of Living in Eastern Europe', took a less sympathetic view, arguing for the mainten- ance of a hierarchical global division of labour. Non-western development need only be agricultural, he argued, and necessitate support only in so far as the alle- viation of rural poverty would help promote the creation of markets for western industry: 'the primary needs of the two-thirds of the world's people in Eastern Europe, Asia, Latin America and Africa...represent an immense potential mar- ket for the industries...of Western civilization.'[44]

Smaller Eastern European countries, with elite cultures of expertise already infused with anti-imperialist thinking, were quicker than the Soviets to reconcep- tualize their place in this world and engage with international development. *Political* arguments highlighting the necessity of economic solidarity between non-western peripheries in the face of such plans came not from Moscow, but the countries on the western fringes of the bloc. Here more globally connected experts were linking their firsthand experience of interwar western intervention, and then suppression in a German-dominated economic occupation, with a ris- ing anti-colonial tide. The idea of a historical interconnectedness between a fra- gile Eastern Europe and a world now challenging empire in the South had its roots in the Marxist conviction that these world regions emerged historically from the same system of monopoly capitalism. As Juliusz Katz-Suchy, the Polish delegate at the United Nations, declared in a speech in 1951: 'the unity of the world, its oneness, consists in the international unity of capital, the common sub- jection of the peoples of the home and the colonial and dependent countries to

---

[41]   Rosenstein-Rodan, 'The International Development', 164.

[42]   On Mandelbaum, see the recollections of Janosz Stanovnik, the Yugoslav expert who played a major role at the UN Economic Commission for Europe: UN Oral History Project.

[43]   Kurt Mandelbaum, *The Industrialisation of Backward Areas* (Oxford: Basil Blackwell, 1945), 1.

[44]   F. L. McDougall, UN Interim Commission on Food and Agriculture, to W. Reifler, Institute of Advanced Studies, Princeton, 15 January 1945 (United Nations Archives Geneva (UNOG), League of Nations Secretariat, Financial Section and Economic Intelligence Service, Princeton Office, Box C, 1739/No. 1/7.

finance capital.'[45] Polish economist Oskar Lange co-opted the nineteenth-century concept of 'hinterland' to describe a form of western economic penetration. This had afflicted Eastern Europe both as post-1918 sovereign nations and then under Nazi occupation, and still survived in a world of colonial possessions after it, Lange argued: 'Profits generated by foreign capital are not generally reinvested in the backward countries, but sent abroad (a typical practice of foreign capital in interwar Poland)....Foreign capital transforms backward countries into "hinterland", an agricultural and raw material extraction annex of a metropolitan economy. Once deprived of their competitive advantage, backward countries are drained of their production surplus.'[46] Lange became socialist Poland's first ambassador to the United States and the United Nations, played a significant role in developing the Polish party's response to decolonization, and acted as an advisor to independent India's first leader Jawaharlal Nehru between 1955 and 1959. He compared India's situation of 'rural backwardness' 'to the one we had here in the thirties' and referred to the status of 'backward countries' as an illustration of the fate Poland would have met had it remained capitalist.[47] He argued that Eastern Europe and colonized countries outside Europe were equally peripheralized victims of capitalism and hence had a shared interest in building an alternative world economic system.

Experts from the western fringes of the bloc, able to relate back to cosmopolitan networks established prior to the Second World War, were often much more comfortable navigating a decolonizing world. Polish economists with an interwar Oxbridge educational background easily mingled with African economists who had also been trained in the UK. By the late 1950s, Warsaw became an important international hub for developmental economics. The Economic Commission for Europe supported the Advanced Course in Planning for Economists from Developing Countries there: almost two hundred experts from Africa, Asia and Latin America attended it annually between 1962 and 1968; the US was concerned at its global popularity, due to its 'lack of dogmatism'.[48] The United Nations Conference on Trade and Development (UNCTAD) organized yearly study tours for Latin American and African economists to Yugoslavia and Poland: they were presented as two countries whose successes in rapid modernization rendered them the most relevant European exemplars for global development.[49] Soviet science, which had been far more isolated, and even in the 1960s had had to draw

---

[45] Juliusz Katz-Suchy, 'National Liberation and Social Progress in Asia', *Annals of the American Academy of Political and Social Science*, 276 (1951), 49.

[46] Oskar Lange, *Dlaczego kapitalizm nie potrafi rozwiązać problemu krajów gospodarczo zacofanych* (Warsaw: Książka i Wiedza, 1957), 746.

[47] Cited in Małgorzata Mazurek, 'Polish Economists in Nehru's India: Making Science for the Third World in an Era of De-Stalinization and Decolonization', *Slavic Review*, 77/3 (2018), 594–5.

[48] Cited in Mazurek, 'Polish Economists', 609. See also European Commission for Europe, UNOG, GX 22/46, where the Central Planning School in Warsaw was termed a 'theoretical lighthouse'.

[49] UNOG, GX22/48, ARR 14/160/file 165.

on the knowledge of sympathetic African, Asian and other Eastern European economists, given their own experts' lack of mobility, often lagged behind.[50] Returning from a tour of institutes across Poland, Hungary, Czechoslovakia and the GDR in 1965, the leading Soviet Africanist Vasilii Solodovnikov admitted that "African Studies in other socialist countries are more advanced in comparison to our field". A report on the visits noted that Soviet scholars were isolated, still ill-informed even about socialist brother states, and lagged in training, fieldwork and publication in foreign languages.[51]

The Soviets had indeed been slower to recognize the opportunities presented by postwar decolonization. Already in the 1930s, Soviet international influence had subsided. Stalin's 'socialism in one country' had provincialized the Union; for Moscow, large parts of Africa and Asia were still seen as static appendages of imperialism and largely irrelevant to global dynamics of economic development. Moreover, with wartime victory they no longer considered themselves peripheral but rather a great power, in a world where imperial ambition still appeared possible. They unsuccessfully argued—for reasons of geostrategic advance, and not anti-colonial development—that they should be granted the former Italian colonies of Libya, Somalia and Eritrea.[52] Some argued that the Soviets had gained imperial desires whose contours were less and less distinct from those of the West—as their refusal after the war to withdraw from either Iran or Eastern Europe demonstrated.[53] Its lack of response to a growing postwar anti-colonialism was made worse by the lack of regional specialists, many of whom had been purged in the late 1930s: area studies would only be rebuilt in the late 1950s under Khrushchev. So far as the Stalinist elite were concerned, Africa was not yet sufficiently proletarianized for revolution—a view that angered the continent's Communist parties. The colonized world remained a 'backwater of capitalism', was not ready for development, its nationalist movements the tools of imperialism, and modernization was thus unlikely in the short term.[54] Indian independence was little remarked on in the Soviet press: Nehru might

---

[50] Steffi Marung, 'Entangling Agrarian Modernities. The "Agrarian Question" through the Eyes of Soviet Africanists', in James Mark, Artemy M. Kalinovsky and Steffi Marung (eds.), *Alternative Globalizations. Eastern Europe and the Postcolonial World* (Bloomington, IN.: Indiana University Press, 2020), 159.

[51] Vasilii Solodovnikov, 'Dokladnaia zapiska o nauchnych zviaziakh Instituta Afriki AN SSSR s tsentrami Afrikanistiki sotsialisticheskich stran', Archive of the Russian Academy of Sciences (ARAN), F.2010, O.1, D.76; 'O nekotorykh formakh organizatsii nauchno-issledovatel'skoĭ podgotovki kadrov spetsialistov po problemam Afriki v Pol'she, GDR, Chekhoslovakii i Vengrii', ARAN, F.2010, O.1, D.76.

[52] Sergei Mazov, 'The USSR and the Former Italian Colonies, 1945–50', *Cold War History*, 3/3 (2003), 49.

[53] W. E. B. Du Bois, *Color and Democracy: Colonies and Peace* (New York: Harcourt, Brace and Company, 1945), 114–15. See also the idea of the 'imperial scavenger state': Austin Jersild, 'The Soviet State as Imperial Scavenger: "Catch Up and Surpass" in the Transnational Socialist Bloc, 1950–1960', *The American Historical Review*, 116/1 (2011), 109–32.

[54] Arthur J. Klinghoffer, *Soviet Perspectives on African Socialism* (Rutherford, N.J.: Fairleigh Dickinson University Press, 1969), 42–4, 57.

have turned to central planning and looked for Soviet assistance, but India was considered a bourgeois democracy, and its planning was associated as much with capitalism as socialism.[55]

Rather than join the growing anti-colonial struggle, the Soviets initially only committed to the expanding world of fraternal Communist states in East Asia. The Soviet 'Marshall Plan' to modernize China, 'history's biggest foreign assist-ance programme', grew from the early 1950s, and fully took off two months after Stalin's death in 1953.[56] Tens of thousands of advisors and technicians from Eastern Europe flocked to all parts of the country. One third of all projects in China's first five-year-plan was financed and executed by the USSR and East European states.[57] Technological expertise on the western fringes of the Eastern Bloc was in advance of the Soviets: Moscow thus saw China as an opportunity to learn more about western technology through exchange with Czechoslovak and GDR specialists.[58] This engagement revealed tensions that would later re-emerge. By the early 1950s, many bloc specialists were already critical of the Soviets' inter-war rapid forced industrialization, and later condemned both China's Great Leap Forward and North Korea's attempts at accelerated autarchic development, argu-ing that extraction and the export of raw materials would remain important.[59] Rejecting the opinion of Soviet and East German advisors, Kim Il Sung argued that anything but autarchic self-reliance (*juche*) based on heavy industrialization would enshrine the constraints of the economic and trade structure inherited from the period of Japanese colonialism—which had reduced North Korea to a 'raw material extraction annex of a metropolitan economy'.[60]

Given the Soviets' initial distrust of non-Communist anti-colonialism, it was often African and Asian leaders who drove the establishment of new interconnec-tions. Leading Bandung states Egypt, India and Indonesia had been trying since the early 1950s to diversify their trade away from an over-reliance on the West by reach-ing out to Eastern Europe.[61] As the decolonization of sub-Saharan Africa gained momentum in the late 1950s, some of the region's leaders encouraged Soviet elites

[55] Alessandro Iandolo, 'De-Stalinizing Growth: Decolonization and the Development of Development Economics in the Soviet Union', in Stephen J. Macekura and Erez Manela (eds.), *The Development Century: A Global History* (Cambridge: CUP, 2018), 203.

[56] Odd Arne Westad, *The Global Cold War: Third World Interventions and the Making of Our Times* (New York: CUP, 2005), 69; idem, *Restless Empire. China and the World since 1750* (London: Vintage/Random House, 2013), 304.

[57] Austin Jersild, *The Sino-Soviet Alliance: An International History* (Chapel Hill: University of North Carolina Press, 2014), chapter 2.

[58] Ibid., 61–3.

[59] Jan Zofka, 'China as a Role Model? The 'Economic Leap' Campaign in Bulgaria (1958–1960)', *Cold War History*, 18/3 (2018), 328. He notes that heavily agricultural regions of the bloc were attracted by East Asian models to escape their marginalization within Comecon.

[60] Young-Sun Hong, *Cold War Germany, the Third World, and the Global Humanitarian Regime* (New York: CUP, 2015), 56–8.

[61] 'State Rapidly Expanding Foreign Trade', Warsaw, 29 December 1954 (Foreign Broadcast Information Service, henceforth FBIS).

to see themselves as part of a broader anti-colonial world of development. Interested in expertise and resource transfers, and distrustful of the strings invariably attached to western aid, Guinea's Sekou Touré, Ghana's Kwame Nkrumah and Mali's Modibo Keïta all claimed that their version of development was infused with socialist content, as they strategically turned to Eastern Europe to tap into resources and adapt their models of agricultural development.[62]

These initiatives coincided with a fundamental reassessment of Soviet commitments in the wake of Stalin's death and the rise of Nikita Khrushchev. By the late 1950s, with the acceleration of decolonization in Africa, developing relations with India, and increasing distance from the Chinese Communists, reformist economists in particular began to provide theoretical arguments to underpin a more flexible strategy. Questioning the Stalinist orthodoxy that anti-colonial nationalist revolutions were inevitably bourgeois and capitalist, Polish economists and Nehru-advisors Michał Kalecki and Oskar Lange developed the idea of 'intermediate regimes', while Soviet economist A. I. Levkoskii formulated the theory of 'multistructurality' (*monogoukladnost'*). Both concepts, developed in parallel in relation to the Indian economy, disturbed the easy teleology of Marxist development theory, proposing that many post-colonial states were not dominated by one economic system—capitalism or socialism—but rather contained several coexisting kinds of economic relations, with neither being expected to fully replace the other in the short term. Albeit subject to the fierce criticism of orthodox scholars, Lenin's 1920s theory of the non-capitalist path to development was recovered by Soviet area specialists to bolster the concept of multistructurality—which then provided a theoretical basis for those who favoured a more flexible approach to winning hearts and minds outside Europe.[63] For reformers, unorthodox mixed 'Arab' and 'African socialisms' ought not to be dismissed.

Indeed, it was not Communism per se which attracted many post-colonial states to the bloc. African-American W.E.B. Du Bois may well have called for a decolonizing world to ally itself to the Soviet ideological position: 'to learn of the progress of the Soviet Union and of how far Lenin was responsible for the world revolution which is today transforming civilization'[64]—but the reality was more complex. In 1953, Indonesian president Sukarno lauded the Soviet Union's 'heroism of construction' which had transformed it 'from a feudal and backward country into a state'. Eastern European countries too appeared to be escaping its position as dependent periphery; rapid industrialization was being achieved by

---

[62] Keri Lambert, '"It's All Work and Happiness on the Farms": Agricultural Development Between the Blocs in Nkrumah's Ghana', *The Journal of African History*, 60/1 (2019), 25–44; Marc Frey, 'Doctrines and Practices of Agrarian Development: The Case of the Office du Niger in Mali', *Comparativ*, 27/2 (2018), 24; Alessandro Iandolo, 'The Rise and Fall of the "Soviet Model of Development" in West Africa, 1957–64', *Cold War History*, 12/4 (2012), 683–704.

[63] Engerman, *Price of Aid*, 366; Marung, 'Entangling Agrarian Modernities', 148.

[64] W.E.B Du Bois, 'W. E. B. Lenin and Africa', February 1959. W. E. B. Du Bois Papers (MS 312). Special Collections, University of Massachusetts.

strong planning states without the support of the West, and against the backdrop of wartime occupation and economic devastation. Yet Sukarno positioned his country between the world's leading powers, also lauding the United States' path to prosperity.[65] Like other post-colonial leaders, he valued the defence of their newly won economic sovereignty over strict Cold War ideological allegiances. Recipes for development of divergent ideological lineages were creatively drawn upon. The bloc was important to them in so far as it helped the development of the economic sovereignty of new nations: both in acting as counterweight to western neocolonial influence, and as a guide to developing a cohesive, unified developmental state from within.

Eastern European leaders encouraged the perception that post-colonial elites' struggles echoed the developmental dilemmas they had faced in the wake of their own earlier independence. They too had faced the question of overcoming the role as a dependent post-imperial agricultural periphery in an industrializing world: the modernization of agriculture, often as a prelude to industrialization, was in fact the more substantial area of exchange between Eastern Europe and its post-colonial partners—as it was for the United States too.[66] Trinidadian intellectual C.L.R. James for example considered the Soviets' identification of the peasantry as the crucial group for development and education as the central lesson for Africa; yet as some Western African states turned to collectivization and nationalization, he warned their leaders not to follow Stalin in his use of violence.[67]

It was mainly advice and education that the bloc could offer. After all, it was economically weak and did not have the West's financial leverage. Even after its rapid industrialization, the Soviet economy was approximately the same size as that of France or Britain. The US economy, by contrast, made up over a quarter of the world's economic output by the 1950s. A Soviet report acknowledged that their country could not compete with American finance in the developing world; rather, it concluded the best way to propagandize was to offer advice about how to control western interventions so that post-colonial countries might maximize their economic sovereignty.[68] In a 1957 report entitled, 'Who needs Eurafrica?', Moscow pitched itself as protector of North and West Africa from the 'neocolonial' Eurafrican plans of the nascent European Community. Western European attempts to build an interdependent economic bloc that spanned the Mediterranean to supply Europe's raw material needs as their formal empires collapsed, Moscow argued, would strangle emerging national industries across North and West

---

[65] Jakarta Indonesian Home Service, 'Sukarno Speech Highlights Heroes Day', 10 November 1953, FBIS-FRB-53-221.

[66] Nick Cullather, *The Hungry World: America's Cold War Battle Against Poverty in Asia* (Cambridge, MA: Harvard University Press, 2010).

[67] C. L. R. James, 'Lenin and the Problem' in idem., *Nkrumah and the Ghana Revolution* (London: Allison & Busby, 1977), 195–6.

[68] Russian State Archive of Economics (RGAE), F. 9480 O. 9 D. 489 L. (1968), 102–9.

Africa and keep these countries as producers of raw materials.[69] Only through protective tariffs, and support from the socialist world for generating agricultural surplus to invest in industrialization, could dependency be avoided. Cameroonian economist Osendé Afana came to Moscow, as did many other African experts, to explore how overdependence on the capitalist market had held back the promise of decolonization. He sought to understand how the Soviet strategies of land reform, cooperatives, and the confiscation and nationalization of their land might help former colonies escape dependence on the exports of monocultural crops and extract surpluses that might be used to promote industrialization.[70]

Those European socialist states which had become multiethnic federations, integrating minorities into new national projects, sought to display this dimension of their model to a decolonizing world. This was a key point for new countries for whom the attraction of planned development lay in its promise of a common economic uplift that could transcend ethnic divisions to build a cohesive unified nation state.[71] Yugoslavia sent Bosnian Muslims across the Islamic world as diplomatic, trade and economic experts. Its seemingly successful postwar policies of integration following the violent ethnic cleansing of interwar Yugoslav developmentalism, and wartime inter-ethnic violence, appeared for a time an important argument to refute western criticisms that decolonization in Africa and Asia was simply a repeat of late nineteenth-century Balkanization, that would similarly incite nationalistic feuds and division.[72] The Soviet Union frequently brought anti-colonial leaders to Central Asia and paraded the development of their Islamic republics as evidence of their supposed commitment to the uplift of minorities in less industrialized peripheries.[73] The Armenian Anastas Mikoyan became Khrushchev's key representative in Third World outreach in the

---

[69] The Soviets commissioned a report on the Eurafrican project: see Georgy Skorov, *Who Needs Eurafrica?* (Moscow: State Publishing House of Political Literature, 1957), 31. Thanks to Peo Hansen for a translation. On the concept, see Peo Hansen and Stefan Jonsson, *Eurafrica: The Untold History of European Integration and Colonialism* (London: Bloomsbury, 2014).

[70] Osende Afana, *Ėkonomika Proizvodstva Kakao v Zapadnoĭ Afrike* (Moscow: Academy of Sciences, Africa Institute, 1961); See also Steffi Marung, 'Out of Empire into Socialist Modernity: Soviet-African (Dis)Connections and Global Intellectual Geographies, *Comparative Studies of South Asia, Africa and the Middle East*, 41/1 (2021), 56–70.

[71] Antony Anghie, *Imperialism, Sovereignty and the Making of International Law* (Cambridge: CUP, 2005), 205–6; Partha Chatterjee, *The Nation and Its Fragments: Colonial and Postcolonial Histories* (New York: OUP, 1994), 205.

[72] Benyamin Neuberger, 'The African Concept of Balkanisation', *Journal of Modern African Studies*, 14/3 (1976), 523.

[73] On a decolonizing Africa as echo of pre-revolutionary Russia and contemporary Central Asia, see 'Otchety o komandirovke sotrudnikov Instituta za granitsu za 1961–1962 gody', ARAN, F.2010. Op.1. Delo No. 20. Also: Artemy M. Kalinovsky, 'Writing the Soviet South into the History of the Cold War and Decolonisation', in Mark et al. (eds.), *Alternative Globalizations*, 189–208; Artemy M. Kalinovsky, *Laboratory of Socialist Development: Cold War Politics and Decolonization in Soviet Tajikistan* (Ithaca: Cornell University Press, 2018); Yakov Feygin, *Reforming the Cold War State: Economic Thought, Internationalization, and the Politics of Soviet Reform, 1955–1985*, PhD dissertation (University of Pennsylvania, 2017), 273. On the Soviet rural periphery, including Moldova, as a model for Congo, see Philippe Boko Missikala, *Sel'skokhoziaĭstvennaia Kooperatsiia v Moldavskoĭ SSR: Ėtapy*

early 1960s in part because his path to power from the periphery to First Deputy Chairman represented this story of ethnic uplift. This was less the case in central-eastern European states whose increased homogeneity was the result of the Holocaust and the postwar expulsion of German minorities—and the elites of which silenced such histories in their interaction with a post-colonial world (see *Race*). Indeed, some Asian and African governments utilized experts from the socialist Europe to develop impoverished ethnic minority regions that the post-colonial state sought (sometimes violently) to integrate. In Vietnam and Ethiopia, such experts supported economic schemes or advised resettlement programmes that targeted specific ethnic groups and incorporated them, sometimes forcibly, through developmentalist measures that extended the state's control over peripheral regions and populations.[74]

Although Eastern European Communists might have considered themselves 'more developed developing countries'—as the Yugoslav formulation had it—their sense of superiority did not obviate the possibility that economic development outside Europe might inform the bloc's development too. Indian economist V. B. Singh observed that 'no impact [...] is a one-way traffic' and noted how much the Soviets had benefited from Indian experiments with high-yielding wheat designed in the Himalaya for wintry conditions.[75] For more mobile Eastern European economists, it also brought them into contact with a wider world of development that helped stimulate disruptive economic thinking within the bloc. Lange and Kalecki used arguments about the mixed economy in India to help reverse Poland's Stalinist collectivization of agriculture, arguing for a recognition of the importance of a smallholder peasantry for economic development, and for market-oriented planning mechanisms in a 'mixed socialist economy'.[76] Romanian economists used anti-colonial critiques of the inequalities in the global division of labour to highlight their own peripherality within the bloc. It also helped to establish expert schools of globalized economic thinking that would eventually play important roles in detaching the region from the South and move it westwards. After reading 'State Planning in Hungary' (*Tervgazdaság Magyarországon*) by Hungarian József Bognár, the first post-independence Ghanaian leader Kwame Nkrumah invited him to assist in drawing up the country's first Seven-Year Plan (1961).[77] In Accra, Bognár worked alongside, and learnt much from, the renowned

Razvitiia I Aspekty Ispol'zivaniia Sovetskogo Opyta v Preobrazovanii Sel'skogo Khoziaĭstva Narodnoĭ Respubliki Kongo (Moscow: Ministry of Agriculture of the USSR, 1982).

[74] Iris Borowy, 'Medical Aid, Repression, and International Relations: The East German Hospital at Metema', *Journal of the History of Medicine and Allied Sciences*, 71/1 (2016), 76; Sylvie Doutriaux et al., 'Competing for Coffee Space: Development-Induced Displacement in the Central Highlands of Vietnam', *Rural Sociology*, 73/4, (2008), 528–54.

[75] V. B. Singh, 'Soviet Impact on Indian Economic Development', ARAN F. 2010 Op. 1, D. 291.

[76] Mazurek, 'Polish Economists', 599–600.

[77] József Bognár, 'Összefoglaló jelentés Ghanában végzett munkámról és ennek során szerzett tapasztalataimról', 1962. MNL OL XIX-A-90-c box 153 (National Archives of Hungary, Budapest).

British-Saint Lucian economist Arthur Lewis. Bognár's experiences in Ghana would lead to the foundation of the Afro-Asian Centre in Budapest, which in turned spawned over three decades of heterodox thinking about development, interdependence and global divisions of labour that would help underpin Hungary's economic reorientations long before 1989, as will be shown below.[78] The potential for global economic engagement to boomerang back would only accelerate as Eastern Europe experienced multiple economic crises towards the end of the Cold War.

Eastern European Ambivalence and Anti-colonial World-making

Yet for all this commitment to post-colonial projects of national development, most—but not all—Eastern European states were reluctant to support progressive plans to create a more just international system.[79] Inheriting the nationalizing impulses of their own post-independence forebears—and viewing the collapse of European empires equally as an opportunity to overcome the region's longer-term exclusion from an imperial world economy—many elites perceived such projects as much through the lens of national advantage as they did through anti-colonial solidarity.

The collapse of Western European empires offered a way to overcome the region's long marginal position within a world economy that had been dominated by imperial and transatlantic linkages. In the late nineteenth century, international trade had expanded only slowly: despite a revival in its established role of supplying agricultural products to an industrialized West, Eastern Europe struggled to compete with US farms, and its global share declined.[80] It received only a quarter of Western Europe's investment, and German capital, although the most significant, was increasingly targeted at its own extra-European colonies, Latin America and China.[81] Not everything here was peripheral, however: regional enterprises fought to be competitive in a transatlantic economy.[82] From the late nineteenth century, the scattered industrial centres in the region—such as textiles in Łódz

Zoltán Ginelli, 'Opening the Semi-Periphery: Hungary and Decolonisation', Research Report for the Vera and Donald Blinken Open Society Archives, July 2017, 28.

[78] Valeska Huber, 'Planning Education and Manpower in the Middle East, 1950s–60s', *Journal of Contemporary History*, 52/1 (2017), 116.

[79] On this, see Adom Getachew, *Worldmaking after Empire: The Rise and Fall of Self-Determination* (Princeton: Princeton University Press, 2019).

[80] Uwe Müller, 'East Central Europe in the First Globalization (1850–1914)', *Studia historiae oeconomicae (Poznań)*, 36 (2018), 73–4.

[81] Ibid., 78–9.

[82] Cf. Mária Hidvégi, 'A Ganz-Jendrassik dízel motorkocsik Argentínában', *Aetas*, 29/4 (2014), 45–64.

(Russian Empire) or oil in Galicia (Habsburg Empire)—were already developing trade links across the Atlantic and towards Africa and India.[83]

In the interwar period, Eastern Europe's new nation states faced further obstacles: global imperial networks were either difficult to penetrate, or enforced rules that hampered smaller European states.[84] Business circles in Hungary and Romania supported Mussolini's expansion in East Africa in the late 1930s precisely because he promised access to new markets in a way other Europeans had not.[85] A more industrialized Czechoslovakia did manage to develop export markets across Africa, notably in glassware and in arms—an industry expanded also to protect its western borders from Germany.[86] It supplied weapons to Abyssinia both before and during the Italian occupation.[87] The later presence of Communist-era Czechoslovak industries—notably in arms in East Africa and footwear across the global South—was built on these interwar foundations. Following the Communist takeovers, Eastern European states would be organized into an economic bloc—and their Western markets were blocked through embargoes and sanctions. Between 1947 and 1953, Czechoslovakia's trade with Western Europe declined by two thirds. The founding of the European Community further restricted access: UNCTAD dubbed Eastern Europe a 'closed second world market'.[88]

For smaller Eastern European states, the accelerating collapse of European empires offered not only an opportunity for the expansion of trade, but also an escape from the economic dominance of the Soviet Union—which sold them highly priced raw materials and did not fully compensate them for produced goods.[89] In Hungary, the search for extra-European markets accelerated from mid-1953, when trade experts were sent to Arab countries, India and Indonesia. Newly independent states likewise sought to diversify exports beyond still powerful imperial networks. Indonesia promoted its low-quality rubber—which could not be sold on the capitalist world market—to Eastern European socialist

---

[83] Uwe Müller, 'Transnationale Verflechtungen der Wirtschaft in Ostmitteleuropa während der, ersten 'Globalisierung', in Frank Hadler and Matthias Middell (eds.), *Handbuch einer transnationalen Geschichte Ostmitteleuropas. Band 1* (Göttingen: Vandenhoeck & Ruprecht, 2017), 255–321; Alison Fleig Frank, *Oil Empire: Visions of Prosperity in Austrian Galicia* (Cambridge, MA: Harvard University Press, 2007).

[84] David Dobrovoda, *Czechoslovakia and East Africa in the Late Colonial and Early Post-Colonial Period: The Case Studies of Kenya, Uganda and Tanzania*, PhD thesis (SOAS, 2016), 55; Hidvégi, 'A Ganz-Jendrassik', 45–64.

[85] Balázs Szélinger, *Magyarország és Etiópia. Formális és informális kapcsolatok a 19. század második felétől a II. világháborúig*, PhD thesis (Szeged, 2008), 138.

[86] Dobrovoda, *Czechoslovakia and East Africa*, 50–3.

[87] Abadi Woldekiros, 'Tendenční neutralita. Československý zbrojní průmysl a italskohabešský', *Soudobé dějiny*, X/1–2 (2003), 27.

[88] UNCTAD, Preparation for 3rd preparatory meeting, 1963/4, Myrdal Papers, General Files, GR9395 (UN Archive), 4.

[89] Jersild, 'The Soviet State as Imperial Scavenger', 116–117.

countries at the 1952 International Trade Fair in Moscow.[90] In the mid-1950s, Hungary imported Egyptian cotton following its failure to grow the crop domestically, in exchange for engineering expertise to build bridges over the Nile.[91] And as socialist states paid more attention to consumerism from the 1960s, their experts concluded that heightened societal expectations of material plenty would inevitably require the further expansion of trade with developing countries.[92] This dovetailed with intentions like those of Tanzanian President Julius Nyerere who encouraged his officials not to 'ignore the possibilities of new markets in the East' and to identify these countries' resource needs in their plans in order to 'break out of the straitjacket of inherited trade patterns'.[93]

Yet how would such expanding links at the end of European empire be organized? In the late 1950s, UNCTAD became the most important space to discuss the project to remake the world economy after empire. Eastern European states publicly supported initiatives that attempted to break the power of former imperial trading networks. Conceptualized by UNCTAD's leaders as a system of both regional integration to prevent dependency on the West, and by the same token an opening up to multidirectional, multilateral trade across regions, and often beyond the West, free trade quickly became viewed as the cause of a progressive world. At the UN, every socialist country voted in favour of these principles, while the United States voted against or abstained on nearly every point.[94] Soviet newspapers made the (misleading) claim that Khrushchev had inspired UNCTAD's foundation: in fact it had been a combined initiative of Brazil, Ethiopia, India, Senegal and Yugoslavia.[95]

The acceleration of decolonization, and the stark exclusion of socialist countries from western markets, rendered such anti-colonial visions attractive. A commitment to solidarity reflected a relatively short-lived belief that future convergence

---

[90] Broadcast from Damascus in French to Europe, 21 January 1953, FBIS-FRB-53–014; 'Sumanang predicts expansion of trade', Broadcast from Jakarta, 17 April 1952, FBIS-FRB-52–077. See also Sanchez-Sibony, *Red Globalization*, 141–2.

[91] Item No. 476/54; Closer Economic Links between Hungary and Egypt, 20 January 1954; Item No. 792/54. Item No. 6818/55. Hungary hopes to get a contract to build Egyptian Bridge. 12 August 1955; HU OSA 300-40-4: 15/3. 751.1 Foreign Trade: Egypt, 1954–1956 (Open Society Archives, Budapest).

[92] A 1965 executive report produced for Alexei Kosygin in the wake of Khrushchev's ouster by the Academy of Sciences noted that the USSR would need to be a net importer of commodities to satisfy the USSR's growing consumer demands. ARAN, F. 1849 0. 1 D. 51.

[93] Julius Nyerere, *Freedom and Unity. Uhuru na Umoja. A Selection from Writings and Speeches, 1952–1965* (London: OUP, 1967), 321–2.

[94] James Mark and Yakov Feygin, 'The Soviet Union, Eastern Europe, and Alternative Visions of a Global Economy 1950s–1980s', in Mark et al. (eds.), *Alternative Globalizations*, 37.

[95] TASS International Service, 24 March 1964. On the Hungarian commitment to support free trade advantageous to Africa, see: 'Afrika a mai világban –kapcsolataink Afrikával', *Nemzetközi Szemle* (1966), 86. Non-aligned Yugoslavia played a larger role in its establishment in the early 1960s: Diego Cordovez, 'The Making of UNCTAD', *Journal of World Trade*, 1/3 (1967), 258–60.

between the post-colonial world and the European socialist camp was possible, and would eventually benefit both: successful business was simply not possible as long as post-colonial nations were dependent on the western capitalist world. However, such commitments were still marked by an economic nationalism that had been forged decades before. The processes developed to cope with the break-up of imperial markets and disruption of interwar trade in Eastern Europe—the defensive autarchy of the depression era, and the development of bilateralism and barter in trade in the absence of regional cooperation—fore-shadowed the parochial bilateralism of the postwar bloc. Whilst proclaiming internationalism, Communists embraced schemes only when they could bolster *national* economic sovereignty, and did not come at the expense of other advantages.[96] Bloc states were not as enthusiastic about building an alternative global economic order as UNCTAD's non-aligned founders, including Yugoslavia. Raúl Prebisch, its intellectual spearhead characterized this disruptive force as 'Second World bilateralism': Eastern European countries were not even able to integrate amongst themselves to defend their interests from the West.[97]

Comecon, established in 1949 to coordinate economic planning across the bloc, developed a Commission for Technical Assistance that endeavoured to present a united regional front to the decolonizing world; however, its coordinating initiatives were in practice ignored.[98] The more 'conservative' Soviet trade institutions, hangovers from the Stalinist era, were reluctant to embrace initiatives that threatened their economic independence. Romania or Yugoslavia were the most enthusiastic about an alternative economic world orders yet even here, bilateralism served as a way to work with states of a similar size freer from the influence of the world's superpowers, including the Soviet Union. Thus Eastern European states competed against each other for trade and developmental cooperation with the Third World.[99] Initially, this was not a disadvantage. Nationalism and bilateralism that undermined efforts at Comecon integration proved attractive to newly decolonized nations seeking to establish their own economic sovereignty and resist regional integration in their own neighbourhoods; nevertheless, as we

---

[96] In its preparations for UNCTAD II (February–March 1968), the Hungarian Ministry for External Trade was critical of developing countries' economic progress, and deeply sceptical that advances could be made, given representatives' 'lack of realism' (Report to Government from KKM, April 1968).

[97] Raúl Prebisch, 'Statement at Informal Meeting of the Second Committee' (1963) Report. Myrdal Papers–General Files–UNCTAD 1963-4, GF 93 95 (UN Archive); 'UN Conference on Trade', Moscow TASS, 24 March 1964.

[98] Sara Lorenzini, 'Comecon and the South in the Years of Détente: A Study on East–South Economic Relations', *European Review of History*, 21/2 (2014), 185; Max Trecker, *Red Money for the Global South. East-South Economic Relations in the Cold War* (London: Routledge, 2020).

[99] Łukasz Stanek, 'Socialist Networks and the Internationalization of Building Culture after 1945', *ABE Journal*, 6 (2004) http://abe.revues.org/1266 (last accessed 16 June 2015).

shall see, this would eventually foil attempts to develop an alternative financial architecture to challenge the capitalist globalism of the 1970s.[100]

Moreover, UNCTAD was attractive because it offered the possibility of developing western trade and technology exchange too. At its first conference in 1964, the USSR, Hungary, Poland and Bulgaria expressed their concern that there was too great a focus on the 'developing world'. This risked undermining attempts to open up trade with Western Europe. While supporting UNCTAD, several smaller eastern European socialist states were simultaneously trying to join The General Agreement on Tariffs and Trade (GATT)—viewed by the Soviets and UNCTAD supporters as a club of rich capitalist countries. Poland joined in 1967, Romania in 1971, and Hungary in 1973, partly to increase access to global trade in the face of the European Economic Community's continued restrictions on the bloc.[101]

This deeply embedded economic nationalism within the bloc restricted its capacity to conceptualize issues necessary for the contemplation of a compelling vision of an alternative global economic order. As Comecon attempted (unsuccessfully) to integrate bloc economies in the 1960s, Moscow resisted the investigation of inequality. It blocked the collection of comparative statistics which might be marshalled to underpin arguments about coloniality and dependency in their own neighbourhood, fearing that they would then lead to politically problematic discussions over economic transfers.[102] The poorer and less industrialized countries in the south-east of the bloc, which would later be the most receptive to 'Third World' calls for global economic justice, noted this early. The Romanian economist Costin Murgescu rejected what he dismissively called the Soviet international socialist division of labour as a 'pseudo-theory' which served to keep Romania and Bulgaria as subservient agricultural economies within Comecon.[103]

Given this institutionalized ignorance close to home, it was thus often left to delegates from poorer post-colonial governments to point out to their reluctant

---

[100] The economic crisis of the 1930s brought hard currency shortages, and countries resorted to the most basic statist bilateralism to organise trade. By 1938, more than 75% of Hungarian, Yugoslav and Romanian foreign trade took place using state-controlled barter and clearing agreements. Ivan Berend, *Decades of Crisis: Central and Eastern Europe Before World War II* (Berkeley: University of California Press, 2001), 270.

[101] Aleksandra Komornicka, "'The Unity of Europe is Inevitable": Poland and the European Economic Community in the 1970s', *Cold War History*, 20/4 (2020), 492. Lucia Coppolaro, 'East-West Trade, the General Agreement on Tariffs and Trade (GATT) and the Cold War: Poland's Accession to GATT (1957–1967)', in Jari Eloranta and Jari Ojala (eds.), *East-West Trade and the Cold War* (Jyväskylä: University of Jyväskylä Press, 2005), 77–93. Indeed, Eastern Bloc states competed against each other for the best terms with GATT: János Nyerges, 'Magyarország teljes jogú csatlakozási szándékának hivatalos bejelentése a GATT Szerződő Feleinél', 31 July 1969. OL XIX-A-90-c box 153 (Hungarian National Archives MNL, Budapest).

[102] Simon Godard, 'The Council for Mutual Economic Assistance and the Failed Coordination of Planning in the Socialist Bloc in the 1960s', in Michel Christian, Sandrine Kott and Ondřej Matějka (eds.), *Planning in Cold War Europe: Competition, Cooperation, Circulations* (Berlin: De Gruyter Oldenbourg, 2018), 187–210.

[103] Zbigniew Brzezinski, *The Soviet Bloc, Unity and Conflict* (Cambridge, MA: Harvard University Press, 1967), 444–5.

European socialist counterparts the necessity of developing relationships that avoided the reproduction of dependence on a global scale. In 1963, Julius Nyerere charged that 'the rich socialist nations' were 'now beginning to use their wealth for capitalist purposes, that is, for the acquisition of power and prestige' rather than tackling issues of development and poverty.[104] A Tanzanian aid-shopping delegation which toured several Eastern Bloc countries in 1964 returned almost empty-handed, disappointed in the salesman-like attitude encountered in Warsaw and Prague, and by Moscow's argument that every machine exported to Africa was a machine less for the USSR.[105] In the same year, Fidel Castro complained about Poland's 'unwillingness to negotiate', Romania's misguided attitudes, and Czechoslovakia's sending of obsolete equipment.[106]

Thus new economic partners were quick to pressurize their Eastern European partners to take the demands of anti-colonial economic solidarity seriously. Many new nations, faced with the withdrawal of European or American capital, needed even the limited resources the Soviets or Eastern Europeans held, but requested it be provided in such a way as to assist eventual economic convergence. When Che Guevara toured Eastern Europe in 1961 as head of the Cuban National Bank, he requested funds that the young Cuban revolution might use to buy advanced industrial, medical and agricultural technology from the bloc, to be paid back initially in raw materials. Yet in order not to keep Cuba in its subordinate role as a primary producer, such 'solidarity loans' should not be repaid until the economic base of the revolution was sufficiently built up. Eastern European socialist states would provide experts, free of charge. Cubans saw such principles as proper marks of 'mutual respect' between socialist nations: flexible repayment terms avoided the practices of western banks, which had used debt to keep primary producers in subservient positions.[107]

Many Eastern Europe states offered such economic support for a short time. Yet the performance of solidarity that this involved—offering loans 'without economic conditions'—was also in part a consequence of the bloc's relative economic weakness. Without generously foregoing ownership or profit-seeking in the name of ideological solidarity, experts concluded, they could easily be passed over for other collaborators, whether from the socialist or the capitalist worlds.[108] The split

---

[104] This charge was made initially in 1960 and repeated in 1963: Nyerere, *Freedom and Unity*, 208.
[105] Cranford Pratt, *The Critical Phase in Tanzania, 1945–1968: Nyerere and the Emergence of a Socialist Strategy* (Cambridge: CUP, 1976), 159–61.
[106] Jarowinsky to members and candidates of the SED Politburo, 'Information – Bericht über die Kuba-Reise', Berlin, 9 November 1964, DY 30/48813, (SAPMO collection in the German Federal Archives, Berlin, henceforth SAPMO-BArch).
[107] 'Guevara reports on Trade Tasks with Bloc', *Cadena de la Libertad*, 7 January 1961.
[108] Main principles of Czechoslovak loan policy when extending and receiving foreign loans: Fond 02/1, sv. 17, ar.j. 50, bod 2, 12 February 1966 (Czech National Archive NAČR, Prague); see also Oscar Sanchez-Sibony, 'The Cold War in the Margins of Capital: The Soviet Union's Introduction to the Decolonized World, 1955–1961', in Mark et al. (eds.), *Alternative Globalizations*, 63–4.

between Moscow and Beijing around 1960, and the competition for leadership in the post-colonial world that ensued, demonstrated how a globalization based upon competitive bilateral solidarities was not conducive to the construction of an alternative socialist world system. Economists stationed in Africa often implored their states, as a matter of *realpolitik*, to offer loans on ever more favourable terms in order to head off the Chinese.[109] Mali's Modibo Keïta and Guinea's Sekou Touré, in their negotiations with the Chinese over investment, complained that Soviet 'interest on loans was high, the salaries of their specialists were high, and their efficiency was low', in order to sweet-talk Beijing into a better deal.[110] China too engaged in this high stakes competitive generosity, proclaiming its 1964 'Eight Principles' for aid to outbid European socialist states. It included respect for national sovereignty, loans with no interest, exclusively supporting projects that fostered self-reliance, and having its experts work under the same conditions as their local counterparts of equal status—the latter point often impressed in African countries where Eastern European experts were accused of coveting working conditions similar to those of former colonialists.[111]

Already by the mid-1960s, critical attitudes towards solidarity-based developmentalism were hardening in some quarters. There was increasing evidence of the failure of ambitious plans for socialist modernization, most notably in Ghana and Mali, which had contributed to the fall of Nkrumah (1966) and Keïta (1968), abandoned by an urban population disenchanted with the ailing economy and cash crop farmers frustrated with the state's monopoly on marketing. The increasing scepticism within the Soviet Union that accompanied Khrushchev utopian Third Worldism was one of the factors that had him removed from office.[112] With the non-repayment of solidarity-based loans that had been extended to 'progressive' regimes across Africa, Asia and Latin America since the late 1950s, Comecon ministers, in a series of meetings between 1967 and 1969, questioned both the wisdom and affordability of such support.[113] Those institutions that had long

---

[109] On the Chinese threat to GDR influence in East Africa, see Flegel, 'Bericht einer Regierungs delegation in die VRT aus Anlass des 5. Jahrestages der sansibarischen Revolution', Berlin, 22 January 1969, DC 20/11525 (German Federal Archives, Berlin – BArch); Büttner (GDR Consul Zanzibar), 'Abschlussbericht Juli 1967 – Juni 1970', Berlin, 30 June 1970.

[110] Cable from the Chinese Foreign Ministry, 'Situation of the Premier's visit to three West African countries', 1 February 1964 (Wilson Center Digital Archive). https://digitalarchive.wilsoncenter.org/document/165408 (accessed 16 June 2015).

[111] The Chinese Government's Eight Principles for Economic Aid and Technical Assistance to Other Countries, January 15 1964 (Wilson Center Digital Archive). http://digitalarchive.wilsoncenter.org/document/121560 (accessed 16 June 2015); Eric Burton, *In Diensten des Afrikanischen Sozialismus. Tansania und die globale Entwicklungsarbeit der beiden deutschen Staaten, 1961-1990* (Berlin: De Gruyter, 2021), 319–20.

[112] Marung, 'Entangling Agrarian Modernities', 158–9.

[113] At a meeting of Eastern European solidarity movements, the representative of Poland's Afro-Asian Solidarity Committee expressed scepticism regarding anti-colonial solidarity, arguing that leaders of liberation movements in exile were self-interested bourgeois. Untitled stenographic transcript of the meeting of Afro-Asian solidarity committees, Berlin, 28–29 June 1966, DZ 8/32 (SAPMO-BArch), 29.

been suspicious of ties not based on immediate economic advantage—most notably trade ministries—increasingly got their way: the Czechoslovak ministry, for example, removed political supervision from commercial trade in the mid-1960s, thereby enabling arms export to non-socialist countries without the oversight of the Ministry of National Defence.[114]

This was also a generational story. In Yugoslavia, for instance, the first real opponents of a 'Third World' orientation came from a rising generation of elites in the richer northern republics from the late 1960s: they were the most strident advocates for increasing trade westwards as tensions relaxed in Europe. They considered the previous assumptions of older Yugoslav Communists, steeped in mythologies of the partisan struggle and heroic postwar reconstruction, to be too romantic.[115] Younger reform economists across the western fringes of Communist Europe who supported the introduction of market mechanisms and a materialist consumerism at home complained of the poor quality of post-colonial trade. One Yugoslav newspaper argued in 1966 that 'for first class Yugoslav merchandise we get second class bananas' and informed their readers that 'customs officers threw away thousands of crates of tropical fruit that didn't meet even the basic standards.'[116] Such discourses anticipated 1980s claims that excessive connections were holding Eastern Europe back from western levels of material consumption.

A new generation also valued a more managerial socialism: their campaigns against solidarity-based economics focused on technocratic issues, such as the fixed preferential prices that had been guaranteed for raw materials such as Cuban sugar. Generous agreements would not help independent states overcome unequal past relationships, they claimed. Such guarantees were a spurious kindness that did not enforce competitiveness, the lack of which would be revealed through eventual exposure to the world market.[117] Over the next decade, economic criteria came to dominate the political: the claims of economists successfully sidelined a language of socialist humanism, which had played a prominent role in justifying assistance.[118] Solidarity did not disappear, however: the new criteria of 'mutual advantage' and 'optimization' were supposed to sustain economically rational projects that would bolster progressive development on both sides, and European socialist states continued to compete in public over which of them was more authentically committed to inscribing socialist values into these increasingly complex relationships.[119] Nevertheless, this shift also paved the way

[114] MNO 1953, box 410 (Central Military Archives VÚA, Prague).

[115] See the work of development institutes in Zagreb and Ljubljana in the 1970s and 1980s.

[116] 'Zašto jedemo loše banane', Vjesnik u srijedu, 29 June 1966.

[117] Az 1972/73 évi magyar-kubai kulturális együttműködési munkaterv. TESCO Nemzetközi Műszaki-Tudományos Együttműködési Iroda iratai. MNL OL XXIX-G-21-b 19.d.direc.

[118] György Péteri, 'Contested Socialisms: The Conflict between Critical Sociology and Reform Economics in Communist Hungary, 1967–71', Social History, 41/3 (2016), 264–6.

[119] For an article extolling Romania's non-exploitative trade relations in the Global South, see Ion Rachmuth, Traian Silea and Spiridon Manoliu, 'Relațiile economice și tehnico-științifice ale RSR cu țări având sisteme social-politice diferite', Revista Română de Studii Internaționale, 3/14 (1971), 7–14.

to an international divisions of labour that reinscribed hierarchies and undermined mid-century visions of convergence.

An Alternative World System?

In 1976, at the fourth meeting of UNCTAD, the Group of 77 (G77) developing
states called for a 'New International Economic Order' (NIEO). They reimagined
the world divided between a rich North and a marginalized South: speaking on
behalf of the latter, G77 leaders called for their right to development, the regula-
tion of capital flows so as not to reproduce the injustices of colonialism, and the
redistribution of global wealth. This global imaginary was also an accusation
against Eastern European Communists, who were no longer considered natural
partners in a common anti-colonial project. Rather, détente with the West had
rendered them part of an ever less differentiated northern industrialized world.
After all, East-West European economic partnership had been partly discovered
through cooperation in the South:[120] Czechoslovak and Romanian enterprises
had begun working with West German firms in Africa and Middle East from the
early 1970s, followed by East German enterprises in the late 1970s. The Western
partners sought to exploit their Eastern colleagues' high political standing with
post-colonial elites—whilst the representatives of European socialist states
endeavoured to gain technological and business know-how.[121]

Although some eastern European economists did support the aims of the
NIEO,[122] many rejected its reconceptualization of the world as 'fallacious'.[123] In
the Polish party daily, *Trybuna Ludu*, Maciej Perczyński was sympathetic but
critical:

> The basic criterion for this homogeneity is the level of income per capita. This is
> obviously false—these groups are not homogeneous either in political or in
> socio-economical terms .... Therefore, dividing a group (the rich 'North') ... from
> developing countries (the so-called poor 'South') is devoid of any basis. The
> responsibility of the capitalist and socialist countries for the situation in the
> 'Third World' is radically different. No one can accuse socialist states of
> exploiting them... it was not the source of their accumulation. The imperialist

---

[120] Patrick Gutman, 'West-östliche Wirtschaftskooperationen in der Dritten Welt', in Bernd Greiner,
Christian Müller and Claudia Weber (eds.), *Ökonomie im Kalten Krieg* (Hamburg: Hamburger Edition,
2010), 395–414.

[121] Lorenzini, 'Comecon and the South', 187; Burton, *In Diensten*, 176.

[122] Eastern European developmentalists did contribute to the NIEO's conceptualization: e.g.
Bognár, *Struggle for a New World Economic System*. Ervin László too was involved, as the coordinator
of a global UNITAR research network on international development.

[123] 'Proceedings of the United Nations Conference on Trade and Development Fourth Session',
Nairobi, 5–31 May 1976, Volume I Report and Annexes, 72.

metropolis, whose moral obligation is to compensate for long-term colonial and neocolonial exploitation, is the one to accuse. Not long ago socialist countries broke free from imperialist exploitation and have sought to develop...Despite not having either moral or material responsibility for the colonial past of the 'Third World', the socialist states do feel responsible for its future.[124]

The Hungarian UN delegation acknowledged that developed capitalist countries wanted to hamper the influence of the international organizations that protected the 'South' in favour of private capital, and that developing countries needed the bloc's support; but, dependent itself on western loans, decided not to issue a separate socialist declaration of support for the NIEO.[125] Only Romania and Yugoslavia— one a renegade member of the Eastern Bloc and the other a nonaligned state outside the Soviet sphere that saw in it the chance to recharge its global role—firmly supported it. Indeed, as one of the bloc's least industrialized countries, Romania took this new global imaginary to heart, reconceptualizing itself as part of this peripheralized world of the global South. At UNCTAD III, its delegation defined Romania as a 'developing country' (soon to be affiliated to the Latin American group in the Group of 77) in an attempt to recover losses incurred through changes in capitalist countries' currency exchange rates.[126]

For the Soviets, by contrast, the NIEO was an unrealistic utopian response to the troubles of building a new world economy: their experts were particularly critical of plans to redistribute global wealth to developing countries.[127] Oleg Bogomolov, the director of Moscow's Institute of Economics of the World Socialist System (IMÈSS), considered it an error to gather up all 'developed' states into one category: 'No one', he argued, 'could accuse the socialist countries of exploiting the developing world and contributing to the misdistribution of global profits.'[128]

For a moment in the 1970s, the Soviets half-heartedly attempted an alternative. Comecon expanded beyond Europe with the accession of Cuba and Vietnam. The Soviets promoted it as a model of equitable international economic integration that could reshape the world order by enabling industrial cooperation and the

---

[124] Maciej Perczyński, 'Nowy międzynarodowy ład ekonomiczny (2): Realistyczne Spojrzenie', *Trybuna Ludu*, 299 (December 20 1977), 2. On Polish reactions, Mieczyslaw Szostak, 'Polish Scientific Literature on the New International Economic Order', *Economic Papers*, 14 (1982), 226–41.

[125] 'Directives for the delegation to the UNIDO 2nd General Meeting in Peru (Lima)', 12–26 March 1975-2283-1975-24, Nemzetközi Gazdasági Kapcsolatok Osztálya.

[126] 'Participarea RSR la III-a conferința a Națiunilor Unite pentru comerț si dezvoltare', 1 March 1972, ANIC (Arhivele Naționale Istorice Centrale), CC (Comitetul Central) al PCR (Partidului Comunist Român), Cancelarie 24/1972 (Romania), 16.

[127] Elizabeth Kridl Valkenier, 'Revolutionary Change in the Third World: Recent Soviet Assessments', *World Politics*, 38/3 (1986), 423–4.

[128] O.T. Bogomolov, *Socializm i perestroika mezhdunarodnykh èkonomicheskikh otnosheniakh* (Moscow: Mezhdunarodnaia Otnosheniia, 1982), 140–1.

international division of labour in a 'socialist world system'.[129] They attempted to build an alternative financial system to underpin it, paralleling the attempts of other post-colonial groupings to create regional 'clearing houses' and credit arrangements that sidelined the dollar. Moscow developed the transferrable rouble as an alternative to western hard currency, and an International Investment Bank (IIB), founded in January 1971, to lend it. Cuba used its structures to ensure the successful and rapid expansion of its citrus fruits industry, built with machinery from the GDR, irrigation from the Soviets and Hungarians, and packaging from Poland.[130] But the rouble fostered dependency and limited trade. Developing countries were paid for primary products in roubles that were in reality unconvertible and thus had to be spent on Soviet goods: it was thus unable to underpin multilateral trade across an expanding socialist system.[131] The rejection of Mozambique's bid to join Comecon in 1981 marked the end of its expansion to the extra-European world. The organization's smaller members saw the war-torn country as a liability,[132] even as President Machel continued to urge its members to invest in Mozambique as a 'Comecon laboratory for socialism in Africa'.[133]

Bilateral Interdependence

Contemporaries noted that the failure of the Soviets to imaginatively construct new forms of effective international infrastructure capable of overcoming the nationalizing impulses of Communist states would prove their eventual undoing.[134] Although relations remained mainly bilateral, connections nevertheless continued to expand. Eastern European states took seriously the UN's claims that developing countries would gain an ever-growing share of world industrial production, and continued to target markets and assist development projects.[135] Facing a domestic coffee crisis, the GDR helped launch the coffee industry in Vietnam, which after 1989 became the second largest exporter of the product in

---

[129]   Proceedings UNCTAD 1976, Annex C, 150. Lorenzini, 'Comecon and the South', 189.

[130]   Anne Dietrich, 'Bartering Within and Outside the CMEA: The GDR's Import of Cuban Fruits and Ethiopian Coffee', in Anna Calori et al. (eds.), *Between East and South: Spaces of Interaction in the Globalizing Economy of the Cold War* (Berlin, Boston: De Gruyter Oldenbourg, 2019), 197–216.

[131]   Ruben Berrios, *The Political Economy of East-South Relations* (Oslo: International Peace Research Institute, 1983), 243.

[132]   Schürer, 'Information zur Frage der Mitgliedschaft der VR Mocambique im RGW', Berlin, 13 June 1981, DY 3023/1471 (SAPMO-BArch), fol. 358.

[133]   'Information', Maputo, 23 May 1986, DY 3023/1472 (SAPMO-BArch), fol. 345.

[134]   George Modelski, 'Communism and the Globalization of Politics', *International Studies Quarterly*, 12/4 (1968), 393.

[135]   2283-1975-24—NGKB Meeting (UNIDO, Cuba); Directions for the delegation to the UNIDO 2nd General Meeting in Peru (Lima); 2312-1976-17 Hungarian Foreign Trade Strategy (1976), 8.

the world.[136] The increase for the smaller socialist states was also due to Moscow's fears that the Soviet Union was becoming economically peripheral within a bloc it politically dominated, confined to the role of a primary extraction economy supplying subsidized energy to the westernmost states of the socialist camp to develop their already more advanced industrial bases. To this end, the Soviets encouraged bloc countries to integrate further with the energy-producing states in the Middle East and North Africa, and to look to sub-Saharan Africa for raw materials. This only accelerated in the late 1970s, as the Soviet Union sought higher prices and hard currency from selling oil on the world market, and reduced their supply to the 'satellite states'—which had to find new ways to purchase it.[137] From 1979, the GDR began exporting arms to Iran, including re-exported Czech tanks, in part as barter for over one billion dollars of oil.[138] Hungary collaborated with non-aligned Yugoslavia to build the Adria Pipeline to bring Middle Eastern oil to Eastern Europe—after multiple setbacks it came into operation only in 1989.[139] Trade continued to increase: non-aligned Yugoslavia was a particularly striking case, where trade southwards increased fivefold across the 1970s, and then doubled in the 1980s.[140]

This expansion occurred under new ideological conditions: the relationship with what Eastern European economists now increasingly called the 'Third World'—albeit always in scare quotes—was shaped by Eastern Europe's gradual loss of faith in a socialist world system. The world economy, undivided, was analysed as an increasingly complex network of interconnections.[141] Soviet economists acknowledged in 1976 that 'in the contemporary world, the progress of each country is inseparable from its participation in the global exchange of material and spiritual values, reflecting an interdependence of all countries...A mass of visible and invisible threads links the economic development of separate countries with those changes that take place in the world economy.'[142] Economists and economic historians in Poland and Hungary formulated the idea of one

---

[136] Andrew Kloiber, 'Brewing Global Relations During the Cold War: Coffee, East Germans and Southeast Asia, 1978–1990', in Heather Merle Benbow and Heather R. Perry (eds.), *Food, Culture and Identity in Germany's Century of War* (Cham: Palgrave Macmillan, 2019), 247–70.

[137] Steffen Wippel, *Die Außenwirtschaftsbeziehungen der DDR zum Nahen Osten: Einfluss und Abhängigkeit der DDR und das Verhältnis von Außenwirtschaft zu Außenpolitik* (Berlin: Das Arabische Buch, 1996), 29–31, 35.

[138] Schalck to Mittag, Berlin, 23 January 1989, DL 226/4 (BArch).

[139] Ljubica Spaskovska, "Crude' Alliance—Economic Decolonisation and Oil Power in the Non-aligned World', *Contemporary European History* (2021).

[140] Paul Marer et al., *Historically Planned Economies: A Guide to the Data* (Washington, DC: World Bank, 1992), 224–5.

[141] See e.g József Bognár, *The Global Problems in an Interdependent World* (Budapest: Institute for World Economy, 1984).

[142] Nikolaj Shmelev, 'Ėkonomicheskie sviziazi Vostok-Zapad', *Institut Ėkonomiki Mirovoĭ Sotsialisticheskoĭ Sistemy*, 12–13, 14 (1976).

'world system'—an idea made famous by Immanuel Wallerstein, who acknowledged his debt to Eastern European thinkers, most notably Marian Małowist.[143]

The United Nations Industrial Development Organization (UNIDO), in its 1975 Lima Declaration, encouraged developed countries to shift some of their industry southwards in the name of the NIEO. Although Eastern European states were often wary of exporting jobs, some at the western fringes of state socialist Europe followed such seemingly progressive initiatives, but with an eye to bettering their own position within the 'new international division of labour'—a term that took off in the early 1980s. With the failure of Comecon in the 1960s to integrate the bloc based on complementary specialisms, some of its states more proactively worked to insert themselves between West and South. Hungary for instance identified its textile industry as a potentially successful exporter to Western Europe, the hard currency profits from which would enable investment in higher-value sectors such as computing, to move up the 'global value chain'. Western expertise was brought in: Levi's established a large jeans factory in Szeged, alongside collaborations with nine other western firms. It had become too expensive to employ Hungarian labour to weave and dye: hence the outsourcing of the initial production stages to cheaper labour at factories in ideologically sympathetic Syria and Egypt. High-quality fashionwear, marketed with advice from London advertising firms, would be sold in western markets.[144]

Older solidarity relationships could be leveraged for gain in this more interdependent world. A comparison between the reaction of bloc states to the accelerated collapse of the British and French Empires from the late 1950s, and the response to the opportunities provided by a collapsing Portuguese Empire in Africa from 1974, was telling. Czechoslovakia used political trust, forged in support for liberation struggles, to gain access to an independent Angola's enormous reserves of oil and diamonds, alongside its highly valued coffee, cocoa and cotton. It also harvested hard currency by selling arms to the Luanda government, which was bringing Angolan territory under its control. This built on Prague's earlier collaboration (officially denied) with Portuguese imperial authorities in mining and business ventures in Angola, and in the construction of the Cahora Bassa dam in Mozambique.[145]

Eastern European states attempted to preserve a commitment to socialist values as they developed new economic infrastructures to cope with interdependence. József Bognár, now head of a new Institute of World Economy in Budapest—replacing his Afro-Asian Research Centre—argued that the modern carriers of economic development were multinationals, and thus socialist enterprises should

---

[143] Theda Skocpol, 'Wallerstein's World Capitalist System: A Theoretical and Historical Critique', *American Journal of Sociology*, 82/5 (1977), 1081.

[144] HU OSA 300-2-5 Box 46 Textiles (Open Society Archives, Budapest).

[145] Pavel Szobi, 'Czechoslovak Economic Interests in Angola in the 1970s and 1980s' in Calori et al. (eds.), *Between East and South*, 171.

be given monopoly positions within the domestic economy to develop economies of scale.[146] Yugoslav experts recommended copying the Brazilian petroleum multinational *Petrobras'* strategy of merging domestic enterprises to become large enough to compete effectively in the global South.[147] The Slovene pharmaceutical enterprise *Krka*, together with the Kenyan government, and some commercial funds, developed the largest medical conglomerate in sub-Saharan Africa in the 1980s.[148] At home, multinational enterprises had an ever greater hold on politics: the Yugoslav Constitution of 1974 had weakened the federal centre, and strengthened smaller republican units which were now home to outsized global enterprises. Nevertheless, such enterprises were still expected to inscribe socialist or non-aligned values into 'mutually beneficial' undertakings in the South.[149] Yugoslavia and Hungary campaigned for an international ban on exploitative western practices of the very long term licensing of technology to skim profit from the South (although Eastern Europe states often enabled freer use of their products out of self-interest, in order to be competitive against more technologically advanced, but user-restricted, western equivalents).[150]

An accommodation with a new international division of labour nevertheless eroded earlier commitments to convergence—and undermined the bloc's own hopes of catching up with the West. Ideologically friendly developing countries were targeted as outlets for poorer goods: the GDR computing industry used lower-quality Czechoslovak components for its exports to Africa, and higher-speed Belgian equivalents when western customers paid in hard currency. However, some customers even preferred the lower-quality goods. Cheaper industrial products, or turnkey projects, could prove very attractive: in the late 1980s, Arab states returned to their suppliers from eastern Europe as collapsing oil prices made it difficult to afford western assistance and goods.[151] Nevertheless, poorer quality bilateral trade based on undercutting the West was not conducive

---

[146] József Bognár, *A magyar gazdaságpolitika és a világgazdaság kapcsolata. Kézirat* (Budapest: Világgazdasági Kutatóintézet, 1976), 150.

[147] Strategija razvoja saradnje sa zemljama u razvoju do 1990. odnosno 2000. godine. IV. Jugoslovensko savetovanje o ekonomskoj saradnji sa zemljama u razvoju, 3–5 October 1984, AS, AS 1134, b. 9, f. 134 (National Archive of Slovenia, Ljubljana).

[148] Marjan Svetličič and Matija Rojec, *New Forms of Equity Investment by Yugoslav Firms in Developing Countries* (Ljubljana: Center za proučevanje sodelovanja z deželami v razvoju, 1985).

[149] Anna Calori and Ljubica Spaskovska, 'A Non-Aligned Business World? The Global Socialist Enterprise between Self-Management and Transnational Capitalism', *Nationalities Papers* (2020), 1–15.

[150] Discussion with Mr Dagomir Cemalovic, 21 March 1975, 'Country Study—Yugoslavia. Transfer of Technology' ARR 1929 006 (UN Archive). Generally, there was a 'fade out' clause on royalties for using eastern European technology: UNCTAD Report, Hungarian Technological Transfer, ARR40 1929 005 (UN Archive). On freer use, see e.g. Victor Petrov, 'The Rose and the Lotus: Bulgarian Electronic Entanglements in India, 1967–89', *Journal of Contemporary History*, 54/3 (2019), 681–2.

[151] Massimiliano Trentin, '"Socialist Development" and East Germany in the Arab Middle East', in Mark et al. (eds.), *Alternative Globalizations*, 136.

to developing higher-level specializations that could push countries of the socialist camp up the 'global value chain'.[152]

Losing Control, and Reperipheralization: The 1980s Debt Crisis

By the end of the 1970s, ideas of development that had been nurtured within postwar UN institutions played an ever less important role in shaping the global economy. Other prominent transnational institutions committed to global planning—such as the International Institute for Applied Systems Analysis or the Club of Rome—lost influence too.[153] This shift reflected another consequence of decolonization: the collapse of financial controls, as western states led the construction of a new global economic architecture to enable the easier withdrawal of capital from the clutches of ideologically unsympathetic post-colonial states.[154] This development was accelerated by the oil crisis in 1973: members of the Organization of Arab Petroleum Exporting Countries (OAPEC) announced an oil embargo against those states which supported Israel during the Yom Kippur War. Prices rose by nearly 300%, and oil-rich states looked to recycle their enormous profits. As cross-border capital flows began to overtake industrialization as the main concern of global development, the management of the world economy shifted from the UN—where Eastern Europe and the global South had greater influence—to the 'Bretton Woods' institutions such as the IMF and World Bank which managed the financial side of the economy, such as debt repayment. And in the early 1980s, UK Prime Minister Margaret Thatcher and US President Ronald Reagan resisted any attempts to bring the World Bank or IMF under the control of the UN—fearing that eastern and southern debtor countries would take advantage in an institution in which they had greater clout.[155]

Foreign direct investment into specific projects was increasingly replaced by portfolio investment.[156] Now mostly arranged on the bond markets, Eastern European bilateral funding and development was outdated. The Tanzanian ruling party's Foreign Affairs Department concluded in the mid-1980s: 'All these socialist nations like to conduct their relations through any number of agreements;

---

[152] On the problems of socialist cooperation being confined to less developed and less technological sectors, see Svetličič and Rojec, *Equity Investment*, 49.

[153] Eglė Rindzevičiūtė, *The Power of Systems: How Policy Sciences Opened up the Cold War World* (Ithaca: Cornell University Press, 2016), Chapter 2.

[154] Vanessa Ogle called them 'late colonial money panics': '"Funk Money": The End of Empires, The Expansion of Tax Havens, and Decolonization as an Economic and Financial Event', *Past & Present*, 249/1 (2020), 213–49.

[155] John Toye, *UNCTAD at 50: A Short History* (New York and Geneva: United Nations, 2014), 63.

[156] Michael Pettis, *The Volatility Machine: Emerging Economies and The Threat of Economic Collapse* (Oxford: OUP, 2001).

[these] are preceded by long and oftentimes cumbersome negotiations...'.[157] Even the leverage that socialist states had used to counter their lack of capital—expertise—yielded diminishing returns. Moscow's Institute of World Economy and International Relations (IMEMO) reported their ever-decreasing influence over changes in the global economic system.[158] Socialist specialists observed that western colleagues became educated in the round through working for both international organizations and private donors, whilst they were limited to involvement in state-led developmental projects. As one GDR economist put it, recalling his stay in 1970s Dar es Salaam, 'as an *Ostmensch* one had no idea about the role of the World Bank and the IMF'.[159]

The collapse of capital controls led many Eastern European states down the road to indebtedness. To render their industries competitive, many had borrowed petrodollars that had flowed out of energy-producing states at low rates of interest after the 1973 oil price spike. The expected revolution in productivity and quality never occurred, and debt could not be paid back. Obligations rose tenfold in the 1970s; a decade later, Hungary had the world's third highest per capita debt.[160] Increasingly funds were borrowed simply to maintain standards of living.[161] With the spiralling cost of raw materials and rising interest rates in 1980—the so-called Volcker Shock—many Eastern European states became ever more mired in debt, which in turn brought them closer to the West. The Polish and Hungarian governments soon announced that they were no longer able to fulfil their obligations to international creditors, and joined the IMF.[162] Debt operated as a 'school for capitalism': Hungarian national banks in particular, which managed loans from both western and Middle Eastern sources, became very well versed in international finance long before 1989.[163]

Pressures to repay debt undermined earlier ideological commitments. In 1977, the Hungarian Central Committee officially abandoned the prioritization of trade with socialist-oriented countries.[164] Its multinationals, removed from the

---

[157] Foreign Affairs Department of CCM Headquarters, Brief of Socialist Federal Republic of Yugoslavia, no date [ca. 1985], (Chama cha Mapinduzi Archives CCMA, Dodoma), CMM/OND/183/36 Yugoslavia, Vol. 1 (Chama cha Mapinduzi Archives CCMA, Dodoma).

[158] Russian State Archive of Contemporary History (RGANI) F. 5, O. 76, D 246 L. 5–20.

[159] Interview with Hans-Joachim Wienhold, conducted by Eric Burton, Leipzig, 17 July 2014.

[160] Debts in Eastern Europe rose from $20 billion to $200 billion between 1971–9. Adam Fabry, 'The Origins of Neoliberalism in Late "Socialist" Hungary. The Case of the Financial Research Institute and "Turnabout and Reform"', *Capital & Class*, 42/1 (2017), 77–107.

[161] Of Hungary's 20 billion dollar debt, only $4–5 billion was invested in increasing productivity: Ivan T. Berend, 'Global Financial Architecture and East Central Europe Before and After 1989', in Ulf Engel, Frank Hadler and Matthias Middell (eds.), *1989 in a Global Perspective* (Leipzig: Leipziger Universitätsverlag, 2015), 56–7.

[162] André Steiner, 'The Globalisation Process and the Eastern Bloc Countries in the 1970s and 1980s', *European Review of History*, 2 (2014), 174–5.

[163] Rezső Nyers (ed.) *Külső eladósodás és adósságkezelés Magyarországon* (Budapest: Magyar Nemzeti Bank, 1993).

[164] On preliminary discussions, including the need for hard currency, see 2312-1976-17 Hungarian Foreign Trade Strategy, Documents of the Hungarian National Planning Office, 1974–1976

supervision of the Ministry of Foreign Trade, were enabled to reach out covertly to a range of partners that from a political point of view were potentially problematic.[165] Its bus enterprise Ikarusz sought (unsuccessfully) to outsource the assembly of parts to a cheaper Cuban labour force, in order to then export these to Latin American markets under right-wing dictatorships.[166] In the GDR in the same year, a special Politburo commission under Günter Mittag was established to consider how to maximize hard currency and profitability.[167] From 1978, they teamed up with Libya—also unsuccessfully—to invest in development schemes in sub-Saharan Africa. In Iraq, a joint GDR-Indian scheme used cheap Chinese labour to build railways for hard currency.[168] The Soviet Union imported substantial amounts of grain from, and shared military technology with, the Argentinian dictatorship—whilst investing in the Brazilian military regime's energy infrastructure.[169] Despite claiming to sever ties with South Africa, Moscow continued to very profitably process its diamonds with De Beers; in the 1980s it expanded its Afrikaans language programmes, and supplied arms and military electronics to the apartheid regime.[170] The GDR provided arms to both parties in the Iran–Iraq War (1980–88).[171] While publicly condemning Pinochet, it secretly expanded its trade volume with the Chilean dictatorship too.[172] Such political promiscuity usually required that these economic relationships be hidden from home populations.

Eastern European countries not only owed significant sums to western creditors, but were themselves owed huge sums they had loaned at low interest rates to Middle Eastern and African states. In 1974, for instance, Comecon states lent $16

(Hungarian National Archive, Budapest), 14, 31; Pál Germuska, 'Failed Eastern Integration and a Partly Successful Opening up to the West: The Economic Re-orientation of Hungary during the 1970s', *European Review of History*, 21/2 (2014), 278.

[165] Balázs Szalontai, 'The Path to the Establishment of Hungarian-South Korean Diplomatic Relations: The Soviet Bloc and the Republic of Korea, 1964–1987' (unpublished manuscript).

[166] Jelentés a PB részére a Magyar-Kubai Gazdasági és Műszaki-Tudományos Együttműködési Bizottság Tárgyalásairól, Budapest, February 1 1977. OL XIX-A-90-c 161. d. A Nemzetközi Gazdasági Kapcsolatok Bizottsága Titkárságának iratai (MNL).

[167] For an early account of this shift, see László Csaba, *Eastern Europe in the World Economy* (Cambridge: CUP, 1990), 127–9.

[168] 'Auskunftsbericht an den Staatssekretär Genossen Nendel zum Vorhaben Nussayeb—Kerbala—Najaf—Kufa—Damawa Railway Project', Sections 3 & 4, 26 January 1984, DN 1/20698 (BArch). Thanks to Max Trecker for this reference.

[169] Tobias Rupprecht, 'Socialist High Modernity and Global Stagnation: A Shared History of Brazil and the Soviet Union during the Cold War', *Journal of Global History*, 6/3 (2011), 526.

[170] Hennie van Vuuren, *Apartheid, Guns and Money: A Tale of Profit* (London: Hurst, 2018), 269–71; Paul Betts et al., 'Race, Socialism and Solidarity: Anti-Apartheid in Eastern Europe', in Anna Konieczna and Rob Skinner (eds.), *A Global History of Anti-apartheid: 'Forward to Freedom' in South Africa* (Cham: Palgrave Macmillan, 2019), 153, 174–5.

[171] Hans-Joachim Döring, *Es geht um unsere Existenz: Die Politik der DDR gegenüber der Dritten Welt am Beispiel von Mosambik und Äthiopien* (Berlin: Links, 1999), 44; Schalck to Mittag, Berlin, 23 January 1989, DL 226/4 (BArch).

[172] Georg J. Dufner, 'Chile als Partner, Exempel und Prüfstein', *Vierteljahreshefte für Zeitgeschichte*, 61/4 (2013), 513–48.

billion dollars to forty-two developing countries, the most favoured recipients being Egypt (15%) and India (15%).[173] But these partners also owed money to the West, and preferred to pay the 'Paris Club'—an informal group of (mainly western) major creditor countries with whom states needed to remain in good standing. Eastern European states simply had little power to enforce repayment: in March 1975, members of the Romanian Politburo were vexed by African states' outstanding debts and criticized Vietnam, which 'unacceptably' re-exported products offered by Bucharest in lieu of currency, to repay western creditors.[174] Oil states flush with petrodollars prioritized trade with western partners; Libya for instance refused to repay socialist countries, whilst spending hard currency extravagantly on western and South Korean firms.[175]

Eastern European states did the same, however: in the 1980s, when their socialist ally Mozambique could no longer service the credit they had been extended to buy East German products, the GDR demanded a share of its black coal, which it immediately sold on the world market for hard currency, before the ships had even reached the Baltic Sea. Czechoslovakia was a distinct case as it was not indebted to the West—but had nevertheless lent copiously to the South. Faced with high debts unpaid, Prague accepted an offer from South Korean company Daewoo in the late 1980s to take on Libyan debt repayment in oil in exchange for market access for South Korea's car industry. Seoul would become a major investor in Eastern Europe from the early 1990s.[176] Indebtedness was key to the disintegration of solidarity-based relationships, and the further integration of Eastern Europe into complex interdependent globalizations.[177]

In the 1980s, only Yugoslav and Romanian elites, still committed to the principles of the NIEO, were prepared to criticize the use of debt to force privatization and the shrinking of the state in Africa and Latin America.[178] At the 1989 Belgrade Summit of the Non-Aligned Movement, Yugoslavs called for debt write-offs for the least developed countries.[179] Few Eastern European countries supported debt forgiveness because they were owed significant sums too. GDR

---

[173] Loans provided by Comecon countries (2312-1976-17) Országos Tervhivatal, Nemzetközi Gazdasági Kapcsolatok Osztálya (MNL). Following Saddam Hussein's fall in 2003, Iraqi accounts revealed that approximately two thirds of the country's $130 billion foreign debt was owed to non–Paris Club states, including former Comecon members Poland, Czechoslovakia, and Bulgaria.

[174] 'Stenograma sedinţei Biroului Permanent al Comitetului Politic Executiv', 25 March 1975 ANIC, CC al PCR, Cancelarie 32/1975, 17.

[175] GDR embassy Tripolis to Streletz, Koenig, Gnedt, 26 March 1984, DY 3032/1469 (SAPMO-BArch), fol. 317-318.

[176] Klára Mészáros, *Business Opportunities for Korea in Hungary* [pamphlet] (Budapest, 1997), 13.

[177] On the western side, see Michael Franczak, 'Losing the Battle, Winning the War: Neoconservatives versus the New International Economic Order,1974–82', *Diplomatic History*, 43/5 (2019), 889.

[178] Mugur Isărescu, 'Criza monetar-financiară internaţională', in Costin Murgescu (ed.), *Criza economică mondială* (Bucureşti: Editura Ştiinţifică şi Enciclopedică, 1986), 91.

[179] Final Document—Declaration, 9th Summit Conference of Heads of State or Government of the Non-Aligned Movement, Belgrade, 4–7 September 1989, 87–90.

advisors publicly railed against the 'imperialist' IMF in Africa,[180] but they remained guarded in their criticism as they hoped that economic reform would increase the probability of repayment.[181] This increasing indebtedness had reshaped the region's position in the world economy, drawing it closer to the West and further from the South, while reducing its agency in the global economic order.[182]

The End of the Eastern European Model? Learning from the 'Semi-Periphery'

Until the late 1970s, it was still possible to believe that advances in socialist systems in Eastern Europe—notably market socialism in Poland and Hungary, or workers' self-management in Yugoslavia—could compete as viable models for economic development outside Europe. Following the assumption of power by Deng Xiaoping in China in 1978, market socialism became of interest to touring Chinese experts who travelled regularly to Romania, Hungary and Yugoslavia.[183] Likewise, Tanzanian economists looking for a counter-model to IMF-imposed market reforms in the mid-1980s looked across the socialist world—from China to Eastern Europe—for market-based socialist alternatives to financialized capitalism.[184] Nevertheless, these vistas and visits did not have long-term impacts; an economically liberalizing China turned its attention to the export-driven models of Japan and the 'East Asian Tigers' by the mid-1980s; Tanzania gradually embraced trade liberalization and privatization between 1985 and 1990.

In Eastern Europe, reform-minded economists reimagined the economic system—from being a two-world model in which Eastern Europe was a core socialist player, to a 'one world' capitalist system in which the region was 'semi-peripheral', sandwiched between the already highly industrialized core, and poorer peripheries—and was capable of swinging between either.[185] This shift was rooted in the gradual abandonment of the commitment to convergence with peripheries that could not overcome their 'backwardness'. Hungarian experts for instance presented their market socialism as the highest stage of development

---

[180]   Kurtz, 'Jahresanalyse 1986/87', Dar es Salaam, 20 July 1987, DR 3/2. Schicht/1514 (BArch).

[181]   Rudolph, 'Information über die von der Weltbank vorgenommene Einschätzung der Entwicklung der Zahlungsbilanz Tansanias in den Jahren 1989–1999', Dar es Salaam, 5 May 1989, DE 1/57846 (BArch).

[182]   Mark Mazower, *Governing the World: The History of an Idea, 1815 to the Present* (New York, NY: Penguin Books, 2013), chapter 12.

[183]   Péter Vámos, 'A Hungarian Model for China? Sino-Hungarian Relations in the Era of Economic Reforms, 1979–89', *Cold War History*, 18/3 (2018), 362–70.

[184]   C. G. Kahama, T. L. Maliyamkono, and Stuart Wells, *The Challenge for Tanzania's Economy* (London: James Currey, 1986).

[185]   Iván T. Berend, *History in My Life. A Memoir of Three Eras* (Budapest, 2009), 152. Adam Kola, 'A Prehistory of Postcolonialism in Socialist Poland', in Mark et al. (eds.), *Alternative Globalizations*, 278–9.

and as incompatible with those stagnant and crisis-ridden African economies with which trade was in decline. Structural explanations, based on the negative impacts of IMF conditionality, or the long-lasting legacies of Western European imperialism 'on the cheap' as regards the weakness of African states, were in decline; rather, the explanation for persistent inequalities was reduced to racialized points about irreconcilable cultures and mentalities. Persisting in this 'irrational' engagement, it was argued, would further hold back the more 'advanced' socialism found on the western fringes of the European socialist camp.[186] Africa was no longer seen as a respectable destination for the region's developmental experts, and higher salaries could be garnered elsewhere.[187] This erosion of faith in convergence had serious impacts in the bloc's poorer peripheries too. For instance, as the promises of development for the Soviet Union's southern republics faded, the same anti-colonial language that had been popularized in the 1960s could be turned back against the Soviet state. Assertive and increasingly nationalist Central Asian elites now characterized Moscow as an imperial metropolis whose policies had confined their republics to the periphery, and were now abandoning them, just as they were the Third World in the global system.[188]

Peripheral thinking had not disappeared; rather, Eastern European experts looked to successful experiments on the global margins to address their own economic crises. Latin America had long been seen as occupying a structurally similar position in the world economy, meriting attention and exchange.[189] In the 1960s, Eastern European economists undertook ambitious research projects on Brazil, Bolivia, Peru and Chile; Latin American economists studied the 'socialist market' in Hungary, Poland and Yugoslavia. By the 1980s, it was Chile's privatization that provided a model for those who wanted to smash state-led developmentalism at home. Like Pinochet, their Communists could use autocratic powers to cut down planning bureaucracies.[190] Marketizing dictatorships in the global South thus provided inspiration for possible elite-led economic transitions in Eastern Europe that avoided 'bothersome' democratic procedures. Such fantasies endured: as severe economic crisis hit Russia in the 1990s, a few economists called for a Russian Pinochet to rescue their country from becoming an impoverished Latin America.[191]

[186] Sz. Besszonov, 'A 'tervezési válság' kérdéséhez a gazdaságilag elmaradott országokban', *Közgazdasági Szemle*, 11 (1971), 710–29.

[187] Svetličič and Rojec, *Equity Investment*, 130; Landolf Scherzer, *Bom dia, weißer Bruder: Erlebnisse am Sambesi* (Rudolstadt: Greifenverlag, 1986), 146.

[188] Kalinovsky, 'Soviet South', 201–5.

[189] Béla Kádár, 'Main Phases of Development in Latin-America', *Acta Oeconomica*, 13 (1974), 89–115.

[190] For the Polish case, see M. Dzielski, 'How to Perpetuate Power in People's Poland?', in *Merkuryusz Krakowski i Światowy*, Samizdat, 1980.

[191] Tobias Rupprecht, 'Formula Pinochet: Chilean Lessons for Russian Liberal Reformers during the Soviet Collapse, 1970–2000', *Journal of Contemporary History*, 51/1 (2016), 165–86.

The dynamic authoritarian 'semi-peripheral' East Asian 'Tiger states' became potential models too in the 1980s. These countries had thrown off Japanese rule—just as Eastern Europeans had done with Nazi imperialism—but had much more successfully integrated into the world economy. Underestimating the extent to which they had been helped by the opening of the US market to East Asian capitalism—primarily to stem further Communist expansion—many eastern European states saw in the Malaysian, Korean, Taiwanese or Singaporean experience important and transferrable lessons.[192] The 'Tigers' had focused on building up export industries, and thereby shown how smaller countries could specialize in certain sectors, and resist their stagnation as peripheral, low-value locations in the emerging 'global factory'. By the late 1980s, as democracy movements prevailed in East Asia, reformists used these examples to argue for the necessity of democratization for development in Eastern Europe too.[193] The attraction of this model survived Communism's collapse, as leftist economists sought an alternative to European Union accession, which, they feared, would once again relegate the region to a hinterland of Western Europe.[194]

The Communist collapse is often seen as the starting point for the region's real internationalization. Yet this moment should be more accurately understood as the high point of a gradual, stuttering and often contradictory readjustment to a particular form: Euro-Atlantic capitalist globalization. And this journey had not always run through the West: decolonization had exposed the region's elites and experts to new ways of conceptualizing the future of peripheries in the global economy. Through such engagements, their experts had engaged with, and contributed to, the practices of a new financialized capitalist globalization. Orthodox Communist elites' long-feared corruption of experts who spent too long in North Africa, the Middle East and East Asia in the increasingly interdependent global economy of the 1970s and 1980s came to appear prescient.[195]

This adjustment occurred at varying speeds across states, and its differing forms were a matter of debate between ministries, industries, republics and political factions. The western fringes of the socialist camp, namely Hungary, the GDR, Czechoslovakia and Poland, had already significantly reorientated in the 1980s: their exports to the West amounted to two to three times their exports to

---

[192] Interview with economist Béla Kádár, conducted by James Mark and Zoltán Ginelli, 9 March 2017.

[193] László Zuglói, 'Mit tanuljunk Ázsiától?', in Fanny Havas (ed.), Beszélő összkiadás (Budapest, 1992), 722–3. For the Soviet turn to East Asia, see Chris Miller, The Struggle to Save the Soviet Economy: Mikhail Gorbachev and the Collapse of the USSR (Chapel Hill: University of North Carolina Press, 2016), 20–3.

[194] Sándor Kopátsy, 'Új világrend felé. Vissza és előre ötven évet', Társadalmi Szemle, 5 (1992), 13–23; Adam Lipowski and Jan Kulik, Państwo czy rynek ? Wokół cudu gospodarczego w Korei Południowej (Warsaw: Poltext, 1992).

[195] On Romania's fears of their international experts' 'capitalist dehumanisation' in 1976: 'Raport privind activitatea delegaţiei Ministerului Sanatatii care a vizitat Libia, 19 februarie–1 martie 1976', MS (Ministerul Sănătăţii)-DCCPI (Direcţia Coordonare, Control Personal şi Învăţământ)-Relaţii Externe 2–1984 (Romania), 14.

the South in 1980, and four to five times by 1989. In the late 1980s, UNCTAD campaigned for them to renew their trade outside Europe.[196] For others, 1989 represented a moment of starker deglobalization; in Bulgaria, Romania and Yugoslavia, southern markets were still of greater importance than western ones; for the Soviets, western trade stagnated in the 1980s, and southbound trade increased by 60%, to equal around 60% of that exported westwards by 1989.[197] During that decade, Yugoslav energy, construction and medical multinationals had successfully built new markets in the Soviet Union, the Middle East and Africa. The Bulgarian computing industry effectively positioned itself between West and South, copying western technology at lower prices, exploiting the absence of western computing firms from India, and developing large trade surpluses there.[198] The Soviet Union massively expanded arms and energy trade across the developing world.[199] The collapse of Communism in Europe from 1989 brought many such projects to a halt. Developmental workers became private contractors. Eastern European states generally lost the 'Third World' as export markets for their cheaper goods, as supplier of raw materials, or as sites for production. Legions of western advisors, business consultants and volunteers arrived, willing to develop Eastern Europe itself. The region became, as it had been in the interwar period, the subject of an external economic intervention that its own worldly economic elites would vigorously enact. Some international arms enterprises, such as the Czech Omnipol or Serbian Zastava Arms thrived; but in general neither western investors nor local neoliberals viewed the region's large multinational enterprises as viable global players, and split them up into constituent parts. The region was reorientated to its continental locale, and for at least two decades visions of alternative non-western economic globalizations were sidelined.

Conclusion

Even during the heyday of rapidly expanding contacts between Eastern Europe and the post-colonial world from the 1950s onwards, alternative economic visions based on anti-colonial solidarities had never been undisputed among the region's elites. Since the interwar period, efforts to overcome a position of peripherality and dependency had turned towards economic nationalism rather than seeking to build an alternative regional or transregional system from the margins. While

---

[196]   ARR 40/1929/545; UNCTAD Liason with Office of Secretary-General Folder—GTD 802/1 (UN Archives Geneva).

[197]   Marer et al., *Historically Planned Economies*, 2–220.   [198]   Petrov, 'The Rose', 666–87.

[199]   Mark Kramer, 'The Decline in Soviet Arms Transfers to the Third World, 1986–1991', in Artemy M. Kalinovsky and Sergey Radchenko (eds.), *The End of the Cold War and The Third World: New Perspectives on Regional Conflict* (Abingdon: Routledge, 2011), 56–7; Engerman, *Price of Aid*, 304–10.

there were a number of significant ruptures, the expanding world of postwar Communism echoed these contradictions. Even as Eastern European politicians and economists came to understand the region as central to global debates about development and the achievement of economic sovereignty in the postwar period, Asian, African and Latin American contacts had to remind them of their pledges to abolish hierarchies that hampered national development strategies. While these commitments thus at least partially shaped trade policies and development work for several decades, their appeal faded as Eastern Europeans sought to cope with the experience of once again becoming part of the West.

The journey back to an integration into Euro-Atlantic capitalism may have been accelerated by the collapse of Communism, but also had roots in an earlier crisis of development outside the West.[200] In the 1970s, a western-led financialized globalization, which had in part emerged as a reaction against the economic claims of a decolonized periphery, liberated capital flows and offered cheap credit. This placed Africa, Latin America and Eastern Europe in debt to the West: a process which undermined bonds of solidarity which had underpinned this interconnected progressive developmentalism. And excessive anti-colonial commitments were increasingly seen as re-peripheralizing Eastern Europe itself; the practices of a new financialized capitalist globalization learnt in encounters from the Middle East to East Asia. Thus even the reorientation towards western capitalism needs— at least in part—to be seen as the result of a deepened encounter with the world's peripheries that had begun half a century earlier.

---

[200] On Communism as the route to capitalism in the periphery: Branko Milanović, *Capitalism, Alone: The Future of the System that Rules the World* (Cambridge, MA: Harvard University Press, 2019), 221–6.

3

War and Peace

Péter Apor

Wars of anti-colonial liberation linked the 'Second World' with Africa and Asia in the postwar period. This chapter traces how both sides recognized commonalities of purpose and shared military histories. It also explores how this relationship was beset by ambiguity: how violence which had once been accepted as legitimate by a generation who had lived through the Second World War was more and more associated with the supposedly excessive demands of liberation movements, or with the threatening terrorism of Islamic groups. To assess the ideas of legitimate violence and connected military histories, this chapter focuses on the experiences of military cooperation in training camps and peace missions, as well as those advisors who engaged in professional diplomacy and military leadership.

A first generation of postwar Eastern European elites, many of whom had experienced the violence of the fight against Fascism in Europe, claimed that they had a responsibility to extend their support for progressive armed struggles beyond Europe. Weapons were delivered in the name of solidarity and later became business opportunities; training camps for liberation movements were established across the Eastern Bloc and beyond.[1] Eastern European soldiers also took part in peace missions,[2] engaged in reconstruction efforts and resettled

---

Although the final text is the product of a single author, this chapter is the result of a genuine collaboration. Assistance with archival research, translation and interpretation was given by Alena K. Alamgir (Czechoslovakia), Eric Burton (GDR), Maria Dembek (Poland), Bogdan C. Iacob (Romania), Mikuláš Pešta (Czechoslovakia), Nemanja Radonić (Yugoslavia) and Natalia Telepneva (Czechoslovakia, East Germany, USSR). Without their generous cooperation, this chapter would have looked very different.

[1] Sergei Mazov, 'Soviet Aid to the Gizenga Government in the Former Belgian Congo (1960–1) as Reflected in Russian Archives', *Cold War History*, 7/3 (August 2007), 425–37; Vladislav Zubok, 'The Soviet Union and Détente of the 1970s', *Cold War History*, 8 (November 2008), 434–5; Jeremy Friedman, *Shadow Cold War: The Sino-Soviet Competition for the Third World* (Chapel Hill: University of North Carolina Press, 2015); Natalia Telepneva, 'Mediators of Liberation: Eastern Bloc Officials, Mozambican Diplomacy and the Origins of Soviet Support for FRELIMO 1958–1965', *Journal of Southern African Studies*, 43 (January 2017).

[2] J.G. Hershberg, 'Peace Probes and the Bombing Pause: Hungarian and Polish Diplomacy During the Vietnam War, December 1965–January 1966', *Journal of Cold War Studies*, 5/2 (2003), 32–67. For the equivalent position in Romania, see M. Munteanu, 'Over the Hills and Far Away: Romania's Attempts to Mediate the Start of U.S.-North Vietnamese Negotiations, 1967–1968', *Journal of Cold War Studies*, 14/3 (2012), 64–96. For an account, see J.G. Hershberg, *Marigold: The Lost Chance for*

Péter Apor, *War and Peace* In *Socialism Goes Global: The Soviet Union and Eastern Europe in the Age of Decolonization*. Edited by James Mark and Paul Betts, Oxford University Press. © Oxford University Press 2022. DOI: 10.1093/oso/9780192848857.003.0004

populations after ceasefires.[3] During the 1950s and 1960s, philosophies of legitimate violence both within and outside Europe were similar in spirit, in part due to the legacies of the Second World War: both a postwar European socialist elite and those fighting for independence against empire instinctively understood the necessity of violence as a constitutive part of political struggle. Legitimate violence, thus, embraced armed struggle that aimed to establish independent nation states. These experiences were by no means uniform though: the USSR, East Germany and Yugoslavia actively engaged in war-making, whereas Poland and Hungary were more concerned with mitigating the effects of war and positioned themselves as experts in peacekeeping.

Eastern European participation in extra-European theatres of conflict changed over the course of the Cold War, reflecting shifting ideas about the centrality of violence. From the mid-1950s onwards the ideology of peaceful coexistence replaced earlier Manichean logics of confrontation inside the Soviet Bloc, which in the next decade fed increasing pragmatism towards supporting revolutionary wars. From the late 1960s with the rise of a new generation of more technocratic leaders with ever weaker connections to the wartime anti-fascist struggle, the shared transregional understandings of legitimate violence began to diverge. On the one hand, a new commercial language increasingly permeated Eastern European arms deliveries and military contracts. On the other, Eastern European Communists started to distance themselves from the espousal of violence associated with Maoist radicalism, political Islam and international terrorism. These transformations eventually contributed to the disintegration of the broader anti-imperialist alliance. With Eastern Europe's growing perception in the 1980s that the global South—and especially southern Africa and the Middle East—was a 'hotbed' of excessive violence, the debate over what constituted the appropriate use of violence became understood in civilizational terms.

Sharing Histories, Sharing Weapons

Nicholas Nkomo, leader of a liberation unit in Zambia who had been trained in the USSR, admired the Red Army mostly for what he understood as its 'war of liberation' in Eastern Europe. The group of Africans in this Soviet military training camp, of which Nkomo was a member, was particularly moved by films documenting the committed resistance of Soviet soldiers and citizens against Nazi Germany, which eventually resulted in hard-fought victory in the war. In fact the

Peace in Vietnam (Washington, DC and Stanford, CA: Woodrow Wilson Center Press with Stanford University Press, 2012).

[3] Charles K. Armstrong, "'Fraternal Socialism': The International Reconstruction of North Korea, 1953–62', *Cold War History*, 5 (May 2005), 161–87. Young-Sun Hong, *Cold War Germany, the Third World, and the Global Humanitarian Regime* (Cambridge: CUP, 2015), 51–82.

idea of Soviet soil as the heroic epicentre of a global struggle had already achieved a mythological status in many parts of Africa by the end of the war: medical aid had been collected and Friends of the Soviet Union associations established across the southern part of the continent.[4] For Nkomo a generation later, the dramatic images of turning back the Germans in the suburbs of Moscow or the life-and-death combat of small partisan units were still powerful.[5] The liberation fighters from Africa did not interpret the lessons of the Soviets' Great Patriotic War primarily in terms of Communist ideology or proletarian class struggle. For them, the power of patriotism and disciplined self-sacrifice was paramount. The trainees from Africa appropriated the lesson of the Great Patriotic War as a model of the legitimate use of armed violence—a war of national liberation.[6]

Africans joining the armed wings of anti-colonial movements arrived in socialist Eastern Europe to learn tactics of armed violence that were appropriate and practical for national liberation. The recognition that violence was a prerequisite for effectively combatting colonialism inspired many Africans to join insurgent resistance armies.[7] Fighters from the developing world considered socialist Eastern Europe to be an attractive model of anti-imperialist violence which had been successfully deployed in the name of liberation. The South African activist Barry Feinberg recalled why he had been attracted to East Germany: 'So, it was not just the case of the GDR providing hospitality and responding to the shopping lists that were given to them by liberation movements, including the ANC. But it was also a case of having a very, very rich experience in the struggle against fascism, the struggle against racism and giving advice on strategies and tactics.'[8]

National experiences shaped what the individual Eastern European states offered as appropriate and legitimate means of violence. Arms transfers and the types of weaponry reflected national military traditions. For example, the weapons that Yugoslavia exported to Algeria from 1956 to 1957 to fight against French colonial forces had been produced in the early 1950s, when, just after the Tito–Stalin split, the Yugoslav arms industry shifted to manufacturing large quantities of simpler military equipment designed specifically for the guerrilla struggle that would be necessary following an anticipated Soviet invasion.[9] The traditions and

[4] Donal Lowry, 'The Impact of Anti-communism on White Rhodesian Political Culture, ca.1920s–1980', Cold War History, 7/2 (2007), 171.

[5] Jocelyn Alexander and Joann McGregor, 'War Stories: Guerrilla Narratives of Zimbabwe's Liberation War', History Workshop Journal, 57 (Spring 2004), 90.

[6] Jocelyn Alexander and Joann McGregor, 'African Soldiers in the USSR: Oral Histories of ZAPU Intelligence Cadres' Soviet Training, 1964–1979', Journal of Southern African Studies, 43/1 (2017), 59.

[7] Quoted in Alexander and McGregor, 'War Stories', 85.

[8] Quoted in Hans-Georg Schleicher, 'GDR Solidarity: The German Democratic Republic and the South African Liberation Struggle', in The Road to Democracy. Volume 3, Solidarity (Pretoria: Pan African University Press, 2008), 1085.

[9] Leon Mangasarian, Independence or Dependence? The Arms Industry in Israel, South Africa and Yugoslavia during the Cold War (London: LSE, 1993), 212.

capacities of arms industries also played a crucial role in binding socialist Czechoslovakia and Africa—particularly independent Egypt—together in the military domain. The backbone of Czechoslovak heavy industry were the two large machine factories Škoda and Zbrojovka Brno, equipped to produce a range of specialized weaponry including heavy artillery and light machine guns. The newly independent Czechoslovakia, one of the most industrialized countries of the region, had inherited an advanced arms industry after the collapse of the Austro-Hungarian Empire. It developed into one of the most important players in the international arms markets during the interwar period: in the 1930s, Czech arms deliveries amounted to no less than one fifth of the global arms trade.[10] After 1945 socialist Czechoslovakia emerged as one of the most important suppliers of Warsaw Pact armies through the 1950s. Yet as its industry became excluded from western markets in the postwar period, it looked southwards: the country re-entered the international arms trade market in 1955 by signing a treaty with Egypt.[11] Up until the mid-1960s, Czechoslovak elites justified these transactions mostly in terms of solidarity with the common anti-imperialist struggle. Arms deliveries for non-socialist countries in the Third World were generally not supported (even if occasionally permitted) and the final say normally rested with the regime's military and political bodies, most commonly the Ministry of Defence.[12]

Communists also sought to transmit their experience of anti-fascist resistance before and during the Second World War—and regarded liberation wars in the South as an extension of that. A postwar Soviet military elite proudly considered themselves the people who had spectacularly crushed the mighty war machine of an imperialist conqueror, as well as the people who effectively brought liberation to smaller nations suffering under imperial control. Participation in the Vietnam War or support for African liberation movements was simply a continuation of this struggle. As Petr Yevsiukov, who liaised between the anti-colonial fighters in Portuguese Africa and the Soviet military and political leadership, put it in his memoirs:

The October [1917] Revolution, and then the victory of the anti-fascist coalition in World War Two, decisively influenced the balance of forces in the world in favour of progress, struggle for national liberation, especially in Africa and Asia. The 'Cold War' did not stop this process...Assistance to nationalists from

[10] Vladimir Francev, *Československé zbraně ve světě: V míru i za války* (Prague: Grada Publlishing, 2015), 211.

[11] Karel Sieber and Peter Zídek, *Československo a Blízký východ v letech 1948–1989* (Prague: Ústav mezinárodních vztahů, 2009), 57. Petr Zídek, 'Vývoz zbraní z Československa do zemí třetího světa v letech 1948–1962', *Historie a vojenství*, 3 (2002), 523–67. Philip Muehlenbeck, *Czechoslovakia in Africa, 1945–1968* (Basingstoke: Palgrave, 2016), 87–124.

[12] Collection Ministerstvo národní obrany (Ministry of National Defence) 1953, box 410, Vojenský ústřední archiv—Vojenský historický archiv (Central Military Archive—Historic military archive, VÚA-VHA, Prague).

socialist countries, first and foremost the Soviet Union, was a natural reply to their appeal for such help.[13]

And there were indeed many continuities in war-making into the postwar period. The Soviet political and military elite prided itself on having a long and successful track record of anti-imperialist warfare and socialist revolutionary violence. The first major postwar Soviet involvement was the Korean War: in the first month of the conflict, the Soviet leadership and Stalin himself decided to send arms, ammunition and military advisors to the North Korean People's Army.[14] Their aid was presented as an extension of their longer-term anti-imperialist intervention in South East Asia (see *Origins*). The chief Soviet military advisor in Beijing who oversaw Chinese and North Korean operations was Matvei Zakharov, the foremost strategist in planning the Manchurian campaign against Japanese armies at the end of the Second World War.[15] Red Army divisions had entered Korea in 1945 as part of the campaign to break Japanese hegemony in the region, and remained there as occupying forces up until 1948.[16] Zakharov himself had been a revolutionary fighter who had joined the Red Guard in 1917. He became an iconic figure during the 'Great Patriotic War', acclaimed as a brilliant strategic mind. Indeed, as Chief of Staff on various Soviet Fronts, he had made significant contributions to the planning of successful operations against the Germans.[17] Zakharov was not only a veteran of industrial socialist warfare: he also played an important role in developing the myth of the Great Patriotic War, as the author of many articles on Soviet military history and technological warfare, especially regarding Kursk, the largest tank battle of the Eastern Front. The elements of this myth were manifold, including heroic popular support, modern war machinery produced in the USSR (including the T-34 armoured vehicles, the 'Katyushas'), and the resolute leadership of a centralized Communist Party.[18]

The Soviets offered support 'at home' too. They established military training for fighters of national liberation movements in the Third World in specialized training camps.[19] These camps were often located at the actual locations of past struggle: the Perevalnoye training camp, for example, did not simply provide a suitable terrain on which to practice warfare, but was a historical site itself, situated in an

---

[13] Quoted in Vladimir Shubin, *The Hot 'Cold War': The USSR in Southern Africa* (London: Pluto Press, 2008), 3.

[14] 'Telegram from Stalin to Shtykov', 6 July 1950, APRF, fond. 45, opis. 1, delo. 140, list. 140 (History and Public Policy Program Digital Archive) http://digitalarchive.wilsoncenter.org/document/112986.

[15] Zhang Xiaoming, 'China, the Soviet Union, and the Korean War: From an Abortive Air War Plan to a Wartime Relationship', *The Journal of Conflict Studies*, 22 (2002), 73–88.

[16] Charles K. Armstrong, *The North Korean Revolution: 1945–1950* (Ithaca: Cornell University Press, 2004). 251–2.

[17] Richard Woff, 'Matvei Vasilievich Zakharov', in Harold Shukman (ed.), *Stalin's Generals* (London: Phoenix, 1997), 327–41.

[18] Nina Tumarkin, *The Living and the Dead* (New York: Basic Books, 1994).

[19] Vladimir Shubin, 'Unsung Heroes: The Soviet Military and the Liberation of Southern Africa', *Cold War History*, 7 (2007), 251–62.

area of the Crimea where particularly intense Ukrainian anti-fascist partisan activities and heavy guerrilla fighting had taken place. The very location of such camps could be used to transmit the historical experiences of the Soviet War of Liberation. They were even run by wartime military leaders: at Perevalnoye, the commander, Colonel Ivan Nikiforovich Boyko was a 'hero of the Soviet Union', having joined the Red Army as a volunteer in 1930, and had become a legendary figure in the context of the Soviet Patriotic War effort during the war itself.[20] The curricula for trainees from the developing world included excursions to Patriotic War memorials and regular showings of documentary war films. As former train-ees from Africa recalled, the films highlighted the unique loss of life suffered by the Soviet people, which was a crucial element in the myth of the Great Patriotic War. The site of the Katyn massacre, where in fact Soviet NKVD gunmen mur-dered some 22,000 Polish military officers, was used to create emotionally mov-ing images of Nazi imperialism. African trainees were taken there and educated into the Soviet war remembrance myth of Katyn—that it was the result of the cruelty and barbarism of German fascists, who, as official Soviet stories claimed, slaughtered the captured Soviet officers.[21]

The memory of resistance was central elsewhere too: South African activists were taken to visit Buchenwald concentration camp near Weimar, which in the 1950s came to be presented as the mythical site of Communist anti-fascist resist-ance in the GDR. The story of a small group of heroic prisoners who, according to the official GDR narratives, successfully organized an armed revolt against Nazi guards made an impact on one South African activist: 'Our visit was made less harrowing and even inspiring by the guides, who included ex-inmates. They placed much emphasis on the resistance of the prisoners, who eventually over-threw the SS administration and took over the camp.'[22] African National Congress members arriving in Yugoslavia for training were taken to visit sites of the parti-san struggle and museums devoted to the Yugoslav liberation war, including the Military Museum in Belgrade, and the Memorial Cemetery to the Victims of Fascism in Jajinci. They also attended lectures and took part in discussions with members of the board of SUBNOR (The Alliance of the Fighters of National Liberation War), the Yugoslav Second World War veteran organization, and staff of the Institute for Study of the Workers Movement, where former liberation fighters instructed African trainees about how to organize popular armed uprisings.[23]

Appeal could also be made to longer-term military traditions. In East Germany, the expansion of the European anti-fascist struggle was promoted as growing out of a century-long history of (East) German national liberation struggles. When

---

[20] 'Bpata Bouko ha bouhe', Комсомольская правда, 13 August 1944.
[21] Alexander and McGregor, 'African Soldiers', 59–61.
[22] Barry Feinberg, *Time to Tell: An Activist's Story* (Newtown: Real African Publishers, 2011), 115.
[23] Program posete SSRNJ člana izvršnog rukovodstva i predstavnika ANC Južne Afrike u Kairu Mzivandile Pilibo-a, 1965, 1–2 (Archives of Yugoslavia (AJ), 142, 558 I).

the ruling elite of the postwar German socialist state endeavoured to create a national historical legacy for their own political project, they rediscovered the resistance to Napoleon's armies led by Prussia. From the early 1950s, the Prussian generals of the Napoleonic wars, especially Gerhard von Scharnhorst and August von Gneisenau, were praised as predecessors of the East German People's Army. Although the two had certainly been dear to a German right-wing militarist nationalism—two Second World War German imperial battle-ships were named after them—the GDR nonetheless managed to couch their biographies in a powerful anti-imperialist language. Emphasizing the context of Napoleonic expansion and, thus, French imperialist traditions, Scharnhorst and Gneisenau were recast as leaders of Prussia's national liberation struggle.[24] Even if official biographies of the Prussian generals did not strongly connect the nineteenth- century German national liberation wars to anti-imperialist armed movements in the post-colonial world,[25] they were integrated into the military training curricula for African liberation fighters. Doing so created new affinities between hitherto distant histories. East German military traditions were now reworked as a prehistory to contemporary anti-colonial liberation struggles in Africa.

Many African and Asian fighters were also greatly impressed by socialist Eastern Europe's evident success at reconstruction, the healing of traumatized societies and the building of durable and modern political orders after the wars of liberation. Africans who received training in the Soviet Union admired the rapid industrial reconstruction of the country following the devastating fighting on the eastern front. Zimbabwean Stool Matiwaza, for example, was confident that if the Soviets could remake their society and economy virtually from scratch, his country could do the same.[26] Ruth First, a South African Communist activist, reported back home in 1954: 'So it was possible to rebuild Stalingrad, almost completely destroyed in 1942–3 in the fiercest battle of the war, in one-fifth of the time estimated by a visiting American engineer. So Leningrad has been rebuilt and Sebastopol, and new suburbs of new cities are shooting up faster than the first grass-shoots on the new lawns before the apartment buildings.'[27]

Yugoslavia was not only known for its successful partisan warfare but also for its attempts at peace-making and reconciliation. First of all, it had played a role at the United Nations War Crime Commission (1943–48) to put Nazi war criminals

---

[24] Mary Fulbrook, *German National Identity after the Holocaust* (Cambridge: Polity, 1999), 87.
[25] Gerhard Förster and Christa Gudzent, 'Einführung', in August Wilhelm Anton Neidhardt von Gneisenau, *Ausgewählte militärische Schriften*, ed. Gerhard Förster and Christa Gudzent (Berlin: Militärverlag der Deutschen Demokratischen Republik, 1984), 8–49.
[26] Alexander and McGregor, 'African Soldiers', 60.
[27] Ruth First, 'Life in the Soviet Union: Building, Building, Building', *Liberation*, 8 (June 1954), 13.

on trial. Alongside Poland, it had supported Ethiopia's pursuit of justice for crimes committed by Italy after the invasion in 1935. It had also assisted the hunting down of fascists who had fled to North Africa.[28] Over the next decades, relationships initiated at the UNWCC would be further cemented by evoking the common experience of overcoming Italian fascist aggression and the shared efforts to modernize their societies. During his 1959 visit to Ethiopia, Tito evoked the bonds that had been forged by 'the struggle against the forces of aggression on the eve and during World War Two'[29] and their shared struggle for a lasting peace after the war. Second, Yugoslav specialists also claimed expertise in treating conflict-related traumas that arose in the course of the anti-fascist struggle, and attempted to transplant what they referred to as 'transcultural psychology' to post-colonial societies. They pointed to their successful experience in curing 'partisan hysteria', which had been identified among 'primitive' peasant fighters after the Second World War, and was perceived as the outcome of the shock of transition from military life to the radically new experience of modern urbanization.[30] Yugoslav psychologists and psychiatrists, like Vladimir Jakovljević, who worked in post-colonial Guinea, used such experiences to treat the neuroses of those who had been part of liberation wars or were attempting to cope with the demands of rapid socialist modernization.[31] Third, Yugoslavia was perceived to be a very important model for post-conflict reconstruction by post-colonial leaders in Algeria, Indonesia, Nigeria or Burma. These new states—where post-colonial state-building ran parallel with the need to reconcile various ethnic, national and religious groups—discovered in Yugoslavia a model for successfully overcoming a past of intra-state ethnic and religious hostilities under strong centralized leadership.[32]

Poland and Hungary were also involved in post-conflict reconstruction. This was partly a result of their respective wartime experiences, and the way in which those experiences were built into their postwar socialist cultures. Unlike the Soviet Union or Yugoslavia, in neither case had indigenous Communist movements played significant roles in anti-Nazi military resistance. The new elites of Hungary and Poland rather emphasized the experiences of suffering under German occupation and the heroic reconstruction after 1945 headed by national

---

[28] Haile Muluken, 'The Failed Ethio-Polish Cooperation to Prosecute Italian Fascist War Crime Suspects: The UNWCC between Abstract Justice and Political Exigency, 1943–1949', conference paper, 19th International Conference of Ethiopian Studies (Warsaw, August 2015).

[29] 'Marshal Tito, Madam on Second Ethiopian Visit Warmly Welcomed by Government, People', *Ethiopian Herald*, 4 February 1959, 1.

[30] Ana Antić, 'Heroes and Hysterics: 'Partisan hysteria' and Communist State-building in Yugoslavia after 1945', *Social History of Medicine*, 27/2 (2014), 349–71.

[31] Ana Antić, 'Imagining Africa in Eastern Europe: Transcultural Psychiatry and Psychoanalysis in Cold War Yugoslavia', *Contemporary European History*, 28/2 (2019), 234–51.

[32] Alvin Z. Rubinstein, *Yugoslavia and the Non-Aligned World* (Princeton: Princeton University Press, 1970), 203–4.

Communist parties. In postwar Poland, the memories of suffering and victimization were shared by various social and cultural groups and, hence, provided the moral foundation for an emerging socialist identity, one in which the nation was under a particular moral obligation to aid others who had endured similar wartime suffering. By the early 1950s, such historical memories were actively mobilized by Polish Communist authorities concerned to support Pyongyang in the context of the Korean War. In publicity campaigns, the American bombing of Korea was thus compared to Nazi air raids over Poland. Many Poles understood their contribution to the postwar reconstruction in North Korea in terms of easing the suffering of civilian populations at war. As a Polish solidarity delegate to Korea recalled, 'A war was going on in Korea, we were just after the war, and we understood what a war was about; one thing that I learned about the Koreans was that they were the same as us [Poles], and that they fought in the same way like us.'[33] Radio programmes compared American detention camps in Korea to wartime concentration camps: the film, 'Korea. American Auschwitz' declared: 'here is the shocking image of the island of death: the American perpetrators of genocide are attacking the camp of Korean prisoners with tanks and flamethrowers.'[34] Thousands of North Korean schoolchildren, many of whom were war orphans, were educated in Poland, Romania and Hungary, and subsequently in Czechoslovakia and East Germany, throughout the 1950s.[35]

Later, from the mid-1950s onwards, Poland and Hungary represented themselves rather as champions of peace: an expression of those values and roles with which the post-Stalinist Polish and Hungarian elites identified. Previously a militarized confrontational rhetoric had been key: during the Korean War, for instance, the official press in both countries condemned US imperialism in the harshest of terms and accused UN troops of barbaric, fascist-like campaigns against civilians. Their domestic populations were exposed to bellicose reports of the war and were mobilized as a 'homefront', working hard in their factories to support the war efforts of the Korean people.[36] After 1956, however, with the onset of the policy of peaceful coexistence announced by Khrushchev, Polish and Hungarian elites increasingly crafted their countries' self-image as experienced peacemakers, a role which they now were ready to play globally. This was central to the way in which Hungarian elites, re-established in

---

[33] Interview with Helena Krzywdzianka, conducted by Margaret K. Gnoiska, Warsaw, 26 July 2006. Quoted in Margaret K. Gnoiska, *Poland and the Cold War in East and Southeast Asia, 1949–1965*, PhD dissertation (George Washington University, 2010), 79.

[34] 'Korea. Amerykański Oświęcim', PKF, 1952. http://www.repozytorium.fn.org.pl/?q=pl/node/6706 (last accessed 1 June 2020); 'Dżungla i Oświęcim', Polish Radio, 10 min., aired 22 August 1962.

[35] Péter Apor, 'The School. Schools as Liminal Spaces: Integrating North Korean Children Within Socialist Eastern Europe, 1951-1959', in Kristin Roth-Ey (ed.), *Second-Third World Spaces in the Cold War: Global Socialism and the Gritty Politics of the Particular* (London: Bloomsbury, 2022).

[36] 'Celebration day of a heroic nation', *Dziennik Bałtycki*, 15 August 1953, 2; 'Korea hős fiai, veletek vagyunk!' Editorial, *Szabad Nép*, 25 June 1952, 1.

power by Soviet intervention following the Uprising in autumn 1956, made sense of their experience of overcoming the threat to their power. Hungarian Minister of Foreign Affairs János Péter visited India, Indonesia, Ceylon, Burma, Egypt, Sudan and Syria in August–September 1957 to explain to the leaders of these countries how Hungary had restored social peace after what Péter called a civil war planned by the counter-revolutionary revolt. These two countries later played a pivotal role in the International Peace Control Commission following the peace settlement of 1973 in Vietnam.[37] The Polish government's head representative Piotr Jaroszewicz justified his country's participation on the grounds that it was its duty to help to restore peace as the basis of international relations.[38]

The visual representation of liberation wars was a powerful means of con-structing a common understanding of legitimate violence. Both the Eastern European socialist elites and the leaders of national liberation movements sought to render the war of the colonists as unjust and imperialist, whereas the violence of the liberation fighters was depicted as legitimate self-defence. Already during the Algerian War, Yugoslav press coverage, and particularly Stevan Labudović's photographic work, was particularly important in representing French brutality both for Algerian and international media. Labudović, who had been a partisan in the wartime Yugoslav army under Tito, was convinced that the Yugoslav and Algerian popular liberation struggles had much in common.[39] He spent three years in Algeria (1959–62) and documented the life of the insurgent army in photographs and documentary. Eastern Europeans made an even larger impact through photojournalism in Vietnam. Among the socialist photographic chron-iclers were the East German Thomas Billhardt, the Soviet Lev Porter in 1966 and 1967, Stefan Tihov from Bulgaria in 1972 and Endre Friedmann, photojournalist of the Hungarian State Press Agency in 1973. Their photojournalism depicting the fighting Viet-Cong and suffering civilians was also published in the form of coffee-table books, often as multilingual editions aimed in part at western audi-ences.[40] The Eastern European visual representation of the suffering Vietnamese or Algerian people echoed the themes of western anti-war photography, which set

[37] R.C. Thakur, *Peacekeeping in Vietnam: Canada, India, Poland, and the International Commission* (Edmonton: University of Alberta Press, 1984).
[38] 'Poland, Hungary Agree to Take Part in Control Commission', 26 January 1973. RFE-RL Background Report (Open Society Archives, Budapest, henceforth OSA). For a brief account of the Hungarian role, see Z. Szőke, 'Magyar békefenntartók Vietnamban', *Külpolitika*, 5/3–4 (1999), 149–75; '25 éve kezdődött...' A magyarok békeküldetése. A Vietnami háborútól napjainkig (Budapest, 1998); J. Davola, 'Magyar rendfenntartók a világban', *Rendvédelem-történeti Füzetek (Acta Historiae Preasidii Ordinis)*, 23 (2011), 29.
[39] 'It is partizanština [guerilla warfare par excellence], the one and the other'. Interview with Stevan Labudović, conducted by Nemanja Radonjić, Belgrade, 1 December 2016.
[40] György Makai and Pál Schiffer jr., *Száz kép Vietnamról* (Budapest: Országos Béketanács, 1966).

out to convey the horrors of colonial wars and the brutal nature of the assault on civilians. This new Eastern European war photography captured similar experiences, and was circulated in contemporary western media. The jury of the World Press Photo contest regularly included members from the region and photographers from the socialist bloc such as Porter and Tihov often won prizes.[41]

Eastern European war photography was akin to its western counterpart inasmuch as it sought to question western interventionism—but was far removed from much of it insofar as it sought to legitimize anti-colonial revolutionary violence. Photography from post-colonial wars was there to assist in the denunciation of military violence perpetrated by the Americans, the French and the British. Such photographs seemed to depict a brutal campaign waged against civilians, often by linking these new wars to the history of European colonialism and Fascism, and to Eastern Europeans' own recent experiences of violence. Following the suppression of the 1956 revolt in Hungary, the re-established Communist state produced a propaganda booklet on the 'counter-revolution', called the 'White Book'. Here images of comrades brutally murdered by so-called 'counter-revolutionaries' on the streets of Budapest were placed alongside images of slaughtered Algerians: the accompanying text blamed 'fascist French paratroopers who executed masses of people: men, women, children'.[42] For Hungarian Communists these images of brutality revealed the essential similarity of anti-Communist violence in 1956 in Budapest, the result of their own domestic 'Fascism' and of the sinister military reach of the colonial powers. Similar images in the region, which were published in the domestic press and thus were directed at domestic audiences, focused on the suffering of civilians caused by the careless military operations of imperialists or the inhuman treatment meted out to captured fighters of the anti-imperialist movements.[43] Such photography often evoked an earlier iconography of colonial brutality, suggesting powerful connections between western 'neo-colonialism' and the history of European exploitation of the Third World.[44] The historical imagery that permeated the Eastern European representations also sought to reveal the true face of the West by tearing off its false mask of humanist and pacifist rhetoric.

---

[41] *Vietnam War: Photos.* World Press Photo. https://www.worldpressphoto.org/collection (last accessed 4 September 2021); Thomas Billhardt. *Fotografie. Mit einem Essay von Steffen Lüddemann* (Berlin: Braus, 2013); Makai and Schiffer Jr., *Száz kép Vietnamról.*

[42] *Nagy Imre és bűntársai ellenforradalmi összeesküvése* (Budapest: Minisztertanács Tájékoztatási Hivatala, 1958), 75.

[43] 'Die Vergiftung der Gehirne', *Berliner Zeitung*, 2 January 1966, 5. 'Horrible Vietnam War—250,000 Children are Killed', *Borba*, 23 December 1966, 1.

[44] 'Puskával a F105D ellen', *Ifúkommunista*, July 1967; György Máté, *Fények a dzsungelben* (Budapest: Táncsics, 1964). This was also true in Poland, see e.g. Daniel Passent, *Co dzień wojna* (Warsaw: Czytelnik, 1968).

Eastern European leaders continued moreover to support liberation fighters from Africa to South East Asia who emphasized that the armed struggle was necessary to realize their essential human rights, most notably the right to self-determination. Diplomats from North Vietnam spoke the language of humanitarianism and human rights when advocating their cause in Eastern Europe, but not in opposition to violence. They often appealed to the European experiences of the struggles against Fascism, particularly in Spain and the Holocaust, to point out the inherent connection of armed struggle and the successful establishment of national sovereignty, social justice and the right to peaceful development.[45] The legitimization of violence was connected to a similar language of rights in Eastern Europe, which in some contexts persisted until the last decade of state socialism. The East German press, for instance, highlighted in the 1980s that the UN approved the right of the Namibian people to self-determination and national independence, which the illegal South African invasion had denied them.[46]

Appropriate violence leading to national self-determination was understood to be a modern disciplined and militarized kind. In this regard, Eastern Europeans envisaged a special role for themselves: they were to bring advanced modes of warfare and the consolidation of state violence into the Third World. The Soviets considered their military assistance not simply as gifts of economic and military unity from an interested superpower patron: it was also understood as a specific model of socialist war-making. As Sharof Rashidovich Rashidov, the leader of the Soviet delegation at the first Tricontinental Congress in Havana in 1966, put it in an address to the other participants at the meeting:

> The Soviet Union is supplying the fraternal people of Vietnam with the most modern weapons for meeting U.S. aggression. We are doing everything in order that the deliveries of Soviet military equipment—aircraft, rockets, artillery, ammunition, and so on—will get into the hands of the Vietnamese freedom fighters as rapidly as possible. We Soviet people are happy that the military equipment which the workers of the land of Soviets are producing at their enterprises with such great enthusiasm also helps the cause of the victory of our Vietnamese brothers over the aggressor.[47]

The Soviet representative highlighted the use of modern military technology, an industrialized home front, as well as a tightly organized and effective means of transport. The meaning of military modernity had concerned Soviet revolutionary leadership since the Civil War. Commanders of the Red Army including

---

[45] Kim Christiaens, 'Europe at the Crossroads of Three Worlds: Alternative Histories and Connections of European Solidarity with the Third World, 1950s–80s', *European Review of History*, 24/6 (2017), 943.

[46] 'Erich Honecker empfing Militärdelegation der PLO', *Neues Deutschland*, 18 November 1981, 1. 'Impulse für Befreiungskampf', *Neues Deutschland*, 9 March 1982, 2.

[47] Speech by Sharaf P. Rashidov, *The Tricontinental Conference of African, Asian and Latin-American Peoples. A Staff Study* (Washington, DC: US Government Printing Office, 1966), 83.

Trotsky, Tukhachevsky and Stalin had rejected the ideas of a 'proletarian' army consisting of irregular militia units only and advocated setting up disciplined and high-tech army corps that they had seen as most effectively mirroring the organized nature of the working-class and their state.[48] Notably, Rashidov also mentioned the central role of the Vietnamese freedom fighters, which he nonetheless portrayed as a popular mass army trained and headed by a centralized and ideologically driven vanguard party. The Vietnam War was viewed as a template of these Second–Third World military relationships. Across the bloc, the conflict was represented in official socialist media as a defensive war waged by revolutionary armies disciplined by a committed Communist Party, and supplied by the effective and modern military technology of socialist Eastern Europe.[49]

Eastern European media was not shy about glorifying revolutionary violence. Its war photography fondly depicted the use of Eastern European weaponry against American troops in Vietnam. Hungarian propaganda boasted of the effectiveness of anti-aircraft guns produced in Hungarian factories.[50] In so doing these images constructed a visual model of revolutionary violence, one that emphasized the disciplined and responsible use of modern socialist military technology. Photographic coverage of Tito's visits to Africa regularly highlighted the giving of military gifts to leaders of national liberation movements, for instance to Ben Bella and Gaddafi. These images were designed to capture African appreciation of the modern weaponry that Yugoslavia generously provided to their new alliance partners: rifles, cameras and X-ray machines.[51] Furthermore, in marked contrast to lurid socialist representations of imperialist brutality, Eastern European photographic representations of the military actions of anti-imperialist fighters removed the physical acts of killing. Whilst armies of national independence movements were certainly depicted in combat, they were pictured in drill formation or firing their guns.[52] The dead remained invisible, turning military activity into a neutral field of anti-imperial resolve and technological combat.

In other ways, the Warsaw Pact's coordinated strategy of revolutionary warmaking aimed to temper the exercise of violence. At meetings of Eastern European military leaders, the guiding principle was to approach revolutionary wars as an intra-state civil war type struggle that should not escalate into broader international conflict. Soviet officials normally rejected requests for the most

---

[48] Raymond L. Garthoff, *Soviet Military Doctrine* (Auckland: Pickle Partners Publishing, 2019), 26–55.

[49] For Hungary, e. g. Bálint Szabó, 'Két hét Vietnamban', *Ifjúkommunista*, June 1961, 68–70. For Poland, e. g. Daniel Passent, *Co dzien´wojna* (Warsaw 1968).

[50] HU 300-40-2-Box 53 (OSA).

[51] Radina Vučetić, 'Tito's Africa: Representation of Power during Tito's African Journeys', in Radina Vučetić and Paul Betts (eds.), *Tito in Africa: Picturing Solidarity* (Belgrade: Museum of Yugoslavia, 2017), 31–2.

[52] Anonymous photographer, Album of Vietnam Photography. MNL OL XIX-A-33-a, box 193 (National Archives of Hungary, Budapest, henceforth MNL).

advanced military technologies to the Third World and limited Warsaw Pact military aid to mobile combat weapons and necessary ammunition, with only a small number of armoured vehicles included to support infantry. In 1965 the Czechoslovak government approved the delivery of infantry rifles and machine guns with ammunition sufficient for 1,000 men in support of Zimbabwe's ZAPU, whereas it considered the full request of 50,000 items excessive.[53] Likewise, the training of fighters of national liberation movements was limited to the sort of weaponry already supplied to these indigenous movements and never expanded towards the more modern technologies of the Warsaw Pact armies.[54]

The question of how to moderate legitimate revolutionary force was central to bloc attitudes to the anti-imperialist struggle in an era of détente and peaceful coexistence. Such concerns especially worried the Poles and the Hungarians, whose elites were most keen to maintain working relationships with the West. This is not to say that these countries denied the appropriateness of using violence to defeat colonialism. Yet they questioned whether the struggle against a common imperialist enemy necessitated the actual armed involvement of the socialist states of Eastern Europe. Peaceful coexistence, or so they argued, was in fact a battle between capitalism and socialism fought in the guise of bettering societies, improving economies and constructing national communities. Linking up with the national liberation fighters of the Third World would only bring the prospect of global war and total annihilation. In these conditions, the Hungarians and Poles argued that the proper means of combating imperialism and winning the struggle was to share the technologies of social and economic reconstruction and peacetime state-building with the post-colonial world.[55] Some of their citizens did not agree: exposure to the horrors of the Vietnam conflict in particular meant that across Eastern Europe, in Belgrade, Budapest and Berlin, young people became so enraged at what they saw that they volunteered to fight.[56] Indeed, at the time this seemed set to become bloc policy. On 6 July 1966, Warsaw Pact countries issued a joint declaration in Bucharest stating their preparedness to send volunteers to Vietnam—but this was never put into practice.[57] In Yugoslavia,

---

[53]   Presidium of the Central Committee of the CSCP, NA Find 02/1, NAD 1261/0/4. Sv.120, a.j. 126, bod 12 (National Archives of the Czech Republic, Prague).

[54]   Klaus P. Storkmann, *Geheime Solidarität: Militärbeziehungen und Militärhilfen der DDR in die 'Dritte Welt'* (Berlin: Ch. Links, 2012), 157.

[55]   Istvan Kende, 'Peaceful Co-Existence: Its Interpretation and Misinterpretation', *Journal of Peace Research*, 5 (December 1968), 352–64.

[56]   *Ifjúkommunista*, January 1967, 9. The magazine claimed that the Communist Youth was mobilizing effectively, and that 'hundreds' had volunteered to go to Vietnam. Activists from East Berlin's radical scene tried to volunteer for Vietnam; see James Mark and Anna von der Goltz, 'Encounters', in R. Gildea, J. Mark and A. Warring (eds.), *Europe's 1968. Voices of Revolt* (Oxford: OUP, 2013), 161. The Soviet authorities reported that they received 750 requests to fight in Vietnam; Gaiduk argues that this was itself a propaganda ploy to threaten the US, and provide a smokescreen for the introduction of Soviet advisors into Vietnam. Gaiduk, *Soviet Union*, 64.

[57]   Gaiduk, *Soviet Union*, 62–3.

where Maoism had a following of sorts amongst so-called 'anarcho-liberals' and students, many of those who wanted to fight felt they would not be well received by their own equivocating state, and hence went to the Chinese Embassy to volunteer, where it is recorded that they were politely turned down.[58]

Not everyone in the Third World was happy with the new Eastern European terms of engagement. Latin American Communists, and particularly Cubans, were particularly quick to criticize their Eastern European partners. In March 1966 Amando Hart, member of the Cuban Central Committee at the 23rd Congress of the CPSU in Moscow, claimed that the Eastern European model of socialist war was impotent and useless. He upbraided the Soviets for neither protecting Vietnamese fighters from the devastations of American carpet bombing nor helping to liberate the peoples of Asia, Africa and Latin America from imperialist exploitation.[59] The anger of Cuban revolutionaries towards their Soviet and Eastern European partners was in part the result of their heightened expectations. Cuban leaders, particularly Fidel Castro and Amando Hart, often proclaimed the direct lessons they drew from the experiences of the 1917 Russian Revolution. In a September 1966 speech, Hart compared the early revolutionary period in Russia with the challenges that Cuban Communists had themselves faced.[60] An editorial commemorating the 49th anniversary of the Great October Revolution in the official daily of the Communist Party of Cuba, *Granma*, claimed that the most important lesson that revolutionary movements of the developing world should learn from Russia was that revolutionary politics, effective leadership and well-organized armed struggle could win the day for socialism even in highly unlikely revolutionary situations. As *Granma* emphasized, 'Now fifty years later, Lenin's analysis of conditions in Russia and Europe during his time applies with singular precision to Asia, Africa, and Latin America.'[61]

Their disappointment lay in what they perceived as the Soviet retreat from armed liberation struggle, which suggested to them that the Soviets had betrayed their own revolutionary inheritance. As Hungarian Embassy reports highlighted, Fidel Castro liked to satirize the Soviet elite by claiming that they were no longer revolutionaries, but rather coddled functionaries who strove their uttermost to die in a comfortable bed.[62] For the Cubans, the new leaders of the USSR had

---

[58] Interviews with Borislav Stanojević, Belgrade, 2 November 2012; and Tihomir Trivunac, Belgrade, 26 October 2012. Nevertheless, a poll conducted in 1969 revealed that Mao—alongside Lyndon Johnson—was one of the most unpopular political figures amongst Belgrade's students. John F. Kennedy, Indira Gandhi and Lenin were the most popular; 'Zastati znači zaostati', *Borba*, 10 May 1969, 7. HU 300-10-2-49 (OSA).

[59] CIA Intelligence Report. The Sino-Soviet Struggle in the World Communist Movement Since Khrushchev's Fall (Part 3) (Reference Title: ESA U XXXVI), 113–14.

[60] CIA Intelligence Report. The Sino-Soviet Dispute Within the Communist Movement in Latin America, 15 June 1967. (Reference Title: ESAU XXVIII), 39.

[61] 'Our Hommage to the October Revolution', *Granma*, 7 November 1966, 1.

[62] Hungarian Ambassador Lőrinc Soós's report, 9 March 1967. 1. MNL OL XIX J 1 j 61. d.

abandoned the fundamental principle of socialist war-making—armed insurrection. For his part, Castro tried to promote alternative models for socialist war-making in the post-colonial areas. As the former commander of guerrilla fighters in the mountains, he recognized the achievement of the Vietnamese freedom fighters as a victory of revolutionary passion and commitment over industrialized technology-based warfare.[63]

At the 1966 Tricontinental Conference in Havana, Latin American and South East Asian revolutionaries formed a new alliance that excluded Eastern Europe. The Cuban approach to revolutionary violence served as an alternative model that reflected the new insurrectionary forces of the global South. Nguyen Van Tien, representative of the South Vietnamese National Liberation Front at the Tricontinental Conference, boasted of the fighting potential of irregular popular troops in his country.[64] The concerns of Latin American revolutionaries about a growing Eastern European reluctance to engage in military operations abroad created a pretext for Maoist China to challenge Soviet influence and increase its impact by championing an alternative mode of socialist revolutionary war.[65] Instead of restraining violence through developing mighty modern armies as deterrents against imperialist aggression, Chinese propaganda stressed the role of popular masses and insurrections in successful revolutionary wars. Furthermore, Chinese leaders considered this model globally relevant and used it to court potential allies, particularly in Latin America, with messages that emphasized Chinese endorsement of their revolutionary causes. In a 1966 article in the globally circulated *Peking Review*, Latin American popular revolts were praised as a model for anti-imperialist revolution:

> It is necessary to resist counter-revolutionary violence with revolutionary violence. This is the valuable lesson the Latin American people have learnt at the price of much suffering and bloodshed. One of the salient features of the Latin American national-democratic revolution in 1965 was that the idea that salvation lies in armed struggle was taking root in the hearts of an increasing number of people.[66]

There were many among the Eastern European elites who were rather uncomfortable with such ardent celebration of unbridled guerrilla warfare. Eastern Europeans and particularly the Soviets observed Che Guevara's ideas on the

---

[63] Castro speech at the Closing Session of the Tricontinental Conference (University of Texas: Fidel Castro Speech Database) http://lanic.utexas.edu/project/castro/db/1966/19660216.html (last accessed 7 September 2021).

[64] The Tricontinental Conference. A Staff Study, 21–3.

[65] Jeremy Friedman, *Shadow Cold War: The Sino-Soviet Competition for the Third World* (Chapel Hill: University of North Carolina Press, 2015), 12.

[66] Fen Hsi, 'Latin America: The People Fight Ahead', *Peking Review*, 9/28 (January 1966), 15.

expansion of revolutionary war with mounting alarm. Soviet embassy reports from the early 1960s dismissed Guevara's theory of guerrilla warfare as an ultra-revolutionary adventurism predicated upon a grave misunderstanding of the diversity of national liberation struggles.[67] Hungarian elites for their part characterized his politics as 'exaggerated revolutionarism', overly reliant on a voluntaristic use of violence with too little attention paid to peaceful construction at home.[68] When Castro visited Budapest in June 1972, Hungarian officials found Castro 'an anachronism' and his appearance at a parliamentary event in military fatigues and boots a 'quaint foible'.[69]

In this context, the Chinese Revolution of 1949, which had been perceived as an inspiring blueprint for extra-European socialist revolutions in the late Stalinist period, was now depicted as an irresponsible and dangerous use of violence. The Politbüro of the East German Communist Party heavily criticized the Maoist Chinese leadership for overestimating the role of the popular masses and underestimating the importance of modern military technology in a possible war against the US. In its 1966 report to the Central Committee, the East German SED stressed that Mao and his followers had wrongly dismissed those army officers who took seriously the consequences of novel military technologies, such as rockets and nuclear weapons, for modern revolutionary warfare.[70] If it was for tactical reasons that the Soviets, Hungarians, Poles and Bulgarians rejected the way that revolutionary violence was being promoted by the Cuban elite, their misgivings towards African uses of violence were based on cultural (and sometimes racially coloured) arguments about their supposed inability to master modern technology. Soviet Deputy Foreign Minister Yakov Malik described the military thinking and state-building visions of many African leaders as naïve and megalomaniacal, as evidenced in a discussion with Czechoslovak counterparts Jan Pudlák and Jan Ledl on 22 April 1966.[71] And in the first joint meeting of the Solidarity Committees of the Eastern European socialist states on 28–29 June 1966 in East Berlin, several representatives voiced doubts about the capacity of African national liberation movements to wage proper socialist revolutionary war.[72]

---

[67] Soviet Embassy in Cuba, 'Cuba and the National Liberation Movement in Countries of Latin America' (excerpts), 5 December 1963, TsKhSD, f. 5, op. 49, d. 655, l. 127,132, r. 9085. Translated for CWIHP by Gary Goldberg. History and Public Policy Program Digital Archive. https://digitalarchive.wilsoncenter.org/document/117069 (last accessed 9 August 2021).

[68] Gábor Karczag, *Ernesto Che Guevara* (Budapest: Kossuth, 1969).

[69] *The Guardian*, 12 June 1972. On similar tensions when Allende visited Cuba in 1973, see Tanya Harmer, *Allende's Chile and the Inter-American Cold War* (Chapel Hill: University of North Carolina Press, 2011), 199–201.

[70] 'From the Report of the Politbüro to the CC', *Berliner Zeitung*, 18 September 1966, 4.

[71] David to Novotny, 7 May 1966, NA inv. c. 2, ka 3.

[72] *Consultation meetings of the Representatives of the Afro-Asian Solidarity Committees of the European Socialist States* (Konsultationstreffen zwischen den Vertretern Afro-asiatischer Solidaritätskomitees (AASK) europäischer sozialistischer Länder), 28–9 June 1966. BA-SAPMO DZ8/32,1–3, 29, 54, 57 (Bundesarchiv, Berlin).

Such views ran alongside an increasing militarization of Soviet and African contacts in the 1960s. Soviet leaders linked the failures of the African revolutions to their misjudgements regarding the state of their armies. As Soviet Foreign Minister Malik explained to his Czechoslovak partners, the army and the police must be seen as important political actors in the future and socialist political and military policies should have considered them so. From the mid-1960s onwards, Soviet political and military personnel began to develop closer contacts with African military leaders and encouraged their Eastern European allies to provide more advanced training for these soldiers.[73] The Soviet general staff of the Warsaw Pact now began on principle to instruct its allies to send arms together with personnel trained for ideological instruction.[74] Whereas the technique and practices of using combat weaponry could be learned by Africans or Asians, or so the logic went, the strategies of revolution required properly trained minds and should therefore be left to the Europeans.

As a result, some African fighters began to draw closer to alternative models of anti-imperialist violence, particularly those coming from South East Asia. Wilton Mkwayi, a liberation fighter of the South African ANC, who had been sent to China for military training, explained why Chinese traditions of anti-imperialist violence looked more appropriate for them:

> We learnt how to make hand grenades by using readily available resources, for example cow dung, in the manufacture of explosives, Molotov cocktails, etc. The Chinese told us these are indigenous methods that are easier to utilise, particularly in rural areas. According to my observation, the differences between the Chinese and the Russians were a decisive factor in sending MK cadres for military training. In the Soviet Union they were trained to use military hardware, not indigenous materials, which the Chinese taught us to use.[75]

The apparent scepticism of Third World leaders towards the technologies of (East) European socialist warfare and the preference for tactics of irregular assaults ironically reinforced conventional European colonial thinking in a socialist context. Many Eastern Europeans active in the field of military relations believed that their southern revolutionary counterparts were the products of a less politically mature world. The *Vietnam Hungarian News* often complained about locals who tried to exploit the uncertainty following the armistice in 1973, reporting on cases of local banditry or other violent crimes in breach of the rules of civilized military conduct. In these reports, the Hungarian military staff appeared as the responsible authority who tried to keep order among the quarrels of chaotic and disorderly groups in the jungle. It was a tone that recalled the

---

[73] Natalia Telepneva, 'Saving Ghana's Revolution: The Demise of Kwame Nkrumah and the Evolution of Soviet Policy in Africa, 1966–1972', *Journal of Cold War Studies*, 44 (2018), 4–25.

[74] Storkmann, *Geheime*, 165.

[75] Wilton Mkwayi, *The Road to Democracy: South Africans Telling Their Stories*, Volume 1 (Houghton: Mutloatse Arts Heritage Trust, 2008), 269.

self-assured voice of white European colonial officials who considered themselves as sober-minded arbiters mediating between brawling tribesmen.[76] The European who represented the rational, reality-based force of mind and technology and the non-European who, in contrast, was the man of instinct and spirit, perpetuated venerable colonial stereotypes and racist hierarchies. In the long run, the disagreements over proper revolutionary tactics revealed not simply differences of geographical background or social structure, but also entrenched cultural divisions. As the Bulgarian representative Mitkovski bluntly remarked at the meeting of the Solidarity Committees in Berlin, 'Africans…are, indeed, somehow different people, there exists a particular African mentality.'[77]

Military training offered to non-European liberation fighters was intended to mould proper revolutionary subjects who were disciplined, precise and strict in morals and demeanour. Antonín Janovec, the director of the Prague-based Felix Dzerzhinsky Central School of the Ministry of Interior, listed the desirable qualities of anti-imperialist liberation fighters in his report to his superiors. Among them were the ability to recognize 'suitable political conditions for the successful conduct of guerrilla warfare, the importance of central management, creating good material and political conditions in combat, the importance of discipline and alertness in combat, the principles of choosing the correct people for partisan units'.[78] Concerns with discipline regularly featured in the reports about the military training courses sent to the Czechoslovak Ministry of Interior. The officials who oversaw the courses valued modesty, responsibility and diligence in their charges and regularly tried to sanction deviance.[79] A frequent theme in interviews among former participants was alcohol consumption. Beer and liquors, in particular, were openly available and consumed. What former trainees often recalled was not the experience of drunkenness, but rather the personal embarrassment they usually felt as a consequence. The loss of temper, manners and good discipline was what bothered their European supervisors the most. As Lincoln Ngculu, former ANC fighter trained in the GDR remembered, 'There were those who were in the habit of over-indulging and would forget about discipline. When it came to criticism and self-criticism meetings the problems arising from the abuse

[76] *The Vietnam War and the Hungarian Peace Keeping Mission: 'It Started 25 Years Ago'* (Budapest: Hadimúzeum Alapítvány, 1998), 14–16.

[77] 'Wir müssen aber auch die Mentalität der Afrikaner kennenlernen. Sie sind doch irgendwie andere Menschen; es ist eine besondere afrikanische Mentalität.' Zdravko Mitkovski, *Consultation meetings of the Representatives of the Afro-Asian Solidarity Committees of the European Socialist States* (Konsultationstreffen zwischen den Vertretern Afro-asiatischer Solidaritätskomitees (AASK) europäischer sozialistischer Länder), 28–9 June 1966. BA-SAPMO DZ8/32, 3.

[78] Antonín Janovec, 'Final Report on the Portuguese Guinea course', Prague, 22 December 1961, Abs, 11853/102/1/4. 2 (Archives of the Czechoslovak Secret Services, Prague).

[79] Janovec, 'Final Report', Prague, 8 November 1961 and 22 December 1961. Abs, 11853/102/1/4. Jaroslav Kodad, 'Final report about the course of the state security for the students from Portuguese Guinea.' Prague, June 1966, Abs, 11853/102/2/4, 3.

of liquor would be raised and comrades would be told to learn how to behave.'[80] Efforts to limit alcohol and shape morals were not simply a means to discipline trainees. They were also part of a broader programme to shape individuals who would behave responsibly when using violence.

From Solidarity to Profit

From the late 1960s, the economic and trade relationships between the Second and the Third Worlds were increasingly militarized, and military support became less an object of solidarity than a source of revenue. This new wave of militarization was spearheaded by the Soviet Union, which grew into the world's largest arms trader, with roughly three times the size of international trade in arms as that of the US by the end of that decade. Soviet deliveries to the Third World were estimated to have grown by roughly 300% in the 1970s: selling arms produced huge profits for the already otherwise declining Soviet domestic industries. By the end of the 1970s, the bulk of Soviet export to the developing world consisted of weapons. Soviet arms shipments constantly increased over this period straight through to the final years of Gorbachev's tenure as Secretary General.[81] In the course of the 1960s, Czechoslovak arms export to *non-socialist* countries increased enormously, more than doubling between 1964 and 1968.[82] Its Ministry of Trade, which valued profit-making, took over the leading decision-making role from the Ministry of Defence, which had previously held the line on solidarity as a key criterion for the arms trade. Economic experts saw the reform movements of the 1968 Prague Spring as an excellent opportunity to whip up business with non-Communist states as they demonstrated independence from Moscow.[83] The GDR regularly sold weapons to various warring states or irregular armies.[84] The peak of East German arms deliveries was the first half of the 1980s, when its export tripled in comparison to the figures from the late 1970s.[85]

---

[80] Lincoln Ngculu, *The Honour to Serve: Recollections of an Umkhonto Soldier* (Claremont, South Africa: David Philip Publishers, 2010), 90–2.

[81] Mark Kramer, 'The Decline of Soviet Arms Transfers to the Third World, 1986–1991', in Artemy M. Kalinovsky and Sergey Radchenko (eds.), *The End of the Cold War and the Third World: New Perspectives on Regional Conflict* (London: Routledge, 2011), 46; Laura Després, 'Third World Arms Trade of the Soviet Union and Eastern Europe', in Marie Lavigne (ed.), *East-South Relations in the World Economy* (Boulder and London: Westview Press, 1988), 52.

[82] Václav Valeš, 'The Principles of Realization of the Special Material Trade', Ministry of Foreign Trade, Prague, 18 June 1968. VÚA-VHA, MNO 1970, box 254.

[83] Daniela Richterova, Mikuláš Pešta and Natalia Telepneva, 'Banking on Military Assistance: Czechoslovakia's Struggle for Influence and Profit in the Third World 1955–1968', *The International History Review*, 43/1 (2020), 13–15. Some of the research for this was carried out as part of the Socialism Goes Global project.

[84] Hennie van Vuuren, *Apartheid Guns and Money: A Tale of Profit* (London: Hurst, 2018).

[85] Gareth M. Winrow, *The Foreign Policy of the GDR in Africa* (Cambridge: CUP, 1990), 145.

A sizeable weapons industry was also developed in Poland by the 1960s, eventually employing about 150,000 workers and consuming about 10–11% of the Polish state budget.[86] Poland became the world's fifth largest exporter of arms by the 1970s, producing mostly Soviet-licensed weaponry for the Third World in exchange for oil. These new commercial opportunities were based on the re-militarization of Polish industry in the 1950s following Soviet pressure, when several civilian-oriented factories were transformed to produce for the army in case of demand.[87] One of the major partners of Poland in the military field was Ethiopia. From 1977 onwards, Warsaw donated weapons to Mengistu's Communist regime, trained a number of officials of the Ethiopian state security and sent Polish experts to Addis Ababa. Between 1985 and 1987, Polish helicopter units participated in famine relief operations, too.[88] Hungary, which emphasized its contribution to peaceful coexistence, nevertheless also became an important—albeit covert—supplier of arms to the global South. It had inherited considerable capacities from the pre-1945 period, and by the mid-1960s, the FÉG arms company in Budapest had become one of the largest industrial employers in the country with some 4,000 workers.[89] The Hungarian socialist state, which was in need of hard currency, made its first arms deal with Syria in 1967.[90] From the late 1970s Hungarian ships regularly left the Yugoslav port of Kardeljevo with a cargo of guns, rocket-launchers and handguns to Iran, Syria, Libya and Angola. In the 1980s, Hungary's main trading partner in arms, besides the militarized regimes of Iraq and Libya, was India.[91] Yugoslavia also increased its exports to Middle Eastern countries in this period. It delivered weapons and military equipment to Iraq, Iran, Libya, Algeria, Angola, Egypt and Kuwait; it enjoyed a large profit of 8.5 billion dollars between 1975 and 1985, with seventy-three projects in these partner countries that included a chemical weapons complex, a weapons factory, three airports, a tank base and several military hospitals.[92]

---

[86] Norbert Baczyk, 'Polski powojenny przemysł zbrojeniowy. Lata tłuste, lata chude', *Polityka*, 8 November 2016.

[87] Krzysztof Kubiak, 'Między ideologią a komercją' and Tomasz Targański, 'Wydziały S' in *Pomocnik Historyczny nr 5, Dzieje Oręża i Przemysłu Zbrojeniowego*, special edition of *Polityka*, 10 (2016), 65, 71–2.

[88] Przemysław Gasztold-Seń, 'Wywiad PRL a problemy polityczno-gospodarcze Afryki Subsaharyjskiej w latach osiemdziesiątych XX wieku', *Olsztyńskie Studia Afrykanistyczne*, 2 (2011), 151. Przemysław Gasztold, 'Lost Illusions: The Limits of Communist Poland's Involvement in Cold War Africa', in Philip M. Muehlenbeck and Natalia Telepneva (eds.), *Warsaw Pact Intervention in the Third World: Aid and Influence in the Cold War* (London, New York: I. B. Tauris 2018), 214.

[89] Zoltán Sárközi, Gábor Szilágyi and Ferenc Gáspár, 'A Fegyvergyár története 1891–1948', *Tanulmányok Budapest Múltjából*, 22 (1988), 376–7, 429–32.

[90] Pál Germuska, *Unified Military Industries of the Soviet Bloc: Hungary and the Division of Labor in Military Production* (Lanham, Boulder: Rowman and Littlefield, 2015), 162.

[91] Folder 'Rakéta', ÁBTL O-19738 (Historical Archives of the Hungarian State Security Services, Budapest).

[92] Jovan Matović, *Vojni poslovi Jugoslavije u XX veku* (Belgrade: Tetra GM, 2003), 45.

The remarkable size of these Eastern European industries gave rise to constant difficulties associated with sustainability, which in turn generated pressure on their governments. Neither the domestic nor the intra-bloc market proved sufficient for the economic output of the national arms industries. The leaders of socialist Czechoslovakia worried about the apparent waste of one of the countries' potentially most successful industries. The sizeable capacities of these arms industries, which should have served as a source of generating income and facilitating exchange for advanced technologies, remained largely unexploited in the framework of trade with Warsaw Pact partners, which tended to pay well below market prices and mostly in exchange for unwanted agricultural surplus. Military relations, and especially arms deliveries to the global South, were increasingly dominated by commercial concerns. Over time, military agreements more and more took the form of barter, rather than being determined by the demands of socialist solidarity. In 1977–78 the GDR, which constantly struggled to meet the popular demand for coffee, contracted Ethiopia to export it in exchange for East German weapons.[93] The arms race was calculated in economic terms by the mid-1980s, rather than for its potential political capital. Covert shipments of East German weapons to South Africa's apartheid regime in the mid-1980s was a striking illustration. The clandestine Stasi-run trade company IMES sold East German arms worth $20 million to a French middleman, turning a blind eye to the fact that the weapons were to be dispatched to the storage facilities of South Africa's military.[94] According to UN investigations, Romanian, Bulgarian and Yugoslav weapons also found their way to the apartheid government via private arms dealer middlemen in this period.[95]

Socialist managers of the international arms enterprises increasingly behaved liked their capitalist counterparts in terms of their overriding concerns with competition, profit, market share and efficiency. They saw the Third World as a ready market for their products. By the end of the 1980s, the East German Commercial Coordination section, when considering the profitability of maintaining Soviet fighter jets, explicitly suggested ways 'to turn countries like India [into] a market for us.'[96] The proliferation of producers deepened intra-Bloc competition and rivalry for the same markets. In 1988 the GDR had to compete with Hungarian and Chinese

[93] Anna Dietrich, *Coffee for Weapons: The Barter between Ethiopia and the GDR* (Unpublished manuscript, 2017).

[94] van Vuuren, *Apartheid Guns and Money*, 260–2. South African Communists had already suspected as early as 1963, and were indignant at these clandestine arms transfers from Eastern Europe to the apartheid regime. Philip Kgosana, 'Africa Wants an Answer: Are the Communists Trying to Have it Both Ways?', *The New African*, 21 September 1963, 156–7.

[95] Telegramă (New York), nr. 075811, 10 April 1984, MAE (Ministerul Afacerilor Externe)-ONU (Organizația Națiunilor Unite) 2032–1984 (Romania), 7 (Diplomatic Archives of the Ministry of Foreign Affairs, Bucharest).

[96] Standpoint of the section Commercial Coordination.

socialist manufacturers to sell fifty tanks to Iran, a contract that the government proudly won 'after tough negotiations'.[97] The Czechoslovak arms deliveries and military training programmes in Africa were contracted by the Ministry of Foreign Trade through the enterprise Omnipol and the Main Technical Administration. The latter strove for more autonomy in its operations by stressing the profitability of the arms trade and the opportunity to gain hard currency so as to expand military trade partnerships towards the non-socialist countries of the Third World. Arms exports were justified on the grounds that they were more profitable than the export of civilian goods, and customers were willing to pay more in advance and were more flexible with trade terms.[98]

It is important to note, however, that the profits from arms trade accrued directly to the companies involved and not to the state itself, so that by the 1980s the former enjoyed a surprising degree of autonomy. Most of the Hungarian arms trading was organized through publicly registered state-run trade companies, particularly by the Technika Foreign Trade Company and Ferunion Foreign Trade Company. Besides weaponry proper, the greater part of the Hungarian deliveries consisted of military communication devices and particularly electronic equipment. Hungary successfully entered the market of military communications since Soviet producers were reluctant to disseminate modern military electronics to the Third World. In the 1980s the company Videoton's audio-visual electronics proved so profitable that it was able to finance a local soccer team, which even competed against Real Madrid in the 1985 UEFA Cup finals.[99] The companies were run by a new generation of professionals trained in foreign trade colleges who often pursued a career inside the foreign trade branches of their respective states. In marked contrast to the country's military leaders in the 1950s and 1960s, these new men had scant connection with the violence of the anti-fascist struggle. For example, Alexander Schalck-Golodkowski, the powerful leader of the East German foreign trade centre, Kommerzielle Koordinierung (KoKo), began his political career as an FDJ member in 1951 and underwent professional training in foreign trade. Schalck-Golodkowski thus directed his organization more as a businessman than a political commissar.[100] His 1970 PhD thesis explored the possibilities of 'avoiding economic loss and acquiring extra hard currency for the GDR economy through its Commercial Coordination organ.'[101] The Czechoslovak

[97] Uhlig to Schalck, 14 March 1988. DDR u. SBZ. DL 226 Kommerzielle Koordinierung, 4–1980–1989. Folder 467 (Bundesarchiv, Berlin).

[98] Václav Valeš, 'The Principles of Realization of the Special Material Trade', Ministry of Foreign Trade, Prague, 18 June 1968. VÚA-VHA, MNO 1970, box 254.

[99] Pál Germuska, 'L'Industrie de la Défense Hongroise: De la soviétisation à l'occidentalisation', Vingtième Siècle. Revue d'histoire, 109 (Jan–Mar 2011), 96–9.

[100] Matthias Judt, 'Ein kommunistischer Kapitalist: Zum Tode von Alexander Schalck-Golodkowski', Deutschland Archiv, 2 July 2015.

[101] Alexander Schalck-Golodkowski, Zur Vermeidung ökonomischer Verluste und zur Erwirtschaftung zusätzlicher Devisen im Bereich Kommerzielle Koordinierung des Ministeriums für

František Langer, the director of the Omnipol company and one of the most influential figures in shaping Czechoslovakia's arms trade until the late 1980s, also belonged to this generation. Langer was born in 1930 and remained a high-level professional of the Czechoslovak Ministry of Foreign Trade throughout his career.

Debates whether arms transfer was a matter of anti-imperialist solidarity or a revenue generator for socialist industry intensified from the late 1960s onwards. As socialist governments turned toward their foreign trade experts and granted more independence to these companies and agencies, Defence Ministry personnel grew increasingly frustrated by what they saw as a betrayal of the principles of the anti-imperialist struggle. A 1966 Czechoslovak report on 'technical assistance' (i.e. arms deliveries) to post-colonial states and partisan movements sharply criticized the fact that delicate military relationships were being managed by the Ministry of Foreign Trade. According to the report, partners in the Third World were equally disappointed by the prospect that business profit would trump political objectives. The Ministry of National Defence demanded more cautious political consideration of the 'progressiveness' of 'local forces', concluding that 'trade and assistance are not the same.'[102] Yet commercial concerns persisted. A 1966 report from the Czechoslovak-run Cairo-based Military Training College recorded the discontent among the Egyptian military leadership with the interference of 'traders' (Foreign Trade Ministry personnel) in the negotiations between 'soldiers'. The commander of the MTC, General Selim, explained that we are all 'soldiers, open and friendly people' and should not be constricted by issues of trade and finance. He even somewhat awkwardly suggested that this style of negotiations resembled the attitude of capitalist countries and their overriding obsession with profit.[103]

Terrorism, Violence and Civilization

These debates about the relationship between arms commerce and socialist solidarity also took place alongside growing fears of international terrorism. From the early 1970s onward leaders of socialist states in Eastern Europe discovered newer forms of violence to distance themselves from. Besides Maoist radicalism or Che's excesses, terrorist groups and their activities became a mounting concern for socialist states. Since these new forms of cross-border violence seemed to have their roots in the Middle East and

Außenwirtschaft der Deutschen Demokratischen Republik, PhD dissertation, Potsdam College of Law (Potsdam, May 1970).
[102] 'Report about technical help to the developing countries', VÚA-VHA, MNO 1966, box 245.
[103] 'Report of the Head of the Experts', 29 June 1966. VÚA-VHA, MNO 1966, box 243.

were often linked to Islamist ideologies, they prompted a reconsideration of the role of political Islam in Eastern Europe. What had previously seemed a 'progressive force of anti-imperialism' was now conceptualized as dangerously destructive. By the 1980s, fears of Islamic terrorism were linked to other irregular armed movements in Africa or Latin America and in turn generated a profound redrawing of the borders between acceptable and intolerable forms of violence. National liberation movements were now accused of indulging in 'oriental' forms of violence that were allegedly different from non-violent 'European' governance and, thus, marking 'civilizational' differences. Somewhat unexpectedly, the emphasis on non-violent governance inadvertently undermined trust in socialist party-states. The Soviet invasion of Afghanistan in the late 1980s provided the emerging opposition groups in Eastern Europe with ammunition to portray Soviet international policies as crass imperialism. Likewise, in the last phase of socialist dictatorships, the military intervention in Beijing's Tiananmen Square provided the counter-image to non-violent governance that undergirded peaceful reforms in Poland or Hungary and distanced populations from the East German and Czechoslovak party-states that withheld support for popular condemnations of the intolerable use of violence against civilians.

From September 1970, the security services of the Eastern European socialist states began to coordinate operations against international terrorism; the Soviet KGB circulated security information and arranged regular meetings of the Eastern Bloc security organs.[104] Such coordination accelerated when terrorism intensified later in that decade. On 8 January 1977 a terrorist group detonated three bombs in Moscow in a crowded metro train near the KGB and the Communist Party headquarters, killing seven people. Even though the perpetrators were never identified, members of an Armenian nationalist separatist group were arrested and executed.[105] The terrorist attack drove home the point that socialist Eastern Europe might now be a target of extra-European radical nationalist groups. The governments and security services of the smaller Eastern European states also felt vulnerable. On 12 July 1982, First Secretary of the Hungarian Socialist Workers Party János Kádár received a letter from the Organization of the Arab Vanguard. In it the previously little-known group threatened the Hungarian government with terrorist actions against Hungarian embassies, transport lorries and civic aircraft in retaliation against what they saw

---

[104] Jordan Baev, 'Infiltration of non-European terrorist groups in Europe and antiterrorist responses in Western and Eastern Europe (1969–1991)', in Siddik Ekici (ed.), *Counter Terrorism in Diverse Communities* (Amsterdam, Washington, DC: IOS Press, 2011), 58–74.

[105] Christopher Andrew and Oleg Gordievsky, *KGB: The Inside Story of Its Foreign Operations from Lenin to Gorbachev* (London, Sydney, Auckland, Toronto: Hodder and Stoughton, 1990), 456.

as unjustified and unlawful recent actions by the Hungarian police against citizens from Arab countries.[106]

The threat of international terrorism gave rise to new Eastern European understandings of illegitimate violence, and this in relation to the Islamic World. Although forms of 'good terrorism' linked to anti-imperialism continued to garner support, critical voices began to object that this was undermining détente and East–West cooperation. On the one hand, covert solidarity with Third World militants remained an element of Cold War rivalry. The Soviet government cooperated with Romanian intelligence services in a secret operation to produce fake Western European visas for Arab citizens in Libya;[107] Carlos the Jackal and Abu Daoud, two infamous terrorists, resided in Prague in the 1980s, and Carlos also built his temporary headquarters in Hungary. On the other, Eastern Europeans feared the growing impact of international terrorism. In September 1982 the Hungarian Ministry of the Interior established specific anti-terrorist protocols for all armed forces and created a new covert 'Fortress' committee to coordinate anti-terrorist measures in the country.[108] The Hungarian Foreign Ministry informed the Czechoslovak Embassy in Budapest about the danger of terrorism, and the Czechoslovak diplomatic corps, in its turn, promised to share relevant information.[109] From the early 1980s, Hungary, Czechoslovakia and the GDR began to coordinate their activities so as to contain high-profile terrorist groups. In this period, the threat of international terrorism in part pivoted on an imagined Arab identity. Hungarian diplomats suggested that their Czechoslovak counterparts should take extra precautions when dealing with 'Arab clients' in consulates, and asked the Czechoslovaks to pass on news related to 'the activities of the Arabs'. The unruly behaviour of Carlos and Abu Daoud did little to dispel disparaging stereotypes.[110] Security service reports drew a sharp dividing line between the apparently untamed violence of extra-Europeans and the orderly, civilized life in Eastern Europe. In 1985 a Czechoslovak secret police officer explained to Kamal al-Issawe, Carlos's arms supplier, that 'our society considers terror an utterly foreign concept.'[111]

---

[106] Arab Élcsapat Szervezet, 'Utolsó figyelmeztetés. Magyarország tisztelt elnökének', 12 July 1982. Central Organs of the HSWP, Foreign Affairs Department. MNL OL M-KS 288. f. 32/b. cs. 1982/121. ő. e.

[107] Gábor Vásárhelyi, Merényletek Moszkva árnyékában. 2 vols (Budapest: Hamvas, 2004).

[108] No. 28/1982 Command of the Minister of Interior on the Tasks of Preventing, Detecting and Averting Terrorist Threats, 6 September 1982. Records of the Ministry of Interior. MNL OL XIX-B-1-az-10–22/28/1982.

[109] János Kaszner, Hungarian Foreign Ministry, Department of Security, 'Note', 1 November 1982. Records of the Foreign Ministry. MNL OL XIX-J-1-j-005070/25/1982.

[110] Qouted in Daniela Richterova, 'The Anxious Host: Czechoslovakia and Carlos the Jackal 1978–1986', The International History Review, 40/1 (2017), 4.

[111] Ibid., 16.

Such debates over terrorism were linked with changing Eastern European attitudes toward the political role of Islam. In the 1950s and 1960s Eastern European
political cultures had widely recognized nationalism as an important aspect of the
anti-colonial struggle. Arab or Third World nationalisms were understood as a
crucial force that led to a legitimate and progressive use of violence inspiring
national liberation movements in their struggle against imperialism. In the late
1970s, socialist security services concluded that the terrorist threat had emerged
from the Middle East and was firmly linked with the rise of radical Islamic movements. Nationalism represented the most dangerous aspect of these movements,
and the security services pointed to political-religious factors as the main reason
why these groups were turning towards terrorist violence.[112]

The 1979 Iranian Revolution would play an important role in this distancing.
In the wake of the fall of the Shah, Eastern European elites, particularly the
Soviets and East Germans, publicly supported the Islamist movement of the
Ayatollah Khomeini. By the early 1980s, the lack of economic reform in Iran and
the intensified persecution of leftist movements soured their views.[113] Across
Eastern Europe, Khomeini's radical Islamism was seen as embodying violent
fundamentalism. In a public political portrait written for the *Literaturnaya Gazeta*
in 1988, Igor Beliaev, a leading expert in Soviet Middle East studies, pointed to
evidence of the Iranian regime's use of inappropriate violence. He cited the
encroachment upon the Hajj by armed pro-Khomeini activists and the taking
hostage of British journalist Terry Waite in Lebanon, and drew links between the
Iranian state and illegitimate terrorism.[114] Communist authorities sometimes saw
in Arab university students potentially threatening bearers of this ideology within
their own societies: Moscow feared the influence of the Muslim Brotherhood on
Egyptian students,[115] whilst the Securitate sensed a 'predisposition to terrorism'
amongst Arab students in Romania, and turned fellow students into informers in
order to gauge the influence of Al Fatah, The Muslim Brotherhood, and the
Palestinian Liberation Front.[116]

Such views reflected a newly perceived civilizational divide in Eastern Europe
between the traditionalist, pre-modern and religious Islam and modern, enlightened Europe and North America.[117] The growing concern with the violent nature

---

[112] Baev, 'Infiltration'.

[113] Jeremy Friedman, 'The Enemy of My Enemy: The Soviet Union, East Germany, and the Iranian
Tudeh Party's Support for Ayatollah Khomeini', *Journal of Cold War Studies*, 20 (Spring 2018), 3–25.
Alvin Z. Rubinstein, 'The Soviet Union and Iran under Khomeini', *International Affairs*, 57 (Autumn
1981), 599–601.

[114] Igor Beliaev, *Literaturnaya Gazeta*, 10 January 1988.

[115] Constantin Katsakioris, 'Soviet Lessons for Arab Modernization: Soviet Educational Aid to Arab
Countries after 1956', *Journal of Modern European History*, 8/1 (2010), 102–3.

[116] Andra Cioltan-Drăghiciu, ' Between "totalitarianism" and "terrorism"'. An introductory study
about the "Arab" students in the Romanian Socialist Republic', *Caietele CNSAS*, 11-12/1-2 (2013), 328.

[117] 'A testi fenyítések újbóli bevezetése az iszlám országokban', *Módszertani Füzetek* (March 1986), 62.

of Islam generated fears of a large scale 'clash of civilizations'. In 1980 Romanian Secretary General Nicolae Ceausescu warned of 'the intensification of activities by Islamic circles from anti-communist positions'. In his view, the growing politicization of conservative traditionalist Islam represented a serious security threat to Eastern Europe. 'There is the danger that if things continue as they are, Islamic countries, which are quite numerous, will intensify sending forces either directly or in the guise of volunteers. These are a billion and they are fanatic. A long term war may begin.'[118]

Although the Romanian Secretary General's fears may have been exaggerated, they did reflect a growing antipathy toward the illegitimate violence associated with the non-European world. For those Eastern European countries keen to build stronger links with the West, the aversion toward what had once been welcomed as anti-colonial nationalism marked a shift in sensibility toward the violence of Third World struggles.

The threat of international terrorism distanced Eastern Europe from the Middle East. In security analyses that dealt with the social, political and cultural origins of covert paramilitary violence, the Middle East was depicted as a hotbed of terrorism—and Eastern Europe was positioned as a partner of the West in a common struggle to contain terrorism outside of Europe. 'It is known that the different varieties of international terrorism emerge in certain developed capitalist countries, West Germany, Italy, etc., which suffer from domestic and economic hardships, as well as in countries of the developing worlds, which are burdened by social antagonisms', explained Major-General Ferenc Tóth to the 13th International Symposium in Criminalistics in 1981. Tóth characterized West Germany, Italy, Spain and Ireland as societies especially vulnerable to terror actions of separatist and radical groups. Nonetheless, as he stressed, 'The most controversial region is the Middle East where in the last three decades national liberation struggle has been pursued on the part of the Arabs.' In this violence-ridden and terror-threatened world, socialist Eastern Europe appeared as an island of peace and security: 'terrorism is unable to develop in the framework of the socialist social system since its breeding ground, the antagonistic social tensions, do not exist here.'[119] During the 1980s, socialist secret services increasingly participated in international anti-terrorist cooperation around the world, including engagement with non-socialist partners. In the mid-1980s, American diplomats regularly negotiated with Eastern European governments about how to tackle international terrorism. Such overtures were partly the result of American fears of being a principal target country, but they were also motivated by Eastern

---

[118] 'Stenograma şedinţei Comitetutului Politic Executiv al CC al PCR', 12 January 1980, ANIC (Arhivele Naţionale Istorice Centrale), CC (Comitetul Central) al PCR (Partidului Comunist Român), 2/1980 (Romania), 5. Translation by Bogdan C. Iacob.

[119] Ferenc Tóth Major-General, 'Paper delivered at the 13th International Symposium in Criminalistics', March 1981. MNL OL XIX-B-14.

European desires to establish themselves as reliable and non-aggressive partners of the West. US diplomats were particularly exercised by Hungary's alleged role in selling chemical weapons to Libya and Iraq, indirectly contributing to the increasing threat of possible terrorist groups.[120] In numerous bilateral meetings in the 1980s, Hungarian officials routinely reiterated their firm rejection of any and every form of terrorism and their readiness to take part in international cooperation.[121]

By the 1980s imperialism was no longer the common enemy that bound the Second and the Third Worlds together. Now it was the common threat of radical violence that bound the 'civilized world' together. The rejection of armed violence to achieve rightful self-determination shattered the once-shared anti-imperialist bond with some liberation movements. Gorbachev himself in his 'New Political Thinking' advocated non-violent solutions to political conflicts and an end to Cold War rearmament. He often emphasized the need for compromise, and advocated the deradicalization of the left in Latin America as military regimes collapsed: in December 1986 *Pravda* warned against violent revolution in Latin America on the grounds that it could turn from 'midwife to the gravedigger of history…The nuclear age demands of revolutionary forces the most serious consideration of decisions over armed struggle and the definitive rejection of… leftist extremism.'[122] Gorbachev supported the Central American Peace Accords (1987), when the presidents of Costa Rica, El Salvador, Honduras, Guatemala and Nicaragua agreed to end regional civil wars and pursue democratization and free elections.[123]

And in the 1980s, as both dissidents and reform Communists in less hardline states began to entertain the possibility and promote negotiated peaceful transitions out of Communism, so they further distanced themselves from violent revolution, and looked for partners who shared these approaches to transformation elsewhere. Reformist elites in Hungary and Poland—who were already encouraging trade with apartheid South Africa—began to criticize the African National Congress (ANC) as irresponsible radicals. In Hungary, Gábor Búr's 1988 biography of Mandela cast the ANC as a dangerous band of violent fundamentalists detached from Mandela, who remained in prison. Mandela himself was presented as a moderate and politically responsible figure, the 'voice of wisdom', who could lead peaceful change. Búr also suggested that economic conditions were not too terrible for non-whites, who were represented as having nice flats, cars

---

[120] Hungarian Embassy in Washington, Telegraph, 31 May 1981, t.-003070/1985, Records of the Foreign Ministry. MNL OL XIX-J-1-j-TÜK-USA-4-40.

[121] Dr János Görög, International Legal Department, Ministry of Foreign Affairs, 'Report', 22 January 1987, t.-00573/1987, Records of the Foreign Ministry. MNL OL XIX-J-1-j-TÜK-USA-4-312.

[122] Rodolfo Cruz, 'New Directions in Soviet Policy towards Latin America', *Journal of Latin American Studies*, 21/1 (1989), 11.

[123] Roger Hamburg, 'Soviet Foreign Policy toward Different Audiences and with Conflicting Premises: The Case of Nicaragua', *Conflict Quarterly*, 9/1 (Winter 1989), 10–11.

and telephones. In this account, ANC violence was rendered entirely inappropriate. Indeed, Búr concluded that the prospect of democratization was being undermined by an excessively aggressive ANC and an opposition movement which could turn bloody. Only Nelson Mandela was able to ensure reasonable and peaceful transition by serving as the personal guarantor of a truce between the old and the new elite.[124] His seventieth birthday concert 'Freedomfest' at Wembley on 11 June 1988 was widely screened across the region in support of his release from prison.[125] Such changes of attitude paralleled similar transformations in the West. In Western Europe and North America the 1970s rediscovery of a language of human rights focusing on the integrity of the individual took aim at the claims of anti-colonial national liberation movements, which stressed the collective rights of national self-determination. In the western language of human rights, these national liberation fighters were now tarred as terrorists threatening the safety of individual citizens.[126]

This was not true everywhere. In the Soviet Union, Mandela was perceived by the late 1980s an ambivalent figure. His embrace of moderate politics was seen as the symbol of the end of armed struggle and hence of a Communist alternative, and his release was almost entirely ignored in the Soviet press. The GDR, whose very existence was based on the idea that it was a viable alternative to West Germany, continued to give unconditional support to the liberation movements in Southern Africa, the ANC and the South West Africa People's Organisation (SWAPO). The material assistance that these movements received during the 1980s was consistently higher than in the previous decade.[127] In the East German press, the apartheid regime was represented as using brutal violence against its population that it might itself be classified as a 'terrorist'. The use of violence as a form of legitimate struggle against the South African government could thus be promoted.

The Soviet recourse to violence, nonetheless, further distanced socialist citizens from their own states, particularly as it was perceived to run counter to those peaceful approaches advocated in public. The 1979 Soviet invasion of Afghanistan, justified at the time in terms of international socialist solidarity, was read as proof a decade later of the imperial character of Soviet policy in Eastern Europe. The Polish underground movements interpreted Afghanistan as a victim of Soviet

---

[124] Gábor Búr, *Nelson Mandela* (Budapest: Kossuth, 1988).

[125] Paul Betts, James Mark, Idesbald Goddeeris and Kim Christiaens, 'Race, Socialism and Solidarity: Anti-Apartheid in Eastern Europe', in Robert Skinner and Anna Konieczna (eds.), *Global History of Anti-apartheid: Forward to Freedom in South Africa* (New York: Palgrave, 2019), 175–6.

[126] Joseph R. Slaughter, 'Hijacking Human Rights: Neoliberalism, the New Historiography, and the End of the Third World', *Human Rights Quarterly*, 40 (November 2018), 735–75.

[127] A J Temu and Joel das Neves Tembe, *Southern African liberation struggles: contemporaneous documents, 1960–1994* (Dar es Salaam: Mkuki na Nyota, 2014), 526–7; 'SWAPO setzt bewaffneten Befreiungskampf fort', *Neues Deutschland*, 1 September 1986, 7. 'Die SWAPO kämpft an drei Fronten', *Neues Deutschland*, 27 August 1987, 6.

imperialism akin to Poland. Leaflets called for solidarity events, and the oppositional trade union *Solidarność* (Solidarity)—which created its own postal service—used stamps adorned with the images of mujahedeen fighters in Afghanistan. The independent press in Poland compared the war in Afghanistan to Polish suffering during the Second World War.[128] American opinion polls conducted between 1982 and 1984 in Western Europe, which included Eastern Europeans residing in the West at the time, registered growing anti-Soviet sentiment. These people were the professional backbone of Eastern European cooperation with the West—members of the diplomatic corps, economic and technical experts and visiting scholars at western universities. For them, hardening Soviet policies signalled the demise of détente. In the opinion research, they unequivocally identified Soviet rearmament and expansionism as a threat to international peace and security.[129] The war in Afghanistan, taken as evidence of unchanging Soviet imperialism, unwittingly helped Eastern Europeans reinforce their cultural ties with the West.

The Chinese use of brutal violence in Beijing's Tiananmen Square in June 1989 reinforced such an understanding. In Poland, Hungary and Yugoslavia, where processes of political pluralization were already under way by June 1989, the use of militarized violence against peaceful protesters was strongly condemned as unacceptable forms of rule that these reform states could and should reject.[130] It was only the GDR elite, alongside Czechoslovakia, who supported the Tiananmen crackdown; yet East German citizens, many of whom still carried their party cards, dismissed the regime's official support for the Chinese government as blatant hypocrisy. Letters sent to media, public debates and grassroots solidarity movements openly rejected the use of state violence, to the point of describing it as uncivilized and contrasting it with images of non-violent statecraft allegedly typical of European governance. These commentaries often explicitly termed the Tiananmen Square crackdown as the manifestation of 'barbarism'.[131] Such perceived hypocrisy caused East German citizens to feel increasing distrust towards their own government, 'today Beijing, tomorrow Berlin and Leipzig', claimed a telegram sent to Honecker following the Tiananmen demonstrations. Socialist

[128] RFE-RL Press Review 2, 26 February 1987. Polish Independent Press Review, 21–6. HU 300-55-10 Box 1 (OSA).
[129] Who Bears Responsibility for World Tensions? (East European, West European and US Results Compared). RFE-RL East European Area and Audience Opinion Research 694. 11–20. HU 300-6-2 Box 6 (OSA).
[130] Peter Vámos, 'The Tiananmen Square "Incident" in China and the East Central European Revolutions', in Wolfgang Mueller, Michael Gehler and Arnold Suppan (eds.), *The Revolutions of 1989. A Handbook* (Vienna: Verlag der Österreichischen Akademie der Wissenschaften, 2014), 107.
[131] Quinn Slobodian, 'China is Not Far! Alternative Internationalism and the Tiananmen Square Massacre in East Germany's 1989', in James Mark, Artemy M. Kalinovsky and Steffi Marung (eds.), *Alternative Globalizations Eastern Europe and the Postcolonial World* (Bloomington, IN.: Indiana University Press), 318.

Eastern Europe thus reconnected with the liberal West as enemies of 'oriental' modes of violence.

Conclusions

In May 2017, Russian Ambassador to Vietnam Konstantin Vasilievich Vnukov took part in a ceremony staged in Hanoi, Vietnam commemorating the seventy-second anniversary of the Soviet victory in the Great Patriotic War. Vnukov high-lighted the links that tied Russia and Vietnam together: the participation of eleven Vietnamese volunteers in 1941 who fought to defend Moscow and the subsequent Soviet backing of Vietnam in its war against the US.[132]

For many, the era of socialist war- and peacemaking had ended, and the military relationships between Eastern Europe and the global South had also gone. But as the Vietnamese commemoration of the Soviet-Russian Great Patriotic War suggested memories of shared military histories and a sense of comradeship-in-arms persisted. The legacy of an anti-imperialist culture based on common hostility towards the West could sometimes inform the politics of international engagement both in post-Communist Eastern Europe and in the post-colonial global South.

In practice, the socialist way of war was to wage national liberation struggles that challenged the imperialist hegemony of the West. The ongoing fears of west-ern encroachment and the assault on national sovereignty bound the Second and the Third World together during the Cold War, and similar concerns continued to shape their later rapprochement. A resurgent Russian nationalism based on a nostalgia for empire and superpower status, and increasingly embracing Moscow's role as a global centre of alternative illiberal modernity, was ready to capitalize on this apprehension. Russian interventions in regional conflicts were often based on old patterns and alliances inherited from Soviet Era military engagements with the Third World. Just as the USSR once saw Vietnam, so too Russia considered its participation in the Syrian War useful for boosting its status as a global power.[133] And support for intervention, based on older Cold War alliances, ran the other way too: Cuba, Venezuela and Nicaragua, the latter once again ruled by the socialist Daniel Ortega, supported—at least rhetorically—Russia's neo-imperialism in the South Caucasus and Ukraine in the 2010s.

After all, the Soviet Union was the world's largest exporter of weapons to the extra-European world in the last decades of the Cold War. Some of the East European companies that had benefited the most from this international arms

---

[132] 'Victory of Great Patriotic War marked in Hanoi', *People's Army Newspaper*, 4 May 2017 https://en.qdnd.vn/tim-kiem/q/victory-day (last accessed 13 September 2018).

[133] Sergey Radchenko, 'Why Were the Russians in Vietnam?', *The New York Times*, 27 March 2018. https://www.nytimes.com/2018/03/27/opinion/russians-vietnam-war.html (last accessed 8 September 2021).

trade continued to play important roles long after. The Hungarian firm Videoton, which had sold military electronics to the global South, is today among the forty biggest producers of micro-electronics in the world.[134] The Czech company Omnipol, which trades in defence electronics and military technology, sells products to sixty countries and earned a net income of 56 million euros in 2018.[135]

These international relationships had a tangible effect decades later. According to a 2017 report, the overwhelming majority of the weapons used by the so-called Islamic State in Iraq and Syria were produced in the 1980s (40%), with an additional 30% produced in the period 1960–79. One third of these weapons originated from former Warsaw Pact countries outside the USSR, with Romania and Hungary in the top four in the list of suppliers. The major competitor for Eastern Europe was not the West, but rather Communist China, which produced more than half of the weapons available to ISIS.[136] A large proportion of Chinese arms were originally intended for the Mujahedeen in Afghanistan as a Chinese clandestine operation against the USSR. After the Red Army withdrew, the weapons stayed and found their way into the hands of al-Qaeda and then ISIS.[137]

---

[134] The MMI Top 50 for 2015. Manufacturing Market Insider https://web.archive.org/web/20060317151305/http://www.mfgmkt.com/mmi-top-50.html# (last accessed 7 February 2019).

[135] https://www.ceginformacio.hu/cr9210091049_EN (last accessed 7 February 2018).

[136] *Weapons of the Islamic State: A Three-Year Investigation in Iraq and Syria* (Conflict Armament Research: London, 2017), 13–15.

[137] Van Vuuren, *Apartheid Guns and Money*, 402.

4

Culture

Paul Betts and Radina Vučetić

From the early 1950s onward, the Soviet Union and Eastern Europe sought to take advantage of a fast-changing political world by forging cultural relations with non-aligned, decolonizing and newly independent countries in Africa and Asia. By the late 1960s the Union of Soviet Friendship Societies had established contacts with no less than thirty-two African countries, fourteen Latin American countries, and seventeen countries in South East Asia and the Middle East to 'help fortify the spirit of solidarity between peoples of these countries'. According to one 1967 brochure, the Union had held over 16,000 exhibitions, meetings and evening events at its flagship house in Moscow since 1956, with reportedly over 2 million attendees.[1] In the late 1950s the USSR mounted numerous art shows featuring the work of Eastern European artists as well as those from socialist countries such as China, North Korea, Vietnam and Mongolia.[2] Such events were becoming ever more common, serving as they did as the vehicles of Communist cultural diplomacy,[3] a trend worryingly noted by western observers at the time.[4]

Such cultural diplomacy was nothing new to the Communist world. Linking foreign policy and culture formally began with the creation of the USSR's All-Union Society for Cultural Relations with Foreign Countries (VOKS) in 1925.[5] VOKS was set up as an umbrella organization to convey a positive image of the Great Experiment to the West, and brought over foreigners (especially Americans)

We would like to thank Bogdan C. Iacob, Alena Alamgir and James Mark for key research references, and to whole the 'Socialism Goes Global' Team for their constructive feedback on earlier drafts of this chapter. Thanks too to Robert Moeller and Saul Dubow for their constructive criticism on an earlier draft.

[1] B. Smirnov, *To Know Each Other* (Moscow: Novosti Press Agency Publishing House, 1967), 1–8, 36.

[2] *Katalog kvystavke proizvedenii izobrazitel'nogo iskusstva sotsialisticheskikh stran* (Moscow: Sovetskiĭ khudozhnik, 1959).

[3] I. Lavrukhin, *Vo imia mira I progressa [O kul'turnykh svĩazakh SSR s zarubezhnymi stranemi]* (1955) and S.K. Romanovskii's *Mezdunarodnye kul'turnye i nauchye svĩazi SSR* (1966).

[4] Frederick C. Barghoorn, *The Soviet Cultural Offensive: The Role of Cultural Diplomacy in Soviet Foreign Policy* (Princeton: Princeton University Press, 1960) and Yale Richmond, *Cultural Exchange and the Cold War: Raising the Iron Curtain* (University Park: Pennsylvania State Press, 2003).

[5] Jean-Francois Fayet, 'VOKS: The Third Dimension of Soviet Foreign Policy', in Jessica CE Gienow-Hecht and Mark C. Donfried (eds.), *Searching for a Cultural Diplomacy* (Oxford: Berghahn, 2010), 33–49.

Paul Betts and Radina Vučetić, *Culture* In *Socialism Goes Global: The Soviet Union and Eastern Europe in the Age of Decolonization*. Edited by James Mark and Paul Betts, Oxford University Press. © Oxford University Press 2022. DOI: 10.1093/oso/9780192848857.003.0005

to show off the country and its achievements.[6] Yet the end of the Second World War to the death of Stalin was a period of relative isolation for the Soviet Union, as the regime devoted its energies to consolidating Red Army gains in Eastern Europe. The aftermath of the Second World War gave rise to a new 'myth of encirclement' much like that following the Russian Revolution and Civil War, after which the USSR had needed to recover and protect itself after the devastation of war.[7] With the death of Stalin the Soviet Union gradually changed course and looked to expand its influence abroad, often tentatively and through culture. Under Khrushchev, cultural diplomacy was rehabilitated, first as part of the building up of peacetime cultural competition with the West, and then extended toward the wider world in the wake of decolonization.[8] But whereas VOKS had been expressly geared toward showcasing Soviet culture to the West, the Khrushchev era witnessed Eastern Europe's drive southward to the developing world. What further distinguished the post-1945 period from its interwar predecessor was that cultural exchange was bundled together with military, economic and public health assistance as part of a broader package of socialist modernity offered to prospective partners in the Third World. This multi-pronged propaganda campaign was a kind of socialist alternative to the aggressively promoted 'American way of life', complete with housing exhibitions, trade fairs, classical concerts and touring exhibitions. Exporting modern socialist culture from Eastern Europe to Africa, Asia and Latin America helped to give credence to the wider claim that the future belonged to socialism, with the Soviet Union positioned as the polestar of scientific and cultural progress.[9] The sphere of culture played a special performative role in shaping the encounter between distant strangers, one that trumpeted the interwar ideology of socialist humanism to the world in the name of equality, anti-imperialism and even anti-eurocentrism.

At times Eastern European enthusiasm toward creating cultural exchanges became burdensome for receiver countries, largely because their Third World partners lacked the resources to take part regularly. One Ghanaian internal government report warned that 'exchanging performing troupes with socialist countries' may be desirable, but our 'type of economy does not allow' us to 'reciprocate the facilities offered by those countries'.[10] Even so, the frenzy of cultural activity initiated by Eastern Europe generated vital diplomatic capital, and was noted in the West as a dangerous development. A 1966 secret CIA report documented

[6] Michael David-Fox, *Showcasing the Great Experiment: Cultural Diplomacy and Western Visitors to the Soviet Union, 1921–1941* (Oxford: Oxford University Press, 2012).

[7] Elena Zubkova, *Russia after the War: Hopes, Illusions and Disappointments, 1945–1957* (Armonk: Sharpe, 1998), esp. 84–90.

[8] Victor Rosenberg, *Soviet-American Relations, 1953–1960: Diplomacy and Cultural Exchange during the Eisenhower Presidency* (Jefferson, NC: McFarland and Co, 2005).

[9] Tobias Rupprecht, *Soviet Internationalism after Stalin: Interaction and Exchange between the USSR and Latin America during the Cold War* (Cambridge: Cambridge University Press, 2015), 2–4.

[10] F. Morisseau-Leroy, National Organiser, Drama & Literature, Protocol Proposals, 27 January 1965, files pages 269–71, RG 3/7/13, Public Records and Archives Administration Department – PRAAD, Accra.

Communist cultural inroads in Africa, Asia and Latin America, in the form of the dissemination of books, press, radio, film festivals, exhibitions, binational friendship societies and economic aid, concluding that Communists were successfully exploiting 'anti-Western prejudices' and presenting themselves 'with an image of benevolence, and to disguise political indoctrination under a cultural cloak'.[11] What the report plainly acknowledged was that these seemingly benign cultural events became new spaces of socialist influence in the post-colonial world in the name of anti-western globalization.

Hot war and hard power of course continued to shape these encounters, as noted in the other chapters in this volume. Equally significant were peace initiatives, soft power and cultural relations forged in the name of mutual respect and reciprocity. Anti-imperialism became the main ideological bridge between the Second and Third Worlds, serving as a Cold War socialist version of 1930s Popular Front activism. These cultural relations took on a variety of forms and ideological manifestations, both at home and abroad. And while these exchanges were designed to overcome geographical distance and long-standing cultural hierarchies between Eastern Europe and Africa, they sometimes led to tensions and misunderstandings. Cultural diplomacy, the mission of modernism and the defence of tradition became the flashpoints of new alliances of socialist fraternity, and these themes will be the main focus of the chapter.

The socialist mission southward attracted international media attention, due to the flurry of high-profile state visits and ceremonies of official cultural diplomacy. To make good on this newly announced Soviet peace policy, Khrushchev travelled to India, Burma, Afghanistan, Egypt and Indonesia, visiting some thirty-five countries in total. Diplomatic relations with leaders from Africa were further formalized through prize-giving cultural ceremonies. In 1961 the Soviet Union awarded the Lenin Prize to Guinean President Sekou Touré, in 1962 to Ghanaian President Kwame Nkrumah and in 1963 to Malian President Modibo Keïta. In the early 1960s, the Soviet Union became a member of over two hundred international organizations, including the UN, UNESCO, the ILO and the Red Cross. Soviet publishing houses churned out some 100 million books per year to send to the outside world. Significant too is that some 20,000 Soviet artists were sent to sixty countries from 1955 to 1958, more than half to non-socialist lands; from 1961 to 1965 these numbers rose to 80,000 Soviet artists with about as many foreign artists travelling to the USSR in this same period.[12] In 1960 Moscow's Oriental Institute's popular monthly journal *Sovremennyi Vostok* (*Contemporary East*) was renamed as *Azia i Afrika segodnia* (*Asia and Africa Today*), and as such

---

[11] https://www.cia.gov/library/readingroom/docs/DOC_0000313542.pdf (last accessed 9 August 2021).

[12] Rupprecht, *Soviet Internationalism*, 5, and Anne E. Gorsuch, *All This is Your World: Soviet Tourism at Home and Abroad after Stalin* (Oxford: Oxford University Press, 2011); see too Chris Osakwe, *The Participation of the Soviet Union in Universal International Organizations: A Political and Legal Analysis of Soviet Strategies and Aspirations inside ILO, UNESCO and WHO* (Leiden: Brill, 1972).

marked the Soviet Union's shift of geographical attention from the East to the South in this period, as it sought to cultivate relations with independent-minded or non-aligned Third World countries following the 1955 Bandung Conference. This popular journal was intended to whet domestic interest in overseas cultures inaccessible to most Soviet citizens, and to undermine young people's abiding fascination with western culture.[13] Moscow hosted key Youth Festivals as meeting places,[14] while Soviet filmmakers were sent to Africa in the early 1960s to document the friendship of the USSR and newly decolonized countries in a spirit of revolutionary romanticism, such as *Hello, Africa!* (1961) and *We Are with You, Africa!* (1963).

Other Eastern European leaders, such as Yugoslavia's Marshal Josip Broz Tito, the GDR's Prime Minister Otto Grotewohl and Romania's Nicolae Ceauşescu also toured Africa in the 1960s and 1970s, and Ethiopia's Emperor Haile Selassie, Guinea's Sekou Touré and Ghana's Kwame Nkrumah were frequent visitors to Eastern European capitals. Eastern European leaders used these visits to communicate not only good relations between their countries and new African nations, but also to help build a sense of shared interest and political solidarity between countries that otherwise had limited historical relation with one another. Tito's state visits to Africa were notable in this regard—the visual trappings of his visit went far beyond handshakes, fraternal embraces and diplomatic speech-making. Lavish press coverage was devoted to these cultural encounters, with particular focus on giving and receiving gifts, inspecting local crops, signing trade agreements, visiting historical sites and museums, watching traditional dancing and taking part in safari hunts, which Tito characteristically undertook with particular gusto.[15] As early as 1954 Yugoslavia commenced cultural cooperation with Egypt, sending a folklore troupe and art exhibition, while a delegation of Egyptian professors visited Yugoslavia that same summer.[16] Such initiatives were replicated across Eastern Europe. From the early 1960s the Czechoslovak government was arranging economics-for-culture exchanges with Ghana in which economic assistance was sent to Ghana in return for print materials and ethnographic objects for use by Czech Africanists.[17] In 1964 some fifteen Czechoslovak musicians played in the Cairo symphony orchestra, whereas that same year the Czechs

---

[13] Masha Kirasirova, 'Orientologies Compared: US and Soviet Imaginaries of the Modern Middle East', in Kalinovsky and Kemper, *Reassessing Orientalism*, 16–46.

[14] Pia Koivunen, 'The 1957 Moscow Youth Festival Propagating a New, Peaceful Image of the Soviet Union', in Melanie Ilic (ed.), *Soviet State and Society under Nikita Khrushchev* (London: Routledge, 2009), 46–65.

[15] Radina Vučetić, 'Tito's Africa: Representation of Power during Tito's African Journeys', in Radina Vučetić and Paul Betts (eds.), *Picturing Solidarity: Tito in Africa* (Belgrade: Museum of Yugoslav History, 2017), 12–45.

[16] DASMIP, PA, 1955, Egipat, F-13, Pov. 15/55, Izveštaj o protekloj godini u Egiptu, Kairo, 10. januar 1955.

[17] Report 19 April 1963, Fond 02/1, sv. 17, ar.j. 18, 14. Bod, Czech National Archive [hereafter CNA].

welcomed an Indian children's troupe, a Cambodian royal ballet ensemble, a Guinean folkloric troupe and a Nigerian jazz band.[18]

In the 1960s, Eastern European socialist culture primarily promoted the international mission of peace and anti-imperialist solidarity, but was also enlisted to advance a kind of 'unity in diversity' doctrine of political kinship across continents. African political leaders, students and economic experts in turn were invited to Eastern Europe to consult, study and exchange ideas with their Eastern European partner countries. The classic model of interaction between the Second and Third World was one in which Eastern European white-collar labour (such as doctors and engineers) was exported, while students (and later blue-collar labour) from the global South were imported. The field of culture offered the possibility of a more equal exchange, one in which older ideas of European cultural superiority would be rejected as an emblem of anti-imperial fellowship. That Eastern European archaeologists, curators, filmmakers and photographers arrived as anti-western internationalists went some way in holding out the promise of building new networks of Eastern European–African understanding.[19]

But for all the language of equality and fellowship, old European attitudes and prejudices still surfaced. A good example is the way that Cairo occupied a privileged place in the firmament of Second–Third World cultural relations. The Egyptian capital was considered the cultural centre of both the Arabic and African worlds, and the US, Britain, West Germany, the Soviet Union, Eastern Europe and China all vied for influence there. In the 1950s and 1960s Eastern European cultural diplomacy often consisted of exporting high culture to the rest of the world. International tours of the Bolshoi Ballet were used to present a highbrow image of Soviet culture, and the star-studded classical ballet troupe routinely performed around the world.[20] The sold-out coast-to-coast tour of the Moiseyev Folk Dance Ensemble and the Bolshoi and Kirov Ballets in 1959 caused a great sensation across America, whilst American George Balanchine took his New York City Ballet to Leningrad in 1962 to popular acclaim.[21] Plenty of international press covered the Bolshoi Ballet's tour of Egypt in 1958 and 1961, as Soviet composers, violinists, pianists and opera singers performed hundreds of concerts as far afield as Argentina, Chile, Mexico, Cuba and Uruguay.[22] Other Eastern

[18]   Report 15 April 1965, Fond 02/1, sv. 107, ar.j. 110, 6. Bod, CNA.

[19]   Martin Slobodník, 'Socialist Anti-Orientalism: Perceptions of China in Czechoslovak Travelogues from the 1950s', and Agnieszka Sadecka, 'A Socialist Orientalism? Polish Travel Writing on India in the 1960s', in Dobrota Pucherová and Róbert Gáfrik (eds.), *Postcolonial Europe? Essays on Post-Communist Literatures and Cultures* (Leiden: Brill, 2015), 299–314 and 315–336, respectively.

[20]   Cadra Peterson McDaniel, *American-Soviet Cultural Diplomacy: The Bolstoi Ballet's American Premiere* (Lanham, MD: Lexington Books, 2015).

[21]   Richmond, *Cultural Exchange*, 124–5. Clare Croft, *Dancers as Diplomats: American Choreography in Cultural Exchange* (New York: Oxford University Press, 2015) and Penny M. von Eschen, *Satchmo Blows Up the World: Jazz Ambassadors Play the Cold War* (Cambridge: Harvard University Press, 2006).

[22]   Rupprecht, *Soviet Internationalism*, 3 and Ilya Prizel, *Latin America through Soviet Eyes: The Evolution of Soviet Perceptions during the Brezhnev Era, 1964–1982* (Cambridge: Cambridge University Press, 1990).

European regimes followed suit in dispatching their state orchestras to Africa, Asia and Latin America. During Tito's visit to Cairo in 1959, lavish attention was paid to Belgrade Opera performances there, both to showcase Yugoslav high culture and to challenge the predominance of their French and Italian counterparts.[23] Czechoslovak and Polish orchestras performed in the capital as well, though by the end of the 1960s the GDR took the lead in developing the socialist opera business in Egypt.[24] Classical music thus became a means for Eastern Europeans to compete with the West and with each other as the true inheritors of European musical heritage.

Cairo may have played host to socialist rivalry between Eastern European states, but attitudes toward sub-Saharan Africa were even more divergent. The Soviets directed barely any cultural attention toward Africa beyond the Maghreb, and never sent their classical musicians and ballerinas there on the grounds that these sub-Saharan audiences would not appreciate them. Such views were in stark contrast to the Eastern Bloc countries and Yugoslavia, which forged links with Ghana, Mali, Senegal, Guinea and Tanzania across a range of cultural fronts. Moreover, they were all keen to make sure that these new relationships were not unidirectional, as African writers and artists were routinely invited to Eastern Europe as cultural ambassadors.[25] In this sense, the Eastern European cultural encounter with Africa challenged the more typical Soviet formula of exporting its high culture to the rest of the world whilst 'folklorizing' other cultures for their exchange visits to the Soviet Union. Eastern European states by contrast were generally keener to broadcast relations of reciprocity to their Third World counterparts, and there were many joint ventures. These included Romanian–Indian theatre exchanges in the late 1950s and 1960s,[26] and a Cairo puppet theatre troupe that toured Eastern European socialist countries in 1964 showcasing stories from Arab folklore. In 1965 the Ghana Institute of Art and Culture sent its drama students to the GDR, theatre technicians to Czechoslovakia, and a dance band to Romania that same summer.[27]

---

[23] AJ, 559-3-5, Opšti poverljivi materijali IV, 1960, Komisiji za kulturne veze sa inostranstvom, pov. br. 450/1, DSIP; Beograd 18. maj 1960.

[24] 'Bericht über den Aufenthalt der Deutschen Staatsoper Berlin in der VAR vom 1. 3. 1969 bis 12. 3. 1969', DR 1/18881, German Federal Archives, Berlin, hereafter BArch.
Bundesarchiv (BA), DR1 (Ministerium für Kultur)/18881, Bericht über den Aufenthalt der Deutschen Staatsoper Berlin in der VAR vom 1. 3. 1969 bis 12. 3. 1969.

[25] Rossen Djagalov, *From Internationalism to Postcolonialism: Literature and Cinema between the Second and Third Worlds* (Montreal: McGill-Queen's University Press, 2020), chapter 3 and Vijay Prashad, *The East Was Read* (London: Leftword Books, 2020).

[26] Viviana Iacob, 'Caragiale in Calcutta: Romanian-Indian Theatre Diplomacy during the Cold War', *Global Theatre History* 2/1 (2017), 37–46.

[27] F. Morisseau-Leroy, National Organiser, Drama & Literature, Protocol Proposals, 27 January 1965, files pages 269–71, RG 3/7/13 and Tour of Rumania by the Ghana Workers Brigade Band No. 2, Press Release by J. Benibengor Blay Esq M.P., Minister of Art and Culture, 7 June 1965, RG 3/7/13, PRAAD, Accra.

While high culture confirmed distance and difference, traditional folk culture was identified as a key contact point between Eastern Europe and the developing world. The revival of folk music, dance, costume as a sanctioned expression of popular culture across the Eastern Bloc and the Soviet Union was a key feature of socialist society after 1945, and was lauded in international socialist festivals from the 1950s onward. That many of the newly decolonized countries in Africa and Asia championed indigenous culture as the bedrock of post-colonial cultural identities provided Eastern Europeans with the chance to build bridges to the Third World around folk culture celebrations. Dance, art and music were also embraced for their ability to overcome language barriers and cultural divisions in visual spectacles of respect and reciprocity. Over the course of the 1960s, dance troupes from Senegal, Mali, Guinea and elsewhere were regularly invited to tour Eastern Europe in the name of fraternity with their counterparts performing as the representatives of Eastern European folk cultures. Likewise, Eastern European folk ensembles were exported to the Third World. As early as 1958 the Romanian government sent a folk art show to New Delhi, Calcutta, Bombay and Hyderabad,[28] and folk music and dance troupe exchanges took place between Romania and Cuba in 1967, as well as between Czechoslovakia and North Africa.[29] In 1961—the year of Tito's grand African tour to drum up support for his first Non-Aligned Movement Conference in Belgrade that September— Yugoslav folklore groups toured Ghana, Guinea, Mali, Togo, Liberia, Ethiopia and Sudan, as well as in Middle East countries.[30] So whereas high socialist culture tended to accentuate the distance between Eastern Europeans and their cultural partners in Africa and Asia, traditional folk culture was embraced as a means of overcoming distance and cultural hierarchies in an international celebration of socialist unity in diversity.

The Modernism Mission

One of the most prominent areas of Second–Third World cultural interaction was modern architecture, especially concerning the redesign of African cities after decolonization. New architecture was seen as key to nation-building, where new governments would address their countries' underdevelopment through state-led industrial planning.[31] Polish architects built in Ghana, with Hungarian designers

---

[28]   MAE (Ministerul Afacerilor Externe)-India, 120-1958 (Romania), 40–52 and 80–89.

[29]   MAE-India, 600–1966, 6–8 and 124–132, and MAE-Cuba, 340–1967, 54–63, 70–78.

[30]   AJ, 559, F-4, Opšti materijali 1961, Izveštaj komisije za kulturne veze sa inostranstvom za 1960. godinu, Beograd, februar 1961.

[31]   East Bloc modernizers often helped each other—GDR exported prefab technology to Poland, Poland sent conservation experts to other socialist countries; Yugo and Bulgarian architects advised on GDR tourist architecture. Łukasz Stanek, 'Socialist Networks and the Internationalization of Building Culture after 1945', *ABE Journal*, 6 (2014), 1–7.

in Nigeria, East Germans in North Korea, Zanzibar and Syria, Romanians in the Sudan and Libya, Yugoslavs in Libya and Egypt, and the Chinese in Guinea.[32] Yugoslav architecture in particular was a laboratory of industrial modernism in the Cold War. Its leadership in the Non-Aligned Movement provided Yugoslav architects and engineers with a new stage on which to promote their designs and ideas across North–South political borders, as Tito's republic emerged as a pace-setter in disseminating modern architecture to newly independent states.[33] Eastern European architects and urban planners drew on the same tradition of European interwar modernism as their western counterparts, to the point that it was often difficult to distinguish modernist buildings built by Eastern Europeans in Africa, Asia and the Middle East from similar western projects in these regions at the time. A number of African leaders preferred Eastern European architects and urban planners for ideological reasons or because their projects were cheaper to construct; socialist builders also tended to hire local construction workers for their urban renewal projects, and were also more committed to the maintenance of the buildings once they were finished.[34] The breakdown of Communist univer-salism proved advantageous to African leaders, enabling them to devise their own versions of modernity as a combination of old and new, international and national, indigenous and imported.[35] Some African leaders were attracted to Polish engineers for their local policies, while others looked to East Germans and Czechoslovaks for technical expertise.[36] Ghana is a good example of these devel-opments, as Nkrumah was keen to draw on Eastern European socialist modern-ism to promote his new state. In 1961 he visited the socialist 'new towns' of Dunaújváros in Hungary and Nowa Huta in Poland as part of an eight-week tour of the USSR, Eastern Europe and China, and a number of leading Ghanaian architects (such as AW Charaway and EGA Don Arthur) were trained in the

---

[32] Tom Avermaete, '"Neues Bauen in Afrika": Displaying East and West German Architecture dur-ing the Cold War'; Ludger Wimmelbücker, 'Architecture and City Planning Projects of the German Democratic Republic in Zanzibar', and Dana Vais, 'Exporting Hard Modernity: Construction Projects from Ceausescu's Romania in the "Third World"', all in *Journal of Architecture*, 17/3 (2012), 387–405, 407–32, and 433–51, respectively, and Cole Roskam, 'Non-Aligned Architecture: China's Designs on and in Ghana and Guinea, 1955–1992', *Architectural History*, 58 (2015), 261–91 as well as Vladimir Kulić, Maroje Mrduljaš and Wolfgang Thaler, *Modernism In-Between: The Mediatory Architectures of Socialist Yugoslavia* (Berlin: Jovis Verlag, 2012).

[33] Matino Stierli, 'The Architecture of Socialist Yugoslavia as a Laboratory of Globalization in the Cold War', in *Toward a Concrete Utopia: Architecture in Yugoslavia 1948–1980* (New York: The Museum of Modern Art, 2018), 11–26, as well as Vladimir Kulić, 'The Scope of Socialist Modernism: Architecture and State Representation in Postwar Yugoslavia', in Vladimir Kulić, Timothy Parker and Monica Penick (eds.), *Sanctioning Modernism: Architecture and the Making of Postwar Identities* (Austin: University of Texas Press, 2014) and Vladimir Kulić, 'An Avant-Garde Architecture for an Avant-Garde Socialism: Yugoslavia at EXPO '58', *Journal of Contemporary History*, 47/1 (2012), 161–84.

[34] Łukasz Stanek and Nikolay Erofeev, 'African Housing in Soviet Gift Economies', unpublished paper, January 2017.

[35] *Toward a Concrete Utopia: Architecture in Yugoslavia 1948–1980* (New York: MoMA, 2018).

[36] Zbigniew Brzezinski, 'The African Challenge', in his edited *Africa and the Communist World* (London: OUP, 1964), 216.

Soviet Union. Accra's International Trade Fair Centre was designed by Polish architects (opened in 1967) and Ghana's government seat, Flagstaff House, was designed by Hungarian architect Károly Polónyi in 1964. It was after his tour of Eastern Europe that Nkrumah steered the country in a more socialist direction of development, most directly reflected in his Soviet-inspired party programme 'For Work and Happiness' (1962) and 'Seven-Year Development Plan' (1964).[37] The blending of western, socialist and African modernism in the architectural city-scape symbolized a new post-colonial identity in Ghana, and elsewhere around Africa. But what at first looks like apolitical neutral functionalist styling carried a domestic political meaning too. The appeal of modernism was not only because this International Style served as a visual vocabulary of arrival and progress, but also because choosing this foreign style enabled African leaders like Nkrumah to sidestep the architecture styles of rival ethnic groups by placing the state under the banner of international modernism.[38]

Modern architecture emerged as a language of fraternity that could bridge the divergent historical experiences of Eastern Europe and Africa. This may seem puzzling at first. Yet it is worth recalling that Central European modernists used architecture as the visual expression of national arrival after the break-up of the Habsburg Empire, when Polish and Czech architects in particular fused inter-national style modernism with vernacular nationalism after the Great War to help create new cultural identities.[39] In the 1960s East European architects argued that their historical situation was not unlike that of Africans after independence. Hungarian architect Károly Polónyi, for example, wrote that central-eastern Europe shared a common 'colonial experience' with Africa, and that as someone from the Carpathian region he too had experienced colonization by external powers.[40] The Polish travel writer Ryszard Kapuściński expressed similar views in his books, in particular *The Shadow of the Sun*, in which he drew a parallel between the experience of African post-colonial countries and his own upbring-ing in 'colonized' eastern Poland.[41] Such views could be found in the Polish popu-lar press too, for example in the Polish youth magazine, *Dookoła Świata*. One 1963 article, following the long romantic tradition of presenting Poland's historical fate as a series of martyrdoms, compared Poles to African nations, described Poland as 'a European nation, that in its history has played the role of a "White Negro",

---

[37] Stephan F. Miescher, '"Nkrumah's Baby": The Akosombo Dam and the Dream of Development in Ghana, 1952–1966', *Water History*, 6 (2014), 362–3.

[38] Łukasz Stanek, *Architecture in Global Socialism: Eastern Europe, West Africa, and the Middle East in the Cold War* (Princeton: Princeton University Press, 2020), 35–96.

[39] Łukasz Stanek, 'Cold War Transfer: Architecture and Planning from Socialist Countries in the "Third World"', *Journal of Architecture*, 17/3 (2012), 299–307.

[40] Pólonyi, *An Architect-Planner on the Peripheries*, 25–46, 184, in Stanek, 'Ghana', 435. See too Ákos Moravanszky, 'Peripheral Modernism: Polónyi and the Lessons of the Village', *Journal of Architecture*, 17/3 (2012), 333–59.

[41] Ryszard Kapuściński, *The Shadow of the Sun* (New York: Knopf, 2001), 40.

rather than that of a colonialist'.[42] Such imagined cultural affinities were not just European inventions. Ghanaian journalists covering the opening of these Eastern Europe-made buildings in the early 1960s drew links between Ghana's colonial past and Prussian, Russian and Ottoman domination of Eastern Europe.[43] Likewise, African media coverage of Tito's high-profile tours of African countries in 1961 and 1970 routinely stressed the parallels between Yugoslavia's anti-imperial and anti-Soviet past with their own stories of African freedom fighting and non-alignment. During Tito's visit to Ethiopia, for example, local journalists highlighted the shared experience of Yugoslavia and Ethiopia as victims of Italian fascist aggression.[44] In these instances, modern architecture not only made visible post-colonial development, it also provided a shared Eastern European–African visual vocabulary of modernization.[45]

Exporting Eastern European modernism to Africa shaped this cultural encounter too, and on this front Yugoslavia took the lead. It dispatched modernist painting to Egypt soon after the 1952 Egyptian Revolution, and thereafter promoted Yugoslav socialist modernism to the developing world as the art of a socialist state independent of the stifling effects of Soviet-style socialist realism.[46] Tito's first visit to Egypt in 1955 was accompanied by an exhibition of contemporary Yugoslav art in Cairo.[47] That year Yugoslavia enjoyed its big breakthrough on the African cultural scene when it took part in Alexandria's Biennale for Mediterranean Countries, scooping the largest number of prizes for its modernist painters.[48] Follow-up exhibitions of Yugoslav contemporary art were dispatched to India, Indonesia and Tunisia in the early 1960s.[49] There were several exhibitions of Egyptian contemporary art in Belgrade during those same years,[50] along with several exhibitions of Egyptian applied art.[51] Similarly, Poland, Czechoslovakia, Hungary, Romania and the GDR showcased their modern art and design work in various countries across Africa at the time. Ethiopia's first modern art academy, the School of Fine Arts in Addis, reportedly stocked large survey books on *Bulgarian*

[42] *Dookoła Świata*, 44/1963, 3–4, 10. We thank Hubert Czyzewski for this reference.

[43] Stanek, 'Architects', 435.

[44] Paul Betts, 'A Red Wind of Change: African Media Coverage of Tito's Tours of Decolonizing Africa', in Vucetić and Betts, *Tito in Africa*, 77.

[45] Wolfgang Thaler, Maroje Mrdulijas and Vladimir Kulić, *Modernism In-Between: The Mediatory Architecture of Socialist Yugoslavia* (Berlin: Jovis Verlag, 2012).

[46] AJ, 559, Kulturna saradnja sa UAR 1959–1971, Izveštaj o izvršenju program akulturne saradnje za 1964/1965. Godinu.

[47] AJ, 837, I-2/5, Plan propagandnih aktivnosti povodom posete Predsednika Republike Egiptu i Etiopiji, 1955.

[48] AJ, 559, Likovne umetnosti, Bijenale u Aleksandriji 1955–1966, Jugoslovenski informacioni centar, br. 181, Cairo, 11 March 1958.

[49] AJ, 559, Kulturne veze sa Azijom i Afrikom 1965, Kulturno-prosvetne veze i odnosi Jugoslavije sa zemljama Azije i Afrike, 17. juli 1965.

[50] Narcisa Knežević-Šijan, 'Egyptian Art: Important Belgrade Exhibitions of Fine and Applied Arts in the Second Half of the 20th Century', in *Egypt Remembered by Serbia* (Belgrade: Faustral, 2013), 83.

[51] AJ, 559, F-6, Opšti materijali 1965, Izveštaj o radu komisije za kulturne veze sa inostranstvom u 1964. godini, Beograd, 1965. godine.

Graphic Art (1956) and *Graphic Art of Romania* (1963), both of which bore the marks of heavy usage in student studios and influenced Ethiopia's revolutionary poster propaganda in the 1970s.[52]

Theatrical modernism was also a point of contact between the Second and Third Worlds. A telling example was the reception of the renowned East German playwright Bertolt Brecht in South Africa. *The Good Woman of Setzuan* was performed in Johannesburg in 1958 and the Performing Arts Council of the Transvaal produced *The Caucasian Chalk Circle* in 1963. With time, however, the plays were re-politicized in connection to anti-apartheid.[53] All-Black troupes (such as the Serpent Players) performed plays in the early 70s, cementing the South African link of Brecht and anti-apartheid. South African playwright Athol Fugard directed a Brecht-inspired play in East Berlin as part of the GDR's international solidarity with South Africa, while Fana Kekana's anti-apartheid 1976 play, *Survival*, drew on Brecht's epic theatre techniques. Thabo Mbeki, the longtime ANC activist and later second post-apartheid President of South Africa from 1999 to 2008, reportedly had a particular attraction to Brecht's allegorical satire of the rise of Hitler, *The Resistible Rise of Arturo Ui*, which he saw performed by the Berlin Ensemble in London in 1970.[54]

Another dimension of this new solidarity was the recasting of socialist internationalism itself, and international organizations such as UNESCO played a mediating role in championing new and anti-imperial ideas of universalism. After all, UNESCO, founded in 1946, was the sole international agency dedicated to upholding an ideal of a singular secular humanity that transcended both Cold War divisions and Eurocentric hierarchies of culture and civilization. Its efforts to organize initiatives in international education, literacy and heritage management around the world reflected its ecumenical vision of a one-world humanity.[55] This could be seen in its Third World development schemes and preservation projects, as well as its high-profile six-volume *History of Mankind* project, which worked to rewrite world history alternatively as a story of peace, exchange and progress, instead of the conventional narrative framework of war and conflict.[56] UNESCO took the international lead in debunking racism as a specious form of science, proclaiming in a highly publicized 1950 report that race was more 'social myth'

---

[52] Kate Cowcher, 'From Pushkin to Perestroika: Art and the Search for an Ethiopian October', in Mark Nash (ed.), *Red Africa: Affective Communities and the Cold War* (London: Black Dog Publishing, 2016), 57.

[53] Loren Kruger, *Post-Imperial Brecht: Politics and Performance, East and South* (Cambridge: Cambridge University Press, 1994), 238.

[54] Ibid., 236, 286–7.

[55] Laura Elizabeth Wong, 'Relocating East and West: UNESCO's Major Project on the Mutual Appreciation of Eastern and Western Cultural Values', *Journal of World History*, 19/3 (2008), 349–74.

[56] Paul Betts, 'Humanity's New Heritage: UNESCO and the Rewriting of World History', *Past & Present*, 228/1 (2015), 249–85.

than 'biological fact',[57] and the organization enjoyed positive coverage in Eastern Europe and the developing world for its progressive outlook. What is more, UNESCO worked to foster this sense of a new humanity through the media, and in particular through photography. Examples included UNESCO's 1947 photo-book *The Book of Needs* and its 1949 follow-up *Children of Europe*, whose univer-salizing tendency found its most popular expression in the 1955 'Family of Man' photography show, conceived by Edward Steichen in collaboration with the Museum of Modern Art in New York. The exhibition aimed to show what Steichen called 'the essential one-ness of mankind',[58] portraying peoples from across the world in a kind of intimate family album of post-fascist humanity.[59]

But despite UNESCO's best efforts to champion a secular ideal of humanity beyond Cold War antagonism and regional ideologies of difference, the term itself would soon become embroiled in Cold War politics. Initially the USSR maintained its older cynicism toward the term humanity, shaped by Marx's suspi-cion of it as a bourgeois concept that in fact reflected class-based special interests dressed up in universalist guise. The Soviet reaction to the 1955 *Family of Man* photography exhibition was instructive here, as Soviet critics took issue with the guiding ideology of an affirmative universalist human family marked by progress and sameness across continents as perniciously obfuscating class conflict, war and international struggle.[60] For the Soviets the preferred term was humanism, and in particular socialist humanism to distinguish it from its bourgeois counterpart. Humanism was intended as a distinctly this-worldly term that denoted the vic-tory of reason and science over religion and obscurantism, and socialist human-ism was rehabilitated as a term of self-definition for the Soviet Union and the Eastern Bloc after 1945. Yet the term humanity did surface internally in the USSR in the 1960s. It re-emerged in the sphere of space exploration and evolutionary biology, to the extent that it was used to describe a more comprehensive anthropological designation of homo sapiens. But it was in the context of the encounter with the developing world in the early 1960s that socialist ideals of humanity replaced humanism as a more geographical term that conjoined the Second and Third World in a shared zone of anti-imperial endeavour and purpose.[61]

---

[57] Elazar Barkan, *The Retreat of Scientific Racism* (Cambridge: CUP, 1992), 341–43, and Michelle Brattain, 'Race, Racism and Antiracism: UNESCO and the Politics of Presenting Science to the Postwar Public', *American Historical Review*, 112/5 (2007), 1386–413.

[58] Museum of Modern Art, *The Family of Man* (New York, 1955), 4.

[59] Tom Allbeson, 'Photographic Diplomacy in the Postwar World: UNESCO and the Conception of Photography as a Universal Language, 1946–1956', *Modern Intellectual History*, 12/2 (2015), 1–33 and Heide Fehrenbach and Davide Rodogno, *Humanitarian Photography: A History* (New York: Cambridge University Press, 2015).

[60] Eric J. Sandeen, *Picturing an Exhibition: The Family of Man and 1950s America* (Albuquerque: Univ. of New Mexico Press, 1995), 125–54.

[61] V. S. Solodovnikov, 'Opening Address at the Conference on the Historical Relations of the Peoples of the Soviet Union and Africa, May 19, 1965', in *Russia and Africa* (Moscow: USSR Academy of Sciences, 1966), 7–15, as well as the other essays gathered in the same volume. See too Paul Betts,

By the mid-1960s Eastern European regimes were organizing their own distinct ideas of the Family of Man, such as the GDR's 1967 *Vom Glück des Menschen*, or *On the Happiness of People*, though the original English translation of the show was significantly called *The Socialist Family of Man*; many of these Eastern European-sponsored cultural shows and cooperative initiatives with the developing world were designed to give visual form to this ideal of international socialist unity.[62]

In all of these various manifestations, the mission of socialist modernism went beyond high-profile episodes of cultural diplomacy. Many of these cooperative projects were an effort to move beyond an unwanted colonial past, to celebrate a new world of freedom, independence and camaraderie in a spirit of equality with progressive and like-minded Europeans.

The Socialist Defence of Tradition

Second–Third World joint ventures were not limited to state visits, modernist art shows and infrastructure investment. There was another dimension of this Eastern Europe–Africa relationship that goes almost completely unremarked in what little relevant historiography exists, and this is the Eastern European attitude toward African heritage. Eastern Europe's celebration of Africa's indigenous past was not a rejection of modernization, however, but rather an extension of it. Eastern Europe's combined interest in Africa's future and its pre-colonial past was understood as a more humane socialist approach to modernization, one that sup-posedly distinguished it from its western rival.

Decolonization greatly stimulated interest in African history and heritage across the USSR and the Eastern Bloc.[63] This however was not so easy or straight-forward. Part of the problem is that Marx and Engels had virtually nothing to say about Africa, and the same went for Lenin.[64] What little attention was paid to Africa in the Stalin Era was chiefly related to the Comintern, mostly in the form of dissatisfaction at the absence of Communist parties in Africa. Until the late 1950s neither the Soviet Union's Foreign Ministry nor the KGB had developed any departments for African affairs; indeed, there were few experts on Africa or Asia anywhere in the Kremlin.[65] While there is a long tradition of German and

'Universalism and its Discontents: Humanity as a 20th Century Concept', in Mirjam Thulin and Fabian Klose (eds.), *Humanity—A History of European Concepts in Practice from the 16th Century to the Present* (Göttingen: Vandenhoeck & Ruprecht, 2016), 51–70.

[62] Sarah Goodrum, 'A Socialist Family of Man. Rita Maahs' and Karl-Eduard von Schnitzler's Exhibition Vom Glück des Menschen', *Zeithistorische Forschungen/Studies in Contemporary History*, 12 (2015), 370–82.

[63] Walter Markov, 'Erinnerung an den Beginn', *Asien-Afrika-Lateinamerika: Zeitschrift des Zentralen Rates für Asien-Afrika-und Lateinamerikawissenschaften in der DDR* 2/5 (1974), 791.

[64] Pieter Lessing, *Africa's Red Harvest* (London: Michael Joseph, 1962), 25–6.

[65] 'From the History of Studies of African Problems in the Soviet Union', *Africa in Soviet Studies: 1968 Annual* (Moscow: 'Nauka' Publishing House, 1969), 145–52.

Russian scholarship on Africa from the late nineteenth century through to the 1950s, other Eastern European countries had comparatively little expert knowledge of the region. Even those countries with the richest area studies' traditions had to start afresh in rethinking the socialist reinterpretation of African knowledge. At a 1958 conference of Soviet Orientalists, the journalist Georgii Zhukov sounded the alarm that 'Life has left us behind, and we happen to be unprepared for creating a theory of dealing with Asian and African countries', adding that 'We need our Soviet missionaries, our Soviet Doctor Schweitzers.'[66]

The Soviet Union wished to show Africans that it was the only major country genuinely interested in Africa's rich past, culture and achievements.[67] As early as 1954 two leading Soviet Africanists, Ivan Izosimovich Potekhin and D.D. Ol'derogge, published their edited *Peoples of Africa*, which was the first study of Africa written from a Marxist-Leninist perspective. These and other Soviet publications forcefully contended that Africa was a 'flourishing civilization before colonialism intervened'.[68] A number of conferences devoted to the ancient history of foreign lands, especially Asia, the Middle East and Africa, took place in the 1960s, and these, along with the associated publications, were focused on class social structure, slavery and the life of the common people.[69] In part this was a means of distinguishing the socialist world's attitude toward Africa and Asia from the racist frameworks of Western European imperialism or American modernization theory. In his 1960 booklet *Africa Looks to the Future*, I.I. Potekhin pleaded that 'African history and African heritage must be built up so as to destroy the cultural heritage of the imperialists', accusing the colonial powers of having destroyed 'high African civilization, which, with the help of the Soviet Union, is there for the Africans to regain'.[70] His idea that Eastern European archaeologists could help Africans rediscover their own pasts was articulated even more forcefully in a late 1950s radio broadcast. In it Potekhin asserted that post-colonial African scholars, 'assisted by the progressive scholars' from Eastern Europe, are now 'unmasking the lie of imperialistic propaganda' that African people 'do not have a history of their own. The obligation of Marxist historians is to help in the restoration of historical truth.'[71] Other Eastern European countries added their voices to this defence of traditional African cultures.[72]

---

[66] Quoted in S. V. Mazov, *A Distant Front in the Cold War: The USSR in West Africa and the Congo* (Washington: Woodrow Wilson Center Press, 2010), 18.

[67] Alexander Dallin, 'The Soviet Union: Political Activity', in Zbigniew Brzezinski (ed.), *Africa and the Communist World* (Oxford: OUP, 1964), 20. See too Fritz Schatten, *Afrika Schwarz oder rot* (Munich: Piper, 1961), esp. 197–216.

[68] Dallin, 'The Soviet Union', 21.

[69] Horst Klengel (ed.), *Beiträge zur Sozialen Struktur des Alten Vorderasien* (Berlin: Akademie-Verlag, 1971).

[70] Lessing, *Africa's Red Harvest*, 33–4. The French version is the most cited: Ivan Potekhin, *L'Afrique regarde vers l'avenir* (Moscow: Editions de Littérature Orientale, 1962), 70–81.

[71] Quoted in Lessing, 126.

[72] 'Ambasador Gheorghe Popescu către Direcția V-a Relații', 7 February 1963, MAE-Guinea, 70/1962, 1.

Eastern European Africanists thus stepped up their interest in ancient Africa so as to forge new links of solidarity after decolonization for international socialism. To defend the formation of African national cultures as steps toward socialist internationalism did however require some fancy ideological footwork. Socialist Orientalists for their part conceded that much of what was described as tradition was really a defence of national culture in the name of heritage and authenticity, with both progressive and regressive elements.[73] But they also felt that this was a key area of cultural diplomacy by virtue of which bridges between the Second and Third Worlds might be built. Pan-Africanism sat awkwardly with the Communist world's reading of ancient African artifacts as proto-socialist. The point now was to champion Africa's socialist past and potentially socialist future beyond the nation state and beyond pan-Africanism.[74]

The 1960s thus saw the founding of a slew of new archaeological and anthropology institutions devoted to studying Africans and Asians, often in the name of celebrating a new socialist humanity rooted in a shared pre-modern past and modernizing present. Take for example the Polish Anglophone journal *Africana Bulletin*, launched in 1964 at the University of Warsaw and published in French and English. The journal's first issue makes clear why the topic mattered, for in an era of decolonization Polish scholars 'have become increasingly concerned with African history—which has to be freed from the falsifications of the colonialist era'.[75] Special interest was shown in Egyptology and archaeological projects in Egypt and Sudan; Egypt authorized Poland to set up a Centre of Mediterranean Archaeology in 1959 and the journal covered excavations by Polish teams in Egypt and Sudan,[76] as well as joint African-Polish anthropological expeditions across the continent.[77]

Another example was the less academic Czechoslovak magazine, *New Orient: Journal for the Modern and Ancient Cultures of Asia and Africa*, which first appeared in 1960. Published in English, the journal was aimed at the English-speaking world in the West and in Africa and Asia; it covered history, archaeology, the arts, music and theatre, literature and folk tales. Particularly notable was its

---

[73] Martin Robbe, 'Authentizität: Bemühungen in Entwicklungsländern um Selbstverständnis, Selbstbewusstsein, Orientierung und Solidisierung', *Deutsche Zeitschrift für Philosophie* 33/12 (1985), 1057-1067.

[74] Karla Bilang, 'Traditionelle Plastik aus Westafrika: Gedanken zu einer Ausstellung', *Asien-Afrika-Lateinamerika: Zeitschrift des Zentralen Rates fuer Asien-Afrika-und Lateinamerikawissenschaften in der DDR*, 5/3 (1977), 490-2.

[75] Editorial Board, 'Presentation', *Africana Bulletin*, 1 (Warsaw: Warsaw University, 1964), 7.

[76] Albert Szczudłowska and Irena Pomorska, 'Les Fouilles archaeologiques polonaises en Egypte et au Sudan', *Africana Bulletin*, 1 (Warsaw: Warsaw University, 1964), 168–76 as well as Elzbieta Dabrowska-Smektala, 'Polish Excavations in Egypt and Sudan', *Africana Bulletin*, 2 (Warsaw: Warsaw University, 1965), 102–12. and Kazimierz Michalowski, 'La Nubie chrétienne', *Africana Bulletin*, 3 (Warsaw: Warsaw University, 1965), 9–23.

[77] Tadeusz Dzierzykray-Rogalski, 'The Joint Arabic-Polish Anthropological Expedition in 1958–1962', *Africana Bulletin*, 4 (Warsaw: Warsaw University, 1965), 105–7.

preoccupation with the ancient past—the so-called Old Orient; by contrast, the word 'new' in the title 'should express our endeavour to approach the Orient without outdated prejudices, without an exotic, romantic or mysterious veil'. Articles focused on various aspects of world culture, such as Javanese Batik, Vietnamese theatre, Congolese masks, and UNESCO's rescue of Nubian monuments.[78] There was a good deal on Chinese culture too, underlining the extent to which this cultural journal did not in fact reflect growing Sino-Soviet tensions. One 1960 issue featured short statements from experts in 'Eastern Studies' from around the world, East, West and South, with a remarkable degree of consensus about the need to devote more energies toward the appreciation of other civilizations and the development of a UNESCO-inspired 'world civilization'. All of the statements were designed explicitly to combat stereotypical notions of these cultures as belonging to 'peoples without history'. Eastern European Orientalists argued that it was easier for them to appreciate this commonality because of their supposedly non-imperial past: Ananiasz Zajączkowski, Director of the Oriental Institute of Warsaw University, proudly asserted that 'Since the Poles—and the Czechs—bear no trace of colonial psychology and, on the other hand, have much sympathy for the nations of Asia and Africa, they can much more easily find a common language of understanding with the East.'[79] In doing so, Eastern European Orientalists recast the idea of the Orient beyond the framework of western imperialism and even eurocentrism.

In reaction to the West's campaign to develop African rural lands in the name of the magic American formula of modernization theory, Eastern Europeans sought to win over Africans sympathetic to the socialist cause by defending traditional anti-capitalist village life as a means of managing the slow transition to full development. Only socialism, so the argument went, held out the possibility of countering the destructive cultural power of American-style modernization by uniting humanism, internationalism and revolution.[80] Anthropology emerged as a key discipline to communicate this solidarity. Journal articles written by Soviet Africanists extolled the role of folklore as a hybrid cultural form that would help Africans cope with the transition to modernity.[81] As one conference report from 1965 put it: 'We Soviet Africanists' set our task in 'preserving and developing the traditions of humanism and proletarian internationalism with respect to the peoples of Africa, traditions which have always been inherent in Russian

---

[78] Zbyněk Žába, 'Ancient Nubia Calls for Help', New Orient, 1/3 (1960), 5–9.

[79] 'Eastern Studies Today', New Orient, 1/4 (1960), 1.

[80] Jürgen Herzog, 'Das Traditionsproblem und der Neokolonialismus: Bemerkungen zur "Modernisierungskonzeption" der amerikanischen politischen Soziologie', Asien-Afrika-Lateinamerika: Zeitschrift des Zentralen Rates für Asien-Afrika-und Lateinamerikawissenschaften in der DDR, 3/1 (1975), 19–36.

[81] Kirill Chistov, 'Folklore, "Folklorism" and the Culture of an Ethnos', in Ethnocultural Development of African Countries (Moscow: USSR Academy of Sciences, 1984), 119–39.

revolutionary democracy and Marxism-Leninism.'[82] Klaus Ernst's widely cited 1973 book, *Tradition and Progress in the African Village*, was emblematic of this kind of socialist thinking, as pre-modern traditional village life—Mali, in this case—was seen as the building block of Africa's future of indigenous socialism.[83] The intention here was to lend credence to alternative models of managed modernization, as well as accentuating commonalities with Eastern Europe's own regional history of rural development.

Such material was also designed to wean Eastern European populations from older European racist stereotypes about exotic primitive peoples inhabiting the African continent. As in most of Europe, so too in the East there had been great popular interest in Africa since the late nineteenth century, which further intensified with decolonization. In some cases, earlier colonial imagery returned: the late 1950s saw large print runs of travel books on safaris, exotic landscapes and encounters with Africa and Africans.[84] Many of these travelogues sat awkwardly with the proclaimed political values of socialist solidarity, and efforts were made to dispel these stereotypes as unworthy of socialism, especially in the classroom. A good example of the GDR's popularization of anthropology was Rolf Krusche's *Völkerkunde für Jedermann: Ein Kartenbuch*, roughly translated as *Anthropology for Everyone: A Book of Maps*, which enjoyed a print run of 125,000 copies in 1966, and was a fixture in East German classrooms for decades.[85] It touched on the key themes of academic East German ethnography, including the regime's commitment to a more universal, UNESCO-like 'culture of humanity'. At first glance the accompanying illustrations might seem to recall old-style colonial photography, but they also drew on visual representational styles from other sources, most notably the 1955 *Family of Man* exhibition discussed above. What distinguished these socialist images from both their colonial predecessors and the 1955 Family of Man styling was the visual accent on community, labour and modernization. The avowed task of GDR anthropology was not to arrest development, but rather, as Krusche put it, to help develop the continent in line with a 'humane and dignified condition of life'. Tradition was understood as cultural ballast, in that it could help mitigate the destructive legacy of colonialism and strengthen national consciousness in the building of a post-imperial 'humane society'.[86]

[82] VS Solodovnikov, 'Opening Address at the Conference on the Historical Relations of the Peoples of the Soviet Union and Africa, May 19, 1965', in *Russia and Africa* (Moscow: USSR Academy of Sciences, 1966), 7–15.

[83] Klaus Ernst, *Tradition and Progress in the African Village: The Non-Capitalist Transformation of Rural Communities in Mali* (London: C. Hurst, 1976).

[84] Fritz Rudolph and Percy Stutz, *Jambo, Afrika! DDR-Afrika-Expedition zwischen Kongo und Sansibar* (Berlin: VEB FA Brockhaus, 1970).

[85] Dietrich Treide, 'Onwards, but in Which Direction? Anthropology at the University of Leipzig between 1950 and 1968', in Chris Hann, Mihály Sárkány and Peter Skalník (eds.), *Studying Peoples in the People's Democracies: Socialist Era Anthropology in East-Central Europe* (Münster: Lit Verlag. 2005), 133–58.

[86] Rolf Krusche, *Völkerkunde für jedermann: Ein Kartenbuch* (Gotha/Leipzig: VEB Hermann Haack, 1966), 10–14.

Archaeology was even more important in this respect, and from the 1960s on there were a number of East European archaeological projects in Tanzania, Kenya and the Sudan. In this context, archaeology was converted into a socialist political science, and in two ways.[87] First, the literal unearthing of the link between archaeology and colonialism was used to remind Africans of their long-standing oppression by foreigners, and to drive home the point that the same dangers were still around.[88] Secondly, archaeology was used to underpin new narratives for the present. When Tanzanian President Julius Nyerere announced his project of building 'African socialism' in the early 1970s, for example, East German archaeologists strove to show that Tanzania's hoped-for 'non-capitalist' development could be built on its own centuries-old egalitarian traditions.[89] There are echoes of pre-revolutionary Russian populism here, when Russian intellectuals went to the Russian countryside in the middle to late nineteenth century to advise peasants on the virtues of rural socialism, and this old European socialist tradition exerted some influence on the thinking of Cabral, Nyerere and even Fanon.[90] That many Eastern European societies in the 1960s still contained significant rural communities then undergoing modernization allowed for further parallels with their African counterparts to be drawn. But in the case of archaeology, the accent on the distant past brought with it a different sense of historical time. Not only could Africans draw on ancient pre-colonial pasts as they modernized, but the traumatic wave of colonial violence from the nineteenth century through to re-colonization in the aftermath of the Second World War was only a limited phase of African history. A pre-modern African past and non-western present, so these Eastern European archaeologists reasoned, could be joined together in the name of socialist solidarity.

Numerous joint archaeological projects took place between African and European teams dedicated to studying ancient African civilizations, such as the high-profile excavation of the eleventh-century Aoudaghost site in Mauritania in 1961.[91] Peter Shinnie, a Scottish Communist who led archaeological teams at the University of Ghana in the 1950s and 1960s on dozens of excavations, did much to publicize prehistoric Sudan and Meroe as ancient and homegrown African

---

[87] Mikhail Miller, *Archaeology in the USSR* (London: Atlantic Press, 1956), 132–68.

[88] Grenville SP Freeman-Grenville, *The Medieval History of the Coast of Tanganyika, with Special Reference to Recent Archaeological Discoveries* (East Berlin: Akademie-Verlag, 1962). For discussion, Ulrich van der Heyden, 'Tansania in der DDR-Wissenschaft: Eine paradigmatische Untersuchung der Afrika- und Kolonialgeschichtsschreibung in der DDR', in Ulrich van der Heyden and Franziska Benger, eds. *Kalter Krieg in Ostafrika: Die Beziehungen der DDR zu Sansibar und Tansania* (Berlin: Lit, 2009), 149–68.

[89] Dieter Graf, *Produktionskräfte in der Landwirtschaft und der nichtkapitalistische Weg Tansanias* (Berlin: Akademie-Verlag, 1973).

[90] P.L. E. Idahosa, *The Populist Dimension to African Political Thought* (Trenton, NJ: African World Press, 2004).

[91] Augustin F. C. Holl, 'Worldviews, Mind-Sets and Trajectories in West African Archaeology', in Peter Schmidt (ed.), *Postcolonial Archaeologies in Africa* (Santa Fe: School for Advanced Research Press, 2009), 135–9.

civilizations.[92] From 1960 to 1966 Shinnie was director of the University of Ghana's excavations at Debeira West and was part of UNESCO's Save the Nubian Monuments collaborative project, after which he trained generations of African archaeologists.[93] Over the decades he worked closely with prominent East German archaeologist Fritz Hintze, a fellow expert on ancient Meroe civilization.[94] In so doing, East European archaeologists, anthropologists and experts in the field of African art worked to provide an alternative account of African history, stressing that these cultures had rich and vibrant pre-colonial national pasts supposedly characterized by what was called 'non-capitalist development'.[95] However, the real motive was to counter American influence, which was routinely condemned for cutting off these newly decolonized countries from their historical roots. A sinister plot was under way, or so the argument went, to coerce these new states into a cycle of underdevelopment, rendering them beholden to the West. In 1961 the Czechoslovak and Egyptian governments signed an agreement to mount a joint anthropological expedition to Nubia,[96] after which the Czechoslovak Egyptology Institute produced pioneering studies on Sudanese and Upper Egyptian folktales and Arabic folk literature.[97]

A remarkable example of this international good will was UNESCO's 1960 call to rescue the Nubian monuments from the flooding associated with the construction of the new Aswan Dam. No less than forty teams contributed to this rescue initiative, and there was a strong Eastern European presence from the beginning. There were missions from the Soviet Union, East Germany, Hungary, Czechoslovakia, Poland and Yugoslavia; in fact, the Polish mission in particular made some of the most spectacular discoveries relating to the remnants of Christian Nubia.[98] Yugoslav newspapers proudly reported the Nubia campaign,[99] and the Czechoslovak Egyptological Institute and the GDR's Mission in the Sudan crowed about their contribution.[100] Teams from Ghana, Egypt and Senegal also played significant roles. Little wonder that the international spirit of cooperation

[92] P.L. Shinnie, *Meroe: A Civilization of the Sudan* (London: Thames & Hudson, 1967), 168–9. See too https://www.theguardian.com/news/2007/oct/30/guardianobituaries.obituaries (last accessed 9 August 2021).

[93] https://www.theguardian.com/news/2007/oct/30/guardianobituaries.obituaries

[94] Fritz and Ursula Hintze, *Alte Kulturen im Sudan* (Leipzig: Leipzig Verlag, 1966).

[95] Ruth Andexel (ed.), *Nichtkapitalistischer Entwicklungsweg: Aktuelle Probleme in Theorie und Praxis* (Berlin: Akademie Verlag, 1973).

[96] See the report by Evžen Strouhal, Czechoslovak Egyptological Institute at the Charles University Prague to the university's Dean's Office of the Philosophical Faculty (Deputy Dean for Scientific-Research) and Ministry of Education and Culture—Department for Foreign Relations, 4 July 1964, Prague, NA (Czech National Archive), file: Ministerstvo školství a kultury, karton 16, signatura: 35 expedice, unprocessed file.

[97] M. Fiedler, 'Preliminary Outline of the Edition of Sudanese and Upper Egyptian Folk-tales', in *Acta Universitatis Carolinae*, as well as 'Some remarks on the Sudanese and Egyptian dialects in the Arabic Folk-Literature' in *Archiv Orientalni*, both in 1962–63.

[98] Hassan, *Exodus*, 313–14.   [99] 17 March 1964, 4, E1/168, 1947–1966, Press Review, UAP.

[100] Zbyněk Žába, 'Czechoslovak Discoveries in Egypt', *New Orient* 2/2 (April 1961), 6–10 and Friedrich W. Hinkel, *Auszug aus Nubien* (East Berlin: Akademie-Verlag, 1978).

captured the attention of journalists. One *New York Times* reporter in 1961 marvelled at the way that the project had brought together countries that officially did
not recognize each other (such as Spain and the USSR) or were in political conflict (India and Pakistan); as he put it, 'there seemed to be no Cold War in the
Land of Kush.'[101]

However, Eastern Europe's interest in Africa's ancient heritage came at a tricky
time. Decolonization was not only a moment of new political independence, but
also one in which Africans were reclaiming their own national heritage as the
cultural bedrock of newly won sovereignty. The pre-colonial past, which had long
been dismissed and devalued by the colonial powers, was now recast as the living
heritage of modern Africa.[102] Ancient heritage thus became the 'necessary fiction'
of origin and patrimony in writing new histories of new nations.[103] In fact, it is
often forgotten that anti-colonial demands for the return of cultural property
were a key part of the 1955 Bandung Conference's concern to undo what was
called the 'indignity of imperialism's cultural chauvinism.'[104] This often took on
the form of forcing imperial powers to give back their stolen artworks from Africa
and Asia. Some did this as a gesture of post-imperial good will, such as the
Belgian return of Congolese artifacts to Zaire or the Dutch repatriation of colonial objects to Indonesia.[105] Complicating matters was the fact that a number of
West European archaeologists were also engaged with many excavations in Africa
at the time too, and themselves strongly subscribed to UNESCO's broader 'world
civilization' philosophy, often as a means of shedding their own imperial and
Eurocentric traditions. Eastern European Africanists tirelessly condemned their
western rivals for peddling 'neo-imperial' approaches to African heritage, largely
to cast themselves as the more progressive and liberated Europeans open to genuine cultural partnership with the developing world. The larger point is that the
bones and stones of Africa's ancient past were now subject to ideological contention from a variety of perspectives.

The creation of a national museum in independent Ghana exemplified the
thorny issues associated with inventing new post-colonial identities. While
Nkrumah may have found a way of effectively integrating western, socialist and

---

[101] Paul Betts, 'The Warden of World Heritage: UNESCO and the Rescue of the Nubian Monuments',
in *Heritage in the Modern World: Historical Preservation in International Perspective, Past & Present*
Supplement 10 (Oxford University Press, 2015), 100–25.

[102] Frantz Fanon, 'On National Culture', in Patrick Williams and Ian Christman (eds.), *Colonial and
Postcolonial Theory: A Reader* (New York: Columbia University Press, 1994), 37.

[103] Daniel Herwitz, *Heritage, Culture and Politics in the Postcolony* (New York: Columbia Press,
2012), 1–25.

[104] Vijay Prashad, *The Darker Nations: A People's History of the Third World* (New York: New Press,
2007), 45.

[105] Sarah van Beurden, 'The Art of (Re)Possession: Heritage and the Cultural Politics of Congo's
Decolonization', *Journal of African History*, 56 (2015), 143–64 and Cynthia Scott, 'Renewing the
'Special Relationship' and Rethinking the Return of Cultural Property: The Netherlands and Indonesia,
1949-1979', *Journal of Contemporary History*, 52/3 (2017), 646–68.

African modernism in the modern architecture of his new republic, things were far less simple when it came to choosing and displaying the artifacts of the past as the foundation of independent Ghana. While the National Museum of Ghana itself was designed by the British design team of Maxwell Fry and Jane Drew in the spirit of what was called at the time 'tropical modern', the objects on display were designed to connect the new state to its indigenous material culture and pre-colonial roots. The problem was that the new museum's holdings were based on the collection of British colonial ethnographer Charles Thurston Shaw along with various missionary donations from the 1920s, suggesting that Ghana's cultural heritage did not represent a break from its Gold Coast colonial predecessor.[106] No less disquieting was the fact that Nkrumah's opponents, who included several powerful chieftains, were sceptical of his desire to link socialism and national culture, and resisted a political programme whose centralizing impetus was felt by them to be at the expense of regional tribal power.[107] As a result, many chieftains did not wish their regional or tribal artifacts to be subordinated to Nkrumah's larger narrative of a unified socialist nation, or even to pan-Africanism. The difficulties surfaced in Ghana's first show at the new museum, the 'Man in Africa' display in 1957, whose centerpiece was an ensemble of sixty Akan stools as the symbolic centre of the nation, though Akan represented only one of the four ethno-linguistic groups in the country. It was precisely the problem of reconciling tribal, national and pan-African ideologies that bedevilled these new museums across Africa.[108]

Traditional African dance faced the same dilemma. Guinea and Senegal developed the most advanced forms of dance theatre in the 1950s, and these performances became showpieces of political legitimacy for new post-colonial elites. In part this was because traditional dance not only helped bridge the pre-colonial past and post-colonial present, but also urban and rural culture. Guinean and Senegalese regional and tribal styles were thus converted into newly minted 'national heritage', and were exported abroad as proud emblems of new national identities. Nevertheless, there were striking contradictions. For in their broader effort to connect a pre-colonial past with a modern present, these dance troupes reinforced a colonial vision of rural Africa as timeless and unchanging. These performances were also criticized for being placeless, as West and Central African

---

[106] Arianna Fogelman, 'Colonial Legacy in African Museology: The Case of the Ghana National Museum', *Museum Anthropology*, 31/1 (2008), 19–26.

[107] Richard Rathbone, *Nkrumah and the Chiefs: The Politics of Chieftaincy in Ghana, 1951–1960* (Oxford: James Currey, 2000), 89–149.

[108] Mark Crinson, 'Nation-Building, Collecting and the Politics of Display: The National Museum, Ghana', *Journal of the History of Collections*, 13/2 (2001), 231–250, here 244 and Mary Jo Arnoldi, 'Youth Festivals and Museums: The Cultural Politics of Public Memory in Postcolonial Mali', *Africa Today*, 52/4 (Special Issue on 'Memory and the Formation of Political Identities in West Africa', Summer 2006); and Sophie Mew, 'Managing the Past in the Newly Independent States of Mali and Ghana', in Craggs and Wintle, 177–95.

regional styles were depicted as a kind of pan-African essence designed for modern consumption.[109] Given the trumpeted values of post-colonial modernity, traditional heritage and African communalism, Guinean and Senegalese national dance theatres toured Eastern European countries on several occasions to popular acclaim. Such neo-traditionalist presentations generally sat well with Eastern European socialism and its 'unity in diversity' ideology, though some felt it departed too far from a more Marxist framework of change, transformation and modernization. At stake were divergent interpretations of authentic African heritage, based on different versions of the invention of tradition, be it an equally artificial proto-socialism or a proto-nationalism.

For Eastern European Africanists, the danger was not just primordial nationalism, but also racism. In this regard the figure who generated the greatest animus was the poet and first president of Senegal, Léopold Sédar Senghor. Senghor was one of the most influential African intellectuals of his generation, and at first glance should have been a natural ally of Eastern Europe's cultural initiative to extend a helping hand to Africa. After all, Senghor frequently spoke about the importance of socialism, was an inspiring figure of anti-imperialism on the world stage, and often insisted on the need to marry socialism with *négritude*. But to his Eastern European critics—especially those in the Soviet Union and the GDR, to say nothing of his Communist critics within Senegal[110]—Senghor's idea of *négritude* was much too ethnically based. The irony is that Senghor's *négritude* arguably was an African version of Pan-Slavism, which was revived after 1945 (especially in archaeology circles) as a means of linking multi-ethnic communities across Eastern Europe as a cultural expression of transnational ethnic unity.[111] But in this case Eastern European cultural elites rejected Senghor's pan-Africanism as racist and exclusionary, not least because they were the ones being rejected as outsiders. Race trumped class as the vehicle of a shared post-colonial African history and diasporic identity, and helped defend Africa's heritage from socialism's geopolitical agenda.

However, it was Senghor's opening of the high-profile 'First World Exhibition of Black Art' in 1966 in Dakar that alarmed Eastern European critics the most. It was the very first international art show of African art to take place on African soil, and was explicitly designed, as one publicist put it, to allow 'Africans to speak

[109] Hélène Neveu Kringelbach, 'Choreographical Revival, Elite Nationalism, and Postcolonial Appropriation in Senegal', in Caroline Bithell and Juniper Hill (eds.), *The Oxford Handbook of Music Revival* (Oxford: Oxford University Press, 2013), 228–51.

[110] Wilbert J. LeMelle, 'A Return to Senghor's Theme on African Socialism', *Phylon*, 26/4 (1965), 330–43.

[111] Ludomir R. Lozny, *Archaeology of the Communist Era: A Political History of Archaeology of the Twentieth Century* (Berlin: Springer, 2016) and Bruce Trigger, *A History of Archaeological Thought* (Cambridge: Cambridge University Press, 2006 [1989]), 207–42.

with their own voice'.[112] Some 2,500 artists, musicians, performers and writers gathered in Dakar to celebrate 'Black Art' across continents, including Senghor and Aimé Cesaire, Langston Hughes, Josephine Baker, Duke Ellington and Wole Soyinka, along with representatives from thirty African countries. Some six hundred objects from over fifty museums and private collections in Africa, Europe and North America were reunited for the first time, and in this sense the show was an illustration of Senghor's idea of *négritude*.[113] Eastern European socialists were ambivalent toward Senghor's arts festival. On the one hand, the Soviets produced a celebratory documentary film of the event, *African Rhythmus*, the only colour film of the festival produced by any country, and organized an exhibition on 'Russo-Negro Brotherhood' on one of its docked cruise ships.[114] An accompanying exhibition of African masks was mounted in Belgrade, Zagreb and Ljubljana to complement Dakar's 1966 festival, as well as to promote African culture in Yugoslavia more generally.[115] On the other hand, Soviet and East European art critics denounced Senghor's *négritude* as irredeemably western, bourgeois and racist. So even if the Soviet press called the festival 'a significant event in the history of world culture' that 'will play a major role in the cultural revival of Africa', Senghor's name went unmentioned in *Pravda* coverage; attention instead was lavished on 'progressive' Senegalese writer and filmmaker Ousmane Sembène as the more genuine socialist.[116]

Eastern European interest in traditional African art grew in the 1960s. European scholarly curiosity toward African art first developed in the late nineteenth century, and enjoyed popularity after the First World War within the French art world and beyond. Attention to African art took off again across the West after 1945, perhaps best noted in the French journal, *Présence Africaine*.[117] The same renewed fascination was in evidence in Eastern Europe, with the Soviet Union, Yugoslavia, the GDR and the Czechoslovaks leading the way. While international organizations like UNESCO were also interested in indigenous folk culture, particularly with regard to its own role in preserving folklore as a defence against the dangers of modernization, the socialist world

---

[112] Engelbert Mveng, 'Signification africaine de l'art', in *Colloque: Fonction et signification de l'Art nègre dans la vie du people et pour le people, 30 Mars-8 Avril, 1966* (Paris: Presence Africaine, 1967), 8.

[113] David Murphy, 'Introduction: The Performance of Pan-Africanism', in David Murphy (ed.), *The First World Festival of Negro Arts, Dakar 1966: Contexts and Legacies* (Liverpool: Liverpool University Press, 2016), 1–40.

[114] Murphy, 'Introduction', 8, 31–2. Romanian filmmakers V. Calotescu and C. Ionescu-Tonciu also produced a film about the festival in 1968.

[115] AJ, 559, F-6, Opšti materijali 1965, Izveštaj o radu na regionalnom sektoru zemalja Azije, Afrike i Australije za 1965. Godinu, Janet G. Vaillant, 'Dilemmas for Anti-Western Patriotism: Slavophilism and Négritude', *The Journal of Modern African Studies*, 12/3 (1974), 377–93.

[116] G. Abramov, P. Kaminskii, 'Isskustvo Derevnee, Vechno Zhivoe', *Pravda*, 20 April 1966, 5.

[117] See in particular the special *Présence Africaine* issue on 'L'Art Nègre' (10/11, 1951).

devoted great energy to celebrating traditional folk art as a means of connecting Eastern Europe and the developing world, especially Africa.[118]

Eastern Europeans recast African heritage to suit their own anti-imperial agenda. The Czechs had a long-standing interest in African art, most vividly reflected in the Náprstek Museum of Asian, African and American Culture in Prague, founded in 1862. The museum's centenary was celebrated in the pages of *New Orient*, which lauded the museum for preserving 'cultural values threatened with extinction in the rapid changes in civilization in our age', as well as for ensuring the 'mutual appreciation of the cultures of West and East'.[119] Eastern European interest in African art was often tinged with expressions of shame, envy and moral superiority. One 1966 Polish publication on the country's holdings of African art conceded that its collections were weak compared to others, stating:

> Unfortunately, we Poles have played the least significant role in the history of the discovery of Africa. For political reasons this may be to the good, because we did not blemish our reputation with the stigma of colonial ambitions. On the other hand, these exotic lands are poorly represented in Polish museums. When England, France, Germany and Belgium were organizing expeditions of exploration, the Poles were busy fighting for their political existence.[120]

Here the poverty of the museum collection—the result of the absence of imperial history—was converted into a virtue and emblem of moral superiority to the West. In a spirit of decolonization, Eastern European collections were revamped, and some new ones were founded, such as the Museum of African Art in Belgrade in 1977, the first museum in Yugoslavia to be devoted exclusively to African culture. The initial catalogue claimed that while there are 'bigger and richer collections' 'mostly in the capitals of former colonial powers', the Belgrade museum was a unique 'product of friendship' and a 'symbol of non-alignment' inspired by 'a new attitude of appreciation toward the achievements of folk art', and over 45,000 visitors passed through its gates in the first two and a half years.[121] The museum was praised as the first African museum in Europe expressly created as a post-imperial

---

[118] Tibor Bodrogi, *Afrikanische Kunst* (Leipzig: VEB E.A. Seemann, 1967); W. and B. Forman, *Kunst ferner Länder* (Czech). Ferdinand Herrmann, 'Die afrikanische Negerplastik als Forschungsgegenstand', in *Beiträge zur Afrikanische Kunst, Veröffentlichungen des Museums für Völkerkunde zu Leipzig*, Heft 9 (Berlin: Akademie-Verlag, 1958), 3–29; and Burchard Brentjes, 'Menschenbild und bildende Kunst in Europa, Asien und Afrika', *Asien-Afrika-Lateinamerika: Zeitschrift des Zentralen Rates für Asien-Afrika-und Lateinamerikawissenschaften in der DDR*, 1/2 (1973), 131–44.

[119] Erich Herold, 'The Centenary of the Naprstek Museum', *New Orient*, 3/6 (December 1962), 177.

[120] Wacław Korabiewicz, *African Art in Polish Collections* (Warsaw: Polonia Publishing House, 1966), 8.

[121] Živorad Kovačević, 'The Opening of the Museum of African Art—A Significant Cultural and Political Event', *Museum of African Art: The Veda and Zoravko Pečar Collection* (Belgrade, 1977), 1–2.

space of civilizational equality and non-exploitation, and the curators built up a strongly collaborative relationship with museums in Ghana, Nigeria and Senegal.[122] Only in Communist Eastern Europe, so went the logic, could such a progressive museum have been created in the first place, and it was here that Eastern European anti-imperial identities could be claimed and displayed.

By contrast with Eastern European–African joint ventures in post-colonial modernization and modernism, the reinvention of the African past proved difficult. These far-flung cultural relations were designed to close the gap between Eastern Europeans and Africans around the themes of colonialism and liberation, and, where museum and folk dance exchanges were concerned, their efforts met with considerable success. But in other instances, best seen in Senghor's 1966 exhibition, divergent conceptions of antiquity and indigenous identity exposed a distance. In these cases, nation, region and race were not so easily reconciled in a broader master narrative of Popular Front-style international socialism. Anti-imperialism and anti-racism still served as the binding ideology of solidarity, yet the forms they took could either strengthen or undermine their imagined commonalities.

Bridges and Borders

Cultural relations between the Second and Third World continued through the 1970s and 1980s in diverse forms, whose general patterns may be classified as radicalization, reverse direction and growing separation. There were a few notable exceptions, usually related to African countries in political upheaval. First, take the 1971 Soviet–Somali archaeological project, which followed Somalia's Marxist 1969 revolution. While Soviet archaeologists had been active in Africa since the 1960s, this partnership was explicitly designed to help the new state create a heritage on which to build a new post-colonial national identity. Here this was done by documenting Somaliland's historic campaign led by Mohammed Abdullah Hassan against the British, Italian and Ethiopian forces between 1900 and 1920. The undertaking was also used to publicize the prestige of Soviet African Studies, and the joint Soviet-Somali preservation project directly led to Soviet support for Siad Barre's national project to showcase over 3,000 artefacts celebrating the birth of Somali national culture at the Garesa Museum in Mogadishu. Another instance is the construction of the Ethiopian National Museum following the country's 1974 Communist revolution. The Soviets (together with UNESCO) played a key role in helping the new revolutionary regime take advantage of the recent discovery of the earliest known hominid

---

[122] Jelena Arandjelović-Lazić, 'In the Heart of Serbia: A Show-Case of African Art', *Museum*, 33/2 (1981), 75–80.

('Lucy') to claim Ethiopia as the origin of 'human civilization' and site of indigenous cultural achievement.[123] In both cases archaeology was identified as a crucial means of strengthening Soviet–African relations and forging new and revolutionary national cultures around the display of historical remains.

By the late 1970s the enthusiasm for Soviet cultural diplomacy began to cool off; elsewhere the cultural connection with the developing world intensified over the course of the decade, most notably in Yugoslavia and East Germany. The African literary presence in Yugoslavia thus increased in the last two decades of the Cold War. In the period 1960–80 approximately fifteen non-aligned authors were translated and published annually in Yugoslavia. Until 1980 the two most translated 'non-aligned authors' in Yugoslavia were Rabindranath Tagore and Pablo Neruda, followed by Gabriel Garcia Marquez and Miguel Angel Asturias. Through the 1970s a number of African poetry anthologies were published in Yugoslavia as well as numerous books by Senghor, Agostinho Neto and Chinua Achebe,[124] along with wide television coverage in Belgrade.[125] A festival on the 'Days of African Cultures' was organized in Belgrade, Novi Sad and Ljubljana in April 1980, in cooperation with Dakar's *Institut Culturel Africain*, which proclaimed that Yugoslavs and Africans had both suffered 'under the veil of cultural colonization of the colonial conquerors'.[126] For its part, the GDR founded the Centre for Art Exhibitions inside the Ministry of Culture in 1973, whose brief was to set up meetings of professional artists and to mount a range of exhibitions at international venues. The Centre organized dozens of shows in the 1970s and 1980s in the fields of painting, sculpture, photography, theatre and industrial design. In 1974—in commemoration of the twenty-fifth anniversary of the GDR's founding—East Germany sent out no less than 8,000 artists to 72 countries, and sponsored 180 exhibitions abroad.[127] The political power of folk art maintained its presence internationally through the 1970s, especially in terms of political resistance. A 1977 East German catalogue on 'Palestinian Folk Art' claimed that such indigenous art served as resistance 'against the decades long annihilatory campaign of Zionism', and the exhibition of music, dance, dress, jewellery and ceramics was itself construed as an 'act of solidarity'.[128] East German photography

---

[123] Kate Cowcher, 'The Museum as Prison and Other Protective Measures in Socialist Ethiopia' and Natalia Telepneva, 'A Cultural Heritage for National Liberation? The Soviet-Somali Historical Expedition, Soviet African Studies and the Cold War in the Horn of Africa', both in *International Journal of Heritage Studies*, 26/12 (2020), 1166–84 and 1185–1202, respectively.

[124] AMAU, I, Isečci iz štampe 1976–1980, P. Zafirovski, 'Otkrivanje pravog lica', *Komunist*, 4. April 1980.

[125] AMAU, II, Isečci iz štampe 1982–1986, D. Milazzi, 'Uz ciklus Savremena afrička književnost', *Školske novine*, Zagreb, 10.2.1981.

[126] AMAU, Hemeroteka, Isečci iz štampe, 1976–1980, M. Milivojević, 'Dokazivanje identiteta', *Borba*, 12 April 1980.

[127] Christian Saehrendt, *Kunst im Kampf für das "Sozialistische Weltsystem": Auswärtige Kulturpolitik der DDR in Afrika und Nahost* (Stuttgart: Franz Steiner Verlag, 2017), 38–44.

[128] *Palästinensische Volkskunst* (Berlin: Solidaritätskomitee der DDR, 1978), 1–2.

exhibitions were also deployed as political agitprop to support Third World revolutions, perhaps best noted in the work of Heinz Krüger, Thomas Billhardt and Sybille Bachmann, who published eyewitness accounts of the revolutions in Chile, Vietnam, El Salvador and Nicaragua.[129]

Such radicalizing tendencies were even more pronounced in the case of the anti-apartheid movement. As noted in the chapters on Race and Rights, anti-apartheid helped bridge Eastern Europe and Africa, but the campaign also spilled over into the cultural sphere. Two exhibitions on anti-apartheid organized by the GDR—'Struggle Against Racism and Apartheid and Colonialism' (1974)—featured posters, documentary footage and other material for the GDR public. Eighty GDR artists contributed to the 1978 exposition 'Struggle against Racism and Apartheid in Southern Africa' that took place in the UN Palace of Nations in Geneva.[130] A year later the East German Embassy in Nigeria and the Nigerian government jointly organized an anti-apartheid exhibition. Major-General H. O. Adefope, Nigeria's Honourable Commissioner for Ministry of External Affairs, thanked the GDR for its continued political support, and remarked that apartheid 'is not just the problem of our brothers and sisters in Tanzania, Zimbabwe and Namibia who directly bear the cross of it, nor of the rest of Africa that suffers the crushing humiliation of its continued existence on the continent', but that it is a 'shame to all humanity and a threat to world peace'.[131] Eastern Europeans were singled out for their special cultural engagement, and their continued commitment to the filmic and photographic documentation of imperial and racial violence around the world (as discussed in *War and Peace*) helped to strengthen their ideological alliance.

In the 1970s and 1980s cultural traffic began to reverse direction. Where Eastern Europeans had tended in the 1950s and 1960s to export their culture to the global South, the 1970s and 1980s saw growing importation of culture from Africa, Asia and Latin America into Eastern Europe, most notable where writers, filmmakers, dance choreographers and other cultural figures were concerned. The cultural influence of the Third World within Eastern Europe was especially associated with Latin America, which found its way into Eastern European popular culture. By 1970 some 5 million copies of Latin American novels were in circulation in the USSR, and Gabriel Garcia Marquez's *One Hundred Years of*

---

[129] Hans Krüger and Joachim Umann, *Blende auf für Guinea* (Leipzig: Brockhaus, 1961); Thomas Billhardt, Eberhard Hackethal and Eduard Klein, *Chile, Santiago de Chile: Hoffnung eines Kontinents* (Berlin: Volk und Welt, 1972) and Thomas Billhardt and Peter Jacobs, *Als die Muchachos kamen: Begegnungen in Nikaragua* (Berlin: Militärverlag der DDR, 1982); and Sybille Bachmann, *El Salvador: Ein Volk im revolutionären Kampf* (Berlin: Solidaritätskomitee der DDR, 1985).

[130] *Struggle against Racism and Apartheid in Southern Africa*, exh. brochure for Geneva exhibition (Berlin: 1978), 1, DR123/91, BAB.

[131] Remarks by the Honourable Commissioner for Ministry of External Affairs Major-General H. O. Adefope, at opening of one-week anti-apartheid exhibition,. 25 May 1979, DR 1/17804 (BArch).

Solitude sold over one million copies in translation.[132] Dozens of Latin American folklore groups toured the USSR and East Bloc in the 1960s and 1970s. Films from Latin America, including Argentine musicals, and documentary films of Latin America were extremely successful. In 1971 the Mexican melodrama *Yesenia* was shown in Soviet cinemas, and it set new box office records—over 91 million Soviet cinemagoers saw it, making it by far the most popular film in Soviet history. Latin American soap operas like the Brazilian A *escrava Isaura* (The Slave Isaura) and the Mexican *Los ricos tambien lloran* (The Rich Also Cry) were hugely popular in Russia and across Eastern Europe through the 1980s and beyond.[133] Observers interpreted this trend as a turning away from politics and communal engagement. In her elegiac oral history of post-Soviet Russia, *Second-Hand Time*, Belarussian Nobel Prize writer Svetlana Alexievich registered the political power of these television shows, remarking that 'Mexican soap operas were the perfect replacements for Soviet parades.'[134]

By the same token, the once-inspiring secular ideals of socialist humanity—based on a shared vision of modernity and respect for indigenous heritage, and designed to overcome older imperialist cultural hierarchies—were now being hollowed out by new defensive discourses of civilizational difference and hier-archies. Rejections of universalism were happening more generally: from the mid-1970s onward elites in the developing world voiced growing concern that a reactivated discourse of human rights was really a western-driven ploy to chal-lenge the sovereignty of new states; new regional variations of Human Rights Charters were drafted to defend homegrown traditions and cultural autonomy. Even the great international standard-bearer of universal civilization—UNESCO—began in the 1970s to shift its focus toward the celebration of separate regional civilizations around the world.[135] Within Eastern Europe there emerged a new emphasis on protecting and promoting the heritage of socialist nations as part of an inclusive European civilization. For the USSR and most other Eastern European states, the 1970s witnessed growing pessimism about the diplomatic, economic and cultural windfall from these transcontinental links with the developing world. With the consequence that the 1960s efforts to forge East–South bridges slowly gave way to a new concern with East–West relations in an era of détente.

Such Eastern European geopolitical realignments were not sudden or even openly declared, but the ideological direction of travel was now toward the West. The new rallying cry for overcoming Cold War tensions was a very old one—Europe. The Helsinki Accords of 1975 marked a watershed in the new

[132] Rupprecht, *Soviet Internationalism*, 108.   [133] Ibid., 295.
[134] Svetlana Alexievich, *Second-Hand Time*, trans. Bela Shayevich (London: Fitzcarraldo, 2016), 247.
[135] Bogdan C. Iacob, 'Southeast by Global South: The Balkans, UNESCO and the Cold War', in James Mark, Artemy M. Kalinovsky and Steffi Marung (eds.), *Alternative Globalizations: Eastern Europe and the Postcolonial World* (Bloomington: Indiana University Press, 2019), 251–70.

cultural geography of Eastern Europe. It is well known that the Accords bestowed international blessing on the Red Army's military occupation of Eastern Europe (Basket I), as well as giving fresh life to human rights as a language of reform and grievance (Basket III); but it was the agreed set of scientific, cultural and personal exchanges between Eastern and Western Europe enshrined in the Accords (Basket II) that mattered most in the short term, and did much to undermine the power and durability of the Berlin Wall and Cold War division itself. Diplomatic recon-figurations of Europe found new cultural expression. A European Festival of Friendship was organized in Bucharest as a follow-up to the Helsinki Final Act, and featured contingents from all of the socialist countries of Eastern Europe per-forming a mixture of classical and folk music in the name of a Europe committed to equality between nations and against neocolonialism. The late 1970s gave rise to efforts in the Balkans to showcase its regional archaeological ruins as the patri-mony of the 'true Europe', a continent based on diversity and post-imperial values of cultural autonomy. The high-profile celebrations of the 2,050th anniversary of the first centralized Dacian state in Romania in 1980 and the 1,300th anniversary of the first Bulgarian medieval state in 1980–81 expressly asserted the centrality of Romanians and Bulgarians within European culture through the ruins of antiquity.[136] While the turn toward the invention of ancient national pasts (and an anti-Roman one at that, in the case of Romania) was part of the campaign among late socialist regimes to mobilize patriotism as an instrument of popular support in an era of economic downturn, it also signalled the beginnings of a historic turn away from solidarity with the developing world. Eastern European economic, military and cultural support for African state partners began to dry up, as atten-tion shifted to Western Europe, East Asia and Latin America for cooperation and inspiration.

Such trends continued during Gorbachev's perestroika period. With his rise to power there was much talk about his assertion that the Soviet Union needed to link to the rest of Europe as part of a 'collective European civilization'. While the rhetoric of a 'common European home' had already been mooted by Brezhnev during his 1981 visit to Bonn, Gorbachev made it a central element in his policy of cultural reform. He thus proposed a trans-European identity running across the Iron Curtain. As he put it in his 1987 book *Perestroika*, 'the idea of a common European home most all of suggests a degree of unity, even if the countries belong to different social systems and opposing political-military alliances.'[137] Even if Gorbachev's views were primarily designed to lessen the tensions between East and West, African observers were not wrong to interpret his idea of a 'common

---

[136] Denis Deletant, 'Romania's Return to Europe: Between Politics and Culture', in Raymond Detrez and Barbara Segaert (eds.), *Europe and the Historical Legacy in the Balkans* (Brussels: Peter Lang, 2008), 83–99, and Theodora Dragostinova, *The Cold War from the Margins: A Small Socialist State on the Global Cultural Scene* (Ithaca: Cornell University Press, 2021), chapter 3.

[137] Gorbachev, *Perestroika*, 195.

European home' as a new assertion of Eurocentrism and the recasting of interest from North–South relations to East–West relations instead.[138] A striking example of this new geographical imagination was the famous 'Letter of Six' written in the spring of 1989 by a half-dozen former veterans of the Romanian Politburo, who used the occasion to denounce the economic policies, mismanagement and deterioration of Romania's international status under its dictator Nicolae Ceauşescu. In it they upbraided him for having taken their country 'out of Europe' and for having refused to follow the reformist lead set by their westerly East Bloc neighbours, who for their part had embraced the wind of change embodied in the so-called Helsinki process. In particular, they rejected the country's turn towards Africa in the 1970s as a betrayal of its European status and identity: 'Romania is and remains a European country and as such must advance along with the Helsinki process and not turn against it.' 'You', they continued, 'cannot remove Romania to Africa.'[139]

Another factor behind this continental drift between Eastern Europe and Africa was religion, and most notably a resurgent pan-Islamism. The presence of Christianity in Africa had always been tolerated and even embraced by Eastern European Africanists as a potential stepping stone to state formation and national independence; Islam too was countenanced insofar as it might help with the building of non-western post-colonial governments. Already in the early 1920s, the Soviet Union had reached out to Muslims to drive home the message that Communism and Islam were compatible,[140] and for much of the post-1945 period Muslims had been quite well integrated into socialist states and international socialist ideology in the aftermath of decolonization, with high-ranking Communist Muslims enlisted to help propagate anti-imperialist or non-aligned internationalism.[141] The Soviet Union's friendly policy toward Islam intensified after 1945, and was bound up with publicizing the religious freedom and institutional support that its Muslim citizens supposedly received.[142] Pan-Islamism thus

[138] Charles Quist-Adade, 'From Paternalism to Ethnocentrism: Images of Africa in Gorbachev's Russia', Race and Class, 46/4 (2005), 88.

[139] For the English text see https://chnm.gmu.edu/1989/items/show/698 (last accessed 9 August 2021). Vladimir Tismaneanu, Stalinism for all Seasons: A Political History of Romanian Communism (Berkeley, CA: University of California Press, 2003), 227–9.

[140] John Riddell, To See the Dawn: Baku, 1920—First Congress of the Peoples of the East (New York: Pathfinder, 1993).

[141] Ben Fowkes and Bülent Gökay, 'Unholy Alliance: Muslims and Communists—An Introduction', Journal of Communist Studies and Transition Politics, 25/1 (2009) and Michael Kemper, 'Propaganda for the East, Scholarship for the West: Soviet strategies at the 1960 International Congress of Orientalists in Moscow' and Armina Omerika, 'Competing National Orientalisms: The cases of Belgrade and Sarajevo', in Artemy M. Kalinovsky and Martin Kemper (eds.), Reassessing Orientalism: Interlocking Orientologies during the Cold War (London: Routledge, 2015), 170–210.

[142] Yaacov Ro'i, 'The Role of Islam and the Soviet Muslims in Soviet Arab Policy', Asian and African Studies, 10/2–3 (1974/1975) and K. Dawisha and H. Carrere D'Encausse, 'Islam in the Foreign Policy of the Soviet Union', in A. Dawisha (ed.), Islam in Foreign Policy (Cambridge: Cambridge University Press, 1983). See too Eren Murat Tasar, Soviet and Muslim: The Institutionalization of Islam in Central Asia, 1943–1991, PhD thesis (Harvard University, 2010).

remained a minor development in the first half of the Cold War, at a time when post-colonial nationalism and socialism were the dominant political causes.[143]

The Iranian Islamic Revolution and the Soviet invasion of Afghanistan in 1979 that same year proved a turning point in the relationship between Eastern European socialism and Islam. In the case of Afghanistan, the Soviet Union began to lose its credibility among Muslim elites across the region, who increasingly advocated pan-Islamic internationalism as the best means to redress growing Muslim discontent toward socialist regimes.[144] Estrangement between socialism and Islam was noted in Eastern Europe as well. While the Iranian Revolution was initially welcomed by socialist states, not least for developing new economic links, the Afghan War marked a new division between socialism and political Islam in the eyes of Eastern European elites, including Orientalists, who were caught off guard by these events.[145] Ceauşescu saw the growth of radical Islam as a signifi-cant threat to Europe, and the Eastern European press increasingly characterized Libya, Egypt and Iran as backward-looking, traditionalist, violent and inimical to socialism.[146] The surge in pan-Islamism especially spooked socialist regimes with sizeable Muslim minorities, such as Bulgaria, Yugoslavia and the Soviet Union. Suspicion and hostility toward Muslim minorities (as discussed in *War and Peace*) was accompanied by the affirmation of Eastern Europe's Christian heritage. In the late 1980s the Bulgarian government resorted to archaeology in order to identify the origins of Christian Bulgaria in areas of the country populated by Muslims. Here the intention was to support the claim that the area had been Christian long before Muslims inhabited the Ottoman Empire.[147] The politics of trans-European Christian solidarity could be seen elsewhere as well. In June 1987 King Juan Carlos of Spain visited Budapest, and was taken to the sites at which Spanish troops had fought in the liberation of Buda from the Turks in 1686, a ceremony designed to invoke a shared past between two of Europe's borderland nations and by implication a shared responsibility to protect the continent's Christian heritage against the threat of Islam.[148] The politics of religion and distinct regional civiliza-tions was making a comeback, and the secular ideals of socialist humanity that

---

[143] Richard Wright, *The Color Curtain: A Report on the Bandung Conference* (Cleveland: World Press, 1956).

[144] Zahid Malik, *Re-Emerging Muslim World* (Lahore: Pakistan National Centre, 1974) and more recently, Cemil Aydin, *The Idea of the Muslim World: A Global Intellectual History* (Cambridge: Harvard University Press, 2017), 199–226.

[145] Hanna E. Jansen and Michael Kemper, 'Hijacking Islam: The Search for a New Soviet Interpretation of Political Islam in 1980', in Michael Kemper and Stephan Conermann (eds.), *The Heritage of Soviet Oriental Studies* (London: Routledge, 2011), 125–44.

[146] Zachary T. Irwin, 'The Fate of Islam in the Balkans: A Comparison of Four State Policies', in Pedro Ramet (ed.), *Religion and Nationalism in Soviet and East European Politics* (Durham: Duke University Press, 1989), 378–407.

[147] Lolita Nikolova and Diana Gergova, 'Contemporary Bulgarian Archaeology as a Social Practice in the Later 20th to Early 21st Century', in Lozny, *Archaeology of the Communist Era*, esp. 177–88.

[148] 'Használjuk ki az együttműködés tartalékait', *Magyar Hírlap*, 1 July 1987.

had once united Eastern Europe and the global South were disintegrating. Bridges of connections were now being replaced by boundaries of distance and difference.

This rich story of East European–African cultural relations conveys the ways in which these seemingly incongruous zones of the world were imagined as a shared space of anti-imperial allegiance in a broader Cold War cultural geography. The Eastern European redefinition of the much-maligned concept of civilization was an attempt not only to shed old European imperial value judgements toward the rest of the world in the name of equality and mutual respect, but also to place Eastern and Western Europe on an equal cultural footing so as to overcome Eastern Europe's own sense of under-development and isolation, as well as its colonial complex toward its Western European rival. What distinguished the world of culture from some of the other modes of contact between the Second and Third Worlds discussed in this volume are two things. First was the accent on rendering these cultural encounters visible. Unlike economic or military relations, which often took place beyond the glare of the media or were deliberately hidden from view, these cultural events were always performative, visual and closely tied to media coverage. They were designed to visualize solidarity, to bring closer the achievements, struggles and causes of distant strangers in a new politics of proximity. The second unique feature of culture in this Second–Third World encounter was the blending of modernization and heritage, one in which distant pasts and rural traditions were championed as the building blocks of post-colonial societies around the world. The history of Cold War Eastern Europe's cultural engagement with the developing world from the mid-1950s through the 1980s and beyond reflected the region's changing understanding of its place and purpose in a post-imperial world.

5

Rights

Paul Betts

> *The challenge of the twentieth century is the*
> *conversion of nationalism into internationalism.*[1]
>
> Julius K. Nyerere

An enduring topic of Cold War commentary concerned the intrinsic incompatibility of Eastern Bloc socialism with human rights. For decades western publicists criticized the Soviet Union and its satellite states for ignoring or violating human rights in their national territories, dismissing Communism's touted commitment to these international ideals as cheap lip service used to mask the Orwellian unfreedom and flagrant governmental abuse of Second World authoritarianism. Such incompatibility was attributed either to the principles of Marxism itself,[2] or to the draconian practices of the 'communist establishment', whose 'uncivil society' was judged by the frequency with which it trampled individual liberties and civil rights.[3] What coverage is given to the history of rights in Eastern Europe usually focuses on the unexpected consequences of the legendary 1975 Helsinki Accords, which sparked a nascent civil rights movement across the Eastern Bloc. This movement deftly deployed the new lexicon of human rights to challenge the legitimacy of socialist governments across the region.[4] This episode is generally seen as the moment when human rights were given a new lease on life, insofar as the lofty universalist principles of the 1940s thereby regained momentum east of the Berlin Wall.

I would like to thank James Mark for helpful research references, and to the whole 'Socialism Goes Global' Team for their constructive feedback on earlier drafts of this chapter. Additional thanks go to Robert Moeller, Saul Dubow, Steven Jensen, Sebastian Gehrig, Sam Moyn and Ned Richardson-Little for their helpful comments on an earlier draft, and to Giovanni Cadioli for the Russian language sources.

[1] Julius K. Nyerere, 'The Courage of Reconciliation: The Dag Hammarskjöld Memorial Lecture', in *Freedom and Unity/Uhuru na Umoja: A Selection from Writing and Speeches, 1952–1965* (London: Oxford University Press, 1967), 284.

[2] Leszek Kolakowski, 'Marxism and Human Rights', *Daedalus*, 112 (Fall 1983), 81–92.

[3] Stephen Kotkin, with a contribution by Jan T. Gross, *Uncivil Society: 1989 and the Implosion of the Communist Establishment* (New York: Modern Library, 2009).

[4] Daniel Thomas, *The Helsinki Effect: International Norms, Human Rights and the Demise of Communism* (Princeton: Princeton University Press, 2001).

Paul Betts, *Rights* In *Socialism Goes Global: The Soviet Union and Eastern Europe in the Age of Decolonization.*
Edited by James Mark and Paul Betts, Oxford University Press. © Oxford University Press 2022.
DOI: 10.1093/oso/9780192848857.003.0006

Comparatively less attention has been paid to the Communist understanding of such rights, especially in an international setting. This is a pity, for rights issues were hotly debated themes in the Eastern Bloc from the very beginning, reflecting as they did shifting ideals regarding the relationship between socialist citizen and society. After all, the Soviets were present at the human rights discussions at Nuremberg and San Francisco, and played a key if forgotten role in helping shape such documents as the Genocide Convention and Universal Declaration of Human Rights.[5] The common perception that the Cold War was a battle between a US-sponsored 'empire of liberty' and a Soviet-style 'empire of justice' was also reflected in the divergent views of human rights after 1945.[6]

No less striking are the ways in which small countries engaged with human rights issues; recent scholarship has devoted increasing attention to how small states (such as Panama, Cuba, Chile, Pakistan and Jamaica) played a decisive role in shaping the international understanding of human rights from the drafting of the Universal Declaration in 1948 through the creation of various human rights covenants in the 1960s and 1970s, many of which stressed socio-economic and women's rights within these broader agreements.[7] The same went for smaller socialist Eastern European states—and in particular Yugoslavia—which all high-lighted issues of race and gender as well as social and economic rights to publicize the progressive nature of socialist political life in these rights discussions. Alternative geographies of human rights thus emerged along different global axes. At issue here is how human rights became a point of contact between new allies of Cold War politics, namely Second and Third World elites. These interactions helped Eastern European elites reimagine the identity and relationship of their region to the wider world, as they worked to reposition themselves as exponents of an anti-imperialist 'better Europe' in partnership with the developing world.

Rights discourse also enabled Eastern European countries to distance themselves not only from the West but from China as well in an effort to draw the so-called Second and Third Worlds closer together. From the 1950s through the 1980s human rights became, somewhat surprisingly, became a language of convergence for Eastern European and African representatives at the UN and elsewhere to build new alliances beyond superpower antagonism. Above all, it provided them with a novel idiom of transcontinental solidarity anti-imperial activism. International organizations served as key fora for exchanging ideas and building new alliances in the international community around rights advocacy. This essay will concentrate on United Nations debates within the General Assembly and the less high-profile Advisory 'Third' Committee, which addressed human rights issues, with a specific

---

[5] Francine Hirsch, 'The Soviets at Nuremberg: International Law, Propaganda, and the Making of the Postwar Order', *American Historical Review*, 113/3 (2008), 701–30.

[6] Odd Arne Westad, *The Global Cold War* (New York: Cambridge University Press, 2007), 8–72.

[7] Susan Waltz, 'Universalizing Human Rights: The Role of Small States in the Construction of the Universal Declaration of Human Rights', *Human Rights Quarterly*, 23/1 (2001), 44–72.

focus on how three key international controversies—the Hungarian Uprising of 1956, the Congo Crisis of 1960–61 and South African apartheid—led to the recasting of diplomatic relations between the Second and Third World around the issues of anti-imperialism, international justice and political sovereignty.

The Cold War, Communism and Human Rights

After 1945 Communist advocates championed an expansive conception of human rights. However, economic, social and cultural rights were accorded secondary status in the Universal Declaration, as clearly noted in the debates about the ordering of the Articles. The first three Articles reflected the tradition of French liberty, equality and fraternity, with Articles 4–21 on civil and political rights, followed by Articles 22–26 on economic, social and cultural rights. The Soviet Union insisted that rights could not be conceived of outside the state, and that rights were thus coterminous with the state. Eastern European delegates fell in line, arguing in the 1948 UN General Assembly that the 'social status of the individual' was the 'result of the social and economic conditions in which the individual lives. That means that the civil and political status of the individual has become in a very great measure dependent upon his social status.'[8] Various representatives from the developing world, in particular the Chilean and Indian delegates, concurred that self-determination should have its economic and political dimensions as well. On these points Eleanor Roosevelt, who chaired the meetings of the UN's Human Rights Commission, had no sympathy with the Eastern European and Third World positions, countering that the state was not the agent to guarantee the fulfilment of these broader rights, and that social, economic and cultural rights therefore did not enjoy any legal status. Motions to put the set of social and economic rights on an equal footing with political and civil rights were supported by the majority of Latin American states and all of the Eastern European Communist states. They were ultimately defeated, prompting some commentators to describe the Soviet Union and its allies as 'the major losers in the human rights sweepstakes.'[9] That may have been so in this particular vote, but this Second–Third World solidarity intensified with time.

At first the Eastern European countries in particular hardly looked like staunch champions of the Universal Declaration. Leaving aside the details behind the arduous negotiations surrounding the Declaration itself,[10] it was widely noted

---

[8] Mr Radovanovic (Yugoslavia), General Assembly Official Records, Third Committee, 183rd Plenary Meeting, 10 December 1948, 58–9, quoted in Roger Normand and Sarah Zaidi, *Human Rights at the UN: The Political History of Universal Justice* (Bloomington: Indiana University Press, 2008), 190.

[9] Normand and Zaidi, *Human Rights at the UN*, 216–18, 191 and 194.

[10] Daniel Whelan, *Indivisible Human Rights: A History* (Philadelphia: University of Pennsylvania Press, 2010); Philip Alston, 'Does the Past Matter: On the Origins of Human Rights', *Harvard Law*

that all of the Communist countries represented at the UN in 1948 (Belarus, Ukraine, the Soviet Union, Czechoslovakia, Poland and Yugoslavia), together with Saudi Arabia and South Africa, abstained from the final vote on ratifying the document. The Czechoslovak representative airily dismissed the Declaration as 'neither bold nor modern', on the grounds that it was not comprehensive enough.[11] According to Hungarian legal philosopher Imre Szabó, the Eastern Bloc countries abstained not because they were opposed to human rights in principle; rather, it was due to the Declaration's failure to state the explicit duties of citizens along with rights; to the non-binding nature of the declaration; and to the western countries' refusal to condemn Fascism and colonialism in the document.[12] The vote put the East at loggerheads with the West over human rights issues for years to come. In fact, the US and Great Britain blocked the accession of Poland, Hungary and Romania to the UN precisely because they were deemed in breach of human rights in these countries. Bulgaria drafted a new constitution in 1947 in response to the criticisms, and incorporated (albeit vaguely) a number of political, social, economic and cultural rights protections into law. Even so, its admission to the UN was delayed until 1955. And when Bulgaria was finally admitted, there was precious little Bulgarian press coverage or academic commentary about its membership; instead, national coverage of Bulgaria's relation to the UN centred on nuclear disarmament, decolonization, western rights abuses and later anti-apartheid.[13] The ratification of the Universal Declaration enjoyed little resonance in the Eastern Bloc and Soviet Union: it was published in nineteen languages around the world, though Eastern European translations were few among them.[14] UN human rights covenants and provisions also did not exert influence in any East European domestic legal system until the Helsinki Accords, and then only cursorily; nonetheless, they did play a key role in international diplomacy.

By the late 1940s human rights was emerging as a political football of Cold War ideological rivalry between East and West. Tales of injustice, misery and unhappiness were sensationalized on both sides of the Iron Curtain to showcase the superiority of their respective systems.[15] In that decade the Soviet Union showed fresh interest in human rights talk. While Stalin toed a classic Marxist line in

Review, 126/7 (2013), 2043–81 and Glenn Tatsuya Mitoma, 'Civil Society and International Human Rights: The Commission to Study the Organization of Peace and the Origins of the UN Human Rights Regime', *Human Rights Quarterly*, 30/3 (2008), 607–30.

[11] *Yearbook of the United Nations, 1948–1949* (Lake Success, NY: United Nations, 1950), 533.

[12] Gábor Halmai and Eszter Polgári, 'Hungary: The Impact of the Freedom of Expression', in Vinodh Jaichand and Markku Suksi (eds.), *60 Years of the Universal Declaration of Human Rights in Europe* (Antwerp: Intersentia, 2009), 179; Johannes Morsink, *The Universal Declaration of Human Rights: Origins, Drafting, and Intent* (Philadelphia: University of Pennsylvania Press, 1999), 3.

[13] Maria Mandova, 'Bulgaria: Evolving Democracy under the UDHR Template', in Jaichand and Suksi, *60 Years*, 147–60.

[14] Jan Holzer and Hubert Smekal, 'The Czech Republic: From Lip Service to Concrete Application', in Jaichand and Suksi, *60 Years*, 307.

[15] Mary Dudziak, *Cold War Civil Rights* (Princeton: Princeton University Press, 2000), 19–46.

dismissing the UN Declaration as a bourgeois ruse by western states to dress up class-based privileges as universal rights, surprising transformations took place under Khrushchev. The Soviets had initially harboured deep scepticism toward international organizations—not only concerning the League and the UN, but also the ILO, UNESCO, the Red Cross and the WHO. Yet in the course of the 1960s the Soviet Union began to embrace these organizations, seeing them as offering opportunities to build up its international profile and influence international opinion,[16] and the presence of UN literature within the USSR grew with time.[17] The shift of attitude was largely spurred by two developments: the first had to do with the seismic global trend toward decolonization and the emergence of a new language of liberation and rights for all, as the Soviets and Eastern Europeans began to bundle the universalist lexicon of human rights with self-determination and national sovereignty so as to win ideological support in Asia and Africa. Such human rights politicking was particularly prominent through the 1960s, though it faded with détente in the 1970s. The Belgrade editor-in-chief of the Yugoslav party weekly *Komunist*, Gavro Altman, emphasized that support of African and Asian countries was losing its importance because sovereignty no longer needed to be defended in an era of détente.[18] But until that time, Eastern Europeans and Third World rights advocates endeavoured to recast the meaning of human rights in an anti-colonial framework. Secondly, Eastern Europeans warmed to human rights issues precisely at the moment when the US was distancing itself from human rights talk in the 1950s, given its own civil rights problems in the American South. Domestic factors were important too, as the introduction of this new interest in rights was greeted as a welcome manifestation of destalinization. This was particularly so in light of the much-vaunted concept of 'socialist legality'— Khrushchev's rejection of Stalin's abuses and arbitrary rule in favour of a state governed by procedural norms and rationalized rule. Citizens' rights were to play a key role in this new socialist legal culture, signalling that the regime was moving from a state based on terror and coercion to one founded on persuasion and participation. With it, rights claims flourished in the USSR under Khrushchev as never before, and on a range of different levels.[19] A Human Rights Day was even consecrated in the Soviet Union in 1957.[20]

Soviet human rights talk was neither strictly for export nor confined to the UN and the Anglophone international public sphere. The Soviet Union played up international events as sensationalized human right abuses, and covered them

[16] Chris Osakwe, *The Participation of the Soviet Union in Universal International Organizations* (Leiden: AW Sijthoff, 1972).

[17] Alexander Dallin, *The Soviet Union at the United Nations* (London: Methuen, 1962), 88–94.

[18] Gavro Altman, 'Odjek', *Komunist* [Sarajevo], 7 (April, 1972), 1–15.

[19] Benjamin Nathans, 'Soviet Rights Talk in the Post-Stalin Era', in Stefan-Ludwig Hoffmann (ed.), *Human Rights in the Twentieth Century* (Cambridge: Cambridge University Press, 2011), 166–90.

[20] Jennifer Amos, 'Embracing and Contesting: The Soviet Union and the Universal Declaration of Human Rights, 1948–1958', in Hoffmann, *Human Rights*, 147–65.

regularly in *Pravda*. This started in the late 1950s in connection with Soviet peace politics and its support for protests in Africa and Asia against nuclear bomb testing. One 1958 article addressed to the UN Commission for Human Rights showed this early Soviet human rights politicking: 'The peoples of the countries of Asia and Africa are opposed to carrying out such a test anywhere and ever. We appeal to international public opinion, to the UN and to the Human Rights Commission to prevent such tests, especially those expected to be carried out in the near future in Africa.'[21] *Pravda* also reported on the work of the 'International Federation for the Struggle for Human Rights', especially in connection with protests against the arrest of Greek anti-fascist Manolis Glezos. In another 1959 piece *Pravda* reprinted the letter from the Worldwide Federation of Democratic Youth to the Greek Government and the UN Secretary General, condemning Glezos's sentencing as 'a serious attack on human rights'. A few days later *Pravda* dedicated most of its fifth page to an article entitled 'Ideas do not shackle! Greek authorities violate human rights.'[22] Similar press coverage was used to condemn the maltreatment of 'Spanish patriots' incarcerated by Franco two years later.[23] Not surprisingly, trade union rights emerged as a pet human rights issue in *Pravda*'s coverage of international politics too.[24]

By the early 1960s, and in the wake of decolonization, *Pravda* stepped up its coverage of human rights issues. Wide publicity was given to those Third World leaders who at every available opportunity extolled the USSR as the champion of human rights. For example, when Brezhnev—as part of his high-profile tour of Africa in 1964—visited Guinea, *Pravda* devoted a long article to the thanks offered by Guinean president Seko Touré to the USSR for being an 'untiring and consistent champion of our human rights and a natural ally of all oppressed peoples'.[25] Over the course of the decade the coverage shifted more toward anti-colonialism, anti-racism and anti-apartheid, targeting South Africa and the American South as human rights abusers. One 1962 *Pravda* article demanded that 'the United Nations should take effective measures to ensure that the population of South Africa enjoys the basic rights and freedoms, included in the Declaration of Human Rights.' Another 1964 article featured on its first page a letter of Brezhnev to the South African authorities in which the Soviet leader appealed to the Government to 'respect the human rights of the fighters', in reference to a number of activists there condemned to death.[26] In the 1970s *Pravda* further intensified its human rights rhetoric, insisting that 'socialist democracy' was the

[21] 'Ne Dopustit' Ispytanii Iadernogo Oruzhia v Afrike', *Pravda*, 20 May 1958, 3.
[22] 'Protesty protiv aresta Manolisa Glezosa', *Pravda*, 8 December 1958, 5, 'Pokushenie na prava cheloveka', *Pravda*, 31 July 1959, 6, and 'Idei ne zakovat' v kandaly!', *Pravda*, 24 July 1959, 5.
[23] 'V zashchitu ispanskih patriotov', *Pravda*, 27 March 1961, 3.
[24] 'O Sozyve V Vsemirogo kongressa profsoiuzov, *Pravda*, 7 February 7, 1961, 3.
[25] 'Grandioznï Miting v Konakri', *Pravda*, 13 February 1961, 3.
[26] 'Protiv Rasizma i terrora', *Pravda*, 7 February 1962, 6, and 'Spasti bortsov za prava cheloveka', *Pravda*, 20 April 1964, 1.

guarantor of human rights,[27] and focused on international human rights scandals—especially South Africa and Chile—to drive home this point.[28] The new Soviet Constitution of 1977 served as another pretext to broadcast the USSR's commitment to human rights to its domestic audience.[29] The larger point is that human rights discussion in the USSR was articulated and publicized on the pages of the country's major daily newspaper in connection with Third World events, broadcasting these issues and human rights language for a domestic audience long before East–West focus on the Helsinki Accords.

By the end of the 1960s, legal theorists in Eastern Europe had rewritten the history of human rights to portray revolutionary socialism as its mainspring.[30] Official accounts elided the socialist Bloc's abstention on the Universal Declaration as they began to portray socialist states as having been at the forefront of ensuring its passage: 'The imperialist powers consistently did everything they could to prevent the insertion of democratic clauses in the Pacts on Human Rights. With the passage of years, however, the proposals made by the representatives of the Soviet Union and other socialist countries, as well as the non-aligned Afro-Asian countries, gained increasing support.'[31] This reimagining of the recent past coincided with Eastern Bloc participation in the UN's International Year for Human Rights in 1968, which sparked a boom in socialist human rights theorization that carried on into the 1970s.[32]

Nevertheless, it was the international dimension of human rights discourse that mattered most. In this context the United Nations became a key platform to broadcast the socialist cause internationally, and to help forge relationships across continents in the 1960s, embracing Africa and Asia. An early point of contact between the Second and Third World in regard to human rights was gender. To be sure, the relationship between women's rights and human rights long predates the Cold War. It was championed at various moments in the late nineteenth and early twentieth century, and the nexus between socialism and feminism had been a central—if contentious—feature of leftist political thought in the interwar years, associated with Rosa Luxemburg, Clara Zetkin, Beatrice Webb and Margaret Sanger, among others. Gender equality was formally integrated into the Universal Declaration of Human Rights in 1948. To advance the international socialist cause, the Women's International Democratic Federation (WIDF) was

---

[27] 'Sotsialisticheskaia Demokratiia – garantiia prav cheloveka', *Pravda*, 28 September 1973, 3.

[28] 'Zashchit' prava cheloveka v Chili!', *Pravda*, 11 December 1974, 5 and 'Popiraiutsia prava cheloveka', *Pravda*, 2 March 1977, 5.

[29] 'Sotsializm – znamenosets prav cheloveka', *Pravda*, 10 December 1978, 1.

[30] Paul Betts, 'Socialism, Social Rights, Human Rights: The Case of East Germany', *Humanity*, 3/3 (Winter 2012), 407–26.

[31] Anatoly P. Movchan, 'The Human Rights Problem in Present-Day International Law', in G.I. Tunkin (ed.), *Contemporary International Law* (Moscow: Progress Publishers, 1969), 242–3.

[32] Ned Richardson-Little, *The Human Rights Dictatorship: Socialism, Global Solidarity and Revolution in East Germany* (Cambridge: CUP, 2019), esp. 97–178.

founded in 1945 in Paris, with strong links to the Soviet Union. The WIDF was active in organizing congresses in the late 1940s to raise awareness of women's rights internationally. Peace, women's rights, anti-colonialism and anti-racism were its central areas of concern. National chapters of the WIDF hailed from some forty countries in 1945; by 1958 member organizations had been established in over seventy countries, rising to 117 by 1985.

In 1947 the WIDF was granted consultative status within both the UN's Economic and Social Council (ECOSOC) and the Commission on the Status of Women. It organized fact-finding missions to Latin America and southeast Asia to research women's lives there and to make contact with local women's organizations, and engaged in anti-imperial politics around the world.[33] The WIDF even inspired the creation of other national chapters in various countries in the early 1950s to fight for women's rights locally, such as the Democratic Union of Cameroonian Women.[34] And unlike other international women's organizations, the WIDF featured women from all parts of the world in leadership positions from the very beginning, especially from Asia, Eastern Europe and Africa.[35] However, the federation soon fell foul of Cold War politics, and suffered the consequences in terms of publicity and links to the UN. In 1950 it spearheaded a fact-finding mission to investigate war crimes against Korean civilians, especially women and children, committed by American and South Korean soldiers in the conflict. It drafted a high-profile report in 1951 called *Korea: We Accuse!*, which was translated into twenty languages and sent to the United Nations.[36] It caused a furore, and the organization became a target of an anti-Communist campaign within the UN, led by the US and Great Britain. Afterwards it lost its consultative status, and was only readmitted to the UN in 1967.[37] In 1951 the federation was forced to move its headquarters from Paris to East Berlin, and became increasingly linked with the World Peace Council, which strengthened a widespread

---

[33] Celia Donert, 'From Communist Internationalism to Human Rights: Gender, Violence, and International Law in the Women's International Democratic Federation Mission to North Korea, 1951', *Contemporary European History*, 25/2 (2016), 320. Melanie Ilic, 'Soviet Women, Cultural Exchange and the Women's International Democratic Federation', in Sari Autio-Sarasmo and Katrin Miklossy (eds.), *Reassessing Cold War Europe* (London: Routledge, 2010), 163.

[34] Meredith Terretta, *Petitioning for Our Rights, Fighting for our Nation: The History of the Democratic Union of Cameroonian Women, 1949–1960* (Langaa: RPCIG, 2013), 105–8.

[35] Cheryl Johnson-Odim, '"For Their Freedoms": The Anti-Imperialist and International Feminist Activity of Funmilayo Ransome-Kuti of Nigeria', *Women's Studies International Forum*, 32 (2009), 51–9.

[36] *Korea: We Accuse! Report of the Commission of the Women's International Democratic Federation in Korea, May 10–27, 1951* (Berlin: WIDF, 1951). For discussion, Celia Donert, 'From Communist Internationalism to Human Rights', 313–33 and Jadwiga Pieper Mooney, 'Fighting Fascism and Forging New Political Activism: The Women's International Democratic Federation in the Cold War', in JP Mooney and Fabio Lanza (eds.), *De-Centering Cold War History: Local and Global Change* (London: Routledge, 2013), 52–72.

[37] Francisca de Haan, 'The Women's International Democratic Federation (WIDF): History, Main Agenda and Contributions, 1945–1991' http://wasi.alexanderstreet.com/help/view/the_womens_ international_democratic_federation_widf_history_main_agenda_and_contributions_19451991.

perception that the WIDF was a Soviet front organization.[38] Still, it remained engaged in a range of gender issues, particularly in Asia,[39] as well as in relation to the Algerian and Vietnam Wars.[40] The World Congress of Women, held in Moscow in 1962, was another effort to broaden the support for women's rights across the socialist world, and the WIDF continued to do its work in internationalizing the issues of women's rights as human rights in the 1950s and 1960s, though its international impact became much more muted after its expulsion from the UN. Gender equality was very low on the rights agenda for these new Asian and African countries, and gender itself seems to have been less a point of convergence at the UN than other issues, as we shall see. In any case, the chequered response to gender issues underscored the limitations of cooperative rights work between Eastern Europe and the developing world in the early postwar period.

Anti-imperialism and the struggle for sovereignty provided the most powerful platform for co-operation. Early efforts to build alliances between Eastern Europe and the Third World around the issue of rights in the late 1940s at the UN were further galvanized by the brutal western 're-colonization' of Asia and Africa after 1945. This was certainly so with the Dutch East Indies and Indochina, as the period 1945-60 was arguably the most violent period of Dutch 'developmental colonialism'.[41] And in the period 1947–58 France 'invested more public funds in its colonial empire than it had during the entire period from 1880 to the outbreak of World War II'.[42] The Sétif massacre in Algeria on 8 May 1945—the colonial corollary of VE Day—infamously claimed an estimated 15,000–45,000 Algerian lives. The British and Western European defence of empire undermined the hallowed values that supposedly defined the West in its fight against Fascism. Eastern European representatives recognized common interests with the colonized, in part because they belonged to a region which had itself been recently occupied and whose countries' borders continued to be contested by the West even after the Second World War. In a pamphlet entitled *Self-Determination: Good Slogan in Bad Hands*, the Czech Antonín Snejdárek linked the cause of global decolonization

[38] Francisca De Haan, 'Continuing Cold War Paradigms in Western Historiography of Transnational Women's Organisations: the case of the Women's International Democratic Federation (WIDF)', *Women's History Review*, 19/4 (September 2010), 547–73.

[39] Katharine Mcgregor, 'Indonesian Women, the Women's International Democratic Federation and the Struggle for Women's Rights, 1946–1965', *Indonesia and the Malay World*, 40/117 (2012), 193–208.

[40] Katharine McGregor, 'Opposing Colonialism: the Women's International Democratic Federation and decolonisation struggles in Vietnam and Algeria 1945–1965', *Women's History Review*, 25/6 (2016), 1–20.

[41] Osterhammel, *Colonialism*, 37–8.

[42] Fabian Klose, *Human Rights in the Shadow of Colonial Violence: The Wars of Independence in Kenya and Algeria* (Philadelphia: University of Pennsylvania Press, 2013), 54–5.

with the protection of postwar Eastern European borders from western revanchism which, he argued, recalled Nazi-era efforts to conquer the East.[43]

British and French insistence on the so-called 'colonial clause' in the UN Charter as a means of maintaining imperial rule in their dominions helped the Soviet Union and its allies forge new links with the Third World during the early UN General Assemblies, and Eastern European representatives often took the lead in condemning colonialism. Africans and Eastern Europeans also jointly condemned the western-led abolition of the The United Nations War Crime Commission (1943–48). This had once rivalled the Nuremberg Trial as a space for the prosecution of war criminals, and helped Ethiopia in its attempts to obtain justice for war crimes committed by Italy after the invasion in 1935: for this reason, western governments feared that the commission might eventually provide a space for prosecuting their own rights violations in colonies. Such moral alliance-building could be seen in the late 1940s UN discussion of the Convention for the Suppression of the Traffic in Persons and the Exploitation of the Prostitution of Others. These debates brought together Soviet and Eastern European delegates alongside their counterparts from newly decolonized countries (notably India and Pakistan) to secure the passage of the international convention in 1949, which was also notable for being the first international document to remove the colonial clause from its application.[44] In another 1950 UN debate, the Polish representative, for example, pointed out western hypocrisy regarding human rights by saying that

> History is repeating itself: the most ardent defenders of human rights are forgetting those rights when they affect the colonial question. They press for the inclusion of the colonial clause because they wish to perpetuate a position of inferiority, oppression, and arbitrary exploitation in their colonies. It is a joke in bad taste to say that it is necessary to await the opinion of the peoples of the Non-Governing Territories as to whether or not they wish to be granted human rights.[45]

Delegates from the Philippines and Chile added their support, declaiming that the West's 'civilizing mission should finally come to an end.'[46] As early as 1951

---

[43] Antonín Snejdárek, *Self-determination; Good Slogan in Bad Hands* (Prague: Orbis; 1961). Lora Wildenthal, 'Rudolf Laun and the Human Rights of Germans in Occupied and Early West Germany', in Hoffmann, *Human Rights*, 125–46.

[44] Sonja Dolinsek and Philippa Hetherington, 'Socialist Internationalism and Decolonizing Moralities in the UN Anti-Trafficking Regime, 1947–1954', *Journal of the History of International Law*, 21/2 (2019), 212–38.

[45] Mr Altman (Poland), 'General Assembly, Third Committee, Summary Records', General Assembly document A/C.3/SR.295, 1950, 158, cited in Normand and Zaidi, *Human Rights at the UN*, 231.

[46] Normand and Zaidi, *Human Rights at the UN*, 232.

human rights were explicitly used by Egypt and other African and Asian countries to make anti-imperial arguments against the French in Morocco.[47]

In these anti-imperial pronouncements, the universalism of human rights blended with calls for a universal principle of international justice. For anti-colonial elites around the world, the key document was not the 1948 Universal Declaration, but rather the Atlantic Charter of 1941. The electrifying reception accorded the Atlantic Charter in Africa was recounted by Nigerian intellectual and eventual President of Independent Nigeria Nnamdi Azikiwe in his *The Atlantic Charter and British West Africa*.[48] In his memoirs, Nelson Mandela later recalled the power of the Atlantic Charter's affirmed democratic principles and faith in the dignity of every human being for those involved in the South African struggle for freedom; as he put it, 'some in the West saw the Charter as empty promises, but not those of us in Africa', since we 'hoped that government and ordinary South Africans would see the principles they were fighting for in Europe were the same ones we were advocating at home'.[49] The recognition of the revolutionary implications of the Atlantic Charter was hardly limited to African intellectuals. In his 1942 book *The Atlantic Charter*, Polish intellectual Stanisław Stroński also saw the link between people repressed by the Axis Powers and those under the thumb of colonial powers.[50] The Charter inspired widespread commentary, and it was the universalism of its claims that proved so attractive. Its Allied Eight-Point programme was intended to serve as the new foundation for civilization itself,[51] and was to be applied to all regions of the globe.[52] A Committee on 'Africa, the War and Peace Aims' was created in the US, featuring the likes of Ralph Bunche and W. E. B. Du Bois, with the aim of applying the Charter's principles to Africa as well.[53] After the war, its principles were immediately picked up around the world, from Algeria to Indochina. It was no surprise that colonial powers sought to restrict its reach: Churchill had argued in 1941 that the Atlantic Charter should only be applied to those under Nazi rule in western and eastern Europe, and not to Europe's colonies. There was thus a genuine nervousness about the danger of the Atlantic Charter; in one directive for the North African Arabic Services of the BBC, all references to the Atlantic Charter were to be avoided.[54]

[47] Evan Luard, *History of the UN*, vol. 2: *The Age of Decolonization, 1955–1965* (Basingstoke: Palgrave, 1989), 78–9.

[48] Nnamdi Azikiwe, *The Atlantic Charter and British West Africa* (Lagos, 1943), 12.

[49] Nelson Mandela, *Long Walk to Freedom: The Autobiography of Nelson Mandela* (Boston: Little Brown, 1995), 95–6.

[50] Stanislaw Stronski, *The Atlantic Charter* (Bombay: Indo-Polish Library, 1945).

[51] Julia E. Johnson, ed., *The 'Eight Points' of Post-War World Reorganization* (New York: H. W. Wilson, Co., 1942).

[52] Julius Stone, *The Atlantic Charter: New Worlds for Old* (Sydney: Current Book Distributors, 1943).

[53] Committee on Africa, the War and Peace Aims (ed.), *The Atlantic Charter and Africa from an American Standpoint* (New York: Committee of Africa, the War and Peace Aims, 1942), discussion in Klose, *Human Rights*, 23.

[54] Klose, *Human Rights*, 31.

But for activists from the developing world, including those at the UN, self-determination was the universal basis of human rights.

Human rights featured in the debate on colonialism at the famed 1955 Bandung Conference.[55] The years following the conference saw a new link established between human rights and African independence. For example, Kenyan nationalist Joseph Murumbi returned from Bandung to condemn colonialism on the basis of violations of the Universal Declaration.[56] President Julius Nyerere of Tanzania was a key advocate of human rights in Africa, and mentioned them in a number of his speeches.[57] In his Independence Address at the United Nations, Nyerere stressed that 'we shall try to use the Universal Declaration of Human Rights as a basis for both our external and our internal policies.'[58] Tanzania became a leading light of human rights advocacy under Nyerere's leadership.[59] In 1958 Kwame Nkrumah hosted the Accra Conference for independent African states, designed to reverse the legacy of the infamous Congress of Berlin. As Ghanaian diplomat Alex Quaison-Sackey put it: 'The European powers had met in 1885 to dismember Africa; the African states in 1958 to unify Africa.' At the conference human rights was a key point of discussion.[60] By the early 1960s, the UN Declaration had been integrated into the constitutions of more than twenty African states.[61] This was especially notable in newly decolonized countries, such as Cameroon, Chad, Niger, Senegal, Upper Volta, Togo and Mali, though there was a wide variety of rights—social, economic, political, human—featured in the various individual constitutions. There were some interesting constitutional hybrids. While the preamble to the Algerian Constitution of 1962 was modelled on China's, it also incorporated elements from both the French constitution and the Universal

---

[55] Christopher J. Lee, (ed.), *Making a World after Empire: The Bandung Moment and its Political Afterlives* (Athens, OH: University of Ohio Press, 2010) and Roland Burke, *Decolonization and the Evolution of Human Rights* (Philadelphia: University of Pennsylvania Press, 2010), 13–34. See too Robert Vitalis, 'The Midnight Ride of Kwame Nkrumah and Other Fables of Bandung (Ban-doong)', *Humanity*, 4/2 (Summer 2013), 261–88.

[56] Bethwell A. Ogot, 'Mau Mau and Nationhood: The Untold Story', in ES Atieno Odhiambo and John Lonsdale (eds.), *Mau Mau and Nationhood: Arms, Authority and Narration* (Athens, OH: Ohio University Press, 2003), 23ff.

[57] Julius Nyerere, 'Individual Human Rights', in his *Freedom and Unity/Uhuru na Umoja: A Selection from Writings and Speeches, 1952-1965* (Dar es Salaam: Oxford University Press, 1966), 70 and 139.

[58] Julius Nyerere, 'Independence Address to the United Nations (14 December 1961)', 'The African and Democracy (1961)', in *Freedom and Unity/Uhuru na Umoja: A Selection from Writing and Speeches, 1952-1965* (London: Oxford University Press, 1967), 146. See also Samuel Moyn, *The Last Utopia: Human Rights in History* (Cambridge: Harvard University Press, 2010), 110–11.

[59] Meredith Terretta, 'From Below and to the Left? Human Rights and Liberation Politics in Africa's Postcolonial Age', *Journal of World History*, 24/2 (2013), 401.

[60] Alex Quaison-Sackey, *Africa Unbound: Reflections of an African Statesman* (New York: Praeger, 1963), 135, 70–3.

[61] Egon Schwelb, *Human Rights and the International Community* (Chicago: Quadrangle Books, 1963), 51. See too Charles OH Parkinson, *Bills of Rights and Decolonization: The Emergence of Domestic Human Rights Instruments in Britain's Overseas Territories* (Oxford: Oxford University Press, 2008), 17.

Declaration of Human Rights. Other former French colonies, such as Guinea and Mali, explicitly referred to the UNDHR in their constitutions, while socialist ideology influenced the constitutions of Angola, Cape Verde, Mozambique and Vietnam. The Nigerian Constitution of 1960 used the 1950 (West) European Convention as a model, with provisions for freedom from torture, freedom from discrimination and the right to family life. In fact, the conservative and anti-Communist European Convention served as a model of independence constitutions for many new African countries inspired by the Nigerian example, including Kenya, Swaziland and Zimbabwe.[62] Moses Kotane, a South African anti-apartheid activist who also attended Bandung, used rights language to condemn apartheid, and helped draft the ANC Charter. In this case rights were imagined in a more expansive way, stressing the freedom of the individual versus the state, the end of apartheid, as well as social rights predicated on justice and equality—all of which was to contribute to the creation of a new South Africa 'based on the will of the people'.[63] Human rights had become commonplace in anti-colonial political discourse among African elites, and they were integrated into the political constitutions of every newly decolonized country in Africa in the 1960s.

Bandung was significant in other ways, especially in terms of Eastern Europe-Third World relations. For one thing, the conference prompted Khrushchev to go on tour, and his first port of call was Yugoslavia. Tito had good relations with the countries that participated in Bandung, having visited India, Burma, Egypt and Ethiopia earlier that year. Khrushchev was in Belgrade the week before the Bandung Conference, and in a joint declaration in June 1955, the Soviet Union and Yugoslavia noted how the conference strengthened the cause of world peace. The UN was also very important for Yugoslavia. Having been cut adrift by the Soviet Union on the international scene, Yugoslavia looked to the UN as a forum to advance the role of small states. Indeed, it sought to mobilize other small states so as to render the UN a check upon the great powers. In this sense, the UN served as a 'Yugoslav bridge to the Third World'.[64] Khrushchev's well-publicized visit to Belgrade in 1955 and his apology to the Yugoslav leader for Stalin's expulsion of the republic in 1948 did much to boost his prestige in the eyes of the developing world. In the early 1950s Yugoslavia sided with Iran and Iraq in the UN during their oil disputes with Great Britain, and supported Algerian independence against the French. As early as 1947 Belgrade argued in favour of India's resolution to protect the besieged Indian minority in South Africa.[65] Yugoslavia

---

[62] Julian Go, 'Modeling States and Sovereignty: Postcolonial Constitutions in Asia and Africa', in Lee, *Making a World*, 120–2, 128–30.

[63] Text of Freedom Charter reprinted in Thomas Karls and Gwendolyn M. Carter, (eds.), *From Protest to Challenge: A Documentary History of African Politics in South Africa, 1862–1964* (Palo Alto: Stanford University Press, 1987), 205–8.

[64] Alvin Z. Rubinstein, *Yugoslavia and the Non-Aligned World* (Princeton: Princeton University Press, 1970), 37.

[65] Ibid., 17–18.

also highlighted its independent status by criticizing Soviet abuses of rights. In 1950, for example, the Yugoslav UN delegation declared that it would not oppose 'an international investigation into the systematic violations of human rights and fundamental freedoms in Bulgaria, Hungary and Romania'.[66] This version of human rights was adopted by small states in Eastern Europe as a defence of self-determination and sovereignty in the international arena.

It is worth remembering that there was also an anti-Soviet aspect to Bandung. There, a number of delegates criticized the USSR as an imperial power, despite its propaganda to the contrary. Iraqi Foreign Minister Fadhel Jamali claimed that 'Today the Communist world has subjected races in Asia and Eastern Europe on a much larger scale than any old colonial power... Under the old form of colonialism, there is some chance of one hearing the cries of pain of the subjugated peoples. Under Communist domination, however, no such cries are permitted to be heard.'[67] With it Jamail was imagining new symmetries between Eastern Europe and the Third World, and such logic served as a key part of this small state solidarity across continents. For this reason, the conference attendees took Khrushchev's loud claim that the Bandung Conference was really only corroboration of his own anti-colonial views with a large grain of salt.[68] Among many of those Third World UN delegates there was widespread scepticism regarding the role of the Soviet Union, which they saw as simply an imperial power in disguise.

Hungary 1956

The Soviet invasion of Hungary in November 1956 only confirmed these suspicions. The Uprising which had provoked it was in part a protest against Soviet control, and brought Eastern Europe to the centre of the global debate about the nature of colonialism and the right to sovereignty. The Communist leader whose reforms had helped spark the revolt, Imre Nagy, was himself inspired by the reinvigoration of anti-colonialism at Bandung: his 1956 *In Defence of the New Course* featured a whole chapter on the applicability of Bandung's principles, including neutrality. He argued that the 'Panch Shila'—the Sanskrit term for the 'five virtues' of Peaceful Co-existence—needed to be applied to relations within the socialist camp as much as to 'the battle between two systems'.[69] The Yugoslav leader Tito, who had broken with the Soviets eight years earlier, also saw what

---

[66] United Nations, General Assembly, Ad Hoc Political Committee, Official Records, Fifth Session (1951), 34, cited in ibid., 125–6.

[67] Opening Address of Iraq, in Hassan, Collected Documents from the Asian-African Conference, 65, quoted in Burke, Decolonization, 28.

[68] Nikita Khrushchev, 'On Peaceful Coexistence', Foreign Affairs, 38/1 (October 1959), 10.

[69] Imre Nagy, On Communism, in Defense of the New Course (New York: F. A. Praeger, 1957), 20, 23.

advantage there might be in applying the main principles of the 1955 Bandung Conference to Eastern Europe. Yet eventually he would temper his initial enthusiasm toward the 1956 Uprising, mindful of its potential to inspire nationalist revolts across the Yugoslav federation. In particular, he feared that Hungarian nationalist violence could spread to Yugoslavia's own sizeable Hungarian minority.[70] Over the following decades, the question of how far the principle of self-determination asserted at Bandung applied to the republics within Yugoslavia would prove a source of tension.

The Soviet invasion, and the Uprising's ensuing violent suppression, were first brought to the Security Council by France, Britain and the US, all of whom regarded the stationing of Moscow's forces in Hungary as a 'flagrant violation' of the 1945 UN Charter and the 1947 Paris Peace Treaty. A report on 'The Problem of Hungary' by the UN General Assembly's Special Committee, made up of delegates from Australia, Denmark, Tunisia, Uruguay and Ceylon, acknowledged the difficulty of gathering information, not least because the General Secretary of Socialist Workers' Party János Kádár refused the committee permission to enter Hungary on the grounds that it was an 'internal affair.' Still, the 148-page report was quite thorough in its investigation, based on information gathered from 111 eyewitnesses along with government radio broadcasts. The report concluded that the invasion did indeed represent a violation of human rights, punctuated by 'inhuman treatment and torture' as well as the illegal deportation of women and children to the Soviet Union.[71] The Hungarian Lawyers' Association issued a quick rebuttal, and notably did so in human rights terms. It defended the Hungarian state's action 'in the interest of upholding the guarantee of human rights and basic freedoms of all her citizens under Chapter II, art. 1 of the [1947] Paris Peace Treaty.'[72] The International Commission of Jurists, in a 1957 report, countered that the Warsaw Pact had not provided any justification for intervention. It further judged that the Hungarian government had not respected the Paris Treaty's commitment (Art 2) to 'secure all persons under Hungarian jurisdiction...the enjoyment of human rights and of fundamental freedoms.'[73]

The Soviet invasion had immediately provoked an emergency UN Assembly. The inability of the Security Council to agree a decision (due to the Soviet veto)

---

[70] Johanna C. Granville, *The First Domino: International Decision Making during the Hungarian Crisis of 1956* (College Station: Texas A&M Press, 2004), 100–5. See too Nataša Mišković, 'Between Idealism and Pragmatism: Tito, Nehru and the Hungarian Crisis, 1956', in Nataša Mišković, Harald Fischer-Tiné and Nada Boškovska (eds.), *The Non-Aligned Movement and the Cold War: Dehli-Bandung-Belgrade* (London: Routledge, 2014), 141–2.

[71] *The Problem of Hungary: A Summary of the Report of the General Assembly's Special Committee* (New York: The United Nations, 1957), 3–4.

[72] Hungarian Lawyers' Association, *Some Comments on the Juristic Aspects of the 'Hungarian Question'* (Budapest: Athenaeum, 1957), 24.

[73] International Commission of Jurists, *The Hungarian Situation and the Rule of Law* (The Hague: International Commission of Jurists, 1957), 10–11.

meant that the General Assembly became the forum for discussion of the issue. While the USSR and Hungary insisted that this was a domestic matter and thus irrelevant to the international community, most countries remained unconvinced; even the socialist world was not unified on the issue, as Yugoslavia agreed to call the emergency session.[74] Nor did other countries accept the Hungarian regime's interpretation that their 'victory' had been waged against western imperialists and domestic 'counter-revolutionaries' seeking to spread reactionary capitalism back into Eastern Europe, and that they were thus in natural solidarity, or so they claimed, with Algerians fighting the French state.[75] Hungary's leaders looked to the swelling ranks of decolonized states to support them in their bid for reintegration into the United Nations and other bodies. On extensive foreign policy tours of Africa and East and South Asia in 1957, and then at the UN, Hungarian foreign minister János Péter attempted to convince a number of different countries that they stood on the same side. More specifically, Péter sought to demonstrate the links between the supply of weapons to domestic anti-Communist 'counter-revolutionaries' and the western imperialists who were ravaging South East Asia.[76]

Yet the Hungarian state's overtures to the Third World failed miserably. India and Ceylon took the lead in drafting the UN report demanding immediate Soviet withdrawal, and $20 million of UN relief in the form of food, clothing, medicine and other supplies were distributed to Hungarian refugees, mainly in Austria.[77] Cuba proposed a resolution (adopted 21 November 1956) calling on the Soviet Union to repatriate those who had been deported.[78]

Even so, the Hungarian situation was vexatious for the African and Asian delegates, and many maintained restraint. In part this was because they were relatively few in numbers at this point, and only Iran from their group was a member of the Security Council. Given the circumstances they opted to play a tactical game. While no member of the Afro-Asian group voted with the Soviet Bloc in opposing the resolution condemning the invasion, Afro-Asian delegates were not prepared to line up in the western camp either. In fact, most of them abstained from the American motion condemning the invasion. A measure of anti-colonial solidarity with the smaller Eastern European countries still held firm, particularly so among those countries that proclaimed themselves non-aligned, such as Egypt, India, Libya and Syria. And even if not a member of the UN until 1971, China did not hide its disappointment with UN delegates from Asian countries for their

---

[74] Luard, *History of the UN*, 59–66.
[75] James Mark and Quinn Slobodian, 'Eastern Europe in the Global History of Decolonization', in Martin Thomas and Andrew Thompson (eds.), *Oxford Handbook on Ends of Empires* (Oxford: OUP, 2018), 361.
[76] This argument was used at the UN General Assembly at New York in December 1957. HU OSA 300-40-5 Box 143 (Péter János 1951–1965). See this interpretation also in the so-called White Books: *Nagy Imre és bűntársai ellenforradalmi összeesküvése* (Budapest, 1958).
[77] Luard, *History of the UN*, 69.
[78] Reprinted in *The Hungarian Situation and the Rule of Law*, 51.

lack of solidarity with the Hungarian regime. The western powers were unhappy that these non-aligned countries did not support resolutions of human rights and self-determination, to the point of accusing them of taking to heart these issues when they concerned Asia and Africa, but not Europe. The Suez Crisis also loomed heavily over the deliberations, as some members—including those from Arab countries—voiced their dissatisfaction that France and the UK were not equally branded as aggressors in the wake of the Suez invasion.[79] In the end, the Afro-Asian group did vote with the West and others for humanitarian assistance to Hungary; this then became a point on which the Soviet group was itself divided, as Hungary and Romania voted against the resolution for aid, while other members of the bloc abstained.[80]

The Chinese position on the Hungarian Uprising is particularly interesting here. It is well known that China was critical of Khrushchev's 1956 Secret Speech for its 'disrespectful' characterization of Stalin, and Mao interpreted the Hungarian Crisis as the result of needless reform and a lack of leadership. The events of 1956 emboldened Mao to present himself as the real leader of the international Communist movement. But the Hungarian Crisis had other effects on the Third World's attitude toward China. While China had been working to build relations with Africa and Asia in the 1950s, the Hungarian Crisis shifted sympathies toward the new Communist power. Having initially identified the root of the crisis as Moscow's inability to treat Hungary as an equal partner, Beijing was shocked by the upsurge of anti-Communist violence. Beijing communicated its views to Moscow that a withdrawal of Soviet troops from Hungarian soil would now be a betrayal of the Communist cause, and recommended military force to quell the uprising. China even exerted pressure on the Polish government—which had expressed 'sorrow at the bloodshed and the damages in Budapest'—to alter its position, and in the UN vote Poland ultimately sided with the other Warsaw Pact countries in rejecting the western condemnation of Soviet aggression; Gomułka went so far as to say that 'Western aggression in Suez' was far worse because the USSR—unlike the British in Suez—was not trying to turn Hungary into a colony.[81]

Yet the Uprising also confirmed to Beijing that de-Stalinization was itself a problematic Communist form of decolonization: it had led a bloc country's citizens to revolt in the name of greater independence, and was furthermore enabling a cultural nationalism to flourish in the Soviets' southern republics too—most worryingly in those that bordered China. Beijing feared that this turn in the Communist world was helping ferment rebellions in Tibet—which might become

---

[79] D.N. Sharma, *Afro-Asian Group in the U.N.* (Allahabad: Chaitnya Publishing House, 1969), 74–81, 106.

[80] Sharma, *Afro-Asian Group*, 92.

[81] Granville, *The First Domino*, 120. See too Zhihua Shen and Yafeng Xia, *Mao and the Sino-Soviet Partnership, 1945–1959: A New History* (London: Lexington Books, 2015), 179–80.

'another Hungary'.[82] Mao then launched his Hundred Flowers campaign in the wake of the Hungarian Crisis so as to 'encourage' intellectuals to help the CCP 'correct its mistakes'; a new Anti-Rightist campaign (in response to criticism from some intellectuals) went on to brand some 300,000 intellectuals as dangerous 'rightists'.[83] The Chinese domestic crackdown was a direct response to the Hungarian Uprising, and the clear message to Africans and others was that China represented Communist authoritarianism in a new guise, prompting them to look to smaller Eastern Bloc states as more trustworthy given their geopolitical situation.

The 1960s wave of decolonization transformed everything at the UN. This could first be seen with the organization's changing membership, as seventeen new African countries came into the UN in 1960 alone. By 1965 more than 45% of UN member states had gained independence since 1945. The entry of these new countries meant that the topics of discussion at the General Assemblies changed too. After 1960 decolonization was the main theme by a long way—in fact, decolonization often exceeded by four times the next major theme, economic development—a trend that increased over the 1960s. Human rights were the third most discussed theme, with issues concerning apartheid South Africa growing in importance as well.[84]

In the 1960s self-determination shaped the understanding of human rights for the Third World, and the USSR and the Eastern Bloc responded accordingly. In the GDR, the young legal academic Bernhard Graefrath was inspired by the emerging Afro-Asian bloc and declared that the self-determination of peoples was not just a human right, but the 'most basic human right'.[85] The 1960 *Declaration on the Granting of Independence to Colonial Countries and Peoples* likewise served as an inspiration: the Polish legal scholar Franciszek Przetacznik would later describe the Declaration as 'one of the most important living documents that has come out of the United Nations in the entire course of its life', because it affirmed that 'all peoples have the right to self-determination, by virtue of which they should determine their political status and freely pursue their economic, social and cultural advancement'.[86]

While the Soviet Union's advocacy of anti-imperialism had been a central plank of socialist internationalism since the 1920s, this ideological campaign

---

[82] Yuri Andropov, 'On the Situation in Tibet', 31 March 1959, Wilson Center Digital Archive.

[83] Chen Jian and Yang Kuisong, 'Chinese Politics and the Collapse of Sino-Soviet Alliance', in Odd Arne Westad (ed.), *Brothers in Arms: The Rise and Fall of the Sino-Soviet Alliance, 1945–1963* (Palo Alto: Stanford University Press, 1998), 264–6.

[84] David A. Kay, *The New Nations in the United Nations, 1960–1967* (New York: Columbia University Press, 1970), 45–50.

[85] Bernhard Graefrath, *Die Vereinten Nationen und die Menschenrechte* (Berlin: Deutscher Zentralverlag, 1956), 54.

[86] Franciszek Przetacznik, 'The Socialist Conception of Human Rights', *Social Research* 38/2 (1971), 344.

intensified under Khrushchev. With the failure of the Soviet Union to win its case about the primacy of socialist human rights internationally (right to work, right to housing) in the 1950s, the USSR and its allies promoted self-determination and anti-colonialism as a way to establish solidarity with newly independent Asian and African countries.[87] In a 1960 speech at the General Assembly, Khrushchev declared that 'the great process of our era, occurring before the eyes of all, is the emancipation and restoration of independent rights to peoples who for centuries have been kept off the high road of mankind's development by the colonialists.'[88] At the UN that year Khrushchev sought to capitalize on the moment by pushing for a resolution to bring an end to colonialism.

African delegates lent their support to this initiative. But in their eyes, the issue was primarily a defence of sovereignty, and some delegates dismissed the Soviet Union's grandstanding.[89] The USSR and its allies were sometimes very heavy-handed in their use of human rights issues to criticize the West, so much so that Guinean President Sekou Touré appealed to the Eastern Bloc not to exploit decolonization for their own political purposes.[90] Other Afro-Asian delegates at the UN baulked at their human rights initiative being taken over by the Soviet Union, and sought to move beyond Cold War squabbling. In the 1960 UN discussion of Resolution 1514, the Republic of Congo delegate Lheyet-Gaboka reopened the issue of Soviet imperialism, saying 'Even in Europe, which prides itself on its civilization, we can count up the people who, at the present time, certainly envy the lot of the African States which have attained independence. We must not forget those countries whose cries are stifled and hence cannot reach us. What are the colonizers waiting for before decolonizing them?'[91] Rights language thus also pointed up the limitations of these partnerships. For that reason, Afro-Asian delegates insisted that they should lead the campaign for the new resolution, after which forty-three African and Asian delegates collectively introduced the 'Declaration on the Granting of Independence to Colonial Countries and Peoples.' They put it in strong human rights language with reference to the UN Charter, whose first point was to overcome the 'subjection of peoples to alien subjugation. Domination and exploitation constitutes a denial of fundamental human rights, and is contrary to the Charter of the United Nations and is an impediment to the

---

[87] Elliot R. Goodman, 'The Cry of National Liberation: Recent Soviet Attitudes Toward National Self-Determination', *International Organization*, 14/1 (Winter 1960), 92–106.

[88] Quoted in Luard, *History of the UN*, 184.

[89] For Soviet efforts to take credit for advancing the anti-racist proposals in the UN's Third Committee, see V. Chkhikvadke, 'The Nations Repudiate Racism', *International Affairs* (Moscow), 12/5 (May 1966), 49–54, which ends with 'Slavery and civilisation cannot co-exist. Mankind must cleanse itself' (54).

[90] A.G. Mezerik (ed.), *Colonialism and the United Nations* (New York: United Nations, 1964), 9, and Normand and Zaidi, *Human Rights at the UN*, 260–9.

[91] Verbatim Records of the General Assembly Plenary Meeting, 938th session, 6 December 1960, A/PV. 938, para. 56, quoted in Burke, *Decolonization*, 53.

promotion of world peace and cooperation.'[92] So whereas the Soviet draft of the Declaration was chiefly intended as an attack on European colonialism, the representatives from the developing world expanded the brief to render it more universal in respect of human rights and the inclusive spirit of the UN.[93]

Such a dispensation was more in keeping with the African and Asian delegates' more universalist attitude toward human rights. So whilst universalism was dying in the West, splintering into regional conceptions of human rights (such as the anti-Communist 1950 European Convention on Human Rights), Third World delegates at the UN campaigned for universal application in the 1940s and 1950s, and identified human rights as the political manifestation of such universalism. As early as 1950 Egyptian lawyer and journalist Mahmud Azmi even argued that the selective application of human rights proposed by the imperial powers was 'only too reminiscent of the Hitlerian concept which divided mankind into groups of varying worth.'[94] The Chinese delegate at the United Nations, P. C. Chang, was also one of the key figures associated with this universalism, and worked to subordinate the inequality inherent in older civilizational models of international development to the more universal, horizontal and inclusive language of human rights.[95] Over the course of the 1960s anti-colonial leaders and UN delegates reconfigured this universalism to their own ends.[96]

Eastern Bloc countries likewise forged new international identities at the UN, in part by defending the UN's universalism in the face of Cold War antagonism. Poland, for example, made much of its commitment to the 'universality' of the UN, which in its case meant campaigning for the admission of Italy, Bulgaria, Hungary, Romania and Finland into the UN in the late 1940s. After 1950 Poland pushed for the admission of Maoist China as well as the GDR in order to challenge West Germany's claim 'to speak for the entire German people.'[97] In part due to the challenges to their own sovereignty—brutally occupied during the war, and then faced in its aftermath with a West Germany which would not recognize its western borders—Poland well understood the struggles of other countries for independence and sought partners to protect its own. It also pushed for Libyan and Eritrean independence, and criticized Spain and Portugal for refusing to submit information to various UN Advisory Committees about alleged human rights abuses in their colonies. Here the discourse of self-determination brought together smaller Eastern European states and a decolonizing Afro-Asian world. The Poles endorsed the Soviet-sponsored Resolution to make self-determination

[92] Burke, *Decolonization*, 50–2.

[93] Steven L. B. Jensen, *The Making of International Human Rights: The 1960s, Decolonization and the Reconstruction of Global Values* (Cambridge: CUP, 2016), 55.

[94] Quoted in Burke, *Decolonization*, 120.

[95] Frédéric Krumbein, 'PC Chang—The Chinese Father of Human Rights', *Journal of Human Rights*, 14/3 (2015), 332–52.

[96] Jensen, *International Human Rights*, esp. 1–17.

[97] Andrzej Abraszewski, *Poland in the United Nations* (Warsaw: Interpress, 1977), 19–31.

a human right, supported UN economic and technical assistance to Third World countries in need, and condemned human rights violations in Chile.

Poland also played a prominent role in anti-racist campaigning, partly the result of the country's experience of Nazi imperialism. By the late 1940s the Polish UN representatives protested against the South African annexation of Southwest Africa (Namibia), and the Polish delegation condemned apartheid as early as 1949. The UN recognized the Polish delegation for its human rights work, as a Polish representative sat on the UN Commission on Human Rights for over twenty years. Much of Poland's work at the UN pivoted on building relations of solidarity with the Third World. Polish UN publicity materials proudly feature photos of Foreign Minister Adam Rapacki shaking hands with Fidel Castro at the UN General Assembly in 1960 and signing the 1966 Convention on the Elimination of All Forms of Racial Discrimination, concluding that the 'standpoint of Poland and other socialist states also corresponded with the interests of the Third World, creating opportunities for undertaking joint action'.[98] What is also especially notable in the Polish UN publicity is the fact that the Soviet Union—and the normally routine expressions of deference—hardly featured at all, as the stress fell on showcasing a modern, open and cooperative Poland for Third World partners. Bulgaria likewise was at pains to espouse solidarity between Communist and post-colonial states, grasping that decolonization might create the conditions of new Second–Third World connections.[99]

From the Congo Crisis to the Algerian War

The Congo Crisis of 1960–61 was an important watershed in relations between the Third World and the superpowers. The crisis took place against the backdrop of the accession of sixteen independent African countries to the UN, and it was the first opportunity for these new countries to voice their opinion at the General Assembly. The atmosphere there in 1960 and 1961 was understandably tense. The Soviets quickly condemned Belgian 'armed aggression' under 'NATO command', and demanded the immediate withdrawal of Belgian troops from the country and in turn stepped up military assistance to the new Congolese government. The Soviet Union's accusation of western imperialism was pretty common by this point: for example, they and the Eastern Bloc countries routinely reported on the Mau Mau uprising in Kenya as a means of attacking British colonialism.[100] Poland was particularly outspoken in its condemnation of the US invasion of Cuba as well as the violation of the Dominican Republic's sovereignty.[101] But in this case,

[98] Ibid., 155, 79–137.
[99] Matei Karasimeonov, *Bulgaria and the United Nations* (Sofia: Sofia Press, 1976), 5.
[100] Klose, *Human Rights*, 199.
[101] Abraszewski, *Poland*, 43–5.

Soviet criticism of both the Belgian government and the UN's handling of the crisis was pointed and widely broadcast. Soviet delegates tried to persuade new African UN delegates to make common cause with them, urging them to abstain from the vote on the UN's conduct of the crisis.[102] Poland and other socialist states condemned UN Director General Dag Hammarskjöld and the UN for 'favouring forces hostile to the Congo's independence'. Socialist governments around the world used the international media to campaign for his removal, and refused to participate in UN operations there. Many Third World countries were sympathetic to the call for immediate Belgian withdrawal, especially left-leaning Egypt, Ghana, Guinea and Mali.[103] But in the 1960 Emergency Special Session of the UN General Assembly, those countries that were wavering opted to align themselves with the majority in supporting the UN mission in the Congo, in effect isolating the Soviet Union and Eastern Bloc.[104] The socialist camp was split, as Yugoslavia sided with the Afro-Asian group, but so were the African delegates. The ex-French colonies in Africa (informally known as the Brazzaville Group, comprising fifteen former French and Belgian colonies) tended to be more pro-western, and abstained on the vote about the Soviet resolution.[105]

The Congo crisis shifted the relationship between the African delegates, the Soviet Union and the UN. In the minds of African elites, the crisis confirmed the pivotal importance of the UN—weak though it sometimes was—for advancing and protecting African independence. By contrast, the UN's ineffectual policy and the subsequent murder of Lumumba convinced Khrushchev that the UN was in the pocket of the United States—colourfully adding, 'I spit on the UN'—and from that point he brazenly strove to replace the UN director with a new troika that would reflect the three power blocs in the world at the time. Having failed to gain support for this coup, the Soviet Union withdrew its funding from the UN's Congo Mission, setting the stage for the even more heightened face-off with the US the next year with the Cuban Missile Crisis. The Congo Crisis served for its part to expose the USSR's manifest inability to act on behalf of African revolution, despite all that it had promised a few months before.[106] And Soviet efforts to exploit these events for the purposes of political propaganda and military posturing toward the Congo led to still more disillusionment even among the more

[102] See the typed letter from Nikita Khrushchev to Kwame Nkrumah about the way in which the West was keen 'to exploit the name of the United Nations in their criminal aims', Moscow, 24 August 1960, 3, RG 17/1/211, Public Records and Archives Administration Department – PRAAD, Accra.

[103] Alana O'Malley, 'Ghana, India and the Transnational Dynamics of the Congo Crisis at the United Nations, 1960–1961', *International History Review*, 37/5 (October 2015), 970–90. See too Samaan Boutros Farajallah, *Le Groupe Afro-Asiatique dans le Cadre des Nations Unies* (Geneva: Librairie Droz, 1963), 285–339.

[104] Thomas Hovet Jr, *Africa in the United Nations* (Evanston: Northwestern University Press, 1963), 88–9.

[105] Sharma, *Afro-Asian Group*, 161.

[106] Alexander Dallin, 'The Soviet Union: Political Activity', in Zbigniew Brzezinski (ed.), *Africa and the Communist World* (London: OUP, 1964), 33.

sympathetic, newly independent African countries. African delegates became increasingly suspicious of Moscow's motives and reckless behaviour,[107] which offered some leeway for the smaller Eastern European countries to work with their counterparts in the Third World beyond superpower conflict. For example, Yugoslavia was viewed very positively—after all, Tito distanced himself from the USSR, did not attack the UN, and earned the trust of African partners.[108]

Significant in this respect is the Algerian War, which became a key issue at the UN.[109] The French colonization of Algeria had been a favourite rallying cause for international justice since the nineteenth century,[110] but its presence in mid-twentieth century international relations was pivotal. The USSR would play a relatively subdued role at the UN on this issue, however, often in the name of diplomacy. In one 1957 UN discussion, for example, the Italian delegation threatened to bring up the situation in Hungary if the Soviet Union made an issue of Algeria, and the USSR accordingly kept quiet.[111] Hungary had tied the USSR's hands on international crises of decolonization; moreover, Afro-Asian delegates had grown tired of the USSR's hijacking of human rights for its own political agenda. One Tunisian representative in the early 1960s complained that he did not want the question of colonialism becoming enmeshed 'within the framework of one in which East and West vie against each other'.[112] These developments thus gave other Eastern Bloc countries some room to forge links (and build credibility) with Third World countries. The GDR, Czechoslovakia and Romania, for example, all sent significant amounts of humanitarian aid to the Algerian National Liberation Front (FLN) in the name of solidarity, and Ben Bella was a frequent guest in Prague, East Berlin and Bucharest in the early 1960s.

Yugoslavia's actions in the Algerian War were crucial for reshaping these Third World politics. Like Nasser, Tito supported the FLN in its liberation struggle with weapons and military assistance; yet he went one step further in dispatching food and medicine as well, a fact never forgotten by Algerian fighters and their political leaders after 1962. The FLN repeatedly argued that the Yugoslavs were their closest non-Arab allies, in marked contrast with India. No less important was the fallout from China's efforts to scuttle these budding Second–Third World relations by stressing racial solidarity for its own purposes. Yet China's efforts to turn Third World politics into a race war never took wing, and non-alignment was built on south-eastern European–African–Indian relations, particularly on the part

---

[107] Ryan M. Irwin, 'Sovereignty in the Congo Crisis', in Leslie James and Elisabeth Leake (eds.), *Decolonization and the Cold War: Negotiating Independence* (London: Bloomsbury, 2015), esp. 212–14.

[108] William E. Griffith, 'Yugoslavia', in Zbigniew Brzezinski (ed.), *Africa and the Communist World* (London: OUP, 1964), 122.

[109] Evan Luard, *History of the UN*, 75–103.

[110] Cheryl B. Welch, 'Colonial Violence and the Rhetoric of Evasion: Tocqueville on Algeria', *Political Theory*, 31/2 (April 2003), 235–264.

[111] Klose, *Human Rights*, 210.

[112] Quoted in Luard, *History of the UN*, 185, 188.

of Tito, Nasser and Nehru. From the early 1960s the Non Aligned Movement supplanted Afro-Asianism as the main organizational concept of the Third World, and helped recast the Third World as a political project with unbounded membership rather than as the expression of a non-western, non-white identity.

This reconfiguration of Third World politics brought neither peace nor harmonious relations. If anything, acrimony within the Communist world between the Soviet Union, China and Yugoslavia about the Third World grew more heated at the various African conferences. Such conflicts thus dominated the proceedings of a number of meetings, including for example the Afro-Asian Peoples' Solidarity Conferences in Moshi, Tanganyika in 1963 and Algiers in 1964. African attendees expressed their displeasure with this constant infighting. One reported in a French newspaper that he couldn't eat in peace without being subjected to endless 'doctrinal quarrels' about Communist politics.[113]

Despite its grandstanding and overbearing presence, the USSR did make inroads among Third World UN representatives. The voting patterns of the Soviet and African factions were often quite similar. As we have seen, the Soviet Union made much noise about its support for African anti-colonialism and self-determination, and effectively used high-profile UN debates to proclaim to the world that the US was no friend of Africa.[114] No less damaging in the eyes of anti-western critics was the fact that human rights were being used to defend white European minorities. After the Algerian War, for example, the French ratified the European Convention on Human Rights in part to protect the French white minority still living in Algeria, and British did the same as a means of protecting themselves in Kenya in the wake of decolonization.[115] Western countries, many of which had played key roles in the postwar the human rights declaration, had become easy targets. In any case, the Soviet Union's considerable success was a great source of consternation for the West. In a 1957 General Assembly the US criticized the USSR for being hypocritical about self-determination, claiming 'The Soviet Union has deprived a large number of countries of the right to self-determination by its resort to force and subversive activities.'[116] And at a 1962 UN General Assembly, the American delegate questioned the USSR's anti-colonial policies in Africa by saying 'where the Soviet Union is master, there is no colonialism; where the Soviet Union is not master and perhaps seeks mastery, there the cry of colonialism is raised.'[117] The UK also railed against Soviet hypocrisy. In

---

[113] D. Kimche, *The Afro-Asian Movement: Ideology and Foreign Policy of the Third World* (Jerusalem: Israel Universities Press, 1973), 185–6, cited in Jeffrey James Byrne, "Beyond Continents, Colours and the Cold War: Yugoslavia, Algeria and the Struggle for Non-Alignment," *The International History Review* 37/5 (2015), 923.

[114] Hovet Jr, *Africa in the United Nations*, 177–83.

[115] Klose, *Human Rights*, 229.

[116] Quoted in Normand and Zaidi, *Human Rights at the UN*, 216.

[117] UN General Assembly, 20 November 1962, quoted in Hovet Jr, *Africa in the United Nations*, 186.

one 1960 UN debate about colonialism, the British delegate felt compelled to interject that

> [s]ince 1939, some 500 million people, formerly under British rule, have achieved freedom and independence, and their representatives sit here. In that same period, the whole or part of six countries, with a population of 22 million, have been forcibly incorporated into the Soviet Union; they include the world's newest colonies: Lithuania, Estonia and Latvia...Countless efforts have been made by national movements in countries under Russian control to gain independence. All have been suppressed.[118]

The Afro-Asian delegates did not warm to Britain's intervention, and even rejected the way in which Cold War issues were being exploited. Soon thereafter Britain learned that such heavy Cold War rhetoric was counterproductive, and subsequently toned down references to Soviet colonialism, focusing instead on the constructive elements of western assistance—the US would for its part adopt the same rhetorical strategy.[119] Even so, such episodes did show how the Soviet Union found it difficult after 1956 to present itself as anti-imperialist, even though the link between the Communist Bloc and the Afro-Asian bloc remained a fairly strong one at the UN.

For this reason, western observers lamented that human rights had only served to strengthen the Third World's attack on colonialism. For them, rights had become hopelessly entangled with the politics of anti-colonialism and self-determination, which shifted the original liberal emphasis of rights from the individual to groups. One American commentator writing in 1965 asserted that

> the struggle to end colonialism also swallowed up the original purpose of cooperation for promotion of human rights...Self-determination was added to the roster of human rights as an additional weapon against colonialism although there was no suggestion that this was a right of the individual that the individual could claim against an unrepresentative government...Human rights was being used as a political weapon against colonialism or economic imperialism, not to enhance the rights of all persons against all governments.[120]

But complain as they might, the momentum of human rights had shifted to the South. In this sense, the Third World had thus turned the language of human rights against the West and the East. As Fabian Klose put it: the 'moral armour for

---

[118] United Nations General Assembly Official Records, 15th Session, 925th meeting, November 28, 1960, para. 19, cited in Kay, *The New Nations*, 159.

[119] Kay, *The New Nations*, 160, 176.

[120] Louis Henkin, 'The United Nations and Human Rights', *International Organization*, 19/3 (Summer 1965), 512–13.

the anticolonial independence movement was hammered out of the ideological answer that the Allies had used against the totalitarian threat.'[121]

The UN was especially important to new and smaller countries concerned that their rights concerns be heard, and as a context where they could forge relations with other like-minded international partners. This point is often lost, however, as most of the commentary on the UN—especially that written in the West at the time—loudly grumbled that with the admission of dozens of new countries following decolonization, the UN was effectively converted into a mouthpiece of Third World grievances mostly directed at western powers. What was really at issue here is that the West was no longer able to control the international understanding of human rights, as its meaning was being expanded and recast by Second and Third World activists for different purposes.

Close readings of the UN debates also indicates that Eastern Europe enjoyed more room for manoeuvre than is generally acknowledged, and often engaged in somewhat surprising ways in bilateral relations and cross-continental alliances. The Soviet UN representatives were generally not very impressive, not least because the Soviet Union tended not to send its best foreign service personnel to the UN.[122] This was not the case with Eastern European countries, as their delegates (especially from Bulgaria and Yugoslavia) were routinely praised for their preparation and diligence. Even the so-called Eastern Bloc was really no bloc at all - as was perhaps most evident in the case of human rights. After all, the Hungarians had to defend 'their' action in the uprising of 1956 along national lines; the GDR—given that it was not formally admitted to the UN until 1973— was absent from all UN deliberations, and thus had to build its international profile as a champion of human rights in the international media and through the platform of its own unofficial UNESCO observer status. Maoist China's non-recognition at the UN was a tricky case too, and its exclusion (until 1971) was a burning issue for the socialist countries in pressing for a more genuine inclusivity at the UN, at least until the Sino-Soviet split in the 1960s. Yugoslavia often tacked close to Eastern Bloc states, but on some key issues took an independent line. If anything, the absence of China and the relentless bluster of the Soviet Union at the General Assembly allowed the Eastern European countries quietly to build small country solidarities around issues of self-determination, development, anti-colonialism and anti-racism. Given Soviet hostility and US indifference toward human rights in the 1950s, human rights debates came to offer an opportunity for small states to discuss politics relatively removed from superpower grandstanding.[123]

---

[121] Klose, *Human Rights*, 232.   [122] Dallin, *The Soviet Union at the United Nations*, 95.
[123] Burke, *Decolonization*, 7 and Andrew S. Thompson, 'Tehran 1968 and Reform of the UN Human Rights System', *Journal of Human Rights*, 14/1 (2015), 84–100.

Race and Rights

The connection between Eastern European and African delegates at the UN was generally strong, but the USSR's heavy-handed politics and imperial presence increasingly complicated their interaction over human rights in the 1960s. However, one issue that helped to fortify their relationship was race. Already the UNESCO 1950 Statement on Race (written in part by Claude Lévi-Strauss) had attracted widespread attention on account of its efforts to debunk race as specious science, and the UN agency devoted great energy to publishing educational materials and organizing teacher conferences that sought to eradicate the scourge of racism from school curricula around the world. By the late 1950s, there was still a sense that the UN should do more to combat racism at a global level, and to this end the General Assembly created a new committee to draft a Resolution on the Elimination of Racial Discrimination. The pretext was the epidemic of swastika-painting and anti-Semitic racial acts in the Federal Republic of Germany in the winter of 1959–60,[124] and there was some real concern abroad about the possible comeback of Fascism. But the perception was that much more needed to be done. In a 1962 special issue of the UN journal, *International Organization*, a number of African heads of state—ranging from Nkrumah to Senghor—identified racial discrimination and apartheid—as well as disarmament—as major problems afflicting the world, and asserted that the UN needed to take a stronger role in addressing the problem.[125] In the early 1960s Egypt, Mali and Liberia took the lead in the discussion of racial discrimination as a human rights issue at the UN. In 1965 this new UN Advisory Committee began its work, and became an important bridge for Second–Third World relations on race and rights.

Opposition to apartheid was in the meantime becoming a galvanizing human rights issue at the UN. Ghana spearheaded the campaign to force anti-apartheid on to the UN agenda in the early 1960s. Support also came from African legal experts, who were quick to link anti-apartheid to human rights and the rule of law. Nigerian Minister of Justice, T.O. Elias, argued that apartheid in South Africa was 'an unparalleled example of the prostitution of the judicial process in recent times', and looked to law as the key to overcoming such injustice. As he put it, 'law is a civilizing as well as a stabilizing influence in human society',[126] and human rights were seen as a possible means of civilizing international relations.

---

[124] Normand and Zaidi, *Human Rights at the UN*, 261.

[125] 'Africa Speaks to the United Nations: A Symposium of Aspirations and Concerns Voiced by Representative Leaders at the UN, with Katema Yifru, J. Rudolph Grimes, Ibrahim Abboud, Mongi Slim, Kwame Nkrumah, Louis Lansana Beavogui, Leopold Sedar Senghor and Alhaji Sir Abubaker Tafawa Balewa', *International Organization*, 16/2 (Spring 1962), 303–30.

[126] International Commission of Jurists, *African Conference on the Rule of Law, Lagos, Nigeria, 3–7 January 1961—A Report on the Proceedings of the Conference* (Geneva: International Commission of Jurists, 1961), 58–9, quoted in Jensen, *International Human Rights*, 58–9.

Senegalese legal scholar Abdoulaye Wade made his case along similar lines, but added that human rights must be linked to legal equality.[127] By 1961 South Africa was feeling more isolated, and even Britain at the UN's 16th Assembly in 1961 joined the rest in assenting that apartheid was 'now so exceptional as to be sui generis', effectively challenging UN provisions regarding domestic jurisdiction.[128]

By the early 1960s it was increasingly common for African leaders to set great store by the UN as perhaps the one place where international justice might be served. Zambian Prime Minister Kenneth Kaunda, for example, was an emerging African leader in the Non-Aligned Movement who devoted a great deal of attention to the apartheid issue. In one speech at the 1964 NAM Conference in Cairo, Kaunda predicted that South Africa would 'reap the whirlwind of disaster' if it continued to defy 'reason and the fundamental principles of civilization and human rights'. However, Pretoria put up stubborn resistance. The Rivonia Trials that year made clear that the National Party would not succumb to the pressure of the ANC and Pan-African Congress. As one journalist reportedly remarked, South Africa was not going to be the 'next Algeria'. For Kaunda and others, the only solution was effective diplomatic action through the UN, not least because they felt that time (and numbers) were on their side. As he put it, 'it is through the General Assembly that the non-aligned nations will be secure until all of the powerful nations are politically, economically and socially just'.[129] Kaunda also played a key role in the campaign by African states (led by Ethiopia and Liberia) to have apartheid tried in the International Court of Justice in 1960, a case that stayed in court until 1966. To the amazement of African observers, the Court struck down the anti-apartheid claim, concluding that the African bloc's arguments were 'based on considerations of an extra-legal character, the product of after-knowledge' best suited to the political realm rather than international law. With it, African representatives lost faith in the legitimacy of the International Court, and instead put their trust in the UN as the sole receptive international body.[130] In fact, this disillusioning verdict led many African activists to push for the ratification of the 1973 Anti-Apartheid Convention as a separate UN convention for specifically African affairs.[131]

---

[127] International Commission of Jurists, *African Conference on the Rule of Law, Lagos, Nigeria, 3–7 January 1961—A Report on the Proceedings of the Conference* (Geneva: International Commission of Jurists, 1961), 45, quoted in Jensen, *International Human Rights*, 58.

[128] Kay, *The New Nations*, 66.

[129] *Conference of Heads of State and Governments of Non-Aligned Countries, Cairo, Egypt, 5–10 October 1964* (Cairo: Ministry of National Guidance, 1964), 149–54, quoted in Irwin, 622. See too Kenneth Kaunda, *Zambia, Independence and Beyond: Speeches of Kenneth Kaunda* (London: Nelson, 1966).

[130] Ryan M. Irwin, 'Apartheid on Trial: South West Africa and the International Court of Justice, 1960–1966', *The International History Review*, 32/4 (2010), 619–42.

[131] Sebastian Gehrig, 'Reaching Out to the Third World: East Germany's Anti-Apartheid and Socialist Human Rights Campaign', *German History*, 36/4 (2018), 574–97.

The struggle against apartheid not only helped bring together Eastern Europe and the Third World in a show of solidarity, it also helped limit China's influence in Africa. At first this may seem puzzling, given that Mao's China had officially broken off all economic links with South Africa in 1960, and had invested heavily in the continent and provided aid for rebel fighters in various countries. However, China resumed commercial relations with Pretoria in the early 1960s, with trade between the two countries actually trebling after 1963. China was also keen to outmanoeuvre the USSR in Africa, but was unable to challenge Eastern Europe's close relations with the ANC. Mandela arranged for the setting up of ANC training sites in Algeria, Ethiopia and Tanzania, and intensified his relations with Eastern European partners, especially the GDR; in fact, all ANC publicity materials were printed and distributed in East Berlin. ANC leaders were frequent visitors to East Berlin, Prague and Belgrade, receiving there badly needed aid and training. Excluded from this network, China turned to the Pan-African Congress as a rival group through which it might hope to win influence in the region, but this too was limited, especially after China turned inward during the Cultural Revolution. With time China's relationship with the ANC grew warmer (Oliver Tambo travelled to Beijing in 1983), but China played no real role in the international anti-apartheid movement in the 1960s and 1970s.[132] In that context Eastern European countries exploited the absence of China on the world stage from the mid-1960s to the mid-1970s to build strong links with liberation struggles in Africa.[133]

The UN Advisory Committee on race is an especially revealing source for those wishing to study how race featured in these Second–Third World relations at the UN. These advisory committees have attracted little attention among historians of human rights, though they served as key sites of international politics precisely because they took place beyond the glare of the world's media. It was also a locus where the superpower representatives could interact with other countries more directly and discreetly. This was certainly the case for the US, which had all but turned its back on the UN after 1953 because of constant Soviet criticism of its chequered civil rights record; the US used the UN advisory committee work to stay engaged in human rights promotion through the 1950s and 1960s.[134] The advisory committees were even more important venues for smaller countries, including Eastern Bloc states looking to forge relations with Third World partners without undue Soviet pressure.[135] For smaller nations, these UN advisory

[132] Ian Taylor, 'The Ambiguous Commitment: The People's Republic of China and the Anti-Apartheid Struggle in South Africa', *Journal of Contemporary African Studies*, 18/1 (2000), 91–106.

[133] P. Costea, 'Eastern Europe's Relations with the Insurgencies of South Africa, SWAPO and the ANC, 1972–1988', *Eastern European Quarterly*, 24/3 (1990).

[134] Carol Anderson, *Eyes Off the Prize: The United Nations and the African American Struggle for Human Rights, 1944–1955* (New York: CUP, 2003), 228–320.

[135] John G. Hadwen and Johan Kaufmann, *How United Nations Decisions Are Made* (New York: Harper & Brothers, 1960), 36.

committees served as contexts in which to explore the meaning of human rights and UN universality in closed-door sessions. The Seminar on Human Rights in Kabul in 1964 is a good example, and it was beyond the glare of the General Assembly that the link between human rights and economic development was first mooted.[136] The newly decolonized countries set great store by the UN and its advisory committees, since they were seen at the time as a way forward for African and East European states in regard to anti-colonialism. As for Second World representatives, these issues could be more quietly explored in these settings, which showed a more informal and private side of UN negotiations.

Take the example of the UN's Third Committee, which was created to handle Social, Humanitarian and Cultural Questions, including Human Rights. It was the place where the meaning of human rights was thrashed out, and where Third World representatives worked to challenge the western hold on the understanding of the concept. This was particularly the case in the 1960s discussions of the Draft Document for the Elimination of Racial Discrimination. In one 1965 exchange, for example, a Venezuelan delegate took issue with a Canadian who insisted on 'the traditional Western concept of human rights' by boldly countering that 'the Western countries had no reason to pride themselves on their advanced moral concepts, since it was in those countries that racial discrimination had originated and still existed.' In the same debate, the Tanzanian delegate acidly added that 'the Western world clearly had nothing to teach the developing countries in the matter of human rights; indeed, it was the Western world that had given birth to colonialism and slavery, while the developing countries had suffered as a result.'[137]

Committee minutes record support from all countries on this issue, especially the Soviet Union, Eastern Bloc and Third World when denouncing racism and apartheid. Portugal (because of its colonial holdings in Angola and Mozambique) became a favourite target of growing criticism at the UN, much like South Africa.[138] Notably, Eastern European countries often took the lead in speaking for the socialist world in these committees, in part due to their own experience of Nazi racism. Poland's judicial apparatus had played a pioneering role in the prosecution of Nazi war criminals, and in 1965, its proposal to the UN Commission on Human Rights to end statutory limitations on international crimes committed by the Axis Powers during the Second World War provoked a wider international debate about the nature of 'crimes against humanity.'[139] By contrast with the

---

[136] Roland Burke, 'Challenging the Universal Declaration: Human Rights and the UN Advisory Services Program', *History Australia*, 9/1 (2012), 27–42.

[137] Quoted in Jensen, *International Human Rights*, 118.

[138] Jamie Miller, 'Things Fall Apart: South Africa and the Collapse of the Portugese Empire, 1973–1974', *Cold War History*, 12/2 (2012), 183–204.

[139] Raluca Grosescu, 'State Socialist Endeavours for the Non-Applicability of Statutory Limitations to International Crimes: Historical Roots and Current Implications', *Journal of the History of International Law*, 21/2 (2019), 239–69.

western states, which wished to confine the debate to those crimes defined at Nuremberg, the Eastern Bloc and states from the South advocated widening such definitions to include 'crimes against peace and...colonialism' and the introduction of 'inhumane acts resulting from the policy of apartheid' as part of this definition.[140] In the early debates about the Draft Document, Yugoslavia and Ukraine led the way in insisting that the final draft should make a strong link between colonialism and racial discrimination.[141] Czechoslovakia then proposed an amendment to make good on this plea, and worked closely with Chile, Nigeria, Ukraine and Yugoslavia on it.

For the Third Committee the main sticking point was not over the general principle of condemning the practice of racial discrimination, which found unanimous support, but rather over enforcement. Here the US, UK and other western powers defended the importance of free speech, to the point of insisting that opinions of racial discrimination—however odious—should not be criminalized *tout court*. In contention was a varied conception of human rights across continents. For the West, human rights were grounded in the right to free expression and assembly, and thus the delegates from the US, UK, Canada and others were wary of the firm application of any human rights proposed ordinance (in this case, Article 9, Paragraph 3) that challenged the sanctity of free speech. For representatives from the developing world, human rights were much more about disallowing racist expressions in any form. These conflicting views created new coalitions, as the delegates from the Third World, the Soviet Union and Eastern Bloc banded together to push for more sweeping measures to criminalize expressions of racism in any form, often referring to the dangers of unchecked Fascism in this regard.[142]

The Soviet Union was less active than the Eastern Bloc countries on this committee. When the USSR delegate did raise his voice, it was generally heavy and long-winded, exploiting every occasion to shame the West.[143] However, such comments rarely made any difference and were ignored in subsequent discussions; what is more, in these Third Committee discussions—unlike in the debates

---

[140] 'UN Convention on the Non-Applicability of Statutory Limitations to War Crimes and Crimes Against Humanity', Adopted and opened for signature, ratification and accession by General Assembly resolution 2391 (xxiii), 26 November 1968.

[141] See the comments by Mrs. Pesic Golubovic (Yugoslavia) and Mr. Polyanichko (Ukrainian Soviet Socialist Republic), *Third Committee, 1213th Meeting, Thurs. 26 September. 1963, Official Records of the General Assembly, 18th Session, Third Committee: Social, Humanitarian and Cultural Questions, 17 September–11 December 1963* (New York: United Nations, 1964), 11–15.

[142] Miss. Addison (Ghana), *Third Committee, 1233th Meeting, Thurs. 16 October 1963, Official Records of the General Assembly, 18th Session, Third Committee: Social, Humanitarian and Cultural Questions, 17 September–11 December 1963* (New York: United Nations, 1964), 101.

[143] Mr. Chkhikvadze (USSR), *Third Committee, 1293rd Meeting, Tues. 14 Dec. 1965, Official Records of the General Assembly, 20th Session, Third Committee: Social, Humanitarian and Cultural Questions, 22-September-15 December 1965* (New York: United Nations, 1966), 501.

at the General Assembly—the Eastern Bloc did not act as a unified front, and clearly the individual Eastern European regimes did not like being spoken for by its overbearing patron. These smaller committees therefore came to offer valuable opportunities for building political bridges to representatives from the developing world. As one commentator put it, at the UN Eastern European voices not only were heard, but in the committee work the 'slavish ritual of reiterating official Soviet positions' was much less apparent.[144]

There were significant moments when representatives from the Second and Third Worlds banded together. In 1965 the US and Brazilian delegates proposed an amendment to the draft that would explicitly include anti-Semitism in its condemnation of noxious practices of racial discrimination to be eliminated. The Afro-Asian delegates thereupon mobilized as a bloc, and at one point in the discussion the Moroccan delegate announced that the 'Afro-Asian group had decided to reject all new proposals' and urged the sponsors of new articles 'not to press them,'[145] to the dismay of Israel, the US, Brazil and other western powers. For the Afro-Asian group it was best to keep the language general and elastic. The Greek representative captured the majority sentiment when he remarked that specifying all forms of racial discrimination would most likely result 'in a series of recriminations rather than a concerted attack on all racial discrimination,'[146] which would only end up undermining the main business at hand. Relevant here is that Greece and Hungary co-sponsored a counter-proposal that expunged reference to the specific forms of racial discrimination featuring in the US-Brazilian proposal. Surprisingly, Hungary did so even though the Soviet Union itself had explicitly endorsed the US-Brazilian version earlier in the discussion, for the Hungarian delegates were keen to include Zionism as another form of racism. The point is that there was no united Communist voice on this matter, by contrast with the more cohesive Afro-Asian group. In fact, Eastern Bloc representatives often expressed quite independent views, and the vitriolic Soviet interventions were left unremarked upon and unsupported by Eastern Bloc representatives in these discussions. While Israel clashed with the USSR over the 'Zionism equals racism' charge, the Soviet Union otherwise did not exert much influence. Instead, Poland, Czechoslovakia, Tanzania and Senegal joined forces in negotiating a

---

[144] Robert and Elizabeth Bass, 'Eastern Europe', in Zbigniew Brzezinski (ed.), *Africa and the Communist World* (London: OUP, 1964), 109. For an expanded argument, see Sebastian Gehrig, James Mark, Idesbald Goddeeris, Kim Christiaens and Paul Betts, 'The Eastern Bloc, Human Rights and the Global Fight against Apartheid', *East Central Europe*, 46/2–3 (2019), 290–317.

[145] Mrs. Warzazi, *Third Committee, 1310th Meeting, Tues. 19 Oct. 1965, Official Records of the General Assembly, 20th Session, Third Committee: Social, Humanitarian and Cultural Questions, 22-September–15 December 1965* (New York: United Nations, 1966), 109.

[146] Mrs. Mantzoulinos, *Third Committee, 1311th Meeting, Wed. 20 Oct. 1965, Official Records of the General Assembly, 20th Session, Third Committee: Social, Humanitarian and Cultural Questions, 22-September–15 December 1965* (New York: United Nations, 1966), 111.

more general language of anti-racism that aligned the Second and Third Worlds, with little input from or reference to the US or USSR.[147]

In the end, the UN Convention on the Elimination of All Forms of Racial Discrimination was adopted unanimously by the General Assembly, and came into force in 1969. It was a significant milestone in the history of human rights at the UN, but also only a qualified success at the time, not least because member states tended to frame rights issues in terms of discrimination, not equality. The ratification of the Covenant was cynically seen by many member states as a way of establishing good 'anti-apartheid credentials', and it was assumed that such racism was only intrinsic to extreme societies, such as Nazi Germany, South Africa or Southern Rhodesia. The result was that the 1966 Convention was treated almost exclusively as a foreign policy matter linked to anti-colonialism, rather than a domestic concern—in other words, racism was elsewhere.[148] In practice many member states failed to report abuses within their own borders. For this reason, anti-apartheid became the human rights issue on which everyone could agree,[149] as apartheid remained at the heart of UN debates from the 1960s through the 1980s.[150] In 1968 alone, Rhodesia and apartheid in South Africa occupied 35 of the 58 meetings of the Commission on Human Rights.[151] Anti-apartheid was also strategically exploited by both superpowers. The USSR used anti-apartheid to deflect attention from problems during the Prague Spring, and the US did the same with regard to Vietnam. Still, the Convention was a breakthrough of international diplomacy, and was publicized as an instance where the socialist world was more progressive than its western counterpart.[152] The Soviet Union devoted a good deal of international publicity to the passage of the Convention, and it was no coincidence that it published its first article on human rights that year in the Soviet journal, *International Affairs*, 'The Nations Repudiate Racism'. Characteristically, the article connected racism to colonialism, Nazism and western machinations, and foregrounded the USSR and the Eastern Bloc states as leading the campaign, even at the expense of the Afro-Asian countries' contribution.[153]

---

[147] UN General Assembly, Third Committee, 20th Session, 1301st meeting, 12 October 1965, 67–73.

[148] M. Banton, *International Action Against Racial Discrimination* (Oxford: Clarendon, 1996), 100.

[149] Daniel Maul, *Human Rights, Development and Decolonization: The International Labour Organization, 1940-1970* (Basingstoke: Palgrave, 2012), 197–208.

[150] Compare *Report of the Expert Committee on Apartheid in South Africa* (New York: United Nations Security Council, 1965) and Maitama-Sule, Alhaji Yusuff, *Struggle Against Apartheid: The work of the Special Committee in relation to the International Year for mobilisation of sanctions against South Africa* (New Delhi: India International Centre, 1982).

[151] Jensen, *International Human Rights*, 176.

[152] Lena J. Kruckenberg, *The UNreal World of Human Rights: An Ethnography of the UN Committee on the Elimination of Racial Discrimination* (Baden-Baden: Nomos, 2012), 101–11.

[153] V. Chkhivadze, 'The Nations Repudiate Racism', *International Affairs*, 5 (May 1966), 49–54, and for discussion, Jensen, *International Human Rights*, 127.

The 1965 Convention established a 'major precedent' that not only helped convert human rights into law. In addition, it paved the way for the passage of the 1966 Human Rights Covenant, and, according to Steven Jensen, it showed how race 'was the issue that forced the hand of the UN member states and came to the rescue of the international human rights project'.[154]

No less significant is that the UN's public campaign against racial discrimination enjoyed influence far beyond the halls of the UN. For example, African Americans carried the UN flag along with the Stars and Stripes in the 1964 Selma marches to protest for the constitutional right to vote, to the consternation of local white Southerners.[155] In Eastern Europe the human rights link with racial equality was a popular cause that attracted widespread publicity. The GDR, for example, issued commemorative stamps featuring all three races (white, black, yellow) as early as 1958 to celebrate the tenth anniversary of the Universal Declaration,[156] and produced a number of books and brochures (often in English) to broadcast the connection between socialism and anti-apartheid more globally. East European countries organized dozens of academic conferences, exchanges and cultural displays of solidarity with the Third World that precisely addressed this nexus of race and rights.

This bundling of human rights, anti-colonialism and economic development assumed increasing international recognition in the late 1960s, as their relationship was recalibrated to suit new political interests.[157] For many in the Second and Third Worlds, the UN's 1966 International Covenant on Economic, Social and Cultural Rights was welcomed for returning to the more ecumenical ethos of the 1948 Declaration and its explicit unity of political and economic rights.[158] Article 11 of the 1966 Covenant for instance stipulated 'the right of everyone to an adequate standard of living for himself and his family, including adequate food, clothing and housing, and to the continuous improvement of living conditions', while Article 12 recognized the 'right for everyone to the enjoyment of the highest attainable standard of physical and mental health.'[159] Nowhere was this

[154] Jensen, *International Human Rights*, 102–3.

[155] Thomas Borstelmann, *The Cold War and the Color Line* (Cambridge, MA: Harvard University Press, 2001), 189.

[156] Ned Richardson-Little, *Between Dictatorship and Dissent: Ideology, Legitimacy and Human Rights in East Germany, 1945-1990*, PhD dissertation (University of North Carolina at Chapel Hill, 2013), 57–9.

[157] Russel Lawrence Barsh, 'The Right to Development as a Human Right: Results of a Global Consultation', *Human Rights Quarterly*, 13/2 (1991), 322–38.

[158] Article 25 of the 1948 Universal Declaration of Human Rights states that 'Everyone has the right to a standard of living adequate for the health and well-being of himself and of his family, including food, clothing and housing and medical care and necessary social services, and the right to security in the event of unemployment, sickness, disability, widowhood, old age or other lack of livelihood in circumstances beyond his control.'

[159] Onora O'Neill, 'The Dark Side of Human Rights', *International Affairs*, 81/2 (2005), 429.

conception of rights more pronounced than at the 1968 UN Conference in Teheran, when human rights talk was effectively subordinated to economic development. Article 13 of the Teheran Conference Proclamation clearly stated that human rights were 'dependent upon sound and effective...economic and social development'.[160] This was a victory for Second and Third World radicalism and small state engagement, and the Final Act of the Teheran Conference was hailed by supporters for having adopted a more 'holistic' vision of human rights as welfare rights for all peoples and political regimes.[161]

But the new conflation of human rights and development contained a hidden dimension, as the once-assumed link between democracy and rights was quietly abandoned. At Teheran two thirds of the delegates did not come from democratic states, and many there wanted to turn the spotlight away from homegrown authoritarianism in these newly decolonized countries. Anti-apartheid again served as a convenient moral common ground across continents. At the Teheran conference the US and USSR—both under attack there as imperialists—developed a new rapport around a tacit agreement to avoid criticizing each other and to 'collaborate to subdue small nation prima donnas' around human rights.[162] Even so, the Teheran Conference of 1968 would prove to be the high watermark of small state power at the international level. With it the Third World's strong advocacy of universalism at the UN faded in the 1970s. For many newer members, universalism was no longer seen as radically anti-colonial, as it had been in the 1950s, but rather was now construed as imperial. The characterization of human rights as crass western colonialism was already present in the controversial 1947 American Anthropology Association statement about the cultural arrogance of the West, and anthropologists such as Julian Steward condemned the Universal Declaration as nothing but 'American ideological imperialism' in the late 1940s. But it was not until the 1970s that these views were picked up by African intellectuals. Makau Mutua, former chair of the Kenyan human rights commission, saw human rights as 'within the historical continuum of the European colonial project'. In a 1977 UN General Assembly, Saudi Arabian UN representative Jamil Baroody even went so far as to say that the contemporary world was without universals, and that human rights did not exist outside specific cultural traditions. In his estimation, the UDHR was simply an 'exclusively Western approach to the human rights question', and that 'Western countries want to impose a concept of those rights shaped according to their own norms of civilization. Those norms had no place in many countries where the concept of

---

[160]   Roland Burke, 'From Individual Rights to National Development: The First UN International Conference on Human Rights, Tehran 1968', *Journal of World History*, 19/3 (2008), 276.

[161]   Gehrig et al., 'The Eastern Bloc', 261–89.

[162]   Roland Burke, *Decolonization and the Evolution of International Human Rights* (Philadelphia: University of Pennsylvania Press, 2010), 94–108.

human rights was based on age-old customs and traditions.'[163] Less remarked is that the new cultural relativism also spelled the end of human rights as a joint venture between the Second and Third Worlds, after which the transcontinental link to Eastern Europe was cut off in the name of regional and even ethnic cultural autonomy. As noted elsewhere in this volume, the 1970s witnessed a growing distance between Eastern Europe and its partners in the global South, and the decline of human rights as a source of socialist solidarity partly reflected this trend as well. So whereas the language of cultural relativism was used by the West in the 1940s to limit the application of human rights to the colonies, best seen with the infamous 'colonial clause' associated with the UDHR,[164] by the 1970s the West and the Afro-Asian bloc had reversed positions. Cultural relativism became the domain of anti-western politics, and human rights once again fell victim to Cold War politics.

By the 1970s, the ideals of socialist internationalism were starting to fracture, and found expression in the discourse of rights. For one thing, self-determination no longer served as the shared rights cause bridging the Second and Third Worlds. The focus shifted instead toward issues of justice in the world economy, best evidenced in the proposals for a New International Economic Order in the mid-1970s by representatives from developing countries at the United Nations to improve terms of trade on the world market. By the end of the decade, Eastern Europe was also embracing cultural relativism in relation to human rights. On the one hand, new oppositional groups, such as Charter 77 in Czechoslovakia and Solidarity in Poland, began to invoke the language of human rights to advance their reform agenda. On the other, socialist regimes, as noted in Bulgaria, defended their positions by developing idea of human rights as gifts from the state in exchange for citizen duties and productive labour, championing a kind of 'labour theory of value' in the realm of socialist civil rights.[165] The fractured understanding of rights was further illustrated in the failure of Eastern Bloc ministers in 1985 to agree a Socialist Declaration of Human Rights. While the declaration was designed to showcase the global relevance of state socialism as an alternative rights culture, its failure effectively underscored the Eastern Bloc's isolation in a changing world of rights claim-making. So at a time when African and Asian elites were recasting human rights as a defence of traditional values, religious heritage and economic development, their Eastern European

[163] Quoted in Burke, *Decolonization*, 137–8. For discussion, see Bonny Ibhawoh, *Human Rights in Africa* (Cambridge: Cambridge University Press, 2018), esp. 173–220.

[164] Burke, *Decolonization*, 113–14.

[165] Todor Hristov, 'Rights to Weapons: Rights as a Resource in Workplace Conflicts in Late Socialist Bulgaria', *East Central Europe*, 46/2–3 (2019), 240–60.

counterparts (especially opposition groups) were reinterpreting human rights as part of a new reform movement linking Eastern and Western Europe.[166]

Conclusion

A few concluding remarks can be made. First, the slow acknowledgement of and interest in human rights across the Eastern Bloc in the 1950s and 1960s took place mostly in relation to developments in the USSR. The Soviet Union was of course one of the main framers of the Universal Declaration in 1948, and the inclusion of more 'material' rights (right to work, housing, healthcare, etc.) was a direct result of its presence there. Even so, it is quite clear that human rights faded in importance in the 1950s across the Cold War divide, as they were treated with indifference by the US, and with hostility by the USSR both before and after 1956. This created a space for small states—in Africa, Asia and Eastern Europe—to discuss and debate human rights issues without an overarching superpower presence. Most of the East European political relations with Asia and Africa were transformed by various hot-button issues—the Congo Crisis, the Algerian War, South Africa and later Chile—wherein bilateral relationships between individual Eastern Bloc countries and individual African/Asian countries were forged as a result.[167] The UN designation of self-determination as a new human right was an obvious means to forge solidarity between Eastern Europe and Africa. However, the conversion of economic and social rights into human rights in the 1966 Covenant and at the UN's Teheran Conference in 1968 did provide another ideological bridge for Eastern Europeans in the 1960s. Emphasis on economic and social rights also became a relatively apolitical means of building solidarity across the continents without direct reference to the USSR, especially for those African countries unsure of the post-1956 Soviet Union. Anti-imperialism and anti-apartheid then became a Détente Era language of fellowship between Eastern Europe and decolonized Africa that sidestepped other delicate issues in the name of international solidarity.

Secondly, the place of the UN underlined how Eastern European–Third World relations were often mediated by international organizations. Much of the action took place in the media and public forums, be it at the UN, in national newspapers, or in brochures and other publications aimed at challenging the evil West and its disrespect for the rights of Africans and Asians. This rights campaign was

---

[166] Ned Richardson-Little, 'The Failure of the Socialist Declaration of Human Rights: Ideology, Legitimacy and Elite Defection at the End of State Socialism', *East Central Europe*, 46/2–3 (2019), 318–42.
[167] Jan Eckel, *Die Ambivalenz des Guten: Menschenrechte in der internationalen Politik seit den 1940ern* (Göttingen: Vandenhoeck & Ruprecht, 2014), 583–710.

geared toward an international public sphere from the beginning, as seen with the crises in Hungary, the Congo, the Algerian War and anti-apartheid. From these international contacts grew strengthening bilateral relations in trade and cultural exchange. This language of solidarity helped build various bilateral relations across Africa, and the USSR seemed prepared to countenance these Eastern Bloc–African relations as long as they remained in an anti-western key; rights became a means of political identity-formation (both at home and abroad) for these struggling Eastern Bloc states, as they all devoted a good deal of publicity to various actions in fraternal African countries. That said, there was little solidarity or networking among other East European countries. On the contrary, there was often a good deal of competition between bloc members in regard to military assistance and economic development. This partly changed with the Helsinki Accords, as new, more connected anti-state human rights groups organized and communicated across the bloc, with the exception of the GDR. Even so, the specific inflections of human rights were predominantly linked to national issues.

Thirdly, the human rights story showed that there was a socialist version of universalism that challenged the standard liberal one. The UN and UNESCO version of universalism held some sway in the 1950s, but much of its touted post-fascist universalism was compromised by Cold War antagonism. Rights language was commonly used as a political weapon to criticize and shame the other side, but also as a means of defining the bloc internationally—i.e., the rights of women under socialism were broadcast as illustrative of progressive socialist culture worldwide. The Non-Aligned Movement was often used as camouflage for Third World regimes susceptible to international criticism on their human rights record. Those countries singled out for criticism in the UN, such as Chile, El Salvador and Guatemala, were typically not NAM members or linked to other international blocs. Arguably, there were more human rights abuses in Vietnam, Iran, Argentina and Cuba at the time, but these countries escaped condemnation largely due to their NAM membership. And since most Third World countries in Latin America were not part of the NAM, most of the UN human rights criticism was effectively aimed at them.

Fourthly, gender made its comeback on the UN and international human rights agenda in the 1970s. The decade witnessed a certain breakthrough in relations between Second and Third World feminists associated with the UN in the 1970s, which was built on some of the initiatives from earlier decades. The creation of the UN's Committee on the Status of Women closely resembled the Resolution to Eliminate Racial Discrimination, as the UN Resolution on the Elimination of Discrimination Against Women was passed in 1975 by the General Assembly. The WIDF played a key role here. After it returned to the UN in 1967, it worked to put gender issues on the main agenda at the UN's 1968 International Conference on Human Rights in Teheran—this was the first time that gender occupied a central topic of discussion in the General Assembly, and the issue gained momentum over the 1970s and 1980s. The WIDF was the driving force behind extending the UN's International Women's Year to the UN's Decade for Women in 1975, and much of this initiative was driven by Eastern European feminist activists.[168] The Mexico City conference in 1975 helped build alliances between Second and Third World feminists, as they linked women's emancipation to the broader struggle against social and economic inequalities. The final report went so far as to identify the root causes of this inequality as 'colonialism, neo-colonialism, Zionism, racial discrimination and apartheid'.[169] It was a landmark moment for international feminism, and moved feminism back on the agenda of the UN.[170] The federation organized a thirtieth anniversary of the founding of the WIDF in East Berlin, and this became a platform for Second and Third World women to discuss the linkage of rights to wider issues of anti-Fascism, colonialism and racism.[171] The WIDF then went on to organize the World Conferences on Women in 1975, 1980, 1985 and 1995.[172] These meetings continue to be important spaces of contact: Eastern European women's groups, such as the Committee of the Bulgarian Women's Movement, helped forge these intercontinental connections, even to the point of organizing so-called 'experience exchanges' between socialist women in Eastern Europe and their counterparts in Tanzania, Syria, Greece, the Congo and Algeria, and delegations from Portugal, Spain and Algeria travelled to Bulgaria as part of these partnerships. The link between human rights and women's rights became a prominent issue at the UN in the 1970s and 1980s, and dovetailed with anti-apartheid issues in the 1980s.[173]

Lastly, these 1960s human rights discussions about Africa and Asia boomeranged back to Eastern Europe in the 1970s. The publication of the Helsinki Accords in all Eastern European national newspapers provided a fresh language

---

[168] Raluca Maria Popa, 'Translating Equality between Women and Men across the Cold War Divides: Women Activists from Hungary and Romania and the Creation of International Women's Year', in Jill Massino and Shana Penn (eds.), *Gender Politics and Everyday Life in State Socialist East and Central Europe* (London: Palgrave, 2009), 59–74.

[169] Report of the World Conference on the International Women's Year, Mexico City, 19 June–2 July 1975, in Women and Social Movements, International http://wasi.alexanderstreet.com, as discussed in Chiara Bonfiglioli, 'The First UN World Conference on Women (1975) as a Cold War Encounter: Recovering the Anti-Imperialist, Non-Aligned and Socialist Geneaologies', *Filozofija i društvo*, 27/3 (2016), 521–41.

[170] For contemporary accounts, Hanna Papanek, 'The Work of Women: Postscript from Mexico City', *Signs*, 1/1 (1975), 215–26, Jennifer Seymour Whitaker, 'Women of the World: Report from Mexico', *Foreign Affairs*, 54/1 (1975), 173–81.

[171] Kristen Ghodsee, 'Rethinking State Socialist Mass Women's Organizations: The Committee of the Bulgarian Women's Movement and the United Nations Decade for Women, 1975–1985', *Journal of Women's History*, 24/4 (2012), 49–73.

[172] Judith Zinsser, 'From Mexico to Copenhagen to Nairobi: The United Nations Decade for Women, 1975–1985', *Journal of World History*, 13/1 (2002), 139–68.

[173] Ghodsee, 'Mass Women's Organizations', 59.

for dissidents to express their rights grievances against the state in new ways.[174] Human rights activism in the Soviet Union is often traced back to the demonstration by a group of intellectuals on Pushkin Square on 5 December 1965, with the slogans 'Respect the Constitution, the Basic Law of the USSR', and the follow-up trials of writers Andrei Sinyavsky and Yury Daniel.[175] But Helsinki internationalized these grievances, even if the movements were mostly national in scope and orientation. Examples ranged from Adam Michnik's condemnation of Poland's martial law (1981) as a human rights violation in his *Letters from Prison* to the new politicization of peace and environmentalism as human rights issues.[176] What is generally forgotten is that this human rights language was also linked to 1960s Third World issues. Steven Jensen has persuasively argued that the 1975 Helsinki Accords cannot be understood outside of these 1960s international human rights discussions. UN rights advocates from the developing world remade human rights based on self-determination and freedom in the Elimination of Racial Discrimination and the UN Covenant of Human Rights, whose rhetoric found its way into the formulations of the Accords.[177] Algeria, Egypt, Morocco, Syria and Israel took part in the Helsinki Accords, despite fierce debate between NATO Warsaw Pact and non-aligned countries.[178] Their success in getting these conventions passed made the Helsinki Accords possible, and the latter even drew on the same lexicon.

Given the way in which this 1960s human rights language shaped the Helsinki Accords, it can be argued that the developing world had a similar effect on Eastern Europe as well. Certainly, a number of human rights committees were formed across Eastern Europe after 1975, focusing on civil rights and linked to Third World issues. The UN's 1966 Covenant on Civil and Political Rights was incorporated in several Eastern Bloc constitutions (such as Hungary's) in the wake of the Accords.[179] Such influences are certainly significant, but they overlook the role that many Eastern European delegates played in the UN debates and UN Advisory Committees in helping draft these conventions, since they it was who carried these experiences and successes back to Helsinki, and helped drive forward these negotiations. Yet this was not limited to international diplomacy. Dissident groups in Eastern Europe would now commonly use the language of

---

[174] Daniel J. Thomas, *The Helsinki Effect: International Norms, Human Rights and Demise of Communism* (Princeton: Princeton University Press, 2001), 165–70 and Snyder, *Human Rights Activism*, 55.

[175] Valery Chalidze, *To Defend these Rights: Human Rights and the Soviet Union* (London: Collins and Harville, 1975), 53.

[176] Adam Michnik, *Letters from Prison* (Berkeley: University of California Press, 1987), 52–3 and Kacper Szulecki, 'Hijacked Ideas: Human Rights, Peace and Environmentalism in Czechoslovak and Polish Dissident Discourses', *East European Politics and Societies* 25/2 (2011), 272–95.

[177] Jensen, *International Human Rights*, 103 and conclusion.

[178] L.V. Ferraris, *Report on a Negotiation: Helsinki-Geneva-Helsinki 1972–1975* (Alphen aan den Rijn: Sijthoff & Noordhoff, 1979), 89–97. See too John Maresca, *To Helsinki: the Conference on Security and Cooperation in Europe, 1973–1975* (Durham: Duke University Press, 1985), 38–42.

[179] Halmai and Polgári, 'Hungary', 182.

apartheid to advance their reform causes. The well-known Charter 77 movement, for example, described the lack of press freedom in Czechoslovakia as a kind of 'virtual apartheid'. What this shows is how these delicate issues of human rights not only provided a vehicle for Eastern Bloc countries to build international identities and bridges to Third World comrades, but also helped forge a new vocabulary of reform that was recast for domestic consumption and internal political change.

6

Race

James Mark

> *I wanted to prove to them there are different white people.*[1]
> Yugoslav traveller, Nikola Vitorović, Congo, 1961

Amongst the records left behind of the encounter between Communist Europe and a decolonizing world, we find ample evidence that in this era Eastern Europeans thought *racially*—not just in terms of nationhood, ethnicity and difference within the region, as is often argued, but in terms of their position in a *global racial order*.[2] Simply put, their commitment to an anti-colonial internationalism had rendered them the better kind of white. The region's populations, Communists claimed, had no meaningful connection with the racist practices of the past. The memory of suffering and violence under Nazi Empire was invoked in many countries to prove that their citizens had been merely the victims of racial ideologies, imposed from outside: the Communist nation was thus unburdened from racial guilt or association. Moreover, in abandoning those capitalist practices which produced racism, Communists argued, its continuation was now a structural impossibility. Racial discrimination would henceforth always be located elsewhere, where fascism, still alive in western capitalist imperialism, reproduced it in the exploitative hunt for profit, whether in America, or resistance to liberation struggles in Africa and Asia.

Eastern Europeans' anti-racist commitments would now be focused beyond their own country or continent, and it was through this internationalist vision

The author wishes to thank Nemanja Radonjić (Yugoslavia), Zoltán Ginelli (Hungary), Alena K. Alamgir (Czechoslovakia), Maria Dembek (Poland), and Eric Burton (GDR) for their material contributions to this chapter.

[1] Nikola Vitorović, *Crne suze Konga* (Belgrade: Izdavač, 1961), 114.
[2] Questioning Eastern European 'racial exceptionalism' has come mainly from scholars of southeastern Europe, see Catherine Baker, *Race and the Yugoslav Region: Postsocialist, post-conflict, postcolonial?* (Manchester: Manchester University Press, 2018); Catherine Baker, 'Postcoloniality Without Race? Racial Exceptionalism and Southeast European Cultural Studies', *Interventions*, 20/6 (2018), 759–84. On the region's 'semi-peripheral racism', see Marta Grzechnik, 'The Missing Second World: On Poland And Postcolonial Studies', *Interventions. International Journal of Postcolonial Studies*, 21/7 (2019), 1010–11.

James Mark, *Race* In *Socialism Goes Global: The Soviet Union and Eastern Europe in the Age of Decolonization*. Edited by James Mark and Paul Betts, Oxford University Press. © Oxford University Press 2022. DOI: 10.1093/oso/9780192848857.003.0007

that a racialized self-image on the global stage could develop. Adopting the popular postwar idea that there were three biologically defined races, none either inferior or superior, Communists discovered whiteness as a mark of progressive commitment. Yet this was often a contested process, as Communist elites sought to close down 'excessive' race talk which undermined a politics of class-based proletarian revolution. Nevertheless, their anti-colonial commitments brought them face to face with a world politics in which increasingly assertive claims to racial liberation were central, and their colour taken as a mark of colonialism: questions around the political implications of their white skin could not be avoided. In many of the cultural texts produced by the anti-colonial encounter—in internationalist propaganda, travel writings and adventure stories in particular—we see Eastern Europeans reimagining themselves. Alongside being Poles, Hungarians, Romanians and so on, whose earlier experience of nationalist struggles against empires in Europe placed them in an authentic solidarity with contemporaneous liberation movements, they were also the better sort of whites, now bestriding the global stage committed to an anti-racist world.[3]

Yet such identities cannot be understood only as a novel product of state socialist claims to political superiority over a racist imperialist capitalism. They were also embedded in a much longer-term history of the racialization of Eastern Europeans: the increasing equivalence between whiteness and European imperial power over the course of the eighteenth and nineteenth centuries was an ambivalent development for those outside a western core.[4] The terms of whiteness were primarily constructed from outside the region, and often meant denigration: Eastern Europeans were those who did not hold colonies—or even for a time their own states—which in turn meant that they would not be considered by Western Europeans fully white.[5] Claims to full access to a European whiteness that relied on the status and power that statehood and colonies conferred thus remained fragile and partial. Nevertheless, by the turn of the twentieth century, some Eastern European nationalists asserted the capacity, on the account of having been colonized themselves, to be able to redeem a European colonial project which had been degraded through violence—and hence superior Europeans who could escape this racialized denigration through this act of imperial redemption

---

[3] On the importance of the cultural archive for tracing race, see e.g. Gloria Wekker, *White Innocence: Paradoxes of Colonialism and Race* (Durham: Duke University Press, 2016), 93–8.

[4] Alastair Bonnett, 'Who Was White? The Disappearance of Non-European White Identities and the Formation of European Racial Whiteness', *Ethnic and Racial Studies*, 21/6 (1998), 1030.

[5] On how Eastern Europeans were seen as lesser whites in imperial Africa, see e.g. Jochen Lingelbach, *On the Edges of Whiteness. Polish Refugees in British Colonial Africa during and after the Second World War* (New York: Berghahn, 2020), 31, 80–2; or regarding their migration to the US, see e.g. David R. Roediger, *Working Toward Whiteness: How America's Immigrants Became White* (New York: Basic Books, 2005); Robert M. Zecker, *Race and America's Immigrant Press: How the Slovaks were taught to think like white people* (London: Bloomsbury Academic, 2013). Also Baker, 'Postcoloniality Without Race?', 772.

(see *Origins*). The Communist era did not in fact mark a clear break with these earlier patterns. The idea of being the better kind of anti-colonial white was still in part a claim to status as equal or superior Europeans that drew on markers of civilizational value derived from European imperialism. As their encounter with the decolonizing world intensified, Communists revived an Imperial Era nostalgia for white hunters, explorers and missionaries, which in turn fed the paternalist civilizing discourses of socialist anti-colonialism.

The fault lines in Communist Europe's anti-racist commitments were spotted from the start: both enemies and friends attacked what they perceived as its hypocrisies and blind spots, claiming that the region's anti-racist commitments on the world stage were merely gestural, a product of only superficially hidden desires for power still shaped by imperial fantasy;[6] or were cynically used to hide the realities of anti-Semitism at home. Indeed, as the power of the anti-colonial project waned in the 1970s, and the status accrued by allegiance to the anti-racist struggle declined with it, so in many places Communists' political commitment faltered. Racially inflected discourses of civilizational difference, which had been reproduced in the cultures of imperial nostalgia that had underlain the anti-colonial project even in the era of high postwar decolonization, roared back much more explicitly into political rhetoric. Both Communists and anti-Communists claimed that internationalism had 'blackened' the region and opened up arguments around whether the difference between a developed Europe and underdeveloped Africa was so great as to be impossible to overcome. Such transformations undermined the appeal of an earlier anti-colonial 'white saviourism' abroad. It also set the scene for increased incidences of racism at home, as foreign students and workers during the 1970s and 1980s were increasingly targeted as alien to a Europe uniting around claims to continental cultural unity, the definition of which even prior to the collapse of Communism often slipped into assertions of racialized difference between white and black continents.

Racial Innocence and Imperial Nostalgia

From early in the consolidation of Communist power, the claim to moral superiority based on the embrace of the global struggle against racism was linked to the *erasure* of concern for the legacies of racism and genocide at home. Those who sought to understand the destruction of the Second World War explicitly through a racial lens—and bring the 'Jewish catastrophe' to the fore—were, after a few years, marginalized. One instructive case was that of the *Liga do Walki z Rasizmem* (League for the Struggle against Racism), which was founded in Warsaw in 1946.

---

[6] Jelena Subotić and Srdjan Vučetić, 'Performing Solidarity: Whiteness and Status-Seeking in the Non-aligned World', *Journal of International Relations and Development*, 22/3 (2019), 722–43.

It was an outgrowth of the wartime *Żegota*—the Polish Council to Aid Jews—and was founded to continue the struggle against racism and anti-Semitism in a country where almost three million Jews, alongside three million non-Jewish Poles, had been killed under Nazi occupation. The League brought together both Jewish and non-Jewish Poles, mainly from the non-Communist left, and was concentrated in Kraków and Łódź.[7] Antedating Communist attempts to externalize the origins of racism, the League presented anti-Semitism as an essentially foreign ideology, implanted first by Tsarist Russia and then by Hitler, which now had infected local populations who after 1945 were still carrying out pogroms against Jews.[8] They thus sought to educate Polish society about continued prejudice and how it was provoking further emigration to Israel. The fight against domestic racism, one 1946 article from their journal argued, was crucial for the re-entry of Poland into the club of civilized nations:

> The necessity to fight racism, both in its broad sense, and with the form of racism occurring among us, anti-Semitism—is dictated by our national interest and by the need of our country [to be] to be part of the family of civilized nations. Hot and eager, we sympathize with every stroke that hits the most unfortunate—our fellow Polish Jews, but we realize that the fight against anti-Semitism is not only a struggle for values and human rights of this earth, but also a fight for the health of the Polish soul, for the honour of the Polish name. The uncompromising enemy of Poland and Polishness—German racism, not only ruined our country and exterminated millions of Poles…but systematically poisoned our thoughts with racial hatred. It has instilled this crime into the instincts of the masses…[9]

With the consolidation of Communist power in Poland in the late 1940s, the position of the League fundamentally altered. As emigration was officially encouraged, Jewish organizations were either dissolved—or Communists claimed the right to regulate them.[10] The Party recognized the League's usefulness: its administrative structures and its journal 'The Rights of Man' were quickly appropriated and its new Communist membership argued its focus should no longer be on anti-Semitism.[11] Across the region, newly installed ruling parties claimed that

---

[7] On its founding, see Władysław Bartoszewski, 'Powstanie Ligi do Walki z Rasizmem w 1946 roku', *Więź*, 4 (1990), 117–28.

[8] 'Current Reflections', *Prawo Człowieka*, 1 (1946), and 'Polish Rationale for Fighting Anti-Semitism' in No. 2.

[9] *Prawo Człowieka*, 1, 15 September 1946, 1.

[10] Władysław Bartoszewski, *Życie trudne lecz nie nudne. Ze wspomnień Polaka w XX wieku* (Kraków: Znak, 2010), 239–40. Protocol nr 4: Minutes from the meeting of the Main Board, November, 22nd 1949, 6–11 ((League Against Racism, Central Archives of Modern Records, Warsaw).

[11] On this closing down, also see The August Trials: Andrew Kornbluth, *The Holocaust and Postwar Justice in Poland* (Cambridge, MA: Harvard University Press, 2021), chapter 8.

Communism rendered racism structurally irreproducible, and hence that institutions to investigate genocide or pogroms, were no longer important. The creation of a unified national proletariat, undifferentiated by race, was the key to revolutionary struggle. In Eastern Germany, race was declared a taboo concept as early as 1946. The Jewish GDR Politburo member Paul Merker put it thus: 'there is neither an Aryan nor a Germanic race biologically speaking...the separation of people into Aryans and non-Aryans was nothing more than dupery.'[12] The idea of a racial hierarchy based on biological difference that had come from German anthropology and had underpinned the practices of Nazi occupation could be put aside. SED leader Walter Ulbricht declared in 1950 that 'there is no longer any racial hatred in the GDR.'[13] The Soviets, after skirting close in the 1920s to arguments for immutability of racial characteristics that could determine behavioral traits, turned against such thinking in the face of Fascism: Soviet *rasovedenie* in the 1930s rejected eugenics as unscientific, and emphasized the equality of all races.[14] Although historians have traced how eugenic thinking survived after the Second World War in Eastern Europe, particularly regarding the disabled and Roma,[15] Communist politicians declared that racial science was unscientific and was a past phenomenon of a now discredited Nazi era. Romanian eugenicists who had supported population exchanges and the deportation of Jews and Roma in Transnistria under the Antonescu government, for example, were marginalized or removed from their posts.[16] In Hungary, elites moved in the mid-1950s against the reactionary geography of the interwar period that had presented Hungary as master race in the Carpathian basin.[17]

Within a few years of the Communist consolidation of power the examination of the persecution of minorities went into abeyance. Three years before the Polish League was eventually wound up in 1951—in part because it had failed to turn itself into a Communist mass organization—its mission was fundamentally altered. No longer was it to address domestic racial prejudice: 'Already, it was decided to focus on the fight against imperialism in general, and American in particular, as the proper source of all manifestations of modern racism.' Its National Delegates' Conference held on 25–6 April 1948, now under the

---

[12] Paul Merker, 'Der Airer-Schwindel', *Neues Deutschland*, 3 September 1947.

[13] Quoted in Quinn Slobodian, 'Socialist Chromatism: Race, Racism and the Racial Rainbow in East Germany', in idem. (ed.), *Comrades of Color: East Germany in the Cold War World* (Oxford: Berghahn, 2015), 26, 31. Heike Hartmann and Susann Lewerenz, 'Campaigning against Apartheid in East and West Germany', *Radical History Review*, 119 (Spring 2014), 191–204.

[14] Francine Hirsch, 'Race without the Practice of Racial Politics', *Slavic Review*, 61/1 (2002), 33–4.

[15] Victoria Shmidt, *The Politics of Disability in Interwar and Socialist Czechoslovakia: Segregating in the Name of the Nation* (Amsterdam: Amsterdam University Press, 2019), chapter 8.

[16] Vladimir Solonari, 'In the Shadow of Ethnic Nationalism. Racial Science in Romania', in Anton Weiss-Wendt and Rory Yeomans (eds.), *Racial Science in Hitler's New Europe, 1938-1945* (University of Nebraska Press: Lincoln and London, 2013), 259–86.

[17] Ferenc Koch, 'A nacionalizmus elleni harc irányelvei a földrajzban', *Felsőoktatási Szemle*, 10 (1960), 593–606.

influence of the party, would ensure that racism was understood as a product of an economic system which could only occur in the capitalist-imperialist world. As one its original founders regretfully noted, it became involved only in issues of racism outside Poland, 'combating American policy towards blacks and British colonialism and imperialism. It completely disappeared from what it was meant to serve.'[18]

The League ceased its cooperation with the church, with which it had been targeting anti-Semitism, and rather focused on anti-imperialist education with working class groups, peasants and youth organizations such as the ZMP.[19] In

'The Rights of Man', Journal of the League for the Struggle Against Racism, 1950.

1949, they began to organize youth camps for 'coloured people' and for students from both capitalist and colonial countries alongside book markets, lectures and screenings of anti-imperialist films.A League questionnaire to uncover 'indigenous racism' amongst youth in Gdańsk was rewritten to explore their knowledge of discrimination abroad.[20]

Just as the Warsaw Communists were substituting the memory of the Jewish catastrophe on Polish soil for the racism of the colonial present, Afro-Asian leaders and African-American intellectuals were beginning to explore the

---

[18] Bartoszewski, *Życie trudne lecz nie nudne*, 239.   [19] Ibid.
[20] AAN, Liga do Walki z Rasizmem, Protocol No. 16 from the meeting of the Presidium of the Board, 20 February 1950, Cat. No. 360/1/8, 35.

connections between the two. W.E.B. Du Bois visited Poland just after the war, and in his writings on the Warsaw Ghetto[21] considered the connections between imperialism and Fascism, and concluded that the suffering of African-Americans could no longer be considered without reference to the tragedy of the European Jews.[22] Leaders from a decolonizing world were surprised when their Eastern European counterparts did not make these same connections. A month after the Bandung Conference in June 1955, Indian Prime Minister Jawaharlal Nehru visited Warsaw with his Polish equivalent Józef Cyrankiewicz. Nehru himself reflected on the fate of Jews at Auschwitz, wondering how India would have fared in the face of Hitler's invasion. According to the transcript, the Polish Prime Minister ignored the invitation to talk about the common roots of persecution: rather, he immediately related the experience of brave Communist prisoners struggling to liberate the camp: 'like many others he had seen everything'. Nehru added that after seeing 'all that' one could have gone mad. Cyrankiewicz replied that indeed, this could have been the case if 'not for his conviction that everything would be over at some point and his faith in a better future that sustained his fighting spirit'.[23] This was an anti-colonialism based on parallel unified national struggles against imperialism that did not foreground questions of race or connect the wartime Jewish genocide to racism globally.

Experts from across Communist Eastern Europe supported UNESCO projects such as the 'Mutual Appreciation of Eastern and Western Cultural Values' that sought to overturn ideas of civilizational inferiority.[24] The 'Great Encyclopedia' of the Soviet Union, published in 1951, claimed that unlike the West, whose continued practice of imperialism reproduced racism, Communists created new cultures of expertise that appreciated all civilizations without racial hierarchy:

> Reflecting the colonialist–racist worldview of the European and American bourgeoisie, from the very beginning bourgeois Orientology diametrically opposed the civilizations of the so-called 'West' with those of the 'East', slanderously declaring that Asian peoples are racially inferior, somehow primordially incapable of determining their own fates, and that they appeared only as history's

---

[21] Michael Rothberg, 'W. E. B. Du Bois in Warsaw: Holocaust Memory and the Color Line, 1949–1952', *The Yale Journal of Criticism*, 14/1 (2001), 172.

[22] Marilyn Lake and Henry Reynolds, *Drawing the Global Colour Line* (Cambridge: CUP, 2012), 347. His way of conjoining such tragedies opened up avenues of solidarity between African-Americans and American Jews too: Clive Webb, 'The Nazi Persecution of Jews and the African American Freedom Struggle', *Patterns of Prejudice*, 53/4 (2019), 337–62.

[23] Archiwum Ministerstwa Spraw Zagranicznych (AMSZ), 12/8/184, Notatka Jerzego Grudzińskiego, ambasadora PRL w Delhi z wizyty premiera Indii w Polsce, [after 23] June 1955, 42.

[24] Hanna Jansen, 'Internationalizing the Thaw: Soviet Orientalists and the Contested Politics of Spiritual Solidarity in Asia 1954–1959', in James Mark, Artemy M. Kalinovsky, and Steffi Marung (eds.), *Alternative Globalizations. Eastern Europe and the Postcolonial World*, (Bloomington, IN: Indiana University Press), 209–10.

object, rather than its subject. Bourgeois Orientology entirely subordinates the study of the East to the colonial politics of the imperialist powers.[25]

Although racial hierarchy based on eugenic ideas was officially rejected, race as a concept defined through biological difference was not. Most Communist states reproduced the idea of three races that was emerging from postwar UN bodies such as UNESCO: the Caucasian, Negroid and Oriental racial types were still distinct, but now part of a 'family of man' within which races were considered equal parts of a common humanity.[26] This tripartite concept would be taught in schools across the region throughout the Communist period, and could lead to the problematic reification of racial difference. Foreign medical students in Yugoslavia in the 1960s for instance objected to an 'excessive insistence' in their textbooks on physiological differences between blacks and whites.[27] Nevertheless, the 'family of man' concept gave Communists a way to embrace the identity of white as a progressive category that might be freed of its former imperialist associations; in much travel writing of this period, we find Eastern Europeans longing for acceptance as a new kind of white on the global stage. Hungarian István Kende, in *Good Morning, Africa!* (1961), related a meeting with an African story teller whose role it was to legitimate his new identity:

> You are a white man who wanted to hear my homeland's history. So far I only knew white men like the ones I had business with…I am happy…This word [tubabu, meaning white man] felt inappropriate. Since this word denoted the concept that for him until now had only represented oppressor, hated alien, equipped with whips and intrigue, and not the sons of those countries, who establish[ed] equality.[28]

However, such travellers were far more commonly disappointed at the reluctance of Africans to accept such claims of anti-colonial whiteness.[29] This was made very explicit in the work of Oskar Davičo, a well-known Yugoslav surrealist writer and revolutionary socialist. In a chapter entitled 'A Former White Man', part of a work of reportage from decolonizing Africa called 'Black on White'

[25] 1951 Great Soviet Encyclopaedia.

[26] For an introduction to race in Soviet period see Nikolay Zakharov, *Race and Racism in Russia* (Basingstoke: Palgrave Macmillan, 2015), 34–45.

[27] Peter Wright, *The Ambivalence of Socialist Anti-Racism: The Case of Black African Students in 1960s Yugoslavia*. Paper presented at the (Re)Thinking Yugoslav Internationalism: Cold War Global Entanglements and Their Legacies conference, University of Graz, 29 September–1 October 2016.

[28] István Kende, *Jóreggelt, Afrika! Guineai útirajz* (Budapest: Gondolat Könyvkiadó, 1961), 69. Quoted in Eric Burton, Zoltán Ginelli, James Mark and Nemanja Radonjić, 'Imagined Spaces of Encounter: Travel Writing between the Colonial and Anti-Colonial in Socialist Eastern Europe 1949–1989', in Kristin Roth-Ey (ed.), *Second-Third World Spaces in the Cold War: Global Socialism and the Gritty Politics of the Particular* (London: Bloomsbury, 2022).

[29] Baker, *Race and Yugoslav Region*, 112.

(1962), he recounted how 'his people' had been victimized by empires themselves, and hence embodied a whiteness untouched by the rapacity of colonial conquest; nevertheless, on encountering Africa, he realized that attempts at anti-racist self-fashioning were in practice an impossible fantasy. He could not escape the political implications of his own colour. He thus wanted to shed his white skin and throw off the marker of the racist and colonial heritage which stuck bodily to him:

> It's pointless, but what can I do, I feel ashamed. My people and my class never tortured, enslaved, killed. For centuries we were slaves ourselves. Yes, but I am white, this is all that passers-by can see. If only I could carry a digested history of my country on my sleeves!...But to them I look like a Frenchman, Belgian, English, Boer, a lyncher from Little Rock. And it's embarrassing to think that in the eyes of an African I can be equated with them, with 'those'. If I could change the colour of my skin, I would do it without hesitation.[30]

Yet it was unclear how deep these commitments to racial equality and mutual learning between civilizations were: a racialized sense of biologically innate superiority and inferiority was gone, but this paternalistic vision of a socialist civilizing mission to aid benighted African blacks stuck in backwardness—now culturally rather than racially defined—could still be commonly found. A 1966 Bulgarian biology school textbook rejected the idea of 'inferior and superior races', but nevertheless emphasized that under Soviet-led socialism 'even the most undeveloped African tribes are capable of producing their own science, culture and art if they are given the opportunity to develop freely and to communicate with the culturally advanced'.[31] And although contemporary internationalist propaganda presented the three races walking hand to hand towards a bright future—the white socialist European man was usually foregrounded, or depicted one step in front.[32]

Such socialist paternalism, whose assertions of cultural difference often skirted around the edges of racialized essentialism, was underpinned by a culture in which images and narratives from the experience of European expansion and imperialism were revived. Such culture had been suppressed for a time under Stalinism, yet with the collapse of Western European empires in the late 1950s, and the attendant internationalization of Eastern European culture, books that placed the reader on the American frontier, or as explorers of Africa, were republished and found a wide readership.[33] Communist regimes did little to

---

[30] Oskar Davičo, *Crno na belo* (Belgrade: Prosveta, 1962), 20.

[31] Quoted in Miglena Todorova, *Race Travels: Whiteness and Modernity across National Borders*, Phd dissertation (University of Minnesota, 2006), 198.

[32] Slobodian, 'Socialist Chromatism', 23–6.

[33] Wladimir Fischer, 'Of Crescents and Essence, Or: Why Migrants' History Matters to the Question of 'Central European Colonialism', in Andrew Colin Gow (ed.), *Hyphenated Histories*.

discourage their citizens from indulging in nostalgic fantasies of involvement in a broader colonial project. Tarzan novels, embodying a fantasy of white defence in the face of racial threat, were so popular in 1960s Yugoslavia that they were sold in weekly instalments.[34] In Hungary the works of P. Howard (Jenő Rejtő, 1905–43) one of the most popular interwar writers of pulp fiction, were republished and became widely read again from the early 1960s. He primarily wrote about Eastern Europeans finding freedom and meaning as European adventurers or as legionnaires, fighting side by side with colonial troops in French colonial Africa and South East Asia. Here Rudyard Kipling was popular too, selling half a million copies in Hungary in the 1950s and 1960s.[35] Across the bloc, Jules Verne, whose works celebrated technological modernity and European mobility, remained the most popular foreign author—by some distance—and his stories were made into films or radio programmes in the 1940s and 1950s.[36] Some travellers were disturbed at the continued hold of imperial thinking within their anti-colonial commitment, and reflected on it in their writing. The Polish author Wiesław Górnicki, for instance, explored his inability to shake his own upbringing in a country which—despite not having extra-European colonies—had not thrown off the legacies of European imperial thinking. He travelled to India in the early 1960s, and his travelogue frequently reflected on the tension between his interwar socialization and the way in which he, as a good socialist, wished to see India. He castigated himself for viewing the world as a white missionary or European Orientalist might once have done: he could only see rural India in terms of its backwardness in relation to western civilization, and could not altogether erase the images of Rudyard Kipling's 'The Jungle Book' that had coloured his views. The failure to cleanse his own 'imperial lens' was central to his account.[37]

To understand the continued hold of this imperial imaginary, we have to turn back to a longer-term history of racialization of Eastern Europeans in an age of European empire. On one hand, lacking imperial holdings, or even their own states, Easterners had long been denigrated in the West as lesser or 'poor whites'— to use a capacious yet malleable imperial term applied from the late nineteenth century that might variously include, for example, the British working class, the Irish or any Eastern European cohorts whose presence in Africa risked

---

Articulations of Central European Bildung and Slavic Studies in the Contemporary Academy (Leiden: Brill, 2007), 84.

[34] Radina Vučetić, *Koka kola socijalizam. Amerikanizacija poularne kulture u socijalsitičkoj Jugoslaviji šezdesetih godina XX veka* (Belgrade: Službeni glasnik, 2011), 319.

[35] Ferenc Erdei (ed.), *Hazánk, Magyarország* (Budapest: Akadémiai Kiadó, 1970), 591.

[36] Stefan Baghiu, 'The Functions of Socialist Realism: Translation of Genre Fiction in Communist Romania', *Primerjalna književnost*, 42/1(2019), 123.

[37] Wiesław Górnicki, *Podróż po garść ryżu* (Warsaw: Iskry, 1964) See the discussion in Agnieszka Sadecka, 'A Socialist Orientalism? Polish Travel Writing on India in the 1960s' in Dobrota Pucherova and Robert Gafrik (eds.), *Postcolonial Europe? Essays on Post-Communist Literatures and Cultures* (Leiden: Brill, 2015), 315–333.

undermining the grandeur of those seen as the full, educated, bourgeois embodiment of white colonial Europeanness.[38] Similar terminology survived the Second World War: the large number of Polish wartime refugees in British colonies in Eastern Africa were ambivalently received because they were seen as 'poor whites' who undermined the social standing of Europeans in colonies.[39]

On the other, long before the Communist era, eastern European nationalists, had claimed the capacity, on the account of having been colonized and marginalized themselves, to be able to redeem a European colonial project which had been degraded through violence. They would thus, replete with their own states and colonies, not only become fully European, but in fact superior to the West, as the more moral civilizing colonialists (see *Origins*). This desire for global status through a 'humane colonization' had driven some to embrace collaboration with Western European empires and to embark upon the search for their own colonies in the interwar period. After the failure of such projects, decolonization opened the door to another variant on this aspiration: an anti-colonial world enabled them to find a global role and thus escape the racialized denigration that had been used to marginalize them as lesser Europeans.[40] Yet this was to be done not only by identifying with an alternative progressive version of whiteness as part of a family of equal races, but also through a mimicry of those earlier imperial aesthetics that white, male and aristocratic Western European imperialists had used to express power. One of the most striking examples was Yugoslav Marshal Tito (see image): as the white European leader alongside Nehru and Nasser in the Non-Aligned Movement, he helped embody the very idea of a newly equitable racial order. Yet when in Africa, he liked to appear in the guise of a European colonial hunter, dressed in a white suit and posing alongside the big game he had shot. Such colonial play acting, of which many examples can be found amongst Communist functionaries in the South, also reflected in part the major role that hunting played in Communist masculine elite political culture, widely used to bond bloc elites or with their counterparts from the decolonizing world.[41] Communists were well aware of the associations of their dress: Tito was warned off—as were others—from publicizing such images for fear of providing the West

[38] For this usage, see Elspeth Huxley, *White Man's Country and The Making of Kenya* (London: MacMillan and Co., 1935), 121. Thanks to Vineet Thakur for this reference.

[39] Katarzyna Nowak, '"We Would Rather Drown Ourselves in Lake Victoria": Refugee Women, Protest, and Polish Displacement in Colonial East Africa, 1948–49', *Immigrants & Minorities*, 37/1–2 (2019), 96.

[40] On non-colonial whiteness, see, Anikó Imre, 'Whiteness in Post-Socialist Eastern Europe: The Time of the Gypsies, the End of Race', in Alfred J. López (ed.), *Postcolonial Whiteness: A Critical Reader on Race and Empire* (Albany: SUNY Press, 2005), 79–102.

[41] Burton et al., 'Imagined Spaces of Encounter'; György Majtényi, 'Between Tradition and Change: Hunting as Metaphor and Symbol in State Socialist Hungary', *Cultural and Social History*, 13/2 (2016), 231–48.

'President Tito with his wife Jovanka hunting in Keekorok, Kenya, 1970 (Museum of Yugoslavia archive)

with opportunities for hostile propaganda that might characterize Communists as the real imperialists.[42]

Safari and hunting books proliferated in the late 1950s, selling the fantasy of escape from a routinized world of socialist modernity into a romantic past that could be play acted in a world opening up. In Hungary, state-sponsored hunting expeditions led by former aristocrats were sent to catch animals under the pretext of replacing the African taxidermy collection at the Natural History Museum, which had burned down during the 1956 revolution.[43] These resulted in not only several travelogues and a TV programme, but also the republication of a number of popular interwar accounts of African hunting.[44] The former nobleman, renowned hunter, and museologist Zsigmond Széchenyi, after a period of marginalization under Stalinism, was allowed to return to Africa: his resulting *African campfires* (1959) sold almost 200,000 copies in 1959—far more than the anti-colonial travelogues of the era.[45] It is striking that these revived images of imperial pastimes were hardly ever challenged across the socialist era. It was only feminist travel writers in the 1970s, in part inspired by their encounter with what seemed to be a more authentic women's liberation in Africa, who criticized the

[42] Radina Vučetić, 'Tito's Africa: Representation of Power during Tito's African Journeys', in Radina Vučetić and Paul Betts (eds.), *Tito in Africa. Picturing Solidarity* (Belgrade: Museum of Yugoslavia, 2017), 42.

[43] For the colonial revivals prompted by these trips, see János Szunyoghy, *Egy év Tanganyikában* (Budapest: Táncsics Könyvkiadó, 1968); István Dénes, *Így láttam Afrikát* (Budapest: Szépirodalmi Kiadó, 1961).

[44] Lajos Horváth, *Háromezer kilométer Afrikában* (Budapest: Gondolat Kiadó, 1963).

[45] Zsigmond Széchenyi, *Afrikai tábortüzek* (Budapest: Szépirodalmi Könyvkiadó, 1959).

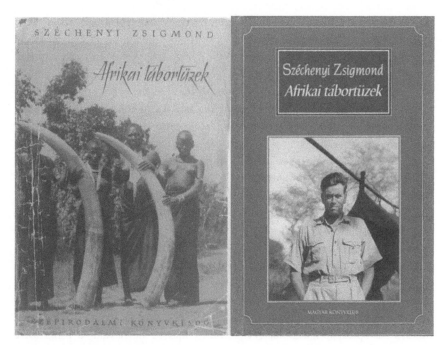

Zsigmond Széchenyi, *African Campfires*. Front covers of the 1959 and 2010 editions.

domineering colonial masculine style of fellow travel writers, and discussed women's economic and social position in Africa to critique implicitly the masculine cultures of state socialism 'at home'.[46]

It was not only that an alternative colonially inspired nostalgic culture existed alongside an official anti-colonialism: it supplied a fantasy that underpinned it. Eastern European state socialism did not reject the idea of the civilizing mission but rather built a variant on it; built out of the belief that it was possible to recover a humane version of European Enlightenment civilization and take it to less developed countries as a paternalistic project of white European anti-colonial 'missionaries'. In this sense, it was a revival of an older claim that Eastern Europeans, given the chance, would be able to redeem a colonial project that Western Europeans had betrayed—now retooled for a world of anti-colonialism and equality. Indeed, exactly this message would be communicated through the revival, in nearly all eastern European countries, of the cult of the 'humane' nineteenth-century national explorer-hero. Each Communist nation had their own, their life stories rewritten in film, novels and biographies from the early 1950s to anticipate the enlightened political and moral values of socialist internationalism. Czechoslovakia had Emil Holub, a progressive 1848-er who, according to the socialist-era framing, wanted to be an anti-colonial David Livingstone

---

[46] Rózsa Ignácz, *Zebradob-Híradó* (Budapest: Gondolat, 1968).

whose science would serve the needs of indigenous peoples, rather than act as a tool of imperial oppression. In such accounts, the invitation of Belgian King Leopold II to oversee the colonization of the Congo alongside Stanley was refused as ruthless exploitation. Holub had then come up against the 'narrow mindedness' of the Czech bourgeoisie, whose institutions rejected the array of ethnographic materials he had recovered to instill a respect for African culture.[47] The Poles had Szolc-Rogoziński, the 'discoverer of Cameroon', who 'did not accept the crown offered to him', dreaming, 'of a free African state that co-habits and cooperates with free Poland'.[48] In the Soviet Union, stories of the Russian explorer as passionate, humane anti-racist proliferated in histories and biopics—their values contrasting with the perceived ruthless and violent colonialism that drew upon racist conceptions of biological and civilizational superiority endemic in the German and British traditions.[49]

Thus the anti-colonial endeavour cannot be said to represent a full overcoming of Europe's attachment to colonialism—but rather rested on the propagation of a possible humane version of it, which would in turn liberate Eastern Europeans from racial denigration as the supposedly only partially realized Europeans. As long as anti-colonialism could garner a previously denied global status, then such Eastern European longings for recognition could be harnessed to progressive projects; yet, as we shall later see, as soon as the power of anti-colonialism on the global stage eroded, so this reproduction of imperial nostalgia would be reworked in the name of return to a bounded white European civilization. Nevertheless, even in the decades which preceded this erosion of political commitment, the claim that Eastern Europeans were the better anti-racist whites was under constant attack, not only by their ideological opponents, but also those friends who observed their practices close up.

Are They White Imperialists?

Foreign critics were quick to claim that just under the surface of the bloc's anti-colonialism lay a desire for global status insufficiently disconnected from a pan-European desire for imperial dominance. Ndabaningi Sithole, who would go on to be a leading figure in ZANU's struggle against Rhodesian rule, argued in the

[47] Dr Emil Holub, 1847–1902, no author listed, published by 'Our science, technology, art and their representatives (materials for bulletin boards)', March 1953; Jiří Baum, *Holub a Mašukulumbové* (Prague: Nakladatelství Československé Akademie věd, 1955).

[48] Janusz Makarczyk, 'Narodziny kolonializmu', *Prawo Człowieka*, 3 (March 1949), 5–7; Jadwiga Chudzikowska and Jan Jaster, *Odkrywcy Kamerunu* (Warsaw: Wiedza Powszechna, 1954), 53–6.

[49] See the biopic of Russian anthropologist and naturalist *Miklukho-Maklai* (1947). For Yugoslavia, see e.g. Rastko Petrović and Aleksandar Deroko; in Hungary, the accounts of János Xantus' expeditions in South East Asia, Ármin Vámbéry's in Turkey and the Middle East and Sámuel Teleki's in East Africa were retold in the 1960s–70s as non-colonial expeditions 'driven only by scientific curiosity': Tibor Bodrogi, *Messzi népek magyar kutatói, II* (Budapest: Gondolat, 1978).

late 1950s that Russians were ' just as white as the French, Belgians, Englishmen'. White Communists, Sithole went on, strove just as much for world domination, 'and that means the submission of Africa.'[50] Moreover, Beijing propagandized that Khrushchev's policy of peaceful coexistence with the West from 1956 meant the reconstitution of an undifferentiated white northern political space detached from the concerns of an Afro-Asian world. In the wake of the Sino-Soviet split, as Moscow and Beijing struggled for a leadership role amongst Third World nations, Mao repeatedly insisted to African leaders, referring to the bloc, that: '[t]hese Europeans are all the same...we non-whites must hold together.'[51] In an attempt to erase a long history of Chinese conceptions of blackness as racial inferiority, Mao now sought to create a category of 'non-whiteness' that would simultaneously bind together east Asia and Africa, and denigrate whiteness by equating it with imperial dominance and exploitation. Beijing thus came to naturalize her new partnerships in racialized terms. 'Our circumstances are fairly similar', Mao Zedong claimed as he reached out to African states, '...so when we talk to you, there is no feeling that I bully you or you bully me, nobody has a superiority complex, we are both of a coloured race.'[52] Chinese elites' claim that 'non-whites' needed to stick together was employed in their attempts to exclude the Soviets from Afro-Asian conferences, particularly in Cairo in 1959.

Many Eastern Bloc elites became concerned with how they were perceived. In 1963, the Czechoslovak Central Committee discussed the deleterious effects of being stereotyped as 'whites' who on account of their skin colour could not express genuine fraternity. Their authorities encouraged domestic publications that explored how the Chinese were neglecting class divisions through their new emphasis on divisions based on colour.[53] At the UN, Czechoslovak representatives refuted the idea that their whiteness barred them from leadership on global racial issues, and presented their support for the developing world in terms of their own country's experience of racial subordination under Nazi occupation in the Second World War.[54] Hungarians conducted international attitudes surveys in order to assess whether their country's youth was affected by such racialized

---

[50] PAAA, MfAA A 15038, fol. 18 (Wilson Center Digital Archive). In the context of détente, the Hungarian-born US scholar John Lukacs recognized the growing political salience of the whiteness of the global North: 'Bismarck was supposed to have said that the most important fact of the twentieth century would be that Americans speak English; it is not impossible that the most important condition of the next hundred years might be that the Russians are, after all, white.' John Lukacs, *The Passing of the Modern Age* (New York: Harper & Row, 1970), 61–2.

[51] W. A. C. Adie, 'China, Russia and the Third World', *The China Quarterly*, 11 (1962), 200–13.

[52] Quoted in Jeffrey James Byrne, 'Beyond Continents, Colours and the Cold War: Yugoslavia, Algeria and the Struggle for Non-Alignment', *The International History Review*, 37/5 (2015), 924.

[53] Fond 02/1, NAD 1261/0/4, sv. 36, ar.j. 39, k info 3 (*Předsednictvo ÚV KSČ*), Presidium of the Central Committee of the Communist party of Czechoslovakia, 1962–66. Presented 'for information' at the Presidium's meeting on 1 October 1963 (National Archive of the Czech Republic, Prague).

[54] Czechoslovak leaders Masaryk and Beneš had in the 1930s called for cooperation to create a consensus on race that would counter Nazi ideology. UN/Geneva So239 (5-1-1)—No 2.473/63.

ideas.[55] The Polish PKS (*Polski Komitet Solidarności z Narodami Azji i Afryki*—Polish Committee for Solidarity with the Peoples of Asia and Africa) was established to bolster the bloc's position within the Third World movement in the face of such Chinese accusations.[56] Area studies institutes in Moscow—and their African specialists in particular—began to argue that race had nevertheless to be taken seriously as category of political analysis. This was not because they considered it to be a term with real ideological content, but rather because peoples across the world took it seriously as a marker of identity, and without such an understanding the anti-imperialist struggle would be undermined.

A potential solidarity based on the shared consciousness of 'being peripheral' was apparent during Ben Bella's discussion with Mali's UN representative, Demba Diallo. Commenting on the protests against Romanian leader Gheorghiu-Dej's presence in New York in 1960, Diallo told his colleague that 'it seems that Americans see you "as black" as well. Only that, obviously, we like the colour black.'[57] Ghanaian leader Kwame Nkrumah sought to undercut the western and Chinese rhetoric that sought to divide the 'East' from the 'South': visiting Hungarian leader János Kádár at his summer residence in Balatonaliga, Nkrumah recalled that Nixon called Eastern Bloc countries 'Communist slaves'—and added: 'if slavery consists of what I saw in Hungary, I am prepared to become a Communist slave', because 'freedom, equality, justice and all what goes with them, that is, humanism, really take shape only in socialist countries.'[58] The Yugoslav press criticized 'Chinese racialism', following a path, they alleged, 'which clearly leads to racial hatred and the implacable enmity of coloured people against the whites'—and for trying to split the working class by colour.[59] In a 1964 meeting with Ben Bella in Belgrade, Tito reportedly railed against China's insinuations that, 'all blacks are good and all whites are bad.' The Algerian leader agreed with him, in no small measure because of the support the FLN had received from Yugoslavia, concluding that 'ideas about continents and skin colour need to be overcome because progressive forces exist all around the world.'[60]

---

[55] James Mark and Péter Apor, 'Socialism Goes Global: Decolonization and the making of a new culture of internationalism in socialist Hungary 1956–1989', *Journal of Modern History*, 87 (2015), 869–70.

[56] On the Polish instrumentalization of anti-apartheid, see the government's response to the International Conference on Economic Sanctions against South Africa, London, 14–17 April 1964, Komisja Współpracy Gospodarczej z Zagranicą, Cat. No. 16/24/3, 1–4.

[57] Stoian Stanciu, 'În legătură cu problema africană abordată la cea de-a XV-a sesiune a Organizației Națiunilor Unite (20 septembrie – 11 octombrie 1960),' CC (Comitetul Central) al PCR (Partidului Comunist Român), Relații Externe, 53/1960, 5. (ANIC, Central National Historical Archive, Bucharest).

[58] Zoltán Ginelli, 'Hungarian Experts in Nkrumah's Ghana. Decolonization and Semiperipheral Postcoloniality in Socialist Hungary', May 2018, mezosfera.org http://mezosfera.org/hungarian-experts-in-nkrumahs-ghana/.

[59] 'Yugoslav Charges Chinese Promote Racism', 30 July 1963. HU OSA 300-8-3-9715; Records of Radio Free Europe/Radio Liberty Research Institute (Open Society Archive, Budapest, henceforth OSA).

[60] Byrne, 'Beyond Continents', 924.

Although China's effort to turn Third World politics into a race war did not take off, it was Beijing's accusations that forced Eastern European governments to play a much more visible role in anti-racist campaigns on the global stage from the early 1960s—so as to substantiate their claims to be a different kind of European whose anti-racism was authentic and the product of commitment unsullied by the remnants of imperial desire. Despite the international outrage in response to the Sharpeville Massacre (1960) of black anti-apartheid protestors, the rapid growth of the international anti-apartheid movement that followed, and Beijing's public severance of links with the South African regime, it transpired that China was in fact secretly increasing its trade with the apartheid state.[61] Eastern European states publicized this hypocrisy, and hoped to gain the moral high ground in their campaigns to marginalize Chinese influence across Africa. Moreover, it was argued, their anti-racist commitments were an authentic outgrowth from their own experience of colonial persecution under Nazi wartime occupation. In 1968, the twenty-fifth UN General Assembly adopted a UNESCO resolution on Measures to be taken against Nazism and racial intolerance, that had been filed by Poland, along with Iraq and the Ukrainian SSR, that sought to widen definitions of 'crimes against humanity' to include racist colonial crimes.[62] Many Eastern European states supported the UN Convention on Racial Discrimination in 1965/66, arguing that the cause of racial equality was a natural pendant to their support for the struggle for self-determination and for the 'equality of peoples'.[63]

And where the bloc led, it was claimed, the West was unable to follow. By the late 1960s, America's war in Vietnam, and continued business links with the apartheid regime, could be presented as evidence that racism still naturally adhered to western capitalism. Addressing the UN Apartheid Committee in 1965, the leader of the Hungarian delegation used his international platform to argue that the West was structurally incapable of confronting such evils:[64]

> one might argue that a considerable part of American public opinion expresses its dissatisfaction with...Apartheid [but], with due respect to the progressive heritage of American history, I should also point out the heritage of slavery, racial discrimination, Jim Crow, and of the heritage of the double exploitation of race and hypocrisy which couch these phenomena in cloudy and pious

---

[61] On support for anti-apartheid as a response to Chinese criticism, as a play for Africa, Paul Betts et al., 'Race, Socialism and Solidarity: Anti-Apartheid in Eastern Europe', in Robert Skinner and Anna Konieczna (eds.), *A Global History of Anti-Apartheid: 'Forward to Freedom' in South Africa* (Basingstoke: Palgrave, 2019), 154.

[62] AAN 1627/88 (UN Archive, Geneva).

[63] Steven B. Jensen, 'Embedded or Exceptional? Apartheid and the International Politics of Racial Discrimination', *Zeithistorische Forschungen/Studies in Contemporary History*, 13/2 (2016), 314–23.

[64] The US recognized the threat its own racial issues posed to gaining trust in the developing world: '[W]e must look to our own salesmanship—in our diplomacy, in our trade policies, in our giving and lending, in our technical assistance programmes, in our attitude towards other nations and particularly towards the coloured races.' 'Nehru—Last Man to Be Fooled', *The Tribune*, 29 November 1955, 5.

announcements from the land of the brave and free. It is not by chance that the country of Birmingham and Selma has until now tolerated Sharpeville, the country of Governor Wallace...has until now tolerated the shame of Apartheid, and a country that...uses Asians as guinea-pigs for experimentation...in Vietnam, does not have the moral standing to admonish South Africa ....These interests are interconnected and motivated by the desire to contain the forces of national liberation in Africa ....to ensure the maximum profit of so-called 'free enterprise'...based on the exploitation of man by man...we bow our heads before the fallen martyrs of the sacred fight against apartheid.[65]

Even so, the US administration was presenting its support for civil rights movements on the global stage as evidence that it could overcome its history of racial discrimination, and thus play an important role in a world of anti-colonial and anti-racist struggle.[66] Such shifts were unsettling in the bloc, where peaceful coexistence, more individualistic consumerism and increasing economic exchange with the West were undermining Eastern European Communist states' claims to distinctiveness.[67] In Hungary, the Communist Youth League were concerned that the American civil rights movement was convincing a younger generation that an 'imperialist America' was capable of overcoming racial divides and were hopeful of a convergence between capitalist and socialist systems.[68] Discrimination against African Americans was much less important than the fear that the young in the Eastern Bloc might believe that the West was capable of humanizing itself, thus depriving Communists of an important propaganda weapon. Vietnam in particular provided the evidence that America's racism was still operative: stories of children's suffering, the brutal interrogations of POWs by US Army officers, popular songs about massacres of innocent Vietnamese civilians, and the widespread publicity afforded the Russell-Sartre Trial (1966–67), which highlight American war crimes, all made this point powerfully.[69] America's domestic racism was emphasized in Polish schools too: eleven-year-olds were required to read texts about American segregation and answer comprehension questions such as 'How would you describe the behaviour of the people belonging to Ku-Klux-Klan? On the basis of the story judge the influence and importance of this organization in America.'[70]

---

[65] Statement of His Excellency Mr Csatorday of Hungary to the Special Committee on Apartheid, 1965. XIS-J-1-j Box 40. Foreign Ministry, Hungarian National Archives.

[66] Mary L. Dudziak, Cold War Civil Rights: Race and the Image of American Democracy (Princeton, NJ: Princeton University Press, 2000), 87–9.

[67] Mark and Apor, 'Socialism Goes Global', 868–9.

[68] PIL 289. f. 13/1963/33. Őe; Jelentés a diákifjúság eszmei-politikai, világnézeti és erkölcsi arculatával kapcsolatos néhány problémáról (The Archives of the Institute of Political History, Budapest).

[69] James Mark et al., '"We are with You, Vietnam": Transnational Solidarities in Socialist Hungary, Poland and Yugoslavia', Journal of Contemporary History, 50/3 (2015), 439–64.

[70] Janina Dembowska, Zygmunt Saloni and Piotr Wierzbicki, Świat i My. Podręcznik do języka polskiego dla klasy 6 (Warszawa: PZWS, 1964), 287.

Are They Anti-racist at Home?

Discussions of race still had been kept at a 'safe distance' from Communist societies. The commitment to the anti-racist struggle on the international stage was often used as proof that such prejudice had been eliminated at home. Yet the relationship was not so simple. Racism that Communists argued naturally adhered to capitalist colonial projects could be brought home to target domestic minorities stereotyped as their local accessories or representatives who became, in the state's view, internal carriers of racist infection. Thus, critics of the bloc argued that their progressive commitments were merely performative, designed to help cover up the realities of discrimination at home.

The peak of Communist states' international anti-racist work coincided with the worst outbreak of postwar anti-Semitism in the wake of Six Day War in 1967. Communist states had supported the Arab forces against Israel; in Poland, against the backdrop of economic crisis, a rising nationalist wing of the party resorted to anti-Semitic rhetoric which had been kept for the most part in abeyance since the Second World War. Suddenly Polish Jews were accused of supporting 'the Zionists', and of having closer links to Israel than Poland. The country's 1968-er student protesters would be condemned as alien Jews and Zionists in attempts to prevent them building working-class support to challenge the degradation of socialism.[71] In the wake of these anti-Zionist campaigns, around 25,000 Polish Jews emigrated to Israel.[72]

Warsaw Communists sought to protect themselves from charges of racism emerging from international bodies such as UNESCO,[73] and from international condemnation of their anti-Zionist propaganda. They refuted the idea that they were anti-Semitic. Rather, they once again externalized the question of racism. Israelis were the real bigots, they claimed. Domestic opposition was the result of 'provocations of the Zionist centre', which, they argued, had unfortunate reverberations in Poland. The Jewish state had supposedly forgotten its origins in racist persecution and become the expression of racist colonialism itself, now supported by an imperialist West. It had now adopted 'Nazi geopolitical concepts with declarations of "historic rights" of the Zionists, including the most extreme concept of "Great Israel" spanning from the Nile to the Euphrates ... It is ironic that the ideological enemy of Palestinians—global Zionism—claims to be a spiritual and theoretical representative of the cultural religious society that felt the

---

[71] Dariusz Stola, 'Anti-Zionism as a Multipurpose Policy Instrument: The Anti-Zionist Campaign in Poland, 1967–1968', *The Journal of Israeli History*, 25/1 (2006), 180.

[72] Ibid., 213.

[73] See the critique of Communist anti-Semitism in Cyril Bibby, 'Race Prejudice and Education', *The Unesco Courier* (October 1960), 10.

practical consequences of racism so drastically.[74] They rather supported the Palestinian struggle, framed as being 'founded on strong and historically justified consciousness of its own national...identity free of chauvinism and racism.'[75] Writers at the Parisian Polish émigré journal *Kultura* were quick to note the hypocrisy. Konstanty Jeleński wrote, '[First Secretary] Gomułka is also a hypocrite when he says that "anti-Zionism has nothing to do with anti-Semitism"...and that racist theories in the style of the Nazi Nuremberg Laws did not exist, and thus on that basis that there is no anti-Semitism in Poland.' He argued that Gomułka was adopting an age-old technique of denying anti-Semitism by claiming that it was Jews' behaviour that marked them out, rather than the Party's assembling of malleable signifiers to formulate an anti-Semitic discourse. This argument culminated in the late 1960s with the claim that Polish Jews were attacked not because of their Jewishness, but because they supposedly identified with a racist project.[76] The Communist policy of externalizing racism—in this case to 'Israeli colonialism'—had been brought home to vilify a domestic minority.

And at the UN, the Polish delegation successfully contributed to the exclusion of anti-Semitism from the International Convention on the Elimination of All Forms of Racial Discrimination, ensuring that only the terms 'apartheid' and 'racial segregation' entered into the convention draft.[77] Critics thus argued that their emphasis on racism in the US, Africa or Israel was a sham, useful mainly to divert attention away from Jewish persecution within the Eastern Bloc.[78] Communists also argued that these novel international agreements to combat discrimination in the 1960s need not apply to them. The response from Minsk to the Convention on Racial Discrimination was typical: despite supporting the 'decisive steps' against South Africa and Rhodesia, it nevertheless concluded that there was 'no need' to implement the Convention within the Belorussian Soviet Socialist Republic, repeating the mantra established in the late 1940s: 'all manifestations of racial discrimination have been completely eliminated.'[79] Socialist countries were wary of giving international bodies openings to interfere with national courts, and feared their potentially destabilizing effects, particularly in states with large minorities. There were a few exceptions: Bulgaria and Hungary both brought the crime of

---

[74] F.J. Kolár, *Sionismus a antisemitismus* (Prague: Svoboda, 1970). See also the discussion in Hana Kubátová and Jan Láníček, *The Jew in Czech and Slovak Imagination, 1938–89 Antisemitism, the Holocaust, and Zionism* (Leiden: Brill, 2018), especially chapter 4.

[75] Alfred M. Lilienthal, *Sionismus* (Prague: Orbis, republished 1988), 6–7.

[76] Konstanty Jeleński, 'Hańba czy wstyd', *Kultura*, 5 (1968). See also Paul Lendvai, *Antysemityzm bez Żydów. Część 1. Komunizm a Żydzi* (Warsaw: Los, 1987), 20–3; Krystyna Kersten, *Polacy, Żydzi, komunizm: anatomia półprawd, 1939–1968* (Warsaw: Niezależna Oficyna Wydawnicza, 1992), 155.

[77] Roger Normand and Sarah Zaidi, *Human Rights at the UN: The Political History of Universal Justice* (Bloomington, IN: Indiana University Press, 2007), 261–9.

[78] Sebastian Gehrig et al., 'The Eastern Bloc, Human Rights, and the Global Fight against Apartheid', *East Central Europe*, 46 (2019), 300.

[79] Comments and Suggestions of Governments Regarding the Draft Declaration and Convention on the Elimination of All Forms of Racial Discrimination SO 239 (5-1-1) Part B (UN archive, Geneva).

apartheid into their domestic law—the former in 1966, the latter in 1978.[80] Yet in both cases this was viewed as moral support for an international campaign against South Africa rather than an initiative that could be used to prosecute discriminatory practices domestically. A commitment to anti-racist work on the global stage was not supposed to come home—indeed, it often functioned to hide domestic discrimination.

Eastern Europe Close Up: The Experiences of Students and Labour Migrants

It was also incomers from the decolonizing world who experienced the effects of a culture than externalized the struggle against racism. African students who arrived in larger and larger numbers from the late 1950s found their presence at new universities—such as at Lumumba in Moscow or November 17th in Prague—publicly celebrated.[81] The Soviet Union, Romania, Poland and Czechoslovakia brought the UN 'International Day for the Elimination of Racial Discrimination' on 21 March—the anniversary of the Sharpeville massacre in 1960 in South Africa—into their commemorative calendars, and publicly paraded their African students on such days as evidence of their authentic commitment.[82] Until the late 1970s, such students suffered no lack of public recognition: their presence confirmed their hosts' newfound status, and moral superiority over the West.

Yet this was an internationalism that was preferred at a distance, even at home. As students and labour migrants from the global South arrived, the prospect of sexual relationships became very real. Those moral panics which arose from the possibility of contacts between white and coloured bodies most often focused on the potentially unsettling effects on Eastern European women—and the threat this posed to the socialist order.[83] The biracial babies that were born after the 1957 Moscow Youth Festival were not celebrated as the result of socialist internationalism: they '[stood] as a mark not of racial tolerance, but of sexual 'looseness'.[84] Appropriate expressions of women's sexuality could be disrupted by

[80] Bulgaria was inspired by the General Assembly resolution 2202 A (XXI) of 16 December 1966 which labelled apartheid as a crime against humanity.

[81] Konstantin Katsakioris, 'Burden or Allies? Third World Students and Internationalist Duty through Soviet Eyes', *Kritika: Explorations in Russian and Eurasian History*, 18/3 (2017), 548–9.

[82] Report of the UN Secretary-General, 'Implementation of the UN Declaration on the elimination of all Forms of Racial Discrimination', 30 August 1967, 34. For Romania: 'Notă de propuneri: răspuns la mesajul celei de-a XXVI-a sesiuni a Adunării generale a ONU privind discriminarea rasială', ANIC, CC al PCR, Cancelarie, 24/1972, 66-7 and 72-74. For Poland: See the annual reports of the PKS in AAN, PKSzNAA(iAŁ) 20 (Central Archives of Modern Records, Warsaw).

[83] Anastasia Kayiatos, 'Pantomimes of Power and Race: Can the Socialist Subaltern Speak?', *Ulbandus Review*, 16 (2014), 24–44.

[84] Kristin Roth-Ey, '"Loose Girls" on the Loose?: Sex, Propaganda and the 1957 Youth Festival', in Melanie Reid, Susan E. Reid and Lynne Atwood (eds.), *Women in the Khrushchev Era* (New York: Palgrave, 2004), 86.

the conflicts such internationalism created: at the height of the Maoist panic in 1963-4 in Hungary, security service reports blamed the fear of war with the 'yellow peril' for a loosening of morals amongst female students.[85] In some cases, black African men were targeted for their supposedly 'promiscuous and illegal behaviour' towards local women, and their refusal to play by the rules of political game was linked to a threatening sexuality. Romania adopted the most severe regulations over desire and association. From 1968, their Communist party intensified its pro-natalist nationalism, which promised a strengthening of the Romanian nation through a policy of 'Romanian women for Romanian men'. As the number of African students increased in this same period, their contact with Romanians was strongly discouraged. By the late 1970s, laws were very draconian— every citizen had to report any and every encounter. Foreign students became known as 'untouchables'.[86] Marriage between African and Romanian students was initially not allowed; by the mid-1970s, the authorities introduced the rule that marriage between a foreign student could be allowed only if, ultimately, the woman received her parents' consent.[87]

Official attitudes were less draconian in Poland, Hungary, GDR and Yugoslavia. Indeed, in the latter two cases there is much evidence that these governments had a relatively relaxed attitude toward mixed marriages; it was often African countries that wanted trained experts to go back home, and who therefore pressed bloc states to reduce the rate of intermarriage.[88] Surveys revealed that many Eastern Europeans welcomed African and other students to the bloc—in part due to the sense of global importance their presence brought—but nevertheless did not support interracial relationships. A 1971 Yugoslav survey revealed that two-thirds of students would not be comfortable with a female relative marrying a 'black man', whilst only a quarter considered it acceptable.[89] In Hungary and Poland, a majority did not consider interracial marriage a good idea—partly out of a resentment at the special privileges supposedly afforded coloured students.[90] African students first appeared in Yugoslav literature in a book published in 1972 called *Onduo, moj crni momak* [Onduo, my black boyfriend]. Written by a popular writer of books for children and young adults, it focused on a Yugoslav girl

---

[85] PIL 289 f. 13/1963/33. Oe (The Archives of the Institute of Political History, Budapest).

[86] 'Anexă privind unele probleme ale activității studenților străini care studiază în țara noastră', ANIC, CC al PCR, Cancelarie 150/1972, 201–2 (Central National Historical Archive, Bucharest). Mihai Dinu Gheorghiu et al., 'Étudiants d'Afrique en Roumanie et en RDA. Les cadres sociaux et politiques de leurs experiences', in Monique de Saint Martin, Grazia Scarfò Ghellab and Kamal Mellakh (eds.), *Étudier à l'Est. Expériences de diplômés africains* (Paris: Karthala, 2015), 106.

[87] Marriages did take place between Soviet women and African students; see e.g. the first wife of the Angolan president, President José Eduardo dos Santos.

[88] Sara Pugach, 'African Students and the Politics of Race and Gender in the German Democratic Republic, 1957–1976', in Slobodian (ed.), *Comrades of Color*, 262.

[89] Ibid., 101.

[90] 'Attitudes to Interracial Marriage in Hungary and Poland', RFE Audience and Public Opinion Research Department, HU 300-6-2 Box 3 (OSA).

Vida who marries a Sudanese student and subsequently goes back home with him; ultimately it emphasized the difficulties of marriage between members of distinct cultures.[91]

International students were quick to critique the racial blind spots of a political system for which discrimination was always elsewhere. Young Kenyans in Budapest in the early 1960s asked why the racism that they suffered at the hands of 'western imperialists' became the stuff of Communist politics, whilst the Jewish friends they made who faced anti-Semitic abuse received no such support.[92] When they themselves were subject to racist incidents in Eastern Europe, they found that authorities, even if they admitted their occurrence, denied that they were victims of a wider problem. African students in Yugoslavia noted the failure of authorities to turn incidents of racial discrimination into a political issue: police and local authorities were prepared to demonize racism at a global level without seeing it as a phenomenon that structured socialist societies too.[93] These students claimed that the violence they had faced during anti-colonial demonstrations—which the police had deemed disruptive and politically excessive— demonstrated that European Communists were insufficiently committed to the struggle.[94] In response, Yugoslav authorities retorted that such students suffered from a 'complex of colonialism' that made them ill-placed to judge such matters owing to an emotional hyper-sensitivity to any incident that might be construed as racially motivated. An overemphasis on négritude—viewed as an excessive attachment to black identity—undermined Africans' capacity to reach out to their 'true allies' in Europe.[95] In an educational pamphlet, 'The Black Tears of the Congo', widely distributed in Yugoslav schools, African students were criticized for being unable to distinguish between countries where racial discrimination

[91] Anton Janko, 'Vida the Beautiful and her Zamorec', in T.E. Knight (ed.) *Broaching Frontiers Shattering Boundaries. On tradition and culture at the dawn of the third millennium* (New York: Peter Lang, 1999), 169.

[92] 'Anti-Semitism Stressed', Hungarian Home Service, 11 November 1959 (Foreign Broadcast Information Service Online Archive).

[93] On this as a 'non-problem' for the state, see Milorad Lazić, 'Neki problemi stranih studenta na jugoslovenskim univerzitetima šezdesetih godina XX veka, sa posebnim osvrtom na afričke studente', *Godišnjijak za društvenu istoriju*, 16 (2009), 73. Julie Hessler, 'Death of an African Student in Moscow. Race, politics and the Cold War', *Cahiers de Monde Russe*, 47/1–2 (2006), 50.

[94] James Robertson, 'Speaking Titoism. Student Opposition and the Socialist language regime of Yugoslavia', in Petre Petrov and Lara Ryazanova-Clarke (eds.), *The Vernaculars of Communism. Language, ideology and power in the Soviet Union and Eastern Europe* (London and New York: Routledge, 2015), 121. When students protested against the death of a Ghanaian student Edmund Assare-Addo in Red Square in 1963, they invoked American racism to describe Soviet practice: 'Moscow, second Alabama'. See Monique de Saint Martin, Grazia Scarfò Ghellab and Kamal Mellakh (eds.), *Étudier à l'Est. Expériences de diplômés africains* (Paris: Karthala, 2015), 90. Abigail Judge Kret, '"We Unite with Knowledge": The Peoples' Friendship University and Soviet Education for the Third World', *Comparative Studies of South Asia, Africa and the Middle East*, 33/2 (2013), 248.

[95] For Yugoslav criticism of négritude, see also Jokica Hadži Vasileva, *Socijalistička opredeljenja u Tropskoj Africi* (Belgrade: Institut za međunarodnu politiku i privredu, 1973) and *Afrika. Ideologije i strategije razvoja* (Belgrade: IMPP, 1987).

was part of the political system (US, Rhodesia, South Africa) and those in which it was a matter only of individual incidents.[96]

The depoliticization of the response to such racist incidents often led Africans to claim that Communist authorities were no better than western imperialists. In February 1963, in Sofia, black students clashed with the authorities after a ban on the Union of African Students, and between 350 and 500 African students fled Bulgaria.[97] The Ghanaian Evening News complained about 'Jim Crowism' in Johannesburg, Mississippi and Sofia, formulating an especially ferocious criticism of socialist Bulgaria where the political system, in contrast to imperialist countries, should have given 'ample opportunities to educate the man in the street against racial prejudice as proclaimed in their socialist manifestoes'.[98] Anti-racism thus appeared hollow: it could be shouted from the rooftops when bloc states wanted allies, but forced very little self-reflection at home. Thus in Ghana, reporters came to see Eastern Bloc anti-racism as simply performative to gain status in the international arena: 'many countries have [the] illusion that it is enough to roar in Africa about friendship and equality, while in their countries the black man is looked down on.'[99]

Abandoning Anti-Racist Whiteness

By the mid-1970s, as eastern European elites began to question the global anti-colonial project and their support of it (see *Development*), the prestige garnered by the presence of people of colour, or by anti-racist internationalism, which had underpinned the sense of being 'better white Europeans', began to decline. Many bloc states sought to distance themselves from the claims to global economic justice advanced by post-colonial advocates of a New International Economic Order (NIEO), whose division of the world into a wealthy global North and poorer global South was interpreted by some as a revival of hostile Maoist attempts to divide the world between white and black to undermine anti-imperialist solidarity.[100] Yet against the background of détente in Europe, and the strengthening of East-West links, those committed to progressive worldmaking in Eastern Europe began to more publicly articulate their fears that Eurocentric worldviews were re-emerging unchecked. A 1973 report on the image of Third World countries in

---

[96] Nikola Vitorović, *Black Tears of the Congo* (Belgrade: Contemporary Education, 1961).

[97] Quinn Slobodian, 'Bandung in Divided Germany: Managing Non-Aligned Politics in East and West, 1955–63', *The Journal of Imperial and Commonwealth History*, 41/4 (2013), 654.

[98] *Ghanaian Times*, 14 February 1963, and Nana Osei-Opare, 'Uneasy Comrades: Postcolonial Statecraft, Race, and Citizenship, Ghana–Soviet Relations, 1957–1966', *Journal of West African History*, 5/2 (2019), 100–1.

[99] Cable from Accra, 14 February 1963. AJ (Archive of Yugoslavia), 559, Opšti materijali 1960–1963, Šifrovani telegram br. 252, 19 February 1963.

[100] András Sugár, *Angolai tükör* (Budapest: Kossuth, 1978), 131.

secondary education produced by Poland's School Textbook Improvement Centre concluded that hierarchies of civilizations and cultures had never been effectively challenged, and were now gaining an ever stronger foothold.[101] Romania, which had supported the NIEO, argued for the urgent necessity of a parallel New International Cultural Order to protect against these ever more visible hierarchical attitudes. At UNESCO, its representatives took their cue from the Cultural Charter of Africa from 1976, which rejected claims to European superiority, and argued for valuing small and marginalized cultures whose achievements had survived against all the odds.[102]

By the 1980s, images of Europe as a racially bounded civilization based on older imperial tropes returned, and the equation between backwardness and race became publicly visible. A report on attitudes towards foreign students compiled by the Angolan P. Carvahlo in late 1980s Poland suggested that the image of Africa had changed from a continent rising phoenix-like, to an older colonial stereotype of the Heart of Darkness, associated with poor living conditions, poverty, illnesses, refugees, humanitarian aid, and intertribal conflicts.[103] One Yugoslav travel writer exemplified this now publishable, essentialized view of Africa as a place where poverty grew ineluctably and development was impossible. Such misfortune was for him 'predestined': 'It is their misfortune that they are born on a black continent, black not because it is the home of the blacks; but because their destiny is black'.[104]

As that promise of prestige derived from anti-capitalist commitment receded, so too did the appeal of being a morally superior white. Instead, this language of racial oppression tapped into the long held fears around the fragility of their status within Europe. Easterners, in this newly emerging imaginary, were whites whose 'unnatural' proximity to anti-colonialism had not rendered them morally superior, but rather degraded their claims on Europeanness. Conservative anti-Communist Andrzej Frycz, in a Polish underground journal issued in 1985, revived the earlier fear of Eastern Europeans becoming 'poor whites'. An internationalist 'multi-coloured socialism' had turned Eastern Europeans into 'white Negroes', he claimed, confined to apartheid-like 'controlled homelands'. The region had thereby been wrenched, Frycz argued, from its true home within a white western civilization:

[101] B. Wrzosek, 'Kraje Trzeciego Świata w polskich podręcznikach szkolnych', *Przegląd Informacji o Afryce*, 2/43 (1976), 109.

[102] Mircea Malița, 'Dimensiunea culturală a noii ordini economice internaționale', *Revista Comisie Naționale a RSR pentru UNESCO*, 19/1–2 (1977), 29–35.

[103] P. Carvahlo, *Studenci obcokrajowcy w Polsce* (Warszawa: University of Warsaw, 1990), 87–8.

[104] Quoted in Nemanja Radonjić, '"From Kragujevac to Kilimanjaro": Imagining and re-imagining Africa and the self-perception of Yugoslavia in the travelogues from socialist Yugoslavia', *Godišnjak za društvenu istoriju*, 2 (2016), 89.

'it is we, the white Negroes, who are supposed to support and strengthen the system of socialist apartheid—the voting regulations preserve class separation between the multi-coloured nomenklatura and the white negroes, several controlled homelands in the form of restricted private property...the Polish white negro may become coloured...provided he swears allegiance to the Polish apartheid'.[105]

Thus colour needed to be purged, the region's true whiteness rediscovered and preserved, in order to complete the journey back to a united Europe. A Pravda headline in the late 1980s declared, 'We are Africans in a European home'.[106] Here the dark continent was backward and a burden: an excessive anti-colonialism had kept the region from its true destiny in 'white civilised Europe'.[107] This racialization was not always explicit—indeed, when Gorbachev spoke of a common European home he meant it as a capacious category that could be expanded to Eurasia —but in the hands of more strident nationalists it became an argument for the detachment from an unwanted Soviet 'Third World' (i.e. Central Asia) and Africa.[108] Facing the diversion of investment from their continent, it was African observers who from the mid-1980s most explicitly characterized the region's geopolitical repositioning as a reconstitution of a white 'Fortress Europe'.[109]

Many Eastern European countries withdrew from international anti-colonial and anti-racist rights work at the UN.[110] Such campaigning was associated with a political lack of moderation and the voicing of excessive claims. By the late 1980s, both reform Communists and dissidents were prepared to embrace the politically tempered and deracialized language of the 'transition paradigm'—which was accused by its critics of marginalizing claims for collective economic and racial justice in its advocacy of individual political rights, market reform and openness to foreign investment.[111] Faced with a weakening apartheid regime in the late 1980s, the Polish and Hungarian governments preferred to support the moderate wing of the apartheid regime and the liberal opposition who advocated technocratic compromise and resisted the 'excessive' claims to racial justice on the part of

---

[105] Andrzej Frycz, 'Socialist Apartheid', *Wola* 24/150 (12 August 1985) [no page].

[106] Quoted in Charles Quist-Adade, 'From Paternalism to Ethnocentrism: Images of Africa in Gorbachev's Russia', *Race and Class*, 46/4 (2005), 88.

[107] Ian Law, *Red Racisms: Racism in Communist and Post-Communist Contexts* (New York: Palgrave Macmillan, 2012), 21–2; Ian Law and Nikolaj Zakharov, 'Race and Racism in Eastern Europe: Becoming White, becoming Western', in Philomena Essed, Karen Farquharson, Kathryn Pillay and Elisa Joy White (eds.), *Relating Worlds of Racism. Dehumanisation, Belonging, and the Normativity of European Whiteness* (Cham: Palgrave Macmillan, 2019), 114.

[108] James Mark et al., *1989: A Global History of Eastern Europe* (Cambridge: CUP, 2019), 143–4.

[109] On the silencing of racialized thought behind late twentieth century conceptions of Europe: David Goldberg, 'Racial Europeanization', *Ethnic and Racial Studies*, 29/2 (2006), 331–64. On the implicit equation between Christian European civilization and race, Ivan Kalmar, 'The east is just like the west, only more so: Islamophobia and populism in Eastern Germany and the East of the European Union', *Journal of Contemporary European Studies*, 28/1 (2020), 15–29.

[110] Gehrig et al., 'Global Fight Against Apartheid', 305.   [111] Mark et al., *1989*, chapter 3.

radicals in the ANC.[112] With the news emerging in early 1990 that Poland and Hungary were moving quickly to deepen economic relations with apartheid South Africa, one black Labour MP in the UK, Bernie Grant, expressed his fears that Europe was witnessing the reconstitution of a 'white men's club'.[113]

The rhetoric of global struggle against racism continued to be drawn upon by emerging dissident movements in the 1980s, but mostly to make sense of their own subjugation under Communism. Polish oppositionists alluded to African-American slavery to describe their nation's own 'capture' by Soviet Communism. Kunta Kinte, the slave hero of Alex Haley's *Roots*, became a popular character after the broadcast on Polish TV of the American miniseries, the meaning of which was re-worked in an anti-Soviet vein in *Solidarność* literature.[114] The Hungarian minority in Transylvania invoked the concept of apartheid to highlight the discrimination they faced at the hands of a nationalizing Romanian Communist state.[115] Both the oppositional group Charter 77 in Czechoslovakia and Polish dissidents used the term to suggest a different form of apartheid, based on political and religious criteria, as they appealed for support from western audiences.[116] These movements deracialized this language, refused connection with ongoing racial struggles, choosing merely to draw on the global power of its vocabulary, and retooling it in the name of anti-totalitarianism. It was difficult for dissidents to identify with anti-colonial movements which were also supported by Communists in Prague or Warsaw, but the lack of empathy was also due to the fact that Eastern Europeans for the most part had not been socialized under Communism to feel that their countries had any connection to the ongoing legacies of European Empire.[117] It was striking that only in the GDR—which had embraced the task of overcoming the legacies of German colonialism in Africa— did a 1980s opposition, mainly around churches, join with the state in anti-apartheid work. In the case of the largest opposition movement in the region, the Polish trade union *Solidarność*, this refusal to express solidarity with anti-apartheid was also rooted in their reliance on donations from Polish emigrés in South Africa who were threatened by the black struggle.[118]

The fantasy of a return to a white continent—rather than to the reality of an increasingly multicultural western Europe—could also be discerned in practices directed towards coloured migrants from the South (see also *Mobility*). In the

---

[112] Betts et al. 'Race, Socialism and Solidarity', 174–6.

[113] BLCSA, MSS AAM, 2075–7, Speech of Bernie Grant, Labour MP, House of Commons, 8 January 1990 (Archive of the Anti-Apartheid Movement, Oxford).

[114] Adam F. Kola, 'A Prehistory of Postcolonialism in Socialist Poland', in Mark et al. (eds.), *Alternative Globalizations*, 279.

[115] Gehrig et al., 'Global Fight against Apartheid', 307.

[116] *Declaration of Charter 77*, 1 (1977). https://www.files.ethz.ch/isn/125521/8003_Charter_77.pdf (last accessed 18 January 2018).

[117] Imre, 'Whiteness', 82, 84.

[118] Kim Christiaens and Idesbald Goddeeris, 'Competing Solidarities? Solidarność and the Global South during the 1980s', in Mark et al. (eds.), *Alternative Globalizations*, 300.

1960s, their presence had been highlighted; yet by the early 1980s, labour migrants from Vietnam, Cuba and Mozambique, who in general received fewer welfare benefits than labour migrants from neighbouring bloc states, were hidden away from the general population and kept in dormitories and factories, often outside cities. In Hungary, it was striking that the official celebrations of Cuban solidarity were not connected to the female Cuban textile workers who arrived in greater numbers from the early 1980s. In the late 1970s, new blocks of flats built in the peripheral eighteenth district of Budapest had been named after the Cuban capital. During the 1980s, it became a space for celebrating Cuban-Hungarian friendship. Despite the proximity of their workplaces, Cubans were never invited to solidarity events in the district.[119] Nor were they offered accommodation in the *Havanna telep* (Havana settlement)—unlike many of their colleagues in the nearby garment factories who were gifted new apartments there as a sign of social mobility.[120] Indeed, Cuban female workers complained that Hungarians confused them with Roma women, and consequently, they were treated unfavourably.[121]

Those who had published on racism in the post-colonial world were forbidden to write about intensifying discrimination against migrants at home. GDR author Landolf Scherzer had written accounts of journeys in both Mozambique and Thuringia, his aim being to look at internationalism as it played out not only in Africa but also in his own country: how did East Germans relate to the Mozambicans with whom they worked and shared public spaces; and with whom they drank and also loved?[122] He had wanted to tackle East German prejudices, but was not allowed to publish because it was thought to be harmful to inter-nationalism.[123] From the early 1980s, some campaigners—sociologists in Hungary, and anti-racist groups in the GDR—tried to make labour migrants of colour visible, their plight known, and presence accepted, although such attempts remained marginal.[124]

As popular support for the Eastern Bloc project in the Third World declined, acts of open discrimination and violence against students and labour migrants increased markedly.[125] Even if students from the global South had been subjected

---

[119] *Peremvidék*, 16 (June 12 1985), 4.

[120] 'Új lakók a Havannán', *Fonómunkás*, 23 (December 21 1986), 3.

[121] 'Kubai lanyok Budapesten', *Mai Magazin*, March 1985, 27.

[122] Interview with Landolf Scherzer, conducted by Eric Burton, 12 December 2018.

[123] See his account in *Die Fremden. Unerwünschte Begegnungen und verbotene Protokolle* (Berlin: Aufbau, 2004).

[124] Mike Dennis, 'Asian and African Workers in the Niches of Society', in Mike Dennis and Norman LaPorte, *State and Minorities in Communist East Germany* (New York: Berghahn Books, 2011), 113; on skinhead attacks on Cubans in Hungary, see James Mark and Bálint Tolmár, 'From Heroes Square to the Textile Factory: Encountering Cuba in Socialist Hungary 1959–1990' (unpublished manuscript).

[125] Maxim Matusevich, 'Probing the Limits of Internationalism: African Students Confront Soviet Ritual', *Anthropology of East Europe Review*, 27/2 (2009), 28–30; Maxim Matusevich, 'Testing the Limits of Soviet Internationalism. African Students in the Soviet Union', in Philip E. Muehlenbeck (ed.), *Race, Ethnicity and the Cold War* (Nashville: Vanderbilt University Press, 2012), 155–9; Weis, 'The Politics Machine', 366.

to racial abuse in the 1960s, they were also widely seen as a source of pride, since their very presence testified to the region's global role. Now, however, 'others' were considered remnants of an evidently failing socialist internationalism and as obstacles to a return to Europe.[126] Minorities within the Soviet Union and Eastern Europe—from Roma to Muslims—became stereotyped as a 'Third World' within, and they too became targets. Voicing their alarm at this shift, commentators, especially those from an older anti-colonial generation, noted the emergence of a new form of 'savage racism' that demonized both labour migrants and domestic minorities as civilizational outsiders.[127]

Some reflected on how socialist societies had not provided their citizens with the tools to combat racism within. György Makai—a journalist who had travelled across and written widely about the decolonizing world—published *Fajelmélet— fajüldözés* (Racial Theory, Racial Discrimination). The impetus for the work had come from an experience in a youth club discussion of the Patriotic People's Front in Budapest in the mid-1970s, in which racism was the key topic. He recounted how to his interlocutors racism was only ever an external occurrence— Communist Youth members knew about The Dreyfus Affair and contemporary cases of racial discrimination across the world, but were simply not aware of Hungary's own traditions of anti-Semitism. For Makai, the externalization of the racial question meant that a younger generation was not well prepared to recognize increasing racism within their own society—or equipped to counter it.[128]

By 1989, the idea of expulsion in the name of joining a white western club was no longer metaphorical: many labour migrants were sent home that same year, representatives of a now demonized socialist internationalism. As many as 80,000 contract workers from Vietnam, Angola, Mozambique and Cuba were forced to leave during the collapse of the GDR, lest they settle in a re-united Germany. Skinhead violence towards Cuban workers in Hungary from late 1988 not only revealed the presence of both a new racist youth culture and a previously concealed migrant community—but would lead to expulsion of the latter in the following year.[129] Attacks against Roma and Vietnamese increased exponentially in Czechoslovakia, leading to a public condemnation from Charter 77 and the Czechoslovak Helsinki Committee, who declared that such violence contradicted

---

[126] On African students' experiences of racism in late socialist period, see Grazia Scarfò Ghellab and Kamal Mellakh (eds.), *Étudier à l'Est. Expériences de diplômés africains*, 117; On racialized prejudice against the 'Soviet South', Jeff Sahadeo, 'Black Snouts Go Home: Migration and Race in Late Soviet Leningrad and Moscow', *The Journal of Modern History*, 88/4 (2016), 797–826.

[127] Andrey Urnov, 'Sovetskii Soiuz i bor'ba protiv rasizma i kolonializma na iuge afriki', *Asia and Africa Today*, 3 (2009), 54–61.

[128] György Makai, *Fajelmélet - fajüldözés* (Budapest: Kozmosz Könyvek, 1977), 7–8.

[129] Mark and Tolmár, 'From Heroes Square'. Against the background of the late 1980s AIDS epidemic, Africans in the Soviet Union were presented in popular culture as alien bearers of this new disease. Matusevich, 'Probing the Limits', 30–1.

the ideals of their democratic revolution.[130] The Czechoslovak government eventually decided to expel 37,000 Vietnamese labour migrants.[131] Tens of thousands of Chinese migrants had been able to come to Eastern Europe, thanks to visa free travel to Hungary, especially after the suppression of the Tiananmen Square protests. From 1992, their entry was barred.[132] Those from the Middle East who remained in Romania, and Vietnamese in Bulgaria, were often the target of racist harassment and criminalized for street trading and black market activities.[133] Racialized others seemed to have less and less of a place in late and post-Communist ideas of Europeanness. This development was not lost on Algeria's representatives at the UN who complained in 1990 that 'racism and xenophobia against migrant workers was in the increase in many host countries, particularly in Europe.'[134] Jan Martenson, the UN Under-Secretary General for Human Rights, offered a sobering view of the global wave of democratization symbolized by '1989': though it had brought about 'amazing changes', it had also triggered 'a resurgence of racial hatred, intolerance, and discrimination.'[135]

In a cartoon composed on 25 October 1989, the Tanzanian David Kyungu related the changing racialized bordering practices that he had observed as state socialism collapsed.[136] Whilst East Germans are welcomed upon arrival on a flight from the East, a black African anti-apartheid activist who has arrived on the same plane is removed, targeted as an economic migrant and then as a drug dealer. In Kyungu's representation, the collapse of state socialism had enabled the reconstitution of a racially bordered continent that embraced only white European freedom of movement; by contrast, networks of solidarity that had previously ensured a certain limited multiracial mobility were now closed down and black faces were targeted as symbols of delinquency and criminality.

---

[130] Intervention of Mr. Slaby (Czechoslovakia), UN Assembly, Third Committee, 9th meeting, 16 October 1989, A/C.3/44/SR.9, 16. David Crowe, *A History of the Gypsies of Eastern Europe and Russia* (New York: St. Martin's Griffin, 1994), 64–5.

[131] Liz Fekete and Frances Webber, *Inside Racist Europe* (London: Institute of Race Relations, 1994), 42.

[132] Pál Nyíri, 'Chinese Migration to Eastern Europe', *International Migration*, 41/3 (2003), 243.

[133] Mark et al., *1989*, 126. Raia Apostolova, 'Duty and Debt under the Ethos of Internationalism. The Case of the Vietnamese Workers in Bulgaria', *Journal of Vietnamese Studies*, 12/1 (2017), 101–25.

[134] Intervention of Miss Boumaiza (Algeria), UN Assembly, Third Committee, 8th meeting, 16 October 1990, A/C.3/45/SR.8, 3 (UN).

[135] Intervention of Mr. Martenson, UN Assembly, Third Committee, 3rd meeting, 8.10.1990, A/C.3/45/SR.3, 15 (UN).

[136] Thanks to Quinn Slobodian for sharing this cartoon, and David Kyungu for granting permission. Reproduced in David Kyungu, *"Mensch guck mich nicht so an!..."*: *Alltagsgeschichten mit spritzer Feder gezeichnet von David Kyungu* (Breklum: Breklumer Verlag, 1991).

David Kyungu, 'Plötzlich passierte es…Deutschland im Herbst 1989', 25 October 1989.

Denigration and Superiority: From Communism to Right-wing Populism

In wake of 1989, Eastern Europeans were once again denigrated as 'poor whites' in the West. In fact, the situation had worsened as they supposedly had been darkened, or orientalized, by an eastern 'Asiatic' socialism which had kept the region in a state of economic backwardness. Fantasies of colonization re-emerged; in a unfied Germany, for instance, Ossis (former GDR citizens) were termed 'east Elbe Negroes', who needed to be improved.[137] And as the fear of being swamped by a poorer East was coded as a racial threat, Eastern European hopes of an unfettered mobility that 1989 had unleashed would at first only be partly realized—and then more fully only after many years. Despite the dissident imaginary that celebrated the fall of the Wall and the possibility of East-West freedom of movement, '1989' in fact led to a less liberal travel environment for some Eastern Europeans.[138] Between the end of Communist rule in the GDR and the unification of Germany, a growing concern in Bonn was how to avoid a mass migration of East Germans to the West and how to halt the flow of migrants from Poland and beyond.[139] Even following the accession of Eastern European states from 2004, the West was perceived as remarkably inhospitable to Eastern Europeans. By the time that the ban on the movement of labour from the East was about to expire, a wave of xenophobic stereotypes arose in many of the countries of 'old' Europe: Eastern Europeans were often racialized as the migrant other rather than as belonging to the same political union with equal rights.[140] The idea that accession would lead to a full public acceptance of Easterners as Europeans was, at the very least, still waiting for its full realization.

At the same time, the idea of being the true or superior Europe returned, this time for an emerging populist right. For them, the post-1968 Western European liberal-left had abandoned a commitment to a white Christian Europe, the return to which, following the collapse of a 'multicoloured' socialist internationalism, underpinned their politics. This notion of supposed reckless abandonment of white Europe for a multicultural one could already be discerned in some conservative dissident writings in the 1980s—which accused the West of ignoring the cause of anti-Communist movements in favour of the anti-racist struggles of the South. Frustrated by the West's supposed privileging of support for the anti-apartheid struggle in the 1980s, right-wing Polish dramatist (and former Stalinist) Sławomir Mrożek wrote a satirical letter to the UN in which he claimed Eastern Europeans had to 'black up' in order to be taken seriously:

---

[137] Anke Pinkert, "'Postcolonial Legacies": The Rhetoric of Race in the East/West German National Identity Debate of the Late 1990s', *The Journal of the Midwest Modern Language Association*, 35/2 (2002), 13–32. See the controversy over Gabriele Mendling's representation of the East in 'Neuland' (1999).

[138] Mark Keck-Szajbel, 'The Politics of Travel and the Creation of a European Society', *Global Society*, 24 (2010), 50.

[139] Ibid., 47–8.

[140] József Böröcz and Mahua Sarkar, 'The Unbearable Whiteness of the Polish Plumber and the Hungarian Peacock Dance around "Race"', *Slavic Review*, 76/2 (2017), 307–14; Philipp Ther, *Europe since 1989: A History* (Princeton: Princeton University Press, 2016), 310–12.

'I should like to report, that the Poles are also Negroes, as they are whites. By virtue of our rights to independence. If the beloved organisation was disturbed by the colour of our skin, or if some kind of difficulty surfaces in this regard, then we can repaint ourselves. To this end we ask the dear organisation to supply us with black Kiwi-branded shoe polish. It's not our fault we are white. This was just how it came to be....We don't ask for the polish for free. For every kilo we receive, we can send in exchange a tonne of red varnish.'[141]

After the collapse of state socialism, these resentments were seldom heard in pub-lic debate. There were those liberals and the left in the region who hoped that westernization would also bring an acceptance of multiculturalism, replacing the Communist insistence on nation and unity, and embracing both long-settled and new minorities. Indeed, post-socialist cities did in many cases become more diverse: socialist-era migrants who remained, especially from Vietnam, and a new post-socialist migration centred on trade flourished.[142] Even though such frustrations remained on the populist right, the requirements of conditionality for those formerly Communist countries seeking to enter the European Union ensured that such discourses were limited to the political margins.

The idea that the West still saw the East as the lesser Europe was weaponized in the context of the arrival of those displaced by the Syrian Civil War from 2015. Populists had long assumed that they had a greater claim on Europeanness—as white Europeans—than post-colonial minorities across the continent. Over time, through the experience of living in societies that promoted multiculturalism, they had also learnt that different groups had to make appeals to identity—often through claims to exclusion—in order to compete for resources. The perception that liberals in Western Europe accepted Islamic migrants with more enthusiasm than they had Eastern Europeans was mobilized by populists, who argued that they were the true victims of a continental project that had given up on the defence of a white Christian Europe. Only those 'Easterners' who had been tempered by the struggle against Communist dictatorship, it was argued, retained a sufficient combative spirit to fight for its civilization. In this sense, populists were the heirs to the Communists, in that they also drew on the idea of the region's racial inno-cence, supposedly untainted by complicity with European colonialism, in order to define their superiority to a debased liberal Europe. Rather than argue for soli-darity, however, such politicians insisted that Eastern European states were not under any obligation to take in refugees from outside Europe. They had not held extra-European empires and hence, by contrast with states in the West of the

---

[141] Sławomir Mrożek, 'To the deeply revered United Nations', reproduced in *A Dél-Afrikai Magyar Egyesület Lapja*, 4/2 (June 1986), 12.

[142] Gertrud Huwelmeier, 'From "Jarmark Europa" to "Commodity City". New Marketplaces, Post-Socialist Migrations, and Cultural Diversity in Central and Eastern Europe', *Central and Eastern European Migration Review*, 1 (2015), 27–39.

continent, neither suffered from a debilitating white guilt, nor had compelling contemporary post-colonial ethical duties.[143] A supposed colonial innocence was invoked in the name of the protection of a racialized conception of Europe.[144] Such assertions conveniently ignored the region's earlier colonial fantasies; Eastern European migration in the context of broader European settler colonialisms; socialist-era migration from Africa and Asia to the region; and the presence of the region's troops in destabilizing conflicts in the Middle East that had helped to precipitate the crisis.[145]

Conclusion

In the nineteenth century, the increasing identification of whiteness with Europe, and with the continent's global imperialism, was an ambivalent development for Eastern Europeans. On one hand, whiteness was constructed from outside the region, and often meant their denigration: not holding colonies—or even for a time their own states—they would be classed as not quite white. Claims on a European whiteness thus remained fragile and partial. On the other hand, many Eastern European nationalisms sought the power that a full identification with an imperial white Europe might confer. From the late nineteenth century onwards, nationalists developed the fantasy of representing the better or true Europe whose own moral sensibilities, heightened by their own experience of colonial subjugation, could be employed to redeem a continent whose global mission had been corrupted through the West's barbaric violence. The Communist anti-colonial project was an extension of this: postwar decolonization in Africa and Asia offered a gateway to status and enabled the claim that they were in fact the better white Europeans on account of their commitment to anti-racism and anti-colonialism. Nevertheless, this was a project with a still ambiguous relationship to European imperialism, critiquing its racist violence, yet simultaneously seeking to imitate, and hoping to redeem, its practices. As long as this imperial longing could be hitched to anti-colonialism it retained meaningfully progressive features; yet as soon as Third World alliances ceased to be perceived as a route to global power, socialist internationalism was deemed to have corrupted or 'darkened' Eastern Europe. Colonial visions, which never fully went away, even at the height of the anti-colonial period, could now be repurposed for the reconstruction of a culturally distinct, securitized, and racially bordered, white Christian Europe.

[143] 'Interview with Gergely Prőhle, former Ambassador of Hungary in Berlin', *Körber Stiftung*, May 2018.
[144] 'By becoming a part of the EU's legal system, the Balkans cannot any longer claim colonial and racial exceptionalism': Dušan I. Bjelić, 'Introduction', in idem. (ed.), *Balkan Transnationalism at the Time of Neoliberal Catastrophe* (Abingdon: Routledge, 2018), 17.
[145] Salman Sayyid, 'Islamophobia and the Europeanness of the Other Europe', *Patterns of Prejudice*, 52/5 (2018), 420–2.

7

Health

Bogdan C. Iacob

Introduction

Eastern Europe played a central role in the politics and practice of post-1945 global health. Socialist states internationalized expertise, institutions and people within the Second World, at the World Health Organization (WHO), or through bilateral relationships with the 'Third World'. These transfers and interactions often—but not always—represented a novel understanding of the improvement of humanity's welfare. The globalization of policies and knowledge from the East adapted to shifts within the camp itself, to interdependencies in international organizations or with the West, and to evolving perceptions of the decolonizing world. These dynamics built on interwar developments and debates at the League of Nations' Health Organization (LNHO), drawing on central and south-eastern European as well as Soviet experiences in disease control and rural welfare. State-socialist approaches to health combined pre-1945 traditions that stressed the social-economic roots of illness with extensive epidemiological surveillance, centralized institutions, and 'Enlightenment' notions of hygiene that rested on authoritarian statecraft. Free access to healthcare merged with 'intervention and control that western public health could only dream about':[1] this was the medical version of 'socialist modernism'[2] that Communist regimes contrasted with the practices of the rival 'capitalist camp'. The rhetoric directed at western health insisted on the latter's profit-oriented profile and history of (neo)colonial interests. Eastern Europeans lambasted the West's assumptions of its racial and civilizational superiority over subject peoples. Nonetheless, the socialist camp developed its own Eurocentric hierarchical vision of the world, which by the end of the Cold

I am grateful for the archival help provided by Alena Alamgir (Czechoslovakia), Eric Burton (the GDR), Nemanja Radonjić (Yugoslavia), and Maria Dembek (Poland).

[1] Elena Izmaïlova, 'The System of Epidemic Control in the USSR: Short Essay on its History', in Anne Moulin (ed.), *Les Sciences hors d'Occident au XXe siècle. Volume 4, Médecines et santé* (Paris: Orstom éditions, 2016), 115.

[2] Dora Vargha, 'The Socialist World in Global Polio Eradication', *Revue d'études comparatives Est-Ouest*, 1/1 (2018), 88.

Bogdan C. Iacob, *Health* In *Socialism Goes Global: The Soviet Union and Eastern Europe in the Age of Decolonization.* Edited by James Mark and Paul Betts, Oxford University Press. © Oxford University Press 2022. DOI: 10.1093/oso/9780192848857.003.0008

War reflected a surprising East–West convergence.[3] Socialist discourse regarding the management of health as both a biological and a social phenomenon occasioned the unprecedented planning and centralization of medical industries and care. These ideas drew on interwar visions regarding the socio-economic embeddedness of disease and the centrality of states to healthcare provision. Growing East–West similarity attenuated the self-proclaimed Eastern European exceptionalism, especially when compared with western welfare state medicine.[4] This overlap sometimes created common ground between socialist representatives and western left-leaning experts who fostered progressive reforms at the WHO.

The integration of Eastern Europe into global histories of health is long overdue: the region was always part of major international debates about the role of the state in the administration of medical assistance. Eastern European public health experts understood the cultural and developmental liminality of the region, and blended ideas of disease control and welfare from both the West and the global South. Their own civilizing missions mixed modern medicine with languages of health self-determination in extra-European territories that challenged western notions of the presumed pathology of 'tropical' peoples and environments. State socialism's global reach forged an unprecedented range of contacts with the developing world, and these efforts to decolonize medical practices helped to shape the WHO's agenda. However, the contrast between Eastern Europe and other socialist alternatives from Cuba and China complicated East–South encounters. By the 1980s the viability of the Eastern European public health alternative imploded because of domestic crisis, competition from other socialist countries and growing East–West convergence. Yet this should not obscure the fact that Eastern Europe had played a key if forgotten role in the globalization and decolonization of public health from the 1950s through the 1980s.

Peripheries Internationalized

During the interwar period, the Soviet Union along with central and south-eastern Europe were at the forefront of experimenting with healthcare reform—in ways that had long-lasting effects on global developments across the twentieth century. The creation of the USSR generated a radical new model of public health based on the social-economic determinants of disease, prevention and universal access, all managed by comprehensive state control.[5] The Soviet Union integrated the Bolshevik critique of what it considered pathological capitalist societies and

---

[3] Young-Sun Hong, *Cold War Germany, the Third World, and the Global Humanitarian Regime* (New York: Cambridge University Press, 2015), 5.

[4] Charles Webster, 'Medicine and the Welfare State 1930–70', in Roger Cooter and John Pickstone (eds.), *Companion of Medicine in the Twentieth Century* (London: Routledge, 2003), 125–40.

[5] Mark Field, 'Soviet Medicine', in ibid., 52.

the destructive effects of imperialism on colonial peoples. During the 1920s, Weimar Germany and the Soviet Union pioneered social hygiene programmes. After the First World War in central and south-eastern Europe, the creation of medical systems was linked to self-determination, and promoted as a model for colonial territories which were denied this right in the peace treaties. Reformers argued that national health management was premised on state-managed education, disease control as well as housing and sanitation reforms.[6] National centralized systems were built around institutes of hygiene funded by the Rockefeller Foundation in Czechoslovakia, Poland, Romania, Greece, Yugoslavia, Hungary and Bulgaria.[7]

The Soviet Union in its first decades also sought to take part in the discussions surrounding these international developments. It cooperated with the LNHO, the Rockefeller Foundation, and endeavoured to establish bilateral links with health researchers and statesmen in 'as many countries as possible'.[8] In the 1930s and the 1940s, dozens of doctors and social reformers from Mexico, Argentina, Chile, Brazil, Columbia, Venezuela and Uruguay travelled to the Soviet Union.[9] Discussions about the Soviet model fuelled the resurgence of social medicine in the US, a trend that was later stifled by the Cold War and 'medical McCarthyism'.[10] In the mid-1930s, the USSR joined the LNHO's coordinated experiments with synthetic anti-malarial drugs, along with Algeria, Italy, the Malay States and Romania.[11] Inspired by French state practices and drawing on pre-revolutionary connections with the Pasteur Institute, the Commissariat of Health pursued mass immunization (rejected in the US) and centralized disease control. It adopted compulsory vaccination against smallpox, a country-wide anti-malarial plan in 1934, and by 1938 had expanded the anti-tuberculosis vaccination of newborns to sixty-five cities and industrial centres.[12] Such plans laid the foundations for

[6] Marius Turda, 'History of Medicine in Eastern Europe, Including Russia', in Mark Jackson (ed.), *Oxford Handbook of the History of Medicine* (Oxford: Oxford University Press, 2011), 216.

[7] Paul Weindling, 'Public Health and Political Stabilisation: The Rockefeller Foundation in Central and Eastern Europe between the Two World Wars', *Minerva*, 31/3 (1993), 243–67.

[8] Susan Gross Solomon, 'Thinking Internationally, Acting Locally: Soviet Public Health as Cultural Diplomacy in the 1920s', in Susan Grant (ed.), *Russian and Soviet Health Care from an International Perspective* (London: Palgrave Macmillan, 2017), 194.

[9] Anne-Emanuelle Birn, 'Public Health and Medicine in Latin America', in Jackson ed., *Oxford Handbook*, 138.

[10] Susan Gross Solomon, 'The Perils of Unconstrained Enthusiasm: John Kingsbury, Soviet Public Health, and 1930s America', 45–64 and Jane Brickman, 'Medical McCarthyism and the Punishment of Internationalist Physicians in the United States', 82–100 in Anne-Emanuelle Birn and Theodore M. Brown, *Comrades in Health: U.S. Health Internationalists, Abroad and at Home* (New Brunswick: Rutgers University Press, 2013).

[11] Edmond Sergent, 'Work of the Malaria Commission of the League of Nations since 1930', 16.09.1938, LN/CH/Malaria/268 (Archives of the League of Nations, Health Section Files-Geneva), 11.

[12] Leonard Bruce-Chwatt, 'Malaria Research and Eradication in the USSR', *Bulletin World Health Organization*, 21 (1959), 739–40; Michael David, 'Vaccination against Tuberculosis with BCG. A Study of Innovation of Public Health, 1925–41', in Francis Bernstein, Christopher Burton, and Dan Healey (eds.), *Soviet Medicine: Culture, Practice, and Science* (DeKalb: Northern Illinois University Press, 2010), 132–54.

postwar disease control policies that enabled the Soviet regime to lay claim to being at the cutting edge of global epidemiology, and served as the template for the USSR's massive post-1945 expansion into global health.

Central and south-eastern Europe along with the USSR were borderlands of European health—spaces where infectious diseases wreaked havoc on the population because of severe poverty, while the standard of infrastructure services (water, electricity, transport and communications, housing, healthcare and education) was often likened to those in what were still colonial territories in Africa and Asia.[13] Intervention in this region, so close to Western Europe, became a priority for the LNHO. This international organization emphasized epidemiological cooperation and social medicine, one which pioneered a social-economic approach to disease and the assistance of impoverished communities. Such international involvement placed the USSR, central and south-eastern Europe at the heart of global public health networks, and at the centre of discussions about global health.[14]

Thus rather than becoming simply a zone of experimentation for an international organization and external expertise, the region itself came to produce many specialists who would help shape its agenda. For instance, the LNHO's Malaria Commission (founded in 1924) became a platform for the international integration of epidemiological knowledge from the USSR and central or south-eastern Europe. Among its original members were Evgheny Martsinovsky (USSR), Andrija Sfarčić (the Kingdom of Serbs, Croats, and Slovenes—after 1929, Yugoslavia), Mihai Ciucă (Romania), and Ludwik Anigstein (Poland). The Commission created a model for scientific cooperation that was emulated by global experts after 1945 and exerted considerable impact on the WHO's eradication programmes. It targeted 'poverty and the environment, rather than a medicalized focus on the vector of transmission [mosquitos], [as] the most sensible approach' to disease control.[15] Central and south-eastern European experts, along with colleagues from Spain, Italy and France, contended that malaria was a social evil, linking it to the much-needed modernization of the countryside, state distribution of medicine, and hygienic education—policies tailored to rural peripheries.[16]

Eastern European health experts' seemingly outsized role in the interwar globalization of health was due to their inbetweenness—occupying a position between the West and the still colonialized world. On one hand, regional medical experts often assumed the superiority of western medicine, as either fellows of the Rockefeller Foundation or as collaborators with institutions such as Pasteur

---

[13] Derek Aldcroft, *Europe's Third World: The European Periphery in the Interwar Years* (Aldershot: Ashgate, 2006).
[14] Iris Borowy, *Coming to Terms with World Health. The League of Nations Health Organisation 1921-1946* (Berlin: Peter Lang, 2009), 85–94.
[15] Sunil Amrith, *Decolonizing International Health: India and Southeast Asia, 1930–65* (New York: Palgrave MacMillan, 2006), 39.
[16] Borowy, *Coming*, 16.

Institutes. They saw themselves as saviours of the nation at home and apostles of modern European medicine abroad, a medical culture that they themselves had helped develop. In 1929, Romanian malariologist Mihai Ciucă, a Pasteurian and the Malaria Commission secretary (1927–38), was part of a LNHO delegation to India. His travel account combined a critique of underdevelopment with the pathologization of the tropics: the Ganges Delta was 'the world's largest hotbed of infection' where in isolated villages locals seemed to 'possess racial immunity'.[17] He argued for reform in India, where 'a sanitary network exists only in the cities…the rest, [is] as it was 500 years ago.'[18] Ciucă exported to India, China, Indochina and the Malay states practices that he had learned and practiced in south-eastern Europe: anti-malarial pilot projects structured around chemotherapy and prophylaxis, the identification of endemic areas, public and specialized education, as well as studies of mosquito types.[19]

On the other hand, Eastern European experts often saw their own region's experience as intimately connected to a non-western world. Long before Eastern European Communists championed a progressive social statist medicine in the South, the LNHO's chairman, the Polish bacteriologist Ludwik Rajchman, had begun to promote expanding the reach of international organizations in ways that linked health concerns in Africa and Asia with those in Europe, and thus indirectly challenged the colonial status quo.[20] He argued that non-European peoples under colonial rule should be helped by the LNHO through centralized national institutions and the training of indigenous experts. The LNHO was most successful in Asia, less so in Latin America because of US hegemony, while in 1935–37 some ideas from the LNHO were transplanted into local health administrations in Africa. Rajchman set about dispatching to colonial territories LNHO experts who had a sympathetic attitude toward local populations—people such as the Romanian Mihai Ciucă or the Pole Ludwik Anigstein. This extension of the boundaries of international health work partially challenged the imperial order; thus British colonial officials loathed Rajchman, as they felt the LNHO was undermining their authority.

Connections also multiplied through a shared interest in tropical medicine that developed with the internationalization of epidemiology. Medicine had been a tool of empire: while colonial administrations attempted to control indigenous populations through medical services, physicians developed knowledge about infectious diseases considered typical of tropical environments.[21] Such practices often reflected western perceptions of 'colonial races' with immutable biological

---

[17]   Radu Iftimovici, *Frații Mihai și Alexandru Ciucă* (Iași: Junimea, 1975), 192–3.

[18]   Ibid., 189.

[19]   Bogdan C. Iacob, 'Malariology and Decolonization: Eastern European Experts from the League of Nations to the World Health Organization', *Journal of Global History* (forthcoming 2022), 17–20.

[20]   Marta Balińska, *For the Good of Humanity. Ludwik Rajchman, Medical Statesman* (Budapest: Central European University Press, 1998).

[21]   Michael Worboys 'Colonial Medicine', in Cooter and Pickstone (eds.), *Companion*, 67–80.

characteristics that made them disease carriers.[22] However, some of these afflictions, such as malaria or smallpox, also devastated Europe's peripheries. Such connections allowed physicians to repurpose tropical medical knowledge for Eastern European nation state–building and for the Soviets' socialist modernization. Its racial premises tended in fact to be transformed into discussions about social practices and cultural traits—rather than biologically determined features—when Eastern European modernizers targeted their own populations. Certain categories of people, especially ethnic minorities such as Jews or the Roma, were deemed 'last bastions' in the fight against infectious diseases, which sometimes echoed the racializing discourse of the eugenic movement, influential during the interwar years and instrumental to legitimizing genocidal policies in the region during the Second World War.[23] Still, mostly assimilationist discourses pervaded medical establishments in Eastern Europe, reflective of public health experts' focus on 'civilizing' the countryside.[24] Tropical medicine could be instrumentalized for national regeneration elsewhere too: models of western tropical governance advocated by the LNHO's Malaria Commission were adapted to suit India, South East Asia and China by local medical elites intent on improving national health of their similarly predominantly rural peoples as an expression of political legitimacy.[25]

Eastern European and Soviet experts' embrace of the cultural and social premises of tropical medicine also bolstered civilizational hierarchies at home and abroad. In the USSR, healthcare acquired a strong neo-colonial flavour as Joseph Stalin moved away from the 1920s 'affirmative action' policies toward Soviet nationalities.[26] The authorities had initially attempted to bring a socialist medicine to Central Asia that synthesized European and traditional medicine. Such syncretism had had an anti-colonial objective, in that the region bordered western empires, China and Japan, and the Soviets wished to demonstrate that they, unlike their neighbouring regimes, could incorporate traditional practices into their version

[22] Pratik Chakrabarti, *Bacteriology in British India: Laboratory Medicine and the Tropics* (Rochester: University of Rochester Press, 2012), 7.

[23] Victoria Shmidt, 'The Politics of Surveillance in the Interwar Czechoslovak Periphery: The Role of Campaigns against Infectious Diseases', *Zeitschrift für Ostmitteleuropa-Forschung* 68/1 (2019), 29–56; Marius Turda, 'Ideas of Racial Purification in Romania, 1918–1944', in Christian Promitzer, Sevasti Trubeta and Marius Turda (eds.), *Health, Hygiene and Eugenics in Southeastern Europe to 1945* (Budapest: CEU Press, 2011), 325–50.

[24] Christian Promitzer, Sevasti Trubeta and Marius Turda, 'Introduction' in Ibid. (eds.), *Health*, 17; Katharina Kreuder-Sonnen, 'Epidemiological State-building in Interwar Poland: Discourses and Paper Technologies', *Science in Context* 32/1 (2019), 59; Victoria Shmidt, 'Race Science in Czechoslovakia: Serving Segregation in the Name of the Nation', *Studies in History and Philosophy of Biological and Biomedical Sciences* 83 (2020), 6.

[25] David Arnold, 'Tropical Governance: Managing Health in Monsoon Asia, 1908–1938', *Asia Research Institute Working Paper Series* No. 116 (National University of Singapore, 2009), 1–21; Warwick Anderson and Hans Pols, 'Scientific Patriotism: Medical Science and National Self-Fashioning in Southeast Asia', *Comparative Studies in Society and History*, 54/1 (2012), 93–113.

[26] Terry Martin, *Affirmative Action Empire: Nations and Nationalism in the Soviet Union 1923–1939* (Ithaca: Cornell University Press, 2001).

of modernity. Yet by the end of the 1930s traditional medicine had been all but eradicated, only to be half-heartedly resuscitated in the late 1950s, when Central Asia was promoted as a showcase to the decolonizing world for socialist modernity's ability to accommodate local knowledge. However, the status of indigenous medicine remained peripheral and gained prominence in the USSR only after the late 1970s as part of the global turn toward more traditional approaches.[27]

In the 1930s, Central Asia in fact became the first testing ground for Soviet tropical medicine[28]—the knowledge gathered would be used after 1945 in the developing world. The Soviet 'civilizing mission' rejected biological determinism and emphasized emancipation. This distinctive interpretation was obvious in the mid-1920s during the Soviet-German expeditions to study the diseases that ravaged the USSR's peripheries. German physicians saw these territories as human laboratories that might replace their country's lost colonies in Africa and the Pacific. In contrast, Soviet experts probed their theory that the aetiology of epidemics had to do with economics, occupation, social class, education, gender, and religion.[29] During the 1930s, health was not an equalizer among Soviet nationalities or between rural and urban populations. Stalinist modernization inflicted levels of destruction comparable to those of western empires in their colonies: Stalin's collectivization in Kazakhstan, for instance, triggered the worst famine experienced in the region and a massive malaria epidemic with a horrific death toll.[30] At the same time, Soviet physicians' critique of the biological determinism inherent in tropical medicine,[31] along with the 'nativization' of medical personnel in Soviet republics,[32] strengthened colonized peoples' fascination with the medical modernization of the USSR. In 1943, in India, the imperial authorities, under pressure from local nationalists, set up the Health Survey and Development Committee. Its report (published in 1946) praised the Soviet system

[27] Ivan Sablin, 'Tibetan Medicine and Buddhism in the Soviet Union: Research, Repression, and Revival, 1922–1991', in Markku Hokkanen and Kalle Kananoja (eds.), *Healers and Empires in Global History: Healing as Hybrid and Contested Knowledge* (Cham: Palgrave Macmillan, 2019), 83–99.

[28] Matthias Braun, 'From Landscapes to Labscapes: Malaria Research and Anti-Malaria Policy in Soviet Azerbaijan, 1920–41', *Jahrbücher für Geschichte Osteuropas*, 61/4 (2013), 513–30.

[29] Susan Gross Solomon, 'The Soviet-German Syphilis Expedition to Buriat Mongolia, 1928: Scientific Research on National Minorities', *Slavic Review*, 52/2 (1993), 212 and 228–30; Elizabeth Hachten, 'How to Win Friends and Influence People: Heinz Zeiss, Boundary Objects, and the Pursuit of Cross-National Scientific Collaboration in Microbiology', in Susan Gross Solomon (ed.), *Doing Medicine Together: Germany and Russia Between the Wars* (Toronto: Toronto University Press, 2006), 162–6.

[30] Paula Michaels, 'Medical Propaganda and Cultural Revolution in Soviet Kazakhstan, 1928–41', *The Russian Review*, 59 (2000), 151.

[31] Susan Gross Solomon, 'Infertile Soil: Heinz Zeiss and the Import of Medical Geography to Russia, 1922–1930', in ibid. (ed.), *Doing*, 240–90.

[32] The nativization of Central Asian healthcare yielded poor results until the 1940s because of Stalin's Russo-centric program of socialism in one country. It was successful from the 1950s, however, when Central Asia regained its status as a showcase for the 'Third World'. Paula Michaels, *Curative Powers: Medicine and Empire In Stalin's Central Asia* (Pittsburgh: University of Pittsburgh Press, 2003), 82–6 and 108; Artemy M. Kalinovsky, *Laboratory of Socialist Development: Cold War Politics and Decolonization in Soviet Tajikistan* (Ithaca: Cornell University Press, 2018), 201–2.

for its provision of free medical care and for placing the control of housing and factories under the authority of the People's Commissariat for Health.[33]

Central and south-eastern Europe's experience with malaria illustrated the complexity of their connections in between European and non-western worlds. On one hand, many countries had their own rural peripheries which would become their internal colonies for experimentation with the control of infectious disease by western experts. Macedonia in Yugoslavia, Dobrudja in Romania, and south-eastern Czechoslovakia were all ravaged by malaria. Between 1929 and 1937, Lewis Hackett of the International Health Board of the Rockefeller Foundation implemented in Macedonia, Bulgaria, and Albania mosquito-centred disease control that had been designed in and for the Philippines.[34] The Foundation's centralized public hygiene developed in the Philippines and Cuba found its way into the programmes of national hygiene institutes in Poland, Czechoslovakia and Romania.[35] On the other, the region developed its own infrastructure for tropical medicine, which brought together concern for its own unhealthy peripheries with aspirations to a more global role in health. Indeed, in Poland, in the context of both the health modernization of its own 'backward' Eastern territories (Kresy), and the desire for its own tropical colonies—an aspiration further fuelled by its League of Nations-sponsored mission in Liberia (1934–38)[36]—tropical medicine became a university discipline at the University of Krakow and an Institute of Maritime and Tropical Hygiene was founded in Gdynia.[37] An Institute of Tropical Medicine was founded in Skopje too, and thirteen similar institutions mushroomed across the USSR from the mid-1920s onwards. These institutes would be later reinvented during the Cold War as training and research centres for students from developing countries, and their colonial origins forgotten. Interwar Eastern European engagements with tropical medicine situated physicians in a grey area of solidarity tinged with civilizational superiority, a mixed legacy that shaped post-1945 socialist internationalism more generally.

Techniques that had been developed on the borderlands of Europe, notably in the sphere of rural health and social medicine, became of global interest well before the Communist period. By 1936, a consensus had developed at the LNHO

---

[33] John Farley, *To Cast Out Disease: A History of the International Health Division of the Rockefeller Foundation (1913–1951)* (Oxford: Oxford University Press, 2004), 258–9.

[34] Warwick Anderson, *Colonial Pathologies: American Tropical Medicine, Race and Hygiene in the Philippines* (Durham: Duke University Press, 2006), 244–5; Patrick Zylberman, 'A Transatlantic Dispute: The Etiology of Malaria and the Redesign of the Mediterranean Landscape', in Solomon et al. (eds.), *Shifting*, 282–3.

[35] Josep Baron, *Health Policies in Interwar Europe: A Transnational Perspective* (New York: Routledge, 2019), 75–8 and 80–4.

[36] Piotr Puchalski, 'The Polish Mission to Liberia, 1934–1938: Constructing Poland's Colonial identity', *Historical Journal*, 60/4 (2017), 1072.

[37] Marek Kowalski, *Dyskurs Kolonialny w Drugiej Rzeczypospolitej* (Warszawa: DiG, 2009), 48–9.

that the best health programme consisted in raising living standards. Ludwik Rajchman sought models for LNHO policies, among them Denmark's welfare system based on a cooperative rural economy.[38] Another crucial case was Yugoslavia, where Andrija Štampar (Minister of Health 1919–31) connected rural medicine with mass education, agricultural extension projects and a cooperative economy.[39] These blueprints along with others in Poland, Hungary, France and Belgium were the bases for the LNHO's programme of health centres integrated into national systems. Such institutions were tasked with preventative care and employed 'polyvalent' (able to implement multiple tasks) rather than specialized medical workers.[40] This initiative set the stage for the European Conference on Rural Hygiene held in Geneva in 1931. Twenty-four countries participated along with twenty-two observers from Bolivia, China, Colombia, Cuba, India, Japan, Mexico and the USA.[41] Inspired by its proceedings, Indian and Chinese delegates proposed a Pan-Asian rural hygiene conference the following year, arguing that the countryside in Europe and Asia faced similar structural problems—the event took place in Bandung, in 1937.[42]

The global focus on the uplift of rural populations was also a consequence of the Great Depression, which created extreme levels of poverty around the world and bolstered the notion of public health as a state responsibility.[43] The LNHO attempted to showcase this approach in China: Štampar designed a 'rural reconstruction plan' for the province of Jiangxi, one deemed too radical by local authorities.[44] However, C.C. Chen, head of the Rockefeller Foundation-funded public health programme in Tinghsien, embarked in 1935 on a LNHO-sponsored trip to the Soviet Union, Austria, Poland and Yugoslavia. Chen was most impressed by Štampar's 'demonstration project' in Mraclin, a village where the community voluntarily engaged in health measures with the help of 'teacher-propagandists' trained in rural hygiene. Chen adapted this model using unpaid but trained village farmers as peasant-medics.[45] The experiments in Mraclin and Tinghsien became the blueprint for Mao Zedong's 'barefoot doctors' scheme.[46]

---

[38] Lion Murard, 'Designs within Disorder: International Conferences on Rural Health Care and the Art of the Local, 1931–39', in Solomon et al. (eds.), *Shifting*, 241.

[39] Amrith, *Decolonizing*, 26.

[40] 'Report on the Conference on Rural Health Centres', Budapest, 27–30 October 1930, League of Nations, C.H.947, 5–12.

[41] Borowy, *Coming*, 337–9.

[42] Tomoko Akami, 'Imperial Polities, Intercolonialism, and the Shaping of Global Governing Norms: Public Health Expert Networks in Asia and the League of Nations Health Organization, 1908–37', *Journal of Global History*, 12/1 (2017), 18.

[43] Murard, 'Designs', 153 and Borowy, *Coming*, 349–52.

[44] Iris Borowy, 'Thinking Big—League of Nations Efforts towards a Reformed National Health System in China', in ibid. (ed.), *Uneasy Encounters: The Politics of Medicine and Health in China 1900–1937* (Frankfurt am Main: Peter Lang, 2009), 205–28.

[45] Murard, 'Designs', 148–50 and 155–8.

[46] Xiaoping Fang, *Barefoot Doctors and Western Medicine in China* (Rochester, NY: University of Rochester Press, 2012), 9 and 139.

The international networks facilitated by the LNHO consolidated this Eastern European consensus over the principle that 'it was up to governments to determine the conditions in which health services and healthy lives could flourish and retain the control and oversight at all times.'[47] In 1936 in Moscow, the LNHO's leadership devised an agenda extolling popular education, culturally acceptable health policies, the convergence of curative and preventative services, and the creation of healthy living environments. In the subsequent two years, Hungary, Poland, Czechoslovakia, Yugoslavia and Romania stood out in their vocal advocacy for such governmental policies, along with francophone nations, where the state's role was similarly influential.[48] After 1945, Eastern European healthcare systems were hyper-centralized as the effects of sovietization were felt across the region; nevertheless, it is important to remember that many of the developments in Cold War socialist health were based on Eastern Europe's pre-1945 integration into global networks of social and tropical medicine, long before Communist takeovers.

The Socialist Alternative

With the takeover of Eastern Europe by Communist parties, and the onset of the Cold War, new medical elites presented themselves as the advocates of alternatives to the dominant forms of western medicine. Although there were in fact similar developments in some non-Communist western countries, state socialist experts showcased centralized, state-funded, universal access healthcare based on preventative medicine, epidemiological surveillance, sanitary education and nationwide networks of primary, secondary and tertiary care units. Moreover, Eastern Europeans associated self-determination with colonial peoples' liberation from the threat of disease. The critique of imperial governance was at the heart of their internationalist solidarity with (former) subject peoples. China, North Korea and Vietnam were the formative locations for medical internationalist engagement from the East that soon expanded globally either through the WHO or bilateral programmes. At the WHO, Eastern European representatives reinforced the distinctiveness of their model by affirming regional solutions within the organization's disease eradication campaigns. They established alliances with peers from newly independent countries that served to shift the power balance within the WHO. However, Eastern Europe, despite its growing stature in global health politics, bore its own civilizational hierarchies, rooted in socialist modernity's perception that post-colonial societies were riddled with social, economic or cultural conditions that determined their resilient 'backwardness'.

---

[47] Borowy, *Coming*, 360.   [48] Murard, 'Designs', 162.

The WHO was a central stage for global health politics, seconded by the United Nations Children's Fund (or UNICEF, founded by the Pole Ludwik Rajchman). Both drew on prewar experiences of the LNHO, and the activities of the United Nations Relief and Rehabilitation Administration, a key UN agency which operated in southern, central, and south-eastern Europe, southern Asia, and China between 1943 and 1947. Eastern European experts prominent in interwar social medicine such as Marcin Kacprzak (Poland), Joseph Cancik (Czechoslovakia) and Andrija Štampar were included in the Technical Preparatory Committee, which drafted the WHO's constitution. The organization's creation was inspired by the pre-war consensus that saw health as a foundation of social life, as noted in the WHO's definition of the concept.[49] The ideological rejection of this consensus came shortly after the founding of the new organization, triggered by the urgency of postwar reconstruction, immunological innovations (antibiotics and DDT), the limited resources of states and empires, and anti-Communist offensives against social medicine. World health thus turned to the problems of infectious disease control in less developed countries, while the earlier emphases on welfare reforms were marginalized.[50] This shift did not go unopposed, as both socialist countries' representatives and left-leaning western experts objected to approaches to disease prevention that saw it as a solely biological issue. The views of western proponents of social medicine such as Norwegian Karl Evang, Belgian René Sand and American Thomas Parran (Surgeon General of the US, who was removed from office for his ideas) overlapped with Eastern European arguments that connected comprehensive healthcare to subjugated peoples' emancipation from poverty and colonialism. However, the US and western empires' early hegemony within the WHO marginalized this approach within the organization's decision-making.[51]

Since the early days of the WHO, Eastern Europe's socialist delegates had insisted that the organization should, in the words of Soviet Deputy Minister of Health Nikolai Vinogradov, 'orientate its efforts…above all for the consolidation and development of national health services'.[52] They argued for international assistance that linked socio-economic development and disease control. The socialist vision for the decolonizing world was of centralized states implementing epidemiological programmes integrated into national health systems managed by local personnel. The task of the WHO was to assist those policies that were the medical equivalent of political self-determination. The breakneck transformation of central and south-eastern Europe under Soviet control seemed to confirm the

---

[49] John Farley, *Brock Chisholm, the World Health Organization, and the Cold War* (Vancouver: University of British Columbia, 2008), 18.

[50] James Gillespie, 'Europe, America, and the Space of International Health', in Solomon et al. (eds.), *Shifting*, 124.

[51] Randall Packard, *A History of Global Health: Interventions into the Lives of Other Peoples* (Baltimore: Johns Hopkins University Press, 2016), 100.

[52] Official Records WHO (World Health Organization) no. 13, 1st WHA (World Health Assembly) (June 24–July 24, 1948), 40.

viability of this approach, obscuring the incompleteness of reforms as Soviet-style state socialism subordinated healthcare to policies such as industrialization or agricultural collectivization.

Despite the gap between discourse and reality at home, Eastern Europe's emancipatory vision placed it at the centre of debates over the welfare of peoples still under western empires. Vinogradov proclaimed at the first World Health Assembly (WHA) in 1948 that 'epidemics are due to poverty and colonial oppression, as well as to the arbitrary exploitation of populations deprived of their rights, and the lack of effective organization of health services in colonial and non-autonomous territories.'[53] Eastern European representatives echoed the voices from newly independent countries in underlining the failure of colonial health governance in Africa and Asia.[54]

Anti-colonialism and Cold War polarization burnished the international image of a socialist health alternative. Already in 1949, Communist-ruled China employed Soviet aid to implement this model—a massive experiment that was closely watched by other decolonizing peoples.[55] Polish delegate Irène Domanska underlined at that year's WHA meeting the existence of two groups in the WHO: 'The camp of peace, standing for the interest of humanity, which demands that the attainment of medical science should serve the whole human race, is represented by the USSR and the People's Democracies, while the capitalist camp represents the interest of a minority who consider science as source of income and as weapon of war.'[56] During that assembly the Ukrainian and Belorussian delegations withdrew from the WHO; a year later, the other socialist countries followed suit (with the exception of future non-aligned Yugoslavia). The withdrawal of socialist governments was not just a Soviet-coordinated decision rooted in Cold War competition. It reflected Eastern Europe's justified accusations of political discrimination, a pro-colonial agenda, and unbalanced budgeting within the WHO. They did not reject the merits of the organization per se, but rather concluded that they could not influence decision-making because of western hegemony and a pro-American voting majority at the WHA. At the end of the 1950s, as decolonization moved up a gear, Eastern European governments returned to the organization in the context of de-Stalinization and peaceful coexistence.[57]

[53] Ibid., 41.
[54] Jessica Pearson, *The Colonial Politics of Global Health: France and the United Nations in Postwar Africa* (Cambridge: Harvard University Press, 2018), 52–60.
[55] Mary Brazelton, 'Western Medical Education on Trial: The Endurance of Peking Union Medical College, 1949–1985', *Twentieth-Century China*, 40/2 (2015), 131–4; Kim Taylor, *Chinese Medicine in Early Communist China, 1945–63: A Medicine of Revolution* (London: Routledge, 2005), 53–5.
[56] Official Records WHO no. 21, 2nd WHA, Rome, 13 June–2 July 1949, 106.
[57] Dora Vargha, 'Technical Assistance and Socialist International Health: Hungary, the WHO and the Korean War', *History and Technology* 34/3–4 (2020), 403–6; Anne-Emanuelle Birn and Nikolai Krementsov, '"Socialising" Primary Care? The Soviet Union, WHO and the 1978 Alma-Ata Conference', *BMJ Global Health* 3: Supplement 3 (2018), 3–4; Farley, *Brock*, 80–2.

Between 1951 and 1957, the West shaped the WHO into an instrument of ideological containment: underdevelopment and the threat of Communism merged, whilst humanitarian crises in Asia and Africa were understood as security problems.[58] Initially, European empires (France, Britain, Belgium and Portugal) perceived the WHO as a threat to colonial rule. During the 1940s, the metropoles designed welfare reforms for their colonial subjects and the organization's inter-ference was proclaimed both superfluous and dangerous. By the mid-1950s, the imperial powers had slowly come to abandon such reform plans, and colonial officials turned to the WHO for resources to implement low-cost disease control. Cooperation with the institution was designed to assuage criticism of colonial governance and to comply with requests from newly independent countries for United Nations oversight in dependent territories.[59]

Socialist countries' withdrawal from the organization served to international-ize Eastern European healthcare in other ways. The camp's wartime medical aid to the Democratic People's Republic of Korea (DPRK) and the Democratic Republic of Vietnam (DRV) (1951–62), countries which were not WHO members and hence did not receive the organization's support, became showcases for their approaches as donors in the post-colonial world.[60] These new links outside inter-national organizations drew on an earlier anti-fascist internationalism. Physicians who had worked in Spain during the Civil War or the Far East during the Second World War played important roles in Eastern European relations with these states. Ianto Kanetti, for example, became Deputy Minister of Health and led the Bulgarian team in the DRV. Stanisław Flato was Plenipotentiary Minister Counsellor of the Polish Embassy in Beijing from 1957 until 1964.[61] Bucur Clejan and his wife, Zhao Jingpu, whom he had met while working for UNRRA in Zhengzhou, coordinated the Chinese edition of *Romania Today*, the regime's magazine for propaganda abroad.[62] Medical teams embodied the new inter-nationalist ethos: a Romanian physician in the DPRK insisted that doctors had to show 'the capacity to make a healthy contribution to the life of the collective, camaraderie, devotion to the cause of the mission, abnegation, conscientiousness, the spirit of sacrifice, discipline, sincerity, initiative, and a healthy morality'.[63] This socialist internationalism also set in motion local variants of self-reliance in

---

[58] Hong, *Cold War*, 25.   [59] Pearson, *The Colonial*, 159–72 and Gillespie, 'Europe', 132.

[60] Vargha, 'Technical', 406; Intervention of J. Plojhar, Czechoslovakia's Minister of Health in Official Records WHO, no. 111, 14th WHA, New Delhi, 7–24 February 1961, 75. Celia Donert, 'From Communist Internationalism to Human Rights: Gender Violence and International Law in the Women's International Democratic Federation Mission to North Korea, 1951', *Contemporary European History*, 25/2 (2016), 322.

[61] Margaret Gnoinska, *Poland and the Cold War in East and Southeast Asia, 1949–1965*, PhD dis-sertation (George Washington University, 2010), 2.

[62] David Iancu, *9 ani medic pe front: Spania-China 1937–1945* (București: Vitruviu, 2008), 76–160 and 238–51.

[63] Quoted in Radu Tudorancea, *Ipostazele 'ajutorului frățesc'. RPR și războiul din Coreea (1950–1953)* (Cluj: Eikon, 2014), 300.

China, the DPRK and the DRV. After 1954, the Chinese Communist leadership began experimenting with traditional medicine, which fostered its own alternative socialist development.[64] DPRK officials likewise aimed at autarky, rejecting, from the early 1960s onwards, integration into a Soviet-centred international division of labour.[65] Around the same time, health authorities in the DRV began to reach out for aid from western progressive circles too.[66]

The Second World also created its own medical transnationalism under the umbrella of the Council for Mutual Economic Assistance (Comecon), founded in 1949: annual conferences for ministers of health, expert exchanges and scientific symposia. Within this framework, each Eastern European country assigned personnel and/or bilateral material aid to the DPRK and the DRV.[67] A socialist commonwealth was manifest on the ground too: teams visited each other, and participated in conferences and multi-national disease control campaigns in China, the DPRK and the DRV.[68] In North Korea between 1951 and 1957, Romanians took over two hospitals in Pyongyang and Nampho, Hungarians worked north of the capital, Poles were in Hynnam then in Hamhyn, Czechoslovaks worked in Chŏngjin and Bulgarians settled in Sinuiju. From 1952 until 1955, the Viet Minh received 100 tons of medical supplies and equipment from China and the USSR along with 40 tons from Poland. The Polish merchant ship *Kiliński* took the leading role in evacuating people from South to North Vietnam.[69] Romania dispatched a sanitary-epidemiological team; Czechoslovaks managed a hospital in Haiphong, while East Germans took over the Phu Doan Hospital in Hanoi, whilst the Soviet Union brought in sixty staff (twenty-seven doctors) to lend assistance.[70] In the DPRK, the first Eastern European medical teams set up field hospitals that often moved or had to be reconstructed because of US bombardment. After the armistice, these institutions transitioned to peacetime medical care, the backbone of the national system.[71] In the DRV, Eastern Europeans worked in towns obliterated by the war of independence or in rural areas without any medical facilities. Improvised hospitals were transformed into brick buildings with services for

[64] Fang, *Barefoot*, 24–9 and Taylor, *Chinese*, 62–5.

[65] Charles Armstrong, '"Fraternal Socialism": The International Reconstruction of North Korea, 1953–62', *Cold War History*, 5/2 (2005), 167–8.

[66] Michitake Aso and Annick Guénel, 'The Itinerary of a North Vietnamese Surgeon: Medical Science and Politics during the Cold War', *Science, Technology & Society*, 18/3 (2013), 298.

[67] 'Prima Consfătuire a Comisiei Ministerelor Sănătății pentru pregătirea și organizarea în comună a manifestărilor științifice, Berlin 18–20 noiembrie', MSPS (Ministerul Sănătății și Protecției Sociale)-OMS (Organizația Mondială a Sănătății) 1958, 38 (Romania).

[68] 'Informace o VDR s hlediska zaravotní péče', 04 July 1958, Státní ústřední archive v Praze, MZdr, Akce V 1956–1958; 'Dodatek ke zprávě o poskytování čs. zdrav. pomoci KLDR v r. 1956', Státní ústřední archive v Praze, MZdr, Akce K, 1955–1957; Pascu Filon, 'Imagini din RPD Coreeană: Pe malul Tedonganului', *Muncitorul Sanitar*, 05 April 1958, 4.

[69] Gnoinska, *Poland*, 82–3 and 253–4.

[70] 'Lékařská pomoc VDR', 27 July 1956, Akce V. 1956–1958, NA, MZd., 14–16.

[71] Tudorancea, *Ipostazele*, 132; Vargha, 'Technical', 6.

multiple purposes.[72] This transformation paralleled similar changes taking place in Eastern Europe, highlighting the convergence between decolonization and building socialism.

The creation of socialist healthcare in the DPRK and the DRV also meant building on pre-existing colonial infrastructures. Many local personnel had been educated under Japanese and French rule. In Korea, the hospital operated by Czechoslovaks in Chŏngjin had been constructed by the Japanese. In Hanoi, the institution founded by Swiss-French bacteriologist Alexandre Yersin was transformed into a surgery-specialized entity that showcased East German technology and know-how.[73] The Pasteur Institute in the North Vietnamese capital was reinvented as a socialist institution with the help of Romanian doctors from the Institute for Epidemiology and Microbiology in Bucharest led by Mihai Ciucă, who had taught in Hanoi in 1932 as a LNHO expert.[74] The repurposing and expansion of former colonial infrastructures underlined the idea that socialism was a catalyst for self-determination in public health. Comprehensive medical systems reflected local needs, departing from past imperial governance that had focused on the wellbeing of colonizers and urban environments.[75]

At the same time, the DPRK and the DRV effectively served as a 'colonial laboratory' for the socialist camp because of the diseases (malaria, yellow fever, kwashiorkor, trachoma, smallpox, schistosomiasis, etc.) that ravaged them.[76] Eastern Europeans developed their own tropical medical practices, which they later presented as alternative expertise to its western counterpart. The latter was described as rooted in the exploitation of and discrimination against indigenous populations. Soviet, East German, Czechoslovak, Romanian and Polish physicians sent to these countries chaired institutions, wrote textbooks, and taught courses of tropical medicine after their return home.[77] Eastern Europeans had already been exposed during the interwar years to this type of medical knowledge; physicians had endorsed the civilizing mission of western bacteriology and virology among 'backward' peoples. This hierarchical underpinning of knowledge could still be witnessed in Eastern European practices in the DPRK and the DRV. While

---

[72] 'Ion Spînu către MSPS, Direcția Generală Sanitaro-Epidemică', 26 May 1959, MSPS, S2, 1960, vol. III, 141.

[73] Hong, Cold War, 123.

[74] Gh. Romanescu and Gh. Zamfir, 'Între prieteni, scrisoare din R.D. Vietnam', Muncitorul Sanitar, 16 January 1960, 4.

[75] Michitake Aso, 'Patriotic Hygiene: Tracing New Places of Knowledge Production about Malaria in Vietnam, 1919–75', Journal of Southeast Asian Studies, 44/3 (2013), 423–43; Mark Harrison and Sung Yim, 'War on Two Fronts: The Fight against Parasites in Korea and Vietnam', Medical History, 61/3 (2017), 401–23.

[76] Hong, Cold War, 124.

[77] 'Instituts et Écoles Européens de Médecine et d'Hygiène Tropicales et leur Coopération avec les Pays d'outre-mer', Acta Tropica, 24/2 (1967), 164–6 and 178–80; 'Lékařská pomoc DRV' 27 July 1956, Akce V. 1956–1958, NA, MZd., 14; Gheorghe Zamfir, Din viața unui medic nonagenar: avataruri și împliniri (Iași: Editura 'Gr. T. Popa', 2004), 6.

publicly rejecting the racial premises of imperial tropical medicine, Eastern European teams in fact still displayed a superiority complex. Local societies were criticized for their lack of education in hygiene, the resilience of superstitious customs, and reactionary social and economic practices. A Czechoslovak report from Chŏngjin noted in 1956 that the team's work 'had been impeded by local habits. Our first task was to teach Korean personnel about cleanliness, sterilization, [proper] communication with the patients'.[78] Two years later, in Vietnam, another Czechoslovak account underlined 'the absence of health consciousness within the population', the presence of 'superstition' and 'charlatans', 'the incorrect use of popular, traditional medicine', 'the inadequacy of qualified doctors and the poor health of the workers'. The prescribed solution consisted in the socialist transformation of the system through state-managed food provision, sickness and disability insurance, retirement benefits, as well as free access to medical services.[79]

The DPRK and the DRV were seen as at the beginning of the road to socialism, despite the fact that Eastern European regimes themselves had only just started to implement the same model. Eastern Europeans' civilizing mission was premised on an idea of indigenous mimesis, that is, the embracing of 'the correct political line [of] the socialist protection of health' that would ensure the clinical and hygienic Enlightenment of North Korean and Vietnamese societies.[80] The superiority complex that characterized Eastern European assistance to these two countries pervaded medical representations across the developing world, and was particularly intense in those African and Asian states which had rejected or were wavering on the path to socialism.

In 1961, a Comecon meeting of Eastern European Ministers of Health decided that all participants should draft plans for assistance to African and other newly independent countries.[81] The recipe was the same as for the DPRK and the DRV: teams operating hospitals and out-patient units, prophylaxis and sanitary education, and the training of local personnel. Socialist countries rejoined the WHO in the late 1950s, and staff with experience in the DPRK and the DRV were dispatched to the WHO or joined bilateral missions across the developing world. Polish physicians who had worked in North Vietnam were recruited by the WHO in 1961 for a mission in Congo-Kinshasa. One of them, Jerzy Ochrymowicz, went on to coordinate the WHO's anti-malarial programs in Cameroon, Togo, Benin, Mali and Sierra Leone.[82]

---

[78] 'Zpráva o činnosti vnitřního oddělení čs. nemocnice v Čondžinu za celé období od r. 1954 do knoce r.1956', MZdr, Akce K, 1955–1957 (Czech National Archive, Prague, henceforth NAČR).

[79] 'Koncept zprávy o činnosti našich pracovníků ve VDR', 2 November 1958, Akce V., 1956–1958, NA, MZd., 2 (NAČR).

[80] 'Informace o VDR s hlediska zaravotní péče'. Similar Romanian account: Ovidiu Popescu, 'Roadele muncii echipei sanitare romîne în R.D. Vietnam', *Muncitorul Sanitar*, 29 September 1962, 4.

[81] J. Plojhar către V. Marinescu, 31 July 1961, Planuri de colaborare, MSPS 1961, 138–7.

[82] Projects Afro-2002, Malaria Consultant Services—West Africa, JKT 1, 1967–1974, WHO 22.0659 (World Health Organization Archives-Geneva).

Eastern European involvement with the WHO's disease eradication campaigns was arguably the most visible opportunity to dramatize the success of socialist health. In 1959, the Soviet Union, Czechoslovakia and Hungary were the first to adopt nationwide anti-poliomyelitis vaccination with live Sabin vaccine, which was the outcome of cooperation between American scientists and their socialist counterparts. These campaigns would inspire Eastern Europeans to advertise the Sabin vaccine as a better option than the Salk virus vaccine, which had been favoured by the US government.[83] Interest from post-colonial states was immediate: in 1961, a Nigerian delegate proposed a review of the WHO's polio vaccination based on 'the remarkable results achieved…in Latvia, Estonia and other parts of the Soviet Union, as well as the spectacular results obtained in Cincinnati [referring to Albert Sabin's experiments].'[84] During the 1960s, polio vaccines from the Eastern Europe were dispatched to North Vietnam and Korea, China, India, Egypt, Mexico, Congo or Mali. With the help of Czechoslovak experts, Cuba developed its anti-polio programme, which became in subsequent decades the basis for Latin American National Immunization Days. Eastern European delegates at the WHO pushed for global eradication, but the project took off only in the 1980s.[85] The organization was preoccupied with its malaria and smallpox campaigns, while the West was reluctant to recognize the East's role in the anti-poliomyelitis struggle.

Eastern European experts challenged the WHO's malaria eradication policy, which relied on DDT spraying and prioritized programmes against the disease at the expense of national health services and social reforms. After surveying several West African countries, Romanian parasitologist Gheorghe Lupaşcu argued that eradication based solely on eliminating mosquitos was doomed to failure, particularly as resistance to DDT had been reported across the world. His alternative harkened back to the interwar LNHO: 'we ought to urgently expand basic sanitary networks in rural areas.' Reminiscent of Štampar's interwar health propagandists, he saw the post-colonial expansion of the school system as an opportunity for teachers to distribute medicine and information about chemoprophylaxis.[86] His observations mirrored African delegations' critiques of the WHO's policy. A speaker from Togo stated in 1964 that 'the most rational method' to combat malaria was 'the development of sanitary infrastructure in parallel with the early phases of eradication.'[87] Some western experts also criticized insecticide-driven eradication, which, as veteran Norwegian public health specialist Karl Evang remarked at the time, 'should [not] be introduced in any country until the

---

[83] Dora Vargha, *Polio Across the Iron Curtain: Hungary's Cold War with an Epidemic* (Cambridge: Cambridge University Press, 2018), 147–79.

[84] Official Records WHO, no. 111, 237.   [85] Vargha, 'Socialist', 81–6.

[86] 'Continentul african şi eradicarea malariei. Interviu cu Gh. Lupaşcu', *Muncitorul Sanitar*, 04 December 1965, 4.

[87] Official Records WHO, no. 136, 17th WHA, Geneva, 3–20 March 1964, 240.

integrated basic health service existed'.[88] In 1966, a meeting of regional WHO malaria experts embraced the reforms spearheaded by Eastern Europeans: the report stressed the importance of rural health centres and polyvalent personnel 'charged with the tasks of both active and passive case detection and the treatment of malaria cases', while being 'deployed…for permanent health protection and promotion'.[89] The same year M. Ciucă and P. G. Serghiev (since 1934 the director of the Soviet Institute of Medical Parasitology and Tropical Medicine, a former member of the LNHO's Malaria Commission) received the WHO's Darling award for outstanding achievements in malariology.[90] This shift did not lead to world eradication, however; many rural areas still did not receive the attention they required, with stalled interventions and limited epidemiological surveillance.[91]

The socialist camp reinforced its position as alternative in world health policies by insisting that smallpox was a 'better candidate' for global eradication than malaria, which since 1950 had received most of the WHO's attention. Soviet officials argued this position based on the disease's unique features and the existence of a vaccine. They contended that an international smallpox eradication programme would cost significantly less than the indefinite continuation of national vaccination programmes.[92] In 1965, President Lyndon B. Johnson announced that the US would dedicate itself to smallpox eradication. In the spirit of détente, a division of labour emerged: the US provided much of the funding and the Soviet Union most of the vaccine.[93] Czechoslovakia provided 9% of the total number of international experts, a by-product of its interwar experience of combatting the disease.[94]

As Eastern Europeans increased their WHO profile and with medical teams scattered across Africa and Asia, Communist regimes competed with the West in the field of tropical medicine. The latter was considered as having been an instrument of neo-colonial influence. Former colonial specialists had been hired by the WHO as experts in newly independent countries. As the socialist critique of WHO's anti-malarial measures shows, this field's preference for disease-focused campaigns at the expense of building national health infrastructures was thought to

---

[88] Quoted in Amrith, *Decolonizing*, 170.

[89] Report of Meeting of Regional Malaria Advisers, 1–7 June 1966, PA/66.125, vol.6, WHO7.0481, 15 and 18.

[90] Official Records WHO no. 152, 19th WHA, 3–20 May 1966, 130.

[91] James Webb, *The Long Struggle Against Malaria in Tropical Africa* (Cambridge: Cambridge University Press, 2014), 98–111.

[92] Official Records WHO, 19th WHA, no. 152, 263 and 281.

[93] Erez Manela, 'A Pox on Your Narrative: Writing Disease Control into Cold War History', *Diplomatic History*, 34/2 (2010), 300–1; Bob Reinhardt, *The End of a Global Pox. America and the Eradication of Smallpox in the Cold War Era* (Chapel Hill: University of North Carolina Press, 2015), 137 and 130.

[94] Bohuslav Chňoupek, 'Koncepce čs. Účasti ve Světové zdravotnické organizaci na léta 1982-1986, 14.10.1981', fond 02/1, sv. 14, ar.j. 21, k informaci 4, 6 (NAČR).

impede post-colonial medical emancipation. In 1962, at the first meeting of European institutes of tropical medicine in Copenhagen, socialist representatives insisted that Asia, Africa, or America needed 'not only tropical medicine but also maternal and child welfare and general medical practice'.[95] Even so, the organization's officials were at times reluctant to hire Eastern European experts due to a 'lack of experience…particularly in tropical areas'.[96] Eastern Europeans countered by emphasizing the assistance they had given in (sub)tropical regions and mentioned their own tradition in the field. In Poland, the Institute of Maritime and Tropical Medicine in Gdynia resumed activities in 1950, but its earlier connection with aspirations for Polish colonial expansionism went unmentioned. In 1962, a Department of Tropical Medicine, with its own hospital, was created in Prague at the Institute for Continued Education of Physicians and Pharmacologists. By 1986, 3,000 Czechoslovak doctors working in developing countries had taken its courses, joined by 1,500 from Lebanon, Syria, Senegal, Costa Rica, Kuwait, Sudan, Cyprus, Vietnam, Laos and Ghana.[97] Soviet experts leaned heavily on their expertise in Central Asia, 'the formerly backward regions of Russia',[98] as evidence of their ability to bring about healthcare modernization to post-colonial states.

A problematic aspect of socialist tropical medicine was its contribution to geopolitical power relations. In 1962, the directors of European institutes of tropical medicine decided that a provisional solution was the training of Asian or African experts in Europe.[99] From a socialist perspective, the policy was integral to strengthening self-determination. This outsourcing of higher education and research continued for decades, as Eastern Europeans seemed more interested in building up the field at home rather than in the developing world. As early as 1960, North Vietnamese representatives proposed at a Comecon meeting the creation in Hanoi of an International Institute of Virology as tropical medicine hub for socialist specialists and others from South East Asia and Africa. This initiative fell through, however, as Eastern Europeans were reluctant to fund it.[100]

The global South's challenge to the political alignment of the field came to a head during the debates over the WHO's Special Programme for research and training in tropical diseases in 1974. The outcome was resolution WHA27.52, drafted by the European socialist countries in cooperation with African ones.[101] African delegates called for the prioritizing of education and research in the South: 'the impetus needed for such work [tropical medicine] could only be

---

[95] Official Records WHO, no. 119, 15th WHA, Geneva, 8–25 February 1962, Part II, 203.
[96] 'Difficulties Faced by WHO in the Recruitment of USSR Nationals', Personnel-Recruitment Correspondence with USSR and Other Eastern European Countries, Microfilm 5, WHO/P3/4/12, 1.
[97] HU 300-30-7 Box 355 (Open Society Archive, Budapest, henceforth OSA).
[98] Statement by R.S. Sagatov, Soviet Minister of Health, in Official Records WHO, no. 111, 308.
[99] 'Instituts', 114. [100] MSPS-OMS 133–1960, vol. III, 27.
[101] Official Records WHO, no. 218, 27th WHA, 7–23 March 1974, 394.

sustained if that work were done in places where the problems existed.'[102] These calls went unheeded. Instead, the Soviet Union created an all-union centre for tropical diseases that aimed to organize research and training at home, and to provide assistance to developing countries.[103] In Romania, the government attempted—but failed—to obtain nearly $1 million for an international higher education centre.[104] These initiatives paralleled the transformation of Eastern European medical schools in the late 1970s into sources of hard currency, as the number of paying students from the 'Third World' grew considerably.[105] This diversion of resources to Europe generated discontent among post-colonial governments. In 1979, an Indian official chafed at the way that WHO funds were being channelled to 'the élite club of permanent members of the Security Council'.[106] The Soviet Union and other socialist countries were lumped together with a North unwilling fully to democratize the field. The distance between the South and the East at the WHO continued to grow.

Competition in Socialist Health

With the acceleration of decolonization, Africa increasingly became a site where different socialist health interventions competed with each other. Initially, this occurred *between* different Eastern European countries. In contrast to aid to the DPRK and the DRV, where cooperation developed through Comecon, Eastern European medical assistance from the 1960s on in Africa reflected the growing reliance on bilateral assistance toward the so-called Third World after de-Stalinization. In 1956, Nikita Khrushchev elaborated on the doctrine of 'active foreign policy': 'the Soviet Union would not always have to be the first to take action', but other Communist countries could take the initiative.[107] Czechoslovakia was at the forefront of socialist aid in Guinea, whereas 400 Bulgarian medical workers took over entire districts in the aftermath of Algeria's independence.

Algeria was initially the most important location. The sheer violence of the struggle against the French for Algerian independence between 1954 and 1962—in which up to half a million died—meant that assistance was of the utmost

---

[102] See the remarks of the Zambian representatives in Official Records WHO, no. 227, 28th WHA, 13–30 May 1975, 683.

[103] 33rd WHA 5–23 May 1980, WHA33/1980/REC/3, 114.

[104] 'Nota de relații participarea delegației române la XXX-a Adunare Mondială a Sănătății, Geneva', MS (Ministerul Sănătății)-DCCPI (Direcția Coordonare, Control Personal și Învățământ)-Relații Externe 17–1977, 21; MAE OMS 241–1979, 4.

[105] Monique de Saint Martin et al. (eds.), *Étudier à l'Est. Expériences de diplômés africains* (Paris: Karthala, 2015).

[106] Official Records WHO, no. 218, 32nd WHA, 7–25 May 1979, WHA32/1979/REC/2, 98–9.

[107] Laurien Crump, *The Warsaw Pact Reconsidered. International Relations in Eastern Europe, 1955–69* (London: Routledge, 2015), 27.

importance. Yugoslavia was at the forefront: Belgrade backed the Algerian provisional government as early as 1959; wounded soldiers were sent to Belgrade for rehabilitation and prosthetic treatment, a programme expanded through the Centre for Rehabilitation in Nahsen (Tunisia). Officials connected solidarity with the Algerian liberation struggle to their own partisan experience during the Second World War.[108] These efforts transformed Algeria into Yugoslavia's gateway to the entire continent. Other socialist governments followed Belgrade's lead: it was here that the GDR initiated its first large-scale humanitarian action in a non-socialist country, which bolstered its international recognition in the context of the isolating effects of West Germany's hostile Hallstein Doctrine.

From the early 1960s, however, Eastern European national teams were working alongside—and in some cases in competition with—other socialist medical internationalisms. Cuba too made its first sorties into health internationalism through Algeria. Between 1963 and 1964, Havana sent 111 medical staff to the country, the opening salvo of what in two decades would become a South–South cooperation that paralleled Eastern European assistance. The Cubans were less hierarchical than their socialist 'brethren', did not charge for services and worked under any conditions. They showed absolute respect for local customs, modesty and self-reliance.[109] This assistance drew on Cuba's experience of revolutionary transformation from the countryside and was often a spontaneous response to decolonization crises (in Congo and Portuguese-ruled Africa) with little consideration of cost (until the 1980s). The Cuban regime envisaged this aid as a means to boost its prestige in the Non-aligned Movement, Comecon, and in its relationship with the Soviet Union.[110]

Beijing likewise used Algeria as a stepping stone for its own foreign policy, building on experience acquired in the DPRK, where Chinese medical schools sent teams to assist Mao's military intervention.[111] Since the Sino-Soviet split, Chinese Communists argued that they were forging a viable alternative to European medical modernity. They rejected 'learning from the Soviets' and fused folk traditions (acupuncture, moxibustion, and herbal medicine) with modern practice; China's hybrid 'new medicine' was supposed to outperform the European one.[112] This turn also dovetailed with an anti-white, anti-imperialist Afro-Asianism

[108] Ljubica Spaskovska, 'The Yugoslav Red Cross and the Algerian Revolution', presented at 'Boundaries of Socialist Medicine' (Exeter, 1–2 June 2017).

[109] Piero Gleijeses, *Conflicting Missions. Havana, Washington, and Africa, 1959–1976* (Chapel Hill: University of North Carolina Press, 2002), 37–8 and 44–8.

[110] John Kirk, 'Cuba's Medical Internationalism: Development and Rationale', *Bulletin of Latin American Research*, 28/4 (2009), 498.

[111] Brazelton, 'Western', 133.

[112] Taylor, *Chinese*, 65 and 135–6; Elisabeth Hsu, 'The History of Chinese Medicine in the People's Republic of China and its Globalization', *East Asia Science, Technology and Society: an International Journal*, 2 (2008), 465–84.

founded on Mao's anti-capitalism and opposition to peaceful coexistence.[113] The Chinese alternative to the Soviet-led camp was on display at the 1964 Peking Scientific Symposium attended by 367 delegates from 44 countries; Eastern Europeans were not invited.[114] The Symposium promoted Beijing as the 'Mecca of science in the East instead of in the West', to quote the leader of Pakistan's delegation.[115] This image was reinforced by the 'Eight Principles' of foreign aid, unveiled by Premier Zhou Enlai in Africa (1963–64). Their focus on equality materialized in engagements on the ground. A diplomat in Guinea remarked that Chinese personnel were 'earning no more and eating no better than the Guineans they work with. They create an impression of frugality and austerity'.[116]

The Chinese model of health for rural and low-income environments reached its climax with the 'barefoot doctors' programme. The policy drew on the Cultural Revolution's assault on the inequalities of socialist life: a programme of training 'half-peasants, half-doctors' operating in cooperative medical service stations that offered curative and preventative care for agricultural collectives and linking these communities to urban facilities.[117] The programme had been initially inspired by interwar Eastern European rural health initiatives. Yet by the 1960s, Eastern European health had lost its earlier commitment to the rural, and now in the domestic context prioritized urban services. In 1965, in the Russian Republic in the Soviet Union only 56% of rural doctor positions were filled. By 1973, in Hungary 2,500 localities were without a doctor.[118] The emphasis on urban health determined their approach in the developing world, with the hospitals they built in African or Asian cities serving as symbols of socialist modernity. Indeed, Eastern Europeans tended to see their own states as developed, industrialized and urban, and to interpret the social conditions in Africa in terms of a backwardness akin to that of the DPRK and the DRV. China's 'barefoot doctor' programme was a direct attack on this approach, epitomized by Mao's accusation that the Chinese ministry of health 'is not a people's ministry. It should be called the Urban Health Ministry'.[119] For developing countries with small budgets and predominantly rural populations, Chinese egalitarian rural medicine for low-income communities held considerable appeal—particularly in Africa.[120]

---

[113] Jeremy Friedman, *Shadow Cold War. The Sino-Soviet Competition for the Third World* (Chapel Hill: The University of North Carolina Press, 2015), 90.

[114] 'New Chapter in World Science', *Peking Review*, 36, 04 November 1964, 11–13.

[115] quoted in C.H.G. Oldham to R.H. Nolte, 'The Peking Science Symposium', 20 November 1964, Institute of Current World Affairs, CHGO-33, 6.

[116] Julia Lovell, *Maoism. A Global History* (London: Bodley Head, 2019), 180.

[117] Fang, *Barefoot*, 30.

[118] Michael Kaser, *Health Care in the Soviet Union and Eastern Europe* (London: Croom Helm, 1976), 67–8, 57 and 180.

[119] Fang, *Barefoot*, 30.

[120] For an overview of Beijing's medical diplomacy during the Cold War and international reactions to the Chinese healthcare model see Mary Brazelton, *Mass Vaccination: Citizens' Bodies and State Power in Modern China* (Ithaca: Cornell University Press, 2019), 153–165.

The Chinese challenge was on display in the United Republic of Tanzania, comprising Tanganyika and Zanzibar. In Zanzibar, East German doctors, who played a significant role in post-independence healthcare there, were criticized by local officials for their quasi-colonial demeanour: they demanded high wages, better living conditions, and acted in an aloof manner. Civilizational hierarchies were reflected in East German expectations: the physicians' status as representatives of a European, higher modernity was embodied in their daily life in Zanzibar.[121] Local authorities compared them to Chinese staff, who by contrast were positively characterized as diligent, modest, disciplined and more empathetic in their response to the realities of post-colonial rural society. In mainland Tanzania, eighty Chinese doctors were by the late 1960s following 'a circuit system': teams were assigned to the country's eight districts, one village at a time, enabling them to treat and educate 'hundreds of thousands'.[122] Chinese socialist solidarity seemed more firmly rooted in similar experiences of rural uplift and decolonization than did that of their Eastern European counterparts. Their vocal Maoism nevertheless sometimes drew local ire. One Dar es Salaam resident remarked that he preferred 'if they...would not mix [the] medical profession with Chinese politics'.[123]

Eastern European physicians claimed to embody the humanism of socialist modernity. During the Congo crisis, triggered by the withdrawal of Belgian personnel after independence, Soviet, East German, Polish and Czechoslovak doctors demonstrated their anti-colonial solidarity.[124] Socialist humanism prioritized building trust by separating medical activity from colonial practices that had discriminated against the indigenous population. East German staff underlined the unethical behaviour of physicians who had deserted and abused the locals, rendering them suspicious of any white personnel.[125] For Poles the ultimate act of solidarity that overcame the colour gap was to donate blood to the Congolese, reminiscent of the blood drives for Korean and Vietnamese war victims: the physical mixing of bodily fluids would be presented in propaganda as a powerful act of socialist fraternity. Such actions were contrasted with the way that the former rulers of colonial territories had treated the locals 'partly as minors, partly as slaves'.[126] Successful surgeries enabled physicians to ascend, as one Polish journalist

---

[121] Hong, *Cold War*, 307 and 316.

[122] Alicia Altorfer-Ong, *A Historical Re-Examination of the Sino-Zanzibari and Sino-Tanzanian Bilateral Relationships in the 1960s*, PhD dissertation (London School of Economics, 2014), 248 and 258–9.

[123] Priya Lal, 'Maoism in Tanzania: Material Connections and Shared Imaginaries', in Alexander Cook (ed.), *Mao's Little Red Book. A Global History* (Cambridge: Cambridge University Press, 2014), 214.

[124] Official Records WHO, no. 111, 240–3.

[125] Walter Bruchhausen, 'Between Foreign Politics and Humanitarian Neutrality: Medical Emergency Aid by the Two German States before 1970', *Social History of Medicine*, 32/4 (2019), 819–42.

[126] Agnieszka Sadecka, 'A Special Mission in Times of Crisis: Polish Doctors in 1960s Congo', presented at 'Africa, East Europe and the Dream of International Socialism' (Oxford, 28–9 October 2016), 2 and 9.

argued, to the status of 'great sorcerers' with 'golden hands and supposedly magical powers', personifying a modernity adapted to local beliefs.[127]

Assistance often took the form of 'gifts': hospitals, medicine, technology and expertise subsidized by Eastern European governments. This was a long-standing practice in the 'Second World': the Soviets had 'gifted' during Eastern Europe's post-war reconstruction, paralleled by East Germany in Albania and Romania—some bloc countries then provided hospitals in the DPRK and the DRV. Internationalism flattened old hierarchies by confirming socialist regimes' anti-colonial credentials, though its implementation became accountable to local needs.[128] In Conakry (Guinea), the USSR built a hospital with 500 beds in the Donka neighbourhood (1962).[129] This monument of socialist modernity stood in contrast with the for-mer colonial hospital in the Ballay district. Until the mid-1960s, the institution in Donka was staffed primarily by Czechoslovaks, Yugoslavs, Romanians and Soviets. As Sékou Touré, the long-serving leader of the country, became frustrated by these socialist countries' reluctance to expand assistance in Guinea, the one-time 'gift' was eventually transformed into a symbol of non-aligned development: over time western, Chinese or national personnel replaced the Eastern European staff.[130]

Adjusting a 'gift' to local needs meant holding socialist donors to their anti-imperialist promises. Yugoslavia built a hospital in Boke (Guinea) to provide medical care to PAIGC who had fought against Portuguese colonialism in Guinea Bissau.[131] Yugoslav physicians came to blows with Cuban doctors working in a nearby hospital because of differing interpretations of the Soviet-led military intervention in Czechoslovakia in 1968. Amílcar Cabral, PAIGC's leader, settled the dispute by reminding Yugoslavs and Cubans that their duty was to show that on anti-colonialism 'two politically, even ideologically different countries can work together.'[132] Developing countries' medical staff sometimes internalized socialist values through the education they received from socialist physicians. In Sierra Leone, personnel trained by Soviet doctors or in the Soviet Union challenged the country's westernized medical culture through their informal clothing, their political outlook, or by practicing medicine collectively.[133] Across West Africa, socialist-educated staff sought to reform 'a decentralized system that no longer met the needs of the people' and criticized profiteering from

---

[127] Marek Regel, 'Munganga Monene—Korespondencja z Afryki', *Dziennik Łódzki*, 155 (1968), 3.

[128] Kalinovsky, *Laboratory*, 10–11.

[129] [no title] *Muncitorul Sanitar*, 9 June 1962, 1.

[130] Deborah Brautigam, *The Dragon's Gift: The Real Story of China in Africa* (Oxford: Oxford University Press, 2009), 34.

[131] Milorad Lazic, 'Solidarité: The Forgotten Story of a Military Hospital in Guinea and Yugoslavia's Aid to the PAIGC', *Journal of Cold War History* (forthcoming 2022).

[132] 'Zabeleška o razgovoru Babić Dimitrija s generalnim sekretarom Afričke partije nezavisnosti 'portugalske' Gvineje i ostrva Kap Ver (PAIGC) Amilkarom Kabralom u Kartumu', 21 January 1969, AJ (Arhiv Jugoslavije), SSRNJ (Savez socijalističkog radnog naroda Jugoslavije), Fond 142, I–452, 3.

[133] Adell Patton, Jr, *Physicians, Colonial Racism, and Diaspora in West Africa* (Gainesville: University Press of Florida, 1996), 238.

the pharmaceuticals trade.[134] Their sense of difference was entrenched by the discrimination they experienced at the hands of fellow countrymen trained in the West.[135]

Despite the closeness implied by solidarity-driven encounters, Eastern European physicians persistently described post-colonial locales as zones of backwardness defined by stagnant cultures and unhygienic lifestyles—a reality explained through incomplete decolonization. In the mid-1960s, Romanian personnel in Guinea painted a picture of unmitigated pathology: 'hospitals do not have separate sections for contagious diseases; paediatrics and internal medicine wards hospitalize cases of typhus, yellow fever, dysentery, malaria, poliomyelitis, parasitoses, hepatitis, eruptive diseases and sometimes even tuberculosis or leprosy.' In quasi-colonial fashion, Romanian doctors held the locals responsible for ill health because of 'poor education [and] the lack of interest shown by the authorities.'[136] Assistance to Guineans was a civilizing mission: the team brought 'better organization of medical practice, a more rational use of local resources and sanitary education.'[137] Transferring socialist modernity remained incomplete because of the class character of local physicians. According to one Romanian account, Guinean doctors were mostly educated in France, at a 'satisfactory' level 'for the requirements here.' In contrast to the DPRK and the DRV, the staff did not embrace socialist health principles because 'their mentality is of capitalist practitioners.' Anti-colonial solidarity supposedly broke down: Eastern European experts in Africa often found it very difficult to cope with having their whiteness equated with colonial attitudes, and they accused Guinean personnel of displaying 'manifestations of racism' towards them.[138]

Eastern Europeans reproduced colonial discourses through their invocations of incompetent indigenous agency and representations of the population as immature germ-carriers.[139] In 1972, Polish physicians in Algeria, Morocco and Libya emphasized the importance of close physical contact with their patients, a marked departure from colonial medicine, which they criticized for distancing itself from the locals once considered 'stinking Arabs'. However, they blamed sickness on retrograde social habits: 'children [were] so emaciated that they were skin and bones. At home they got leftovers of meals consumed by adults, first by men, then by women....We tried to teach mothers how to feed their children.'[140]

---

[134]   Ibid., 245–6.

[135]   Oxfam Case Study, 'Scholarships and the Healthcare Human Resources Crisis: A Case Study of Soviet and Russian Scholarships for Medical Students from Ghana', 16 December 2014 https://policy-practice.oxfam.org.uk/publications/scholarships-and-the-healthcare-human-resources-crisis-a-case-study-of-soviet-a-337500 (last accessed 9 May 2020); Patton, Jr, *Physicians*, 228–43.

[136]   'Raport asupra activității echipei de medici români detașați în Republica Guineea', 26 July 1966, MSPS, S2, 1966, vol. II, 226.

[137]   Ibid., 225.   [138]   Ibid., 224–5.   [139]   Arnold, *Colonizing*, 156; Anderson, *Colonial*, 3.

[140]   Krystyna Raczynska 'Polish Doctors Acquire Experience in Africa', *Tygodnik Democratyczny*, 02 January 1972, HU 300-2-6 Box 103, 6 (OSA).

Despite claims of solidarity, post-colonial societies were presented as being in an inharmonious relationship with socialist modernity, which could be sustained only through the work of Eastern European modernizers. In 1989, an East German doctor reported that the trade union clinics that he managed in Dar es Salaam could be maintained 'as well-organized health facilities...if they were strictly managed by a GDR doctor.'[141]

These quasi-colonial discourses remained ambivalent. Eastern European physicians came from societies riddled with inequalities between city and village, metropole and province. Their countries experienced tremendous upheaval during the postwar period. Doctors sometimes employed this national background to understand the post-colonial situation. In Guinea, Yugoslav psychiatrist Vladimir Jakovljević developed an analysis of 'primitivism' and civilization drawing on his Marxist analysis of backwardness in Macedonia, a 'periphery' of Yugoslavia. He argued that Guineans could overcome psychological breakdowns caused by modernization to achieve a 'progressive' stage of development. Nevertheless, he insisted that the country showed a lower rate of neurotic disorders. This was a trope of colonial psychiatry, which saw psychological illness as characteristic of industrialized, urbanized and cultured nations.[142] Polish doctors in West Africa placed locals on a lower civilizational level due to their supposedly mystical beliefs or because of the un-European, tropical diseases afflicting them. Still, they sought a common ground between medical modernity and local traditions, between antibiotics and 'what is primitive but wise.'[143] Socialist medical anti-colonialism was an uneasy assemblage that both undermined and reinforced the idea of a Eurocentric civilizing mission.

This superiority complex was met with resistance from post-colonial officials especially if it impinged upon the implementation of medical duties. Alpha Diallo, the Guinean Minister of Information and Tourism, argued that 'the absence of enthusiasm and often unethical behaviour' among socialist physicians betrayed their aid mission. The government insisted that complaints about bad working conditions, poor facilities and inferior personnel or limited hygienic education smacked of neo-colonialism.[144] Local authorities used Eastern Europeans' sense of superiority to reaffirm authority. In 1983, a Libyan official lambasted the performance of the Romanian staff by framing it comparatively:

---

[141] Direktor der Juwata-Kliniken in der Vereinigten Republik Tansania OMR Dr. Manfred Weigelt an Abt. Int. Verbindungen, MfGe, 'Halbjahresbericht', Dar es Salaam, 11 April 1989, BArch (Bundesarchiv-Federal Republic of Germany), DQ 1/12533—Tanzania.

[142] Ana Antić, 'Imagining Africa in Eastern Europe: Transcultural Psychiatry and Psychoanalysis in Cold War Yugoslavia', *Contemporary European History*, 28/2 (2018), 248.

[143] Regel, 'Munganga', 3.

[144] Traian Roşca, 'Informare asupra vizitei în oraşul Forecariah cu ocazia zilei mondiale a leproşilor', 03 February 1966, MSPS, S2, 1966, vol. I, 275.

'Libyans consider Romanian doctors average, below Bulgarians and Indians', and they 'do not trust Romanian cadres.'[145]

A Fading Socialist Alternative

From the mid-1970s, the idea of socialist public health as a global alternative began to fade. Eastern European states started to monetize medical interventions in the developing world, and ranked countries according to their economic profitability. This development ran alongside socialist countries' Eurocentric uneasiness with Southern visions of reform. At the WHO, Eastern European countries were increasingly accused of aligning themselves with a hegemonic global North: they paid less and less attention to rural healthcare, focused resources on highly specialized medicine, adopted an ever more exploitative commercialized medicine, and were peripheralizing the South in field of healthcare. According to this critique, during the 1980s they were no longer able—or in some cases prepared—to counterbalance interference from the World Bank and western donors. Eastern Europe's inadequate response to famine in Africa represented a final confirmation of this withdrawal. By the end of the Cold War, this alternative model of public health had collapsed as Eastern Europeans converged with the West in embracing free-market health reforms.

Against a background of disillusionment with the prospects of socialism in the South and the recognition of interdependence in a western-dominated global economy, Communist officials began to prioritize economic rationality and mutual benefit in the developing world (see *Development*).[146] A similar trend can be noted in the medical field: Eastern European pharmaceutical companies—whose leading proponents were Yugoslav, Czechoslovak and Hungarian—focused more and more on profit-making from post-colonial markets. Eastern European countries were primed for an upsurge in health exports: by the early 1970s medical industries and higher education had expanded considerably.[147] Commercialization was accelerated by the lure of petrodollars available in oil-producing countries after the 'shocks' of 1971 and 1973. This development accentuated the competition among socialist governments to obtain health-related contracts in the global South. A Romanian delegation reported in 1976 that the USSR, Bulgaria, Yugoslavia and Hungary vied to enhance their economic relations with Libya by

---

[145] 'Notă de convorbire', MS-DCCPI Relații Externe 2/1984, 2.

[146] Sara Lorenzini, 'The Socialist Camp and the Challenge of Economic Modernization in the Third World', in Juliane Fürst, Silvio Pons, and Mark Selden (eds.), *The Cambridge History of Communism. Volume 3: Endgames? Late Communism in Global Perspective, 1968 to the Present* (Cambridge: Cambridge University Press, 2017), 343, 349 and, 351.

[147] Kaser, *Health*, 3 and 10.

building hospitals, providing staff and engaging in pharmaceutical and medical technology trade.[148]

Commercialization fundamentally shifted Eastern European interests in the global South. In 1975, the Czechoslovak government ranked developing countries according to ideological priority (Angola, Ethiopia, Mozambique, Yemen, Afghanistan or Laos) and long-term economic prospects (Iraq, Syria, India, Mexico, Iran, Libya, etc.).[149] In the second category, medical assistance either brought hard currency or led to contracts in agriculture, construction or the oil industry. By the 1980s, such agreements were preferred for their capacity to alleviate Eastern European debt.[150] Socialist governments considered the arrangement mutually beneficial: the East assisted healthcare as part of post-colonial state-building, while making a profit from staff wages paid by local governments at rates lower than the cost of importing 'neo-colonial' western professionals. Socialist countries exploited the new opportunities for commercial ventures on the pharmaceuticals market. By 1980, the Alkaloida factory in Hungary produced 30% of the world's chloroquine, an anti-malarial drug.[151] The Slovene enterprise 'Krka' together with the Kenyan government and commercial funds established the largest medical venture in sub-Saharan Africa.[152]

The numbers of socialist personnel in countries that had hard currency skyrocketed. In 1972, there were 200 Polish doctors in all of Africa; by 1986, 1,400 Polish medical staff worked in Libya alone.[153] In 1974, there were 500 Yugoslavs in Libya; five years later, 2,000 ran twelve health institutions across the country.[154] Low salaries at home drove many to the global South where wages were higher. The large number of professionals who 'went South' put a significant strain on Polish hospitals and polyclinics, some thirty years prior to the pressures of westwards migration after European Union accession.[155] Across Eastern Europe, ministries of health grew increasingly reluctant to dispatch trained personnel overseas because of shortages at home.[156]

---

[148] 'Raport al delegaţiei Ministerului Sănătăţii care a vizitat Libia, 19 februarie-1 martie 1976', MS-DCCPI-Relaţii Externe 2–1984, 6.

[149] NA, Fond: 966/0/1 Zasedání kolegia ministra, 1969-1986, ev.j. 19. 10 April 1975 (NAČR).

[150] 'West Outstrips East in Aid', 18 January 1984, HU 300-20-1, Box 191, 573 (OSA).

[151] 33rd WHA, 188.

[152] Marjan Svetličič and Matija Rojec, New Forms of Equity Investment by Yugoslav Firms in Developing Countries (Ljubljana: Center za proučevanje sodelovanja z deželami v razvoju, 1985).

[153] Sophia Miskiewicz, 'Health Services in East Europe', RAD background Report/161, 10 November 1986, HU 300-30-7, Box 351, 37 (OSA).

[154] 'Cooperation Planned for Large Hospital Project in Libya', Privredni Pregled, 4 January 1974, HU 300-10-2 Box 245, 77; 31 May 1979, HU 300-10-2, Box 246 (OSA).

[155] Elżbieta Goździak, 'Biała Emigracja: Variegated Mobility of Polish Care Workers', Social Identities, 22/1 (2016), 35.

[156] Pro schůzi Rady pro mezinárodní hospodářskou a vědeckotechnickou spolupráci. Předběžný návrh koncepce technické pomoci rozvojovým zemím a pomoci přijímané od orgánů OSN na období 1981-1985, NA, MF ČSSR, Box 1, signatura: Pomoc rozvojovým zemím 1981 (NAČR).

Subsidized solidarity assistance continued for Vietnam or Cuba and in new socialist states like Laos, Mozambique, Ethiopia, Nicaragua and Afghanistan. There were also hybrid situations such as Algeria or Angola where commercial interest mixed with ideological fraternity. For some countries, international aid retained greater weight. The GDR leadership considered it an essential element for its national identity and international profile. From 1985, the National Volksarmee built a field hospital in Managua, Nicaragua, financed by donations from trade unions, the National Front, and church organizations.[157] In Ethiopia, embarrassed by generous western famine relief, the GDR and Soviet Union were the only Eastern European countries that offered comprehensive medical help.[158] In Mozambique, the Soviet Union provided non-monetized assistance as part of its competition with China in order to obtain influence over the new Afro-Marxist regime. Among other Eastern Europeans interest was selective and limited: there were more Italian physicians in Mozambique than all the staff from East Germany, Bulgaria, Romania and Hungary combined.[159]

Eastern European approaches increasingly parted company from other socialist medical projects. Cuba expanded its global medical engagement, and created five-year plan quotas for medical graduates assigned to Africa or Asia. Health exports became central to the regime's international identity and political legitimacy at home.[160] Additionally, Cubans reimagined communal medicine by positioning themselves as family doctors who combined the work of 'a social worker as much as a medical/technical expert', living alongside the people whom they treated. Physicians acquired multiple skills through continuous training at the institutions where they worked.[161] In comparison with Eastern Europe, Cuba's foreign health assistance preserved its dynamism and communal character through the 1980s. During Comecon meetings, Havana was held up as an exemplary synthesis of 'Second' and 'Third World' medicine, even if Cuban community medicine was never identified as a viable blueprint for Eastern Europe.[162] Cuba's export of medical workers and public healthcare initiatives across the developing world strengthened Havana's prestige in the NAM, to the point that Cuba spearheaded the NAM conferences of health ministers and chaired a working group

[157] Iris Borowy, 'East German Medical Aid to Nicaragua: The Politics of Solidarity between Biomedicine and Primary Health Care', História, Ciências, Saúde -Manguinhos, 24/2 (2017), 411–28.
[158] Iris Borowy, 'Medical Aid, Repression, and International Relations: The East German Hospital at Metema', Journal of the History of Medicine and Allied Sciences, 71/1 (2015), 89.
[159] Bogdan C. Iacob and Iolanda Vasile, 'Agents of Decolonization? Romanian Activities in Mozambique's Oil and Healthcare Sectors (1976–1984)', in Anna Calori et al. (eds.), Between East and South: Spaces of Interaction in the Globalizing Economy of the Cold War (Berlin: de Gruyter, 2019), 153.
[160] John Kirk and Michael Erisman, Cuban Medical Internationalism. Origins, Evolution, and Goals (New York: Palgrave Macmillan, 2009), 85.
[161] Kirk and Erisman, Cuban, 41–2.
[162] 'A 29-a Consfătuire a miniştrilor sănătăţii din ţările socialiste, Havana 1–4 decembrie 1983', MS-DCCPI-Relatii Externe 2–1984, 2–40.

during the WHA.[163] Authorities in Havana also embraced commercialization: teams in Libya, Iran, or Iraq were revenue-generators for the Cuban state. Even in war-torn Angola, half of the Cuban staff salaries were paid in hard currency after 1982. In contrast to their Eastern European peers, Cuban experts were unaware of these payments; they believed their activity was 'altruistic, 'internationalist' support in the spirit of solidarity.'[164]

The rise of primary healthcare (PHC) at the WHO further underlined the distance between Eastern Europe and the developing world. This health paradigm reflected the influence of post-colonial countries within the organisation as well as broader international critiques of conventional approaches to medicine in the global North. It emphasized the social-economic contextualization of ill-health, community participation and traditional medicine; it critiqued medical over-specialization and insisted on the role of auxiliary personnel (assistants, nurses, or midwives) and technology appropriate for rural, low-income countries.[165] Though the Soviet Union and other socialist countries pushed at the WHO for the organization of the 1978 conference on PHC in Alma-Ata (Kazakhstan),[166] their domestic systems stood in sharp contrast with the new ideas advocated at the WHO. European socialist healthcare, paralleling developments in the West, had moved away from community medicine; it relied on mega-hospitals and over-medication, while rural health remained underfunded and understaffed.[167] Eastern Europeans' support for PHC was a response to the rising popularity of China's healthcare tailored to low-income countries because of its reliance on 'barefoot doctors' and traditional medicine.[168] Eastern European states' officials and experts often criticized PHC for its putative de-professionalization of health. Tellingly, there was no coverage of the Alma-Ata conference in the most important Soviet newspapers, *Pravda* and *Izvestiya*.[169]

Over time, domestic crises weakened Eastern Europeans' capacity to sustain and internationalize the distinctive quality of socialist healthcare. During the 1980s, due to rising national debts, socialist governments deemed healthcare a 'non-productive sector' of the economy, leading to drastic budgetary cuts.[170] As a

---

[163] 'Nota de relații participarea delegației române la XXX-a Adunare Mondială a Sănătății, 1–21 mai 1977', MS-DCCPI-Relatii Externe 17–1977, 27.

[164] Christine Hatzky, 'Cubans in Angola: Internationalist Solidarity, Transfers and Interactions in the Global South 1975–91', in Sandra Bott et al. (eds.), *Neutrality and Neutralism in the Global Cold War* (London: Routledge, 2016), 205.

[165] Marcos Cueto, 'The Origins of Primary Health Care and Selective Primary Health Care', *America Journal of Public Health*, 94/11 (2004), 1864–74.

[166] Sung Lee, 'WHO and the Developing World: The Contest for Ideology', in Andrew Cunningham and Bridie Andrews (eds.), *Western Medicine as Contested Knowledge* (Manchester: Manchester University Press, 1997), 40.

[167] Packard, *A History*, 244–6.   [168] Cueto, 'The Origins', 1866–7.

[169] Birn and Krementsov, '"Socialising"', 11–12.

[170] Eva Orosz, 'Health and Development under State Socialism. The Hungarian Experience', in David Phillips and Yola Verhasselt (eds.), *Health and Development* (London: Routledge, 2003), 283;

result, Eastern European medical systems stagnated in the face of collapsing investment, undermining the region's international appeal.[171] No less significant was the fact that World Bank directives began to trump those of the WHO, whose loans to the global South were conditional upon the adoption of structural adjustment, forcing cuts in health budgets and favouring privatized medical care. In 1982, a US-led coalition of western states that included the UK, France, Belgium, and the Netherlands decided to freeze their contributions to the WHO, advocating 'zero growth' for the institution's budget[172]—a decision endorsed by all Eastern European delegations because of their own economic crises. Since the WHO's inception socialist representatives had criticized its budgetary policies, arguing that they burdened post-colonial economies, which were compelled to increase their dues. In the last decade of the Cold War, this reasoning was repurposed by a new consensus across the global North that, to quote one Soviet representative, 'financial resources must be spent in the most rational way…and stabilization of the budget [is] now necessary for the organization.'[173] This 'zero growth' approach facilitated the stepped-up interference of the World Bank and western donors in WHO activities. Many of the organization's activities were now supported through extra-budgetary funds which these 'investors' controlled. They influenced their disbursement, using the WHO's agenda to shape post-colonial governments' policies. A year before the USSR's collapse, the Soviet Minister of Health Igor Denisov criticized the extent to which the WHO's programmes were influenced by outside donors. But as the Soviet system experienced deepening economic crisis, Denisov's government refused to pledge money to the WHO: 'the principle of zero real-growth budget…should continue to be applied in the future.'[174]

Socialist international humanitarianism was further compromised by Eastern European regimes' ambivalent reactions to famine in East Africa. They refused to take part in the two International Conferences on Assistance to Refugees in Africa (ICARA) in 1981 and 1984, and instead opted for targeted bilateral assistance.[175] This argument did not convince their African counterparts since famine aid from Eastern Europe was limited and the socialist camp's presence at ICARA could have strengthened African governments' negotiating position. In 1981, an Ethiopian official proclaimed that socialist countries' absence from ICARA showed that they 'deserted [Africans] exactly when they need most support. Now

Mateusz Zatonski and Witold Zatonski, 'Health in the Polish People's Republic', *Journal of Health Inequalities*, 2/1 (2016), 7–16.

[171] Kaser, *Health*, 20–1.

[172] Theodore Brown, Marcos Cueto and Elizabeth Fee, 'The World Health Organization and the Transition from "International" to "Global" Health', in Alison Bashford (ed.), *Medicine at the Border Disease, Globalization and Security, 1850 to the Present* (London: Palgrave MacMillan, 2007), 152.

[173] 34th WHA, Geneva, 4–22 May 1981, WHA34/1981/REC/2, 64.

[174] 43rd WHA, Geneva, 7–17 May 1990, WHA43/1990/REC/2, 138.

[175] 'Comecon Aid in Line with Africa's Needs', *Pravda*, 14 January 1985, HU 300-30-12, Box 7 (OSA).

[Africans] are alone to face the West.'[176] Socialist states' reluctance and incapacity to continue with their earlier health internationalism was visible when 7.9 million Ethiopians were threatened by starvation between 1984 and 1986. The famine was a great embarrassment to the European socialist camp because the Soviets had claimed that the Derg regime in Ethiopia was committed to 'the principles of Marxism-Leninism 'in pure form', instead of following the 'invented variations' of so-called 'African socialism'.[177] But despite significant involvement on the part of the Soviet Union, East Germany, Czechoslovakia, Poland, and Cuba, western food and logistical relief constituted the majority of support provided to Ethiopia.[178] In 1984, the Czechoslovak ambassador in Addis Ababa admitted the inability of Eastern European regimes to address the crisis: 'whatever we do, we won't be able to feed this nation.'[179] In contrast, China used the famine to publicize its humanitarianism; it was the only socialist state that provided grain in all the three years of the relief operations.[180] An OECD study (1984) listed Beijing as 'the eighth-largest bilateral donor in Sub-Saharan Africa, with commitments very close to those made by Norway, and not far below Japan and the United Kingdom'.[181]

Though the numbers of medical professionals remained high in certain countries and socialist pharmaceutical enterprises thrived, Eastern European internationalism had lost its anti-western thrust by the late 1980s. In 1988, when famine once again struck Ethiopia, Mikhail Gorbachev approved the delivery of 250,000 tons of wheat purchased on the open market and worth $80 million. Two years later, he and US president Ronald Reagan jointly pledged to assist in the operation to alleviate starvation.[182] Soviet efforts symbolized Gorbachev's desire to have the USSR recognized as part of a post-Cold War common European home. In 1989, socialist delegates at the WHA emphasized their Europeanness too; solidarity with the South was secondary. Judit Csehák, Hungary's Minister of Health proclaimed that 'for us European countries, regional European problems and programmes are just as important as global and interregional ones....if we wish to remain part of an integrated Europe in social and economic terms, we must do our best in this regard.'[183] This Europeanization of public healthcare was founded on the transition from a state-led health sector to privatization. Even Yugoslav delegates conceded their country's alignment along a policy of this sort:

---

[176] 'Telegramă, Ambasada României la Geneva', 08 April 1981 MAE (Ministerul Afacerilor Externe)-ONU (Organizația Națiunilor Unite) 2180–1981 (Romania).
[177] Radoslav Yordanov, *The Soviet Union and the Horn of Africa during the Cold War* (Lanham: Lexington Books, 2016), 214.
[178] Ghaji Bello, *The International Politics of Famine Relief Operations Ethiopia: A Case Study of the 1984–86 Relief Operations*, PhD dissertation, (London School of Economics, 1990).
[179] Yordanov, *The Soviet*, 244.   [180] Bello, *The International*, 90.
[181] Brautigam, *The Dragon*, 54.   [182] Yordanov, *The Soviet*, 296 and 289.
[183] 42nd WHA, 8–19 May 1989, WHA42/1989/REC/2, 80–1. Similar remarks from the Polish Minister of Health and Social Affairs, Izabela Planeta-Malecka (145).

'Yugoslavia has opted for a market economy…health will share the destiny…of the economy as a whole.'[184] According to a Romanian participant at the WHA in 1990, this 'restructuring' brought ex-socialist countries 'into line with the rest of modern Europe.'[185] When the Berlin Wall fell, the East's 'return to Europe' marked the end of its alternative vision of international welfare.

Epilogue

The East's medical internationalism alleviated post-colonial states' dependency on the West and was central to challenging colonialism's medical legacies. Eastern European contributions to global disease control and eradication were distinctive. Their impact at the WHO can be traced to principles such as the integration of epidemiological programmes into national health services, mass vaccination and the state's role in ensuring affordable care. Simultaneously, Eastern Europeans maintained old civilizational hierarchies that further intensified with state socialism's economic crisis in the late Cold War and its incorporation into a western-driven global healthcare regime. Over time, anti-imperial solidarity was replaced by medical Eurocentrism, as personnel and governments distanced themselves from the South. The success of the Cuban and Chinese socialist alternatives lay in their ability to preserve their internationalism by adapting to conditions prevailing in the newly independent states.

The memory of an Eastern European presence in developing states was eclipsed by the collapse of healthcare across the global South during the 1980s and the 1990s.[186] Scarcity of investment effaced the physical traces of socialist assistance. The Soviet-built hospital in Kisumu, Kenya (called by locals 'Russia') was renovated only in 2015.[187] The former Soviet-Khmer Friendship Hospital in Phnom Penh was salvaged by the Australian Rotary Club in 2017.[188] Another legacy of East–South medical entanglements was training local personnel. One Ghanaian physician stated in 2013 that 'without Soviet education, the Ghanaian medical system would have been in a terrible state' because of the massive out-migration of local staff.[189]

By contrast, Cuba and China maintained sizeable medical footprints in the global South. The government in Havana, after severe difficulties in the 1990s, resuscitated and even expanded its medical internationalism, which became central

---

[184] Ibid., 114.   [185] 43rd WHA, 7–17 May 1990, WHA43/1990/REC/2, 202.

[186] Patton, Jr, *Physicians*, 42.

[187] Ruth Prince, 'From Russia with Love: Medical Modernities, Development Dreams, and Cold War Legacies in Kenya, 1969 and 2015', *Africa: The Journal of the International African Institute*, 90/1 (2020), 51–76.

[188] 'Russian Hospital Hygiene Project in Cambodia', *Applecross Rotary*, 27 June 2018 http://www.applecrossrotary.org/stories/russian-hospital-cambodia-hygiene-project-2017 (last accessed 9 May 2020).

[189] Oxfam, 15, 13, and 23.

to its post-Cold War identity. Earnings from the medical trade (higher education, pharmaceutics, and treatment) became essential to Cuba's national budget.[190] Since the 1980s, the government in Beijing revitalized projects that had been faltering in the previous decade. China experienced its own commercialization of medical exports during the 1990s, yet a sense of solidarity remained. In Tanzania in the late 1960s, Chinese experts had built a factory for vaccines and medicine, to combat smallpox. By the end of the Cold War the enterprise was failing; in 1997 it was transformed into a joint venture that in 2006 became Tanzansino United Pharmaceuticals Ltd, which produces anti-malarial remedies derived from Chinese plants.[191] Chinese physicians continue to benefit from the goodwill amassed before 1989. As one Tanzanian put it: 'in Nyerere's times there were many Chinese doctors here, we trusted them more than our local doctors.'[192]

Some Eastern European pharmaceutical companies survived state socialism's collapse. The Hungarian company 'Alkaloida' was bought in 2005 by an Indian pharmaceutical company, Sunpharma[193]—an East–South connection within a global order where Cold War hierarchies are now obsolete. By 1989, the Romanian factory 'Antibiotice', a Comecon project originally designed to provide penicillin for member states, had exported its antibiotics to thirty countries, with sales of 150 million dollars per year. After failed privatizations and pressed by Chinese competition, the company crumbled in the 1990s. In the 2000s, its activities were diverted into the production of nystatin, essential for cosmetics and pharmaceuticals. By 2018, the state-owned 'Antibiotice' enjoyed 60% of the world market thanks to its old Second World networks, with representations in Hanoi, Novi Sad and Kiev, while covering China's entire national demand.[194]

In the early 1990s, the East and the South came together along an unexpected trajectory. Foreign observers and local analysts described the 'third worldization' of Eastern European healthcare. In January 1990, a French relief worker argued that 'Romania has all the health problems of a Third World country, combined with all those of early industrialization.'[195] Previously eradicated infectious diseases (poliomyelitis and measles) made a comeback to the extent that the UN child immunization campaign designed primarily for Africa, Asia, and Latin

[190]   Kirk and Erisman, *Cuban*, 97–120.   [191]   Brautigam, *The Dragon*, 71–4 and 118.
[192]   Elisabeth Hsu, '"The Medicine from China Has Rapid Effects": Chinese Medicine Patients in Tanzania', *Anthropology & Medicine*, 9/3 (2002), 295.
[193]   http://alkaloidazrt.hu/en/introduction (last accessed 9 May 2020).
[194]   https://economie.hotnews.ro/stiri-companii-23140894-video-reportaj-povestea-antibiotice-iasi-una-dintre-putinele-industrii-din-perioada-comunista-care-scapat-privatizare-reusit-aduca-romania-locul-lume.htm and https://economie.hotnews.ro/stiri-companii-23184852-video-reportaj-cum-face-penicilina.htm (last accessed 9 May 2020).
[195]   Patricia Clough, 'Romania Wracked by Disease', *The Independent*, 19 January 1990, HU 300-60-1 Box 757 (OSA).

America now had to turn its attention to the region.[196] According to WHO estimates, in 1990 'the chances of a 15-year-old Polish boy...to survive to 60 years of age were lower than that of a teenager living in China, Latin America, or India.'[197] With the end of the Cold War, Eastern Europe was once again turning into a global periphery. It forfeited its alternative medical modernity once states across the region had abandoned their pioneering role in public healthcare in the developing world in favour of Europeanization.

[196] 'UN-Child Immunization Campaign Succeeding', 08 December 1991, HU 300-20-1 Bulgarian Unit, 1951–1995 (OSA).
[197] Zatonski and Zatonski, 'Health', 16.

8

Mobility

Education and Labour

Alena Alamgir

In the mid-1980s, Mr Tuan[1] worked as a blacksmith for a company in the Moravian city of Brno and Ms Mai was employed by an enterprise making ball bearings in the Slovak town of Skalica, some 100 kilometers to the east. Both were part of the migrant Vietnamese workforce in state-socialist Czechoslovakia, which, at that point, comprised some 12,000 people. They had known each other already in Vietnam, having lived on the same street. At one point, they decided to defect from Czechoslovakia. Mr Tuan had relatives in France, Britain, Canada and the United States and figured one of the countries would take them in as refugees fleeing from behind the Iron Curtain. For two years, he saved money and worked on a plan. The plan involved a Bulgarian man who made a living buying goods in Dresden and selling them in Budapest, Brno, Bucharest and Sofia, and vice versa. He knew how to move things, and, once in a while, if asked, he helped move people too. On the big day, the couple took a train from Brno to Budapest, where they rented a room in a cheap hotel while waiting for the Bulgarian to finish his business in Dresden. The Bulgarian then took the couple first to the Romanian city of Timișoara, then the trio continued on to Belgrade. The Bulgarian said that his mission would be completed once he led the couple to a refugee camp on the outskirts of the Yugoslav capital. Once there, the Vietnamese were told that the camp was not for them, but for Eastern Europeans, that they should try their luck in Hong Kong. The embassies of the western countries where they wanted to apply for asylum told them the same thing. And all turned them away.

In the camp, they met another Vietnamese couple who had previously worked in Eastern Europe. This couple had been stuck in the limbo in the refugee camp for four years by then, and advised them that they were better off crossing the Yugoslav border on their own, to head to either Austria or Italy. While at the

I would like to thank Bogdan C. Iacob for bringing several primary and secondary sources to my attention, as well as James Mark, Bálint Tolmár, Nemanja Radonjić, Peter Wright and Bogdan C. Iacob for sharing their (at the time) unpublished manuscripts with me.

[1] Interview with Mr Tuan, conducted by Alena Alamgir, Vienna, 14 November 2010. The names are pseudonyms.

Alena Alamgir, *Mobility: Education and Labour* In *Socialism Goes Global: The Soviet Union and Eastern Europe in the Age of Decolonization*. Edited by James Mark and Paul Betts, Oxford University Press. © Oxford University Press 2022. DOI: 10.1093/oso/9780192848857.003.0009

camp, Mr Tuan marvelled at the Czechs, Poles and Romanians he met there. He was shocked by how easy they had it: his head spun imagining that all defecting involved *for them* was getting in their cars and driving off. He and Ms Mai, not having a car, decided to take a train to a Slovenian border town at a foot of a big hill under which two tunnels ran: one to Italy, the other to Austria. Mr Tuan chose Austria as he heard that the refugee processing system was better there. After several hours of nerve-racking trekking through the very narrow tunnel (there were only about 30 cm between a passing train and the wall, and so, every time they heard a train approaching, they hid in small alcoves, spaced roughly 300 m apart), they finally emerged on the other side. At first, they were not sure if they had really made it to Austria. But soon, Mr Tuan spotted a sign with a word on it. He did not speak German but, while in Czechoslovakia, he became an amateur photographer and subscribed to an East German magazine for photo enthusiasts, so he felt confident that the word he saw was indeed German and that they therefore had reached Austria. Describing the atmosphere in the tunnel, he spoke about eerie light that made them think it might have come from the devil. Talking about the moment they approached the opening on the Austrian side of the tunnel, he recalled the feeling of fresh air on his face and the sense of freedom that enveloped him.

This is not the archetypal story of escape from oppression to freedom. Mr Tuan and Ms Mai decided to make a run for it mainly because they were in love. Mr Tuan was Catholic, and Ms Mai was not. Moreover, she was two and half years older than him. Mr Tuan believed that his mother would never consent to their marriage in Vietnam. He had not come to Eastern Europe because his government forced him to go. Before he decided to take the job in Czechoslovakia, he turned down the offer to go to the Soviet Union, thrice, without any repercussions (in fact, such jobs were coveted and some resorted to bribery to get them). Originally, he was not interested in going abroad because his family owned a popular restaurant in Hanoi; he helped his father run the business, and the family was doing well financially. But the war with Cambodia broke out and he wanted to avoid the draft (though, he noted, he would have gladly taken up arms during the American War). When asked about his stay in Czechoslovakia, he said that he'd enjoyed it. He made very good money, though noted that not all of his friends were paid as well as he was. Czechs were mostly kind to him, and he picked up photography as a hobby along the way. When asked how he would assess his stay in Czechoslovakia as a migrant Vietnamese worker, he said: 'Very positively... not just because of the money, also because of the culture, we learned things, the experience enriched us'. In fact, he mentioned in passing that living in Czechoslovakia equipped him with cultural competency that came in handy later when starting his new life in Austria. He even praised the factory cafeteria food as 'fantastic' ('You'd get half a grilled chicken!'). And finally, this Austrian citizen of Vietnamese origin noted: 'I must say: the Czech Republic is partly my homeland too.'

State-Socialist Europe as a Mobile Space

As unique is this story sounds, its contours hint at several features that character-ized mobility in state socialism. The story certainly makes visible what is normally seen as its main (and often the only) feature: the barriers to it that existed and the regulations that limited it—that is why the couples' move to the West was a clan-destine escape. However, the story also hints at the robustness of mobility within the state-socialist camp. On the one hand, it was the movement of insiders, which the mysterious Bulgarian embodied in an archetypal way. He clearly belonged to the group of people whom the Czechs called *šmelináři*, or black marketeers, for whom traveling, buying and selling all throughout the socialist camp was a recog-nized occupation. There were also those for whom such travel and shopping (though usually not selling) was a hobby, that is to say, people who engaged in what Alenka Švab called shopping tourism.[2] In the mid-1970s, for example, some 25% of Poles travelled outside the country, and when cross-border travel reached mass scale, it wasn't unusual for 2,000 Poles to board a train bound for Budapest, several times more than the regulations permitted.[3]

However, visitors from the Third World travelled as well. The Vietnamese in particular were known for the intensity of their mobility. A Czechoslovak man-ager who was in charge of Vietnamese workers in his company wrote in his recol-lections: 'It was immediately clear just how clever the Vietnamese were. They figured out train and bus schedules and travelled all around the country on the weekends to see their friends'. The manager was astounded by how fast the newly arrived Vietnamese workers could orient themselves and undertake these trips in a country completely foreign to them, one whose language they did not speak. Vietnamese workers stationed in different European state-socialist countries sometimes even travelled to visit each other, such as when a Vietnamese worker in Czechoslovakia scrambled, upon being arrested for a crime, to make sure that his friend employed in the USSR, who was scheduled to visit him, would be taken care of since he was in jail and could not receive him personally.[4]

Angolans and Mozambicans who worked in the GDR also remember the 1980s there as 'a time of mobility in a society that supposedly restricted [their] freedom of movement'. They contrast this mobility with the 'present-day freedom', which they experience 'as stasis'.[5] State-socialist mobility was made possible for these

---

[2] Alenka Švab, 'Consuming Western Image of Well-Being—Shopping Tourism in Socialist Slovenia', *Cultural Studies*, 16/1 (2002), 63–79.

[3] Jerzy Kochanowski, "Pioneers of the Free Market Economy? Unofficial Commercial Exchange Between People from the Socialist Bloc Countries (1970s and 1980s)', *Journal of Modern European History*, 8/2 (2010), 196–220.

[4] Case number VV-17/10-82 investigated by the KS SNB Ostrava (Archive of Security Forces, ABS, Prague).

[5] Marcia C. Schenck, 'A Chronology of Nostalgia: Memories of Former Angolan and Mozambican Worker Trainees to East Germany', *Labor History*, 53/3 (2018), 352–74.

workers through 'reliable wages and functional public infrastructure' that were available to them in the GDR, but are absent from their current lives in Mozambique and Angola. Thus, an Angolan man remembers wistfully: '[w]hen we were in Germany, I'd just buy a ticket to see my brother-in-law in Czechoslovakia and [after German reunification] I went from Berlin to Munich, but since I returned, I have not left this place [Luanda] and that makes me feel as if I am imprisoned.'[6] Thus, the conceptualization of the state-socialist era as a time of immobility characterized by 'isolation and the reduction of cross-border contact to a minimum'[7] is a simplification and a product of Cold War propaganda battles, whereby Second World realities were judged in terms of idealized First World expectations. The usual focus on immobility glosses over the robust and 'oft-overlooked circulation of people, goods, knowledge and capital'[8] that took place both between the state-socialist countries and between these states and a number of developing countries. The socialist world, far from being immobile, was instead, as Susan Bayly put it, 'crosscut and interconnected by agreements under which scientific and technical specialists in their thousands were continually on the move to distant places'.[9] The specialists were not the only ones on the move; indeed, numerically, they constituted a minority. Aside from the shoppers, and vacationers, the most mobile were students, and—especially in the 1970s and 1980s—blue-collar workers.

State-Socialist Visions of Mobility

To understand state-socialist mobility, we need to take seriously the ideological underpinnings of the state-socialist project, and seek to understand this mobility on its own terms. This is because

[w]hat meant success from the socialist point of view—nationalization and the creation of a state-led economy, for instance—would be a failure from the liberal one. The socialist model of modernization furthered the quest for [national] sovereignty and advocated state control over production and foreign exchanges, while the liberal one promoted free enterprise, individual agency and the integration of the national economy into the world market.[10]

---

[6] Cited in ibid., 360.

[7] David Turnock, 'Cross-Border Cooperation: A Major Element in Regional Policy in East Central Europe', *Scottish Geographical Journal*, 118/1 (2002), 19, 20.

[8] Christina Schwenkel, 'Rethinking Asian Mobilities: Socialist Migration and Post-Socialist Repatriation of Vietnamese Contract Workers in East Germany', *Critical Asian Studies*, 46/2 (2014), 235–58, 236.

[9] Susan Bayly, 'Vietnamese Intellectuals in Revolutionary and Postcolonial Times', *Critique of Anthropology*, 24/3 (2004), 321, 334–6.

[10] Constantin Katsakioris, 'Soviet Lessons for Arab Modernization: Soviet Educational Aid to Arab Countries after 1956', *Journal of Modern European History*, 8/1 (2010), 105.

Similarly, in the liberal (capitalist) framework, 'proper migration' is envisioned as *individual* migration and ideal migrants are those who decide to migrate on their own, which is to say 'free' of the pressures of family, community and institutional networks.[11] This is because the liberal version of mobility and migration reflects 'the fantasies of a free market where workers [can] sell their labour without constraint and on equal bargaining terms with employers'.[12]

The state-socialist version of mobility reflected a very different sort of fantasy (or vision) and hence revolved around different priorities. Paramount among these were economic development and modernization (i.e., state-building in the *economic* sense) and state-building proper (i.e., state-building in *political* sense). Accordingly, these state-socialist migratory schemes were conceived as important tools for achieving developmental goals. That is to say, *socialist mobility was not conceived as an end in itself but as a means of development.* The notion of development referred primarily to states, but that does not mean that individuals' development did not matter; it was rather that the fate of individuals was seen as inseparable from, and embedded in, the development of states. This meant that spheres of life, and types of travel, which in the liberal-capitalist context are kept separate, overlapped in the state-socialist context. The tourist cruises between the GDR and Cuba, organized by the East German trade unions from 1961 all the way through to 1989,[13] illustrate this issue vividly. There was no thick wall separating tourism from politics since 'tourism was supposed to serve the immediate needs of workers, reproducing—through rest and relaxation—[their] labour power.' It, therefore, made perfect sense that, on the return leg of the journey, a cruise ship carried from Cuba not just the suntanned East German tourists, but also wounded Cuban fighters who sought hospital treatment in the GDR.[14]

Greek, Korean and Vietnamese Children: Developing the Mobility Infrastructure

This overlap between leisure and politics is evident in the earliest forms of mobility within the state-socialist camp, specifically in the relocations of Greek political refugees and Korean and Vietnamese children (often, but not always, orphans of the eponymous wars). The first consisted primarily of some 100,000 Greek citizens who sought refuge in several different people's democracies in the

---

[11] Adam M. McKeown, *Melancholy Order: Asian Migration and the Globalization of Borders* (New York: Columbia University Press, 2008).

[12] Tara Zahra, 'Travel Agents on Trial: Policing Mobility in East Central Europe, 1889–1989', *Past & Present*, 223/1 (2014), 161–93.

[13] George Bodie, '"It is a Shame We Are Not Neighbours": GDR Tourist Cruises to Cuba, 1961–89', *Journal of Contemporary History*, 55/2 (2020), 411–34.

[14] Ibid., 416.

wake of the Greek Civil War. Their main destinations were Albania, Bulgaria and Yugoslavia, but they headed also to Czechoslovakia, Romania and Poland. By December 1950, there were 12,095 Greek refugees reported as living in Czechoslovakia, of whom 5,185 were children.[15] Most Greeks chose to repatriate in the early to mid-1970s, after the fall of the Colonels' dictatorship.[16]

In the case of the Greek refugees, children had been evacuated first and parents followed them into exile months later. Due to what was essentially a context-contingent complication, the host countries had to create a network of institutions for housing and educating the unaccompanied children. In Czechoslovakia, chateaux, spas and other recreational spaces were converted into orphanages for the children. These had been recently expropriated, and, when not used as havens for refugee children, they 'were part of the Communist Party's efforts to provide workers with 'purposeful tourism'—a variety of 'virtuous' leisure',[17] whose rationale resembled that of the GDR Cuba cruises. Consequently, the chateaux and spas were implicated in two different sorts of mobility—one internal, one external— and both saturated with meaning. Through the two different ways in which the buildings were put to use, the early socialist Czechoslovak state was constructing its identity as a provider of welfare. In the case of the migrant refugee children, the welfare it provided was of an emergency-and-basic-needs sort; in the case of its own citizens, welfare was of the leisure-and-self-actualization sort. This was observable more broadly: as the states—embodied in its administrators and mid-level officials—were tackling the various logistical challenges that arose from having to transport and house relatively large groups of people, they were simultaneously also working out their identity. Hence, they were quite literally engaging in the process of their own state-building while contributing toward the state-building efforts of their foreign guests and their respective governments. Besides Czechoslovakia, at least six other state-socialist countries—China, the USSR, the GDR, Romania, Poland and Hungary—ran special programmes for children from war-torn areas. Reportedly,[18] as of 1952, Poland, Hungary, Czechoslovakia, GDR and Bulgaria each hosted 200 Korean children, China purportedly invited 30,000 Korean families and 30,000 orphans for long-term stays, and 'USSR's assistance [was] so vast that it's impossible to express it in numbers.'[19] Estimates are that Romania took in anywhere between 1,000 to 3,000 Korean

---

[15] Konstantinos Tsivos, *Řecká emigrace v Československu (1948–1968): Od jednoho rozštěpení ke druhému* (Prague: Dokořán, Univerzita Karlova, Fakulta sociálních věd, 2011).

[16] By 2018, there were only 862 Greeks left in the Czech Republic.

[17] Cathleen M. Giustino, 'Open Gates and Wandering Minds: Codes, Castles, and Chateaux in Socialist Czechoslovakia before 1960', in Cathleen Giustino, Catherine Plum and Alexander Vari (eds.), *Socialist Escapes: Breaks from Ideology and Everyday Routines in Eastern Europe, 1945–1989* (Oxford, New York: Berghahn Press, 2013), 50.

[18] Korea, TO-T [Teritoriální odbory, tajné] 1945–1954, carton 1: 'An overview of current situation in Korea', 24 March 1953. (AMZV. Archive of the Ministry of Foreign Affairs, Czech Republic).

[19] Ibid.

children,[20] and Czechoslovakia accepted an additional 700 Korean children in a second wave of the programme.

The broad outlines of the story of the Vietnamese children sent to the GDR and Czechoslovakia resemble those of their Korean counterparts, except that they were sent abroad primarily to receive education that upon their return they would use to rebuild their homeland. The importance accorded to the project by the Vietnamese side can be gleaned from the fact that the children were received by Hồ Chí Minh before their departure; the Vietnamese president stopped by to spend an afternoon with them during his trip to Czechoslovakia in July 1957. Both the programmes acquired informal nicknames referring to the name of the town in which the children were housed: *chrastavské děti*, after the Czech town of Chrastava, and the *Moritzburger Kinder*, after the East German town of Moritzburg. The one hundred Chrastava children, who were between six and thirteen years old, were sent there by the DVR government in July 1956. After arrival, they were housed in an orphanage that was already sheltering Greek refugee children.[21] The 149 *Moritzburger* children, between the ages of nine and fourteen, had reached the GDR a year earlier, in September 1955. The trip took roughly two weeks on the train, with several day-long stopovers in Beijing and Moscow.[22] Once in Moritzburg, they were welcomed by the 'boys and girls from the Greek colony in Dresden-Radebeul'.[23] Whether by coincidence or design, the two governments formulated very similar projects and came up with the same institutional solutions to the logistical problems they were facing. In 1959, the Vietnamese government recalled the children, reportedly out of concerns that, due to their youth and the length of their stays, they might lose their cultural identity,[24] leaving only the fifteen oldest to pursue higher education and training. This step exemplifies two other features typical of state-socialist mobility, which became even more pronounced in the case of student and blue-collar worker migrations, namely their temporary and goal-oriented nature: once the aim was accomplished, it was time to return.

Another notable aspect of these war migration projects was their emotional resonance, which surfaced when the former participants were asked to recall their experiences. They uniformly remember their stays exceedingly fondly,

[20] Radu Tudorancea, *Ipostazele 'ajutorului frățesc'. RPR și războiul din Coreea (1950–1953)* (Cluj-Napoca: Eikon, 2014), 96, thanks to Bogdan C. Iacob for bringing the material to my attention.

[21] Šárka Martínková-Šimečková, 'Chrastavské děti', *Klub Hanoi*, http://www.klubhanoi.cz/view.php?cisloclanku=2006071101 (last accessed 26 October 2016). Unless noted otherwise, I rely on Martínková-Šimečková's account throughout in my reconstruction of the Czechoslovak programme.

[22] 'Vietnamese Children Accepted into the GDR', reprinted in Deniz Göktürk, David Gramling and Anton Kaes (eds.), *Germany in Transit Nation and Migration, 1955–2005* (Berkeley: University of California Press, 2007).

[23] 'Warm Welcome for 200 Korean Children', reprinted in Göktürk, Gramling, and Kaes (eds.), *Germany in Transit*.

[24] Martínková-Šimečková, 'Chrastavské děti'.

revisiting with great affection the loving orphanage staff, or the families of local police officers who 'adopted them' and hosted them during holidays such as Christmas.[25] Before we write these emotions off as mere nostalgia, we should note that similar sentiments appear not just in post facto musings, but also in contemporaneous texts. In a 1961 magazine interview, a Korean girl residing in Romania since she was ten, described Romania as her 'second motherland' and the representatives of the Red Cross as her parents who 'did everything so that [she and the other Korean children] would be happy'. She said that her 'mothers', by which she meant the Red Cross personnel, were so good to the Korean children that they 'spoiled [them]'. Finally, she said she had yet to come to terms with the idea that she would 'be separated from the Romanians to whom [she owed her] intellectual upbringing, who loved and helped [her] as if [she] were theirs, with no profit for themselves'.[26] The framing used by Moroccan students in the Soviet Union was strikingly similar, one said: 'The [male] teachers, but especially the [female] teachers were like mothers, like parents to us. We would spend weekends with them, and they took care of us. They took us out for walks. As if we were their children'. Another one is quoted as saying: 'The professors were like parents to us. When we would be absent from class, they'd come to our room to see if we were sick. And if that happened to be the case, they would give us extra lessons! The big professors, even the academicians, in my room!'[27] This suggests that it was not only the host *states* that developed (facets of) their state-socialist identity through such mobility projects, but that 'ordinary people', too, were building a specific sort of state-socialist identity, one that revolved around caring for the needs of others. It is important, however, that this identity originally evolved specifically through the process of caring for destitute *children*, i.e., a situation whose structure naturally invited paternalist and patronizing attitudes. This, combined with the economic differences between the state-socialist 'core' and 'periphery' fed into the framing of both the educational and later labour programmes as a state-socialist civilizing mission of sorts.[28]

Thus, these early migrations of people, especially children, affected by wars already exhibit several of the main features of state-socialist migrations: (1) they are not ends in themselves, but the participants are to receive training that they will later put to use in post-war reconstruction and development of their home countries' industries, i.e., *their main purpose is state-building*; (2) the children travel and stay in groups: i.e., *they are collective, not individual*; (3) their travels as

[25] See the 2006 documentary directed by Martin Ryšavý, 'He Who Teaches Me Half a Character', (Kdo mě naučí půl znaku) http://www.ceskatelevize.cz/ivysilani/1131721572-babylon/407235100152019 (12:08).

[26] Edmond Frédéric, 'Enquête sur 4 continents à Bucarest', *La Roumanie d'aujourd'hui*, 6 (1961), 19, thanks to Bogdan C. Iacob for bringing the material to my attention.

[27] Ghellab, '"Les meilleures années de notre vie"', 196.

[28] Alena Alamgir, 'Race Is Elsewhere: State-socialist ideology and the racialisation of Vietnamese workers in Czechoslovakia', *Race & Class*, 54/4 (2013), 67–85.

well as stays are *brokered and organized by states and organizations*; and finally, (4) the stays are conceived of as *temporary and purpose driven*: once the goal is reached or job is completed, the migrants return home. The temporary migrations of students and workers are paragons of such state-socialist migration projects, but note that all four features are easily discernible even in trade union–sponsored *tourism*, whether it be of the exotic sort as the Cuba cruises, or more mundane in-country week-long recreational trips to the mountains.

State-Socialist Educational Mobility as Means of Development

The first state-socialist migration projects were launched after the Second World War. The receiving states used the projects to pursue two sets of inter-related goals. On the one hand, they were internal projects of working through what being a state-socialist country meant. At the same time, they were external projects of involvement in global decolonizing processes. The idea was to help former colonies build up their economies, especially heavy industry, and thus enable them to sever economic ties with former colonial powers. Decolonization also meant an 'exodus of colonial officials and other expatriate staff' as a result of which, 'the political elites of African states were confronted with a serious lack of qualified personnel to run the newly independent states.'[29] For example, at the dawn of independence, in 1961, Tanganyika only had sixteen African doctors (out of a total of 164), two African lawyers (out of fifty-seven), and only a single engineer (out of eighty-four).[30] Even more starkly, at the moment when Mali gained its independence, in September 1960, there were *no* institutions of higher learning on its territory.[31] Accordingly, visions of mobility espoused by political leaders of European state-socialist countries revolved around education and development, both of which, in turn, were conceived of as means to support the global spread of the state-socialist model of modernization.

A point to be emphasized here is that these projects were not simply manifestations of the unilateral exercise of Eastern European initiative and power, far from it. They were responses to real needs of decolonizing countries, and, especially early on, the projects got off the ground only after persistent urging by the potential sending countries' representatives. 'While much historical literature tends to over-emphasize the initiative and perspectives of European socialist states in hosting "Third World" students, these exchanges largely came about through the

---

[29] Eric Burton, 'African Manpower Development during the Global Cold War: The Case of Tanzanian Students in the two German States', in Andreas Exenberger and Ulrich Pallua (eds.), *Africa Research in Austria: Approaches and Perspectives* (Innsbruck: Innsbruck University Press, 2016), 102.

[30] Ibid., 103.

[31] Tatiana Smirnova and Ophélie Rillon, 'Quand des Maliennes regardaient vers l'URSS (1961–1991)', *Cahiers d'Études africaines*, LVII (2), 226 (2017), 331.

lobbying of post-colonial states and national independence movements, and sometimes even through the independent initiatives of students from developing states'.[32] When, in 1951, a high representative of the Nigerian trade unions asked Soviets for scholarships—being happy with the scholarships already granted by the GDR—his request was rejected, just as many others made by representatives of other African countries. But 'the issue of scholarships was repeatedly raised by delegations from colonial Africa, which had started visiting the USSR, after the death of Joseph Stalin' until 1958, when the Communist Party of the Soviet Union finally decided 'to foster political and cultural ties with Sub-Saharan Africa and to offer Africans scholarships for study at Soviet universities'.[33] The inauguration of Vietnamese vocational training into state-socialist European countries was initially also marked by ambivalence: East German officials' first reaction was to state that the Vietnamese proposal was 'rather complicated...due to language problems [and because]...an absolute majority of the Vietnamese citizens who were likely to be sent [had] only low levels of education', and finally, because they thought 'that the proposed two-year-long training period [was]... too short for successful instruction, or the acquisition of true professional qualifications'.[34]

Thus, Eastern European governments were initially wary of the commitments asked of them. Nonetheless, in most cases, the projects were eventually launched, despite the initial hesitation. It is hard to judge whether the eventual impetus for accepting and endorsing these projects came primarily from geopolitical calculations or whether they were genuine expressions of socialist and internationalist solidarity. It is likely that in many cases they were both. Arguably, however, the answer to this question ultimately was not what mattered most. Rather, it was the *effect* that the development assistance (mobility-based or otherwise) had on the ground, i.e., the role played by the myriad of industrial projects in postcolonial countries' development. Also immensely important was *the mere existence* of these projects, that is to say, the possibility of an alternative, which created space for decolonizing countries' governments to exercise power. Their leaders 'could play off the two superpowers and so strike the best deal for themselves...The existence of another source of funding gave...leaders [of developing countries] some power to negotiate with donors and so shape their own destiny'.[35]

[32] Peter Quinnan Wright, 'Between the Market and Solidarity: Development Aid and International Higher Education in Socialist Yugoslavia'. The manuscript was later published, in slightly different form, as ' Between the Market and Solidarity: Commercializing Development Aid and International Higher Education in Socialist Yugoslavia', *Nationalities Papers* 49/3 (2021), 462–482. My quotations come from the earlier unpublished version and hence do not always appear in the same form in the published article.

[33] Constantin Katsakioris, 'Creating a Socialist Intelligentsia. Soviet Educational Aid and its Impact on Africa (1960–1991)', *Cahiers d'études africaines*, LVII (2), 226 (2017), 259.

[34] NA, Letter from the Foreign Ministry to the State Commission for Economic and Scientific and Technical Cooperation, 'Zaškolování občanů VDR', dated 10 June 1966.

[35] Jude Howell, 'The End of an Era: The Rise and Fall of GDR Aid', *The Journal of Modern African Studies*, 32/2 (1994), 305–28.

The same dynamics were evident in the educational migratory schemes, where Cold War competition between the two camps led to global educational expansion. Seeing the Soviet and East-Central European educational initiatives as a 'Communist threat', former colonial powers, as well as the United States, Canada and other liberal-capitalist countries also dramatically increased the number of scholarships for students from Third World countries. The result was a growth of education in the economically less developed countries so substantial that it was later described as a 'world educational revolution'.[36] In short, while Eastern European development assistance projects did not quite manage to upend global hierarchies, they provided more breathing space for the decolonizing and economically less developed countries.

Yet, especially in the case of student mobility, the impact of state-socialist interventions went beyond just providing greater breathing space. Here, they managed to disrupt existing hierarchies in significant ways. The principal method was recruitment. As a general rule, when selecting candidates for education overseas 'academic merits and modest social background were the most important criteria of selection' leading to the recruitment of youth from 'rural, socially disadvantaged backgrounds'.[37] Through their introduction of quotas geared toward children from poorer families, state-socialist countries were trailblazers of affirmative action. The Soviet government, after first conceptualizing their partner countries' societies as consisting of 'the upper, middle, and lower strata' and further subdividing those 'into social groups depending on ... political, economic or social/cultural privileges, power, and resources' (so that, e.g., the families of political establishment or clergy were classified as 'upper', those of farmers or intellectuals as 'middle', and workers and peasants as 'lower' classes), sought to reserve 70–80% of scholarship places for foreign students from lower classes, 15% for the middle strata, and 5% for upper-class students.[38] This effort to prioritize the education of foreign students from modest socio-economic backgrounds was enhanced further by what occured in the sending countries. For example, most of the Moroccan engineers who graduated from Soviet schools came from relatively modest families, those of blue-collar workers, small farmers, and low-level administrators, and 'often the belief [in the value of] education was the only type of capital their families could extend to them'.[39] In this situation, the scholarships offered by the Soviet Union and other European state-socialist countries were the only way these people could (afford to) obtain university degrees. Similarly,

---

[36] Katsakioris, 'Creating a Socialist Intelligentsia', 260–1.
[37] Hauke Dorsch, 'Black or Red Atlantic? Mozambican Students in Cuba and their Reintegration at Home', *Zeitschrift für Ethnologie*, 136/2 (2011), 296.
[38] Natalia Tsvetkova, 'International Education during the Cold War: Soviet Social Transformation and American Social Reproduction', *Comparative Education Review*, 52/2 (2008), 203.
[39] Grazia Scarfò Ghellab, '"Les meilleures années de notre vie." Des ingénieurs marocains formés en URSS', in Monique de Saint Martin, Grazia Scarfò Ghellab and Kamal Mellakh (eds.), *Étudier à l'Est. Expériences de diplômés africains* (Paris: Karthala, 2015), 191, translation from French mine.

several Beninese students claimed that attending the university would have impossible for them without Second World scholarships and support.

These recruitment practices turned the programmes into 'a large-scale intervention in established patterns of access to and participation in university education'. While affirmative action-style programmes are commonplace today, 'in the late 1950s, a program to radically expand university education for previously excluded populations takes on greater historical significance' since it amounted to 'a systematic intervention that directly subverted established patterns of unequal access to education based on geographical location within the world economy'.[40] In (very) rare cases, the access to education was expanded extremely radically and the programmes drew into their orbits rather unconventional students: consider Minabe Diarra, from Mali, who graduated from Leningrad's Ethnographic and Anthropological Institute, a part of the Soviet Academy of Sciences, in 1972, without ever having completed secondary education in Mali, except for undergoing 'traditional' education, specifically that of a hunter.[41] A similar case was documented also in Czechoslovakia, where it was discovered that an African student who just completed his university studies had never actually graduated from high school (he then had to pass the Czechoslovak high-school leaving exam after having completed all his Master's degree graduation requirements).[42]

At the same time, the Second and Third World understanding and expectations of what socialist development entailed sometimes differed quite markedly. For example, the Soviets, in keeping with *their* goals, were primarily interested in training 'qualified and progressive specialists... required in the sphere of administration', particularly, 'economists, administrative staff, military officers, legal experts, philosophers, journalists, propaganda experts, teachers and professors', whom the Soviets saw as 'the principal pool, from which upper and middle rank state employees are recruited'.[43] However, many of the sending states saw their priorities differently and wanted their citizens trained primarily in engineering and natural sciences. Eventually, it was the sending states that prevailed: in 1991, 53% of all foreign students in the Soviet Union were enrolled in engineering schools.[44] The Romanian case was similar, though there, the favoured field was medicine. On average, 38% of foreign students in Romania were enrolled in medicine and pharmacy higher education programmes, but the figure was sometimes as

[40] Tom G. Griffiths and Euridice Charon Cardona, 'Education for Social Transformation: Soviet University Education Aid in the Cold War Capitalist World-System', *European Education*, 47 (2015), 232.

[41] Anna Siim-Moskovitina and Nikolay Dobronravin, 'Des élites africaines entre deux mondes. Impact de la formation en URSS ou poids du milieu social d'origine?', in Saint Martin et al. (eds.), *Étudier à l'Est*, 278.

[42] Marta Edith Holečková, *Univerzita 17. listopadu a její místo v československém vzdělávacím systému a společnosti*, PhD dissertation (Charles University, 2018), 109.

[43] Katsakioris, 'Creating a Socialist Intelligentsia', 272.   [44] Ibid., 273.

high as 64.1%, in 1988.[45] The conflict between the different ideas of what constituted socialist development can be seen in particularly sharp relief in Soviet-
Malian educational cooperation. The fact that some scholarships for Mali were
brokered by the Soviet Women's Committee, opened the door to higher education
for Malian girls and women. The Malian women recruited to Soviet universities
in the 1960s became the first generation of female Malian physicians in what had
previously been an all-male profession.[46] However, Soviet priorities did not overlap with those of the Malian state. The Malians preferred educating women to a
secondary technical level to prepare them to be, for example, midwives and kindergarten teachers. In 1981, the Soviet Ministry of Secondary Technical and
Professional Education issued an internal memo, in which it vowed not to accept
more than 20% of candidates from each country in secondary educational programmes. This provoked an angry reaction on the part of the National Union of
Malian Women, the partner of the Soviet Women's Committee. As an attempt at
compromise, 30% of Malian women receiving education in the Soviet Union in
the 1980s pursued secondary technical degrees. This, however, still did not satisfy
the Union of Malian Women, which continued to try, unsuccessfully, to increase the
number of scholarships for secondary technical education.[47]

In the Malian instance, the Soviet Union, though admittedly culturally insensitive as it was pushing its conception of 'proper socialist development' and gender
roles, contributed, through its scholarship policy, toward a disruption of gender
hierarchies. Ironically, the labour migration projects tended to do the opposite
and reaffirm the traditional gendered division of labour and hence also gender
hierarchies. The case of Cuban workers in Hungary exemplifies this. The other
foreign contract workers in 1980s state-socialist Europe (primarily the Vietnamese
in Czechoslovakia, USSR, GDR, and Bulgaria, and Mozambicans and Angolans
in the GDR) were overwhelmingly male (in Czechoslovakia, at any time, women
comprised at most 25% of Vietnamese contract workers). 60% of Cuban workers
employed in 1980s Hungary, by contrast, were women.[48] And while the Cuban
men worked in metallurgical plants in Dunaújváros and Székesfehérvár (home of
the bus company Ikarusz), Cuban women were primarily placed in textile factories. Thus, the Hungarian government, in accordance with its own conservative
gender turn in the 1980s, allocated Cuban workers so as to reflect the division
between 'male work' and 'female work', which was further mapped onto the division of the economy into high-priority and low-priority sectors.[49]

---

[45] Valentin Maier, 'Foreign Students Enrolled in the Medicine and Pharmacy Higher Education in
Romania (1975–1989)', *Clujul Medical*, 89/2 (2016), 307–12, 308.
[46] Smirnova and Rillon, 'Quand des Maliennes', 339.   [47] Information from ibid., 343–4.
[48] James Mark and Bálint Tolmár, 'From Heroes Square to the Textile Factory: Encountering Cuba
in Socialist Hungary 1959–1990' (unpublished manuscript).
[49] Joanna Goven, *The Gendered Foundations of Hungarian Socialism: State, Society, and the Anti-
Politics of Anti-Feminism, 1948–1990*, PhD dissertation (UC Berkeley, 1993).

Learning from the State-Socialist (Semi)Periphery

Temporary migrations of school children did not end with the Greek, Korean, and Vietnamese children in the 1950s. They reappear in the late 1970s in Cuba, and throughout the 1980s in the GDR and Czechoslovakia. As before, the projects pursued joint political and educational goals. The Czechoslovak scheme, the planning for which started in late 1985, was modelled on a similar undertaking by the GDR, which hosted some eighty young (four- to six-year-old) Namibian children in the village of Bellin, starting in late 1979. The children arrived with several Namibian women, who, together with their East German colleagues were to care for them, and simultaneously obtain training to be kindergarten teachers.[50] Similarly, the South West African People's Organization (SWAPO) asked for Czechoslovakia to provide first elementary and then secondary education to fifty to sixty Namibian children.[51] The educational goals included the objective that the children 'become acquainted with the cultural, historical, and revolutionary traditions of *their nation*, and *not lose the sense of belonging to their motherland*.'[52] To help with this goal, the children were to be accompanied by African educators (who, however, unlike in the GDR case, were to be men) who would be responsible for civic education classes taught in the children's native tongue.[53] There were other adjustments made to the curriculum to cater to the needs of the children, who were to return home upon graduating from high school. One was that instead of taking Russian as a foreign language, which was compulsory for all Czechoslovak students, they were to learn English. Finally, the Namibian children's fifth grade geography was to have an expanded focus on Africa.

Similar, but much larger in scope, was the GDR project of the *Schule der Freundschaft*.[54] The school was opened at the request of the Mozambican government and educated primarily Mozambican children, more than 4,000 of them by the end of 1981. The state-building focus is very clear in this project as the Mozambican state requested general education for younger kids and vocational training for older children, and, in addition, asked the GDR to build technical schools for another 700–1,000 students in Mozambique.[55] The latter request was not unusual and constituted another major form state-socialist mobility: the temporary stays of experts, academic and otherwise, abroad. Already in 1957, Egypt invited a group of seven Soviet professors to teach at the Suez Oil Institute.

---

[50] Jason Verber, 'True to the Politics of Frelimo? Teaching Socialism at the *Schule der Freundschaft*, 1981–1990', in Quinn Slobodian (ed.), *Comrades of Color: East Germany in the Cold War World* (New York: Berghahn Books, 2015).

[51] Czech National Archive (NA): Fond: KSČ, Ústřední výbor 1945–1989, předsednictvo, 1981–1986, sv. P142/85, k info 3.

[52] Ibid. (NA), italics mine.

[53] In Czech, it was literally called patriotic education (*vlastenecká výchova*).

[54] Verber, 'True to the Politics of Frelimo?'   [55] Ibid.

Between 1960 and 1964, the USSR established the Polytechnic Institute of Conakry, in Guinea, with an enrolment capacity of 300 students per year. In Mali, between 1963 and 1966, the Soviets founded the Higher Administrative School of Bamako with a capacity of 250 students per year, as well as a school for medical assistants and a centre for agricultural training. Responding to a request from the Algerian government, the USSR also created the African Centre of Hydrocarbons and Textiles in Boumerdès, in 1964, with a sizeable community of Soviet professors.[56]

If Czechoslovakia looked to the GDR for logistical tips on how to set up its school for Namibian children, the GDR, in the planning stages for the school for Mozambican youth, looked to Cuba.[57] This is because, between 1959 and 1981, Cubans built no fewer than fifty-six secondary schools on the Island of Youth (La Isla de la Juventud) off the coast of Cuban mainland, and 37.7% of the student body (or 10,468 students) there was non-Cuban in 1982.[58] Some schools specific-ally served students from particular countries: for example, in 1987, there were seven Angolan schools educating 3,581 students, and four Mozambican schools in which 2,231 children were enrolled.[59] It is here that we find the prototype of the joint local–foreign teaching staff model, which the GDR and Czechoslovakia copied. Mozambican students on La Isla de la Juventud were taught by both Cuban and Mozambican teachers, and the latter taught them—exactly as in the *Schule der Freundschaft*—the Portuguese language, Mozambican history, geog-raphy with a focus on Africa generally and Mozambique specifically, and political education.[60] So here was a diffusion of institutional practices not, as one might expect, from the state-socialist core to the state-socialist periphery, but in the opposite direction: from the periphery to the core. Thus, one of the remarkable features of state-socialist migrations is that some of the non-European socialist countries—Cuba most prominently—were simultaneously both recipients and providers of educational and professional training. Cuba had a number of its citizens employed and educated in various European state-socialist countries—in 1983, for instance, there were 362 Cubans who earned their PhDs in the Soviet Union, 126 in Czechoslovakia, 95 in the GDR, 49 in Bulgaria, 22 in Poland, 19 in Hungary and 4 in Romania.[61] But at the same time, between 1961 and 2004, Cuba provided both secondary and university education to 30,000 sub-Saharan Africans (of whom 8,053 were Angolans and 3,764 Mozambicans).[62] Similarly, Vietnam sent tens of thousands of its students and workers to be trained in European state-socialist

[56] Katsakioris, 'Creating a Socialist Intelligentsia', 262.

[57] Verber, 'True to the Politics of Frelimo?'.

[58] Elena Fiddian-Qasmiyeh, 'Education, Migration and Internationalism: Situating Muslim Middle Eastern and North African Students in Cuba', *The Journal of North African Studies*, 15/2 (2010), 137–55, 139.

[59] Ibid., 140.   [60] Dorsch, 'Black or Red Atlantic?', 298.

[61] Menja Holz, 'The Cuban Experience in East Germany: Academic Migration from 1960 to 2000', *Bulletin of Latin American Research*, 33/4 (2014), 473.

[62] Dorsch, 'Black or Red Atlantic?'.

countries, but it also sent thousands of its own experts to train technicians and scientists in Africa.[63]

Another remarkable instance of a state-socialist educational migration project that occurred entirely without any input from the camp's European core, and in which students were accompanied by their own educational staff to a foreign country was the Chinese-Vietnamese educational assistance cooperation.[64] This programme was unique in that the host country, China, provided land, facilities and funding, but the curriculum and the *entire* teaching and administrative staff was Vietnamese. In essence, Vietnam relocated entire teaching facilities to China to continue educating its youth in times of war. A central campus was established in Nanning, the capital of Guangxi province, for several Vietnamese educational institutions, including the Pedagogical Institute, the Science University, and several secondary schools. The undertaking was launched in 1951 and comprised 2,000 people, both students and staff. The programme was expanded to include an additional 3,000 or so military students. In 1953, the DRV Education Ministry added the School for Children and Adolescents of Lushan, a nine-year general education school, in which 200 Vietnamese teachers were in charge of some 1,000 students. In 1957, two more were added: a school in Nanning City, Guangxi province, with a total of 3,000 people including students, and teaching and administrative staff, and another school in Guilin City, also in Guangxi Province, with a total of a 1,000 people. In 1965, the Vietnamese government again asked its Chinese counterpart for this form of cooperation and their agreement paved the way for project '92', referring to 2 September, the day when Vietnam proclaimed its independence in 1945. By December 1967, three schools were constructed and became part of the Vietnamese Southern School District, which eventually included seven schools, and served as a place of study and work to more than 2,000 students, teachers and administrators. Many of the students were children of cadres and party members killed during the Resistance Wars against the French and the Americans, from both South and North Vietnam. Despite various logistical difficulties, the system remained in place until mid-1975, that is, the conclusion of the American War.[65] This scheme exemplifies particularly clearly that state-socialist governments systematically used educational mobility as a policy for development, or in this case even self-preservation. It, therefore, makes sense that in the same year, 1966, when the DRV government signed the agreement on launching the second phase of relocating its educational facilities to China, it also approached several East-Central European governments with a request that they provide vocational and on-the-job training for its citizens.[66]

[63] Susan Bayly, 'Vietnamese Intellectuals', 320–244.

[64] Olga Dror, 'Education and Politics in Wartime: School Systems in North and South Vietnam, 1965–1975', *The Journal of Cold War Studies*, 20/3 (2018), 57–113.

[65] All information is from ibid, op. cit.

[66] NA, uncatalogued, Letter from the Foreign Ministry to the State Commission for Economic and Scientific and Technical Cooperation, 'Zaškolování občanů VDR', dated 10 June 1966.

State-Socialist Cosmopolitanism and Transnationalism

As we have just seen, in state-socialist migratory projects care was taken to ensure that key components of national belonging and identity be cultivated while abroad. This happened not only as a result of the formal institutional features put in place precisely for that reason (teachers and staff from the country of origin and adapted curricula), but also informally and organically, such as when African students in Cuban schools started to 'reflect on their own national identity' as they observed 'the Cubans'...strong patriotism'.[67] Yet, at the same time, an opposite, and complementary, process was also taking place. State-socialist migrations also produced what Gertrud Hüwelmeier aptly called *socialist cosmopolitans*, or people who 'experienced a kind of global socialist life and were engaged in forms of a cosmopolitan sociability by creating overseas friendship relations, economic ties and networks of exchange and reciprocity'.[68] Susan Bayly offers a brilliant ethnographic portrayal of socialist cosmopolitanism when recounting the life story of Professor Le, a Vietnamese woman who received her university education in the Soviet Union and later found herself as an expert in Algeria. When feeling homesick, 'what made all the difference were her *Russian-speaking* colleagues, especially two *Poles*, with whom she discussed books and music, and visited local archaeological sites. Thanks to them, she says, she was able to carry on living a proper intellectual's life'.[69] Somewhat along similar lines, 'Africans who studied in the USSR...learned Russian as an international and inter-ethnic *lingua franca*'.[70] International marriages were a more concrete expression of cosmopolitanism. Thus, in a group of forty Moroccans, thirty married Soviet partners.[71] Interestingly, high rates of intermarriage have been reported even in cases where the general relationship with the local population was described as rocky, such as in the case of Syrian students in Czechoslovakia: one third of the 105 who graduated from universities in 1966 married Czechoslovak women.[72] Finally, an education in Eastern Europe could be a springboard to a transnational professional career that transcended the Cold War divide. This was the case of Nigerian scholar Omotoso Eluyemi, the Director-General of Nigeria's National Commission for Museums and Monuments, who, upon first graduating, in 1968,

---

[67] Dorsch, 'Black or Red Atlantic?', 300.

[68] Gertrud Hüwelmeier, 'Socialist Cosmopolitanism Meets Global Pentecostalism: Charismatic Christianity among Vietnamese Migrants after the Fall of the Berlin Wall', *Ethnic and Racial Studies*, 34/3 (2011), 440.

[69] Bayly, 'Vietnamese Intellectuals', 334–339, italics mine.

[70] Anna Siim-Moskovitina and Nikolay Dobronravin, 'Des élites africaines entre deux mondes. Impact de la formation en URSS ou poids du milieu social d'origine?', in Saint Martin et al. (eds.), *Étudier à l'Est*, 281.

[71] Ghellab, '"Les meilleures années de notre vie"'.

[72] Daniela Hannova, 'Arab Students inside the Soviet Bloc: A Case Study on Czechoslovakia during the 1950s and 60s', *European Scientific Journal*, 2 (2014), 375, 377.

from the Lomonosov Moscow State University with a degree in archaeology, proceeded to study at the University of Birmingham in the United Kingdom, only to return for his PhD to the Academy of Sciences in Moscow.[73]

Technical Expertise and Propaganda

Eluyemi's trajectory not only illustrates the cosmopolitanism engendered by state-socialist migrations; it also indirectly speaks to the disputes over the quality of training provided by state-socialist universities. That is to say, if, as appears to be the case, Eluyemi was able to move smoothly back and forth between Second and First World universities, and then go on and have an illustrious career in his home country, the education he received in Moscow must have been at the very least adequate. Oral histories suggest as much. This is how Senegalese students, for example, talked about their education: 'Education was excellent insofar as that the professors made themselves available. They would even come to your place for tutoring. They were very available.'[74] A Beninese (female) student in Bulgaria also appreciated the conditions for studying and the accessibility of professors: 'We had everything we needed to be able to devote ourselves to our studies... equipment, books... we could meet with professors without any limitations or problems... The difference between what we had there and in Benin is that the theory was always accompanied by practice at the same time.'[75] Latin American students' recollections echo those of the African students: 'From the first day, everything was different from what I was used to in Bolivia, but in a positive sense. Teachers took care of each of us personally, they were excellent academically, we got any help and assistance we needed.'[76]

One reason why this issue is difficult to assess is that both sides used disputes over superiority of their respective educational systems as weapons in Cold War propaganda. To wit: a 1965 review of a book about fictionalized experiences of foreign students at Eastern European universities written by a Black American activist Jan Carew published in *The New York Times*. The *Times* review, which claimed to be describing the content of the book, made it seem like the life of these students was nothing short of hell. 'The review, however, gave simply an incorrect impression of Carew's book' as it ignored completely 'the fact that the book is also full of positive remarks about the Soviet Union, about great teachers

---

[73] Siim-Moskovitina and Dobronravin, 'Des élites africaines', 285.

[74] Boubacar Niane and Manétou Ndiaye, 'La langue russe, un palimpseste pour les Sénégalais formés en URSS/Russie?', in Saint Martin et al. (eds.), *Étudier à l'Est*, 254.

[75] Élieth P. Eyebiyi, 'La formation des cadres béninois dans les pays de l'Est. Expériences biographiques en URSS et en Bulgarie entre 1980 et 1994', in Saint Martin et al. (eds.), *Étudier à l'Est*, 237.

[76] Tobias Rupprecht, *Soviet Internationalism after Stalin: Interaction and Exchange between the USSR and Latin America during the Cold War* (Cambridge: CUP, 2015), 208.

and acquaintances and about the hospitality and solidarity towards people from Third World countries.[77] Thus, just as we do not take self-congratulatory proclamations of state-socialist governments about their successes at face value, we should be similarly circumspect when evaluating their contemporary western critiques.

Beyond conscious distortions in the service of propaganda, however, there is another issue that makes comparative evaluations difficult: the issue of framing and criteria of what constitutes good education. Specifically, one of the frequent lines of criticism was the dismissal of Soviet and Eastern European educational systems and institutions as sites of and tools for indoctrination. However, explicitly political classes, such as courses on Marxism-Leninism, were optional for foreign students in the Soviet Union, and indeed, most did not attend them—in universities in Moscow and Leningrad, participation was somewhere between 25 and 50%.[78] Indeed, some of the revolutionary African governments were quite displeased with the situation. A Ghanaian official, for example, berated representatives of the Soviet Education Ministry in 1965 thus: 'It is inconceivable for us that in the country of Marxism and of socialism our students are exempted from the study of social and political disciplines and that often they know much less about Marxism than our students in Manchester...You say you give the students the right to decide whether to study Marxism or not. We do not agree with this. And we are not interested in what the students prefer.'[79] In part as a response to such complaints, Soviet universities added political courses to foreign students' curricula in 1968. A Moroccan engineering student at a Soviet university summarized the situation: 'As far as politics is concerned, there was no pressure, no obligation. Of course they taught you Marx, political economy, but it was very light, it was not the core of the studies.'[80]

If we want to understand the state-socialist educational and migratory projects, the insistence on maintaining a dichotomy between 'ideology' and 'technical expertise' is unproductive. That is because '[e]ducating professionals and experts to drive rapid economic development was a priority, and political formation was in part shaped by these commitments. Socialism was presented as a superior way of identifying and developing expertise through its universal and more authentically meritocratic models of public education, to in turn contribute to development in a more egalitarian society.'[81] In other words, the issue was not that politics was absent from the technical education foreign students were receiving; indeed 'the Soviet program both incorporated an overt dimension of political formation, and explicitly politicized the development project in terms of overcoming colonial

---

[77] Ibid., 191–2.   [78] Katsakioris, 'Creating a Socialist Intelligentsia', 268.
[79] Ibid., 268–9.   [80] Ghellab, '"Les meilleures années de notre vie"', 198.
[81] Griffiths and Cardona, 'Education for Social Transformation', 237.

and capitalist underdevelopment.'[82] Socialist universities understood technical training as an intrinsic part of a *political* economy, which therefore required that explicit attention be paid to the political ramifications of technical expertise. In other words, in the state-socialist framing, *a lack of* political dimension would have *undermined* technical expertise. The two were not understood to be opposites, but constituent parts of each other.

Indirect evidence suggests that, at the very least, the political dimension did not detract from technical expertise, the contemporary claims to the contrary notwithstanding. In 1968, *The Ghana News*, issued by the Embassy of Ghana in the United States, printed the following: 'The Ghana Government is aware of the current public interest and concern over the case of the first batch of Ghanaian doctors trained in the Soviet Union who returned to Ghana a few months ago. It became obvious shortly after the return of these doctors that their knowledge and skill did not fit them to shoulder adequately all the responsibilities that a young doctor in Ghana is of necessity called upon to discharge.' To what extent this was actually the case is difficult to evaluate directly. However, we can make some indirect inferences when we juxtapose this account to an Oxfam case study,[83] which reported that, in 2014,

Soviet-trained doctors still comprise[d] 11.3 per cent of all permanently registered doctors in Ghana... All of the doctors interviewed... shared the view that the Soviet programme played a crucial role in averting a catastrophic shortage in the system... there was a time when almost all the regional hospitals were run by Soviet-trained doctors... The scheme was thus able to reduce the impact of migration by domestically trained staff. Nevertheless, the scale of migration was such that, even with the Soviet-trained doctors, the doctor-to-population ratio in Ghana actually decreased between 1965 and 1989, from 1:13,740 to 1:20,460. *Without the scholarship scheme, the human resources catastrophe would have been even larger.*

While the report does not explicitly speak to the quality of these doctors' training, it certainly suggests that they are competent and have been performing absolutely crucial services in Ghana's healthcare system. To Ghanaian doctors, we can add 43% of Moroccan pharmacists who have been trained in Eastern European countries,[84] or the fact that, in 1988, 30% of professors at the three largest universities

---

[82] Ibid., 238.

[83] Jeremy Holt, Samuel Newhouse and Daria Ukhova, *Scholarships and the Healthcare Human resources Crisis: A case study of Soviet and Russian scholarships for medical students from Ghana* (Oxfam International, December 2014), italics mine, thanks to Bogdan C. Iacob for pointing me to this text.

[84] Kamal Mellakh, 'La formation des pharmaciens marocains dans les pays de l'Est. Enjeux et expériences', in Saint Martin et al. (eds.), *Étudier à l'Est*.

in Hanoi had been trained in the Soviet Union,[85] in addition to those trained other state-socialist countries. The sheer numbers and the importance of the positions that these experts and professionals occupied implicitly but definitively puts to rest the allegations about a lack of technical rigor in Eastern European state-socialist educational systems.

Sometimes the problems that did arise seem to have been caused not so much by too much Marxism in state-socialist higher education, but too little of it. Specifically, by the movement away from internationalist assistance and toward marketization of their higher education. This primarily took the form of the recruitment of self-financing students, especially from wealthy Middle Eastern countries. Thus, for instance, in 1983, a series of articles was published in the Jordanian press complaining about the quality of teaching practices in Romania and about the low level of the medicine and pharmacy higher education (MPHE) of Jordanian graduates of Romanian universities.[86] However, the steps that were agreed upon by the representatives of the two countries to remedy the situation made it clear that the root of the problem was Jordanian students' performances, not the Romanian curriculum or instruction. At the time, Romania, like several other state-socialist countries, started to rely heavily on the convertible-currency income generated by self-financing foreign students. In Yugoslavia, at its peak, in 1987, the 'self-financing international students...made up approximately 97% of all international students...and roughly 5% of total student enrolments at the country's institutions of higher education.'[87] The marketization of higher education offered to foreign students was one of the ways the state-socialist countries dealt with the slowdown in their economic growth that started in the mid-1970s.[88] Arguably, this move away from socialist and internationalist commitments was counterproductive. The desire to pocket as much hard currency as possible incentivized universities to be lenient when it came to enrolling and passing academically-poor-but-paying-customer foreign students, and so also became detrimental to universities' reputations.

Second World Seen from a Third World Vantage Point

More importantly, this partial withdrawal from commitment to the socialist project undermined the very reasons that made state-socialist East-Central European

---

[85]   Buu Hoan, 'Soviet Economic Aid to Vietnam', *Contemporary Southeast Asia*, 12/4 (1991), 367–8.

[86]   Bogdan C. Iacob, 'A Babel in Bucharest: "Third World" Students in Romania, 1960s-1980s', *Cahiers du monde russe* (forthcoming 2022), 12.

[87]   Wright, 'Between the Market and Solidarity', 2.

[88]   Ivan Szelenyi and Balazs Szelenyi, 'Why Socialism Failed: Toward a Theory of System Breakdown—Causes of Disintegration of East European State Socialism', *Theory and Society*, 23/2 (1994), 211–231.

countries attractive destinations for migrants from postcolonial countries in the first place. Citizens of various Latin American countries pursuing higher education in the Soviet Union recalled that 'they could easily afford the inexpensive tickets for cinemas and sports stadiums. Theatres, operas, ballets and museums, affordable only for the upper classes in their home countries, were cheap, too.'[89] Not unlike Mr Tuan from the beginning of this chapter, who while working his blue-collar job in a Czechoslovak factory was also able to became an amateur photographer, a Moroccan student took full advantage of all that was available to him: 'When I arrived in the USSR, I played the lute, but no one there played the lute. But one [female] musician, who helped me a lot, suggested that I play the piano. I even bought a piano for my room. I did theatre at school, I acted and I sang. As soon as I arrived in Kyiv, I immediately found out where I could pursue my study of piano. I even obtained a certificate at the end of my six years. The culture over there, it's really good!'[90] At the same time, the temporary migrants from the Third World read the daily realities they encountered in the Second World in nuanced and contextual ways. A former student from Chile noted: 'Everyone in the Soviet Union lived the living standard of the middle class in my country. There was a shortage of some products, but there was no poverty.'[91] The main gist of this assessment is strikingly similar to that of a Somali man who studied civil engineering in Czechoslovakia in the early 1960s. When asked whether he thought that he might have learned more had he pursued his degree elsewhere, he replied: 'It is true that much of your new construction lacks courage, ambition, colour, and imagination. What you are concerned with is making sure that all people have access to a good home as fast as possible. And we [in Somalia] will face the same issue. So that's why I can learn a lot of things here.'[92] What makes both of these assessments compelling is that they eschew the oneupmanship that was characteristic of the Cold War discourse. From the vantage point of Third World observers, the comparison between the 'first two worlds' was not seen as an invitation to give a definitive answer as to who was 'better' and who 'worse', but rather as a consideration of trade-offs whose meaning and significance depended on the countries' individual socio-economic contexts.

In part, Third World actors' vantage point was shaped by the differences in the material wealth between their home countries and their East-Central European hosts. Thus, a Vietnamese man who arrived in Czechoslovakia as a student in the 1980s was stunned when he was given a brown paper bag with 'cold dinner' (i.e., sandwiches) that included five hard-boiled eggs when, in Vietnam, an entire family would have had to share two eggs.[93] Seen from the point of view of the global

[89] Rupprecht, *Soviet Internationalism*, 210.
[90] Ghellab, "'Les meilleures années de notre vie'", 197.
[91] Rupprecht, *Soviet Internationalism*, 120.
[92] Jindřich Lion, *Od Limpopa k Vltavě* (Prague, 1963) cited in Holečková, *Univerzita* 17, 37.
[93] Interview, Prague, 23 April 2010.

periphery, the European state-socialist countries were desirable destinations both because of their greater material wealth and because they were seen as sites of successful modernization campaigns. Like Mr Tuan, other Vietnamese who worked in Czechoslovakia in the 1970s and 1980s talk about having been struck upon arrival by it being 'a very modern country' that produced 'industrial products of high quality', exhibited 'social order', enjoyed 'high standards of living', and boasted 'modern transport'.[94] Vietnamese workers in the GDR expressed identical sentiments, commenting on GDR's wealth compared with Vietnam, its advanced and functional infrastructure, its high standard of living, and its clean and orderly streets.[95]

The Third World observers' vantage point was also shaped by the political and historical trajectories of their homelands. The effect of a collective historical experience is evident, for instance, in the framing used by Angolans and Mozambicans who chose to take up jobs in the GDR. These migrant workers contrasted the state-socialist temporary labour migration experience with the connotations that labour migration held for their parents, namely the association of migration with 'forced transportation of slaves to the Americas, Europe and Asia, and of historical ties between European colonial powers, including Germany, and sub-Saharan Africa, based to a large extent on labour exploitation'.[96] By contrast, African workers described their labour migrations into the GDR not just as voluntary but also as 'the best possible choice for a better personal future'. Indeed, the Mozambicans preferred the state-socialist semi-peripheral location over the traditional migrant destinations: 'My father went to South Africa, my uncles, my grandfather. All the men in my family went to South Africa, I went to [East] Germany. [East] Germany was definitely better because I amassed much more in a shorter time. My cousin left before me to South Africa and we returned at the same time, only I had been able to afford much more than him. The work in the mines is also harder and paid worse.'[97] As far as these migrant workers were concerned, '[t]his was another Europe, but also another paradise.'[98] Moroccan students also read Soviets' attitudes toward them through their collective experience as former colonial subjects: 'The Soviets are not like the French.

---

[94] Tereza Kušníráková, 'Vztah vietnamských navrátilců předlistopadové imigrace k československému státu a jeho společnosti', *Český lid*, 99/1 (2012), 45-66.

[95] Alena Alamgir and Christina Schwenkel, 'From Altruistic Assistance to National Self-Interest: Vietnamese Labor Migration Into CMEA Countries' in James Mark, Steffi Marung and Artemy M. Kalinovsky (eds.), *Alternative Globalizations: Eastern Europe and the Postcolonial World* (Bloomington, IN: Indiana University Press, 2020), 103.

[96] Marcia C. Schenck, 'From Luanda and Maputo to Berlin: Uncovering Angolan and Mozambican Migrants' Motives to Move to the German Democratic Republic (1979–1990)', *African Economic History*, 44 (2016), 207.

[97] Ibid., 211.

[98] Andrew Hardy, 'From a Floating World: Emigration to Europe From Post-War Vietnam', *Asian and Pacific Migration Journal*, 11/4 (2002), 463–84.

They are welcoming, humble, they encourage you. We did well.'[99] In short, from the vantage point of the Third World observers, the countries of the socialist camp were places that made development—of individuals and through them of states—possible.

There is an additional aspect that affects whether the Third-to-Second World migration projects, both educational and labour-based, are assessed—and remembered—as successful. That is, the trajectories of former migrants after the return back to their home countries, which depended, in turn, on the political and economic situation in the country of origin *both* at the time of departure *and* later. The contrast between the Ethiopians and Vietnamese is instructive here. Ethiopian graduates of *Western European* universities opened restaurants and cafes bearing the names of the cities in which they studied, such as 'la Parisienne', 'London café', 'Restaurant Amsterdam', 'Oslo café' or 'Swiss café'. Yet, there was not a single establishment in Addis Ababa carrying the name of a Russian or Eastern European city despite the fact that Ethiopians studied in state-socialist countries as well.[100] By contrast, in Hanoi, there were no fewer than four Czech-Slovak beer pubs and restaurants (three bearing names evoking Czech beer and landscape directly—GoldMalt, Gambrinus and PraGold, the fourth one has a Vietnamese name, Hoa Viên), all founded by Vietnamese who had spent considerable periods of time in Czechoslovakia as students, vocational school trainees or workers.[101] Abye explains the 'collective amnesia'—which extends so far as some of the Ethiopians deleting the degrees and credentials acquired in Eastern Europe from their CVs, and not socializing with the people they met during their stays there (in a sharp contrast to the Vietnamese who maintain incredibly strong networks)—by the fact that their educational stays were arranged by the *Derg* military government, which was overthrown and whose policies have been renounced. Intriguingly, this collective amnesia does not extend to Cuba, which also educated Ethiopians during the *Derg* era (and continues to do so to this day). The contrast between how Angolans and Mozambicans remember their temporary labour migrations to the GDR is less dramatic but demonstrates well the importance of the current political situation. While Angolans see their identity as former GDR workers as a private matter, the Mozambicans use it to organize themselves and push for their rights (primarily, pensions accrued to them through their work in Germany but not paid out to them by the Mozambican government).[102] The more explicitly socialist the home country was when students and trainee workers returned, the more upward mobility they would experience.

[99] Ghellab, '"Les meilleures années de notre vie"', 196.
[100] Tassé Abye, 'Les élites éthiopiennes formées en URSS et dans les pays du bloc socialiste: une visibilité éphémère?', *Cahiers d'études africaines*, LVII (2), 226 (2017), 289–311.
[101] Alena Alamgir, *Socialist Internationalism at Work: Changes in the Czechoslovak-Vietnamese Labor Exchange Program, 1967-1989* (Ph.D. Dissertation, Rutgers University, 2014), 3–4.
[102] Schenck, 'A Chronology of Nostalgia'.

Vietnam is exemplary in this regard: at least six members of the Vietnamese cabinet obtained their university degrees in state-socialist Czechoslovakia and have occupied such high-profile posts as deputy prime minister, foreign affairs minister, and finance minister. Numerous senior government officials were likewise awarded their degrees in East Germany, including a deputy prime minister and a minister of education.[103] When that was not the case, mid-level technical and managerial careers would be more typical, exemplified best perhaps by the Moroccan pharmacists.[104]

The Scope of the Projects and Conclusion

By the end of 1989, the Soviet Union educated 39,675 Latin American students (26,439 of whom were Cubans), 39,223 students from Arab countries, 21,615 from the rest of non-Communist Asia, and 36,146 from sub-Saharan Africa. Of these, 88% earned higher degrees and 12% attended secondary technical schools.[105] The statistics available for other state-socialist countries are less complete, but they provide us with at least a partial sense of the extent of educational mobility. Romania, for its part, graduated over 23,500 foreign students between 1974 and 1988.[106] In Yugoslavia, the numbers of foreign students grew at a breathtaking pace: while in the school year 1951/52, there were only four foreign students enrolled at Yugoslav universities, by 1959, there were 229 citizens from forty-two different countries. By 1970, the number rose to 6,000 people, only to reach 13,000 students hailing from one hundred countries by the mid-1980s, the majority from the Middle East and Africa.[107] Czechoslovakia offered roughly 500 scholarships to students from developing countries annually,[108] and among them, the Vietnamese comprised the largest group. Some of these students studied at institutions set up specifically for foreign students, such as the People's Friendship University (PFU), which became also known as Patrice Lumumba University, in Moscow. Modelled on it was the University of 17th November (USL) in Prague,

[103] Alena K. Alamgir and Christina Schwenkel, 'From Socialist Assistance to National Self-Interest: Vietnamese Labor Migration into CMEA Countries', in Mark et al. (eds.), *Alternative Globalizations*, 118.

[104] Mellakh, 'La formation des pharmaciens marocains'.

[105] Constantin Katsakioris, 'Burden or Allies? Third World Students and Internationalist Duty through Soviet Eyes', paper presented at the workshop 'Racism in the "Land of People's Friendship": Racisms under State Socialism's "Internationalism" and its Aftermath' (Södertörn University, Sweden, 28–9 January 2016).

[106] Computed from data included in Maier, 'Foreign Students', 307–12.

[107] Nemanja Radonjic, 'A Socialist Shaping of the Postcolonial Elite: Students from Africa in Socialist Yugoslavia', unpublished manuscript.

[108] Barbora Buzássyová, *Fenomén Univerzity 17. novembra: Zahraniční študenti na Slovensku v rokoch 1961—1974*, BA thesis (Comenius University, Bratislava, Slovakia, 2017), 21.

and the Gamal Abdel Nasser Foreign Students Institute in Sofia. The founding of these universities expressed the commitment that the host countries were making to the education of students from developing countries. This was clearly conveyed, among many other proclamations, by the speech given by Nikita Khrushchev at the university's opening ceremony, when he stated that the Soviet Union 'sympathized with the aims of Asian, African, and Latin American peoples to develop their economies and to train their own engineers, agronomists, doctors, and scientists'.[109] The message was heard loud and clear around the world, as the initial number of applicants was enormous: 43,500 applied, the admission committee invited 1,200 to Moscow, and half would later travel home, their return journey paid for by Moscow.[110] Nonetheless, while the symbolic meaning of these special universities was great, the vast majority of foreign students pursued their degrees at the European state-socialist countries' regular universities.

Compared to student migratory projects in which a large number of postcolonial countries as well as all European state-socialist countries took part, labour migrations were much more limited in scope and concerned (if we are to talk about more than just a few dozen individuals) only four major postcolonial sending countries: Vietnam (most prominently), Cuba, Mozambique and Angola. Between 1967 and 1989, Vietnamese headed primarily to four Comecon countries: about 103,000 to the USSR, about 72,000 to the GDR, some 50,000 to Czechoslovakia, and probably about 17,000 to Bulgaria.[111] Additionally, between 1978 and 1989, Czechoslovakia employed some 23,160 Cubans.[112] The GDR's overseas foreign worker schemes were more extensive: 'In 1988 alone, more than 78,000 [workers] from Vietnam, Mozambique, Angola and Cuba' were employed in GDR enterprises.[113] Of these, roughly 20,000 were Mozambicans, who worked in the GDR between 1979 and 1990;[114] Angolans started arriving after March 1985.[115] In April 1980, Hungary, too, signed an agreement that launched a labour exchange programme with Cuba.[116] Its structure bore striking resemblance to the Vietnamese labour programme: hundreds of young Cubans were expected to receive a six-month vocational training, which would be followed by a three and a half year placement in Hungarian factories.

[109] Katsakioris, 'Creating a Socialist Intelligentsia', 260.

[110] Rupprecht, Soviet Internationalism, 199.

[111] Alamgir and Schwenkel, 'From Socialist Assistance', 108–9.

[112] Petra Boušková, 'Pracovní migrace cizinců v České republice v 70. až 90. Letech', in Národní diskuse u kulatého stolu na téma vztahu mezi komunitami 19. února 1998, sborník dokumentů, 36.

[113] Howell, 'The End of an Era', 310.

[114] Eric Allina, 'Between Sozialismus and Socialismo: African Workers and Public Authority in the German Democratic Republic', in Mahua Sarkar (ed.), Work out of Place (Berlin: De Gruyter Oldenbourg, 2018), 87.

[115] Marcia Schenck, 'Between Hammer, Machete, and Kalashnikov: Contract Labor Migration from Angola and Mozambique to East Germany, 1979–1990', EuropeNow 15 (2018).

[116] Mark and Tolmár, 'From Heroes Square'.

The specificity of labour migration in the state-socialist context is its close connection to, and partial overlap with, educational migration. In contrast to capitalist guest worker schemes, the Eastern European temporary migration programmes were not originally envisioned or articulated as a strategy for economic growth in the receiving countries. Rather, they were framed as acts of solidarity and fraternal aid. If labour schemes in Western Europe were conceived as a means of rebuilding post-war Europe, and hence the *receiving* countries, labour migration schemes in Eastern Europe were originally conceived of as projects revolving around the training of labour and thus the means of rebuilding the *sending* countries.[117] Technological transfer became central to this effort to populate newly independent socialist countries with skilled workers and usher in socialist modernity.[118] Thus, in the mid- to late 1960s, at the initiative of Vietnamese government officials, schemes for vocational training of technicians and blue-collar workers were devised and implemented in the USSR, GDR, Czechoslovakia, and Bulgaria. This training, which consisted of both educational and factory-floor paid work, constituted both a structural-institutional and a conceptual bridge between educational temporary migrations and contract-work-based labour migrations, which appeared throughout East-Central Europe and the Soviet Union in the 1980s. It was a structural-institutional bridge in that: the receiving state relied on the institutional knowledge it had accumulated through the administration of the student migrations, and before that, the migration of war-refugee children, when implementing the apprenticeship form of work-training migration. Since the training either took place in factories or was followed by 'practice labour' in local enterprises, during which the trainee workers received regular wages and were incorporated into standard production processes, the apprenticeship projects, which were defined mainly in educational terms, nonetheless, constituted the earliest form of state-sponsored labour migration into state-socialist Europe. For ideological reasons, the administrators of the temporary labour migration schemes, from both the sending and receiving countries, hung tenaciously to the notion that some elements of learning and education were present in the employment of temporary foreign migrant workers. This remained the case when the formal apprenticeships were no longer part of the contracts. This was even true in the cases of Cubans, Mozambicans and Angolans, who neither went through apprenticeship model nor attended vocational schools. Nonetheless, GDR state planners still talked about 'an ambitious economic, political, and cultural program that served the interests of all partners', one whose 'objective was *to train the future vanguard* of Mozambique and Angola's working class'.[119]

---

[117] Alena Alamgir, *Socialist Internationalism at Work*, 38–40.

[118] See Katherine Pence and Paul Betts (eds.), *Socialist Modern: East German Everyday Culture and Politics* (Ann Arbor: University of Michigan Press, 2008).

[119] Schenck, 'Between Hammer, Machete, and Kalashnikov', italics mine.

Yet, an out-and-out cynicism is not warranted since at least some of the workers themselves conceptualized their stays along roughly similar lines (Mr Tuan being one example).

In a parallel fashion, in the 1980s, both the educational and labour migratory schemes made a decisive turn toward marketization, that is to say, a withdrawal from socialist and internationalist commitments. In both cases, the move amounted to what a Slavic proverb describes as 'sawing off the branch on which one is sitting'. When it comes to educational migrations, Yugoslavia exemplifies this perhaps in the starkest terms: 'In their attempt to compensate for funding deficits by recourse to the market, Yugoslav faculties...had inadvertently priced out Yugoslavia's own scholarship students from developing countries, thereby undermining a long-standing feature of Yugoslavia's foreign policy of non-alignment.'[120] In the case of labour migratory schemes, Czechoslovakia is the paragon: having eliminated the vocational school-based apprenticeship training along with most of the language training for which the Czechoslovak state used to pay, Vietnamese workers at first appeared to have become a bargain-priced solution to the endemic labour shortages. The 'bargain', however, came with the unanticipated costs of industrial unrest. As the Czechoslovak state started to commodify Vietnamese workers, that is, to treat them primarily as a convenient source of 'fully mobile' labour power, the workers responded with resistance, often in the form of strikes, usually protesting their wages and compulsory monetary transfer (a roughly 10% cut the Vietnamese government took from their wages). The events of 1989–90 meant either sudden and complete termination of the projects, or else a drive toward commodification of foreign labour on steroids. With one exception: Cuba, which continued to engage in internationalist educational and medical assistance. By the year 2000, Cuba had educated some 35,000 students from thirty-seven Third World countries and over the last half century, it has signed agreements on receiving students in Cuba with the governments of *practically all* sub-Saharan countries.[121] It thus, for now, carries on the torch of internationalist transnational engagements whose purpose is (economic) state-building carried out through migratory projects that are brokered and managed by the state, privilege the collective over the individual, are temporary in nature, do not operate on the core–periphery principle, and foster cosmopolitanism.

---

[120] Wright, 'Between the Market and Solidarity', 2–3.
[121] Dorsch, 'Black or Red Atlantic?', 295.

9

Home Front

Péter Apor and James Mark

Socialist internationalism meant not only the repositioning of Eastern Europe on the global stage: it also reshaped political and popular cultures at home. Solidarity with a range of national liberation and socialist movements fighting 'western imperialism'—from Cuba to Vietnam to Chile—became commonplace across all countries within the region. For the most part, this has been understood through the prism of dictatorship: expressions of solidarity were politically instrumentalized and essentially inauthentic top-down initiatives that imposed an alien culture on reluctant populations.[1] Here we argue differently: postwar socialist solidarity generated widespread domestic activism that was the outcome of both centralized and grassroots initiatives at the same time. It extended well beyond the state, deep into intellectual and popular cultures, and was capable of bearing unorthodox political meanings that were often a challenge to Communist elites. To understand this, we have to broaden our vision. Extra-European solidarity in the region was not new, having been present in various nineteenth-century nationalist movements which had recognized themselves in others' struggles for liberation, and in the anti-fascist movements of the interwar period (see *Origins*). Traditions of solidarity were never simply the preserve of the Communist left, and, as western European empires began to fall, groups from varying political traditions sought to recast their global sympathies.

And shows of solidarity often proved popular. This is firstly because they were in part a way of narrating national pride: most solidarity propaganda encouraged local populations to see revolutions happening across the world as the replication of their own histories of liberation. National struggles against the German, Russian, Austro-Hungarian or Ottoman Empires before the First World War, or against German or Italian occupation in the Second World War, were seen as part of a process that now extended beyond Europe. In this sense, the anti-colonial culture that these states encouraged was still deeply Eurocentric, albeit one whose

The authors wish to express their gratitude for the material provided for this chapter by Radina Vučetić (Yugoslavia), Maria Dembek (Poland), and the GDR (Eric Burton).

[1] See e.g. Toni Weis, 'The Politics Machine: On the Concept of "Solidarity" in East German Support for Swapo', *Journal of Southern African Studies*, 37/2 (2011), 351–67.

Péter Apor and James Mark, *Home Front* In *Socialism Goes Global: The Soviet Union and Eastern Europe in the Age of Decolonization*. Edited by James Mark and Paul Betts, Oxford University Press. © Oxford University Press 2022. DOI: 10.1093/oso/9780192848857.003.0010

narrative followed a Marxist developmental timeline. Second, Communist infrastructures often provided space to develop critical agendas and subversive readings in which the language of anti-colonialism was turned against the Soviet Union, or eventually led to a new internationalism based on a common rejection of authoritarian rule. As such, this language provides an insight into a peculiar and understudied form of transnational identification: one produced under regimes which allowed their citizens very limited mobility or opportunities to build political connections across borders. It nevertheless constituted a very powerful set of transnational images and discourses, which in turn provided an important set of resources through which alternative visions could be articulated—ones that both critiqued existing state socialism, and, at times, bolstered their state's own recourse to internationalist appeals.

Origins of Solidarity

The concept of solidarity in Eastern Europe did not begin with the Communists. Nineteenth-century nationalist movements often linked their own suppression under the Russian, German or Habsburg Empires to struggles against the British in Africa and campaigned against slavery in America or the Caribbean. Leaders of the labour movement, and social democratic and Communist party elites, had used solidarity as a means of political organization since the late nineteenth century. In the interwar period, international solidarity was effectively used by Communist parties to mobilize working-class activism on behalf of their cause. The institutionalization of solidarity emerged from broader grassroots social practices: working-class movements across Europe participated regularly in donations for starving fellow workers in Russia in 1921, in Germany in 1923, as well as organizing mass appeals for imprisoned labour movement activists.[2] The International Workers' Relief (*Internationale Arbeiterhilfe*) in Weimar Germany, which had been the main vehicle to support strikes in the 1920s, subsequently became one of the most important organs for internationalizing anti-fascist solidarity. By the mid-1920s, their campaigns had extended beyond Europe and America to China: they first organized solidarity donations for the victims of the 1924 flood there; then protested against the shooting of workers on strike in Chinese harbours by British troops in April 1925; then collected funds for the Chinese revolutionary organization, the Thirtieth of May Movement.[3] Solidarity with non-European causes expanded significantly in Eastern Europe in the late 1930s as some citizens recognized the equivalences between the threat of Nazi

---

[2] Kasper Braskén, *The International Workers' Relief, Communism, and Transnational Solidarity: Willi Münzenberg in Weimar Germany* (Basingstoke: Palgrave, 2015), 48–63, 147–54.
[3] Ibid., 145–50.

ambitions in their region and a revived Italian imperialism in Africa. In the Kingdom of Yugoslavia, anti-Italian sentiment fed sympathy for the plight of Abyssinia across both left and right.[4] Soviet support for Abyssinia in the wake of Mussolini's invasion was, by contrast, muted at best, and here popular solidarity movements were still focused on Europe, being chiefly preoccupied by the Spanish Civil War (see *Origins*).

International solidarity after the Second World War initially developed through an engagement with the Far East. The first mass solidarity campaigns in the German Democratic Republic followed the foundation of the People's Republic of China on 1 October 1949.[5] Elites of the new state—including Wilhelm Pieck and Walter Ulbricht—were veteran leftist activists, who had opposed Nazi Germany as illegal resistance fighters or in exile, worked for the Communist International, and now saw their struggle extended further on the world stage.[6] Their enthusiasm to create a culture of support—through film festivals, art exchanges and solidarity shifts to raise funds to send to Beijing—derived in part from the fact that China provided much-needed evidence that their efforts to establish an anti-imperialist state based on Soviet military and political power was not a contingent act produ-cing only political dependence, but a globally viable model of state-building.[7] Such an orientation would only be consolidated once many bloc states offered North Korea their support in the Korean War. They encouraged a form of militar-ized identification amongst their populations, who were instructed not to think of themselves as benevolent outsiders providing support for a distant war, but rather as members of a global anti-imperialist army, as warriors on the home front. A speaker at the demonstration of the Hungarian Women's Federation against the Korean War in 1950 claimed that 'we stand our ground in the "peace front". We battle for each and every seed of grain.'[8] The war in the Korean penin-sula was often related as the possible prelude to a forthcoming global war between the socialist bloc and the imperialist camp. 'The masters of Wall Street want to hurl us into a Third World War', one Czechoslovak worker wrote in a ritualized letter to represent proletarian opinion in the party press.[9] Given such mobiliza-tions, many studies of solidarity have lent credence to an image of a top-down state-driven solidarity that contrasted with the extra-parliamentary, rowdy, threatening Third Worldist solidarity in the West from the late 1950s.

---

[4] See for example, Dušan Timotijević, 'Egipat ne želi rat, ali ga očekuje svakog trenutka', *Politika*, 11 October 1935.

[5] 'Volkschina bahnt sich den Weg zum Sozialismus', *Berliner Zeitung*, 1 October 1949, 1. 'Mit Chinas Volk auf dem Marsch in den Frieden', *Neues Deutschland*, 2 October 1949, 5.

[6] 'Das Kampfprogramm der deutschen Demokratie', *Neues Deutschland*, 13 October 1949, 5.

[7] Quoted in David G. Tompkins, 'The East is Red? Images of China in East Germany and Poland through the Sino-Soviet Split', *Zeitschrift für Ostmitteleuropa-Forschung*, 62/3 (2013), 395–6. By the late 1950s, Maoism had come to be embraced as a bulwark against de-Stalinization in the GDR.

[8] 'A magyar asszonyok a koreai nép ügye mellé állnak', *Szabad Nép*, 14 July 1950, 5.

[9] Lajos Brezina, 'Félre az árulókkal és a háborús uszítókkal!', *Új Szó*, 3 February 1951, 3.

The relatively high level of workers' participation in the solidarity campaigns of the 1950s did not necessarily reflect blind adherence to the party line; it was also the outcome of familiarity with certain practices. Just as in prewar leftist proletarian culture, workers were called to gather at mass rallies to condemn the invasion of socialist countries, and collected donations through working extra solidarity shifts in their factories. In June 1950, East German Peace Committees organized mass demonstrations of 50,000 in Halle, 60,000 in Dresden and 100,000 in Leipzig, and launched campaigns to collect medical supplies for the Korean People's Army.[10] In Budapest a mass rally was organized in July 1950.[11] The Polish Peace Committee organized a similar demonstration of 10,000 Warsaw citizens on 9 June 1951. The professional journal Teacher's Voice (Głos Nauczycielski) called for educational solidarity: high school students from Myślibórz funded a plane of health supplies; whilst university students for their part collected scrap metal in Szczecin, and potatoes in Stargard Szczeciński, to raise funds.[12] Following the armistice, the Czechoslovak Communist Party launched the 'Let's Help Korea!' action. The programme included raising funds via cultural performances and street and factory collections.[13]

And such solidarity activities were often as much the product of grassroots activism as they were party initiatives. A confidential note to the Central Leadership of the Hungarian Workers Party in July 1950 complained about the failures of the respective party organs to take full control of solidarity meetings on the shopfloor, and criticized factory party activists for lagging behind the enthusiastic masses.[14] Demonstrating solidarity with North Korea—and later with Vietnam—appealed to many who had witnessed the horrors and destruction of the Second World War.[15] Anti-Fascism was still a living ideology, and in East Germany in particular, memories were still all too raw of the bloody battles there between the Red Army and the last remnants of the Wehrmacht just five years before. The suffering of the civilian population had been far greater in the Eastern parts of the country, and the razing of cities like Dresden or Berlin was still a powerfully present reminder of the massive destruction wreaked by modern warfare. Achim Reichardt, who later was to become the leader of the GDR Solidarity

---

[10] 'Mit Koreas Freiheitskampf solidarisch', Berliner Zeitung, 30 June 1950, 2.

[11] 'El a kezekkel Koreától!', Hungarian Newsreel, 29 (July 1950) http://filmhiradokonline.hu/watch.php?id=10362 (accessed 10 March 2019).

[12] 'List ZG ZNP do nauczycieli koreańskich', Głos Nauczycielski, 34 (1953). Krzysztof Grudnik, 'Wychowanie ideologiczne w szkole polskiej w latach 1945–1953', Przegląd Historyczno-Oświatowy, 3–4 (2004), 59–67. Życie Warszawy, 10 June 1951, 2.

[13] István Gyurcsó, 'Korea újjáépítésére', Új Szó, 8 December 1953, 2.

[14] Meeting of the Secretariat of the Hungarian Workers' Party, 17 August 1950. Magyar Nemzeti Levéltár Országos Levéltára (MNL OL) 276/54/113, 40–1. Károly Fendler, 'The Korean War (1950–1953) in the Foreign Affairs of Hungary: Forms of Hungarian Assistance', Korea Journal (November–December 1990), 53.

[15] James Mark, Péter Apor, Radina Vučetić and Piotr Osęka, '"We Are with You, Vietnam": Transnational Solidarities in Socialist Hungary, Poland and Yugoslavia', Journal of Contemporary History, 50/3 (2016), 445–6.

Committee, remembered how he had been moved by the great loss of men in his home village in Thüringen and how similar memories led many of his compatriots to demonstrate against the war of the French and then Americans in Southeast Asia.[16] Polish Communists made sense of the conflict in Korea through the images of mass destruction and extermination that were all too familiar to their citizens. An August 1952 Polish newsreel entitled 'Korea: American Auschwitz' used images of barbed-wired POW camps, attacks on civilian population and burning human corpses to relate the distant war to the familiar imagery of Nazi occupation in Poland.[17]

Such activism often involved social organizations beyond party and state and, hence, had the capacity to mobilize broader social groups. Most notably in the GDR and Poland, churches played an important role through the launching of their own solidarity drives. Although the Christian language of solidarity differed from its socialist counterpart, emphasizing religious obligation over revolutionary promises, in many ways it also shored up the anti-imperialist message of the party-state. In the GDR, the Protestant-led solidarity movement 'Bread for the World' (*Brot für die Welt*) began in the late 1950s, and thenceforth always remained separate from the party's solidarity organs: their rhetoric combined long-established discourses on the deserving poor with a new focus on the condemnation of colonialism for creating such poverty, and claimed that 'Christian Europe' had a particular responsibility to address the inequalities bequeathed by empire. They collected money from congregations to support flood relief in Algeria, earthquake assistance in Skopje, and healthcare in Latin America and India.[18] There was widespread identification with the Chinese revolution too, most notably in Poland where, following Mao's supposed role in dissuading the Soviets from intervention in 1956, friendship associations sprung up 'from below', first in Gdańsk amongst dockyard workers employed in Polish-Chinese shipping, then in the guise of a wider membership, growing to some 300,000 in the space of a couple of years.[19]

New Generation, New Internationalism

By the end of the 1950s, the meaning of solidarity had shifted substantially. The Sino-Soviet split had put an end to Chinese-Eastern European friendship

---

[16] Achim Reichardt, *Nie Vergessen! Solidarität üben* (Berlin: Kai Homillius Verlag, 2006), 39.

[17] 'Korea. Amerykański Oświęcim', PKF 33/52 (6 August 1952) (Archiwum Polskiej Kroniki Filmowej) Available at http://www.repozytorium.fn.org.pl/?q=pl/node/6706. It should be remembered that under the Communists, Auschwitz was a symbol of the victimization of the Polish nation by fascist imperialism, and the specificity of the site for Jewish extermination not examined. James E. Young, *The Texture of Memory: Holocaust Memorials and Meaning* (New Haven and London: Yale University Press, 1993), 128–33.

[18] Gregory Witkowski, 'Between Fighters and Beggars: Socialist Philanthropy and the Imagery of Solidarity in East Germany', in Quinn Slobodian (ed.), *Comrades of Colour: East Germany in the Cold War* (New York, Oxford: Berghahn, 2015), 80–9.

[19] Tompkins, 'The East is Red?', 406–7.

organizations, but solidarity had nevertheless expanded its geographical reach: in 1960, the Moscow Declaration of eighty-one Communist Parties of the world emphasized the solidarity of the European socialist camp 'with all the peoples of Asia, Africa, Latin America and Oceania who are carrying on a heroic struggle against imperialism'.[20] This expansion of the anti-colonial world coincided with concerns about political socialization at home. Solidarity initiatives would no longer be primarily directed at the working class or the 'masses' per se, but rather at a younger generation born during or after the war. From the late 1950s, a more internationalist education was introduced in schools: in Poland, a 1964 textbook for civic education asked twelve-year-olds to 'Answer the following questions: 1. What is the meaning of the expression *colonial oppression*? Why do we speak about African countries as *economically backward*? 3. In what way does Poland help young African countries?' They were then to 'compose a sentence about Africa, using the word *independence*'.[21] In Hungary, 'World Map Circles' (*Világ terkép elött körök*) became a regular feature of a new anti-colonial education directed at all high school and university students. These sought to instil in youth an awareness of the geographical extent of the non-capitalist world and the belief that socialism was on its way to becoming the dominant world system.[22]

Communist youth organizations made tremendous efforts to generate genuine cultural activities: solidarity performances, art events, pol-beat concerts and political debates about the new revolutions outside Europe were at the heart of the burgeoning university and factory youth club movements, such as the Soviet Clubs of International Friendship.[23] Internationalist magazines directed at youth such as the Soviet *Around the World* (*Vokrug sveta*) and the Hungarian *Country-World* (*Ország-Világ*) were established. A new wave of socialist travelogues were targeted particularly at the younger generation, deemed to be particularly receptive to anti-colonial ideas.[24] In Poland, *Spark* (*Iskry*), which had previously published literature aimed for the most part at children and teenagers, became the main publisher of foreign travelogues, including the popular *Around the World* series. Yugoslav Nikola Vitorović's *Black Tears of Congo* (*Crne suze Konga*), which concerned the Congo Crisis and murder of Patrice Lumumba and Hungarian Endre Barát's 1962 novel *Burning Spear* (*Égő lándzsa*), a fictionalized account of

[20] 'Statement of 81 Communist and Workers Parties Meeting in Moscow, USSR, 1960', *Political Affairs* (January 1961).

[21] Janina Dembowska, Zygmunt Saloni and Piotr Wierzbicki, *Świat i My. Podręcznik do języka polskiego dla klasy 6* (Warsaw: PZWS, 1964), 274, 281–7.

[22] *Kézikönyv. A Kisz Politikai Körök Vezetői Részére 1960–61* (Budapest: Ifjúsági Lapkiadó Vállalat, 1960). On the role of geographers in conceptualizing this new anti-imperialist world, see Ferenc Koch, 'A nacionalizmus elleni harc irányelvei a földrajzban', *Felsőoktatási Szemle*, 10/9 (October 1960), 605.

[23] Yulia Gradskova, 'The Soviet Union: "Chile is in Our Hearts." Practices of Solidarity between Propaganda, Curiosity, and Subversion', in Kim Christiaens, Idesbald Goddeeris and Magaly Rodríguez García (eds.), *European Solidarity with Chile, 1970s-1980s* (Bern: Peter Lang, 2014), 337–8.

[24] Aleš Bebler, *Putovanja po sunčanim zemljama* (Belgrade: Štampa Kultura, 1954), 5.

Kenyan liberation, were given as prizes to the best students at schools.[25] Later in the decade literary competitions on themes such as 'People's Struggle in Vietnam', letters to Vietnamese pen pals, Christmas solidarity concerts and collections of presents for Vietnamese children became part of everyday life.[26] A popular Yugoslav television show, A Concert for a Crazy Young World (Koncert za ludi mladi svet) featured popular music that captured the anti-imperialist mood: its most famous performance was an anti-Vietnam protest song about the US soldier Bobby Smith, delivered by a Yugoslav and an African singer together.[27]

This new generational focus arose out of a concern that youth might be undergoing a political demobilization. As the founding myths of Eastern European socialism faded, elites feared that the postwar generation, having had no direct experience of the anti-fascist fight, might struggle to identify with the socialist cause. From the late 1950s, party organs, the Communist Youth, and the secret police regularly produced surveys on youth attitudes—a phenomenon that reveals much about this anxiety. As a KGB report noted, Soviet youth was becoming disillusioned with the CPSU and was losing their faith in the prospects of Marxism-Leninism as the guiding theory of future revolutionary action.[28] One youth survey from Hungary in 1963 concluded that the experience of the privations and terror of Stalinism made others skeptical about the future of the project at home and might explain their growing attraction towards the lifestyles and values of contemporary western youth and pop culture.[29] In this context, the heroic struggles of the decolonizing world, and the seemingly successful expansion of socialism globally, offered a powerful propaganda tool to regenerate the domestic project too.[30]

---

[25] Nikola Vitorović, Crne suze Konga (Belgrade: Školska knjiga, 1961). Endre Barát, Égő Lándzsa (Budapest: Móra Ferenc Könyvkiadó, 1962). Barát dedicated his book to, and on one occasion presented a copy to, Jomo Kenyatta, see N.G., 'A címzett: a főhős', Ország-Világ, 6/48 (1962), 15.

[26] Informacija o politič̆koj aktivnosti u SR Srbiji u toku 'Nedelje solidarnosti sa borbom naroda Vijetnama', January 1968 (Arhiv Jugoslavije (AJ), 142–457). Interview with Géza Takács. Monor, conducted by Péter Apor, 10 November 2008. Bernd Schaefer, 'Socialist Modernization in Vietnam: The East German Approach, 1976–1989', in Slobodian (ed.), Comrades of Color, 95–114.

[27] 'Nedelja solidarnosti sa borbom vijetnamskog naroda', 15–22 November 1969 (AJ), 142–465.

[28] Jeremy Friedman, Shadow Cold War: The Sino-Soviet Competition for the Third World (Chapel Hill: University of North Carolina Press, 2015), 171–2.

[29] 'Jelentés a diákifúság eszmei-politikai, világnézeti és erkölcsi arculatával kapcsolatos néhány problémáról' (PIL) 289. f. 13/1963/33. Őe (The Archives of the Institute of Political History, Budapest, henceforth PIL).

[30] Anne E. Gorsuch, '"Cuba, My Love": The Romance of Revolutionary Cuba in the Soviet Sixties', American Historical Review, 120 (April 2015), 462–96. Tobias Rupprecht, Soviet Internationalism after Stalin: Interaction and Exchange between the USSR and Latin America during the Cold War (Cambridge: CUP, 2015), 73–127. James Mark and Péter Apor, 'Socialism Goes Global: Decolonization and the Making of a New Culture of Internationalism in Socialist Hungary 1956-1989', Journal of Modern History, 87 (2015), 857–9. Jennifer Ruth Hosek, Sun, Sex and Socialism: Cuba in the German Imaginary (Toronto: University of Toronto Press, 2012), 55–89. Gerd Horten, 'Sailing in the Shadow of the Vietnam War: The GDR Government and the "Vietnam Bonus" of the Early 1970s', German Studies Review, 36 (October 2013), 557–78.

The Cuban revolution of 1959 was the first to provide this sense of renewal. As the powerful Soviet Presidium member, internationalist and Cuban envoy Anastas Mikoyan explained to US Secretary of State Dean Rusk: 'You Americans must realize what Cuba means to us old Bolsheviks…. We have been waiting all our lives for a country to go Communist without the Red Army. It has happened in Cuba, and it makes us feel like boys again.'[31] For the Soviets, it became the most powerful evidence that their national story was still relevant. Cuba—and later the Vietnamese struggle—were places where socialism appeared truly homemade and not a Stalinist export.[32] Across the bloc, socialist culture was saturated with all things Cuban: Spanish language programmes at universities proliferated, and Red Army choir learnt to sing in Spanish. It also helped Soviet urban youth define themselves against Stalinism: socialism was indeed able to rejuvenate, and did not have to mean repression, rigidity and greyness in everyday life. Soviet visitors to Cuba in the 1960s, like cinematographer Alexander Calzatti or aviation engineer Rostislav Rokitianski, often discovered a humanist, non-violent face of revolution and presented it as having a genuine popular backing. Renewing socialism and creating a more equal, abundant and human socialism was understood by many of them as their generational duty, and global anti-imperialist solidarity was conceived as the evidence that this was viable. It also rekindled a fascination with the Russian Revolution, and young intellectuals and activists advocated a return to the allegedly authentic internationalist ideals of the 1920s.[33]

Inculcating an anti-colonial internationalism was also considered to be an answer to excesses of nationalism amongst the young. In Hungary, for instance, the 1956 Uprising was blamed on the impact of an inward-looking anti-Communism. Most of the post-1956 elite concurred that the 'national Communism' espoused by Imre Nagy—Prime Minister from 1953 and during the 1956 revolution itself—was a 'bourgeois deviation' that had in effect stoked reactionary nationalist resistance to Communism and opened up the country to the influence of 'counter-revolutionary forces'.[34] This ideology, it was commonly argued, had particularly affected youth, who, as a consequence, had taken part in the 1956 Uprising in large numbers, supposedly 'tricked' into believing that the presence of the Soviets and the Red Army was inimical to the interests of the Hungarian nation.[35] From 1959 onwards, there was an increasing interest in how

---

[31] Quoted in Gorsuch, '"Cuba, My Love"', 505.

[32] Rupprecht, *Soviet Internationalism*, 4. Robert Hornsby, 'The post-Stalin Komsomol and the Soviet fight for Third World Youth', *Cold War History*, 16/1 (2016), 97.

[33] Igor Torbakov, 'Celebrating Red October: A Story of the Ten Anniversaries of the Russian Revolution, 1927–2017', *Scando-Slavica*, 64/1 (2018), 17.

[34] See the position of First Secretary János Kádár in M-KS 288/5/113, 3–4., 5., 14 (Magyar Nemzeti Levéltár).

[35] On the link between youth, nationalism, and involvement in the 1956 Uprising, see e.g. Martin Mevius, *Agents of Moscow. The Hungarian Communist Party and the Origins of Socialist Patriotism* (Oxford: Oxford University Press, 2005), 267. Nóra Dikán Némethné, Róbert Szabó and István Vida

'bourgeois nationalism' could be countered through a reinvigorated 'socialist patriotism'.[36] From the early 1960s, the party's propaganda section, branches of the Communist Youth League, and public educational institutions began to promote a socialist patriotism that consciously linked contemporary anti-imperialist struggles to the progressive national tradition that the socialist state had been promoting in education and culture since the late 1940s.[37]

It was commonly asserted that Hungarians 'instinctively' understood contemporary movements of revolutionary national liberation, as they could recognize similar experiences in their own country's past. When Che Guevara visited Hungary in December 1960, he went straight to Budapest's Heroes Square to lay flowers at the memorial to those who had fought for Hungarian independence in the nineteenth century—here the traditions of anti-imperialist revolutionary struggle of the Hungarian and Cuban nations came together. And as with movements across the region, solidarity was envisaged as a bilateral connection between two national revolutions occupying different stages on a Marxist developmental timeline—a simple transnational imaginary, unencumbered by the more complex nature of global interconnection, and one that would animate internationalism in mass culture until the end of the socialist period.[38] The country's history—typically for the region—was rewritten in anti-colonial terms. The liberation of Cuba from US imperialism was seen to echo Hungarians' own efforts against the Austrians and Russians in 1848. Che Guevara was commonly depicted as a successor of Sándor Petőfi—the Hungarian revolutionary poet who was probably 'martyred' at the hands of the Russian army in 1849. Petőfi's poetry had in fact been popular in Cuba since the nineteenth century, and the Hungarian Communists took the opportunity to promote him once again.[39] A contemporary

---

(eds.), *Vidéki diákmozgalmak 1956-ban* (Budapest: Nagy Imre Alapítvány, 2004); and László Eörsi, *Corvinisták, 1956. A VIII. kerület fegyveres csoportjai* (Budapest: 1956-os Intézet, 2001). On this connection between youth and 1956 in elite minds, see László Kürti, *Youth and the State in Hungary* (London: Pluto Press, 2002), 100–2. Milán Pap, '"A nép és a szülőföld igaz szeretete"—A szocialista hazafiság fogalma a Kádár-rendszerben', *Politikatudományi Szemle*, 1 (2013), 72.

[36] MNL OL 288/5/118, 4, 61. 'A burzsoá nacionalizmusról és a szocialista hazafiságról (Tézisek)', *Társadalmi Szemle*, 14 (July–August 1959), 11–39. 'A nacionalizmus elleni harc néhány kérdéséről (Tézisek)', MNL OL M-KS 288/5/113, 42–54.

[37] József Révai, *48 útján* (Budapest: Szikra, 1948). Mevius, *Agents of Moscow*, 111–262. Péter Apor, *Fabricating Authenticity in Soviet Hungary: The Afterlife of the First Hungarian Soviet Republic in the Age of State Socialism* (London, New York, Delhi: Anthem Press, 2014), 34–8.

[38] Quinn Slobodian refers to this type of national-historical parallelism as 'socialist multilateralism', a 'means of representing the world without disrupting the primacy of the nation-state container....depicting national contexts as discrete entities rather than attempting to portray an entangled reality....struggles happen[ed] simultaneously and in parallel, untroubled by extensive border-crossing.' Quinn Slobodian, 'The Uses of Disorientation. Socialist Cosmopolitanism in an Unfinished DEFA-China Documentary', in Slobodian (ed.), *Comrades of Color*, 222.

[39] The Cuban poet Diego Eliseo claimed that 'Cubans have always felt great sympathy with the works of Petőfi. Beginning in the last century they knew his works and spoke about them. José Martí often mentioned them in his writing. In the last century one of the most significant Cuban poets, Diego Vicente Tejera, translated some of his poetry...we feel the same about him as they did, there are certain interesting connections between José Martí and Petőfi, both were exceptional poets and

writer, András Simor, observed that the stubborn decades-long belief in the nineteenth century that Petőfi had not died but would return to save the nation found a new form resurrected as a Latin American freedom fighter.[40] He asserted, in a rhetorical flourish of mind-boggling anti-imperialist speculative retrospective futurology: 'If he [Petőfi] had looked into the future, he would he have commented: In Cuba, I will be Che Guevara.'[41] In this sense, solidarity was the expression of a progressive Eurocentric national pride: it celebrated each Eastern European nation as a true forerunner of the astonishing changes that were happening across the globe.

Cuba also enabled Eastern European elites to tell a story of the common defense of revolution, as attacked by the ever-shifting forces of international counter-revolution. Hungarians, in this view, had long fought foreign invaders to maintain their progressive traditions. The 1956 Uprising was presented by the re-established Communist regime as its latest reactionary manifestation. The so-called White Books—lengthy pamphlets that served to propagate the official version of the 'counter-revolution', and were widely used in Hungarian schools—claimed an equivalence between the struggles in Algeria and Cyprus against the French and British and the struggle of Hungarian socialists against 'reactionaries' supported by imperialist elements abroad.[42] The authorities hoped to connect these events by manifesting an enhanced sensitivity to the threat of foreign intervention. Indeed, it was in response to the CIA-backed invasion of Cuba at the Bay of Pigs that the Hungarian state launched its first major national solidarity campaign—'El a kezekkel Kubától!' (Hands Off Cuba!) Demonstrations were held across the country, including on Heroes Square in central Budapest.[43] Hungarian schools were named after the heroes of the Cuban revolution, and Debrecen twinned with Santa Clara. Opponents of the regime, however, according to Radio Free Europe's respondents in Hungary, expressed incomprehension at a second instance of insufficient American support for an attempt to overthrow a Communist regime.[44]

---

each one of them devoted their energies, enthusiasm, love and their lives to the cause of their country's revolution......beyond this the connection is still greater in the expressive forms of the two poets, additionally these days the works of Petőfi are particularly relevant, not just in our country but they are known in all of Latin America.' In János Horvát, Kubai Riport (Budapest: MRT-Minerva, 1974), 57–8. See his later recollection of his Cuban experiences in János Horvát, Kubai retro (Budapest: Geopen, 2013).

[40] András Simor, 'Kaland, Megváltás, Forradalom. Che Guevara naplója', Új Írás (October 1967), 102. András Simor assisted Cuban poets with the translation of Petőfi into Spanish.

[41] Ibid., 95.

[42] Nagy Imre és bűntársai ellenforradalmi összeesküvése (Budapest: Magyar Népköztársaság Minisztertanácsa Tájékoztatási Hivatala, 1958), 140–52.

[43] Népszabadság, 20 April 1961, 3, 4.

[44] Radio Free Europe X/CURT 'Hungarian Reactions to Cuba', 24 April 1961. HU OSA 300-40-1— box 898 (Open Society Archives, Budapest).

Placing Eastern Europe as the true successor of European anti-colonialism also required careful acts of erasure. Solidarity movements and their proponents were not overly concerned to explore the legacies of colonialism of states already gone: the Tsarist Empire, the German Reich or the Habsburg Monarchy. Rather, social- ist states, in these accounts, simply became the inheritors of progressive anti- colonial traditions which had often lain submerged, on occasion erupted to the surface, but, whether once visible or not, were somehow always core to the mod- ern identity of the region. The growing number of histories of the anti-imperialist struggles of the Third World normally ignored the presence and contribution of Hungarian, Czech or Polish forces or experts in these areas—or claimed their nation's explorers as having been humane anti-colonial heroes 'in advance'. The GDR, for its part, rejected any sort of continuity between the new state and the old German Reich. Their historians uncovered the German colonial past in order to reject it, depicting the new socialist state as ' the first truly anticolonial state in German history' and as such, the heir to German anti-colonial voices, the critic August Bebel amongst them.[45] All was externalized to the West, which was not 'unburdened by colonialism'—a term favoured in the diplomatic circles of the Federal Republic that was constantly criticized by the GDR. East Germans were keen to discredit West Germany's claim that it was itself 'an anti-colonial state and therefore could not pursue political and predatory goals in other countries'.[46] They pointed first to the fact that Germany had lost its colonies 'against its will' and it was disingenuous for West Germans now to employ the early end to German Empire as a positive story to win favour in former European imperial markets. Rather, West Germany was subsidizing what was pithily called 'collective colonialism' through their support it had offered since 1958 to the development fund of the European Economic Community. From the East German perspective, West Germany was thus bankrolling the maintenance of empire.[47] East German crit- ics also sought to connect the legacies of Nazism to the contemporary behavior of West German business. Capitalist firms that had been central to Nazi imperialism— Krupp, DEMAG, Daimler Benz, Bosch and Siemens, all of which had profited in the Third Reich-were leading the African and Asian export offensive in the 1950s. The socialist poet Volker Braun, in *The War Faraway* (Der Ferne Krieg, 1966) and a literary photobook *War Stories* (Kriegs Erzählungen, 1967), sought to find evidence of trade contracts between two West Berlin chemical factories and the US Department of Defence for transporting war material to Vietnam in 1966.[48]

---

[45] Hartmut Schilling, 'Der Bonner Neokolonialismus—Feind der Völker', *Einheit*, 16 (January 1961), 135–53. *Afrika im antiimperialistischen Kampf. Probleme eines Kontinents* (Berlin: Akademie Verlag, 1978). László Salgó—András Balogh, *A gyarmati rendszer története, 1870–1955* (Budapest: Kossuth, 1980).

[46] Katrina Hagen, *Internationalism in Cold War Germany*, PhD dissertation (University of Washington, 2008), chapter 1.

[47] Ingo Oeser, 'Die Konferenzen von Accra und Kairo', *Deutsche Aussenpolitik*, 4/3 (1959), 284.

[48] Volker Braun, *Wir und nicht sie: Gedichte* (Halle, Leipzig: Mitteldeutscher Verlag. 1979), 74.

Although the object of Braun's criticism was the greed of Wall Street, his approach was typical of the GDR's mainstream readings of Nazism, whereby big industries, especially the arms producer Krupp and chemical plants like Leuna and BASF, were in league with military elites who allegedly cultivated interests in imperialist expansion. Peaceful coexistence, in this reading, did not mean that the West had abandoned the legacies of Nazism.

The conscious choice to forget the region's ambiguous relationship to European imperialism—and their eager externalization of all its legacies to the West—was at the core of the Eurocentrism of the bloc's anti-colonialism. Imagining themselves unburdened by a colonial heritage, they could more easily uncritically entertain the idea that they, being on a putative developmental timeline the more advanced Europeans, had the right and duty to take a leading role. This sense of superiority was challenged most commonly in the Caribbean and Latin America, where national liberation had already been achieved in the nineteenth century, and its Cold War revolutionaries preferred to relate the growing relationship between Latin America and Eastern Europe in terms of entangled revolutionary traditions rather than through a Eurocentric Marxist timeline. Indeed, the Cuban essayist and poet Roberto Fernández Retamar, writing in 1965, suggested Eastern Europe had followed Latin America. He explored how the nineteenth-century Cuban revolutionary José Martí had been connected with 'similar Europeans' in 'the "backward", semi-feudal European countries' whose 'national independence lay ahead of them'. In particular, he picked out 'the great poets and political leaders' Sándor Petőfi (1823–1849) in Hungary, and Hristo Botev (1848–1876) in Bulgaria, who both died, like Martí, fighting for the liberty of their people, and who both supported 'a position of maximum radicalism in their respective historical circumstances.' According to him, they were revolutionary democrats who 'were no longer bourgeois ideologues, who openly censured the evils of the developed capitalism of the "West", without becoming spokespersons of a proletariat that was still incipient in their respective countries. It is proper to compare Martí with such Europeans.'[49]

It was striking that *the* instance of non-European anti-colonial rebellion that long preceded the Russian *October*—namely, the Haitian Revolution, received very little exposure. Its memory was celebrated in the Harlem Renaissance and in the anti-colonial milieu of interwar 'black Paris': indeed, this is where Soviet director Sergei Eisenstein became inspired to make a film about it, to star Paul Robeson. His best efforts fell foul of the turn to socialist realism in Moscow in the mid-1930s, however.[50] African-American activist and writer W. E. B. Du Bois did

---

[49] Reproduced, and translated into English as Roberto Fernández Retamar, 'Martí in His (Third) World'. Translated by John Beverley, with Miguel Llinas, *boundary 2*, 36/1 (2009), 68–9.

[50] Charles Forsdick and Christian Høgsbjerg, 'Sergei Eisenstein and the Haitian Revolution: The Confrontation Between Black and White Explodes Into Red', *History Workshop Journal*, 78/1 (2014), 157–85.

try to position Haiti as the forerunner of socialist nations in Europe: in his 1945 *Color and Democracy* he connected 'the dream of…a world filled with peaceful but independent nations…proclaimed by Toussaint and Dessalines in Haiti; it was even planned in the Balkans and Far Asia'.[51] And at decolonization's height there were a few historians in the bloc, such as Tadeusz Łepkowski in his 1964 work on the Haitian Revolution, who challenged a hitherto prevailing Eurocentric revolutionary history. Nevertheless, even here, the project was partly motivated by the desire to include accounts of those Poles who had been brought there by Napoleon to suppress the revolution, had switched sides, and remained in Haiti.[52] It placed Europeans at the start of black revolution, and hence was used to underscore the special capacity of Poles to work with a wider anti-colonial world. Nevertheless, for the most part, there was little use for histories of black rebellion preceding the Russian Revolution in postwar Communist memory culture.[53] In both Poland and Hungary, the Haitian Revolution in fact first entered school curricula through history textbooks in the 1980s. Its uniqueness as a black revolution was acknowledged, but greater stress was placed on its its character as a class-based, grassroots social revolution. In other ways, however, it was rendered marginal: it was linked to the French Revolution as its imperfect imitation, and the textbooks left no doubt that the important historical transformation happened in Europe.[54]

Unsuprisingly, it was the October Revolution which provided the key origin story of self-determination that linked Eastern Europe and a wider Afro-Asian world. In 1967—at its fiftieth anniversary—Communists celebrated the common root of progressive self-determination in Eastern Europe, Africa and Asia alike: Vietnam's revolutionary leader, Ho Chi Minh, spoke about the 'beacon of the Russian revolution'.[55] Echoing Ho, the South African Communist J. B. Marks wrote, 'The October Revolution and the epochal events connected with it—the growth of the might and influence of the USSR, the defeat of Fascism, the emergence and development of the socialist world system—vastly contributed to the

---

[51] W. E. B. Du Bois, *Color and Democracy: Colonies and Peace* (New York: Harcourt, 1945), 69.

[52] Jan Pachonski and Reuel K. Wilson, *Poland's Caribbean Tragedy: A Study of Polish Legions in the Haitian War of Independence 1802–1803* (Boulder, CO: East European Monographs, 1986). Tadeusz Łepkowski, *Haiti. Początki Państwa i Narodu* (Warsaw: Państwowe Wydawnictwo Naukowe, 1964). On the Polish and German troops' defection during Haiti's war of independence, see C. L. R. James, *The Black Jacobins: Toussaint L'Ouverture and the San Domingo revolution* (New York, NY: Vintage, 1963), 258: 'A regiment of Poles, remembering their own struggle for nationalism, refused to join in the massacre of 600……later, when Dessalines was reorganising the local army, he would call one of his regiments the Polish regiment.'

[53] On the post-Communist revival of the memory of the Haitian Revolution in Poland, see Magdalena Moskalewicz (ed.), *Halka/Haiti 18°48'05 "N 72°23'01 "W"* (Warsaw: Zachęta-National Gallery of Art, 2015). See also the staging of the classical Polish opera *Halka* about Russian occupation in the village of Cazale in Haiti in 2016.

[54] Géza Závodszky, *Történelem III.* (Budapest: Tankönyvkiadó, 1982).

[55] Hammond Rolph, 'Ho Chi Minh: Fifty Years of Revolution', *Studies in Comparative Communism*, 1 (July–October 1968), 92.

rise of the African revolution and accelerated the advance of our peoples.'[56] In central Europe, the popular memory of US President Woodrow Wilson as the 'true liberator' of the region's nations had to be marginalized too. In Poland and Czechoslovakia, two countries where Wilson's intervention had been particularly important in the establishment of statehood after the First World War, aspersions were cast on the role that the American President had played. Their interwar predecessors had exaggerated his role, Communists claimed. The West had abandoned the region in the late 1930s; rather, it was Bolshevik leaders who had demonstrated the greatest commitment to meaningful national self-determination.[57]

Controlling Solidarity

Even if cultures of solidarity were not only the result of initiatives from above, it was certainly the case that states attempted to control them. After the Sino-Soviet split, authorities across the region increasingly feared the influence of Maoist propaganda on youth: it was this threat, along with the expansion of socialism across Africa, which accelerated the appropriation and coordination of solidarity through governmental organizations. National solidarity committees were established: the Afro-Asian Solidarity Committee of the GDR in 1963,[58] the Hungarian Solidarity Committee and the Polish Committee for Solidarity with the Peoples of Asia and Africa (PKS) in 1965. Multiple organizations came together to organize campaigns: in Poland, for instance, pro-Vietnam activities were coordinated by the National Unity Front, the Socialist Youth Association, the Polish Committee of Solidarity, the National Peace Committee, the Association of Combatants for Freedom and Democracy and the Central Council of Trade Unions. Similarities in solidarity across countries have also led some scholars to place great emphasis on transnational synchronization from above.[59] The precise level of coordination is hard to ascertain, however, in particular because the state institutions charged with organizing such activities were required to represent them as 'organic'. Nevertheless, we know—for Warsaw Pact countries at least—that Moscow would regularly issue instructions to mobilize trade union, youth, women's and student

---

[56] J. B. Marks, 'October, Africa and National Liberation', *African Communist*, 31/4 (1967), 21. Terence Africanus, 'Shaking the World', *African Communist*, 31/4 (1967), 37.

[57] Jiří S. Hájek, *Wilsonovská legenda v dějinách ČSR* (Prague: Státní nakladatelství politické literatury, 1953); 'Stalin and our Nation's Right to an Independent National and Political Life', Prague, Czech Radio, March 8 1953.

[58] *Die afro-asiatische Solidaritätsbewegung. Dokumente* (Berlin: Deutsches Institut für Zeitgeschichte, 1968), 22.

[59] For an emphasis on controlled solidarity from above, see Ilya V. Gaiduk, *The Soviet Union and the Vietnam War* (Ann Arbour: I. R. Dee, 1996), 64. X. Liu and Vojtech Mastny (eds.), *China and Eastern Europe, 1960s-1980s*. Proceedings of the International Symposium: Reviewing the History of Chinese-East European Relations from the 1960s to the 1980s. Beijing, 24–6 March 2004, Zürcher Beiträge zur Sicherheitspolitik und Konfliktforschung 72 (Zürich, 2004), especially 56–7, 62.

movements for campaigns.[60] Coordination often took place at the level of youth organizations too: the resolutions of the 9th Congress of the International Union of Students, which was held in Ulan Bator 26 March–8 April 1967, called upon all their affiliates to organize meetings, marches, demonstrations, petitions, exhibitions and film screenings for Vietnam with titles such as 'the Mekong on Fire' and 'Children Accuse...'.[61] The World Youth Festivals, which in the early postwar years had been subjected to increasing Soviet domination, were occasions to harmonize the central solidarity initiatives of individual socialist countries at an international level. At the 1968 World Youth Festival in Sofia, for instance, the Bulgarian Communist Party worked in concert with their Soviet counterparts to exclude the 'heretical' Cuba, China and Albania, while the Soviet organizers carefully selected their own trainees from Iran or Greece.

States sought to enforce a tempered peaceful domestic solidarity in which western imperialism was criticized—but only to a certain extent. Communist elites in Eastern Europe had come of political age during the anti-fascist struggle of the 1930s and the Second World War: the constant fight against western reactionary politics—which they viewed as an outgrowth of Fascism—was central to their understanding of how a socialist system had been established and maintained. Such elites feared that the policy of peaceful coexistence between East and West, initiated by Khrushchev in 1956, was leading youth to believe that distinctions between socialism and capitalism were lessening, to seek out similarities between these systems, and to value the humanization of the capitalist West.[62] They expressed the fear that the class struggle in the West was not understood[63] and that the civil rights movement—supported by President Kennedy—had led to an unquestioning idealization of the United States as capable of promoting peace and equality.[64] Young people 'born into socialism' appeared particularly liable to entertain the illusions about capitalism contained in bourgeois

[60] Ilya V. Gaiduk, 'The Soviet Union Faces the Vietnam War', in Christopher Goscha and Maurice Vaisse (eds.), *La Guerre du Vietnam et L'Europe* (Brussels: Bruylant, 2003), 195–6. László Nagy, 'La Hongrie face á la guerre du Vietnam', in Goscha and Vaisse, *La Guerre*, 203–12.

[61] Važnije rezolucije IX Kongresa Međunarodnog saveza studenata koje su donesene prilikom održavanja Kongresa u Ulan Batoru. AJ, 145–12, 1967.

[62] On this tension, see: György Péteri, 'Introduction. The Oblique Coordinate Systems of Modern Identity', in György Péteri (ed.), *Imagining the West in Eastern Europe and the Soviet Union* (Pittsburgh: University of Pittsburgh Press, 2010), 1–12, 8. On using divides to discipline domestic populations in the Cold War, see: Mary Kaldor, *The Imaginary War. Understanding the East-West Conflict* (Hoboken: Blackwell, 1991).

[63] See, for example, the report on a youth survey of 125 seventeen- and eighteen-year-olds in Hungary. Vilmos Faragó, 'A Small Country', *Élet és Irodalom*, 7 January 1967. For Yugoslavia, see the Conference of the Ideological Commission of the Central Committee of the League of Yugoslav Communists, *Komunist* (October 1963), *Borba*, 29 January 1964. On Poland, Emilia Wilder, 'Impact of Poland's "Stabilization" on Its Youth', *The Public Opinion Quarterly*, 28 (1964), 450.

[64] Communist Youth Federation. Report on a Few Problems Concerning the Ideological-Political, World View and Moral Outlook of Student Youth (Hungary). PIL 289. f. 13/1963/33. Öe.

propaganda because they had no first-hand experience of it.[65] The idea that socialism necessitated a constant struggle against 'fascistic' western capitalism no longer seemed powerful. As a Communist Youth political instructor in the Hungarian capital complained in 1962: 'The old comrades participating in political instruction had experienced the privations of capitalism and the horrors of Fascism. The previous regime left its imprint much more deeply on them than on the young, who were only children in those years.'[66]

In the context of this anxiety, the struggles of the newly decolonized and independent states of the extra-European world furnished stories through which the supposedly immutable differences between these ideological systems could be reaffirmed. Whereas peaceful coexistence and growing economic cooperation in Europe were considered to have hidden the realities of the differences between capitalism and socialism close to home, the 'Third World' exposed the real distinctions between the systems that an older generation knew from its own experience but the young had yet to learn. Solidarity activities were designed to unmask the true face of western capitalism: it was America's brutal intervention in Vietnam that once again proved its unworthiness to represent civilization, and the Eastern Bloc was shown to be its true bearer. Strikingly, writers in these debates did often allude to the use of violence during the Stalinist period as contrary to the values of the modern world as well; nevertheless, these instances were presented as short-term aberrations that did not fundamentally call into question socialism's superior claims to represent civilization. They were much quicker to draw direct links between their struggle against Nazism in Europe and the present-day technological, medical, and economic aid they provided to the North Vietnamese in order to assert the longer-term commitment of socialism to the defence of humanity.[67]

At the same time, most states wanted to curb unrestrained critiques of the West. During the Vietnam War, Yugoslav, Polish and Hungarian elites had played important roles as peace-making global go-betweens who—as advocates of non-provocation, and a peaceful settlement—could help prevent a further escalation of the conflict.[68] Moreover, growing economic cooperation with, and the necessity of technological transfer from, capitalist countries, gave elites cause to fear that an unduly combative rhetoric would impede the western relationships

---

[65] György Aczél's report concerning the youth politics of the HSWP, Central Committee meeting, February 18–19, 1970. MNL OL 288/4/104–5, 42.

[66] Ervin Várkonyi, 'Forradalmi romantika a KISZ politikai körben', Ifjú Kommunista (December 1962).

[67] Vietnam. Szemünk láttára (Budapest, 1973).

[68] J. G. Hershberg, Marigold: The Lost Chance for Peace in Vietnam (Stanford, CA: Stanford University Press, 2012); Gaiduk, The Soviet Union, 86–7; L. Nagy, 'La Hongrie' in Goscha and Vaisse (eds.), La Guerre, 203–12.

needed to modernize the domestic economy.[69] From 1965, the US threatened to disrupt their export of grain and cotton at subsidized rates to Yugoslavia, so as to exert pressure on elites to tone down their anti-US and anti-war rhetoric.[70] Although western capitalism remained officially an ideological enemy until the end of the Communist period, elites increasingly promoted a 'responsible' or 'tempered' confrontation with the capitalist world—or the 'anti-imperialist politics of peace'.[71] They were critical of the Chinese, who believed that the future of socialism lay in direct confrontation with the West. Writing in Pravda a year after the Sino-Soviet split, in December 1961, Hungarian leader János Kádár criticized the Chinese rejection of peaceful coexistence, suggesting that the true interests of workers were wages, paid holidays and social security, and that socialist states had a responsibility to protect them from the 'fatal consequences of war' which was 'a thousand times more important'.[72] Given the international and domestic contexts, authorities often reminded the younger generation of their obligations to display only a tempered solidarity that paid heed to the requirements of 'peaceful coexistence' and economic development. In January 1967, an international seminar in Prague was convened to present Vietnam in terms of non-radicalization and coexistence to a student audience.[73] In Yugoslavia too, elites made it clear that the necessity of good relations with the United States meant that only a 'responsible anti-Americanism' would be tolerated and excessive anti-imperialist sentiments suppressed, violently if need be. When President Nixon visited Warsaw in 1972, the Polish government sent African, Latin America and Arabic students to Poznań to avoid anti-war street protests.[74] Only in Romania in 1965–66 did socialist elites encourage radical anti-American and pro-Vietnamese demonstrations in public. This was to demonstrate their agreement with Chinese criticism of the allegedly limited material solidarity offered by the Soviet Union, and in so doing encourage their population to identify with a struggle that echoed their own attempts to assert independence from Moscow.[75]

[69] On softening one's line on Vietnam as a quid pro quo for greater economic integration into the US market, see M. Gasiorowski and S. W. Polachek, 'Conflict and Interdependence: East-West Trade and Linkages in the Era of Détente', The Journal of Conflict Resolution, 26/4 (1982), 713.
[70] Memorandum from the Under Secretary of State for Economic Affairs (Mann) to the President's Special Assistant for National Security Affairs (Bundy), Washington, 22 July 1965, FRUS, 1964–1968, Vol. XVII, Eastern Europe, 178; Pregled spoljno politic̆kih informacija 3/67, KPR, IV-7 (AJ).
[71] Gábor Karczag, Ernesto Che Guevara (Budapest: Kossuth, 1969), 163–4.
[72] He continued: 'Some people....confuse...civil war, the liberation struggle against colonizers and imperialist war...We communists have always shown full solidarity with workers waging a revolutionary struggle against capitalist slavery, and with the oppressed peoples fighting for liberation from the colonial yoke, but we have always fought and will fight to avert imperialist, aggressive wars...A change in the social system depends entirely on the will of the people of the country concerned...', Speech reported in Pravda, 26 December 1961.
[73] 'Coexistence and the Third World' conference, Prague.
[74] Piotr Długołęcki, 'Nixon i Gierek—pierwsza wizyta amerykańskiego prezydenta', Polityka, 15 February 2021.
[75] Laurien Crump, The Warsaw Pact Reconsidered: International Relations in Eastern Europe, 1955–1969 (London: Routledge, 2017), 179.

Communist states had long sought to confine activism to particular spaces. On an everyday level, it was a a responsible solidarity in professional settings that was most widely encouraged. Socialism had already been 'consolidated' in Eastern Europe, and had surpassed the first flush of heroic socialist construction. In this context, valiant and exaggerated deeds that might have been appropriate in the period of postwar reconstruction were no longer necessary. Simply by working in a factory in Budapest, Belgrade or Warsaw one could be contributing to the anti-imperialist struggle: this idea was made most explicit in so-called 'solidarity shifts', where workers would undertake extra hours and 'voluntarily' donate their overtime pay to the Vietnamese people. During 'Solidarity Week' in 1967, over a million Yugoslavs made donations, with many workers offering 2% of their earnings to the 'Vietnam fund'. The workplace was also the focus for actual encounters: in the late 1960s, twinning between Hungarian and Polish, and Vietnamese, 'sister factories', was established. Exchanges took place, for instance, between the workers of Budapest's 'Red' Csepel works and Hanoi's Trang Hung Dao machine plant in 1968 and 1970.[76] Public demonstrations were expected to take place only in officially supported events such as May Day parades or World Youth festivals.[77]

Untempered, Heterodox Anti-Colonialism

Yet not all anti-imperialist solidarity initiatives conformed smoothly to the expectations of party-states. Yugoslav youth protest was particularly striking for its preparedness to go beyond the state's endorsement of a tempered and peaceful anti-Americanism in schools or at the workplace. Here there was a longer tradition of aggressive public anti-imperialist protest which stretched back to 1961, when, in the first big public demonstrations in Yugoslavia since the Second World War, called in response to the execution of Patrice Lumumba in the Congo in February 1961, an official rally of 150,000 people on Marx-Engels Square developed into an aggressive mob which threatened violence in front of the embassies and libraries of western countries. Eventually, protesters succeeded in breaking through the police line in front of the Belgian embassy, burning cars and then wrecking the building.[78] Then, after the Bay of Pigs Invasion on 18 April 1961, a group of students in Belgrade smashed the windows of the American Library,

---

[76] HU 300-40-2-Box 53 (OSA).

[77] Nick Rutter, 'Look Left, Drive Right: Internationalisms at the 1968 World Youth Festival', in Anne E. Gorsuch and Diane Koenker (eds.), *The Socialist Sixties: Crossing Borders in the Second World* (Bloomington, IN: Indiana University Press, 2013), 193–212. Interpersonal relations frequently escaped these bounds. Young-Sun Hong, *Cold War Germany, The Third World, and the Global Humanitarian Regime* (Cambridge: Cambridge University Press, 2015), 52.

[78] Predrag J. Marković, 'Najava bure: studentski nemiri u svetu i Jugoslaviji od Drugog svetskog rata do početka šezdesetih godina', *Tokovi istorije*, 3–4 (2000), 59.

which brought about an official protest from the American Embassy.[79] In the context of the Vietnam War, this 'tradition' of popular anti-imperialist violence manifested itself again first in Zagreb, on 20 December 1966, as a Yugoslav Student Association (SSJ) protest of 10,000 students attracted locals whose presence raised numbers to 20,000. Seemingly provoked by the Yugoslav media which had stoked anti-war feelings that week with a number of extremely anti-American articles that focused on the brutalization of children,[80] the demonstrations turned aggressive. Violence in the following weeks was directed at symbols and institutions of American power; in Zagreb, protesters attacked the American Consulate throwing bricks and stones, breaking windows, pulling down the American coat of arms and trying to burn the American flag.[81]

These extensive and violent forms of Yugoslav youth protest were not reproduced in bloc countries. Nevertheless, elite universities, which were becoming sites for the incubation of alternative politics across Eastern Europe in the early to mid-1960s, provided spaces where dissenting forms of solidarity could be generated.[82] The role of foreign students in fomenting unorthodox solidarity was a key challenge to authorities. The protests in Bucharest following the murder of Patrice Lumumba were led by students from countries in Africa, Asia and Latin America, including speakers, reports noted, from Sudan, Zanzibar, Rwanda, Algeria, India, UAR, Indonesia, China and Somalia.[83] In Hungary, Communist Youth 'mood reports' often noted that foreign students were less likely to toe the ideological line, praising instead Chinese assistance in Vietnam or criticizing the bloc's commitment to peaceful coexistence. This was particularly troubling as the Hungarian Communist Youth League often sent foreign students to the countryside—in their hundreds—to spread the message about internationalist solidarity.[84]

At the Universities of Warsaw and Budapest in the mid-1960s, various student circles were beginning to criticize their system for having betrayed left-wing ideals. One of these groups was known as the 'Vietnamese': it was centred around Henryk Szlajfer, a student of economics since 1966, who drew on the

---

[79] Radina Vučetić, *Koka-kola socijalizam: Amerikanizacija jugoslovenske popularne kulture šezdesetih godina XX veka* (Belgrade: Službeni glasnik, 2012), 67–8.

[80] On the day of the scheduled protest of 23 December in Belgrade, the Party daily Borba published an article 'The Terrible Vietnam War—250,000 Children are Killed' on the front page, *Borba*, 23 December 1966, 1.

[81] Informacija o demonstracijama u Zagrebu, 23 December 1966, AJ, KPR, II-4-a.

[82] On recovering the importance of the university as a site of intellectual ferment,, see Zdenek Nebrensky, 'Early Voices of Dissent: Czechoslovakian Student Opposition at the Beginning of the 1960s', in Martin Klimke, Jacco Pekelder and Joachim Scharloth (eds.), *Between Prague Spring and French May, Opposition and Revolt in Europe, 1960–1980* (New York and Oxford: Berghahn, 2011), 32–48. On the importance of intellectual clubs and committees in generating alternative politics in Poland and Hungary, see Robert Gildea, James Mark and Anette Warring (eds.), *Europe's 1968. Voices of Revolt* (Oxford: OUP, 2013), esp. 53–4, 174, 176.

[83] 'The Colonialists' Lawlessness Must be Punished!', *Scanteia*, 17 February 1961.

[84] Tájékoztató a Gyarmati Ifjúság Napjának megünnepléséről, Budapest, 29 August 1966, KISZ KB Agitprop. Osztály, PIL 289 f.8/857 őe.

internationalist tradition of the International Brigades during the Spanish Civil War—which his friends' families had been involved in.[85] His group recalled traditions of radical international solidarity from the 1930s, and, and on May 1 1966 used the May Day commemoration to demand that the Polish state lend meaningful support to the people of Vietnam; the following year his group arranged pickets at US and Greek embassies (in protest against the dictatorship of the colonels). This network would eventually form a nucleus for a group called the 'Commandos', who would help initiate the major protests of March 1968.

Some groups were frustrated by the absence of real solidarity and military support. For them, state-led solidarity was not enough: it neither provided sufficient support at an international level, nor did its domestic institutional forms allow the expression of the anger that exposure to the horrors of the Vietnam conflict had generated. Some radical youth responded to these contradictions by offering to fight in Vietnam. Indeed, at the time this seemed set to become bloc policy. On 6 July 1966, Warsaw Pact countries issued a joint declaration in Bucharest stating their preparedness to send volunteers to Vietnam—but this was never put into practice.[86] Across Eastern Europe, young people wanted to fight.[87] Some of these were attracted to Maoist China because of its promises of a more radical support for Vietnam: in Hungary there is evidence that official solidarity movements grew in part out of the need to counter Chinese influence on foreign students and Hungarian youth, who used Maoist arguments about the bloc's insufficient military support for the anti-American struggle.[88] In Yugoslavia, where Maoism had a following of sorts amongst so-called 'anarcho-liberals' and students, many of those who wanted to fight felt that their gesture would not be well received by their own equivocating state, and hence went to the Chinese Embassy to offer themselves.[89]

Such refusals to conform to states' conceptions of solidarity were doubly threatening in that they were used to point to the abandonment of progressive

[85] Interview with Henryk Szlajfer, conducted by Piotr Osęka, Warsaw, 27 September 2012.

[86] Gaiduk, Soviet Union, 62–3.

[87] Ifjú Kommunista (January 1967), 9. The magazine claimed that the Communist Youth was mobilizing effectively, and that 'hundreds' had volunteered to go to Vietnam. Activists from east Berlin's radical scene tried to volunteer for Vietnam; see James Mark and Anna von der Goltz, 'Encounters' in Gildea et al. (eds.), Europe's 1968, 161. The Soviet authorities reported that they received 750 requests to fight in Vietnam; Gaiduk argues that this was itself a propaganda ploy to threaten the US, and provide a smokescreen for introduction of Soviet advisors into Vietnam. Gaiduk, Soviet Union, 64.

[88] 'Jelentés a diákifjúság eszmei-politikai, világnézeti és erkölcsi arculatával kapcsolatos néhány problémáról', 3 February 1964. KISZ Középiskolai és Iparitanuló Egyetemi és Főiskolai Osztálya: PIL 289. f. 13/1963/33. őe.

[89] Interviews with Borislav Stanojević, conducted by Radina Vučetić, Belgrade, 2 November 2012; and Tihomir Trivunac, conducted by Radina Vučetić, Belgrade, 26 October 2012. Nevertheless, a poll conducted in 1969 discovered that Mao—alongside Lyndon Johnson—was one of the most unpopular political figures among Belgrade's students. John F. Kennedy, Indira Gandhi and Lenin were the most popular; 'Zastati znači zaostati', Borba, 10 May 1969, 7. HU 300-10-2-49 (OSA).

ambition 'at home' too. Eastern European states' claim that the expansion of the socialist world represented the renewal of their project internationally was taken by a younger generation as a call for domestic renewal too. In East Germany, intellectuals, artists, film directors and poets were moved by the extra-European revolutions since they opened up authentic visions through which they pursued their own anti-consumerist, anti-capitalist projects. In his 1962 film *And Your Love Too*, the younger director Frank Vogel compared the lessons of Fidel Castro's revolution in Latin America with those drawn from their East German experiences.[90] For GDR artists Ingo Arnold and Siegfried Ratzlaff, Cuba represented the power of revolution to change the world, and functioned as a utopian space through which to critique the realities of GDR socialism.[91] Like Allende's Chile a decade later, it played a role as a surrogate land of idealized socialism far from their own homeland—yet produced no actual social or political alternative.

In Hungary, the seeming authenticity of Third World revolution was used to critique the 'bourgeois values' of consumerist 'goulash Communism'—across multiple political traditions. One of the first alternative readings came from Sándor Csoóri, a young populist intellectual from a peasant background, who in 1961 travelled to Cuba for the first time. His account of this trip—recounted in the youth, intellectual and popular press, and eventually published as his Cuban Diary (*Kubai napló*) in 1965, would be influential in shaping the broader cult of the Cuban revolution in the early to mid-1960s.[92] Csoóri was one of the many populist intellectuals who had made their peace with the regime following the defeat of the 1956 revolution, viewing western forms of individualistic capitalism as the greater threat to rural Hungary and the state-socialist status quo as the lesser evil. In Cuba, Csoóri found an imaginative and inspiring space through which he could rethink the national project at home. Rejecting the Hungarian party's official image of Cuba as a land of modern socialist construction, Csoóri rather represented her as an idealized peasant society in an independent country which had now chosen—through its revolution—to resist the materialism of the modern world. The Cuban Revolution could be celebrated as anti-capitalist, free from the technological over-sophistication and acquisitiveness of the capitalist West, and valuing 'genuine community'. The construction of this new transnational culture cannot be reduced to new elite strategies; it was also encouraged by those from other intellectual traditions, whose unconventional contributions could simultaneously reinforce and critique the party leadership's transnational appeals.

---

[90] Hosek, *Sun, Sex, and Socialism*, 5, 16.

[91] Marcus Kenzler, *Der Blick in die andere Welt: Einflüsse Lateinamerikas auf die Bildende Kunst der DDR* (Münster: LIT Verlag, 2012), 305.

[92] Sándor Csoóri, *Kubai napló* (Budapest: Magvető, 1965). See also the earlier serialization; Sándor Csoóri, 'Kubai útinapló', published as three parts in *Új Írás*, 3 (September 1963), 1030–41; (November 1963), 1287–99; (December 1963), 1458–72.

By the mid-1960s, male university activists in particular were critiquing a consumerist 'frigidaire socialism' as emasculating: it had denied them, by contrast with their fathers' generation who had experienced war and postwar rebuilding, involvement in heroic revolutionary work.[93] Che Guevara became *the* figure against which men could lament their contemporary revolutionary shortcomings. In the wake of his death in Bolivia, the November 1968 issue of New Writing (*Új Irás*) called upon Communist, anarchist, populist and 'proletarian' poets to respond to his 'martyrdom'. One response came from working-class radical poet Zoltán Soós, who was critical of the failure of Hungarian socialism to throw off the residues of bourgeois living even after the economic construction of socialism. His 'Death of a Doctor. A Subjective Funeral Oration in the Memory of Che Guevara' related his disappointment with a contemporary materialism that had emasculated former heroes, for whom slippers, and encounters with authoritarian party technocrats all too ready to clamp down on outbursts of revolutionary romanticism, now dominate their lives. In this world, only a continual erotic merry-go-round could compensate for what was lacking. 'Doctor' Guevara, by contrast, represented a radical masculine authenticity which was unknown in a system where the 'Gods' of real socialist ambition had been defeated. Hence a funeral oration from a distant Budapest could only be a 'stuttering' parody of authentic solidarity:

My Doctor, we have become hen-pecked husbands (papucshősök, literally 'slipper heroes'); if our melancholy band sometimes gets together, in soft flats, as shabby heroes, sipping extra booze from our Frigidaires,

I roar as the world guffaws

I will be proud, brave, a comrade of Titans,

singing 100 revolutionary songs, until a piercing voice explodes,

'The Owner of X. pullover factory wants to sleep!'

We play the hero 'in peace'—The booze has run out—and in the end we stay, continually exchanging our 'little cuties', we are bleeding under the lovely buttocks of the night, squatting on us...

A TV-break, on flat feet in our slippers...

Doctor! I suppose that your heroic obstinacy is not in style here,

Is it only licentiousness that these 'zigzag years', and our defeated gods have sculpted?

To your memory, with raised fists, our consciences can only stutter: FREEDOM!'

---

[93] On this appeal to Soviet masculinity, see Gorsuch, "'Cuba, My Love'", 513–14.

This anti-colonial critique of the limited ambitions of bloc socialism was the starting point for many who would later become leading figures of liberal or leftist dissidence—although this period later became politically problematic and thus rendered marginal in their life stories. In Poland, the rise of a generational opposition who would go on to become leading figures in the largest opposition movement in the Communist bloc—the trade union *Solidarność*—started in such milieux. A founding document was Karol Modzelewski and Jacek Kuroń's 'Open Letter to the Party', which aimed to stir up an internal party debate about the bureaucratic nature of the Communist system in Poland and elsewhere in the Soviet Bloc. Written in 1964, the letter was radical, revolutionary, anti-Soviet and anti-colonial in its spirit.[94] By deploying a term 'colonial revolution' (*rewolucja kolonialna*), the 'Open Letter' framed 'the anti-bureaucratic revolutions' in Communist Eastern Europe and Third World liberation movements as part of one and the same struggle. In their view, 'Soviet bureaucracy' echoed the politics of imperialist countries: both used the rhetoric of peace to keep masses in subjugation and did not shy from military interventions where liberation struggles had occurred: Greece, Korea, Vietnam, Algeria, Cuba and Hungary, were named. 'International bureaucracy, led by the Soviet Union hampers in fact the anticapitalist revolution, it fears 'authentic revolutions' around the globe, because they endanger a bipolar world of stabilized spheres of influence', wrote Kuroń and Modzelewski. Their message was overtly internationalist: 'Anti-bureaucratic revolution is not just a Polish problem. Anti-bureaucratic revolution is…a movement in the name of colonial revolution in African, Asian and Latin American countries.…Our allies against the Soviet tanks are the Russian, Ukrainian, Hungarian and Czech working class. Our allies against imperialist pressures are workers in the industrial West and colonial revolution in the backward countries.' This broad, not specifically Eastern European, spectrum of revolutionary references might have contributed to its success and wide circulation in the West: it was translated into French, English, Italian, German, Swedish and Japanese. French students compared Kuroń and Modzelewski to black Americans in the United States and Vietnamese partisans.[95]

Anti-colonialism and Soviet 'Empire'

The reinvigoration of anti-colonialism not only opened up unsettling questions about the conservative turn in Eastern European socialism: it also served to forge

[94]   See the English translation: Jacek Kuroń and Karol Modzelewski, 'An Open Letter to the Party II', *New Politics*, 5/3 (1966), 79.
[95]   Martha Kirszenbaum, '1968 entre Varsovie et Paris: un cas de transfert culturel de contestation', *Histoire@Politique. Politique, culture, société*, 6 (September–December 2008) www.histoire-politique.fr.

a revived political language of empire through which to critique Moscow as occupier of the region. The question of whether the Soviet Union was a new form of imperialism was there from its very foundation (see *Origins*). Such questions acquired fresh urgency with the Red Army occupation of Eastern Europe after the Second World War—but became part of a global conversation over what constituted imperialism in the mid-1950s. Prior to the Bandung Conference, which marked an important turning point in the creation of the idea of an anti-imperialist Third World, Ferenc Nagy, the leader of the last democratic government in Hungary prior to the Communist takeover, had toured Asia. He sought to convince the Philippine, Pakistani, Sri Lankan and Thai governments to support the idea that Soviet Communism too was colonialism—and that decolonization was thus equally a question for Eastern Europeans.[96] He claimed to have convinced Ceylonese Prime Minister Sir John Kotelawa to introduce the issue of 'Soviet colonialism' at Bandung (1955): 'If we are united in our opposition to colonialism, should it not be our duty openly to declare our opposition to Soviet colonialism as much as to Western imperialism?'[97] Although vocally supported by Pakistan's Mohammed Ali, Indian Prime Minister Nehru and Chinese Premier Zhou Enlai rejected this formulation. The simultaneous occurrence of the Soviet intervention to suppress the revolt in Hungary in 1956 and the British intervention at Suez once again placed this question of who should be considered colonialists at the forefront of international debate: both invasions were judged by Nehru to be revivals of 'old colonial methods, which we had thought, in our ignorance, belonged to a more unenlightened age.'[98] Frantz Fanon was initially silent, being reluctant to undermine the Soviets' moral authority on decolonization; W. E. B. Du Bois saw the invasion as a necessary intervention and later would be rewarded by the Hungarian Academy of Sciences, which appointed him as an honorary member. Fanon later shifted his position, using the violence of Soviet suppression to justify the armed struggle against empires, whichever ideological mask they adopted: 'But it is above all Suez and Budapest which constitute the decisive moments of this confrontation.'[99]

[96] Ferenc Nagy, 'The Bandung Conference. Report and Recommendations', 10 May 1955, 3–4. 3566, Box 59 (Ferenc Nagy archive, Columbia University). See also Zoltán Ginelli, 'The Clash of Colonialisms: Hungarian Communist and Anti-Communist Decolonialism in the Third World', online essay https://www.academia.edu/41405321/The_Clash_of_Colonialisms_Hungarian_Communist_and_Anti-_Communist_Decolonialism_in_the_Third_World (last accessed 15 September 2021).

[97] Nagy, 'Bandung', 7.

[98] Most Indian newspapers accepted that 1956 was a suppressed national uprising. 'Reactions to the Report in India', 1 July 1957. Records of the UN Special Committee on the Problem of Hungary: UN Documents. HU 398-0-1-1413 (OSA). Nehru quoted in Nataša Mišković, 'Between Idealism and Pragmatism: Tito, Nehru and the Hungarian Crisis, 1956', in Natasa Mišković, Harald Fischer-Tiné and Nada Boskovska (eds.), *The Non-Aligned Movement and the Cold War. Delhi—Bandung—Belgrade* (London: Routledge, 2014), 125.

[99] Franz Fanon, *The Wretched of the Earth* (New York: Grove Press, 1963), 38.

The breadth of the definition of anti-colonialism thereby became a key struggle for those who sought to throw off Soviet rule in Eastern Europe.[100] Despite Eastern European states' attempts to forge an internationalist anti-colonial patriotism in which their Communism was part of a wider global past and present of liberation, many saw in this revived anti-colonialism as offering an opportunity to attack Soviet occupation in Eastern Europe—and to present it as such to international audiences. The anti-Communist 'Assembly of Captive European Nations' drew on such language in the late 1950s, displaying posters and billboards close to the UN Headquarters in New York that drew attention to ongoing 'Soviet imperialism'. It was striking that even anti-Communist conservatives could imagine themselves in solidarity with those fighting US, British or French imperialism— in the name of a common struggle against imperialism in all its guises.[101] In 1961, the security services reported that the then twenty-nine-year-old József Antall, who would later become the first post-Communist Hungarian Prime Minister as leader of the centre-right Hungarian Democratic Forum, cultivated sympathies for Fidel Castro. Antall was at this time a member of anti-Communist middle-class agrarian intellectual networks. For him, Cuba was inspirational as a small country fighting for independence against a great power, an idea that resonated with the anti-Soviet sentiments of the fifty-sixer groups to which he belonged.[102] This was not a one-off: surveys of Hungarian youth discovered that although a negative image of the United States had been effectively reasserted as a threat, such a feeling was seldom accompanied by a 'pro-Soviet mentality'.[103]

Maoist China also propagated internationally a critique of the Soviet Union as imperialist. Following the Sino-Soviet split of 1960, Beijing challenged the Eastern Bloc's rhetorical division of the world into an anti-imperialist socialist camp on one hand, and an imperialist-capitalist one on the other. According to China's quite distinct version of the Three Worlds Theory, the Soviets became the aggressive superpower alongside the United States in the 'First World'; Western Europe, Eastern Europe and Japan became the developed but colonized regions of the

---

[100] See also the work by Mate Nikola Tokić on Croatian right-wing exiles: 'The End of "Historical-Ideological Bedazzlement": Cold War Politics and Émigré Croatian Separatist Violence, 1950–1980', *Social Science History*, 36/3 (2012), 421–45.

[101] In the 1960s Csoóri was critical of the Soviet 'occupation' of 1945 and attempted to bring Red Army atrocities to public attention: Feljegyzés a 'Tiszta Szívvel' című folyóirat vitájáról, Budapest, 6 March 1965. Lajos Gál KISZ KB Egyetemi és Főiskolai Osztály. PIL 289. f. 13./1965/53. őe. He was one of the few cultural elites to criticize publicly the Soviet occupation of Czechoslovakia in August 1968.

[102] The security report: (ÁBTL) TH O-11386, "Kátai", 8 May 1961, 193 (Állambiztonsági Szolgálatok Történeti Levéltára, Budapest). See also János M. Rainer, 'Egy "kompromisszum" hétköznapjai—jelenetek a hatvanas évekből. Antall József és az állambiztonság embere', in idem. (ed.), *Múlt századi hétköznapok. Tanulmányok a Kádár-rendszer kialakulásának időszakáról* (Budapest: 1956-os Intézet, 2003), 270–98.

[103] See Faragó, 'A Small Country'. Communist Youth reports often assessed youth sentiments with regard to international affairs. See the Communist Youth Executive Committee Report of 1967, which asserted that while youth were firmly behind Vietnam solidarity, they were nevertheless too easily influenced by 'bourgeois propaganda' concerning western societies. PIL 289/3/210.

'Second World'; and the rest, including China, were the 'Third World'.[104] Policy pursued through such an ideological lens was designed to isolate the Soviets from both Eastern Europe and the Afro-Asian bloc and to undermine Moscow's conception of a unified anti-imperialist world under its own leadership. Some opposition in Eastern Europe drew on Maoist framings: those Polish citizens who typically had been members of the substantial Sino-Polish Friendship Society in the 1950s, kept sending letters to the Chinese Embassy in Warsaw during the early 1960s supporting the Maoist revolution and accusing Moscow of imperialism. A number of these letters considered Chinese revolution in terms of Polish nationalism and saw Mao as a potential ally for reclaiming the eastern lands of pre-1945 Poland lost to the Soviet Union.[105] And the reach of China's propaganda grew: following the split, Radio Peking had begun broadcasting to Eastern Europe, and by the end of the decade was producing programmes in Albanian, Czech, Polish, Romanian, Russian and Serbo-Croatian.[106] In November 1963, the Political Club of Polish Socialist Youth debated the Sino-Soviet conflict and praised the Chinese position.[107] Some left-leaning Polish emigrés in Belgium and France, in response to the Year of Africa celebrations in 1960, articulated similar sentiments, producing brochures that drew equivalences between histories of slavery ('Pologne-esclave') and the Soviet capture of Poland: 'Communisme? Absent! Imperialisme? Present!'[108]

The plight of Vietnam, and its prosecution of a 'just war' as a small nation against an imperialist superpower, also became a way of articulating criticism of Soviet control. Student groups such as the Polish Commandos distributed leaflets at Warsaw University in 1967 in which they identified the Vietnamese cause with Polish revolutionary and national interests, equating Soviet superpower politics with western imperialism.[109] Following the Soviet invasion of Czechoslovakia in August 1968, the Chinese compared the act to 'Hitler's invasion of Poland, to the US aggression in Vietnam, and to Japanese imperialism in China thirty years earlier'.[110] GDR dissident groups, such as the one led by student activist Frank Havemann, took this line too. In previous years, he had boycotted official Vietnam

[104] Péter Vámos, 'The Soviet Bloc and China's Global Opening-Up Policy during the Last Years of Mao Zedong', in James Mark, Artemy M. Kalinovsky and Steffi Marung (eds.), *Alternative Globalizations: Eastern Europe and the Postcolonial World* (Bloomington, IN: Indiana University Press, 2020), 90.

[105] Informacja1/70/63, IPN, 0296–61 t.1, tajne, Dept. III, 12 listopada 1963, MSW, 61–2 (Instytut Pamięci Narodowej, Warsaw).

[106] The external information and cultural relations programmes of the People's Republic of China, United States Information Agency, 1973, 50.

[107] Informacja1/70/63, IPN, 0296–61 t.1, tajne, Dept. III, 12 listopada 1963, MSW, 60.

[108] Jerzy Jankowski, 'L'Afrique s'inspirera-t-elle de l'experience communiste de la Pologne?', *Les cahiers africains*, 4 [after 1960; no date].

[109] James Mark, Nigel Townson and Polymeris Voglis, 'Inspirations', in Gildea et al. (eds.), *Europe's 1968*, 101, 109.

[110] Vámos, 'The Soviet Bloc', 85.

solidarity meetings in his school and had organized unofficial voluntary work shifts for Vietnam. His group now produced leaflets condemning the Soviet invasion of Czechoslovakia, comparing it to the American intervention in Vietnam ('Prague—no second Saigon!' or 'Don't create a second Vietnam!'), and calling for a common solidarity with Ho Chi Minh *and* Dubček.[111]

The vocabulary of anti-imperialist self-determination was also commonly used by exile groups which had left multi-ethnic socialist federations in Eastern Europe. Slovenian dissident émigré communities launched the journal *Slovenian Freedom* in Munich in 1964.[112] Combining their lawful political activism with violence and terrorism, Croatian far-right militants urged the UN to endorse the creation of a 'free and independent Croatian state' against 'Yugoslavian violence and imperialism'.[113] Croatian nationalists in Australia complained in a pamphlet about the pusillanimous conduct of their exiled political leaders while 'in the African Continent, actual freedom has been achieved by practically all the Negro tribes whose structure has hardly any national characteristics'.[114] Kosovo Albanian nationalists too drew on the language of anti-imperialism and self-determination to challenge what they perceived as their status as second-class citizens. In November 1968, hundreds of protesters took to the streets of the Kosovan regional capital Prishtina, chanting slogans of 'self-determination', 'We want a republic', 'We want a university', and 'Down with colonialism'.[115] Calls for national self-determination were intertwined with demands for social and economic prosperity in 'an economy free of colonial characteristics'.[116] The language of socialist internationalism pervaded the political rhetoric of Armenians who struggled for a greater measure of sovereignty within the Soviet Union.[117] These calls would return again in the 1980s, albeit stripped of their internationalism—as we shall see below.

---

[111] Stasi report, file RH 173, 385 (Archives of the Robert Havemann Gesellschaft, Berlin).

[112] Jure Ramsak, 'Neodvisna Slovenija do konca leta 1964! Kritika polozaja Slovenije v Jugoslaviji in zgodnje ideje o samostojnosti', in Mitja Ferenc, Jurij Hadalin and Blaž Babič (eds.), *Osamosvojitev 1991: država in demokracija na Slovenskem v zgodovinskih razseznostih* (Ljubljana: Univerza v Ljubljani, 2011).

[113] Secretary-General Kurt Waldheim (1972–1981), S-0904-0051-04, 'Freedom for Croatia' (United Nations Archive, Geneva).

[114] Tokić, 'The End of "Historical-Ideological Bedazzlement", 421–45.

[115] Mary Motes, *Kosova, Kosovo: Prelude to War 1966–1999* (Homestead, Fla: Redline, 1999), 103–4. Sabrina P. Ramet, *Nationalism and Federalism in Yugoslavia, 1962–1991* (Bloomington, IN: Indiana University Press, 1992), 296. Dennison I. Rusinow, *Yugoslavia: Oblique Insights and Observations* (Pittsburgh, PA: University of Pittsburgh Press, 2008), 267.

[116] Gazmend Zajmi, 'Kosova's Constitutional Position in the Former Yugoslavia', in Ger Duijzings, Dušan Janjić and Shkëlzen Maliqi (eds.), *Kosovo-Kosova: Confrontation or Coexistence* (Nijmegen: Peace Research Centre and Political Cultural Centre, 1996), 95–103.

[117] Maike Lehmann, 'Apricot Socialism: The National Past, the Soviet Project, and the Imagining of Community in Late Soviet Armenia', *Slavic Review*, 74/1 (2015), 9–31.

Clamping Down

By the late 1960s, many Communist states were clamping down on the diverse cultures of anti-colonialism that had to a degree sustained solidarity as a living ideology. In its variety of forms it had had the power to reinvigorate socialist culture and commitment, but had also provided a language through which a new generation could make sense of a world of interconnectedness in ways unanticipated by their states, and could lead to authentic outbursts of political fervor—whether in support of a growing socialist world or, conversely, directed against Soviet imperialism in Eastern Europe itself.[118] Surveillance systems were thus established to regulate and control heterodox internationalisms. Multiple surveys were conducted in the mid-1960s to assess a younger generation's worldviews.[119] In Hungary, in reaction to the perceived threat of Maoist ideology, 'mood reports' focusing on the influence of foreign policy on youth started to be regularly produced by the Communist Youth League.[120] The GDR's Stasi regularly reported not only on their own radical left, but followed their links to west Germany and across the bloc.[121]

But by the late 1960s authorities began to take much more direct action. Hungarian authorities placed a so-called 'Maoist conspiracy' on trial in the spring of 1968, making it clear that domesticating Chinese or other excessive forms of revolutionary behavior would not be tolerated any more.[122] Writings that advocated such radicalism were placed on 'closed circuit' (zárt kiadvány) lists made available only to party elites: only 300 copies of the Hungarian translation of Che Guevara's Bolivian Diaries were produced for this purpose.[123] Anti-imperialism too was blamed for providing a younger generation with the materials for wider socialist visions that could be used to attack on the home front. Mass student demonstrations for the renewal of both university democracy and Yugoslav socialism more generally started with the occupation of Belgrade University in June 1968, and involved many of those who had taken part in earlier anti-imperialist protest.[124] Although Tito initially recognized the validity of their

---

[118] See also Christina Schwenkel, 'Affective Solidarities and East German Reconstruction of Postwar Vietnam', in Slobodian (ed.), Comrades of Color, 267–92.

[119] Faragó, 'A Small Country'. Communist Youth Executive Committee Report, 1967. PIL 289/3/210.

[120] See the many reports in KISZ KB Nemzetközi Kapcsolatok Osztálya. PIL 289.

[121] See for example the fear of Maoism spreading in Stasi report, 27 January 1968. MfS, no. 276/68, file RH 173, 337 (Archives of the Robert Havemann Gesellschaft).

[122] On the trial, see Gábor Murányi, 'Tévelygők, avagy a maoista összeesküvés', in Sándor Révész (ed.), Beszélő évek. A Kádár-korszak története 1957–1968 (Budapest: Stencil Alapítvány, 2000), 578–81. The press communique was in Népszabadság, 9 June 1968. The defendants rejected the label of Maoism, preferring to view themselves as 'authentic Marxist-Leninists'.

[123] Kossuth Könyvkiadó for MSZMP KB. Closed circuit list for 1970. MNL OL 288/41/167. On this, see also: Anonymous, 'Kommentár', Mozgó Világ, 26/3 (March 2000) http://epa.oszk.hu/01300/01326/00003/marciu3.htm (accessed 1 October 2013).

[124] Boris Kanzleiter, '"Yugoslavia" in 1968', in Martin Klimke and Joachim Scharloth (eds.), Europe: A History of Protest and Activism, 1956-1977 (Basingstoke: Palgrave Macmillan, 2008), 223–4.

claims, this moment also came to mark the end of even a limited tolerance for unofficial anti-war demonstrations. This fear of public protest only hardened after the Prague Spring, and the Soviet-led intervention in Czechoslovakia in August 1968. Those anti-imperialist demonstrators who had initially exposed the system's fragility continued to be dealt with harshly: in 1974, the 'Belgrade Eight' were dismissed from the University of Belgrade because of their dissident activities. The charges levelled at them included taking part in anti-American Vietnam protests in December 1966 and the critical student demonstrations in June 1968.[125]

Anti-colonialism did briefly retain its capacity to inspire, despite post-1968 crackdowns on unofficial activism. Many analyses focus on the Prague Spring as the moment when a socially widespread belief in the possibility of reformed socialism was fatally undermined. These interpretations, however, ignore the significant power that global anti-imperialist politics could still hold for the forging of political identity even in the early 1970s. Indeed, the Chilean revolution reactivated the hopes of a progressive wing of a younger generation.[126] In Hungary between 1968 and 1973, in Budapest, Debrecen and Szeged, new movements grew within the Communist Youth League that called for universities to democratize and to address the stagnation in social mobility that they blamed on the regime's abandonment of class-based university quotas in 1962. They had held ambivalent views of the Prague Spring, and had not sought to replicate the radical heroism of the Cuban revolution, Che Guevara, or the Vietnamese struggle: none of these issues appeared relevant to their goal of responsible and sober institutional democratization of the revolution.[127] Chile was the first foreign revolution that really appealed to them.[128] It was not reliant on a violent vanguard role for the working class or peasantry, and for a short time it appeared to offer the possibility of a consensual incremental accommodation between parliamentary democracy and socialism that would be internationally recognized in an era of détente. Chile could be harnessed to reject the stance of older elite conservatives

---

M. Arsić and D. Maković, *Studentski bunt i društvo* (Belgrade: ICC SSO, 1985), 36. Boris Kanzleiter, '1968 u Jugoslaviji—tema koja čeka istraživanje', in Đ. Tomić and P. Atanacković (eds.), *Društvo u pokretu. Novi društveni pokreti u Jugoslaviji od 1968. do danas* (Novi Sad: Cenzura, 2009), 41.

[125] These were university professors Mihailo Marković, Svetozar Stojanović, Ljubomir Tadić, Dragoljub Mićunović, Zagorka Pešić-Golubović, Miladin Životić, Trivo Inđić and Nebojša Popov.

[126] For a further discussion of how in the late 1970s the Prague Spring was constructed as a symbol that represented the end of the possibility of reformed socialism, see Péter Apor and James Mark, 'Mobilizing Generation: The Idea of 1968 in Hungary', in Anna von der Goltz (ed.), '*Talkin' 'bout My Generation': Conflicts of Generation Building and Europe's '1968'* (Göttingen: Wallstein Verlag, 2011), 110–11.

[127] On the failure of KISZ to integrate the radical anti-imperialist left in this period, see György Kalmár, 'Az ifjúság politikai beilleszkedése', *Társadalmi Szemle* (May 1973), 60–8.

[128] 'Nyilatkozat A Latin-Amerika Ifjúsága Harcával Vállalt Szolidaritásról', 8th KISZ Congress, 8 December 1971, Budapest. The declaration gave its support to all progressive forces in Latin America, but it dealt mostly with Cuba and Chile. There were also demonstrations of solidarity for Chile at the local level; see e.g. 'Székesfehérvár gyűlés: Latin amerikai népek melletti szolidaritás'. PIL 289/1/88.

and their view that one-party centralized state socialism was the only possible model.

The abrupt end to the Chilean experiment—as Pinochet's coup overthrew the Allende government—coincided with clampdown on domestic opposition in many Eastern European countries. As such, it was an important moment for the genesis of a new kind of opposition, one that no longer sought to work within the regime's language of anti-colonial socialist internationalism. In Czechoslovakia, following the suppression of 'socialism with a human face' reformism in 1968, Allende's Chilean experiment from 1970 onwards had provided a space for critique of the hardliners' normalization and suppression of reformists, in part because alternative reformist values could be articulated under the cover of official solidarity actions for Chile. Allende's fall thus confirmed that an era of reformism had indeed come to an end: dissidents such as Jiří Pelikán, the exiled 1968-er director of Czechoslovak television, and underground press outlets such as *Narodni Noviny*, linked the terror unleashed against Allende's former followers with the persecution of the Czechoslovak reform left.[129] Pelikán argued that a people whose reformism had been suppressed by an imperialist Soviet intervention had a duty to express solidarity with the victims of a similarly violent putsch against a similar reformist socialism: 'President Allende, the Chilean Dubček, is dead.'[130] In East Germany, the collapse of Chilean democratic socialism cut the ground from under the feet of critics who had previously contrasted Allende's ideals with the reality of official socialism.[131] In Hungary, the fall of Allende coincided with a clampdown on non-conformist politics at home. The rise of the hardline 'Workers' Opposition' in the Hungarian Central Committee thus quashed hopes for even a limited democratization and destroyed the spaces available to unorthodox Marxists such as György Lukács's Budapest School.[132] The movement to humanize and democratize socialism appeared defeated both at home and abroad.

Questioning Third Worldist Internationalism

Some bloc states saw the hollowing out of the political infrastructure that had generated official solidarity. Some Communist Youth Leagues, notably in Poland, Czechoslovakia and Hungary, which had played a leading role in promoting this

---

[129] David Featherstone, *Solidarity: Hidden Histories and Geographies of Internationalism* (London: Zed Books, 2012) Chapter 5.

[130] Jiří Pelikán, *Socialist Opposition in Eastern Europe: The Czechoslovak Example* (New York: St. Martin's Press, 1976), 208–9. For its importance in Hungary, see James Mark and Bálint Tolmár 'Connecting the Peaceful Roads to Socialism? the Rise and Fall of a Culture of Chilean Solidarity in Socialist Hungary 1965–1989', in Christiaens et al. (eds.), *European Solidarity with Chile*, 301–27.

[131] Kenzler, *Der Blick*, 317.   [132] Mark and Apor, 'Socialism Goes Global', 886–7.

culture in the 1960s, no longer served as its incubator. They shifted their attention away from international agitation and, in becoming party cadre schools rather than political movements, lost the influence they had once had over some segments of youth.[133] Reports of campaigns in the late 1970s and 1980s often suggest an empty ritualization accompanied by little fervor even from above—where Communist youth leaders simply recycled the already existing discursive repertoire of anti-imperialism, which was no longer capable of sparking off non-state instigated political projects.[134] New critical movements of the 1980s—such as environmental and peace activism—did not emerge from the structures of anti-imperialist solidarity, as earlier non-conformism had.[135]

It appeared that many socialist states were turning away from a committed Third Worldism too. That which had once provided space and language to criticize both capitalist and state-socialist modes of exploitation and hegemony increasingly appeared as ideologically empty propaganda of one-party elites. In other cases, elites realigned their countries with a broader vision of European belonging; Gorbachev adopted the rhetoric of a 'Common European Home', and replaced the theory of two ideologically opposed camps which had perpetuated a divided Europe. By the second half of the 1980s, Hungarian reform Communists presented themselves as the representatives of a 'small country' strategically placed between the Soviet Union and the West: a loyal ally in the East, and a responsible partner in the West ('*keleten lojális szövetséges, nyugaton megbízható partner*'), as the regime routinely put it.[136]

This was not true everywhere. Yugoslavia stood out as a socialist country where Communist youth infrastructures were still producing meaningful activism in the 1980s: activists used these platforms to campaign against their state's hypocritical profit making through selling arms across Africa—with the 'roses of non-alignment' on them, as one magazine editorial sarcastically put it.[137] In the GDR, infrastructures remained, and anti-imperialist activism was still backed by significant institutional commitment. Even in the 1980s, solidarity committees were 'spontaneously' raising donations for Nicaragua and elsewhere.[138] Factory trade union organs still reported on their voluntary solidarity shifts and the training of

---

[133] Kürti, *Youth and State in Hungary*, 170, 179.

[134] On this paradigmatic shift, see Alexei Yurchak, *Everything was Forever, Until it was No More: the Last Soviet Generation* (Princeton, NJ: Princeton University Press, 2006), 24–6.

[135] Vladimir Tismaneanu (ed.), *In Search of Civil Society: Independent Peace Movements in the Soviet Bloc* (London, New York: Routledge, 1990). See also the dominance of non-institutional oppositional activity related in Padraic Kenney, *A Carnival Of Revolution: Central Europe 1989* (Princeton and Oxford: Princeton University Press, 2002).

[136] Csaba Békés, 'A helsinki folyamat hatása a magyar külpolitikai gondolkodásra. Az európai biztonsági folyamat előzményei', *Magyar külpolitikai gondolkodás a 20. században* (Budapest: Magyar Történelmi Társulat, 2006), 155–69.

[137] Ljubica Spaskovska, *The Last Yugoslav Generation: The Rethinking of Youth Politics and Cultures in Late Socialism* (Manchester: Manchester University Press, 2017), 74, 138.

[138] Reichardt, *Nie vergessen!*, 315.

workers from Mozambique and Cuba in important industrial centres such as Karl-Marx-Stadt in the mid-1980s.[139] And in response to the decline late in that decade, the GDR's Solidarity Committee were still being set serious targets to increase solidarity donations through trade union organizations.[140] The GDR also retained its visible public commitment to the violent struggle in southern Africa: there was widespread media coverage in the 1980s of injured African National Congress (ANC), uMkhonto we Sizwe (MK) and South West Africa People's Organisation (SWAPO) rebels, who had been flown to East Berlin hospitals for convalescence.

Nevertheless, even in this most committed of bloc states, there was evidence of hollowing out. Certainly the GDR's material support for the armed struggle was part of a vehement anti-westernism that continued in this frontline Cold War state to the end: such commitments still usefully distinguished the German people's state from its western counterpart, whose flourishing anti-apartheid movement, which favoured political compromise over militant struggle, was presented as a sell-out. Yet economic problems at home during the 1980s meant that elites were reluctant to publicize the amount of aid being sent to South Africa, for fear of their legitimacy being undermined if their supposedly irresponsible squandering of resources was known about. The fact that milk powder was being sent to liberation movements to feed refugee children was kept a secret, since it was in short supply back in GDR.[141] Even supporters of continued solidarity seemed to have internalized ideas of civilizational difference, and of wasteful spending in a supposedly less economically responsible developing world: Trade Union members wrote to the presidium in November 1989 demanding that donations no longer be wasted.[142] Travel writer Landolf Scherzer complained that solidarity no longer moved the populace, and that only 'church people' and 'jazz musicians' still volunteered to go abroad without material incentives.[143] Churches certainly supported the official commitment to anti-apartheid, although they found themselves more and more uncomfortable with the state's anti-colonial framing of the violent struggle, and preferred to stress campaigns against the violations of civil and religious rights.[144]

[139] Proposal for awarding the flag of honour of anti-imperialist solidarity. 4 January 1985. BA DY 34/14140 (SAPMO-Bundesarchiv, Berlin).

[140] Seibt, 'Letter'. DY 34/14140 (SAPMO-BArch).

[141] Hans-Georg Schleicher and Ilona Schleicher, *Special Flights: The GDR and Liberation Movements in Southern Africa* (Harare: SAPES Books, 1998), 190.

[142] Letter from the trade union members of the Institute for Rationalising the Trade with the Means of Production to the presidium of the Free German Trade Unions, 29 November 1989. Information for the Presidium and Secretariat of the Board of Free German Trade Unions. BA Sapmo DY 34/14038.

[143] Landolf Scherzer, *Bom dia, weißer Bruder: Erlebnisse am Sambesi* (Rudolstadt: Greifenverlag, 1986).

[144] Heike Hartmann and Susann Lewerenz, 'Campaigning against Apartheid in East and West Germany', *Radical History Review*, 119 (2014), 191–204.

The Transformations of Anti-colonial Internationalism

In the 1960s, even conservatives had seen their anti-Communist struggle against Moscow as part of a wider global anti-imperialism that might equally be directed against the US. By the 1980s, Eastern European oppositional movements still drew upon anti-colonial language, albeit in a provincialized form, stripped of its earlier Third Worldism—an ideology they had come to associate predominantly with the hollowed-out rhetoric of their own socialist systems. Anti-colonialism was now directed mainly against the Soviet Union, deployed in the name of escaping their region's subservient geopolitical status through a 'return to Europe'. Mainstream voices in the ten-million strong independent trade union *Solidarność*— the largest opposition movement in the history of the Eastern Bloc—presented themselves as part of a national tradition of resistance against centuries-old invaders, whether Prussian, Austrian, German, Russian or now Soviet. African and Asian post-colonial movements' attempts to shake off western dominance had less and less relevance to their cause. *Solidarność* were reluctant, for instance, to lend full-throated support to the anti-apartheid struggle of the ANC, despite the commonalities in their struggles as trade unions fighting for workers' rights— both because the later struggles of decolonization in Africa were supported by Warsaw Communists, and because right-wing Poles in exile in South Africa gave generously to support its anti-Communism.[145] Polish, Czechoslovak and Hungarian dissidents in fact drew on the term apartheid to describe their own exclusion by a privileged nomenklatura—but in so doing they were instrumentalizing a term that had global resonance to describe their own persecution at the hands of a Communist state, rather than expressing any sense of solidarity beyond their own national struggles.[146]

This is not to say that all international solidarity disappeared: the notion of the anti-colonial struggle that had long shaped nationalist movements in the region, and had been revived and remoulded under Communism, found new expressions in the 1980s. Internationalism survived in the guise of a common resistance to the Soviet Union. In an article entitled 'Colonialism Caught in a Trap' published in a Warsaw *Solidarność* weekly in May 1988, the author explained that Soviet internationalism was only 'an elegant way of describing age-old, greater Russian colonialism aimed at dominating the nations of Asia, Transcaucasia, the Baltic States, the Crimea, and Central Europe. The tragedy of the Soviet Union is

---

[145] Kim Christiaens and Idesbald Goddeeris, 'Competing Solidarities? Solidarność and the Global South during the 1980s', in Mark et al. (eds.), *Alternative Globalizations*, 301.

[146] Charter 77 charged that Czechoslovak dissidents had become "victims of a virtual apartheid". *Declaration of Charter 77*, 1. https://www.files.ethz.ch/isn/125521/8003_Charter_77.pdf (accessed 7 September 2020). Sebastian Gehrig et al., 'The Eastern Bloc, Human Rights, and the Global Fight against Apartheid', *East Central Europe*, 46/2–3 (2019), 291, 307.

that it has realized too late that the era of colonialism is well and truly over.'[147] The Soviet invasion of Afghanistan in 1979 was of particular importance in reviving the idea of the Soviet Union as an empire, not only among anti-Communists, but also within the western left, across the global South and for a wider range of oppositional movements in Eastern Europe.[148] The USSR claimed their presence was justified as they were there not only to protect the internal politics of Afghanistan from western interference and imperialism, but also to ensure the future of a vision of socialist developmentalism and post-colonial territorial sovereignty.[149] In Poland, the underground press constantly depicted the war in Afghanistan as a fight against a common enemy. The story of a 'Polish Mujahideen'— the exiled activist Lech Zondek who had left Australia to fight in Afghanistan and had been killed there in 1985—was used to mobilize opposition at home.[150] The year after, an independent Poland-Afghanistan society was founded, and Radosław Sikorski, at the time a student in Oxford and later Polish Foreign Minister, travelled to Afghanistan to report on the struggles there for a Polish and international readership.[151] Later in 1986, the left-wing 'Peace and Freedom' movement within Solidarność raised 130,000 zloty for medical aid for Afghan refugees. They also produced Afghan-fighter-themed postage stamps for Solidarność's mail system, and in February 1987 gathered in Kraków publicly to protest against the torture of prisoners in the war.[152]

Older analogies between a colonized Eastern Europe and the oppression of blacks and Native Americans in the New World returned. From this perspective, the region was part of a wider leftist shift away from stories of anti-fascist struggle to political cultures based around suffering, in this case drawing on black experiences in order to highlight victimization as Europeans.[153] This was most apparent in Poland, where parallels between, and connections to, the history of

---

[147] 'Armenia and the Polish Opposition Press', *Polish Independent Press Review*, 4, 18 May 1988, HU300-55-9, Box 1 (OSA).

[148] 'Resolution ES-6/2', *Security Council Report* http://www.securitycouncilreport.org/atf/cf/%7B65 BFCF9B-6D27-4E9C-8CD3-CF6E4FF96FF9%7D/Afgh%20ARESES6%202.pdf (accessed 10 January 2019).

[149] Timothy Nunan, *Humanitarian Invasion: Global Development in Cold War Afghanistan* (Cambridge: Cambridge University Press, 2016).

[150] An incomplete bibliography of the contents shows that war in Afghanistan was discussed 400 times in 1985, and 300 times in the first half of 1986. 'Afghanistan: Polish Views and Hopes', RFE Press Review, 26 February 1987, 5–9. 'Afghanistan: Polish Views', 5–9. HU 300-55-9 Box 1 (OSA).

[151] Radosław Sikorski, *Dust of the Saints: a Journey to Herat in Time of War* (London: Chatto & Windus, 1989).

[152] 'Opinion polls Radio Free Europe; Afghanistan: Polish Views', 5–9. In Hungary, the avant-garde art group Inconnu organized a solidarity with Afghanistan exhibition in December 1988. HU 300-6-2 (OSA).

[153] Enzo Traverso, *Left-Wing Melancholia: Marxism, History, and Memory* (New York: Columbia University Press, 2017), 29: 'The memory of the Gulag erased that of revolution, the memory of the Holocaust replaced that of anti-fascism, and the memory of slavery eclipsed that of anticolonialism: the remembrance of the victims seems unable to coexist with the recollection of their hopes, of their struggles, of their conquests and their defeats.'

African-American and Caribbean slavery had long been employed in the struggle for national independence. Indeed, in the late seventeenth century, the situation of Polish serfs were already being compared to African slaves in the Caribbean; this only accelerated at the time of the partitions of Poland in the late eighteenth century, as Polish elites nationalized the struggle, equating the situation of 'negro' slaves with Polish serfs now living under Russian domination.[154] Sidelining the profound differences between economic oppression and poverty on one hand, and the extreme brutality and dehumanization of chattel slavery and its cultural erasure on the other,[155] romantic Polish nationalists such as Polish-Lithuanian poet Adam Mickiewicz nevertheless found it useful to draw on the rhetoric of enslavement when advocating the cause of Poland's independence. There were solidarities too. Abolitionism was popular within Polish national movements in the mid-nineteenth century: in Galicia a Catholic foundation of Maria Teresa Ledóchowska collected funds for the purchase of African-American slaves out of bondage.[156] Such connections continued into the twentieth century. Following the Communist takeover in the late 1940s, exiled leaders were quick to refer to the new political system as enslavement and Poles as 'half slaves'.[157] Communist education itself too kept up this interest in slavery, but usually taught it through histories of the Roman Empire, and focused on popular slave rebellions.[158] And by the mid-1960s it was already becoming a coded language at home to refer to anti-Sovietism. Julian Stawiński, in his 1966 introduction to the Polish translation of Harriet Beecher Stowe's *Uncle Tom's Cabin*, was already hinting at a link between slavery in the United States and Moscow's oppression of the Poles. He noted that the book had been published in Russia only after the enfranchisement of Polish peasants, because previously the Tsar's censors had been afraid of the comparisons that could be drawn between the plight of the Polish peasantry and that of African-American slaves.[159] By the late 1970s, the idea that a Moscow-dominated bloc had enslaved Poland became much more explicit in the language of the region's largest opposition movement, *Solidarność*. Alex Haley's book *Roots: The Saga of an American Family*, which told the story of slave Kunta Kinte, brought from the Gambia to the US, was published in Polish in 1976 and was turned into an American TV series the following year; then screened in Poland,

---

[154] Paweł Zajas, 'Polskie postcolonial studies?: przypadek południowoafrykański', Materiały z konferencji 'Słowa ponad granicami. Literackie świadectwa kontaktów kulturowych', *Napis*, 11 (2005), 218.

[155] Catherine Baker, 'Postcoloniality Without Race? Racial Exceptionalism and Southeast European Cultural Studies', *Interventions*, 20/6 (2018), 768.

[156] Maciej Ząbek, *Biali i Czarni. Postawy Polaków wobec Afryki i Afrykanów* (Warsaw: DiG, 2007), 54. Mieczysław Haiman, *Historia polaków w amerykańskiej wojnie domowej* (Chicago: Dziennika Zjednoczenia, 1928), 8.

[157] Stanislaw Mikolajczyk, *The Rape of Poland: Pattern of Soviet Aggression* (New York: Whittlesey House, 1948), Preface.

[158] Marian H. Serejski (ed.), *Historia. Dla klasy V* (Warszawa: PZWS, 1951), 119–41.

[159] Julian Stawiński in his introduction to H. B. Stowe, *Chata Wuja Toma* (Warszawa, 1966), 15.

its popularity lay in the fact that the struggle against slavery appeared to echo the fight against the dominance of Moscow. The story was repeatedly recalled in popular culture: First Secretary Gierek was understood to be the slave-owner on the 'Communist plantation' where Poles were raped by forces from the East.[160] This conception of the victimized nation instrumentalized the brutality of African-American experience through a Eurocentric framing of the barbaric Orient, viewed as a threat to the borderlands of European civilization. As such, it marked the rise of a particular ideological assemblage—a right-wing post-colonialism drawing on subaltern stories to reclaim the full power of white Europeanness—which would become central in the rise of the populist politics of the post-socialist right.[161]

A provincialized anti-colonialism could also be found on the peripheries of the Soviet Union. In the 1960s a common anti-colonial politics had been used to bring Soviet Central Asia and the Caucasus into a closer relationship with the global South. These regions were used by the Soviet authorities to demonstrate that their cultural and economic model could provide meaningful development to areas formerly marginalized within empires. Yet by the 1980s, as the promises of development for the Soviet Union's southern periphery faded, the same anti-colonial language that had been popularized in the 1960s could be turned against Moscow. Increasingly assertive Central Asian elites who had once embraced their role as exemplar for Soviet anti-colonialism, and had viewed their own regional story as part of the wider global uplift, now characterized the Soviet Union as an imperial power that had confined Central Asia to the periphery, rendering its position akin to that of the Third World within the global system.[162] More surprisingly perhaps, such anti-colonialism was also to be found at the heart of the Soviet Union. The Soviet retreat from Eastern Europe and the Third World was accompanied by the emergence of a specific Russian nationalism that—at least for a few vital years—celebrated the notion of a nation stripped of any imperial pretentions. Just as Polish nationalists revived the image of the threat from the East, so their counterparts in Moscow compared the putative exploitation of 'Mother Russia' by the Soviet Union to the depredations of the Mongol Empire.[163] For them, the Soviet South—now viewed as the country's 'backward' 'Third World'—was both a financial burden for the centre and a civilizationally distinct Islamic space which held Russia back from its own modernization. The corrosive effect of the traumatic Afghanistan War had been chipping away at many Soviet citizens'

[160] Adam Kola, 'A Prehistory of Postcolonialism in Socialist Poland', in Mark et al. (eds.), *Alternative Globalizations*, 273–4, 279.
[161] James Mark, Bogdan C. Iacob, Tobias Rupprecht and Ljubica Spaskovska, *1989: A Global History of Eastern Europe* (Cambridge: CUP, 2019), chapter 6.
[162] Artemy M. Kalinovsky, 'Writing the Soviet South into the History of the Cold War and Decolonization', in Mark et al. (eds.), *Alternative Globalizations*, 204–5.
[163] Helmut Altrichter, *Russland 1989. Der Untergang des sowjetischen Imperiums* (München: C.H. Beck, 2009), 37.

desire for imperial adventures. Economic decline, combined with the new opportunities to give voice to extreme discontent, led many during Perestroika to
inveigh against the spending of 'Russian money' on and in the 'Third World'. An
old Soviet internationalist complained in 1991:

> I speak of the foreign debt, the lack of food, infant mortality, the political repres-
> sions in many Latin American countries, and the answer is: 'Enough of feeding
> these wogs. They are ungrateful cattle. Remember Indonesia—we fed them, fed
> them; Egypt, we fed them, fed them, and then they all showed us their
> arses'...All these opponents of mine had the same solid conviction: the lack of
> sausage at our shop counters is to be blamed on the Cubans, the Vietnamese, the
> Ethiopians and all the other scum from the 'Third World'.[164]

Yet even if solidarity with the extra-European world could no longer be effectively built through a leftist anti-colonialism, a common anti-totalitarianism provided the building blocks for a new internationalism within dissident circles. The
revival of the early Cold War idea of Communism as all-powerful totalitarian
dictatorship was the outcome of the failures to reform and democratize the
system from the late 1960s. It expressed dissidents' attempts to reinterpret the
sources of party-states' resilience and their means of social control, and to counter the claims of reforming elites in the 1980s that their systems would eventually
be capable of incorporating pluralism while maintaining the party's leading role.
Some of those who had once seen themselves as part of a wider anti-colonial front
came to embrace the idea of a new international anti-dictatorial front extending
from Latin America to East Asia to Europe that transcended Cold War bipolar-
ism and could include support for leftist struggles against military dictators too.
Resistance against right-wing General Pinochet was a case in point: the proclamation 'Solidarity with Chile', written by US and Chilean intellectuals, was signed
in 1987 by Czechoslovak, Polish, Hungarian and Yugoslav dissidents. The introduction to this proclamation epitomized the new transregional anti-totalitarian
ethos of the times: 'We express our support to all liberation and social justice
movements of the world, regardless if they are in South Africa, Poland, Turkey, or
the USSR.'[165] Such commitments demonstrated that they had outgrown the previously dominant left versus right division of the Cold War and that they supported struggles for democracy and human and civic rights against all kinds of
authoritarianisms, whatever their political hue.[166]

---

[164] Aleksandr Snitko, 'Skol'ko stoit nasha sovest' v Latinskoĭ Amerike? Zametki eshche bolee ner-
avnodushnye', *Latinskaia Amerika*, 4 (1991), 38–44.
[165] *Infoch*, no. 7, 1987.
[166] Christiaens and Goddeeris, 'Competing Solidarities?', 297.

Dissidents and the Communist states could find themselves supporting the same causes, albeit through very different ideological frames. Solidarity with Nicaragua remained an integral part of official socialist campaigning up until 1989: Eastern European Communist parties, trade unions and youth organizations continued to organize support for Daniel Ortega's Sandinistas, who were classified as Marxist revolutionaries struggling against US imperialism.[167] Dissidents, however, spoke a very different language, using terms such as freedom and democracy to criticize those who were failing to address the political rights or material needs of their populations. In February 1986, prominent Eastern European oppositionists, including former 1968er activists Petr Uhl, Gerd Poppe and Gábor Demszky, together with leftist intellectuals from all around the world, such as Isabel Allende or E. P. Thompson, joined an international protest declaration initiated by American intellectuals against the military support that Ronald Reagan's government provided for anti-Sandinista insurgents in Nicaragua. The declaration superficially seemed to echo former anti-imperialist protests against US imperialism, demanding 'an immediate end to the United States' growing intervention in Nicaragua'.[168] Nevertheless, this was not like an earlier socialist anti-imperialism:

the fight for human dignity and freedom, the fight for social justice and the fight for equal rights of peoples and nations, are one and the same struggle: the emancipatory battles in Eastern Europe and Latin America are part and parcel alike of that struggle. And it is out of our feelings of solidarity...in the field of human rights and regarding the future of democracy in your country.[169]

Still, these connections often did not come easily, because many of the movements in the global South embraced a Marxism that dissident groups were increasingly distancing themselves from. Often voices from the South criticized Eastern Europeans' reliance on liberal and right-wing supporters in the West who provided succour to their own opponents.[170] And whereas the languages of anti-imperialist solidarity had once linked Eastern Europe to Africa, Asia and Latin America by suggesting a natural alliance among these regions against the imperialist core, solidarity based on rights could also loosen such ties and bind parts of Eastern Europe more tightly to the West. By the late 1980s, anti-apartheid was

---

[167] Ádám Anderle, 'Forradalom és ideológia Nicaraguában', *Társadalmi Szemle*, 40 (December 1985), 74. Klaus Storkmann, 'East German Military Aid to the Sandinista Government of Nicaragua, 1979–1990', *Journal of Cold War Studies*, 16 (Spring 2014), 56–7. 'Szolidaritás Nicaraguával', *Magyar Ifjúság*, 16 March 1984, 3. *Új Szó*, 16 November 1984, 3.

[168] *The New York Times*, 1 December 1985.

[169] *New York Review of Books*, 13 February 1986.

[170] Kim Christiaens, 'Europe at the Crossroads of Three Worlds: Alternative Histories and Connections of European Solidarity with the Third World, 1950s–80s', *European Review of History*, 24/6 (2017), 947.

being embraced both by reformist Communists and by dissident groups not out of a Communist anti-imperialism—an ideology which belonged to a world that was dying—but rather as an aspect of their participation in a common culture of rights-based solidarity across the global North. The 1988 Free Mandela concert at London's Wembley Stadium was shown across the region, and was accompanied by demonstrations in Prague, Budapest and Warsaw. If the shortcut to Cold War home-front solidarity had been Korea and the one leading to global anti-imperialist solidarity had been Vietnam, the new rights-and-needs-based solidarity was represented by the mass pop culture of stadium festivals. The model for the 1985 Budapest Live Aid for Africa[171] was the London/Philadelphia Live Aid concert beamed across the world, initiated by rock star Bob Geldof. These parallels helped Eastern Europeans recognize that their political activism was assuming very similar forms to those of western human rights activist and democratic movements. It was thus not only so as to make common cause with the disadvantaged of the imperialist world order that Eastern Europeans came to support selected extra-European struggles. It was increasingly commonly the recognition of the difference between a disadvantaged South and a relatively developed, modern and free Europe that motivated these gestures of support and aid. An anti-authoritarian internationalism, which had in many ways been incubated within an earlier Communist-sponsored anti-colonialism, then became an important part of the creation of a liberal western-facing identity in the first decades after the fall of Communism. Committed to the struggle to expand the reach of liberal democracy and civic rights—and grateful for the support that the West had offered to Eastern Europe— one-time dissidents and then post-Communist elites such as Czech Václav Havel or Poland's Adam Michnik would go on to support enthusiastically the anti-Communist struggle in Cuba and the US-led intervention in Iraq in 2003.[172]

Epilogue

After 1989, a right-wing anti-Communist anti-colonialism made its way into the mainstream, accelerating after the global financial crisis of 2008, with the entry of populist parties into government. On one hand, such political movements defined themselves against socialist internationalism: for them, the product of an inauthentic totalitarian ideology imposed on unwilling populations that threatened to wrench the region from its true European home. Yet on the other, many

---

[171] *Mondd, mit ér egy falat kenyér?* (LP: Favorit, 1985).

[172] Maria Mälksoo, *The Politics of Becoming European: A Study of Polish and Baltic Post-Cold War Security Imaginaries* (London: Routledge, 2010), 125, 128–30. On support for Cuba, see Mark et al., *1989*, 242–3.

notions of the region's place in the world embedded in Communist solidarity did go on to influence post-Communist politics. This should not be surprising: as we have argued here, it is far more illuminating to interpret anti-colonial solidarity as a much longer-term historical phenomenon, the pre-Communist forms of which would ensure that solidarity was a living ideology that extended well beyond the control of the Communist state—and would mean that aspects of its ideology were destined to outlive it. We can recognize the legacies of Communism in the present-day struggle against a 'dissolute' West: whilst the Communists had once defined the region against the West's imperialism and racism, populists would define themselves as protectors of a region from liberal western Europe's multi-culturalism and progressive 'gender ideology'. The Communist-era lack of curios-ity about the region's complex relationship to imperialism had given rise to a Eurocentric anti-colonialism that in turn laid the ideological foundations for a later right-wing populism intent on claiming an anti-colonialism in the name of the defence of white Europe. Supposedly unburdened by colonial guilt—as Communists too had once argued too—Eastern Europe in populists' visions did not have a duty to address global inequalities, or to take post-colonial populations into their countries. For such forces, anti-colonialism now meant the absence of any responsibility to take in non-European migrants, and an overriding concern to preserve a white, Christian conservative vision of the continent.

Index